RACE AND GENDER
IN THE
AMERICAN ECONOMY

RACE AND GENDER IN THE AMERICAN ECONOMY

Views from Across the Spectrum

Edited by

Susan F. Feiner

Hampton University

Prentice Hall
Englewood Cliffs, New Jersey 07632

Library of Congress Cataloging-in-Publication Data

Race and gender in the American economy : views from across the
  spectrum / edited by Susan F. Feiner.
      p. cm.
    Includes bibliographical references and index.
    ISBN 0-13-670092-6
    1. Equality—United States.   2. United States—Social
conditions—1980-   3. United States—Economic conditions—1981-
4. Racism—United States.   5. United States—Race relations.
6. Sexism—United States.   I. Feiner, Susan.
HN90.S6R33   1994
305′.0973—dc20   93–38937
                                                    CIP

This book is dedicated to my parents, Irving and Trudy Feiner

Acquisitions editor: Stephen Dietrich
Editorial assistant: Elizabeth A. Becker
Editorial/production supervision: Mary McDonald
Interior design: Peggy Gordon
Copy editor: Sherry Babbitt
Cover design: Maureen Eide
Production Coordinator: Patrice Fraccio

© 1994 by Prentice-Hall, Inc.
A Paramount Communications Company
Englewood Cliffs, New Jersey 07632

Printed in the United States of America
10 9 8 7 6 5 4 3 2

ISBN 0-13-670092-6

Prentice-Hall International (UK) Limited, *London*
Prentice-Hall of Australia Pty. Limited, *Sydney*
Prentice-Hall Canada Inc., *Toronto*
Prentice-Hall Hispanoamericana, S.A., *Mexico*
Prentice-Hall of India Private Limited, *New Delhi*
Prentice-Hall of Japan, Inc., *Tokyo*
Simon & Schuster Asia Pte. Ltd., *Singapore*
Editora Prentice-Hall do Brasil, Ltda., *Rio de Janeiro*

CONTENTS

PREFACE

FOUNDATIONS

For much of the history of the United States, race, sex, and ethnic origin have been good predictors of economic and social status. Yet despite much legislation and many policies designed to eliminate economic inequality stemming from unfair treatment based on personal characteristics like skin color or sex, Americans of color and women from all racial and ethnic groups are far more likely to be poor, unemployed, or underemployed than are men of European descent. The purpose of this book is to present the three competing economic explanations of this situation: conservative, liberal, and radical.

In the liberal view, the persistence of economic inequality along the lines of race, ethnicity, and sex suggests that these patterns result from the normal workings of the U.S. economy. It is believed that race, ethnicity, and gender must be influencing the decisions of some economic actors some of the time, or else the incidence of poverty and other economic ills would be roughly the same across demographic groups. Since this "equality of inequality" is not typical in America, significant numbers of economists, public-policy makers, and citizens have reached the conclusion that political forces, social attitudes, and structural impediments, originating in racial prejudice, gendered occupational stratification, and an intolerance of difference, constrain the economic achievements of women and minorities.

In the liberal view, overt and covert discrimination, as well as continued occupational segregation by race and sex, combine with racist and sexist hostility to produce work environments, social climates, and community behaviors that limit the economic success of minority racial and ethnic groups and women from all groups. Conservatives argue from a very different position, one that stresses the *individual* and not the *social* situation. From this perspective, individual behavior reflects underlying choices, and these choices are directly or indirectly responsible for the observed disparities in income, wealth, educational attainment, housing, and familial support. Radicals argue that racial and sexual inequality are functional for the U.S. economy. From this position, racial and sexual inequality protect the underlying patterns of economic power, ownership, wealth distribution, and production for private profit.

Given these very different initial premises shaping how economists, policy makers, social scientists, and citizens analyze race, gender, and ethnicity, a good deal of conflict in interpretation, analysis, and even definition is inevitable. In fact, every attempt to begin a discussion of the economic effects of, for example, racism, sexism, discrimination, or oppression generates controversy for two inescapable reasons: first, these words themselves evoke stong feelings; and second, there is so much at stake. Consequently, discussions of race, sex, ethnicity, and public policy are frequently fraught with disagreement, hostility, and sometimes even violence. One of the major objectives of this volume is to help move beyond the negative experience of such disagreements and instead establish the reasons for the disagreements. In this process, however, we will find that dispassionate objectivity may not be possible.

It is a commonplace of social science to note that people have different perspectives on social life. It is thus important to understand both the origins of these perspectives and their consequences. A good place to begin this inquiry is to acknowledge that everyone has an outlook on society, and that points of view shape and are shaped by different experiences of race, sex, class, and power. In addition, perspectives on society reflect perspectives on social justice: for some the problems of discrimination, oppression, and exploitation are pervasive and harmful precisely because these people place high personal and social value on equality and fairness. Perspectives that downplay these problems have a different vision of social justice, one in which issues of personal merit and competitiveness dominate the view of fairness. In consequence, it is not possible to offer definitions of terms like "racism," "sexism," or "oppression," that do not embody some *preexisting* perspective on the subjects discussed in this volume.

INSIGHT

Does the discussion of these topics cause you some discomfort? Do you find yourself responding emotionally to them? If so, you are probably not alone. We have all grown up in a world in which the color of our skin, our sex, and our religious beliefs have played a significant role in shaping our life opportunities; the places in which we live, the schools we attend, and the occupations we choose are all influenced by personal characteristics over which we have had little control. Consequently, the discussion of issues relating to race, discrimination, ethnicity, gender, and inequality generate much heated debate. Indeed, try to remember a single classroom discussion of these topics that did not quickly become a hostile confrontation of opposing points of view. The different points of view are in many respects inevitable. We can, however, strive for open and informed discussion of the sources and consequences of our disagreements. And one way to begin the movement toward this type of positive dialogue is by openly and frankly examining our own feelings about race, gender, and ethnicity.

Economists working to incorporate issues relating to women and minorities into the economics curriculum have been supported in their efforts by the National Science Foundation. Through the NSF Division of Undergraduate Science Enhancement, a project titled "Improving Introductory Economics Education by Integrating the Latest Scholarship on Women and Minorities," directed by Professor Robin Bartlett (Denison University) and this author, has provided an opportunity for economists from across the United States to work on teaching strategies appropriate for bringing these sensitive content areas into the classroom. Our work, and the experiences of a growing pool of economics educators, confirms the important role attitudes and emotions play in shaping our understanding of race and gender in the American economy.

The importance of exploring emotional, subjective feelings about race, ethnicity, and gender became very clear to me when I was a participant in a faculty development project titled "Black Students, White Teachers: Exploring Assumptions and Practices." This path-breaking project, supported by the U.S. Department of Education's Fund for the Improvement of Post-Secondary Education, and directed by Jack Noonan, James Cones, Denise Janha, and Adelaid Simpson (Virginia Commonwealth University in Richmond), involved faculty from across the campus in a three-year exploration of the ways in which our own preconceptions, misconceptions, expectations, and day-to-day classroom practices affected the classroom experiences of minority- and majority-race students. As colleagues, we visited each others' classrooms to see how we interacted with students of different races: Were all students asked questions and given an appropriate time to answer? Did teachers make eye contact with minority and female students as frequently as they did with white male students? Which students tended to sit front and center, thereby assuring attention from the professor? Did other students respect the contributions of minority students, or were they interrupted when speaking in class? As we worked together to make these observations and make sense of the data we collected, all of us became aware of the frightening power of the hidden assumptions we all have about race and appropriate behaviors. We discovered that a surprisingly effective way to disarm these assumptions was to talk frankly about our private feelings about race.

Some of the questions that were most helpful in initiating positive discussions were: Do you remember the first time you became aware of yourself as a boy or a girl? When did you first realize that you are a person of color or a member of the majority race? Where were you? What events or personal interactions brought you to this awareness? How did you feel when you realized you were in some sense "different"? Do you remember people in your family or neighborhood telling you about people who were "different"? Did they use pejorative language? How did this make you feel? These are difficult and probing questions, but because the topics so frequently cause our emotions to leap to the surface, it is important to reflect on our earliest and most deeply held beliefs about race and sex.

As you explore your feelings, it will be helpful to sit down with a friend, classmate, or roommate, and try to express your feelings honestly. An important goal of these first private dialogues is to share your emotions while remaining respectful of, and sensitive to, others. Can you, with a close and trusted friend, explore your deeply held attitudes and beliefs? As you are talking, see if you can answer these questions: Why is it important for me to question the origins of my feelings about women's roles in society? Why should I think about the sources of my impressions about the social and economic status of people of color? What effects are my feelings likely to have on others?

As you become comfortable with this exercise, it will become easier to participate in the classroom discussions stemming from this volume of readings. Since each chapter includes contrasting views on how race and gender affect various spheres of the U.S. economy, you will undoubtedly find yourself sympathetic to some positions and antagonistic to others. One of your principal jobs as a reader will be to find the similarities in the kinds of arguments you find appealing and to determine how these arguments differ from those that you reject. Classroom discussions will provide an opportunity to "try on" different positions and explore new points of view. Hopefully, this process will lead to a wider appreciation of diversity at both the social level of diverse racial, sexual, and ethnic experiences and the intellectual level of diverse economic, political, and cultural points of view.

STRUCTURE OF THE BOOK

Part I, "Views from Across the Spectrum," consists of three chapters. Chapter 1 contains four brief essays, written specifically for this volume, which lay out the major points of view on questions of economic inequality. The authors are some of the most influential economists writing on these topics, and their contributions greatly enrich this volume. Chapter 2 lays out the main paradigms, or points of view, that shape economic approaches to questions of race and gender. Chapter 3 relies heavily on data to sketch the range of competing interpretations of the recent history of race- and gender-linked economic inequality in the United States. You should not be surprised to find that a principal point of contention concerns the impact of the twelve years of economic and social policy administered by Ronald Reagan and George Bush.

Part II, "Employment and Education," explores the relationship between work and school. Chapter 4 examines changes in the composition of the working population. These articles discuss the likely impact of these demographic changes on employer–employee relations, public policy, and educational reform. Chapter 5 presents opposing arguments concerning the need for and likely effects of government intervention in labor markets. Chapters 6 and 7 address the connection between education and economic well-being. The belief that education provides a path to economic advancement has been a constant theme in the dialogue between generations. Recently, however, this claim has come under close scrutiny. The readings in Chapter 6 focus on the relationship between access, earnings, and education to offer insight into the observation that similar investments in education may yield different patterns of incomes. The articles in Chapter 7 discuss aspects of discrimination in education to ask if the system of schooling in the United States contributes to or helps to overcome race and gender bias. This issue is separate from the argument that even with equality of educational opportunity, some may experience greater economic and social success than others.

Part III, "Households, Habitats, and Health," provides a comprehensive view of how some of the most private aspects of our lives are shaped by economic forces. The articles are arranged in five chapters. Economic and social changes influencing American families are discussed in Chapter 8. The many ways in which children are affected by economic processes are discussed in Chapter 9. The complex interconnections among culture, behavior, and the economy are explored in Chapter 10. Chapter 11 takes up questions relating to racial segregation. And Chapter 12 discusses some of the ways in which race and sex interact with the U.S. health care industry.

Part IV, "Evaluating Fairness, Eliminating Inequality," turns our attention to the future. Chapter 13 presents a variety of interpretations of the economic and social status of women and minorities. Comparing the different points of view will help to clarify the consequences of adhering to competing social visions. Chapter 14 offers a series of arguments calling for widespread attention to the problems of race and gender in the American economy.

LEARNING OBJECTIVES

For students of economics and for noneconomists, finding information on the economic status of women and minorities can be surprisingly difficult. One might think that a good starting place would be economics textbooks. These, however, would not prove to be too helpful. Introductory textbooks in both micro- and macro-economics contain very little on the economic status of women and minorities, and a similar situation characterizes the majority of texts used in intermediate and advanced economics courses. Frequently, the little that is found is of dubious quality: women and people of color are typically presented in stereotypical roles and situations, while the competing explanations for differences in unemployment, poverty, or earnings are rarely given; in most instances, the relevance of race and/or gender to economic activity is minimized, despite the centrality of these topics in current policy debates. (These findings have been extensively documented in a variety of articles. See, for example, Feiner and Morgan, 1987[1]; Feiner, 1993.[2]) The principal objective of this volume is therefore to present and foster an understanding of the major points of view on these pressing issues. In this process, students and professors will have the opportunity to share thoughts, feelings, and experiences in a constructive fashion. For some, this will be a time to find out how very different life experiences can be. For others, this will be a chance to recognize and appreciate the diversity of American social relations. For all, this will be an opportunity for emotional and intellectual growth rooted in the study of economics.

This is a book about economics, and the absence of graphs, equations, and data sets is deliberate. This book presents arguments, and its most important goal is to create an environment in which students learn to move from the "facts" to an evaluation of complex arguments. But evaluation, like most aspects of learning, is an active process. Hence it will be useful to have on hand a model of learning that makes the activities of learning explicit. Then we will share a common standard for judging progress toward a critical appreciation of our thoughts on such controversial subjects as race, men and women, exploitation, discrimination, family life, and segregation.

Figure 1 presents a useful framework for viewing cognitive development. Notice the ladder-like quality of the stages, or levels, of thinking. Oddly, we find the term "knowledge" at the lowest, or earliest, level. Specific tasks that can be completed when you "know" the material will include recognizing definitions, describing concepts, and labeling positions—in short, this stage of learning involves "getting your facts straight." This, however, is a rudimentary task, expected of all students. In each chapter, you are likely to find facts that challenge your ideas about such issues as the causes of poverty or the effects of welfare policy on incentives. The second rung of the ladder is comprehension, which involves tasks such as giving examples, paraphrasing, and explaining. A good exercise to ensure comprehension is to write a brief paragraph summarizing an article. Such summaries could include your interpretation of an author's school of economics, and a defense or critique of the position advocated.

The next two steps on the learning ladder are application and analysis. These two categories of thinking and learning are closely intertwined, since analysis (breaking a problem down into its component parts) often involves application (applying concepts to a new situation). To test your ability to work at these levels, see if you can: (1) show how basic economic concepts like supply and demand, elasticity, or business cycles are used in the different arguments; (2) use basic economic concepts to illustrate the points made by various authors; or (3) demonstrate how the economic arguments in two or more articles relate to each other. Your mastery of work at these stages will be demonstrated by your ability to discriminate among competing arguments, relate one argument to another,

[1]Feiner, Susan, and Barbara Morgan, 1987. "Women and Minorities in Introductory Economics Textbooks, 1974 to 1984." *The Journal of Economic Education* (Fall), 376–392.

[2]Feiner, Susan, 1993. "Introductory Economics Textbooks and the Treatment of Issues Relating to Women and Minorities, 1984 to 1991." *The Journal of Economic Education* (Spring), 145–161.

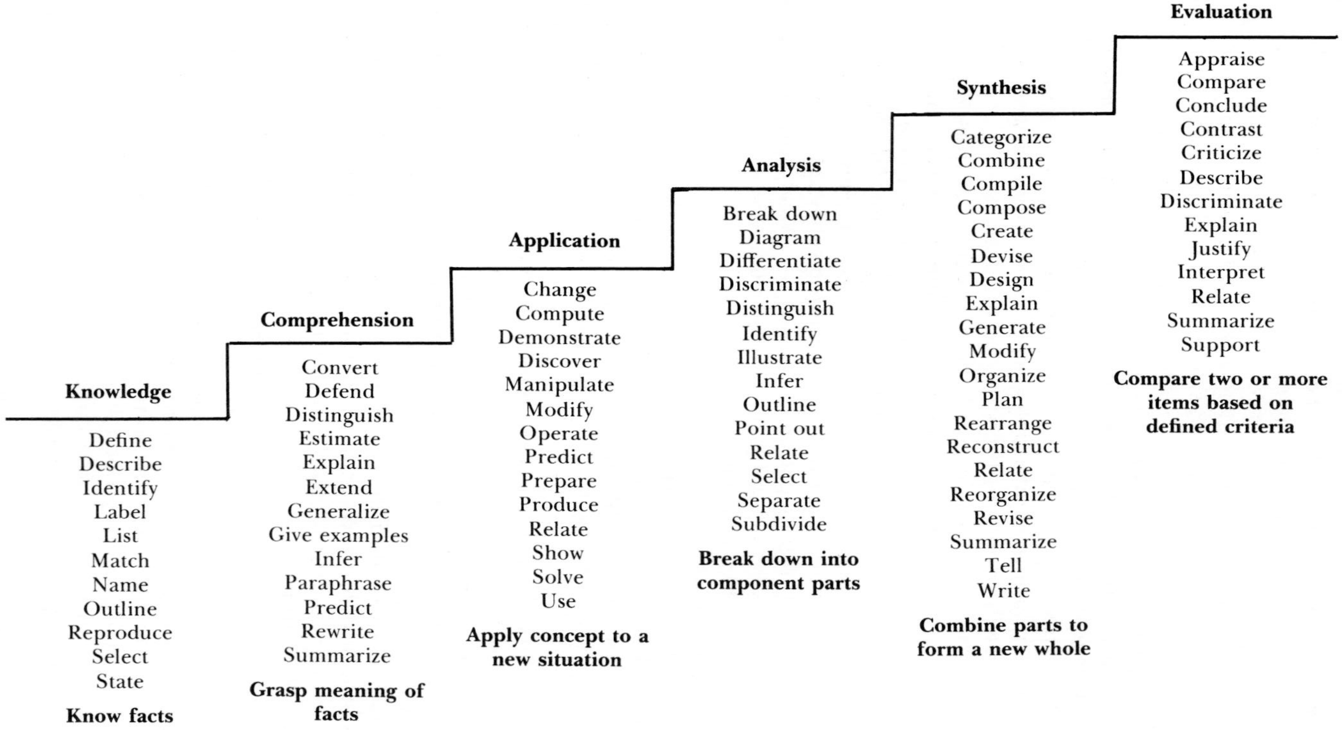

Knowledge

Define
Describe
Identify
Label
List
Match
Name
Outline
Reproduce
Select
State

Know facts

Comprehension

Convert
Defend
Distinguish
Estimate
Explain
Extend
Generalize
Give examples
Infer
Paraphrase
Predict
Rewrite
Summarize

Grasp meaning of facts

Application

Change
Compute
Demonstrate
Discover
Manipulate
Modify
Operate
Predict
Prepare
Produce
Relate
Show
Solve
Use

Apply concept to a new situation

Analysis

Break down
Diagram
Differentiate
Discriminate
Distinguish
Identify
Illustrate
Infer
Outline
Point out
Relate
Select
Separate
Subdivide

Break down into component parts

Synthesis

Categorize
Combine
Compile
Compose
Create
Devise
Design
Explain
Generate
Modify
Organize
Plan
Rearrange
Reconstruct
Relate
Reorganize
Revise
Summarize
Tell
Write

Combine parts to form a new whole

Evaluation

Appraise
Compare
Conclude
Contrast
Criticize
Describe
Discriminate
Explain
Justify
Interpret
Relate
Summarize
Support

Compare two or more items based on defined criteria

Figure 1. Bloom's taxonomy of educational objectives in the cognitive domain.

Source: Adapted from Bloom, Benjamin, 1956. *Taxonomy of Educational Objectives: The Classification of Educational Goals.* New York: Dave McKay, Inc.

or predict how authors from the various perspectives will treat particular problems.

The final two rungs of the ladder are synthesis and evaluation. Mastery of these skills is essential to a full appreciation of the competing positions on race and gender in the U.S. economy. When you can work at these levels, you will be able to argue creatively, both for and against the positions you favor. You will be able to construct logical explanations of novel social situations and tell convincing stories about how a situation can be changed. A closely related skill involves the ability to compare and contrast competing interpretations of the economic status of women and minorities. A fine exercise to develop this capacity would be to establish criteria that you would then use to evaluate and critique various articles in the volume. (For example, do assumptions about human behavior allow for diversity or do they restrict behavior to one type only, and then label that behavior "good?")

At first, it might seem that this volume is far removed from the world of supply and demand, marginal productivity, preferences, price indices, demand multipliers, and the myriad other tools and theories studied in economics classes. But the distance is not so great at all. Ultimately, economic tools are always used within conceptual frameworks, and the conceptual frameworks of economics, like economists themselves, interact with and help to produce the world in which women and men of all colors and ethnic backgrounds struggle to make life meaningful. It is my hope that this volume will contribute to that process.

ACKNOWLEDGMENTS

A very special debt of gratitude is owed to Professors Robert Solow, Glen Loury, June O'Neill, and William Darity, Jr. Each took valuable time from pressing schedules to prepare the excellent essays which open this volume. No finer introduction could be envisioned. Bruce B. Roberts, my husband and colleague, also played an instrumental role in the preparation of this book. Without his encouragement and support this work would not yet be complete. Professor Peter Bell, Executive Director of the New York Council for Economic Education, carefully read and commented upon the introductions to Parts I–IV. His remarks invariably helped me to improve the clarity of the presentation. Ms. Claretta Daniels, my student assistant at Hampton University, worked diligently, efficiently, and cheerfully on the endless correspondence required to secure permissions to reprint the many articles comprising this collection. Her assistance was invaluable. I also extend thanks to my enthusiastic editor at Prentice Hall, Mr. Stephen Dietrich, for keeping me on track during the many years of this project. And finally, Ms. Mary McDonald provided wonderful guidance in the final stages of editing and producing this book. I of course am fully responsible for any and all of the problems which remain.

Susan F. Feiner

VIEWS FROM ACROSS THE SPECTRUM

The three chapters in Part I will introduce you to the major positions in economics. The first four readings, written by four prominent economists specifically for this book, provide examples of the dominant positions on the economics of race and gender: the conservative/free market school, the liberal/imperfectionist school, and the radical/exploitation school. Even before you begin reading, however, you are probably aware of the controversial nature of the topics related to discrimination and economic fairness.

Most of us have argued, at one time or another, not just about the existence or extent of discrimination, but also about the most appropriate ways to redress the problem. The opinions of economists are often fuel for the contending sides in these debates. Moreover, some observers think that the persistence of disagreements on questions of discrimination or on other issues relevant to the economic position of women and people of color is a weakness of the discipline. As you work through the readings in this volume, however, you will see that controversy of this sort is not a sign of confusion or muddled thinking. Instead, the reality of economic disagreements follows directly from the existence of different ways of thinking about the social world. As you evaluate the different positions represented in this book, you will come to recognize the very different logics of cause and effect that animate the three main paradigms in economics: the conservative, liberal, and radical schools. In each chapter, these paradigms are represented. The existence of these paradigms, and the interpretations of the economic conditions facing women of all races as well as men from diverse racial and ethnic backgrounds, pose a challenge the claims of objectivity and value neutrality often advanced by economists and economic textbooks.

While the ideal of the objective mind making unbiased inquiries into the nature of things represents one view of economic science, other views of the scientific enterprise call this ideal into question. The alternative to "objectivity" is not, however, a free-for-all of equally subjective claims. The rules of logic and consistency of course still hold. But even more importantly, we need to keep in mind that all sciences necessarily have implications for the ways we see, and hence want to shape, society. For this reason, it is extremely important to be aware of the presuppositions about social life that undergird competing paradigms in economics.

Like Chapter 1, Chapter 2 is original to this volume. Here you will find a brief outline of the three major approaches to economic science: the conservative/free market, the liberal/imperfectionist, and radical/exploitation schools. To enrich your understanding of the points at issue across economic paradigms, you might consult the following: Robert Carson, *Economics Issues Today: Alternative Views* (New York: St. Martin's Press, 1987); Thomas Schwartz and Frank Bonello, *Taking Sides: Clashing Views on Controversial Issues*, 5th ed. (Guilford, CT: Dushkin Publishing Group, 1990); and Stephen Resnick and Richard Wolff, *Economics: Marxian versus Neoclassical* (Baltimore: Johns Hopkins University Press). Each contains essays that compare and contrast the different theoretical positions in economics.

Chapter 3 is the first chapter of collected readings. These articles provide an overview of the recent changes in the structure and functioning of the U.S. economy that have affected the economic status of women and minorities. The chapter juxtaposes competing economic, political, and social perspectives on the patterns and causes of race- and gender-linked economic inequality. This set of readings provides an excellent opportunity to develop critical thinking skills, since the positions of the various authors are easily compared. Readers are encouraged to reflect on why extensive and heated disagreements are the norm on virtually every topic relevant to the economic status of minorities and women.

To a very large extent, the widespread interest in the economic status of women and minorities arises as a response to both the striking inequalities associated with race and gender in the United States and the perception that these inequalities are not fair. Racist and sexist behaviors will limit peoples' opportunities and experiences without regard for individual talents or desires. Since discriminatory behaviors target people based on characteristics over which they have absolutely no control—one can choose neither one's parents nor one's biology—discriminatory social forces are generally considered to be unjust. At the same time, ideals of fairness, equality and democracy have a long and important history in America. Consequently, observers who "see" race- and gender-linked inequality as the result of unfair practices feel that it is important to correct such injustices. Economic and political disagreements arise precisely because not everyone "sees" the same forces at work producing inequality.

A clash of viewpoints is unavoidable. Probably most of us would agree that characteristics such as skin color or gender ought *not* play a significant role in how one is treated. On the other hand, there is no widespread agreement that the economic status of women and minorities follows from racism or sexism in the economic system or in the individual behavior of employers, teachers, co-workers, or real estate agents. Our concern in Chapter 3 is to understand the conservative, liberal, and radical interpretations of recent trends in race- and/or gender-linked inequality.

It is generally agreed that structural changes in the U.S. economy since the 1970s have had profound consequences for all phases of economic activity. The interconnected processes of production, distribution, and consumption are carried out today in quite different institutional settings than they were fifty years ago. It is not so generally agreed, however, that the long-term effects of these changes are responsible for the continued secondary position of women and minorities in the economy. Before turning to the set of articles representing the different points of view on the changing patterns of income distribution, let us first review the major structural changes of the last two decades.

Economists use the term "structural" to refer to changes in the geographic location of production; the technologies employed in production; the composition of the bundle of commodities demanded by consumers; and the demographic composition (racial, sexual, age, and educational level) of the work force. Structural changes in one or all of these may occur in response to forces at work within or outside the U.S. economy. For example, soon after the end of World War II, manufacturing firms moved out of the unionized Northeast and Midwest to the Sun Belt states. Structural changes may also occur in response to changes in the competitive pressures in the international marketplace. A quick summary of recent changes in the U.S. automobile industry will illustrate this source of pressure for structural change and simultaneously highlight some important asymmetries in the U.S. economy.

Initially, because of both union and employer discrimination, African American employment in the automobile industry was limited to menial tasks. But this changed dramatically after World War II. By the 1970s, direct black employment in the auto industry accounted for an extremely large share of all stable, high-paying jobs held by blacks. In 1979, for example, the Chrysler payroll to black workers was $800 million, or approximately 1 percent of the total income earned by African Americans. African Americans accounted for 25 percent of the work force at Chrysler, 15 percent at Ford, and 14 percent at General Motors. (Cited in Richard Child Hill and Cynthia Negry, "Deindustrialization and Racial Minorities in the Great Lakes Region, U.S.A." Paper presented at the International Conference on Racial Minorities, Economic Restructuring and Urban Decline. University of Warwick, Coventry, England (September 1985). Reprinted in D. Stanley Eitzen and Maxine Baca Zinn, *The Reshaping of America: Social Consequences of a Changing Economy.* (Englewood Cliffs, NJ: Prentice Hall, 1989), pp. 175–76.)

Now consider the effects on black income and employment of the massive decline in auto production that has occurred since the mid-1970s. It is obvious that with such a high concentration of African American employees, any reduction in the size of the auto industry would disproportionately effect African Americans. We can profitably employ a tool from macroeconomics to understand this situation: the movie *Roger and Me* dramatically illustrates the negative multiplier effects that have virtually dismantled the region's economy. The salient point, though, is that these structural changes, which include the declining auto industry, the expansion of foreign auto consumption, and the rise of service sector employment, have not had an equal impact on all members of the economic community. Those who were most dependent on the payrolls of the auto makers and their suppliers have seen their incomes and standards of living decline precipitously.

Another example of structural change demonstrates some of the problems confronting female workers from all racial and ethnic traditions. Before 1970, most jobs provided full-time, year-round employment. Since 1970, there has been a huge increase in the number of part-time jobs and of "contingent workers."

In fact, in the 1970s the number of part-time jobs increased 68 percent, and by 1980 almost one-fourth (25%) of all jobs were part-time. Women hold almost one-half (50%) of these jobs. Changes of this type, when combined with the expansion of employment in the low-wage "female" occupations, suggest that for women, as for African Americans, structural change can hurt a lot. The readings that follow offer competing interpretations of these trends and their effects.

CHAPTER 1

My View

1

How Race and Gender Issues Arise in Economics

Robert Solow

Are questions about the economic status of women and minorities important? They certainly are if you are a woman or a member of a minority group. That covers a lot of people. Even if you are not, I should think that any decent and curious person would want to know the facts about group differences in economic outcomes and then understand why things happen as they do.

There is something wrong with a society that punishes some people and rewards others just because they have personal characteristics for which they are not responsible and cannot control. When there are gross differences in the economic status of identifiable groups, the reason may be simple discrimination—in education, in health care, or in the labor market itself. Often, however, the chain of cause and effect will be quite complicated. Some social institutions may work in almost invisible ways, even across

generations, to create or preserve group differences. This is worth puzzling out, and for economists this means investigating the behavior of markets in competitive economies. There are other ways of organizing economic activity, but they seem to be vanishing quickly. So the market is the main environment worth considering. (The others involve the relationships within business firms and within families.)

An ideal market is anonymous. Goods and services are bought and sold for money. A dollar is a dollar, a pound of sugar is a pound of sugar, and the names of the buyers and sellers are irrelevant. There are markets like this. To take an extreme example, if you have the wherewithal, you can buy one hundred shares of a listed stock at the quoted price in a completely impersonal way; or, if you own the shares, you can sell them for the quoted price. The brokerage

Professor Solow is professor of economics at the Massachusetts Institute of Technology. He was awarded the Nobel prize in economics in 1987.

Robert M. Solow

charges are standardized too. Some markets for ordinary goods and services come close to this idealized notion of anonymity, and more come tolerably close. You would not go far wrong in analyzing them as if the personal characteristics of buyers and sellers do not affect the outcome.

Obviously some markets are very far from anonymous in this sense. The market for bank vice presidents will do for an example. You would have to be very naïve to believe that the race and gender of the buyers (the bank officials doing the hiring) and the sellers (the job applicants) have nothing to do with outcome, that is, prices and quantities. The same could be said about the market for condominiums in fancy neighborhoods. Careful investigation would undoubtedly turn up a lot of less obvious instances. So here are two important ways in which race and gender influence market outcomes. Recognizing the pervasiveness of these types of influences should affect the ways in which economists think about such markets.

It is worth being a little more formal about this. Everything, or nearly everything, that matters about the market for a well-defined commodity can be summed up in the supply-and-demand schedules for that market. We could say that a race or gender issue arises in a market when race or gender affects either the supply or demand in that market in a manner fundamentally irrelevant to the commodity being traded. The phrase "fundamentally irrelevant" invites nitpicking, of course, but that cannot be helped. There are true borderline cases.

I chose bank vice presidents and fancy apartments as examples a moment ago because it is obvious that the race and gender of buyers and sellers are "fundamentally" irrelevant to the demand and supply. If race and gender have *any* effect at all, there is an "issue." I could have gone to the opposite extreme. If race and gender affect the demand and supply of sumo wrestlers and Tina Turner look-alikes, one would not be inclined to suspect that race or gender were problems in these instances. No doubt there are borderline cases where legitimate questions can arise: is there a race or gender issue here, or is the influence of race or gender on supply and demand reasonable in the sense that it is genuinely a matter of muscular strength or eye-hand coordination or resistance to panic or something else that is "technologically" relevant to the market and is, for whatever reason, correlated with race or gender? Those cases can be discussed one by one. There is no general rule. My own inclination is to be pretty cynical: if there is genuine doubt as to whether race or gender enters the supply-and-demand picture legitimately or illegitimately, I would at least tend to be suspicious.

Some economists believe that the income inequality correlated with race and gender is not a "problem" but just the inevitable fact of life in a competitive economy. I do not think this is a valid distinction. Disease and family violence and political corruption are facts of life in most societies, but that doesn't keep them from being problems. Societies are what they are because many different institutions—legal, political, economic, and still other kinds—work the way they do. Some of those institutions would be very hard to change, but most of them can be influenced by policy, and sometimes even by understanding and publicity. It is certainly a mistake just to assume that such problems are necessarily permanent.

I believe that the large and persistent differences in the economic status of women and minorities is a problem for policy makers, since these differences arise from the normal workings of the U.S. economy and society. To understand these forces, we have to understand the way our economy grinds out its ordinary, daily results. If women are paid less than men for doing the same work, that is a consequence of the everyday operation of the labor market. If we want to learn how and why this happens and how it can be changed, we have to understand everything that happens in the labor market.

But there is a general lesson here for analytical economics. It is not enough to think that race or gender issues are undermining the anonymity or impersonality of market outcomes. Race and gender work through supply and demand (and so do all the other forces). It should always be possible to trace the route through which prejudice or discrimination affect the demand for something or the supply of the same thing, and thus its market price, and the quantity actually bought and sold. Without this link, nothing can be settled. With it, we are on firm analytical ground.

This sounds more straightforward than it is. Causal chains in economics are often several links long, and it can be misleading to stop too soon. It is not so hard to work out whether women or members of particular ethnic groups are denied access to credit or to certain jobs even when they meet the financial or education criteria that seem appropriate to the loan or to the job. (I mean

it is not conceptually difficult; actually finding data suitable for the task may be difficult indeed.)

There is a more subtle point, however. Economists and other scholars may get into the habit of analyzing the labor market or the housing market in terms of averages. They may not think about inequalities, or may prefer to imagine that most inequalities reflect random differences rather than the systematic working of market institutions. They may get into the habit of adopting assumptions that seem to give pretty good answers about averages but are quite incompatible with the persistence of systematic inequalities. These assumptions are just wrong. They are not wrong when it comes to particular topics; they are wrong in general. My guess is that most of the time those inappropriate assumptions will be found to give biased answers even about averages.

But what practical consequences follow for public policy? Would it be a good idea to force or subsidize lenders to provide credit for women who fall below the "objective" cutoff? Or would it be better not to interfere in the credit market, which is functioning anonymously, after all, and to focus entirely on eliminating discrimination in the labor market? Nature would then take its course. And suppose nature required a generation to take its course? This is the dilemma of affirmative action. I am not about to settle the public policy question, which may depend on noneconomic factors as well as the narrowly economic question of the functioning of markets. The point is rather to emphasize the importance of tracing the influence of race and gender on supply and demand, both for analysis and for policy.

This line of thought suggests a further conclusion about the practice of economics. Because race and gender can influence market outcomes in subtle and indirect ways, they are easily ignored. Economic events ranging from occupational choice to business-cycle fluctuations can be described and analyzed without any reference to gender or ethnic differences. That omission has two negative consequences. At the most superficial level, it is descriptively false, simply because it ignores facts that are important to the people involved and intrinsic to the workings of the economy. At a slightly deeper level, it is analytically misleading, because it leaves out of the account a whole set of influences on demand and supply, and provides at best a partial understanding of market outcomes.

A more complete account would be not only fairer economics but better economics. It would be a lot truer to life in the United States in the 1990s if we saw clearly the many ways that race and gender help to determine market outcomes. That would be a first step toward equity.

Sometimes the question of how best to increase economic equity for women and members of minority groups is posed as a question of *either* government intervention *or* market competition. This is a false dichotomy. Sometimes market forces may work against discrimination or disadvantage, but sometimes they will not. Government intervention may be required, but there is a lot of experience to suggest that direct intervention, attempts to change behavior by command, work badly, even perversely. Obviously some forms of behavior are so wrong that they should simply be forbidden. But if we think of disadvantage and inequality as arising through the normal working of the market system, then one effective form of intervention will often be to operate *through* the market, by changing the previous rules of the game.

This approach may have political advantages too. In a market economy, reforms that are explicitly intended to make markets work fairly may often be politically acceptable when reforms through direct intervention will arouse resistance. Notice that this is not an argument against policy intervention, but an argument that policies that work through the market will often be more effective and more successful than others. Perhaps it needs to be said explicitly that some persistent inequalities may not be the results of direct or indirect discrimination built into the way markets operate. Those inequalities may have to be dealt with in some other way. But we will not know which they are unless we understand the normal working of the economy and the society at large.

Most of us, of course, think that simple discrimination is wrong. Complex and unintended discrimination is wrong too, but in order to correct it we need to understand how it comes about and whether apparently innocuous patterns of behavior are behind the things we observe. Economics does provide much of this understanding. Why then is it so hard to eliminate discrimination? There are probably many reasons. Some people profit from discrimination; they would not be glad to see it go. Besides, the economy is a very complicated piece of machinery. It is not easy to see exactly how it produces the results it does. For the same reason, policies often have consequences that were not intended when they were adopted. Finally, most members of the majority, who do not profit perceptibly by the existence of inequalities and discrimination, are fully preoccupied with keeping their own heads above the water, trying to get ahead, or merely surviving. They may not be prepared to spend a lot of effort or accept a lot of uncertainty to make changes in a familiar system. In some moods, I think the chances to make further progress are pretty bleak. In other moods, however, I am amazed that we have made as much progress as we have.

2

Racial Inequality in the American Economy Today

Glen Loury

One important measure of the health of an economy is the degree of inequality in its distribution of income. Although experts do not agree about what constitutes an ideal distribution, most people acknowledge that too much inequality is unjust, inefficient (since the potential productivity of the disadvantaged is impaired by their lack of resources), and threatening to the political stability on which everyone's prosperity depends. Understanding the nature and causes of inequality is therefore among the most important tasks of economics.

Because of the peculiarities of American history, racial inequality between blacks and whites has a particular significance in our society. That history, directly stated, involved chattel slavery, and after that the adoption of a thoroughgoing social caste system that for centuries kept blacks at the margins, and bottom, of the nation's economic life. A half-century ago, the Swedish economist Gunnar Myrdal surveyed the status of blacks in his classic study *An American Dilemma*. It is sobering to reread that work today. Myrdal graphically revealed the material consequences of racial caste exclusion in this study, as they played themselves out in the lives of black Americans. Poverty was the state of the vast majority of black families; the primary occupations were farm laborer for men and domestic servant for women; malnourishment was commonplace; participation in the professions was very limited; political influence was virtually

nonexistent. Myrdal chronicled the widespread practice of racial discrimination in employment; education; housing; politics; the military; social intercourse; the provision of health care, public services, and amenities; and the like. He concluded that these conditions stood in stark contrast to the professed values and beliefs of most Americans, thus constituting a profound dilemma for the nation.

Things began to change in the decades following Myrdal's work. The civil rights movement remade the moral, legal, and political landscape. The Great Society ushered in sweeping programs of social and economic activism. The federal courts revolutionized constitutional jurisprudence by reinterpreting the meaning of the Reconstruction Amendments so as to move black Americans closer to an estate of genuinely equal citizenship. While there is plenty of dispute about just how much progress has occurred, it seems safe to say that two things are true: there has been enormous improvement, and there remain enormous problems.

Some current trends are very discouraging: sustained higher unemployment among blacks; falling labor force participation rates, especially among black men; the increasing number of black children being raised in single-parent households; the poor and deteriorating quality of public education in the large cities, where many blacks live; the growing problems of crime, violence, drugs

Professor Loury is professor of economics at Boston University. His critical analyses of issues such as affirmative action, social welfare, and civil rights policies have been noticed and discussed by opinion leaders in business, politics, and the legal community.

Glen Loury (Boston University Photo Services)

economists consider how investments in education and other forms of human capital might result in differences between the groups in the skills that workers bring to the labor market. Both supply and demand factors seem to have a role in accounting for inequality between blacks and whites in the United States, but the relative importance of the two factors has been changing over time.

Studies suggest (although not without some exceptions) that demand-side factors have declined significantly in importance. Economic discrimination (different pay for the same work, or refusal to hire qualified blacks for available jobs), while it still exists, seems less important today than it was twenty years ago, and is certainly far less important than it was forty years ago, in accounting for the gap between black and white wage earners. But there have been other trends that are much less encouraging. The unemployment rate among black workers is twice as great as it is among whites. This difference has remained stable, or worsened, since the 1960s. Moreover, the labor force participation rates of black men have declined much more rapidly than those of white men in the last quarter-century. As a consequence, blacks are more sensitive to cyclical swings in the macroeconomy. The income difference between black and white households tends to grow during an economic downturn.

Another area of concern is the stability of families and the living conditions of children. Over 60 percent of black children did not live in households with both parents present in 1988, as compared with just over 20 percent of white children. These numbers for both races have approximately doubled since 1960, although the scale of the phenomenon is vastly greater among blacks. About two-thirds of the black children living in single-parent households are poor. Among black women ages fifteen to forty-four, fewer than three in ten were married with a spouse present in 1988, and nearly 60 percent of men in the same age range reported that year that they had never been married. Family life has changed dramatically among blacks since 1960. Of course this is

and other ills that are especially severe in urban black communities. On the other hand, there are some encouraging trends as well: over the long term we have witnessed rising relative earnings of fully employed black workers; the level of educational attainment in the black population has increased substantially in the last thirty years; there is a sizeable and growing black middle class, which barely existed a generation ago; blacks are present and influential in many professions that had been closed to them until recent years.

With social forces of this breadth at work, you may well ask what role economics might play in the analysis of racial inequality. Put in very simple terms, economics tries to explain racial earnings inequality by applying the concepts of supply and demand in the context of the labor market. On the demand side, economists worry about discrimination against blacks by employers who face black and white workers offering essentially the same quality of labor. On the supply side, true for the society as a whole, but the scope of these developments among blacks is much greater. The reasons for this are hotly disputed; nobody really knows why. But the implications for the poverty and impaired development of children are clearly substantial, and negative.

Now if one wants to address the racial inequality problem of our time, one must take seriously the trends that I have been discussing. While they do not involve "discrimination" as conventionally understood, and as conveniently analyzed by economic theorists, they nevertheless engage fundamentally our concerns about economic fairness and about economic efficiency. Unabated continuation of these trends offers the prospect that millions of Americans will be unable to fully participate in our economy and society. It is imperative, as a matter of justice and of national economic competitiveness, that these matters be addressed.

Yet the conventional way in which economists think about racial inequality—in terms of labor market discrimination—is not very helpful for understanding these trends. I believe that social discrimination, not in the labor market but in the choice of neighbors, friends, and associates, has become a very important cause of racial inequality in our time. It is evidenced by segregation of residential neighborhoods and public schools, and by the social isolation of the inner-city poor. Its effects are more likely to be seen on the supply side, rather than the demand side, of the labor market, due to the poorer skills that those from socially isolated communities bring to the competition for jobs. Unfortunately, this is not a problem to which economists have, as yet, given much attention.

That is, I would argue that today's racial inequality problem is not nearly so much a demand-side discrimination matter as it is a supply-side concern. It is not the result of a "no blacks need apply" mentality or a "lower black pay for the same work" attitude. Rather, it is more a matter of kids being poorly educated and having little work experience, few work skills, damaging peer influences, unstable family lives, and so on.

These matters deserve a more prominent place in economic analysis, because the full economic opportunity of any person does not just depend on his or her own income, but is also determined by the incomes of those with whom he or she is socially affiliated. The patterns of such social affiliation in our society are not arbitrary, but derive in part from ethnic and social class identity.

We are, of course, intimately familiar with these affiliational behaviors because we all engage in them daily. We choose our friends and neighbors, decide upon our business partners and professional associates, select the schools our children will attend, influence (to the extent we can) the prospective mates of our children, and, of course, choose our own mates. For the great majority of us, race, ethnicity, social class, and religion are factors involved in these discriminating judgments. The preservation of our distinct ethnic communities, once thought to be a parochial, even reactionary objective, has, in the wake of the black power movement, the "rise of the unmeltable ethnics," and the advent of multiculturalism, become the respectable (and sometimes government-aided) pursuit of pluralism.

Economists should begin to make use of the fact that societies are not simply amalgamations of individual agents pursuing exogenously determined goals. Rather, all societies, and therefore all economies, exhibit significant social segmentation. Various groups of individuals and families are tied together in various ways as a result of their historically derived commonalities of language, ethnicity, religion, culture, class, geography, etc. These networks of social affiliation among families and individuals, most often not the consequence of overt economic decisions, nevertheless exert a profound influence upon the allocation of resources, especially those important to the development of the productive capacities of human beings.

Think of the development of a skilled adult worker in analogy with a production process where the output, a skilled worker, is produced by inputs of education, parenting skills, acculturation, nutrition, and the

like. Some of these inputs are readily acquired through markets to which all agents
at least have access, although they may be
without the financial resources to acquire
them. But many of the relevant inputs cannot be obtained via such formal economic
transactions at all. Instead they become
available to the developing person only as
the by-products of noneconomic activities.
Parenting services, for example, are not
available for purchase on the market by a
developing person, but accrue as the consequence of the social relations that obtain
between a mother and a father. So the allocation of parenting services among the prospective workers in any generation is the indirect consequence of the social activities of
members of the preceding generation.

I recognize that this is an odd way to think
about human development, but it is very
natural for an economist, and useful too. For
thinking in this way underscores the critical
roles played by inalienable, nonmarketed,
social and cultural resources in the process
of human development and therefore in the
creation of economic inequality. The relevance of such factors is beyond doubt. *Whom*
you know affects *what* you come to know,
and what you *can do* with what you know.
The evidence for this maxim is incontrovertible; the importance of networks, contacts, social background, family connections,
and informal associations of all kinds has
been amply documented by students of social stratification.

Through such network ties flow important information about economic opportunities. They form the basis for nepotism,
which, in large ways and small, plays a role
in advancing for some and hindering for
others the attainment of economic success.
The status of sons varies systematically with
the occupation and education of fathers; the
"company you keep" as a youngster has been
shown to affect subsequent success in school
and at work. Attitudes, values, and beliefs of
central import for the development of economically relevant skills are shaped by the
milieu in which a youngster develops. Parents' time and effort, a family's traditions
and reputation, ethnic identity and loyalty,

adolescent peer groups and friendship networks, religious affiliations—these things influence how individuals develop and what
becomes of their God-given potential. They
determine to a large extent what an individual brings to the supply side of the labor
market.

Now consider all of these processes associated with naturally occurring social relationships among persons, which promote or
assist the acquisition of skills and traits valued in the marketplace. They constitute an
economic resource that I have called *social
capital*, an asset that may be as significant as
financial bequests in accounting for the
maintenance of inequality in our society, especially inequality between ethnic groups.
Because of historic racial discrimination,
black families on the average are endowed
with less social capital than are white families. Therefore black youngsters, again on
the average, begin life at a disadvantage in
the competition for success in the labor market, even if they encounter no discrimination of the conventional sort from employers. But it is social discrimination, of the sort
I have been describing, which is by and large
not illegal and which is universally practiced, that accounts for the perpetuation
from one generation to the next of this inequality of social capital resources.

Thus, I think it is especially important
that, when we talk about racial inequality
and discrimination, we broaden our definitions. This will also imply that we may need
to broaden the remedies that are considered
necessary. In the past, civil rights legislation
has been seen as a primary tool for fighting
discrimination. But, if I am right, it will
probably be much less important to pass another civil rights bill than to address directly
the limited resources available to low-income black children trapped in isolated
inner-city communities through enhanced
programs of education, health care, and the
like. In any case, viewed from the perspective that I advocate, one can see that the racial inequality problem is much more intractable than many economists would be
inclined to suggest.

3

Discrimination and Income Differences

June Ellenoff O'Neill

Most people would agree that income inequality is unjust when it is based on discrimination against particular groups because of their race, ethnicity, gender, or religion. The controversial issues are the extent to which discrimination is in fact an important source of inequality and the role that government should play in enforcing nondiscriminatory behavior.

Discrimination has existed throughout history and in all kinds of societies. Totalitarian regimes have the power to discriminate effectively against a group, and, not surprisingly, some of the most brutal examples of discrimination have been perpetrated by czars, dictators, and commissars. In a capitalist democracy, prejudice can also be translated into discrimination. But unlike the czar or the commissar, an entrepreneur in a free-market economy will face a penalty in the form of lower profits if he or she allows prejudice and preferences to take priority over worker productivity in making hiring and other employment decisions.

Suppose, for example, that a company employing computer programmers prefers male workers to equally skilled women workers and is willing to pay a wage premium to attract an all-male staff. If many firms share these preferences, the demand for male programmers will rise, pushing up men's wages. These firms will pay higher wages than they would if they were willing to hire women programmers, and as a result their money profits will be lowered. If a firm has very strong negative feelings about women programmers, it may be content to indulge its feelings and accept the lower profits. But the situation is not stable. Employers without a gender preference would have an incentive to enter the market hiring only women at a lower pay rate. With its lower labor costs, the nondiscriminating firm would produce its output at a lower cost and could sell it at a lower price, thus taking away business from the discriminating firms. The expansion of nondiscriminating firms would increase the demand for women programmers and eventually bid up their wages, a process that would narrow and potentially eliminate a discriminatory wage gap.

In theory then, prejudiced attitudes can result in employment discrimination against groups in competitive markets, but at the same time the profit motive provides a self-correcting mechanism, giving firms a strong incentive to reduce discriminatory behavior. Yet discrimination may persist, and the extent to which it does will be influenced by the degree and the pervasiveness of discriminatory attitudes and by the size of the penalty for discriminating.

So far I have stressed the penalty that arises naturally in the market in the form of reduced profits. But government has also played a major role in determining the effects of discrimination. For example, the federal civil rights legislation introduced in the 1960s significantly increased the penalty to firms for discriminating against minorities and women. Yet government actions at times have reversed the process, imposing penalties for nondiscrimination. Thus the

Professor O'Neill is professor of economics at Baruch College, City University of New York. She is former director of the Civil Rights Commission, Office of Research; former senior staff economist for the President's Council of Economic Advisors; and current director of the Center for the Study of Business and Government.

June Ellenoff O'Neill

Jim Crow laws and regulations, introduced by southern states and localities around the turn of the century, not only mandated the segregation of blacks and whites in the use of public services, but also limited the employment of blacks, actually barring blacks and whites from working under the same roof in certain industries. Moreover, by maintaining racially segregated schools with substantially poorer resources for black children, the southern states sharply limited the opportunities of blacks to acquire educational skills and created a powerful barrier to their advancement.

I suspect that a major force behind the Jim Crow laws governing employment was the fear of many white southerners that market forces would inevitably bring racial integration to the workplace as employers sought to take advantage of the large supply of black workers. It is noteworthy that al-most immediately following the passage of the Civil Rights Act in 1964, which in effect abolished Jim Crow, southern white employers greatly increased their employment of blacks in industries such as textile manufacturing.

HOW MUCH DOES DISCRIMINATION AFFECT INCOME?

Although it is now almost thirty years since passage of the Civil Rights Act, differences, sometimes of significant magnitude, still exist between the incomes of different ethnic and racial groups and between men and women. But it is extremely difficult to unravel the role that labor market discrimination plays in these differentials, because groups also differ significantly in their work-related skills and other factors that influence their productivity and therefore their earnings.

A significant proportion of Hispanics, for example, are recent immigrants with relatively little schooling. About 30 percent of Hispanic men in the U.S. labor force have not gone beyond the eighth grade of school, while only 6 percent of all white male workers have such little schooling. These differences in education appear to account for about 40 percent of the difference in earnings between Hispanics and non-Hispanic white men. The differential may be accounted for, partly or wholly, by productivity differences related to being an immigrant and lacking the kind of knowledge that comes with long-term familiarity with a country. Particularly important is the ability to speak English fluently. In 1980, the vast majority of adults who had migrated from Mexico over the past ten years reported that they could not speak English well or at all. Moreover, even second and later generations of Hispanics continue to speak Spanish at home and, more pertinent for their assimilation in U.S. labor markets, tend to remain less fluent in English than other groups. Of course persons of Hispanic origin are not a single, homogeneous group. Those from Cuba, for example, have considerably higher educational attainment and earnings than those from Mexico. The length of time it takes to adapt to U.S. labor markets may then depend a great deal on specific cultural traditions and other background characteristics.

Asians are also a large population of recent immigrants to the United States. And they have experienced considerable overt discrimination over the years, including government restrictions on their mobility (for example, the Chinese Exclusion Act of 1882, which specifically curtailed the immigration of Chinese laborers, and the internment of Japanese Americans in World War II). Even today, Asians in America are subject to racially motivated acts of violence. Yet Asians, on average, actually earn more than whites. However, they also have more education. When Asian and white workers with the same years of schooling are compared, the earnings of Asian men are found to be somewhat less than those of white men, but Asian women earn somewhat more than white women, even after controlling for education. Since these comparisons do not take into account the special language and other handicaps of recent Asian immigrants, one can only conclude that Asian groups are doing relatively well economically in the United States despite discrimination. This is a pattern followed by some other minorities, notably Jews, who seem to have earned more than other whites, even early in the century when anti-Semitism ran high, and Jews were openly excluded from certain firms and industries. In recent years, Jewish men have attained an extremely high level of education, but even after controlling for differences in schooling, geographic residence, and other factors, Jews are found to earn 16 percent more than non-Jewish whites.

Perhaps the most serious concerns about the effects of labor market discrimination on earnings relate to black males. Over the years, blacks have made substantial gains in income, narrowing the differential with whites. In 1940, the weekly earnings of black men were only 44 percent of the earnings of white men. This huge gap was due in part to a lack of skills and the concentration of blacks in the low-wage South, and in part to pervasive discrimination in hiring and employment, particularly in the South. The acquisition of education by blacks, the great migration of blacks from farm to city and from South to North, the economic development of the South, where half of blacks still live, and an erosion of discrimination all contributed to a narrowing in the wage gap since 1940. Nonetheless, black men still earn less than white men—about 20 percent less after taking account of differences in years of schooling completed.

However, years of schooling is a crude measure of academic competence. Cognitive skills are learned at home, and children with more educated parents are known to be better prepared before they enter school. Schools also vary in quality. Black children have been at a disadvantage on both counts. Not surprisingly, substantial differences between blacks and whites have been found in scores on tests measuring school achievement. For example, at the same age and schooling level, black men score well below white men on the Armed Forces Qualification Test (AFQT). My own research suggests that most of the racial differential in earnings between blacks and whites with the same educational level can be explained by the AFQT differential. After controlling for AFQT differentials by race, as well as by years of schooling and region, the earnings gap is virtually eliminated.

These results suggest that deprivation related to school, home, and neighborhood are more serious obstacles to the attainment of black-white equality in earnings than current labor market discrimination. These current problems of a disadvantaged background are undoubtedly a legacy of past discrimination, which created institutional barriers for blacks seldom faced by other groups, the most important of which may have been the deprivation of educational resources.

A significant gap in earnings also remains

between men and women. However, this gap has been shrinking rapidly over the past decade, as younger generations of women have entered the labor force with a stronger career orientation than their mothers and grandmothers before them. Women now are much more likely than past generations to continue working after they marry and bear children. And, expecting a career, women have dramatically changed the focus of their schooling. They not only have caught up to men in terms of years of college training, but they are much more likely than before to train for more highly paid jobs in business and the professions.

It is difficult to assess the extent to which labor market discrimination accounts for the gender gap in earnings, because data on career orientation are difficult to obtain. But I doubt whether discrimination was ever the dominant factor, since the underlying forces affecting a woman's decision to work, and the kind of work to do, were rooted in real economic contingencies affecting the family, not merely prejudice. Nonetheless, women in the past who chose to have full careers may well have found their paths filled with obstacles based on the customs and attitudes that society may have erected to maintain woman's role in the home. These attitudes have changed considerably as the economic realities of work in the home have changed—such as fewer children and more mechanical substitutes for housework—and as market work became a more highly paid alternative.

I draw several lessons from this brief review of group differentials in incomes. The first is that it is difficult to use income statistics to determine the extent of discrimination. Groups vary considerably with respect to their advantages and disadvantages—factors such as educational attainment and family background—and these factors may swamp the effects of discrimination on income. It is also possible that groups with greater resources, in terms of both human capital and physical capital, can avoid the effects of discrimination through segregation. Jews, for example, when barred from some economic activities, may have organized predominantly Jewish business structures that could then trade in more impersonal markets. Consumers are not likely to know who manufactured the goods that they buy.

The experience of blacks has been on a different plane than that of other groups. At the time of emancipation, most blacks lived in the poorest areas of the country—southern rural counties—where they received a small share of a very low level of educational resources. In addition, until the passage of the Civil Rights Act of 1964, blacks were second-class citizens under Jim Crow laws in the South. Despite these handicaps, blacks made considerable progress even before the Civil Rights Act, through immigration to the North, increases in schooling, and, likely, some decline in discrimination. Substantial progress was also made after the Civil Rights Act, in which the ending of institutionalized racism legislated by the act undoubtedly was an important factor.

Although it has not disappeared, discrimination appears to be less of a factor affecting incomes now than in the past. Generally speaking, I believe that the civil rights movement of the 1960s played a positive role. During the 1970s, however, antidiscrimination policy took a more militant and, in my opinion, a destructive turn as the policy known as affirmative action took center stage. At the federal level, the policy requires that firms holding federal contracts set numerical hiring goals for women and minorities with the threat of loss of their federal contracts if they fail to meet these targets. The setting of hiring goals requires the estimation of available pools of qualified minorities and women that in practice cannot be done with any precision. In consequence, the original standard of the Civil Rights Act, which made discriminatory behavior by employers illegal, has given way to a new standard based almost entirely on numerical results. A firm that does not have the proper composition of women and minorities can be found in violation, even if it has not engaged in any discriminatory act.

There are several things wrong with this new direction. One is that it is a serious departure from the principle of equal treatment under the law, which requires that a person's race, religion, national origin, or gender should not be the basis for preferential treatment. Affirmative action is intended to help disadvantaged groups overcome the effects of past oppression. But in violating principles of justice and individual freedom to enforce equality, it employs tactics that become reminiscent of a Maoist "cultural revolution." Moreover, it is not likely to be genuinely helpful. Some who obtain a job through affirmative action may be pleased. But if the job is viewed as undeserved, the process will generate ill will and divisiveness, and perhaps a loss of self-image on the part of the protected minority. Finally, affirmative action has misplaced the emphasis on what is really needed to improve economic status, and in so doing it has given young people the wrong message. In the long run, it is hard work and the acquisition of job skills that ensure success, not jumping ahead in the queue. A better direction for public policy is to provide the resources that are needed to acquire these skills.

4

Loaded Dice in the Labor Market: Racial Discrimination and Inequality

William Darity, Jr.

Discrimination as an economic phenomenon is pervasive and persistent. It occurs in all ethnically and racially heterogeneous societies. Its wellspring is the existence of hierarchy, which means that there are preferred niches in the occupational and social ladder, niches that groups will seek to secure and reserve disproportionately for members of their own. And its presence can be detected and documented in *direct* fashion across countries. The most persuasive evidence of discriminatory activities comes from audit studies performed in a variety of locations. Three examples will be mentioned in what follows.

In 1973 and 1974, the Gulbenkian Foundation funded an experimental study in Britain in which "white and Asian and West Indian testers [applied] for jobs and homes in person, by telephone and by letter in a set of carefully controlled situations, so that the success rate can be compared for the different racial groups."[1] This was a follow-up to a similar study, conducted in 1966 and 1967 using the correspondence method developed by Jowell and Prescott-Clarke that relied upon personal and telephone testing, that identified high levels of discriminatory

behavior toward Asians and West Indians in Britain.[2]

The technique was to pair professional actors, one always British by birth and white, the other either West Indian, Pakistani, or Greek. The pair, whose credentials were artificially designed to be similar, would simultaneously apply for jobs, home purchases, or rental accommodations. An instance of discrimination was defined as a case "where one tester was made an offer, while the other was made none, or one where a better offer was made to one tester than to the other."[3] Because there were some instances in which discrimination, based upon these criteria, occurred against the white British tester and in favor of the immigrant, whether white or nonwhite, the researchers developed a measure of "*net* discrimination against the immigrant ... [that was defined as] the gross number of cases in which there was discrimination against the immigrant *less* the number of cases in which there was discrimination against the white British tester."[4]

High levels of discrimination were found

---

[1]Neil McIntosh and David J. Smith, *The Extent of Racial Discrimination*, vol. 40, Broadsheet no. 547 (London: PEP, September 1974), p. 2.

[2]Roger Jowell and Patricia Prescott-Clarke "Racial Discrimination and White-Collar Workers in Britain," *Race*, vol. 11 (April 1970).

[3]McIntosh and Smith, *Discrimination*, p. 13.

[4]Ibid.

Professor Darity is Boshamer professor of economics at the University of North Carolina at Chapel Hill. He is former president of the National Economic Association, former vice-president of the Southern Economic Association, and current member of the executive committee of the American Economic Association.

against the immigrants, especially the Asians and West Indians, in all the cases. The net discrimination calculation indicated that in the case of unskilled jobs, Asians and West Indians would "face discrimination in at least one-third and perhaps as much as half of all cases."[5] Across all situations, net discrimination against Greek testers was 11 percent, while it was 24 percent for Asian and West Indian testers, suggesting that race played a role independent of immigrant status in affecting the responses to these minority groups in Britain.[6]

Direct evidence of discrimination against immigrants and nonwhites was also found in an Australian audit study done by Riach and Rich in the late 1980s.[7] And in the United States, the Urban Institute conducted an audit study of access to entry-level jobs in Chicago and Washington, D.C. Young black and white males (19–24 years of age) with manufactured identical résumés applied for the same jobs, with a total of 1,052 applications made. Black males were three times as likely as white males to face job bias.[8]

Indirect evidence of racial and ethnic discrimination also exists in abundance. Numerous studies have shown that earnings and employment status differentials persist across ascriptively different groups, after controlling for differences in productivity-linked characteristics. The residual gap in these studies has been taken as evidence of discrimination against the group that suffers the loss.

Representative of this type of study is Reynolds Farley's investigation of economic outcomes for fifty mutually exclusive racial/ethnic groups in the United States using the

William Darity, Jr. (Photo © 1993 M. McQuown)

1980 decennial census. Farley found that virtually all of the white ethnic minorities in his sample received a rate of return for their own characteristics (such as years of schooling) above the national average, while all of the nonwhite ethnic minorities in his sample faced negative rates of return for their own characteristics relative to the national average.[9]

---

[5]Ibid., p. 15.

[6]Ibid., p. 16.

[7]Peter Riach and Judith Rich, "Testing for Racial Discrimination in the Labour Market," *Cambridge Journal of Economics*, vol. 15, no. 1 (September 1991), pp. 239–56.

[8]The Urban Institute, *Confirming Evidence* (Washington, D.C.: The Urban Institute, forthcoming).

[9]Reynolds Farley, "Blacks, Hispanics and White Ethnic Groups: Are Blacks Uniquely Disadvantaged?" *American Economic Review*, vol. 80, no. 2 (May 1990), pp. 237–41.

Indirect evidence of this type is always subject to the charge that a factor that is relevant to gauging individual productivity that might differ systematically across groups has been omitted. June Ellenoff O'Neill has made the strongest case against studies like Farley's that offer indirect evidence of discrimination against blacks and other non-white minorities in the United States (see Reading 3). She argues that all black-white differences in earnings are due to human capital differences, contending that the omitted factors in previous studies are school achievement and school quality, which cannot be captured by the traditional years-of-schooling measure employed to calculate educational attainment. O'Neill uses scores on the Armed Forces Qualification Test (AFQT) as a proxy for school achievement and school quality; she proceeds to show that taking into account AFQT scores removes all unexplained differences in earnings by race.

It is my speculation that O'Neill's results are attributable to the fact that, for a number of reasons having little to do with ability and motivation, blacks tend to have lower scores on standardized tests than whites, whether the AFQT, the CAT [College Aptitude Test], the SAT [Scholastic Aptitude Test], or the GRE [Graduate Record Examination]. Had O'Neill had a sample that included any standardized test score with other characteristics of blacks and whites, the inclusion of any standardized test score in the analysis probably would have eliminated the unexplained portion of the racial earnings gap.

But the direct evidence of discrimination is incontrovertible. If we were to take O'Neill's results seriously, despite the persistence and universality of the phenomenon, we would have to conclude that discrimination exercises no significant effects on labor market outcomes. That would be a reassuring conclusion for proponents of orthodox/neoclassical economics, whose theoretical apparatus leads them to doubt that discrimination can persist in a world of profit-seeking entrepreneurs. But it would also be an instance where the logic of traditional theory is incompatible with and unable to explain a real world phenomenon.

In the real world many studies (several are described above) amply demonstrate the extent to which discrimination exists in a wide array of settings (including housing markets, job markets, credit markets and healthcare markets). Thus it may be hard to see why traditional economic analysis tries so hard to show that discrimination is not a significant social problem. To resolve this puzzle we need to take a close look at the principal objectives of this approach to economics.

In neoclassical analyses arguments which attempt to minimize the importance of discrimination proceed on two fronts. First, empirical work is done in support of the idea that even though discrimination may exist, discrimination does not play a critical role in explaining income inequality along racial, sexual or ethnic lines. Second, theoretical models are developed to show that discrimination and competition cannot coexist. Yet both approaches—the quantitative and the qualitative—are incompatible with and unable to explain real world phenomena. Thus, arguments "proving" that discrimination doesn't significantly explain the wide variances in income by race, sex and ethnicity are actually saying that markets work so well that everyone's income is fully accounted for by factors relating to their individual productivity. As a result there is no need to attempt to redistribute income or to realign markets so that they are fairer—instead policy makers, and those who have historically suffered most from discrimination, need only wait for markets to ride to the rescue. Similar results follow from the theoretical work produced by orthodox economists. Once again, competitive market forces will penalize discriminating firms to such an extent that they will wither away under price pressure emanating from the non-discriminating competitors. In short the conclusion—laissez faire—is guaranteed by the assumptions of the analysis.

Neoclassical theory starts from premises

which assure that market generated outcomes for all prices, quantities and the distribution of income embody the principles of free choice, efficiency (maximum output at minimum costs), and equity (incomes received by producers and households are symmetrically determined by supply and demand; i.e., there is no significant difference between profits and wages). It is no accident then that traditional economic theory reaches the conclusion that discrimination is not a problem—when and if markets are seen as essentially just then this fairness will of course be reflected in the outcomes which the market produces. In short, the empirical and theoretical work of neoclassical economics which dismisses discrimination as a significant force in the life of the economy is yet another defense of the American status quo as a social system in which there is an essential harmony of interests.

The inability of orthodox/neoclassical economics to construct a convincing explanation for the persistence of discrimination under competitive conditions has led a small group of researchers to chart a fresh investigation of both the theory of discrimination and the theory of competition. This new body of research is informed by the nontraditional premises of classical political economy and Marxist theory, rather than the premises of neoclassical economics. I would include in this group Rhonda Williams, Jeremiah Cotton, Patrick Mason, Howard Botwinick, and Steven Shulman.[10]

At the core of this work is the adoption of the classical, rather than the neoclassical, concept of competition and the notion that in hierarchical societies there is a "reason" (a rationale) for ethnic inclusion of one's own and exclusion of others. This body of

work views as artificial the distinction frequently made between in-market versus extra-market discrimination; traditional theory finds it hard to believe that the former can persist and places all weight on the latter, to the extent that it countenances the existence of discrimination. The new work views the dividing line between the two types of discrimination as murky, and sees both processes as interactive mechanisms for inclusion of one's own and exclusion of others.

As long as the structure of the social ladder is highly unequal, there will be a strong motivation to preserve the amenity-laden rungs of the ladder for your own tribe. Hence, general inequality lays the basis for the processes that generate racial inequality. From this perspective, unless and until general inequality is markedly reduced, one cannot expect discrimination to diminish into unimportance. Correspondingly, unless and until general inequality is markedly reduced, one cannot expect racial inequality to come to an end.

[10]See, e.g., William Darity, Jr., and Rhonda Williams, "Peddlers Forever? Culture, Competition and Discrimination," *American Economic Review*, vol. 75 (May 1985), pp. 256–61; Jeremiah Cotton, "Labor Markets and Racial Inequality," in William Darity, Jr. (ed.), *Labor Economics: Problems in Analyzing Labor Markets* (Norwell, Mass.: Kluwer Academic Publishers, 1993), pp. 183–208; Patrick Mason, "Inter-Industry Wage Differentials and African-American Employment: An Alternative Theory of Discrimination," *Cambridge Journal of Economics*, in press; Howard Botwinick, *Wage Differentials and the Competition of Capitals: A New Explanation for Inter- and Intra-Industry Wage Differentials Among Workers of Similar Skills* (Princeton: Princeton University Press, forthcoming); and Steven Shulman, "Racial Inequality and White Employment: An Interpretation and Test of the Bargaining Power Hypothesis," *The Review of Black Political Economy*, vol. 18, no. 3 (1990), pp. 5–20.

CHAPTER 2

Three Economic Paradigms

5

The Conservative/Free Market, the Liberal/ Imperfectionist, and the Radical/Exploitation Schools

Susan F. Feiner

THE CONSERVATIVE/FREE MARKET SCHOOL

The conservative/free market approach to economics is closely associated with, although not identical to, politically conservative analyses. Economists working within this perspective insist on an orthodox treatment of issues relating to the economic status of women and minorities. (This analytical framework is confined to the consideration of individual choices and their effects.) All people are seen as free, rational choosers, and consequently the observed economic outcomes of poverty, unemployment, or occupational segregation are seen as the result of choices. The individuals comprising various racial and ethnic groups, and women from all backgrounds, exist in an economic climate that is seen as essentially the same as that in which white males find themselves. As all people have unlimited wants yet live in a world of scarcity, it simply is not pos-

sible to distinguish (in an economically meaningful way) between doctors, lawyers, and business managers, on the one hand, and nurses, secretaries, and janitors, on the other. Each individual has simply chosen an occupation that most satisfies his or her tastes and preferences. This focus on individual behavior and choice makes it possible for conservative economists to take market-produced inequalities as an inevitable feature of society, one that is determined by innate qualities of all human nature.

Foremost in the orthodox handling of race and gender is the view that individuals are essentially separate, competitive atoms animated solely by the rational search for personal satisfaction. Springing directly from this is the view that competitive markets are the best possible social arrangement for allowing individuals to exercise their choices freely. (It is crucial to be sure you understand how the supply and demand curves found in your economics textbooks embody these free choices.) It follows then that the equilibrium prices and quantities established in the markets for final goods and services, as well as in the markets for factors of production, necessarily reflect the underlying voluntary actions of free, rational individuals. Any interference with market outcomes is a direct threat to freedom and a sure recipe for reducing economic efficiency.

Analysts operating from this perspective are deeply suspicious of programs that tamper with markets, and since they see the status of women and minorities as simply the result of so many individual choices, they see really no call for government intervention to improve the economic status of disadvantaged groups. Affirmative action, minimum wage, rent controls, prohibitions on discrimination by race and sex, publicly financed education, subsidized health care, low-income housing, and social security are seen as counterproductive for two reasons. First, they interfere with the market, which will distort prices. People will make the "wrong" choices, since the information transmitted by the market will be "wrong" (remember: prices are the signals that consumers and firms rely upon as they make decisions about the quantities to supply and demand).

Second, discrimination is seen as economically costly, and because it is of no benefit, it is destined to wither away. Firms that discriminate will have higher costs either because they have to pay higher wages to attract workers with the desired racial or sexual characteristics, or because they are willing to employ workers with lower productivity if they have the desired racial or sexual characteristics. Firms that discriminate will thus be less competitive, since their profits will be reduced relative to firms that do not discriminate. In other words, discrimination imposes monetary costs for which there are no corresponding monetary benefits. There is therefore no *economic* incentive to continue to discriminate. In this competitive world, the hunt for profits will eliminate discriminatory behavior.

On the other hand, conservative economists argue that policies designed to improve the economic status of women and minorities may be well intentioned but are misguided. Minimum wages will reduce the number of job opportunities for low-wage workers, thereby inhibiting the development of the labor market skills needed for advancement to better jobs. The use of tax dollars to support public schools limits individual choices, reduces incentives, and rewards inefficiency, because sending a child to private school involves two payments: a tax payment to the public school system that is not used and the tuition payment to the private school. This double payment reduces choices while minimizing the incentives for public schools to increase the quality of their outputs or to hold the line on costs. Policies like affirmative action interfere with productivity since those less qualified will receive preferential treatment.

In short, the orthodox school sees in the market forces of supply and demand the essential ingredients for individual freedom and happiness. Although conservatives disagree about the extent to which discrimination may in fact limit free choice, there is general agreement that competitive market forces will tend to reduce such impediments to individual advancement. As individuals from disadvantaged groups succeed, more upward mobility will occur.

At the same time, conservatives believe that even if discrimination is a serious problem, the government has no business meddling with people's attitudes. Since the main problems for members of minority groups and for women arise from their own lack of education, drive, poor behavior, or failure to respond to competitive incentives, any successful policy will simply try to correct these individual flaws. This point of view structures the conservative economic and social vision: to conduct a successful analysis of the economic status of women and minorities, one need look no further than the market and individual free choice. Constraints imposed by unequal relations of power, ties to community, class, race, or family, fall outside the vision of conservative economists. As you read the articles in each chapter, see if you can identify the way that conservative views of people and society enter the analysis as assumptions about the inevitability of economic relations.

THE LIBERAL/IMPERFECTIONIST SCHOOL

The liberal/imperfectionist approach to economics offers a different perspective on the causes of the secondary economic status of women and minorities than does the conservative view and puts forward different policy recommendations. One of the most important differences lies in the interpretation of the causes of individual behavior. Conservatives look to individuals and their free choices for the full explanation of why people live where they do, why they do (or don't) go to school, why they take jobs, and what kinds of jobs they take. Liberal analysts look beyond individual choices to include social structures and patterns of culture to determine why women and minorities are so susceptible to poverty and unemployment.

The liberal view has its roots in the moral outrage against the virulent racism that was so prevalent in the United States during the early part of this century. The eugenics movement (frequently called "scientific racism" by scholars today) explained the inferior socioeconomic status of immigrants, blacks, and women by referring to their genetic inferiority. The liberal view offers an alternative analysis. While acknowledging that undesirable traits are sometimes exhibited by members of disadvantaged groups, liberals argue that these traits are socially determined and that they can therefore be ameliorated by social policy.

If there is widespread belief that minorities or women are inferior, employers and educators will limit their access to both formal education and on-the-job training, essential ingredients for gainful, rewarding employment. This in turn will tend to lower the productivity of individuals in these groups and reinforce their assignment to low-skill, high-turnover jobs. As people in these groups recognize their lack of opportunity for advancement, this will produce bad work attitudes, habits, and behaviors that reinforce the tendency to hire them for relatively unskilled jobs. Then, if their skill levels remain low and if their adaptation to these conditions continues to be "dysfunctional," stereotypes will be further fueled and discrimination by employers and segregation in communities will increase. This process will strengthen the barriers to the social and economic advancement of women and minorities. Liberals believe that this cycle is much stronger than the countervailing market forces.

Analyses that proceed from these premises come to specific conclusions regarding the need for government programs aimed at breaking this negative cycle. First among the recommendations is education. It is considered to be very important to provide excellent education to members of the discriminated groups in order to improve their labor market skills and make it possible for them to get jobs with advancement potential. But education aimed at reducing bigotry is seen as essential too; since everyone's opinions are shaped by society, government has a responsibility to try to correct misperceptions derived from ignorance. In addition to education, liberals advocate government action to prohibit discriminatory behavior.

"Imperfectionist" is coupled with "liberal" here because a large part of this analysis concerns inadvertent discrimination stemming from structural changes in the economy and the society. In other words, change in the real-world economic structure of society is never as smooth and perfect as suggested by textbook models. One example illustrates this logic. Changes in mass production and transportation technologies since World War II encouraged firms to relocate from the central urban areas (where railroad and shipping services had been efficiently located) to the outer suburbs, which have easier access to interstate truck traffic. This reduced the incomes earned and the dollars spent in the center city, which helped create persistent urban unemployment. As incomes fell, it became harder and harder for cities to raise enough taxes to pay for decent schools. As urban education deteriorated, the skills of the emerging workers suffered, which made their unemployment or underemployment inevitable. Informal information about job opportunities became even more scarce, thus further exacerbating problems of joblessness.

Liberal/imperfectionists advocate government policies to help people cope with such changes. Some of the types of programs advocated are increased production of low-cost housing closer to entry-level jobs; enhanced educational services for inner-city residents; more federal funding for education; and improved communication about jobs, education, and housing to residents of the areas where such information is most needed.

In the chapters that follow, many of the articles are written from the liberal/imperfectionist perspective. As you read, you should identify the liberal assessment of the costs and benefits of discrimination and segregation, since the idea that they have no real beneficiaries is a belief that liberals share with conservatives. You should also pay careful attention to the ways that liberal/imperfectionists link the behaviors of disadvantaged groups to broad trends within the society. The concept that structural changes in the economy are not the result of choices made by those most adversely affected by such changes is also important in the radical/exploitation school.

THE RADICAL/EXPLOITATION SCHOOL

The radical/exploitation approach to economic analysis is least familiar to Americans. One of the conclusions reached by scholars and activists working within this tradition is that the U.S. economy thrives upon and nurtures racial and sexual discrimination. Because discrimination is seen as "beneficial" to the continuation of the existing system of economic, social, and political power, eradicating racial and sexual discrimination and inequality would require a

thoroughgoing change in the social structure. Radical economists argue that racial and ethnic groups, men and women, working classes and owning classes, have different relationships to the sources of economic prosperity, political power, and cultural legitimacy. These different social relationships will powerfully influence political and economic perspectives.

A fundamental part of this analysis includes the proposition that the realms of politics and culture are not outside the legitimate scope of inquiry for economists. Following the general mode of argument first developed by Karl Marx, radical economists (also known as "political economists") in the United States today typically believe that economic domination and control shapes and is shaped by attempts to dominate and control political and cultural institutions as well. When thinking about the economic status of women and minorities, proponents of the radical/exploitation approach always examine the extent of political power wielded by each of these groups as well as the extent to which cultural norms for their behaviors reinforce the prevailing distribution of economic power. These themes can be woven together to produce an interesting explanation of the socioeconomic positions defined by race, gender, ethnicity, and class in the U.S. economy.

One of the enduring contributions of Marxian economic theory is the notion that business cycles are a necessary part of any capitalist system. Capitalist economies experience periodic episodes of expansion (boom) and contraction (recession) because there are many tensions in market economies between, for example, consumption and production, wages and profits, and capital goods and consumer goods. At the same time, there is no conscious coordinating mechanism for aligning economic activities. Sooner or later, every expansion comes to an end. In the contraction phase of the cycle, much human suffering is caused as a direct result of unemployment. Rising cynicism and despair are also associated with falling standards of living. Radical economists recognize conflicts of economic interest as inherent in capitalism (and in other economic systems too). The participants in the economic system—workers and bosses; men, women, and children; majority race and subordinated races—do not equally share in either the fruits of expansion or the pains of economic contractions. Race, ethnicity, class, and sex are understood as ways to allocate the benefits and costs of capitalism's instability. For radical economists, this instability and the mechanisms for allocating its costs and benefits can be explained by reference to the need for low wages, which are the key to more and larger profits.

All economists agree that profitability is the first necessity for capitalist firms. Radical economists argue that in capitalist firms profits arise because the firms do not pay workers for all the work they do—the concept of "surplus labor" or "surplus labor time." This is easily illustrated by reference to the slave-based economic system of the antebellum South. Virtually all marketed goods and services were produced by African Americans, who received only the barest necessities of clothing, shelter, and food. The rest of what was produced belonged to their white exploiters, even though they (as the *owners* of other people) did not contribute to the production of goods and services. Radical exploitation analysis always focuses on such asymmetries in social relationships.

The first asymmetry we note in the class relationships that define the pre–Civil War South is the distinction between doing—an act of physical or mental exertion—and owning, which involves no action. The next asymmetry follows from the first: the share of output received by the slave owners came from the "surplus labor" performed by African Americans, since this output represented the fruit of labor above and beyond that necessary to reproduce the people who did the work. To clarify this central idea, look at the opposite case: imagine what would have happened if the slave population in the antebellum South first set aside enough raw materials (seed, livestock, tools, etc.) to continue production and then consumed everything else, could the owners of the slaves survive?

Radicals make a similar argument regarding the source of capitalist profits. Workers, whether taken in the aggregate or individually, perform more labor than is necessary to produce the goods and services they need to achieve their society's "normal" standard of living. The calculation goes like this: first determine a society's *gross product* (this is a physical, not a dollar, measure), and subtract the portion that is needed to replace the worn-out tools and other means of production. The remaining *net product* is divided between the workers who produced it and all the members of society who did not produce it. The portion to the nonworkers is the *surplus product*, and it exists because the workers performed *surplus labor*. The portion to the producers is the *necessary product*—necessary for the workers' physical, material, and psychological sustenance. We can use these concepts to paint a preliminary picture of how racism and sexism benefit the capitalist system.

From the end of the Civil War to 1900, the organization of production in the United States changed in many ways. You are probably familiar with the term "robber baron," which refers to the major industrial capitalists of that era. Under their control, firms became larger and more impersonal. Steam power was introduced in virtually all lines of manufacturing, thereby ushering in mass production techniques for almost all commodities that were widely bought and sold. Although many workers had very little bargaining power because both the federal and state governments put severe restrictions on the scope of labor organizations, some privileged workers with high skill levels were able to use the exclusionary practices of craft unionism to protect their wages. These workers secured for themselves a "family wage" when they forced their bosses to pay them a real wage high enough to allow one wage worker to earn enough to support several nonworkers (wife and children). The first to earn the family wage were Anglo American workers, not the new immigrants from southern and eastern Europe. Earning a family wage rapidly became an important economic and cultural status symbol that was easily displayed by having a dependent wife and children outside the paid labor force.

This economic change had important political and cultural counterparts. Politically this period saw the beginning of protective legislation that limited the extent to which female and male workers could do the same jobs. This has had a long-term effect on the pattern of sex stratification in the labor market. In the South, Jim Crow laws were passed to prohibit integrated work spaces and enforce occupational segregation, thereby excluding people of color from the best jobs. On the cultural front, we see the emergence of the notion of the housewife. Social policy encouraged women to leave the paid labor force and "specialize" in caring.

African American, Hispanic American, Asian American, and Native American men almost never had access to jobs that paid a family wage. Nor did women. Frequently government "protective" legislation or union policies prevented women and non-white males from entering occupations that paid a family wage. Members of the ethnic groups from southern and eastern Europe were also excluded until the expansion of industrial unions during and after World War II. Surplus labor enters the picture when we understand that the high family wage secured by many white males occurred at the expense of nonwhite, nonmale workers. The family wage was, in effect, a way to transfer income derived from surplus labor from one group of workers to another, without reducing capitalists profits.

The groups that were excluded from the family wage system belonged to what radicals call the "reserve army of the unemployed." This term refers to the pool of workers whose standard of living is so precarious that they are virtually always ready and available to go to work regardless of work conditions or pay rate. This helps keep wages down and keeps workers divided along racial, ethnic, and sexual lines. The irony is this: as capitalists succeed in earning profits, industrial expansion is encouraged. As business expands, more workers must be

hired. Firms compete for workers, and wages start to rise. Once this happens, profits fall. In the face of falling profits, the expansion phase of the business cycle ends, recession sets in, and the conditions are ready again for recruiting the reserve army of the unemployed. The radical/exploitation school argues that if all workers were equally likely to fall victim to recession and unemployment, the system of production and power would be destabilized.

Thus in the United States, the historical presence of racial, ethnic, and sexual diversity has provided a unique way of allocating the social and economic benefits and costs of business cycles. It is obvious that men and women who are African American, Hispanic American, Asian American, or Native American, as well as women who are European American, are far more likely to be poor, unemployed, and underemployed than are males of European descent. This is a tremendously stabilizing fact, since those who suffer most acutely from bouts of economic instability are the least powerful politically, while those with relative economic security have a vested interest in perpetuating the very inequalities that are the precondition for their comparative economic success.

This situation is in marked contrast to that in other advanced industrial nations with far more homogeneous populations. In Western Europe, there has been a general movement since World War II to let the central government use activist policies, including income policies as well as the more traditional tools of monetary and fiscal policies, to disburse the effects of business cycles more equally. Radical economists do not believe that the current economic status of women and minorities in the United States is some vast conspiracy. It is rather the specific result of 200-plus years of this nation's history. As you read the essays in this book, try to identify historical arguments that link race, ethnicity, and gender to the broader fate of the economy. This is generally a reliable sign that a radical economist is at work.

CHAPTER 3

Women, Minorities, and the Recent Economic History of Inequality

6

Untouched by the Rising Tide

David M. Cutler and Lawrence F. Katz

This article compares the distribution of benefits from economic growth of the 1980s with the distribution during other periods. The authors begin with an analysis of the historical relationship between economic expansion and the decline in both the incidence of poverty and the degree of income inequality. Then the roles of the structure of families and of income distribution are assessed to see how well these factors explain the condition of the poor in the 1980s. The authors conclude that monetary and fiscal policies to increase the aggregate demand for labor will no longer be an effective antipoverty policy. New policies must instead directly counter urban deterioration and include provisions for well-designed transfer programs.

Reprinted by permission of *The Brookings Review*. Winter 1992. pp. 41–45.

Exercises to Guide Your Reading

1. Define the following terms: economic growth; correlation; trickle-down economics; income distribution by quintile; income shares to capital and labor; real wages; primary and secondary earners; unearned income; monetary and fiscal policies; aggregate demand for labor; and in-kind transfer.
2. Use the data in Tables 1 and 2 to discuss the difference between the 1960s and the 1980s.
3. Predict what will happen when labor demand shifts away from young and unskilled workers.
4. Use words and graphs to explain how macroeconomic policies can increase the aggregate demand for labor.

Economic growth has traditionally been seen as the dominant source of gains for the poor. From World War II through the early 1980s, economic data showed a positive and steady correlation between overall economic growth and the well-being of the poor.

During the 1960s, for example, rapid economic growth and a relatively stable economy dramatically reduced the share of Americans living in poverty by 10.3 percentage points. During the 1970s, a period of unstable economic conditions and slow growth, poverty rates were relatively constant. Although the recession of the early 1980s saw an almost 4 percentage point increase in poverty, an analyst in 1983 would have expected six years of sustained economic expansion to lead to another surge in the well-being of the nation's disadvantaged.

The anticipated benefits for the poor failed to materialize fully. The overall poverty rate in 1989, after the record-breaking six-year expansion, was 12.8 percent, 1.1 percentage points higher than it was in 1979 and 1.7 points higher than the all-time low of 11.1 percent reached in 1973 (see figure 1). If the "trickle-down" mechanism that had worked so well during the 1960s had been as effective in the 1980s, poverty would have fallen below 11 percent by 1989.

The story is equally true of overall family income inequality—again, the 1980s are a sharp break with historical experience. Ordinarily during an expansion, the share of income going to families in the lower half of the income range increases at the expense of those in the upper half. During the decade of the 1960s, for example, the share of total income received by the lowest quintile grew about 1 percentage point, with a similar drop in income shares among the highest quintile. If historical relations had held up through the 1980s, the 1983–89 period would have seen roughly similar changes in income distribution. In fact, the income share of the lowest quintile actually fell 0.1 percentage point, while the share of the highest quintile grew almost 2 percentage points (see Figures 2 and 3). Income inequality increased substantially in the 1980s, belying more than 30 years of macroeconomic experience.

For both the poverty rate and the income shares, these divergences are getting larger over time. The gap between predicted and actual income shares has widened every year since 1983, as has the gap between predicted and actual poverty rates.

WHY DID IT HAPPEN?

Analysts are now busy trying to explain why the 1980s expansion conferred so few benefits on its traditional recipients. One explanation is the shift in the population from traditional two-parent families into single-parent, particularly female-headed, families.

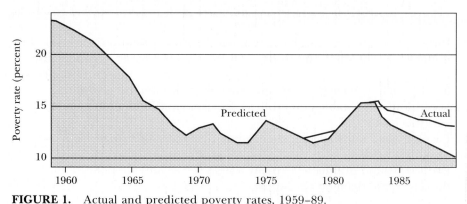

FIGURE 1. Actual and predicted poverty rates, 1959–89.

Source: Authors' calculation based on Current Population Survey and *Economic Report of the President*.

Note: Predicted poverty rates based on data through 1983.

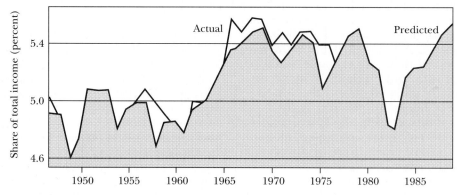

FIGURE 2. Actual and predicted income share, lowest quintile, 1947–89.

Source: Same as figure 1.

Note: Predicted income share based on data through 1983.

The shift is indeed large. In 1963, for example, 65 percent of Americans were in husband-wife families with children. By 1989 that figure had dropped below 45 percent. In 1963 only 5.7 percent of people were in families with a single parent and children; by 1989 the percentage had doubled. Because poverty rates are higher for single-parent families, shifts in the population toward these households will necessarily be associated with increases in poverty.

This change is not particularly important in explaining poverty trends of recent years, however. First, most of the change in family composition occurred in the 1970s, not the 1980s. While the increase in poverty rates in the 1970s was thus greater than macroeconomic conditions would warrant, this is much less true in the 1980s. Indeed, poverty reduction was sluggish for all family types in the 1980s. For married-couple families with children, for example, the poverty rate went from 7.0 percent to 7.6 percent between 1979 and 1989. We estimate that if

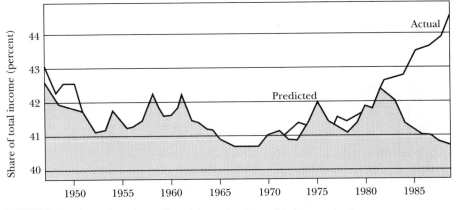

FIGURE 3. Actual and predicted income share, highest quintile, 1947–89.

Source: Same as figure 1.

Note: Predicted income share based on data through 1983.

family composition had remained unchanged since the 1960s, the increase in the poverty rate between 1979 and 1988 would have been smaller—0.7 percentage point, rather than the actual 1.1 percentage points. But still—and this is the puzzle—poverty would have worsened rather than improved.

CAPITAL INCOME

A second explanation for increased inequality in the 1980s and the failure of expansion to reduce poverty significantly is that the expansion conferred most of its benefits on capital rather than on labor. As Lawrence Mishel and David Frankel have put it, "a major reason for the unequal growth in family incomes is that, in recent years, a greater share of national income has been in the form of capital incomes (such as rent, dividends, interest payments, capital gains) and a smaller share has been earned as wages and salaries." It is true that capital incomes (particularly personal interest and dividend income) grew faster than wages and salaries from 1979 to 1989. But these statistics are incomplete on two counts. First, the increase in dividend and interest incomes does not mean that more of national income was paid

to capital. Appropriately measured, labor's share of income was constant or increased slightly in the 1980s. Rather, the increase in dividend and interest income reflects a shift within the corporate sector from undistributed profits (which do not show up in measured family incomes) to dividends (which do) and an increase in government interest payments. The first of these is a labeling change rather than an increase in economic disparity. The second is potentially a large change in economic resources, but without knowing who will bear the ultimate burden of debt reduction, it is difficult to determine the winners and losers. In any case, the effect of the increase in capital income is small.

WAGE INEQUALITY

A much more important explanation for family income inequality is increasing wage inequality. The real (inflation-adjusted) weekly wages of workers in the top tenth of the work force rose 5 percent from 1979 to 1988, while the wages of those in the bottom tenth fell 12 percent. Wage inequality increased along three primary dimensions. First, the return to education increased sub-

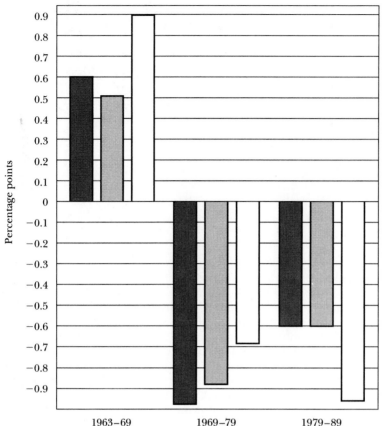

FIGURE 4.   Components of change in share of family income going to lowest quintile.

Source: *Current Population Survey.*

stantially, particularly for young workers. From 1979 to the late 1980s, the weekly earnings of young male college graduates increased by some 30 percent relative to those of young men with a high school education or less. Second, among less educated workers in particular, older workers did much better than younger workers. Third, there were sharp increases in wage dispersion within narrowly defined demographic groups.

Figure 4 shows the importance of the increasing inequality of the wage distribution to the income of the lowest quintile. We show the distribution of adjusted family in-come—family income scaled by the needs measure in current poverty guidelines. We divide family income into three compo-nents—earnings of the primary earner, earnings of the secondary earners, and un-earned income, primarily government trans-fers and capital income. As the figure shows, a narrowing of the distribution of primary-earner income increased the share of in-come going to the lowest quintile by 0.6 per-centage point from 1963 to 1969. But a wid-ening of the distribution of primary-earner income caused that share to fall in both the 1970s (1.0 point) and the 1980s (0.6 point). Wages of secondary earners did not change the lowest quintile's income share in 1979–89. Changes in nonlabor income exacerbated the trend for primary earners, with the income share of the lowest quintile falling another 0.4 point in 1979–89. Thus, while unearned income is important in accounting for increased family income inequality in the 1980s, the dominant source of the change in family income inequality is shifts in the distribution of primary-earner income.

IS THE RISE IN INEQUALITY AN ILLUSION?

Although government statistics on family income clearly suggest a deterioration in the standard of living for a large share of American families over the past two decades, some researchers have begun to challenge these income statistics. One objection is that annual income fails to capture income received through in-kind transfers. This is important for the measurement of poverty since families with low money incomes often receive a variety of in-kind transfers including food stamps, housing assistance, and medicaid. Many of these programs expanded rapidly in the 1970s, suggesting that official poverty rates overstate the level and exaggerate increases in poverty during the 1970s. But since these programs did not expand greatly during the 1980s, it is unlikely that imputing a value to in-kind transfers would have any significant effect on poverty trends during the past decade. In fact, according to the U.S. Bureau of the Census, while the official poverty rate increased by 1.8 percentage points (from 11.7 percent to 13.5 percent) from 1979 to 1987, a poverty rate adjusted for the value of in-kind and noncash transfers increased by a slightly larger 2.1 percentage points (from 8.9 percent to 11.0 percent) over the same period.

A second argument, suggested by Christopher Jencks and Susan Mayer among others, is that more direct measures of material well-being, such as crowding, adequacy of housing, and access to medical care, indicate that living standards continued to improve over the 1970s. Mayer and Jencks argue, using this evidence, that income may be a poor measure of trends in economic well-being over the past two decades. Indeed, Dale Jorgenson has suggested that economic welfare is more appropriately measured by consumption than by income, and Jorgenson and Dan Slesnick have argued that income-based measures of poverty are "severely biased" measures of the level and trend of poverty.

In table 1 we show income- and consumption-based poverty measures. In both cases we employ a poverty line updated using the Personal Consumption Expenditure deflator rather than the standard Consumer Price Index. We also use the needs level in the current poverty scale in all years.

At any particular point in time, income- and consumption-based measures provide quite different pictures of poverty. As table 1 shows, the poverty rate measured using family consumption is substantially lower than is the poverty rate measured by income. Such findings are consistent with the view that lifetime resources (measured by consumption) are more equally distributed than are resources at particular times (measured by annual income).

But as the table also makes clear, trends in economic well-being appear quite similar regardless of whether resources are measured by income or by consumption. Poverty rates calculated using both income and consumption fell sharply from the early 1960s to the early 1970s, by 8.4 percentage points in the case of income and 6.8 points in the case of consumption. Both measures have increased since the early 1970s, however. Income-based poverty rose 0.4 percentage point from 1972–73 to 1988, and consumption-based poverty rose 2.4 points.

Table 1 also shows one other disturbing trend. Almost all of the recent success in the war on poverty has been in poverty rates for the elderly. According to both income and consumption measures, the poverty rate for the elderly was lower in 1988 than in 1980. For working age adults, and particularly

TABLE 1   Poverty Rates and Resource Shares as Measured by Income and Consumption.

	Income-Based Measures				
Group	*1963*	*1972–1973*	*1980*	*1984*	*1988*
Poverty Rates					
All	20.0%	11.6%	11.9%	12.6%	12.0%
Adults, 18–64	15.2	8.7	9.2	10.3	9.6
Elderly, 65+	32.6	17.3	13.6	10.0	10.2
Children, 0–17	23.5	15.0	16.9	19.1	18.3
Quintile Shares					
Lowest	4.9%	5.3%	5.0%	4.4%	4.4%
Highest	43.1	42.6	41.5	44.1	44.1
	Consumption-Based Measures				
Group	*1960–61*	*1972–73*	*1980*	*1984*	*1988*
Poverty Rates					
All	13.0%	6.2%	7.5%	8.7%	8.6%
Adults, 18–64	9.5	4.8	6.0	7.2	6.7
Elderly, 65+	13.6	7.0	6.2	5.4	3.8
Children, 0–17	17.9	8.9	11.1	13.5	15.2
Quintile Shares					
Lowest	8.1%	9.0%	8.2%	7.5%	7.3%
Highest	36.6	35.1	36.2	37.4	37.5

Source: Authors' calculations from the Current Population Survey (for income) and the Consumer Expenditure Surveys (for consumption).

children, however, the reverse is true. Both groups had substantial increases in poverty in the 1980s. Indeed, the consumption data suggest that poverty in the United States is concentrated almost exclusively on those aged 64 and below, and particularly on children. Poverty rates for children are four times those for the elderly. The nonelderly population has also been the hardest to reach with income transfers, however.

The same is true for the share of income or consumption received by the lowest quintile of the distribution. The share of income to the poor fell by almost 1 percentage point from 1972–73 to 1988; the share of consumption fell more than 1.5 percentage points. The data send a very clear message: changes in income inequality are indicative of large and important changes in total resources. Both measures of economic hard-

ship suggest a deterioration at the lower end, even in the face of rapid macroeconomic expansion.

WHO WAS LEFT BEHIND IN THE 1980S?

Traditionally, economic expansions help the disadvantaged in two ways. First, increased labor demand creates jobs for the unemployed. Second, strong growth changes the nature of jobs available to workers. During expansions, low-wage workers can get higher-paying jobs than are available during economic downturns. But as table 2 shows, the gains traditionally conferred by expansions were largely absent during the 1980s. In the 1960s, economic gains were widespread. Young families (generally poorer)

TABLE 2 The Expansion of the 1960s and 1980s: Changes in Family Income.

| | 1988 Dollars | | | | | |
| | 1960s | | | 1980s | | |
Group	1963	1969	Annual Change	1983	1989	Annual Change
Age of Family Head						
Under 25	$ 8,561	$11,726	5.2%	$ 9,568	$ 9,834	0.5%
25–34	10,413	13,900	4.8	14,689	15,904	1.3
35–44	11,044	14,212	4.2	17,548	19,889	2.1
45–54	13,778	17,825	4.3	21,300	24,534	2.4
55–64	14,059	18,156	4.3	20,629	22,383	1.4
Education of Family Head						
Less than high school	8,984	11,055	3.5	10,345	10,309	−0.1
High school	12,068	15,268	3.9	16,011	17,250	1.2
College or more	17,077	22,053	4.3	26,546	30,269	2.2
Family Head Aged 25–34						
High school	10,824	13,864	4.1	13,452	14,486	1.2
College	14,476	19,628	5.1	22,420	26,550	2.8
Family Head Aged 45–54						
High school	15,376	19,131	3.6	20,772	22,747	1.5
College	22,120	25,784	2.6	31,270	36,731	2.7

Source: Authors' calculations using Current Population Survey.

did better than older families, and family income increased evenly at all education levels. Among older workers, the less educated did even better than the more educated. In the 1980s, the reverse was true. Young families, and particularly the less educated, fared much worse than older, more educated families. The adjusted income of families headed by individuals with fewer than 12 years of schooling, for example, fell more than 2 percent a year relative to families headed by a college graduate.

The economy of the 1980s is clearly different from that of the 1960s. Labor demand has shifted because of increased international trade competition, the decline of unions, and improved technology. Manufacturing employment grew during the 1960s and fell equally dramatically during the 1980s. Economists have tried to assess formally the extent to which industrial and occupational shifts can explain changes in the

wage structure in the 1980s, but such research is as yet inconclusive.

POLICY IMPLICATIONS

In many respects, the problems of sustained poverty and rising inequality are not macroeconomic in nature. Increased economic growth and job creation still boost the welfare of the poor, and policies to promote economic growth are clearly an important part of the war on poverty. But strong economic performance is not the panacea many claim it to be. The conventional wisdom that macroeconomic growth is the most important source of benefit to the poor and that industrial and occupational upgrading will necessarily boost young, less educated workers during an expansion is contradicted by the experience of the 1980s. Large and sustained shifts in labor demand away from the young and poor can more than offset improvements from increased job availability.

Indeed, the consequences of such labor demand shifts, if prolonged, may be even more severe than their effects on poverty or the distribution of income. William Julius Wilson, Richard Freeman, and others have argued that a decline in job availability for disadvantaged youths carries with it a deterioration in the social conditions in inner cities, an exodus of the middle class, and an increased incidence of behavior harmful to future earnings prospects—crime, drug use, dropping out of school, and teen childbearing. Such effects imply that even demand shifts that are reversed in several years may have long-term effects on living standards of the poor. Indeed, in the booming Boston labor market of 1989, the fraction of young blacks from poor neighborhoods who perceived more earnings potential in crime than in legitimate jobs had increased substantially from the late 1970s, a time of much greater unemployment and much weaker earnings prospects. The Boston experience suggests that strong labor markets alone may not stop social disintegration in poor neigh-borhoods. Policies designed to directly offset adverse neighborhood and peer influences and to keep young people in school may be far more important.

The 1980s also suggest that well-designed transfer policies may affect the welfare of the disadvantaged more than previously thought. The contrast between the experience of Canada and that of the United States is instructive. Between 1979 and 1986, pre-transfer poverty rates increased even more in Canada (1.9 percentage points) than in the United States (1.7 percentage points). As Maria Hanratty and Rebecca Blank document, however, differences in the generosity of the Canadian and U.S. government transfer payments led to very different changes in post-transfer measures of poverty. Post-transfer poverty actually fell 0.7 percentage point in Canada from 1979 to 1986, while it increased more than 2.6 points in the United States. The ultimate lesson of the 1980s may well be that renewed efforts to fashion appropriate transfer policies for the disadvantaged, both when economic performance is weak and when it is strong, can be an important component of the war on poverty.

Contrary to Popular Belief, the Economic Boom Did Trickle Down

Gary S. Becker

This article argues that African Americans, women, teenagers, and other less advantaged workers did benefit from the economic policies that Ronald Reagan used to create economic growth. The author points to a number of measures that support this conclusion and claims that these facts reveal the political and ideological biases of those who detract from the effects of Reagan's policies.

Exercises to Guide Your Reading

1. List the benefits experienced by African American workers.
2. Discuss the improvements in women's economic situation.
3. Give examples of different causes of the economic expansion of the 1980s.
4. Infer the author's position on government intervention in the economy.

It is widely believed that the Reagan years have been good for the middle class and the rich but not for the poor. This perception probably reflects the influence of David Stockman's famous accusation in *The Atlantic* magazine that supply-side economics should be seen as a Trojan horse in which the rich's taxes are reduced with the hope that the effects "trickle down" to the poor.

But Bureau of Labor Statistics and Census Department data for employment and earnings of blacks, teenagers, and women in 1976 (the last year of Gerald Ford's Administration), 1980 (the last year of Jimmy Carter's), and 1987 show these impressions of the record of the past eight years are largely mistaken.

Young and unskilled workers and minorities suffer much more from unemployment than older and skilled white workers. Yet not only is the overall unemployment rate down, from 7% at the end of the Carter years to 5.4% in July, but unemployment rates among blacks and teenagers are much lower than they were at the end of the Carter

Reprinted by permission of *Business Week*. September 19, 1988. p. 20.

Administration. For example, the unemployment rate for blacks, although still much too high, has declined to 11.4% from 14.3% in 1980.

Fast Rise. The trend in earnings of employed blacks has been less favorable. After rising sharply during the 1970s, wage rates of black males in the early 1980s fell compared with those of whites. However, earnings of black men have been rising faster during the past three years along with the sharp decline in black unemployment.

Unemployment rates could have declined because some of the unemployed withdrew from the labor force after becoming discouraged by the difficulty of finding jobs.

But the record shows the contrary: Employment rose while unemployment fell. From 1980 to July, 1988, 15 million more people got jobs, and the black employment-rate increase of 4.5 percentage points exceeds the 3.1 percentage point increase for all workers.

Is the decline in unemployment and the growth in employment due to a fall in real wages over this period, encouraging employers to hire cheaper workers? No, real hourly earnings rose slightly from 1980 to 1987. The connection between falling real earnings and a decline in unemployment is, in any event, hard to prove. From 1976 to 1980 unemployment remained high even though real earnings fell by more than 5%.

The Reagan Administration has been criticized by many women's groups, partly because it opposes the Equal Rights Amendment and comparable-worth laws. Paradoxically, female workers did very well during the past eight years. Unemployment rates of both white and black women declined, and the differential between the median earnings of full-time employed men and women fell, from 39 percentage points in 1980 to 32 points in 1987.

This strong improvement in the position of women is all the more remarkable since the gender wage gap remained fixed at about 40 percentage points from the late 1950s to the end of the 1970s, and many people believed the gap would never shrink without extensive government help.

Yet it did become a great deal smaller—under a government opposed to affirmative action. The full employment environment, the shift toward a service economy, increased training, and higher labor-force participation all contributed to women's economic advancement.

Some critics of the Reagan Administration concede the great expansion of jobs, but contend that the new jobs generally require little skill and pay badly. We are becoming a nation of hamburger grillers, the argument goes.

However, in an article in the winter issue of *The Public Interest*, Marvin Kosters of the American Enterprise Institute closely examines job creation in recent years and finds the distribution of jobs between high-, low-, and middle-paying levels remained approximately the same during the 1980s as it was in the decade before.

Contentious. Indeed, the economic growth of the Reagan years favored educated and skilled workers, not the less educated and unskilled. Current Population Survey data show that the gain in earnings from going to college has been much higher in recent years than during the 1970s.

Professors Kevin Murphy of the University of Chicago and Finis Welch of the University of California at Los Angeles show that a college education is worth more now than at any time in the past 30 years.

These findings indicate that for the most part, blacks, women, teenagers, and other less advantaged workers have participated fully in the economic boom of the past six years. This conclusion is based on the facts, and stands apart from the contentious and politically loaded issue of whether the boom was caused by tax cuts, budget deficits, the declining dollar, or whether Murphy and Welch are correct in their assessment that the changing importance and structure of exports and imports during the 1980s greatly affected the wages of women, blacks, college graduates, and young people.

Family Trends: What Implications for Family Policy?

Shirley L. Zimmerman

The author summarizes and describes changes in family patterns associated with marital status, births to unmarried women, women's labor force participation, and later life families. The relationships between these trends and economic well-being are then discussed. Particular attention is paid to the role of social policy in correcting race, gender, and class differences in the economic outcomes of families.

Exercises to Guide Your Reading

1. Describe relationships between the following: marital status and family households; racial or ethnic background and births to unmarried women; and labor force participation rates and marital status.
2. Identify and discuss the relationship between economic variables (like unemployment and financial instability), and marital stability.
3. Summarize the earnings differential between males and females, and discuss the consequences of this inequality for families supported by women.
4. Compare, contrast, and evaluate arguments for viewing trends in family status as important objects for social policy with arguments for regarding these trends as the outcome of individual choices and therefore not appropriate objects for social policy.

The meaning of current family trends is a subject about which there is considerable controversy. While some interpret such trends as threats to the family as traditionally understood, and by extension, to society itself (Glenn, 1991), others regard them as signaling the need for a paradigm shift from marriage and family to close relationships (Scanzoni, Polonko, and Teachman, 1989). Whether marriage and family are viewed as "folk concepts" or ideal types, Edwards (1991) argues that they represent distinct types of close relationships that continue to have meaning for the individual and the larger society. Regardless of legal status, Edwards (1991) advises, they are a means of cataloging and ordering a set of relationships about which there is some shared understanding in the larger society. Indeed, the courts and some employers have been conferring some of the rights and privileges associated with marriage and family on persons involved in family-like arrangements that have no legal status. Illustrative is the extension of health benefits and housing to unmarried partners, and more recently, guardianship rights to a lesbian partner of a 35-year-old woman left brain damaged and

Reprinted by permission of *Family Relations*. October 1992. pp. 423–29.

quadriplegic in a 1983 car accident; for all practical purposes, such rights are considered the same as those of a spouse.

These developments would seem to enlarge the concept of family, in keeping with Scanzoni et al.'s (1989) point concerning the range of personal relationships that traditional views of marriage and family tend to obscure. But they also are in keeping with Edwards' (1991) view as to the usefulness of family as a concept. With this in mind, this discussion examines selected family trends, those pertaining to marriage and divorce, women's participation in the labor force, unwed parenthood, and life expectancy in terms of what they might mean for family policy. Family policy which is concerned with the problems of families in relation to society (Zimmerman, 1988, 1992) is defined here as an agreed upon course of action with respect to the pursuit of individual and family well-being as a value and goal (Aldous and Dumon, 1990; Zimmerman, 1988, 1992). The question is: Do these trends represent problems that family policy can and should address, or do they merely reflect preferences as to how people choose to live their lives in the late 20th century, and therefore fall outside the purview of collective political choice? The discussion focuses primarily on the period between 1970 and 1988–89, taking a longer look backward from time to time for historical perspective. Although probably familiar to most readers, these trends are reported here as context for reviewing findings from selected research that bear on the trends so as to better assess whether they do in fact represent problems that have implications for family policy.

FAMILY TRENDS

Marital Status and Family Households. Despite differences as to the meaning of family trends, it is of interest to note that in 1990, families of all types—married-couple, female householder, and male householder families—constituted 71% of all households in the United States. Families are defined here as the Census Bureau defines them: a group of two or more persons related by birth, marriage, or adoption and residing together in a household. Included among its members is the householder, that is, the first adult member of the household listed on the census survey questionnaire. Prior to 1980, the husband was always considered the household head or householder in married-couple families. Although married-couple families represented a declining share of U.S. households in 1990, they constituted the largest share of households in this country (56%) and accounted for most of the nation's household population (69%) (U.S. Bureau of Census, 1991c) as compared to 74% in 1980 and 82% in 1970. The rate of growth in nonfamily households slowed at the same time by 50%, from 5.7% during the 1970s to 2.5% during the 1980s, as did the rate of growth in family households maintained by women, from 5.1% during the 1970s to 2.3% during the 1980s. This was not the case for unmarried cohabiting couples. Their numbers grew to 3 million in 1990, an increase of 80% over the previous decade (Barringer, 1991), cohabitation among persons 25–44 years of age increasing 15 fold between 1970 and 1988 (U.S. Bureau of Census, 1990).

A longer time frame provides a better historical perspective for viewing these data. Here, it is of interest to note that in 1940, 30% more of the population was single than in 1988; a smaller percentage was married, only 59.6% in contrast to 65% in 1988; about the same percentage was widowed (7.8%). Parenthetically, the percentage of widowed has remained more or less steady over time, approximately 8% in 1900, and a slightly larger proportion in 1970 (8.9%). The biggest change has occurred in the percentage of divorced persons in the population. In 1940 they constituted only 1% of the population but almost 8% in 1988, reflecting a long-term trend that could be discerned as early as 1900 (U.S. Bureau of Census, 1975). Between 1966 and 1976 the divorce rate doubled, from 2.5 to 5.0 per 1000 population in 1973 and then reached an all-time high of 5.3 in 1979 and again in 1981. Divorce rates declined during the mid-1980s and from 1988 to 1991 have hovered around 4.7 (National Center for Health Statistics, 1991a).

Trends in marital status vary for different groups. While the percentage of marrieds declined for all three groups—whites, blacks, Hispanics—between 1970 and 1988, the rate of decline was sharpest for blacks, 27% compared to 11% for whites and only 1% for Hispanics (U.S. Bureau of Census, 1990). Similarly, although the rate of increase in the percentage of divorced was almost the same for all three groups, more than doubling for each during this period, trends in singlehood among the three showed much more variation. While the percentage of single blacks increased a dramatic 66% and whites, 29%, the percentage of single Hispanics *decreased* 8% over this period.

Births to Unmarried Mothers. As to birthrates for unmarried women, these have increased as birthrates overall have declined. Since 1940 when the birthrate for unmarried women 15 to 44 years of age was 7.1 per 1000 unmarried women (U.S. Bureau of Census, 1975), the birthrate for unmarried mothers has more than quintupled. Between 1980 and 1987 alone, the percentage of births to unmarried women 15 to 44 years of age increased 33%, from 18.4% to 24.5% (U.S. Bureau of Census, 1990).

Over the years, however, patterns of unwed childbearing for black and white women have diverged. During the 1950s, the birthrate for unmarried white women increased 80%, from 3.6 in 1940 to 5.1 in 1950 and continued to increase during the 1960s, from 9.2 in 1960 to 13.9 in 1970. Then between 1971 and 1974, it declined a bit only to resume its upward course, reaching a high of 26.6 in 1988 (National Center for Health Statistics, 1990). Although the birthrate for unmarried black women also increased during the 1950s, doubling from 35.6 in 1950 to 71.2 in 1960, unlike the birthrate for unmarried white women, it declined during 1960s, from 98.3 in 1960 to 89.9 in 1970. Until 1976, it continued to decline, and then,

after 1980, it declined again to 76.8 in 1984 before it too took an upward turn. Nonetheless, between 1970 and 1988, when the trend in birthrates for unmarried white women was upward, the trend for unmarried black women was downward, 95.5 in 1970 and 88.9 in 1988. However, in 1989, birthrates increased for both groups of women, but more for white than black women, 10% and 5% respectively (National Center for Health Statistics, 1991b). Thus although differences in birthrates for unmarried white and black women are still considerable, the gap between them has narrowed from being almost 7 times wider in 1970 to being only 3 times wider in 1989.

Just as birthrates for unmarried women 15 to 44 years of age have increased, since 1970, they also have increased for unmarried teen girls 15 to 19 years of age, from 22.4 per 1000 unmarried girls in that age group to 27.6 in 1980 to 36.8 in 1988. By 1989, that rate increased to 40.6 (National Center for Health Statistics, 1991b). This same trend pertained to 18- to 19-year-old unmarried women whose birthrate in 1988 reached an all-time high of 52.7 only to increase to 57.4 in 1989 (National Center for Health Statistics, 1991b). Having said this, it is important to point out that relative to all births, the percentage of births to teen mothers declined by 20% between 1980 and 1988, from 15.6% to 12.6% (U.S. Bureau of Census, 1990). Whether this continues to hold in light of the more recent upward trends in birthrates for unmarried teens remains to be seen.

The Participation of Women in the Labor Force. The rates of labor force participation of women have steadily increased for all women, from 34.8% in 1960 to 55.9% in 1988, or by 61% (U.S. Bureau of Census, 1990). However, just as marital status varies among groups, the labor force participation of women varies with marital status. Although increasing at a faster rate for married women, actual participation rates are higher for divorced women, 71.5% in 1970 and 75.7% in 1988. This same pattern holds for married and divorced mothers of young children, the rate of increase being higher for married mothers, 30.3% in 1970 and 57.1% in 1988, although actual participation rates are higher for divorced mothers, 63.3% in 1970 and 70.1% in 1988.

Never-married mothers constitute the smallest proportion of working mothers, 53% in 1986, as contrasted with 60% for married mothers and 80% for divorced mothers (U.S. Department of Labor, 1987). In March 1986, their unemployment rate was almost 5 times higher than married mothers', 28.5% as contrasted with only 6.0% for the latter, and was appreciably higher for black than never-married white mothers, 34.4% and 19.3% respectively. For black mothers with children under age 3, the unemployment rate was about 50%. Never-married mothers tend to be younger than married mothers, 43% being younger than age 25 as contrasted with only 9% of the married mothers. Seventy percent had preschoolers as contrasted with only 49% of the married mothers. Over twice as many were high school dropouts as mothers who were married, 36% and 16% respectively, and whereas 18% of the married mothers had college degrees, only 5% of the single mothers did.

Later Life Families. The one trend that pertains universally to all of us is the increase in life expectancy. Increasing from 54.1 years in 1920 (U.S. Bureau of Census, 1975) to 75 years in 1988 (U.S. Bureau of Census, 1990), life expectancy at birth is projected to increase to 77 years by the year 2000 and to 78 years by the year 2010. Women, though, are projected to continue to outlive men by about 7 years and whites to outlive blacks by 3 to 4 years. As a result, the proportion of persons over 65 years of age in the population has increased 33% since 1960, from 9.3% to 10.5% in 1975 to 12.4% in 1988 (U.S. Bureau of Census, 1983, 1990), and by the year 2030, it is projected that 20% of the population will be 65 years of age and older. Thus, just as there were fewer widowers in 1988 than in 1970 and

1960, there also were fewer widows, a trend that can be expected to continue, given advances in medical technology. Nonetheless, whereas three fourths of all men 65 years and older were married with spouse present in 1986, only 38.3% of women 65 years and older were, attributable in part to the fact that women outlive men, and in part to the increased numbers of women over 65 who are divorced. Counting both widowed and divorced, the number of women 65 years and older living alone increased 22% between 1970 and 1986. Indeed, in 1985, the percentage of women 65 years and over who were divorced exceeded the percentage of 65-year-old divorced men, the opposite of 1980 and previous decades. The U.S. Bureau of Census (1990) estimates that by 1995, 60% of women 75 years and older will be living alone—and poor.

ANTECEDENTS AND CONSEQUENCES OF FAMILY TRENDS

Of what relevance are these trends for family policy? Do they constitute problems that ought to evoke some kind of policy response? Or do they merely represent the choices and preferences of diverse populations in a free society? Although answers to these questions would seem to depend on how these trends are perceived and defined, findings from selected research may help in this regard. Since space does not allow for a complete review of all of the research that could shed light on the antecedents and consequences of these trends, or their correlates, such a review must be partial at best. Nevertheless, it could be a basis for drawing some tentative conclusions as to their relevance for family policy.

Marriage and Divorce

With respect to marriage, for example, nationally representative polls would seem to confirm what many may hope—that marriage as an institution continues to be a satisfying option for most. In a Harris poll taken in 1987 (Harris and Associates, 1987), most respondents reported being very satisfied with their marriages, 85% saying they would marry their present spouses again. A Gallup poll taken in 1989 (Colasanto and Shriver, 1989) found a similar preponderance of respondents to be very satisfied with their marriages, 84%, although men expressed higher levels of satisfaction than women. Even among those who once had considered divorce but remained married, 93% were convinced they had made the right decision by staying together. Being a good wife and husband ranked highest as an important aspect of success in a 1991 Roper poll of 2,000 people (Hall, 1991).

Other evidence, however, is of a different sort. The U.S. General Social Surveys from 1972 to 1988 show a decline in the probability of attaining marital success in a first marriage, if at all (Glenn, 1991). Bumpass (1990) estimates that 56% of recent first marriages are likely to disrupt within 40 years of marriage. Also, responses to the Gallup poll (Colasanto and Shriver, 1989) were not as rosy as appears at first glance in that although most respondents reported being very satisfied with their marriages, when questioned further, many said they either had experienced or were experiencing a serious marital problem. Nearly 40% said that either they or their spouse had seriously considered leaving their partner at some point. Twenty percent said that in the last 6 months their marriage seemed bad at least half of the time. Particularly at risk were persons 35 to 54 years of age, 64% saying their marriages were marked by serious discord, marital instability for this age group being two-thirds higher than for those 55 years and older. Of those who decided to divorce, the overwhelming majority thought they had made the right decision. Despite the emotional strain associated with divorce, respondents rejected the notion that things would have been better for them if they had remained married. Of the divorced women who were interviewed in the survey, 55% said that it was their idea to separate; only

44% of the divorced men said it was their's. The latter findings were thought to be directly attributable to the generally lower levels of satisfaction and contentment that women experience in their marriages.

To help account for these findings, Glenn (1991) advanced such reasons as increased expectations of marriage, a breakdown in consensus concerning marital and gender roles, and a decline in the degree to which the ideal of permanence in marriage is held. Gallup poll respondents' accounts of their own divorces add greater specificity to these reasons: infidelity, alcohol and drug abuse, incompatibility, physical and emotional abuse, sexual incompatibility, and financial problems (Albrecht, Bahr, and Goodman, 1983; Kitson and Sussman, 1982). Reasons vary with gender and education (Colasanto and Shriver, 1989). College educated respondents cited incompatibility as a reason for divorce more frequently than noncollege educated respondents, the latter citing drug and alcohol problems more frequently than college educated respondents. Also while wives cited substance abuse more frequently than husbands as a reason for the divorces that they initiated, husbands cited infidelity more frequently than wives as a reason for the divorces that they initiated.

Conger et al.'s (1990) observations are relevant here. Like Bakke (1940), Conger et al. found that the risk of marital dissolution increases with increasing economic pressures. So does family disorganization and the risk of physical abuse and child neglect (Kadushin and Martin, 1981; Straus, Gelles, and Steinmetz, 1980), all of which are a part of the legacy of the Great Depression of the 1930s (Bakke, 1940; Elder, 1974) and the economic crises of the 1980s (Dooley and Catalano, 1988). As Liker and Elder (1983) explain, financial worries are likely to generate frustration, anger, and depression among family members which then may be manifested in family violence. Indeed, Conger et al. (1990) were able to show the processes by which economic conditions adversely affect marital interactions and stability in their study of 76 white middle-class couples.

South's (1985) time series analysis also speaks to the adverse effects of economic hard times on marriages and marital stability.

Such effects also evidenced themselves in the strong positive relationship that was found between states' unemployment and divorce rates (Zimmerman, 1991). Indeed, in 1985, the divorce gap widened between states with high and low unemployment rates. Although the unemployment rate in 1992 (7.3%) was not as high as in 1982 when it was 9.7%, the official unemployment rate is only a tip of the iceberg so to speak. It does not include people who need and want to work, but have become discouraged from actively seeking it. It also does not include people who in 1992 have been victims of massive layoffs in both the private and public sectors. High unemployment rates not only were strongly related to high divorce rates in 1985, but they also were indirectly related to high suicide rates via divorce rates: The higher states' unemployment rates, the higher their divorce rates and the higher their divorce rates, the higher their suicide rates (Zimmerman, 1987, 1990, 1992). Ahlburg and Schapiro (1982–83) estimated that 45% of the suicides of men between the ages of 45 and 64 years could be attributed to the loss of a job, each percentage increase in unemployment resulting in 320 additional suicides.

All of this seems to suggest that for couples to reap the benefits of marriage, circumstances must operate so as to favor it. Indeed, some very practical benefits seem to accrue from married life. Compared to others, married couples consistently seem to enjoy a higher overall sense of well-being. Marriage is associated with better physical health, higher levels of psychological well-being, and lower mortality for partners (Ross, Mirowsky, and Goldstein, 1990). Also, although the relationship between marital happiness and overall happiness may have weakened in recent years, the two continue to be strongly related (Glenn and Weaver, 1988), attributable Hughes and Gove (1981) and Umberson (1987) say, to the social support and stable, coherent, and regulated environment that marriage provides. Because of this, married persons are more likely than others to report that they have someone to whom they can turn for support and understanding in times of trouble (Ross et al., 1990).

Although applicable to men more than women (Zick and Smith, 1991), the social support that marriage provides also contributes to the health of partners by encouraging and reinforcing protective behaviors. Because women in general tend to use preventive and curative medical services more than men, this applies less to married women than to married men who are less likely than nonmarried men to engage in such risky health behaviors as smoking, drinking, and poor eating (Verbrugge, 1985; Wingard, 1984). Depression and anxiety are less prevalent among married women than widows, and the risk of illness is lower for married than divorced persons (Ader, Cohen, and Felton, 1990; Calabrese, Kling, and Gold, 1987).

The risk of mortality also is lower for married persons than others, which again is largely attributable to the social control and behavioral regulation inherent in marriage (Anson, 1989; Umberson, 1987). Death rates are lower for married than unmarried women (Bowling, 1987; Helsing, Moysen, and Comstock, 1981). For causes of death that have a large behavioral component, such as lung cancer, cirrhosis of the liver, suicide, and accidents, the ratio of nonmarried to married persons is especially high (Litwak and Messeri, 1989; Smith, Mercy, and Conn, 1988). The risk of mortality increases for men who are widowed, partly because of the loss of access to networks of social support previously maintained by their wives (Zick and Smith, 1991). Nonetheless, regardless of marital status and gender, the risk of mortality is higher for persons who are poor.

Marriage also is a factor in the economic well-being of partners, even when adjusting for age, minority and employment status, and education (Ross, 1989), although here the situation is more applicable to women than men (Bianchi and Spain, 1986; Cherlin, 1981). Because economic well-being has a large positive effect on health and mental health (Hollingshead and Redlich, 1964; Kessler, 1982; Kessler and Cleary, 1980; Pearlin, Lieberman, Menaghan, and Mullan, 1981), the positive effects of marriage on physical and mental health are thought to be partly economic in nature, just as life itself is, as shown above. In a similar fashion, couples in two-earner families and married women with higher incomes report higher levels of satisfaction than others ("Poll: Married Women's Lives," 1988). Thus, economic well-being is both antecedent to and a consequence of marital stability.

Because divorce is now such a widely shared experience, and not simply a period or cohort phenomenon of the baby boom generation (White, 1990), concern about its economic, social, and psychological implications for individuals and society has heightened (Kitson and Morgan, 1990). For many, the decision to divorce creates a period of dislocation and problematic functioning, as may be surmised from the strong positive relationship between states' divorce and suicide rates cited earlier (Zimmerman, 1990, 1992, in press). Also, with the advent of no-fault divorce, the economic consequences of divorce have changed (Weitzman, 1985). Financial settlements are now less advantageous to women. Alimony is not awarded as frequently, is of shorter duration when it is awarded, and assets and liabilities are divided more equally between spouses than was the case prior to no-fault divorce. Still, the proposition that no-fault divorce contributes to divorce is not supported by empirical evidence (Weitzman, 1985; Wright and Stetson, 1978), or by the long-term trends cited earlier. Nonetheless, White (1990) contends that no-fault divorce has undermined norms of lifetime obligation and the expectation that individuals will be rewarded for fulfilling normative roles.

Of particular concern is the decline in the economic well-being of children following divorce. A study based on data from the Census Bureau's Survey of Income and Program Participation (U.S. Bureau of Census, 1991a) shows that the percentage of children living in poverty increases from 19% to 35% (or by 89%) 4 months after parents divorce. One of the reasons that their economic situation deteriorates so quickly is that noncustodial fathers fail to pay the child support they owe, only 44% paying child support 4 months after divorce and also a year later. According to another Census Bureau study (U.S. Bureau of Census, 1991d), the likelihood that absent fathers will meet their child support obligations increases when they share joint custody with the mother, or at least have visitation privileges. Ninety percent of those with joint custody and 79% of those with visitation rights paid child support. However, only 7% had joint custody, and only 55%, visitation privileges. Of the 38% who had neither joint custody nor visitation privileges, only 45% met their child support obligations.

Earnings of Working Mothers

Although mothers work more after marital breakup, their efforts do not compensate for the loss of the fathers' income, family income declining by 26% after divorce, even when taking smaller family size, attributable to fathers' absence, into account (U.S. Bureau of Census, 1991a). Earnings differentials between men and women are pertinent here. Despite their increased representation in the labor force, women not only are not rewarded the same as men for their work effort, but the gap in average weekly earnings between men and women as heads of family households increased during the 1980s (U.S. Bureau of Census, 1990). The problem becomes even more acute when the costs of child care are calculated into the equation. While almost 22% of the average monthly income of working mothers below the poverty line goes to pay for child care, only 6.2% of the average monthly earnings of mothers above the poverty line does (U.S. Bureau of Census, 1989).

The earnings differential between men and women pertains regardless of education. A Census Bureau study ("Paying Field," 1991) shows that women at every level were paid less than men with the same amount of schooling in 1989. Although more recent reports show that some of this earnings differential declined in 1991, women with 4 years of college earned roughly the same as men with a high school diploma in 1989. The pay gap between men and women widens with age with obvious implications for retirement income. While some of the pay differential may be due to the fact that jobs in fields dominated by women tend to command lower salaries, some of it also is due to the "glass ceiling" that women encounter when attempting to break through barriers to higher paid positions.

During the 1980s, the earnings gap widened as earnings became more concentrated at the top and average earnings declined. This trend was exacerbated between 1989 and 1991 with the slowdown in the nation's economy, average hourly wages declining by a percentage point for all the nation's workers. This was in addition to the decline in earnings they suffered throughout the 1980s. Thus while the share of aggregate earnings received by the highest paid one fifth of male workers increased from 37.3% to 40.4%, full-time year-round workers in the lowest quintile received only 6.7% (U.S. Bureau of Census, 1991b). Reasons advanced for divergent trends are well known: the continuing shift in employment from the goods-producing sector of the economy to the service sector where the pay is generally lower and the financial rewards accrue to persons with a college education, particularly beyond the 4-year bachelor's degree. For those with a high school education or less, wages have declined or remained the same. But this is not the whole story, since as has been shown, women, regardless of education and position, are paid less than men for their work.

Unwed Parenthood

What about unwed parenthood? How should these trends be viewed? Here the evidence is more ambiguous, since again, much de-

pends on views about the link between marriage and childbearing, and childbearing itself for that matter. Larry Bumpass (1991) conducted a study based on interviews with persons in 57,400 randomly selected households which showed that while over two thirds of the babies born out of wedlock were unplanned, about one fourth were really children of two parent families in that the parents, although not married, were living together. Thus, according to Bumpass, the increase in births to unwed women is the consequence of an accidental pregnancy coupled with the decision not to marry. Also, the fact that women are delaying marriage while pursuing a higher education and careers, he says, means that they have a longer period during which they might accidentally become pregnant.

Delayed timing of marriage shows up in the median ages of persons who marry. In 1990, the median age of first marriages for women was 23.9 years and 26.1 years for men, about where it was 100 years ago (U.S. Bureau of Census, 1975), but 3 1/2 years older on average than in 1970 when women's average age at first marriage was 20.6 years and men's, 22.5 years ("U.S. Household Patterns," 1991). This same pattern of later first marriages pertains to remarriages, for both men and women, regardless of prior marital status, divorced or widowed (U.S. Bureau of Census, 1990). It also is reflected in the increasing proportion of never-marrieds among both men and women, in all age groups until ages 55 to 64 when the percentage of never-marrieds declines (U.S. Bureau of Census, 1990).

While delayed timing of first marriages may help to explain increases in unwed parenthood, and perhaps dampen concerns as to the severing of the link between marriage and parenthood, trends in teenage parenthood are another story and the subject of much more argument. Although the increase in teenage childbearing in 1974 gave the impression then that teenage childbearing was a growing problem, it in part was attributable to the size of the baby boom cohort (Furstenberg, 1991). Increases in teenage childbearing in 1989 to levels not seen since 1974 similarly are attributable in part to the increased proportion of teenagers in the population since 1986 (National Center for Health Statistics, 1991b). Between 1980 and 1988, the percentage of women 15 years of age increased 52% (from 17% to 26%) and for girls 17 years of age, 44% (from 36% to 52%).

Nonetheless, according to Furstenberg (1991), the weakening of cultural norms relative to marriage and childbearing has served to weaken the motivation of men to prevent a pregnancy from occurring, an attitude that he says could change if child support enforcement efforts were to become more effective. Just 14% of unwed mothers collected any child support in 1989 (Dugger, 1992). At the same time, for teens whose future prospects are bleak, having a child offers certain immediate rewards such that many drift into parenthood before they are ready or adequately prepared to assume the responsibilities of parenthood—financially, socially, or psychologically. As in the case of divorce whereby unhappy partners have the choice of remaining in or exiting from unhappy marriages, pregnant teens, just like their older sisters, have the choice of marrying or not. Still, according to Bumpass (1991), one third marry within 5 years after the child is born.

Whether or not early childbearing adversely shapes the course of later life is the subject of some debate. Luker (1990), for example, holds that many early childbearers would fare poorly in any case. Indeed, evidence shows that those who have early sex and fail to contracept, or abort, differ from later childbearers in a number of ways: social background, schooling, family influences, cognitive abilities, and motivation. Furstenberg (1991) argues, however, that while the postponement of early childbearing may not guarantee disadvantaged teens a way out of poverty, it increases the odds of their doing so, adding that it also might prevent some of the indirect effects of premature parenthood on children who would otherwise suffer the costs of being born into

an unstable family situation. Yet, evidence suggests that teen parenthood need not be the end of a dead-end line that leads to nowhere if second-chance opportunities are made available to young teen mothers (Hayes, 1987).

Nonetheless, aggregate state level analyses of teen birthrates for 1960, 1970, 1980, and 1985 (Zimmerman, 1992) support the inferences Furstenberg (1991) draws from his and others' work. These analyses show in addition that high teen birthrates must be seen in the context of the environment in which they occur. States having higher teen birthrates are states that have higher poverty rates, higher unemployment rates, higher divorce rates, and lower rates of school completion. They also are states that do less to foster the well-being of families. Thus it may be hypothesized that fewer second-chance opportunities will be available to teens in these states than to teens in other states, supporting Furstenberg's contention that persistent inequality and growing social isolation, especially among blacks, are a part of the context in which early childbearing is likely to occur.

Increased Longevity

In so far as increased longevity is concerned, the data show that for married couples, family relationships in later life are an important source of satisfaction (Aldous, 1987), spouses being seen as sources of support and companionship (Brubaker, 1990). Given this, increased longevity would seem to be an advantage, in that couples after retirement are able to focus on their relationships more fully. Those who have vital, rewarding relationships generally experience continued positive marital interactions (Brubaker and Kinsel, 1985). When the husband retires first, however, couples often experience lower levels of marital satisfaction (Lee and Shehan, 1989). Trends in male and female employment in later years are relevant here in that the proportion of men ages 60 to 69 who work has declined while the proportion of women ages 55 to 64 who work has increased (Tuma and Sandefur, 1988). Dating back to 1900, the decline in male work effort is attributable not only to the availability of income from Social Security and other sources, but also to the availability of work opportunities, or lack thereof, in the event of layoffs or compulsory retirement, as well as a desire for leisure (Ross, Danziger, and Smolensky, 1985). More important for marital satisfaction than retirement in later life, however, are changes in partners' health status, health being the primary predictor of psychological well-being in the later years (Quinn, 1983).

Findings from a nationally representative telephone survey conducted by Belden and Russonello for the Alliance for Aging Research in 1991 ("Most Want to Live," 1991) are illustrative. Most respondents (75%) said they worried about losing control of their lives and nearly 80% said they were more afraid of ending up in a nursing home than dying a quick death from the sudden onset of disease. The most pessimistic about these matters were those who were poor, uneducated, black, or from the South.

The fallout of increased longevity in the face of declining parent health and fewer children to share the care of older parents has begun to be seen in hospital emergency rooms. A recent survey of hospital emergency room workers revealed a phenomenon called "granny dumping" ("Dumped Elderly, Grandmas," 1991). Although still relatively rare, the phenomenon is more prevalent in states that have many large retirement communities such as California, Texas, and Florida. Based on 169 responses, the survey revealed an average of 8 such abandonments per week. In Tampa, one woman was found sitting in a wheel chair with a note pinned to her dress that said, "She's sick. Please take care of her." Another, in North Carolina, was dumped in a hospital driveway—literally. Survey respondents ranked the problem as 4 or higher on a severity scale from 1 to 6. The most common reason for family abandonment, they said, was the depletion of emotional, not financial, resources. At the same time,

the newspapers are filled with daily accounts of family impoverishment attributable to the costs of long-term care for elderly family members, but this also pertains to situations requiring long-term care for younger family members.

News accounts also report an increase in the financial exploitation of vulnerable elderly by family members, neighbors, and also health aides and household workers (Nordheimer, 1991). In Canada, a confidential survey of a representative sample of older persons in 1989 showed that a small percentage of those surveyed (2.5%) had been the financial victims of someone they knew. As the ranks of impaired elderly persons continue to grow, however, the problem of their financial abuse is expected to increase accordingly. Mental impairment, loneliness, and the fear of becoming a burden on families make some accomplices in their own victimization. Often the victims are women living alone, a consequence of the longer lives of U.S. women compared to men. As noted earlier, it is expected that by 1995, 60% of all women 75 years and older will be living alone.

CONCLUSIONS AND IMPLICATIONS FOR FAMILY POLICY

In light of the evidence that has been presented, what are the implications of the family trends that have been reported for family policy? Do they represent problems that call for a policy response, or do they simply represent preferences in the ways in which people choose to live their lives in a free society?

A few summary comments may be helpful here before answering these questions. In general, it would seem that marriage is an important source of well-being for people along several dimensions: financial, psychological, and social. This is not to say that other kinds of close personal relationships are not as well. Also, for some, marriage is a source of ill-being and dissatisfaction, depending on gender, race, social class, general economic conditions, and the interactions of these with other social and psychological factors. The economic difficulties that women and their children experience subsequent to divorce are compounded by the fact that women are disadvantaged in the work place, both with respect to earnings and advancement, and that noncustodial fathers often fail to meet their child support obligations. Thus, trends in marriage and divorce must be seen not only as a reflection of options that people exercise in how they choose to live their daily lives, but also as the outcome of structural and economic conditions affecting their personal lives and relationships. Some of these same conditions pertain to trends in unwed parenthood although here, other factors seem to be at work as well, such as changing cultural norms in relation to unwed parenthood and demographics. As to increased longevity, the conditions that make for a satisfying life in the later years would seem to depend in part on economics and the good fortune of remaining mentally and physically healthy. One of the greatest fears for many is that they may not be so lucky ("Most Want to Live," 1991).

To the extent that the economic and structural conditions antecedent to both marital status and family well-being are amenable to policy choices, it would seem that trends in marriage and divorce do have implications for family policy and hence, for family policy specialists. Thus, to the extent economic conditions are perceived as problematic for marital and family stability, family policy specialists might do well to attend to proposals for stimulating the economy that go beyond raising and lowering interest rates. Such proposals might be concerned with the creation of jobs, job training and education programs, investing in the nation's infrastructure, and making our tax laws more progressive. They also might do well to attend to the role of the Federal government as an instrument for effecting a more equitable distribution of resources among states and enlarging the economic base from which poor states can derive the

resources they need for stimulating economic growth and renewal within their borders.

In so far as structural conditions underlying marital status are perceived to be a problem as manifested by the effects of gender, race, and social class, and are amenable to policy efforts, it would seem that some family policy specialists may want to focus their attention here. In particular they may want to attend to affirmative action and comparable worth measures, not only to reduce earnings disparities between men and women and among racial groups, but also to increase the resource base for families presently penalized because of these structural barriers. They also might want to give special attention to the equalization of educational opportunities for women and minorities to better prepare them for higher paying jobs to enable them to better support their families. Along this same vein, they might advocate for the enactment of family and medical leave legislation, or as a way of reducing the earnings gap, for a cap on the earnings of corporate executives that many, if asked, would probably regard as excessive.

In so far as the problem is seen in terms of the failure of divorced fathers to conform to parental norms of child support, perhaps some family policy specialists would want to focus their attention here. Clearly, if joint custody and visitation privileges are so central to divorced fathers' compliance with child support obligations, it would do well to explore why these are not used more widely. The issue of child support also applies to unwed fathers whose record in this regard is so abysmal. Critical to child support collection from unwed fathers is the early establishment of paternity and simplification of the process of doing so, as for example, a voluntary consent procedure that bypasses the judicial system. Also to reduce the burden of child care for low-income mothers and to facilitate a more equitable distribution of its costs, perhaps some family policy specialists might want to focus their attention on measures designed to do this: child care subsidies for low-income mothers comes to mind, or a refundable child care tax credit.

If the problem is perceived in terms of the increasing rates of childbearing by unmarried women, particularly teens, many of the measures already mentioned would be applicable here as well. In particular, family policy specialists might want to attend to the forces that give rise to high teen birthrates in the first place: cultural norms, family instability, academic failure, and individual motivation within a context of persistent inequality and growing social isolation of poor families.

To the extent that physical and mental deterioration coupled with the high costs of health care are seen as problematic in the later years, hopefully some family policy specialists may want to attend to the different health care reform proposals that have been put forward and how these might affect families of different marital and income statuses. They also might want to work to ensure the availability of certain social provisions, such as respite care and adult day care, to help families better cope with the demands of elder care. In addition, they also may want to question the indiscriminate application of medical technology whose personal, social, and financial costs are about on a par, especially in situations where quality of life is and can be no more. In this regard, the issue of euthanasia is ripe for policy debate. In the meantime, efforts also might be directed at improving services to better protect mentally impaired older persons from unscrupulous others.

Depending on what the problem is perceived to be, the above are only some of the policy and programmatic implications gleaned from the evidence related to the family trends reported here. Clearly, not all of these trends are reflective of the preferences in the ways people choose to live their lives in a free society. Rather, they are the outcomes of interacting influences that lead to higher levels of well-being for some than others. Thus gender, race, and social class interact with economic conditions so as to promote higher levels of well-being for white

males via marital status and occupational position and lower levels of well-being for women and minorities. If this is deemed to be one of the central problems associated with family trends in the 1990s, and if families are as important as politicians say they are, then the implications for family policy are clear. While family policy cannot address all of the problems associated with family life in the 1990s, it certainly can be fashioned in ways to make the playing field more even so that all families, regardless of type and however defined, have a chance to acquire their fair share of well-being. To make sure that happens, this is where I think family policy specialists ought to focus their attention for the rest of the decade.

REFERENCES

Ader, R., Cohen, N., and Felton, D. (Eds.). (1990). *Psychoneuroimmunology* (Vol. 2). San Diego: Academic Press.

Albrecht, S., Bahr, H., and Goodman, K. (1983). *Divorce and remarriage: Problems, adaptations, and adjustments.* Westport, CT: Greenwood Press.

Ahlburg, D., and Schapiro, M. O. (1982–83). Suicide: The ultimate cost of unemployment. *Journal of Post-Keynesian Economics,* **5,** 276–280.

Aldous, J. (1987). New views on the family life of the elderly and the near-elderly. *Journal of Marriage and the Family,* **49,** 227–234.

Aldous, J., and Dumon, W. (1990). Family policy in the 1980s: Controversy and consensus. *Journal of Marriage and the Family,* **52,** 1136–1152.

Anson, O. (1989). Marital status and women's health revisited: The importance of the proximate adult. *Journal of Marriage and the Family,* **51,** 185–194.

Bakke, E. W. (1940). *Citizens without work.* New Haven, CT: Yale University Press.

Barringer, F. (1991, June 7). Changes in U.S. households: Single parents amid solitude. *New York Times,* p. A1.

Bianchi, S. M., and Spain, D. (1986). *American women in transition.* New York: Russell Sage Foundation.

Bowling, A. (1987). Mortality after bereavement: A review of the literature on survival periods and factors affecting survival. *Social Science and Medicine,* **24,** 117–124.

Brubaker, T. (1990). Families in later life: A burgeoning research area. *Journal of Marriage and the Family*, **52**, 959–982.

Brubaker, T., and Kinsel, B. (1985). Who is responsible for household tasks in long term marriages of "young-old" elderly? *Lifestyles: A Journal of Changing Patterns*, **7**, 238–247.

Bumpass, L. (1990). What's happening to the American family? Interactions between demographic and institutional change. *Demography*, **27**, 483–498.

Bumpass, L. (1991). The role of cohabitation in declining rates of marriage. *Journal of Marriage and the Family*, **53**, 913–927.

Calabrese, J., Kling, M., and Gold, P. W. (1987). Alterations in immunocompetence during stress, bereavement, and depression: Focus on neuroendocrine regulation. *American Journal of Psychiatry*, **144**, 1123–1134.

Cherlin, A. (1981). *Marriage, divorce, and remarriage*. Cambridge, MA: Harvard University Press.

Colasanto, D., and Shriver, J. (1989, May 2). Problems plague even happily wed. *Star Tribune*, p. 1E.

Conger, R., Elder, G., Lorenz, F., Conger, K., Simons, R., Whitbeck, L., Huck, S., and Melby, J. (1990). Linking economic hardship to marital quality and instability. *Journal of Marriage and the Family*, **52**, 643–656.

Dooley, D., and Catalano, R. (Eds.). (1988). Psychological effects of unemployment. *Journal of Social Issues*, **44**(4), 1–191.

Dugger, C. (1992, January 4). Settling paternity earlier for child support later. *New York Times*, p. A12.

Dumped elderly, grandmas abandoned on hospital doorsteps. (1991, November 28). *Star Tribune*, p. 1A.

Edwards, J. (1991). New conceptions: Biosocial innovations and the family. *Journal of Marriage and the Family*, **53**, 349–360.

Elder, Jr., G. H. (1974). *Children of the great depression: Social change in life experience*. Chicago: University of Chicago Press.

Furstenberg, F. (1991). As the pendulum swings: Teenage childbearing and social concern. *Family Relations*, **40**, 127–138.

Glenn, N. (1991). The recent trend in marital success in the United States. *Journal of Marriage and the Family*, **53**, 261–270.

Glenn, N., and Weaver, C. (1988). The changing relationship of marital status to reported happiness. *Journal of Marriage and the Family*, **50**, 317–324.

Hall, T. (1991, March 5). New emphasis on family dims lure of divorce. *Star Tribune*, p. 1E.

Harris and Associates. (1987). *Source Document, Harris Survey, July 7*. The Roper Center for Public Opinion Research. Storrs, CT.

Hayes, C. D. (Ed.). (1987). *Risking the future* (Vol. 1). Washington, DC: National Academy Press.

Helsing, K. J., Moysen, S., and Comstock, G. W. (1981). Factors associated with mortality after widowhood. *American Journal of Public Health*, **71**, 802–809.

Hollingshead, A., and Redich, F. (1964). *Social class and mental illness: A community study*. New York: Wiley and Sons.

Hughes, M. M., and Gove, W. R. (1981). Living alone, social integration, and mental health. *American Journal of Sociology*, **87**, 48–74.

Kadushin, A., and Martin, J. A. (1981). *Child abuse: An interactional event*. New York: Columbia University Press.

Kessler, R. C. (1982). A disaggregation of the relationship between socioeconomic status and psychological distress. *American Sociological Review*, **47**, 752–764.

Kessler, R. C., and Cleary, P. D. (1980). Social class and psychological distress. *American Sociological Review*, **45**, 463–478.

Kitson, G., and Morgan, L. (1990). The multiple consequences of divorce: A decade review. *Journal of Marriage and the Family*, **32**, 913–924.

Kitson, G., and Sussman, M. (1982). Marital complaints, demographic characteristics, and symptoms of marital distress in divorce. *Journal of Marriage and the Family*, **44**, 87–101.

Lee, G., and Shehan, C. (1989). Retirement and marital satisfaction. *Journal of Gerontology*, **44**, S226–S230.

Liker, J. K., and Elder, Jr., G. H. (1983). Economic hardship and marital relations in the 1930s. *American Sociological Review*, **48**, 343–359.

Litwak, E., and Messeri, P. (1989). Organizational theory, social supports and mortality rates: A theoretical convergence. *American Sociological Review*, **54**, 49–66.

Luker, K. (1990, August). *The social construction of teenage pregnancy*. Paper presented at the annual American Sociological Association meeting, Washington, DC.

Most want to live to be 100, but fear infirmities of age. (1991, November 18). *Star Tribune*, p. 7A.

National Center for Health Statistics. (1990). *Advance report of final natality statistics, 1988* (Monthly vital statistics report: vol. 39, no. 4, suppl.). Hyattsville, MD: U.S. Public Health Service.

National Center for Health Statistics. (1991a). *Advance report of final divorce statistics, 1988* (Monthly vital statistics report: vol. 39, no. 12, suppl. 2). Hyattsville, MD: U.S. Public Health Service.

National Center for Health Statistics. (1991b). *Advance report of final natality statistics, 1989* (Monthly vital statistics report: vol. 40, no. 8, suppl.). Hyattsville, MD: U.S. Public Health Service.

Nordheimer, J. (1991, December 15). A new abuse of elderly: Theft by kin and friends. *New York Times*, p. A1.

Paying field isn't level: Study confirms men earn more than women. (1991, November 14). *Star Tribune*, p. 1A.

Pearlin, L., Lieberman, M. S., Menaghan, E., and Mullan, J. T. (1981). The stress process. *Journal of Health and Social Behavior*, **22**, 337–356.

Poll: Married women's lives more likely to be satisfying. (1988, August 24). *Star Tribune*, p. 3A.

Quinn, W. H. (1983). Personal and family adjustment in later life. *Journal of Marriage and the Family*, **45**, 57–73.

Ross, C. (1989, August). *The intersection of work and family: The sense of control and well-being of women and men*. Paper presented at the Family Structure and Health Conference, San Francisco.

Ross, C., Danziger, S., and Smolensky, E. (1985). *Social security, work effort, and poverty among elderly men, 1939–1979* (Discussion Paper no. 785-85). Madison, WI: Institute for Research on Poverty.

Ross, C., Mirowsky, J., and Goldstein, K. (1990). Impact of family on health. *Journal of Marriage and the Family*, **52**, 1059–1078.

Scanzoni, K., Polonko, K., and Teachman, J. (1989). *The sexual bond: Rethinking families and close relationships*. Newbury Park, CA: Sage Publications.

Smith, J. C., Mercy, J. A., and Conn, J. (1988). Marital status and the risk of suicide. *American Journal of Public Health*, **78**, 78–80.

South, Jr., S. (1985). Economic conditions and the divorce rate. *Journal of Marriage and the Family*, **47**, 31–41.

Straus, M., Gelles, R., and Steinmetz, S. (1980). *Behind closed doors: Violence in the American Family*. Garden City, NY: Anchor Press/Doubleday.

Tuma, N., and Sandefur, G. (1988). *Trends in the labor force activity of the elderly in the United States* (Reprint no. 578). Madison, WI: Institute for Research on Poverty.

Umberson, D. (1987). Relationships with children: Explaining parents' psychological well-being. *Journal of Health and Social Behavior*, **38**, 306–319.

U.S. Bureau of Census. (1975). *Historical statistics of the United States: Colonial times to 1970. Part 1*. Washington, DC: U.S. Government Printing Office.

U.S. Bureau of Census. (1983). *Statistical abstracts of the United States, 1984* (104th ed.). Washington, DC: U.S. Government Printing Office.

U.S. Bureau of Census. (1989). Child care costs hit the poor harder. *Census and You*, **24**(10), 8.

U.S. Bureau of Census. (1990). *Statistical abstracts of the United States, 1990* (110th ed.). Washington, DC: U.S. Government Printing Office.

U.S. Bureau of Census. (1991a). Current Population Reports, Series P-70, no. 3, *Family disruption and economic hardship: The short-run picture for children*. Washington, DC: U.S. Government Printing Office.

U.S. Bureau of Census. (1991b). How did earners fare during the 1980s? *Census and You*, **26**(7), 7.

U.S. Bureau of Census. (1991c). Number of two parent family households still decreasing. *Census and You*, **26**(2), 3.

U.S. Bureau of Census. (1991d). Who's supporting the kids? *Census and You*, **26**(12), 1.

U.S. Department of Labor. (1987). *Employment in perspective: Women in the labor force* (Report 740). Washington, DC: Bureau of Labor Statistics.

U.S. household patterns are changing in the face of divorce, delayed marriage. (1991, June 7). *Star Tribune*, p. 16A.

Verbrugge, L. (1985). Gender and health: An update on hypotheses and evidence. *Journal of Health and Social Behavior*, **26**(1), 156–182.

Weitzman, L. (1985). *The divorce revolution*. New York: Free Press.

White, L. (1990). Determinants of divorce: A review of research in the eighties. *Journal of Marriage and the Family*, **32**, 904–912.

Wingard, D. (1984). The sex differential in morbidity, mortality, and lifestyle. *Annual Review of Public Health*, **5**, 433–458.

Wright, G., and Stetson, D. M. (1978). The impact of no-fault divorce law reform on divorce in the American states. *Journal of Marriage and the Family*, **40**, 575–584.

Zick, C., and Smith, K. (1991). Marital transitions, poverty, and gender differences in mortality. *Journal of Marriage and the Family*, **53**, 327–336.

Zimmerman, S. L. (1987). States' public welfare expenditures as predictors of states' suicide rates. *Suicide and Life Threatening Behavior*, **17**, 271–287.

Zimmerman, S. L. (1988). *Understanding family pol-*

icy: Theoretical approaches. Newbury Park, CA: Sage Publications.

Zimmerman, S. L. (1990). The macro-micro level connection: States' hospital expenditures and their suicide rates. *Suicide and Life Threatening Behavior,* **20,** 31–55.

Zimmerman, S. L. (1991). The welfare state and family breakup: The mythical connection. *Family Relations,* **40,** 139–147.

Zimmerman, S. L. (1992). *Family policies and family well-being: The role of political culture.* Newbury Park, CA: Sage Publications.

Zimmerman, S. L. (in press). Three faces of suicide phenomena: Political culture, public policy choices, and unmet needs. In A. Leenaars, R. Maris, R. Litman, and P. Cantor (Eds.), *Suicidology: Essays in honor of Edwin S. Shneidman.* New York: Plenum.

America's Blacks: A World Apart

This article begins with a statistical portrait of the U.S. black urban underclass. Then, using the arguments developed by Charles Murray, an analysis of the impact of government policies on the problems of African Americans is presented. Next, the problems of segregation and urban economic change are discussed to highlight the explanatory power of the arguments developed by William Julius Wilson. Concluding comments address policies of "empowerment" to underscore the essential role of education in solving the problems of the black underclass. The policy recommendations include finding new ways to motivate inner-city youth to attend school.

Exercises to Guide Your Reading

1. Give examples of behaviors and/or situations that either support or contradict the view that government policies are the root of the problems of black Americans.
2. Give examples of behaviors and/or situations that either support or contradict the view that structural unemployment and changes in urban economies are the root of the problems of black Americans.
3. Identify the strengths and weaknesses of policies designed to foster "empowerment."
4. Construct a set of policies to help alleviate the problems of the black underclass.

Absorb these figures about America's cities. Nearly half of black teenagers in the city of Chicago fail to graduate from high school. In Washington, D.C., in 1989 nearly four times as many black men were jailed in the district's prison as graduated from its public schools; the leading cause of death among young black men is murder. In the country as a whole a staggering two-thirds of black babies are born to unmarried mothers; 43% of black children are, by government criteria, born poor; many do not live to see their first birthday. Last year's unemployment rate among blacks was 10.5%, more than twice that for whites.

Sealed off in inner-city ghettos, by-passed by fly-over freeways, black America is suffering out of sight. Has America turned its back on its inner-city blacks?

Not all of them: a black middle class has mushroomed, from about one in ten blacks in 1960 to more than a third today. But a scissors effect is cutting through America's blacks (see Figure 1). Measured by the government's official poverty line—which counts as poor a family of four with an income below $12,675, in 1989 dollars–the proportion of blacks stuck at the bottom has refused to budge from around a third for the past 20 years, compared with a tenth of all whites.

The plight of inner-city blacks affects the whole of America. The cost of the welfare system has skyrocketed: spending on all fed-

Reprinted by permission of *The Economist*. March 30, 1991. pp. 17–18, 21.

eral programmes more than tripled between 1965 and 1987, from $141 billion to $520 billion (in 1988 dollars). During the rest of the 1990s the number of youngsters entering the workforce each year will be smaller than at any time since the second world war; but two-fifths will be from minorities, mostly Hispanics and blacks.

Corporate America is starting to wake up to all this. Last year a group of 45 *Fortune* 500 chief executives and university presidents, known as the Business-Higher Education Forum, published a report saying that the country could not ignore the growing isolation of its inner-city minorities. The authors, Steven Mason, president of the Mead Corporation, and Clifton Wharton, chairman of TIAA-CREF, the nation's largest private pension fund, say: "The population as a whole is ageing, the growth of the workforce is slowing, and the twin burdens of greater productivity and supporting an ageing population will fall mostly on younger workers. . . . Our society cannot afford to lose a single one of its young people."

True, not all the inner-city poor are black: on the west coast many are Mexican; in New York lots are Puerto Rican. But wholly disproportionate numbers are black, and stuck in the nastiest parts of the most dangerous cities: Washington, D.C., is over 70% black; Detroit 63%. It is difficult to tease apart the chiefly race-caused problems from those caused by inner-city economics. But policies intended for the poor in general, which are politically more acceptable than those designed for specific racial groups, will aim at a big section of blacks too.

CAN'T WORK, WON'T WORK

When Americans talk about an "underclass" in their cities, they do not simply mean the poor; they mean poor but healthy young people who cannot or will not, but anyway do not, get a job. The images are vivid: an unmarried mother who lives off welfare cheques; a young man who drifts from girl-friend to girlfriend, selling drugs to get by.

Estimates of the size of this underclass vary hugely from about 5% to 50% of all the poor—2m–15m people, of whom some two-thirds are black, a tenth Hispanic.

Liberals tend to stress the "cannot" work. Smoke-stack industry jobs that used to pay a decent wage have been wiped out. Twenty years ago mid-western steel workers could earn $20 an hour; today, it is hard to find replacement jobs in the service industries that offer $6–7 an hour. In real terms, median black family income in the mid-west has fallen by nearly a third in the past 20 years, from $24,690 to $17,400. For many young blacks, the only jobs that offer a secure future and steady income are in the armed forces.

Conservatives tend to stress the "will not": jobs exist, but people do not take them; jobs do not pay enough, or people do not try hard enough to find them. Even with the country in recession, suburban papers are filled with wanted ads for waitresses, cleaners and cooks. The view is widespread: a recent poll by the National Opinion Research Centre showed that 78% of whites think blacks are more likely than whites to "prefer to live off welfare."

The truth lies somewhere in between. Hamburger-flipping jobs ("McJobs") that pay the minimum wage ($3.80 an hour in 1990) are fine for teenagers, but not for parents trying to support a family. Inner-city blacks often see better-paid jobs as beyond their reach: they ask for too many qualifications, they are too far away, there is nobody to look after the children.

A HAND UP, NOT A HAND-OUT

What irks conservatives most is their belief not only that inner-city blacks are unwilling to take jobs, but that the government pays to keep them unwilling. The welfare system, runs this view, makes things worse because it discourages people from working and rewards undesirable behaviour.

The welfare hand-out that pains critics most is that given to poor, unmarried moth-

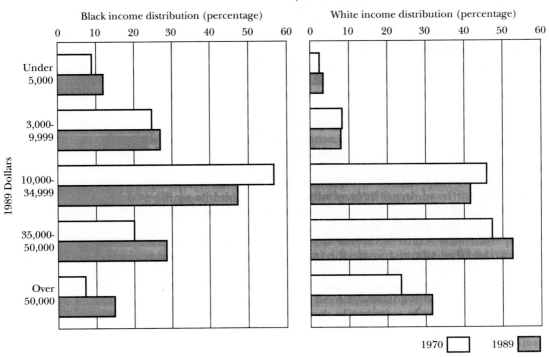

FIGURE 1.   America's Blacks
Source: U.S. Department of Commerce; Bureau of the Census.

ers: Aid to Families with Dependent Children (AFDC). One of the most eloquent critics has been a conservative writer, Charles Murray. He argues that, in seeking to protect children from poverty, AFDC has eased the financial strain of raising children alone; so more women do so. His evidence: more and more babies were born to unmarried women during the past 30 years—which is when social-welfare spending shot up. His prescription: abolish welfare.

Mr. Murray's argument does not fit the facts. First, there is no evidence that in states where AFDC payments are generous more children are born outside marriage. Second, the lion's share of increased welfare spending since the 1960s has been on programmes most people approve of: social security (pensions) financed by tax on earnings, and medical insurance for old people (Medicare). Spending on AFDC, in real terms, fell by nearly a fifth between 1975 and 1989—the

period that saw the biggest growth in illegitimate births.

It is even harder to blame an over-generous welfare system for joblessness among young men. In America, unlike Europe, youngsters who have not paid unemployment contributions cannot claim welfare at all. Many survive by "hustling": doing odd jobs here and there, often illegally. The perverse result, in many poor neighborhoods, is that a young man lives off his mother's or pregnant girlfriend's welfare cheques, or both. Going out with girls who have babies is good news; the more girlfriends the better. On Chicago's south side the day the monthly cheque arrives is nicknamed "mother's day," because that is when absent sons and husbands turn up.

So Mr. Murray's criticism does have an important grain of truth in it. Although AFDC is not generous, it may still be attractive. In 1989, in a state with average AFDC payments, a single woman with two children who took a job at the minimum wage (then $3.35 an hour) would earn a paltry $33 more each month than if she did not work at all and stayed on welfare. Research by David Ellwood, at Harvard University, shows that the surest way for a woman to escape poverty, and get off welfare, is not to work but to get married.

Mr. Murray's solution is drastic. A more measured response is not to abandon welfare but to shift the carrots: make welfare reward work. In current White-House-speak: give people a hand up, not a hand-out. If benefits were not deducted when mothers worked, they would not discourage working; if some benefits were available only for working mothers (child care, for instance), they would encourage it. Liberals and conservatives are beginning to find common ground on one point: welfare should be strictly temporary—a transition back to work. After the 1988 Family Support Act, states must help to provide one year of child care for mothers who leave welfare for a job or training. Nursery education for poor children, like Head Start, undoubtedly improves later school performance.

What about young men (and young women without babies)? Unlike Europe, America is against welfare payments available to everybody without a job, even those who have never worked. Instead, policy concentrates on making work pay. Some suggest tinkering with the tax system: raise the ceiling for tax-free earnings, or boost the earned-income tax credit for low-earners. Others would like the minimum wage raised. However, since young men are largely excluded from welfare benefits, they are best helped by programmes other than welfare reform.

THOSE MEAN STREETS

Five o'clock at State Street station, in downtown Chicago, and the platforms groan with homeward-bound commuters, wrapped up against the winter frost. Peer more closely at the faces: on one side, heading south, all are black; on the other, heading north, nearly all are white.

According to one 1989 study, Chicago is the most racially segregated city in America, just beating Cleveland and Detroit. Ending legal segregation has not been enough to end segregation itself. Rich blacks have indeed moved out of the ghettos; but estate agents, anxious to protect property prices, still steer even rich blacks away from the nicest, lily-white suburbs. For poor blacks, without money to move, living in an inner-city ghetto can mean days without seeing a white face. The scale of segregation stuns: Chicago's black south side covers 50 square miles—bigger than the whole of Paris within the *périphérique*.

This separation breeds prejudice; worse, it isolates young blacks from the white world that will judge them when they leave school. No amount of insisting that black fashion, black history and black speech are as valid as white alters the fact that to get a decent job means to work where being able to "act white" pays. As one suburban employer in Chicago, whose staff deal with clients in the office, comments: "I just can't afford to take on somebody who says the plural of 'woman' is 'womans'."

It is not getting better: a recent study of 60 cities showed that black and white speech patterns are drifting further apart. According to William Julius Wilson, of the University of Chicago, himself black, poor blacks are even more isolated because any rich blacks who can get out do so. Gone are the movie-halls and lawyers' offices on Chicago's south side, once the ritzier part of town for blacks. Shabby brick apartments stretch for block after block, dotted with little more than the odd liquor store, fried-chicken shack and cheque-cashing shop, well buttoned up with wire mesh and bullet-proof glass. Policemen patrol only in cars.

Poor neighbourhoods, argues Mr. Wilson, have lost great numbers of working people who used to set examples to local children. Work habits (such as waking up every day to an alarm clock) that often flow over into responsible social attitudes (such as being a good father) are not being learnt. It is hard for black youngsters, growing up in poor areas where few people have jobs, to see that "making it" requires hard work and discipline. Those who do "make it" and can afford the status symbols—the heavy gold chains, the Nike trainers—are drug dealers; and, in Chicago, most drug traffic is controlled by gangs. Along with rap artists and basketball players, these are the black men the black boys look up to.

Jobs, too, have left the ghettos; new jobs now grow quickest in the (white) suburbs. Northeastern Illinois Planning Commission reckons that jobs in Du Page county, suburban Chicago, will grow by a whopping 120% between 1980 and 2010; in the city of Chicago, by a measly 6%.

Most programmes that try to move people and jobs have little success. Enterprise zones—which seduce businesses into poor areas with attractive tax breaks—are currently back in vogue at the federal Department of Housing and Urban Development. But experience shows that few companies will budge without vast incentives; most firms recruit few local people; some leave when tax holidays end; and zones work only when there are few of them in any one area.

Moving people has also been tried, for instance by giving housing subsidies to poor people so that they can move out of inner-city slums and rent new homes in the suburbs. Research shows this can nudge up work rates; but, like busing schoolchildren from black to white areas, it can be political dynamite. There are few votes to be won in the rich white suburbs by promising to move poor blacks there.

One logical fix to this geographical mismatch is for inner-city blacks to commute out from the ghettos to the suburbs. The snag is getting there: public transport often links up white suburbs with the city centre, but not with poor black segments in between. And few ghetto blacks have cars.

An answer from the private sector: "dedicated" bus routes. Suburban Job-Link, a Chicago employment agency, runs buses from North Lawndale, the city's poorest neighbourhood, where the unemployment rate runs above 20%, out to three western suburbs, where it barely hits 5%. Costs are split between employers and workers; over 600 people travel each day; most work in light-manufacturing jobs, not services; and each earns an average hourly wage above $6—nearly twice the minimum wage. Similar private bus services operate in a dozen cities. The public sector could take note.

FROM THE BOTTOM UP

One of the more curious recent products of the Bush administration has been the hyping up of a new anti-poverty idea in terms that sound more like black radicalism of the 1960s. The buzzword is "empowerment": let people manage their own affairs. It suits the right: it encourages individual responsibility. It suits the left: it hands over control to local people. What does it mean?

A lot of words, and a few concrete proposals. The driving force behind empowerment is Jack Kemp, secretary of housing and urban development. Mr. Kemp has been trying for several years to prod the White House into launching a serious anti-poverty programme. Last autumn he won round one when President Bush appointed him to lead a cabinet "empowerment task force," told to come up with specific proposals.

Take decisions away from bureaucracies and give them to people: that is the principle. The practice is to let parents choose freely their children's schools, let people buy their own homes, let public-housing tenants run their own estates. Admirable goals; but with only a modest prospect of helping inner-city blacks. Critics say Mr. Kemp is an Alice in Wonderland. Buying a house is not high on many poor blacks' shopping lists. Successful tenant-management, like the running of Kenilworth-Parkside, a housing project in Washington, D.C., and one of Mr. Kemp's favourite examples, depends heavily on finding dedicated organisers.

If empowerment means anything, it is economic: empowerment to escape poverty. The classic route, proved time and again by waves of immigrants, is education. America is failing its blacks nowhere more than in its schools. In poor black areas it is common for half the class to fail to graduate (which, in America, means merely failing to stay in school until you are 18—there is no national exam for school-leavers). But no amount of tinkering with parental choice or national testing alters one main problem: many young black children do not even turn up to classes. They cannot see the point. They are distracted by the glamour and excitement of drugs and gangs; they get little discipline at home; they fail to connect getting a good job with finishing high school.

Larry Hawkins, president of Chicago's Institute for Athletics and Education, thinks he has an answer: stop battering on a closed door, and try an open one. If the one thing that inner-city black children will go to school for is sport, use it to keep them there. "It is not sport for sport's sake," says Mr. Hawkins, who is an ex-Harlem-Globetrotter, "but a way of imposing a structure on undisciplined lives: in a sports team they turn up regularly, on time, in uniform, and train hard. This habit spills over into their schoolwork." He and his colleagues coach competitive basketball in schools across the city. They also act as mentors to the children, discussing the pressures of drugs and gangs, and how to cope with schoolwork. The results are persuasive: those who take part regularly in his sports programmes at school are only one-third as likely to drop out as those who don't.

For the droppers-out, there is little choice but to spend more on training. Federal employment and training programmes were sliced in half during the 1980s, from $12.8 billion to $5.6 billion, in real terms.

IF THE WILL FAILS

For all the talk, dishing out control to individuals has its limits. One example: black churches, which organise services from financial credit to remedial education, carry enormous influence in poor black neighbourhoods, and offer the kinds of local leadership that Mr. Kemp so much wants to nurture. More than three-quarters of black Americans belong to a church, and nearly half go to church every week. But if the state supported church groups it would provoke a constitutional row, because the constitution separates church and state.

Another example: the empowerment that cities crave is a share of the taxes raised in their rich suburbs. Suburban schools gleam with modern gadgetry, while inner-city schools lack basic text books. But a proposal to re-draw the tax-boundary line between them would win little favour in the rich suburbs.

The slums in America's great cities are shameful. They are a damning indictment of the richest country in the world. The problems that fester in them are not peripheral: they constitute America's main domestic challenge today. The nation now has a quarter of a century's worth of anti-poverty experiments to draw on. That poverty persists despite these efforts is less a reason to give up than a reason to learn from what works and what does not. George Bush could now cash in on the country's post-war confidence by launching another war on the black home-front. America cannot afford to let down its blacks for much longer.

10

Left in the Dust

Randy Albelda

This chapter compares U.S. antipoverty policies with those of other advanced industrial nations. The author points out that the poor in the United States have benefited significantly less from government policies than have the poor in other countries, that racial and ethnic characteristics are more significantly correlated with poverty in the United States than in other countries, and that poverty is much more severe among American children than among children in other countries. Policy makers in the United States, it is concluded, would do well to learn from the successes of other advanced industrial nations.

Exercises to Guide Your Reading

1. Define the term "regressive tax policy," and explain how such a policy might affect women, children, and minorities.
2. Summarize the comparison of the United States with other countries in terms of: (a) the overall poverty rate; (b) race and poverty; and (c) children and poverty.
3. Compare Albelda's conclusions with those advanced in Readings 7 and 9.
4. Both defend and then criticize the U.S. policy record vis-à-vis poverty.

The United States had steadier growth and lower unemployment during the 1980s than any European industrialized country except Sweden. Nevertheless, by the middle of the 1980s, the U.S. poverty rate was double that of every industrialized European nation except the United Kingdom.

A new study by the Joint Center for Political and Economic Studies [JCPES], an African-American managed think tank in Washington, D.C., attributes this contrast to differences in tax policies and social programs. Years of regressive U.S. tax policies and underfunded social programs have taken their toll. While poverty has also grown in Western Europe, more progressive tax policies and more generous income transfer programs have diminished its severity.

In 1986, the study found, U.S. policies added to the number of America's poor. That is, taxes pushed more people into poverty than income transfer programs pulled out. Surveying 8,000 households, researchers accounted for taxes paid, as well as cash and "near-cash" benefits that added to household income, such as unemployment compensation, disability, food stamps, and Aid for Families with Dependent Children. Instead of decreasing the number of poor

Reprinted by permission of *Dollars & Sense*. December 1991. pp. 20–21.

households, the combination of regressive taxes and inadequate social benefits increased the number of households living in poverty.

In contrast, in the United Kingdom that year, almost half of the households which were poor before subtracting taxes and adding public benefits were no longer poor after paying taxes and receiving income transfers. The Center's Katherine McFate, who coordinated the project along with William Julius Wilson of the University of Chicago and Roger Lawson of England's University of Southampton, points to paid parental leave policies and child allowances as two examples of social programs common in Europe but not in the United States. McFate also notes that a great proportion of America's unemployed receive no unemployment benefits.

The study highlights differences in public attitudes toward taxation and social programs between the United States and Europe. Here, the public views taxes as means to pay for public services. Europeans, however, demonstrate greater commitment to leveling income inequality and ensuring that no one falls too far below a national income norm, McFate comments. Despite the spread of conservatism in Europe, and despite the economic difficulties European nations have had, both tax and income-transfer policies still serve these goals.

"The United States stands in ignominious isolation," the report charges. "Among industrialized countries, the United States has the highest incidence of poverty among the non-elderly and the widest distribution of poverty across all age and family groups." It is also "the only western democracy that has failed to give a significant portion of its poor a measure of income security."

POOR SHOWING

Researchers compared poverty and social policies in the United States, Canada, France, West Germany, Italy, the Nether-lands, Sweden, and the United Kingdom. To compare across countries, they defined a family as poor if its income was half or less of the country's median family income. The official U.S. poverty line is lower than this standard, so the poverty rates reported by JCPES are higher than official U.S. rates. Researchers only studied families headed by someone 20 to 55 years of age.

Researchers found that poverty grew in the early and mid-eighties in every country except France, where the poverty rate stayed the same, and the Netherlands, where it dropped slightly. While family-related changes such as divorce caused some of the increases in poverty, job loss and wage drops were the most common causes. By 1986, 18% of U.S. households and 12.5% of British households studied were poor. The following year, about 14% of Canadians studied were poor, compared to fewer than 8% in the Netherlands and 9% in Sweden.

By using a combination of tax policies and social programs, every country except the United States pulled at least one-fifth of its poor citizens out of poverty during the years studied. (Due to data-collection problems, researchers sampled different years in different countries.) In 1979, government action lifted less than 1% of poor U.S. families studied out of poverty, compared to 33% in the United Kingdom.

KINDER AND GENTLER?
TRY DEEPER AND NASTIER

Not only were more U.S. households poor compared to other countries, but Americans were more likely to be "severely" poor. In Europe and Canada, household incomes hovered close to the median national income. In the United States, more households fell far below the national median.

Researchers also found that the poor in the United States stayed poor longer than poor families elsewhere. More than 14% of all families with children stayed poor for three years in a row. In contrast, 12% in

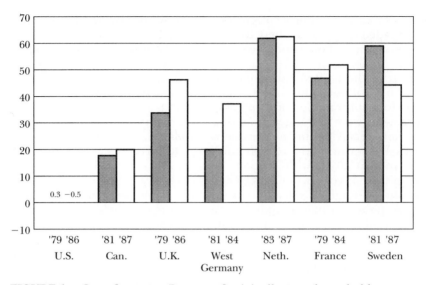

FIGURE 1.   Out of poverty: Percent of originally poor households lifted out of poverty by government programs after accounting for tax payments.

Canada and less than 2% in West Germany, France, and the Netherlands remained poor for three years or more.

Researchers compared poverty rates for blacks in the United States to foreign-born people in West Germany (mostly Turks), many of whom work in low-status industrial jobs. They found that both Turks in West Germany and blacks in the United States were three times more likely to be poor than whites living in the same country. But because U.S. poverty rates were so high, white Americans were about as likely to be poor as were Turks in West Germany. In other words, the poverty rate for Turks in West Germany was only slightly higher than the rate for white Americans—18% for Turks and 15% for U.S. whites. (U.S. blacks faced a staggering 50% poverty rate.)

Even more revealing, almost half of African Americans who experienced poverty stayed poor for three years or more, compared to less than 10% of U.S. whites and only 4% of Turks and other foreign-born families in West Germany.

TREAT YOUR CHILDREN WELL?

Poverty rates for single-parent families were particularly high in the United States, Canada, and the United Kingdom. In each of these countries, such families experienced poverty about three times more often than families headed by married couples. This contrasts markedly with other countries studied, which had lower poverty rates for all families and less difference in the rates for between single-parent and couple-headed families.

Researchers attributed the success of these countries in ameliorating the financial burden of single parenthood to "the combined effects of advance child-support payments, relatively generous income 'support' packages for families with children in general, and support services—particularly publicly funded child care—that allow mothers to remain in the labor force during their child-rearing years."

Sweden succeeded in attaining the lowest poverty rates for both single-parent and couple-headed families. Far more Swedish mothers from both family types worked than in any other country, though most single parents worked only part-time. At the same time, almost all single parents relied on government programs for support. National commitments to full employment, progress in gender pay equity, collection of child-support payments, and publicly supported child care combined to give single mothers a greater measure of income security than in any other nation.

In fact, Sweden's generous child allowances help lift over 80% of poor mothers and their families out of poverty, while U.S. social policies (mostly tax credits for working mothers and Aid to Families with Dependent Children) lift fewer than 5% of poor female-headed families out of poverty.

TARNISHED MODEL

The report concludes that continental European countries have a variety of family-assistance programs that, if copied in the United States, could improve the lives of many Americans. McFate says the jury is still out on whether the United States will go in the direction of its generous European counterparts, or whether European nations will follow the conservative U.S. lead. Despite Britain's "progress" in "catching up" with U.S. poverty rates, many European family-assistance programs have survived the recent spread of conservatism. On this side of the Atlantic, McFate notes that congressional representatives recently introduced several pieces of child-credit and parental-leave legislation.

The U.S. experience has undoubtedly contributed to Europe's rightward shift, in part because the U.S. economy shone in comparison to Europe in the early 1980s. But today, Europeans are less eager to endorse U.S. economic policies. "America," comments McFate, "is looking kind of tarnished as a model."

This perception was borne out, according to McFate, by European researchers who visited Washington, D.C., during the study. Many of them had not visited this country for several years, and the number of people begging on the streets, McFate says, appalled the European researchers.

PART II
EMPLOYMENT AND EDUCATION

The next four chapters describe the dramatic changes in the composition of the U.S. population, and the responses of employers, policy makers, and educators to these changes. The increasing presence in the United States of African Americans, Hispanics, Asian Americans, Native Americans, women from all of these groups, and white women means that by the end of the next decade neither the typical American worker nor the typical American student will be a white male of European descent. While these major population shifts have been widely reported, there is generally little discussion in economics textbooks of their impact on work, labor markets, employment policies, educational processes, or the economic reasons for seeking education. Yet the links between income, employment, and education are vital, and much can be gained by an explicit examination of the different experiences of various subgroups of the population. Taking up these questions will enrich both microeconomic discussions of the process of wage determination and macroeconomic discussions of the determination of the level of unemployment.

Economists commonly refer to the relationship between the value of acquired skills, or "human capital," and the higher labor market rewards that accrue to the owners of such capital. Consequently, discussions of diversity in the world of work need to be juxtaposed to discussions of educational opportunities, since virtually all observers agree that even though education produces different rewards for different groups, the lack of education almost always guarantees low lifetime earnings. That is, equal years of schooling do not generally produce equal income profiles for men and women, and white and nonwhite workers. We should not be surprised to see that economists from the competing schools offer alternative explanations for these outcomes. Similarly, many economists are aware of connections between (un)employment and the extent of schooling, but textbooks rarely take up this discussion. Instead topics relating to unemployment are generally treated in courses on macroeconomics, while discussions of education are traditionally located in the field of microeconomics.

Macroeconomics texts generally do report the widely divergent rates of unemployment experienced by white and black workers, and male and female workers. But very little attention is paid to explaining these observed differences. In fact, many recent treatments of the problem of unemployment are carried out within the context of the "natural rate of unemployment." (This is the rate of unemployment that prevails when cyclical unemployment is zero and all remaining unemployment is either frictional or structural. You can find technical definitions for these terms in any principles of economics textbook.) When, however, the concept of a "natural rate of unemployment" is examined with the variables of race, gender, and ethnicity at the forefront, it is readily apparent that some groups experience much more "natural" unemployment than do others (see Bartlett, 1993).* Since the racial, ethnic, sexual, and educational characteristics of workers expose them to different risks of unemployment, it is important to explore the ways that educational attainment varies by race, gender, and ethnicity. So before describing the next four chapters, it will be useful to review the competing theories of income determination to understand how economists connect income, employment, and education.

Conservative, Liberal, and Radical Models of Income Determination For both conservative and liberal economists, the crucial question is the connection between income, employment opportunities, and the formation of human capital. The important additional concepts needed to understand this relationship emerge from the supply-and-demand approach to wage determination. In this approach, returns to the factors of production (labor and capital) are determined just like all other prices. That is, there are supply-and-demand curves for each factor, and the competitive market sets equilibrium prices (wages and interest rates are the relevant "prices" here). On the supply side, individual choice determines how much of each factor is supplied. This choice follows the rule of utility maximization: individuals simultaneously choose between (1) income (derived from labor) and leisure, and (2) consumption now and consumption in the future (which depends on saving). The demands for labor and capital are related to technologically determined productivity, with firms willing to hire factors of production up to the point where the additional contribution to total output resulting from the extra output produced by that factor just equals the payment for the factor. In capsule form, this constitutes the orthodox textbook theory of factor pricing. The following paragraphs present the arguments more technically and in terms familiar to more advanced students in economics. A very productive exercise for all levels of economics students is to translate the next several paragraphs into the appropriate graphs, diagrams, and equilibrium conditions of neoclassical economics.

In the neoclassical vision, supply-and-demand schedules determine the prices of the factors of production (labor and capital). On the one hand, there are individual choices regarding the decision to supply labor (the income/leisure trade-off) alongside individual choices to supply capital (the "consume now"/ "save now to consume more in the future" trade-off). On the other hand, there are firm choices regarding the decision to demand labor. This choice is directly related to technology since the technique of production is assumed to determine the value of the marginal contribution to total output of each factor. The equilibrium prices of each factor (assuming that rents are not being discussed) then reflects: (1) tastes and preferences, since these underlie the decision to supply

*Robin Bartlett, "Macroeconomics: An Introductory Lecture Integrating the New Scholarship on Women." In Janet Bauer, Jane Bransburg, and Elizabeth Maher (eds.), *Teaching Differently* (Feminist Studies in Education [SUNY at Albany], forthcoming).

labor or capital as well as the decision to demand particular final goods and services; (2) each individual's holdings of endowments (labor and capital), since these also shape the factor supply decision; and (3) technology, since the marginal contribution to production of each factor follows directly from the engineering relationship between inputs and outputs.

In this scenario (and assuming perfectly competitive markets for both inputs and outputs), the payments to each factor of production will just exactly equal their contributions at the margin. Thus, one of the major debates in economics is over the extent to which the wages actually received by women and minorities deviate from those predicted by the theory of marginal productivity (to sharpen your understanding of this, review the arguments in Chapter 1).

The conservative position seeks to prove that differences in pay that follow lines of race and gender reflect either the free (occupational or educational) choices of women and minorities or the differences in productivity of these groups. And, according to this view, productivity differences themselves reflect choices about the acquisition of "human capital."

The liberal position seeks evidence for the argument that differences in pay follow from structural problems in labor markets. Your economics textbook probably discusses the idea that there are nonmarket forces, or "imperfections," that distort the market/wage-setting process depicted by the simple supply-and-demand model. Here textbooks usually discuss the ways that discrimination may establish different wages for men and women, or whites and nonwhites. Two frequently discussed models are the dual labor market model and the crowding model.

In the former, worker characteristics relating to sex, race, ethnicity, and age are used to assign some workers to the primary sector jobs, which offer security, advancement potential, high pay, and benefits. Workers with different characteristics are channeled into secondary sector jobs, which do not offer security, advancement, high pay, or benefits. These primary and secondary jobs constitute the dual labor market. In sympathy with this approach is the crowding model, which argues that access to the most preferred jobs is restricted to a very narrow part of the population. Restrictions of this sort artificially raise the wages of this group, and since everybody else is "crowded" into the less preferred jobs, those wages are artificially depressed. It is useful to examine the policy implications that flow from these two visions of labor markets.

In the conservative, free-market view, markets work very well to set wages, since marginal productivities and individual choices undergird supply and demand. Although there may be considerable problems of discrimination and access in the *prelabor* market processes of education and training, the market for labor itself is seen as fair and efficient. Interventions like minimum wages, unionization, or affirmative action, which are supposed to increase the equality of outcomes in labor markets, will instead cause distortions that impede efficiency and so make everyone worse off. From this perspective, exogenous forces like government legislation or unionization are the *source* of labor market problems. The liberal, imperfectionist position reverses this argument, and holds that since impediments like imperfect competition and discrimination mar the wage-setting process, government intervention and unionization are needed to correct the market. Both schools share the view that if markets worked perfectly, a market-determined income distribution would be both fair and efficient. Both schools also share the view that discrimination, to the extent it exists, *does not benefit anyone*. Given these final agreements, it should not be surprising that for both liberal and conservative economists the link between education and economic status is quite similar. Both groups see education as the means to acquire the human capital needed for economic competition. They do of course disagree about access to education and discrimination in education, but they agree about the role of education.

As we would expect, radical analyses are quite different from either the liberal or conservative positions, since economists working within this perspective start from the premise of economic exploitation. (In every situation where production is for profit, the performance of surplus labor must occur for the profits to exist. Hence exploitation and profit making are virtually synonymous in radical analyses.) Radical explanations stress the way that discrimination creates advantages that flow to both the favored groups of workers (usually white and male), and to the owners of profit-making enterprises, since workers divided by race, ethnicity, and gender are easier to exploit. Thus the radical argument about inequality is quite different from both the liberal and conservative arguments. In this view, discrimination is *more* than tastes and preferences, and *more* than irrational behavior. It also yields real material benefits while helping to maintain the underlying exploitation of labor that is essential to the production of profits.

Radicals attempt to show that some members of the community benefit from the intensified exploitation of others. The argument is as follows: since race and sex place some workers in more vulnerable positions, these people will receive lower wages. Then some of what *would have been* their wages can be paid to workers with more bargaining power. As a result, issues of power are closely related to demands for workplace and educational intervention. This argument is strengthened when placed in the context of the theory of imperfect competition.

Recall that in both the liberal and conservative visions of income determination, the assumption of perfect competition is generally maintained. If this assumption is dropped, then firms with *market power* will produce *less output* as compared to perfectly competitive firms. Thus in the aggregate these firms will hire fewer inputs than the perfectly competitive firms. Consequently, an economic environment characterized by imperfect competition will have more unemployment than an economy characterized by perfect competition. (This argument can also be made in terms of the difference between the value of marginal product and marginal revenue product.) Divisions among workers along the lines of race, gender, and ethnicity emerge as ways to allocate this inevitable unemployment (and underemployment). We can now sketch the radical link between education, employment, and income.

First, education acts as a screening process, since students with desired social characteristics are as likely to do better in school as they are likely to do better in labor markets. Indeed, innumerable studies show that the most significant factor in educational success is parents' socioeconomic status. Second, many of our ideas about racial, ethnic, and sexual identity are produced in and through educational processes. The vision of history produced by the education system stresses the equality of the American experience, while downplaying the exploitation of nonwhite, non-European peoples that was indispensable to the economic growth of this nation. Thus education helps to perpetuate divisions among workers along the lines of race, ethnicity, and gender. These divisions are socially created and manipulated in ways that preserve the dominant organizations of power, production, and culture. By presenting positive conceptions of identity and diversity as the basis for united opposition to oppression, radicals pose an alternative to the dominant ideological view of race, gender, and class in which difference is immediately interpreted as a hierarchy of good and bad, better and worse, more and less.

Summary of Part II The first two chapters of Part II focus on employment issues. The readings begin with a discussion of the major demographic changes in the work force and in business ownership, while highlighting the experiences of different groups in the business world. Other articles discuss the roles of culture and tradition in shaping workplace and employment opportunities. Chapter 5 ends with a comparison of approaches to problems of diversity in the work world. Some observers argue for increased government support for programs focusing on the needs of two-career households, since this will more rapidly open the work world to women and minorities. Others, however, stress that the marketplace generates sufficient pressures to wear down traditional barriers to minority and female advancement.

A particularly important perspective on the relationship between work-force diversity and employment holds that future corporate profitability is dependent upon women and minorities rising to greater authority within corporate hierarchies. We can relate this perspective to both the textbook discussion of the role of worker productivity in shaping the cost structure of a firm and the presentation of the dual labor market model. Some management experts argue that policies concerning family/maternity leaves, flex-time, and other adaptations designed to help two-career households juggle their many responsibilities will ultimately increase worker productivity. Firms that make these sorts of innovations will face lower costs of production and there would be less productivity lost due to employee turnover. Although there is debate over the extent to which these innovations should be mandated by government, these are the orthodox economic reasons for expecting improved employer sensitivity to women and minorities.

There are, however, barriers to such innovations. The corporate culture and traditional behaviors within many firms may produce and reproduce ingrained attitudes about women, minorities, and work that make it difficult, if not impossible, for nontraditional workers to advance. Such situations may well be self-perpetuating. That is, when minority or female workers see their chances for advancement as minimal, or when they feel that their creativity is stifled or that their best ideas are either ignored or taken over by others, they will be frustrated and may well leave the firm. Their departure then confirms the expectation that female and minority workers are not committed to corporate careers.

These tendencies may be reinforced by the discrimination that crowds nonwhite, female workers into low-wage, dead-end jobs. Occupational segregation frequently acts to confirm existing stereotypical attitudes about the types of jobs that are appropriate for women of all races and for men of color. Through many subtle and not-so-subtle processes, corporate cultures are viewed as mechanisms for reinforcing occupational segregation that in turn supports race and gender stereotypes. The extent to which people believe in or act on these stereotypes will buttress corporate visions of which jobs are appropriate for whom. Thus, there may well be powerful forces that limit the access of women and minorities to stable corporate jobs while minimizing their opportunities for advancement once they are employed in the corporate setting.

The relationships between social perceptions and meaningful employment are taken up in Readings 17, 18, 19, and 20 in Chapter 5. One of the readings discusses black youth unemployment to show the severity of the labor market problems facing this group. One simple statistic underscores the dramatic nature of this situation: since 1970 the unemployment rate for young black men between the ages of eighteen and twenty-four has never been less than 30 percent! In this reading, we find both documentation of the pervasiveness of this problem as well as substantive discussion of its causes. The emphasis is on the impact of structural change and the shift of urban employment away from low-skill manufacturing jobs to high-skill service jobs. There are, however, reasons to believe that the problems of urban decline are related to the network of racial biases that pervade American society. This link will become clear in Chapter 10, which presents considerable evidence to show that the lending policies of many major metropolitan banks undermines urban employment growth.

Another reading in Chapter 5 draws attention to the close parallel between occupational and residential segregation. Although some economics textbooks mention in passing the distribution of women and minorities across occupations, individual choice is most frequently asserted to be the cause of these employment patterns. A considerable economics literature has grown up challenging this point of view, and the lines of argument developed by economists from this perspective are congruent with the principal themes of Reading 22. The basic point is that every pattern of employment has a history that is inseparable from the processes of racism and sexism that have so significantly shaped social customs concerning job suitability. Just as paternalism produced legislation and union policies that excluded women from virtually all the high-paying trades and manufacturing jobs, so racist attitudes produced discriminatory laws and union policies regarding African American, Latino, and Asian American employment. Taken together, the readings in Chapters 4 and 5 help us to understand how demographic trends interact with personal behavior and corporate culture to limit the economic possibilities of women and minorities. These readings enrich the textbook presentation of labor market issues and the discussion of unemployment by bringing the nuances of perception, stereotyping, and sensitivity to the forefront.

The readings in Chapters 6 and 7 discuss the relationship between education and employment. In these chapters you will find a discussion of work-force diversity in terms of its effects on the supply of and demand for labor services.

Then, culture and tradition (which for conservatives are part of "tastes and preferences" and therefore not appropriate objects of social policy, but for liberals are part of the institutional-social structure and thus amenable to change) are seen as important influences both on the decision to supply labor and on workers' productivity.

Discussions of access to education and discrimination within educational institutions can be grouped into three corresponding positions. In the conservative view, institutions of higher education, like all other institutions in a capitalist society, reflect the purely meritorious reward structure of the market. There is no need for government interference, and if schools are required to reflect social diversity, campus tensions are to be expected as the natural product of unfair advantages that may result from such interference. Liberals argue that equal access to education and equal treatment within schools are necessary antidotes to inequality, since income inequalities reflect different training, human capital, and attitudes toward work. Radicals, however, argue that the educational system functions to reproduce the conditions of inequality in society at large. Let us turn now to the readings.

CHAPTER 4

The Changing World of Work

11

Meet Your New Work Force

Sharon Nelton

This article describes the major trends shaping the racial, sexual, and ethnic composition of the U.S. work force. The advantages of and strategies for managing diversity are enumerated. Special attention is paid to the role of the corporate culture in fostering an atmosphere in which diverse people can flourish.

Exercises to Guide Your Reading

1. Describe the major changes in the U.S. work force.
2. Explain how diversity issues affect business performance.
3. Give examples of "managing diversity."
4. Construct a policy for "managing diversity" for your current (or former) employer.

Brenda L. Roth had high hopes for Mary, a white woman she hired last year as a receptionist for the front office at SBE, Inc., a computer-products manufacturer in Concord, Calif.

Mary was "a mature, articulate, educated, well-put-together, handsome woman," recalls Roth, SBE's vice president of administration. Throughout the new recruit's first day, Roth heard she was doing a good job,

Reprinted by permission of *Nation's Business.* July 1988. pp. 14–17, 20–21.

so at the end of the day, Roth was surprised when Mary, smiling pleasantly, said she was quitting. "I don't like to work with gays, coloreds and boat people, so I won't be back."

"If that's the way you feel," Roth told her, "we don't want you back."

Mary had discovered that the workplace just isn't what it used to be. Nobody's workplace is.

SBE has a multicultural employee mix and likes it that way. Of its 100 workers, 40 percent are women and 23 percent are minorities—blacks, Hispanics or Asians.

SBE's variety symbolizes what is happening all over the United States: The work force is becoming more and more diverse. White males are already in a new minority of their own, representing 45 percent of America's 117.8 million workers in 1986. Over the next dozen years, their share will decline to 39 percent.

"White males, thought of only a generation ago as the mainstays of the economy, will comprise only 15 percent of the net additions to the labor force between 1985 and 2000," says *Workforce 2000*, a report prepared by the Hudson Institute for the U.S. Department of Labor last year. The rest will be American-born white females, immigrants and a rich mix of native minorities that includes blacks and a wide variety of Hispanics, Asians, American Indians and Pacific Islanders.

Little by little, senior executives and management experts across America are recognizing that these vast demographic shifts demand a new way of running things—an approach often called "managing diversity." This means recognizing that diversity is already a fact of life, learning to understand "culturally different" workers and creating an environment in which they will flourish.

"The company that gets out in front managing diversity, in my opinion, will have a competitive edge," says Xerox Chairman David T. Kearns in a three-part series of training videotapes, "Valuing Diversity," produced by Copeland Griggs Productions of San Francisco.

"We want to attract the very best talent available. And talent is gender-blind and color-blind," says James E. Preston, president and chief operating officer of Avon Products, Inc.

Proponents of the new concept say companies stand to gain a number of advantages when they do a good job of managing diversity. Among them are:

The Opportunity to Hire and Keep the Best of the New Labor Pool. Companies with reputations for being good places for women or minorities to work are sought out by those workers.

Greater Innovation. The broader the spectrum of backgrounds in a group, says one executive, the richer the ideas that emerge.

"Without women, *USA Today* would have been '*USA Yesterday*,'" Nancy J. Woodhull, president of Gannett New Media, told participants at a University of Southern California conference. When *USA Today* was launched, she said, readers liked it immediately because they found it interesting. "The reason we were interesting is that there were a lot of ideas from different people with different points of view in our news meetings every day. There were women; there were minorities; there were young people; there were old people. There were people who went to Harvard. There were people who went to Trenton State in New Jersey."

Better Performance among Female and Minority Workers. When only white males have opportunities to attain positions of power in a company, it "diminishes the sense of motivation and commitment of the workers who are underrepresented," says Denise Cavanaugh, an organization-development consultant in Washington.

Ability to Make the Most of Ethnic or International Markets. "We are consumer marketers, and the marketplace is very diverse in this country," says Avon's Jim Preston. "Who best understands the needs of

Hispanics, Asians and women than Hispanics, Asians and women?"

Procter & Gamble has had great success in recruiting minorities and women, according to Calvin A. Harper, who is black and is an officer in the company. "We're convinced that this diversity in our work force can give us a significant competitive advantage if managed or utilized effectively."

But for many companies, success in meeting affirmative-action goals has created a new problem: retaining women and minorities and moving them up through the ranks.

"We tried everything," says Preston. "We tried mentoring, we tried recruiting at black and other minority universities, we had special internship programs, we had internal tracking. You name it, we tried it all."

The problem, Avon found, was not getting minorities and women in the door. It was keeping them.

It was a classic example of what R. Roosevelt Thomas, Jr., calls "the frustrating cycle." A company meets its hiring goals for minor-

ities and women, and it develops high expectations that they will work well and move up in the corporation. "Unfortunately, these expectations are rarely met," says Thomas, director of the American Institute for Managing Diversity, Inc., at Morehouse College, in Atlanta.

"So you have frustration," he continues. "Frustration on the part of people who were recruited because they are not experiencing what they had hoped to have happen, and frustration on the part of managers because they don't understand why these 'right' people aren't moving up the hierarchy and because they are not being given credit for a good-faith effort."

The disappointed minorities or women leave the company. Often, the company will make another recruitment effort, beginning the cycle again.

Avon's Jim Preston and other business leaders find that meeting the challenges of the new work force requires some fundamental changes in corporate culture. Most American businesses have corporate cultures that have "been described and imprinted by white males," he says. "Small wonder, then, that minorities and women have had difficulty over the years in adapting to the climates that exist in these businesses."

Companies can make the culturally different worker feel uncomfortable or alienated by instituting rules that favor traditional white male culture—such as banning corn-row hairstyles popular among black women or setting dress codes that require white shirts and ties.

At more serious levels, companies often inadvertently prevent the advancement of women and minorities. White males may feel they can take the measure of another white male more easily or feel more comfortable with him, says Denise Cavanaugh. They may fear going out on a limb to promote a woman or a minority employee.

Or they may misinterpret the behavior of people unlike themselves. One of the Copeland Griggs videos demonstrates, for example, a scene in which a white male manager questions the wisdom of giving a promotion

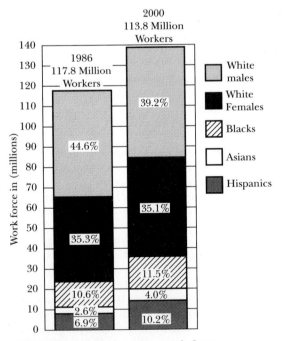

FIGURE 1.   Our changing work force.
Source: Hudson Institute.

to an Asian because the Asian is reluctant to speak of his own personal achievements. In the manager's view, the employee has not shown that he can provide leadership; in the Asian's view, it is inappropriate to toot your own horn.

"Some cultures emphasize working as a team in a group; others emphasize individual pursuits," observes Andrew M. Geller, vice president of the Hay Group, a management consulting company. "Some value consensus-building; others emphasize competition and winners and losers."

The white male system that predominates in American business, many psychologists say, is marked by emphases on objectivity, competition and "getting down to business." "We're trained throughout our education to become critical thinkers and to be hard-nosed and adversarial," says Nancy Rule Goldberger, a co-author of a study called *Women's Ways of Knowing*.

But women tend to gain much of their knowledge subjectively—through intuition, for example. When they get into the business world, they find this kind of knowledge belittled by their male peers. They also are uncomfortable with the adversarial style favored by men. In fact, women and minorities frequently complain of being ignored in business situations even though their ideas may be better than those of their white male colleagues.

Managing diversity means not only tolerating differences but also supporting and nurturing them, says the Hay Group's Geller. One popular assumption has been that women aren't assertive enough and therefore need assertiveness training so that they can be more like men.

"I would prefer to see organizations that instead say there are different ways to make your points around here, and it isn't necessarily by being the most assertive about it," says Geller.

Smaller firms may have the advantage in managing diversity because they are more in touch with their individual workers and are more likely to accommodate their differences.

About 75 percent of the 180 employees at Pace Foods, Inc., in San Antonio are Mexican-Americans. Pace, which makes Pace Picante Sauce, is headed by a white male, President Kit Goldsbury.

Goldsbury has been watching the demographics and knows that, if anything, he can expect still more Mexican-Americans in the company's future. And he's prepared.

"We're a bilingual company," says Goldsbury, who spent much of his youth on a family-owned ranch in Mexico, where he learned Spanish. Publications are printed in two languages, and even meetings are conducted in both Spanish and English.

Pace might have lost a good mechanic had it not been so flexible. One applicant took a company-required test and failed. "We gave it to him again in Spanish, and he scored very, very high," says Goldsbury.

At SBE, where the Asian workers are primarily Filipino, Brenda Roth says, "There was a lot of consciousness-raising when the Philippine government went through a complete change two years ago." The company offered extended leaves of absence to people who wanted to go back to the Philippines to check on their families. Two employees accepted the offer.

SBE is headed by two white males, Thomas C. Anderson, chairman and CEO, and William R. Gage, president. But Roth credits them with creating an environment in which all kinds of people can develop and advance. Roth started as a sales administrator when she was hired five years ago, and she received several promotions before becoming a vice president. One Hispanic and three Asians hold management or supervisory positions. And last year, the company named a woman to its seven-member board of directors.

Does she see the possibility of a minority or a woman ever running the company? "Absolutely," she says.

In large companies, accommodating diversity in a corporate culture is a more deliberate process. And one of the best examples of what a large company can do is Avon, with 30,000 employees worldwide.

Four years ago Avon brought in Roose-

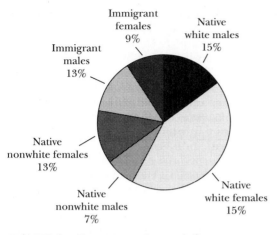

FIGURE 2. Entrants to the work force: 1985–2000.

Source: Hudson Institute.

velt Thomas and a San Francisco consultant, Ron Brown, to help it address its turnover problem. According to Jim Preston, Thomas and Brown first worked with top managers, helping them identify the subtle "negative assumptions" that existed in Avon's culture, such as "Asians generally make good technicians but not good managers," or "blacks inherently aren't as smart as whites." Over the next three years, all of Avon's middle managers were put through seminars that aimed at attacking such biases.

Three years ago Avon also created two positions with the unusual title of "director of multicultural planning," one post for the corporate office and one for the company's beauty-products division, which brings in 92 percent of Avon's $3.2 billion annual revenues.

Daisy Chin-Lor, a Chinese-American born in New York, was moved into the beauty-group post from a marketing job. Top management, she says, wanted someone "who had not only the line-management mentality but could attack this like a business."

One thing that makes Avon's approach unique, says Chin-Lor, who was recently promoted to area director of human resources for continental Europe, is that it ties multicultural planning into its strategic plan.

Representatives of three ethnic networks—black, Asian and Hispanic—meet regularly with Preston and Avon's chairman, Hicks B. Waldron. Once, the minority delegation said Avon's process for selecting people for promotion left too much to the whims of a few people in upper management. In response, Avon last year improved its system of tracking employee skills. When an opening occurs, the candidate slating is done not by line management but by the human-resources department.

Says Preston: "We insist that there be a representation of women and minorities on every slate, and if there is none, we won't look at it until there is one or they tell us that for this particular position there just are no minorities. But we challenge it each time."

Although Preston says Avon is still "far from perfect," its approach is beginning to pay off. The company has increased the number of minorities at the director level from 15 to 22 since 1986. Over 60 percent of its managers are women, and 13 women hold senior management positions.

A company still has a choice. "A uniform set of expectations and rewards makes sense when you've got a fairly uniform work force," says Andrew Geller. Senior management can still insist on uniformity even in a diverse work force. Both diversity and uniformity, he says, are "viable alternatives."

Large or small, if your company chooses the approach of managing diversity, here are some of the measures you can take:

- Aim for an environment where no one has an advantage or a disadvantage because of race, sex, ethnic origin or creed. This includes white males, says Roosevelt Thomas.
- Identify the elements in your corporate culture that prevent you from retaining good minority and female employees. You may find prejudices that serve as deterrents, or that some of your systems, like Avon's promotion system, need to be altered.
- Couple awareness or sensitivity training with action. Accepting and valuing diversity is a formal goal of the Hoechst Celanese Chemical Group in Dallas, and its managers are put

through training to make them aware of prejudices. But, says the group's human-resource manager, R. W. (Bob) Swanbeck, they are also rated on how well they meet employee equality objectives as part of their performance appraisals.

- Take on some of the burden of adjustment. When you expect minorities and women to do all the adapting to your culture, you sap them of energy that could otherwise go into their work. Pace Foods not only offers classes in English to its Hispanic workers, but also provides Spanish lessons for its English-speaking employees.

- Help minorities and women fit in and advance. Make sure they understand the unwritten rules of your organization. Look for development opportunities for them. Some companies this year, for example, will be sending promising women managers to one of six four-day seminars called "Executive Women Workshop: Development for Women as Leaders." They are sponsored by the Center for Creative Leadership of Greensboro, N.C.

Does managing diversity well really help the bottom line? It's too soon to tell, but Brenda Roth says SBE's diverse work force has helped the company grow from 17 employees in 1982 to its present 100 employees and $9 million in annual sales. And Preston says that sales and profits for the Avon beauty group have been "straight up" during the past $2\frac{1}{2}$ years.

When it comes to valuing diversity, Preston is a true believer. Instead of thinking of the United States as a melting pot, he says, "I'd rather view it as a mosaic—composed of many cultures, many races, many colors, many religions. We all have to recognize that America's greatness is a result of the fact that we are this beautiful mosaic, the only one in the world."

12

Discrimination Reflects on You

Ann C. Wendt and William M. Slonaker

This article reports the findings of a study of employment discrimination cases in Ohio, a state with a work force composition quite similar to that of the United States as a whole. The authors found that human resource professionals were more likely than other corporate executives to be cited in discrimination suits. The four behaviors most frequently listed in grievances filed with the Equal Employment Opportunity Commission (EEOC) against human resource professionals are identified and discussed.

Exercises to Guide Your Reading

1. Define the concept "standard occupational classification."
2. List ten of the major occupational classifications.
3. Give examples of the behavior patterns likely to lead to discrimination complaints.
4. Explain why the recruitment, selection, and termination stages of the employment process are frequently involved in discrimination suits.

The relative isolation of small groups, their constant feeling of insecure tenure, imposes upon such groups an attitude of suspicion or even hostility. . . . By this road we drift downwards to . . . a disintegration of a community into an infinity of mutually hostile sections.[1]

Elton Mayo wrote these words in 1941, when war was inevitable. He believed that isolation had triggered the war. In 1945, after the war, he warned that "collaboration in an industrial society cannot be left to chance."[2] The social upheavals of the '50s and '60s led to the passage of the Civil Rights Act of 1964, which eliminated the isolation of certain groups for employment. In fact, the '60s proliferation of federal, state and local equal employment opportunity legislation was a significant impetus for human resources. These departments assumed responsibility for developing policies and practices to comply with these complex laws. While legislation, court decisions and positive responses by organizations have reduced employment discrimination, we still have a long way to go.

Two 1990 national surveys reported that nearly one-third of employers admitted that discrimination is still a problem in their organizations.[3] One-fourth of American workers reported experiencing some form of employment discrimination.[4] With the increasing diversity of the workforce, human resource professionals often stand alone between Mayo's collaboration and unlawful discrimination.

Reprinted by permission of *Human Resources Magazine*. May 1992. pp. 44–47.

A STUDY OF 2,500 CASES

We have studied 2,500 cases randomly drawn from the files of the Ohio Civil Rights Commission (OCRC) during the years 1985 to 1990. More than 95 percent of these cases were employment-discrimination claims filed under federal (85 percent) or state (15 percent) laws. Men filed 48 percent of the claims; about 10 percent fewer than their representation in the workforce. Women filed 52 percent of the claims; about 10 percent more than their representation in the workforce.

The Ohio workforce participation rates mirror those of the United States. Ohio ranks seventh in employment, and the claimants held jobs in more than 300 of the standard occupational classifications. They filed claims against all types of public and private sector employers, and their sizes ranged from micro-businesses to *Fortune* 500 firms.

The OCRC, established in 1959, received 78 filings its first year, and by 1990, received approximately 6,500 filings per year. Like most state equal opportunity commissions, the OCRC enforces the Ohio anti-discrimination laws and is an EEOC 706 (Equal Employment Opportunity) agency. Employees file discrimination charges with the OCRC. The commission then investigates the charge and determines if there is probable cause. It may attempt conciliation, hold hearings, make findings and issue orders.

SOURCE OF DISCRIMINATION

Avoiding employment-discrimination problems requires identifying potential sources of discrimination. Neither the EEOC, nor the various state agencies, publish data about the persons named by claimants as the source of discrimination. The authors' study, however, included the sources. While their study found that most claimants (71 percent) named a supervisor as the source of the discrimination, 11 percent of the respondents identified human resource professionals (HRPs) as the culprits.

Analyzing these cases involving HR professionals yielded four patterns of behavior that will help prevent discrimination claims that name HR professionals as the source. The four patterns are:

- Sixteen percent of the claims described HRPs as having unfair or ineffective policies.
- Twenty-two percent claimed that they were ambushed by an HRP.
- Twenty percent said that they were the victim of an HR professional "trigger" person.
- Twenty-two percent of the claims portrayed an HR professional who acted without thinking.
- The remaining 20 percent of the claims included a diverse variety of situations involving HRPs.

PATTERN 1: UNFAIR POLICIES

"I am a male. Mr. Smith, director of human resources, fired me for failing to report two tardinesses. I reported them within the required times. The progressive discipline system was not followed. I was supposed to receive a verbal counseling first, a written warning next and a disciplinary hearing for the third occurrence. Females always get progressive discipline."

This example, taken from the study, highlights the first important pattern. The policy was in place, but it was not being consistently used.

Policies Stored on Shelf Are of Little Value. Regular use is the goal and the fulfillment of the written words. Nondiscriminatory policies are carefully formulated and consistently applied by all members of the organization. Human resource policies should be periodically audited to accomplish these goals.

Examine Personal Biases. Everyone has them. But, when formulating and applying policies, be careful to control negative or prejudicial biases so that they do not interfere. Honestly examine your attitudes and behaviors toward minorities, women, disabled persons, older people, religious groups and other diverse groups. Also, review disciplinary, discharge and other relevant records to see how existing policies have been applied.

Gather Current Information. Talk with the people who are most affected by the policies—managers, supervisors, employees and union representatives. Find out:

- Are the policies accepted, or are they circumvented?
- How are the policies interpreted and applied?
- What do they find to be the strengths and weaknesses?
- What are their suggestions for improvements?

Also, compare the HR policies to those of other organizations. Most HR professionals are members of one or more professional associations, and these contacts can be valuable sources of information.

Revise and Communicate. Write policies at a level understandable by those persons with the least education in the organization. Pay particular attention to the following areas:

- Format, make the document user friendly. For example, is discipline discussed in one area, or in several sections of the policy manual?
- Legalese should be avoided, and plain language should be encouraged.
- Good policies are flexible to meet diverse situations.
- Review drafts for clarity with employees from all levels.

For example, the following claim could have been avoided. "I am a black female. I decided to step down from senior cashier to cashier. Several days later, Jane, the HR director, told me that I had lost all seniority. The handbook states that you only begin again if you are transferred or promoted."

How would your employees interpret this policy?

- Remember to check the policies for compliance with all laws. Distribute the policies to every employee and conduct training sessions or meetings as appropriate. Include human resource policies as a topic for new employee orientation.

Implement and Continually Evaluate. Policies and procedures should be continually assessed and adjustments made when necessary. Consider the negative impact projected by this HR professional on the legitimacy of policies in the following case: "I am a 44-year-old woman. Ms. Doe, employee relations manager, told me I was terminated from my job as a teller because I 'violated company policy.' When I asked her what she meant by 'violating company policy' she would not tell me."

PATTERN 2: AMBUSHING EMPLOYEES

"I was on sick leave. During my leave, my paycheck was delayed four times, and Mrs. Doe, manager of personnel, called me requesting my resignation. In a letter dated June 23, Mrs. Doe stated that I missed a doctor's appointment that the company scheduled for me, and that if I didn't explain it by June 30, they would consider me to have resigned. I did not know about the appointment, and I did not receive the letter until July 3."

This was one of the most flagrant ambushes in the study. Nearly one-half of the ambushes were carried out against claimants who were disabled or who had filed previous charges of discrimination against the same employer.

"I am a 43-year-old female, and I worked for the company for 17 years. On August 21, I was fired. Jane, the human resource manager, said I was fired for record falsification. I recorded one day's time in error. I received no warning, as had other younger employees for the same mistake."

This employee was ambushed by the HR professional. It is likely her employer previously had decided to discharge her, and any minor infraction would have been used as the reason. While the letter of the policy may have warranted discharge, the spirit should have considered the length of the claimant's employment and her employment history.

Although the typical claimant in ambush cases had two to five years of employment with the organization, a sizable number had 16 to 20 years of employment. To avoid ambushes, HR professionals should stop, look and listen before they or others take punitive actions against employees. This can be done by following policies that provide notice, an opportunity to correct performance, and subsequent follow-ups between the employee and the human resource professional or supervisor.

PATTERN 3: HR AS THE TRIGGER

"The personnel manager said that they were going to hire 40 females into the plant, and he promised me a job. But instead, he hired 29 males and no females."

Human resources has the most visible role in the recruitment process. They place the advertisements, receive and screen applications, identify qualified applicants, and refer them to line supervisors who make the selection decisions. Unfortunately, line management frequently overrules the HR professional's concerns about discrimination in favor of maintaining the steady state of the office or shop floor. HR must promote the organization's compliance with all antidiscrimination laws.

"I am a 59-year-old male and have worked for them for 24 years. I did not have any problem until Tom, age 33, became my supervisor. He constantly harassed me. Mr. Smith, the personnel manager, transferred and demoted me, and he gave me no reason, only that he hated to do it."

The HR professional was the trigger person for line management. Interestingly, men in managerial jobs were the victims at a rate that was double their representation in the

study. Also, age-discrimination claimants were victims of the HR trigger at two times the expected rate.

Finally, long-term employees (21 to 30 years) were victims at a rate of more than two and one-half times their number in the study. Before punitive action is taken against employees, their employment records should be carefully examined. If there is not just cause for the contemplated actions, then HRPs should be cautious lest they become the trigger person.

PATTERN 4: ACTING WITHOUT THINKING

"I was not hired as machine operator. I believe I was not hired because of my race, black. Mr. Smith, industrial relations director, said that I scored too low on my test. He showed me a list of applicants and their scores. A letter 'W' or 'B' was penciled in next to each name. I believe all the 'W's' were next to whites' names and all the 'B's' next to blacks' names."

Title VII of the Civil Rights Act of 1964 prohibits employment decisions based on race, color, national origin, religion or sex. The Age Discrimination in Employment Act of 1967 prohibits age discrimination. Most states have parallel statutes.[5] Notations in application or employment records that identify any protected group are clear violations of these statutes.

"I am a female. I applied for the position of truck driver that the company advertised in the newspaper. Mr. Smith, personnel officer, told me that I would be considered. I did not get the job. I was later informed that Mr. Smith took my application over to the warehouse and waved it in the air and said, 'I would never hire a woman to drive a truck.'"

The U.S. Supreme Court recently affirmed in *Price Waterhouse vs. Hopkins* (1989), that stereotyping can be employment discrimination. HRPs should make employment decisions by focusing on the job requirements and not on stereotypes.

CONCLUSION

In our study of 2,500 claims, more than 95 percent were employment-discrimination claims. Eleven percent of these claims named the organization's HR professional as the source of the discrimination. Analyses revealed that 80 percent of those cases fit within one of the four distinct patterns described. Some HR professionals were accused of unfairly applied or ineffective policies, some ambushed employees, others acted as the trigger person, and finally, many were perceived as acting without thinking.

In all four patterns, the actions taken against the claimants primarily occurred during the recruitment and selection phase of employment, or in the termination phase.

Therefore, recruitment and selection policies should be carefully audited. Job specifications should be precise and job-related. Position notices should be clearly written. Advertising should be carefully monitored. Many discrimination claimants were told that the position was filled, yet the notice continued to be published. Numerous job applicants were told that the position had been filled and that there was no record of their application.

Discharge policies also should be carefully audited. Common complaints were that this serious action was taken without any warning, discussion or opportunity to be heard. These claimants frequently had no prior production or behavioral problems. Why not afford employees a pre-disciplinary hearing that assures them notice, an opportunity to be heard, the right to question accusers, review by an impartial person and fair procedures to protect these rights? Another frequent complaint was that they were told that their jobs were being eliminated, but a new hire quickly replaced them. Finally, employees who reported discrimination against other employees were often discharged.

While not all discrimination claims have merit, all are important concerns. An employee's perception that something is wrong is real to that individual. When employees have discrimination problems, the human resource department should strive to resolve them internally rather than allowing them to be decided externally.

Once an employee files a claim with an external anti-discrimination agency, human resources and the employer organization are placed in defensive positions.

In the 1990 follow-up report by the Hudson Institute and Towers Perrin to the original *Workforce 2000* study,[6] nearly one-third of 645 surveyed employers admitted that employment discrimination is still a problem in their organizations. Considering that employers are now concerned about the forthcoming labor shortage, skills gap, increases in minority and immigrant workers, increases in working women and the "graying" of the workforce, is it not time that employment discrimination be declared obsolete? Human resource professionals can make that declaration clear and effective in their organizations.

NOTES

1. E. Mayo, in the foreword to F. Roethlisberger, *Management and Morale* (Cambridge: Harvard University Press, 1941).
2. E. Mayo, *The Social Problems of an Industrial Civilization* (Cambridge: Harvard University Press, 1945).
3. R. Samborn, "Many Americans Find Bias at Work," *The National Law Journal* (July 16, 1990): 1. [This research by the *Journal* and by Lexis, Div. of Mead Data Central, surveyed 803 adult Americans.]
4. Hudson Institute & Towers Perrin, *Workforce 2000: Competing in a Seller's Market: Is Corporate America Prepared?* (New York: Towers Perrin, 1990). [Six hundred and forty-five organizations completed the survey.]
5. National Association of Manufacturers, *Employment Law in the 50 States: A Reference for Employers* (Washington, D.C., 1989).
6. Hudson Institute (for the U.S. Department of Labor), *Workforce 2000: Work and Workers for the 21st Century* (Washington, D.C.: U.S. Government Printing Office, 1987).

13

Reaching for the Dream

William O'Hare

This article describes changes in patterns of minority-owned businesses in the 1980s. Particular attention is paid to variations among minority groups themselves. The rates of business ownership and firm size for various subgroups are compared, and characteristics associated with entrepreneurship are discussed.

Exercises to Guide Your Reading

1. Summarize data on minority ownership.
2. Identify recent trends in minority ownership.
3. List the characteristics associated with minority firm ownership.
4. Discuss cultural, sociological, and economic factors that may hinder or enhance a minority group's ownership rate.

The rapid growth of minority populations is changing the profile of America's business owners. In 1987, minorities owned nearly one-tenth of the nation's 13.7 million firms. As a result, businesses that sell to entrepreneurs face a rapidly changing market. Minority business owners are also altering the balance of economic and political power.

The number of businesses owned by various minority groups in 1982 and 1987 is collected in the Census Bureau's Survey of Minority-Owned Business Enterprises. The data reveal wide variations in rates of business ownership among minority groups.*

*The types of firms included in this study are restricted to partnerships, individual proprietorships, and Subchapter S corporations. For large corporations with many stockholders, determining the race of the owners is virtually impossible.

GOOD YEARS

The mid-1980s were good years for minority business owners. Every significant minority group experienced an increase in the number of businesses owned and in rates of business ownership. But some minority groups have much higher rates of business ownership than others, and the increases of the mid-1980s were not evenly shared.

The total number of minority-owned firms grew by nearly half a million during the mid-1980s, from 742,000 in 1982 to 1,214,000 in 1987. This is more than four times the rate of growth for all businesses (64 percent versus 14 percent). By 1987, minorities owned about 9 percent of the firms in this country, up from 6 percent in 1982.

But these overall rates mask important dif-

Reprinted by permission of *American Demographics*. January 1992. pp. 32, 34–36.

TABLE 1   Minority Business Owners

Koreans are the minority group most likely to own a business; American Indians are the least likely.

(Minority-Owned Firms per 1,000 Population, for Minority Groups, and Percent Change 1982–87)

	1987	1982	Percent Change 1982–87
Blacks	14.6	11.3	29.2%
Hispanics	20.9	14.3	46.2
Mexican	18.8	13.7	37.2
Puerto Rican	10.9	6.3	73.0
Cuban	62.9	41.4	51.9
Other Hispanic	22.9	14.2	61.3
Asian*	57.0	43.2	31.9
Asian Indian	75.7	51.3	47.6
Chinese	63.4	49.1	29.1
Japanese	66.1	59.3	11.5
Korean	102.4	68.0	50.6
Vietnamese	49.6	14.6	239.7
Filipino	32.8	25.5	28.6
Hawaiian	21.5	16.6	29.5
American Indian	11.8	8.8	34.1
Aleut	54.0	58.5	−7.7
Eskimo	44.4	36.8	20.7
Native American	10.3	7.4	39.2
Nonminority	67.1	61.9	8.4

*Includes Pacific Islanders.

Source: Bureau of the Census, 1982 and 1987 Economic Census and population estimates

TABLE 2   Asian Profit Centers

The average Asian-owned business makes twice as much as the average black-owned business.

(Total Minority-Owned Businesses, Total Receipts and Receipts per Firm, by Minority Type, 1987)

	Number of firms 1987	Receipts (in $000)	Receipts per Firm
Black	424,200	$19,762,900	$46,600
Hispanic	422,400	24,731,600	58,600
Asian*	355,300	33,124,300	93,200
American Indians**	21,400	911,300	42,600

*Includes Pacific Islanders.

**Includes Eskimos and Aleuts.

Source: Bureau of the Census, 1987 Economic Census

13 percent rate of black population growth between 1980 and 1990.

The rapid growth of Hispanic-owned firms has brought them to parity with the number of black-owned firms. Blacks owned 424,000 U.S. businesses in 1987, and Hispanics owned 422,000. Each group accounts for just over one-third of minority-owned businesses. Asians account for 29 percent; American Indians, 2 percent.

ASIANS HAVE THE EDGE

The raw numbers don't reveal the relative success of various groups. A better measure of success is the business ownership rate, or the number of businesses owned by members of a group relative to their population size. We used decennial census data to estimate the mid-year population of minority groups in 1982 and 1987.

The popular image of Asians as industrious immigrants is true. Asians own 57 businesses for every 1,000 people, by far the highest business ownership rate of the four major groups. Their rate is almost three times as high as the rate for the next-highest minority group (Hispanics), but it is still below the business ownership rate of nonmi-

ferences among subgroups. The number of firms owned by Asians* grew by 89 percent during the five-year period, not far behind the rate of Asian population growth. The number of firms owned by Hispanics grew by 81 percent. The number of firms owned by American Indians grew 58 percent, a rate slightly below the overall average for minorities, but far higher than the group's population growth rate. Business growth was weakest among black-owned businesses, at 38 percent. But that was still faster than the

*In this article, the term "Asians" includes Pacific Islanders, and the term "American Indians" includes Eskimos and Aleuts.

norities, which was 67 in 1987. Blacks have a business ownership rate of 15, slightly higher than the rate for American Indians.

The high rate of business ownership among Asians is due to several factors. First is their high level of educational attainment. In 1990, about 40 percent of adult Asian Americans had completed college, compared with only 23 percent of non-Hispanic whites. Asian Americans also have relatively high incomes, which provide them with more capital to launch small businesses.

A large share of Asian Americans are recent immigrants, many of whom came to the U.S. specifically to go into business. Between 1982 and 1989, 38 percent of immigrants from Asia and the Pacific Islands had professional or executive occupations, compared with only 17 percent of immigrants from other parts of the world, according to the U.S. Immigration and Naturalization Service. And Asian Americans are concentrated in Los Angeles, San Francisco, and other large West Coast cities where local economies were booming during the 1980s.

Minority groups differ from each other in terms of their rates of business ownership, and also in the sizes of the firms they own.

Once again, Asians have the edge. The average income of an Asian-owned firm was $93,200 in 1987, significantly higher than the average for any other minority group. Hispanic-owned firms had the next highest average income, at $58,600, followed by firms owned by blacks ($46,600) and by American Indians ($42,600).

Asian-owned firms have a higher average income, in part, because of the types of firms Asians own. More than 5 percent of Asian-owned firms are partnerships, which tend to be bigger businesses. Just 2.9 percent of Hispanic-owned businesses are partnerships, compared with 2.7 percent of firms owned by blacks and 2.6 percent by American Indians.

The larger size of Asian-owned firms is also reflected in data on the number of firms that have paid employees. Most minority-owned businesses have no paid employees other than the owner (as do nonminority-owned businesses). But 26 percent of Asian-owned businesses had paid employees in 1987, compared with 20 percent for Hispanics, 17 percent for American Indians, and 17 percent for blacks. Among firms with at least one paid employee, the average number of

---

TABLE 3   Blacks Move Over

Blacks are losing their status as the largest group of minority business owners.

(Total Minority-Owned Businesses and Share of All Minority Businesses, by Minority Type, and Percentage Growth in Businesses, 1982–87)

	1987		1982		Percent Change 1982–87
	Number	*Percent of Total*	*Number*	*Percent of Total*	
All minorities	1,213,800***	—	741,600	—	63.7%
Black	424,200	34.9%	308,300	41.6%	37.6
Hispanic	422,400	34.8	234,000	31.5	80.5
Asian*	355,300	29.3	187,700	25.3	89.3
American Indian**	21,400	1.8	13,600	1.8	57.5

*Includes Pacific Islanders.

**Includes Eskimos and Aleuts.

***Numbers do not add to total because firms that were owned equally by two or more minorities are included in the data for each minority group.

Source: Bureau of the Census, Economic Censuses

employees for Asian-owned firms was 3.79, compared with 3.19 for firms owned by Hispanics, 3.11 by blacks, and 2.40 by American Indians.

KOREANS ARE DOING BETTER

Large differences also exist in the business ownership rates of Asian and Hispanic subgroups. In some cases, the differences between subgroups are larger than the differences between races. The clear leaders among minority business owners are Koreans.

In 1982, Koreans had the highest rate of business ownership of any minority group, with 68 businesses owned for every 1,000 Korean residents. By 1987, that rate had gone sky-high. The most recent data show that more than one of every ten Korean Americans is a business owner.

The Korean rate of 102 businesses owned per 1,000 population is higher than the rate of any other racial or ethnic group, including nonminorities. This high rate reflects the selective migration of Koreans to the U.S., and their relatively high levels of educational attainment. It may also reflect certain sociological or cultural traits of the Korean population in America. For example, Koreans show a willingness to pool their resources to help other Koreans start or expand a business.

Several other Asian groups also have high business ownership rates. These include Asian Indians (76 businesses per 1,000 population), Japanese (66), and Chinese (63). All three of these groups are well represented in the U.S. at the beginning of the decade. The 1980 census showed that Asian Indians were 10 percent of all Asians and Pacific Islanders, Japanese were 20 percent, and Chinese were 23 percent.

The relatively high business ownership rates among Eskimos (44 per 1,000) and Aleuts (54 per 1,000) are probably because they live in isolated communities almost totally populated by fellow members of these groups. Business ownership reflects that population distribution.

Among Hispanics, Cubans have by far the highest business ownership rates, at 63 businesses for every 1,000 Cuban Americans. This rate is more than three times that of Mexicans (19) and nearly six times that of Puerto Ricans (11). The high rate of business ownership among Cubans is probably due to the selective migration of former business owners and better-educated adults following Fidel Castro's rise to power in 1959. Another reason is the heavy concentration of Cubans in the Miami area, which had a booming economy during the 1980s. That large, prosperous ethnic enclave provides Miami's Cubans with a potent small business incubator. And 20 percent of Cuban adults have a college education, compared with 9 percent of all Hispanics.

The numbers show that some segments of America's minority population are more likely to own businesses than are non-Hispanic whites. Other groups are catching up fast. Taken together, minorities are rapidly becoming a larger share of America's business owners.

American Indians in the 1990s

Dan Fost

This article describes recent changes in the socioeconomic status of Native Americans. Details of Native American communities and policies for future self-development are discussed. Special emphasis is placed on entrepreneurial ventures.

Exercises to Guide Your Reading

1. List the reasons for the increase in the number of people counted as American Indians in the last three censuses.
2. Explain the difficulties of counting American Indians.
3. Describe the problems confronting economic development of Native American communities.
4. Analyze the concept of "American Indian" as a racial category, and compare it with other racial categories.

When Nathan Tsosie was growing up in the Laguna Pueblo in New Mexico, he was not taught the Laguna language. The tribe's goal was to assimilate him into white society.

Today, Tsosie's 9-year-old son Darren learns his ancestral language and culture in the Laguna schools. He speaks Laguna better than either of his parents. "They're trying to bring it back," says Darren's mother, Josephine. "I'm glad he's learning. I just feel bad that we can't reinforce it and really teach it."

The strong bonds American Indians still feel to their native culture are driving a renaissance in Indian communities. This cultural resurrection has not yet erased the poverty, alcoholism, and other ills that affect many Indians. But it has brought educational and economic gains to many Indians living on and off reservations. A college-educated Indian middle class has emerged, American Indian business ownership has in-

creased, and some tribes are creating good jobs for their members.

The census counted 1,878,000 American Indians in 1990, up from fewer than 1.4 million in 1980. This 38 percent leap exceeds the growth rate for blacks (6 percent) and non-Hispanic whites (13 percent), but not the growth of Hispanics (53 percent) or Asians (108 percent).

The increase is not due to an Indian baby boom or to immigration from other countries. Rather, Americans with Indian heritage are increasingly likely to identify their race as Indian on census forms. Also, the Census Bureau is doing a better job of counting American Indians.

Almost 2 million people say that their race is American Indian. But more than 7 million people claim some Indian ancestry, says Jeff Passel at the Urban Institute. That's about 1 American in 35.

"A lot of people have one or more ances-

Reprinted by permission of *American Demographics*. December 1991. pp. 26–28, 32–34.

(population of the ten states with the largest American Indian populations, in thousands)

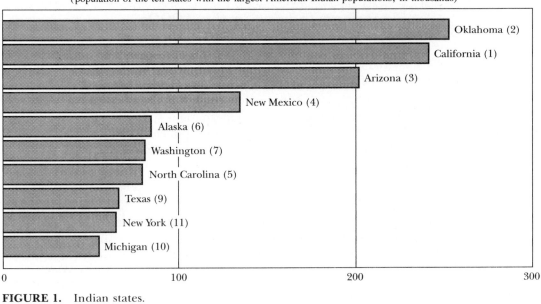

FIGURE 1.   Indian states.
Source: 1990 census.
Note: 1980 ranks in parentheses.

tors who are American Indian," says Passel. "There's a clear trend over the last three censuses for increasing numbers of those people to answer the race question as American Indian. But it doesn't tell you how 'Indian' they are in a cultural sense.

"The strength of this identification in places that are not Indian strongholds is transitory. If it becomes unfashionable to be American Indian, it could go down."

People who try to count American Indians employ many different means that often confound demographers. Tribes keep tabs on enrollment, but the rules vary on how much Indian blood makes one a member. Some tribes are not recognized by the federal government. Local health services may keep one set of records, while federal agencies like the Bureau of Indian Affairs will keep another. Some Indians are nomadic; Navajos, for example, may maintain three residences. Rural Indians can be hard to find, and minorities are always more prone to census undercounts. A growing number of mixed marriages blurs the racial boundaries even further.

"I don't know what an Indian is," says Malcolm Margolin, publisher of the monthly *News from Native California.* "Some people are clearly Indian, and some are clearly not. But the U.S. government figures are clearly inadequate for judging how many people are Indian."

Even those who can't agree on the numbers do agree that Indians are returning to their roots. "In the early 1960s, there was a stigma attached to being American Indian," Passel says. These days, even Anglos are proud of Indian heritage.

IDENTIFYING WITH INDIANS

When white patrons at Romo's restaurant in Holbrook, Arizona, learn that their host is half Navajo and half Hopi, they frequently exclaim, "I'm part Cherokee!" The host smiles and secretly rolls his eyes. More *bahanas* (whites) are jumping on the Indian bandwagon.

"In the last three years, interest in Indian beliefs has really taken off," says Marzenda McComb, the former co-owner of a New Age store in Portland, Oregon. To celebrate the sale of her store, a woman performed an Indian smudging ritual with burnt cedar and an eagle feather. Most of McComb's customers were non-Indian.

Controversy often accompanies such practices. Some Indians bristle at the sharing of their culture and spiritual practices with whites. But others welcome people of any race into their culture. And many tribal leaders recognize that Indian art and tourism are hot markets.

Anglos are not the only ones paying more attention to Indian ways. Indian children are showing a renewed interest in their culture. Jennifer Bates, who owns the Bear and Coyote Gallery in California, says her 9-year-old son has taken an independent interest in Northern Miwok dance. "It's nice, knowing that we're not pushing it on him," she says. "He wanted to dance and make his cape. It's up to us to keep things going, and if we don't, it's gone."

The oldest generation of California Indians "grew up among people who recalled California before the arrival of whites," says Malcolm Margolin. These people have "something in their tone, their mood, their manners—a very Indian quality." Younger generations are more comfortable in the white world, he says, but they sense "something very ominous about the passing of the older generation. It's the sense of the younger generation that it's up to them."

The Zuni tribe is trying to revive ancient crafts by opening two tribal-owned craft stores—one in their pueblo in New Mexico, and one on San Francisco's trendy Union Street. The most popular items are fetishes—small stone carvings of animals that serve as good-luck charms. "After *Dances with Wolves* came out, we weren't able to keep the wolf fetishes in stock," says Milford Nahohai, manager of the New Mexico store.

JOBS ON RESERVATIONS

Many Indians on and off the reservation face a well-established litany of problems, from poverty and alcoholism to unemployment.

Many tribal leaders say that only jobs can solve the problem. Promoting Indian-owned businesses is their solution.

The number of Indian-owned businesses increased 64 percent between 1982 and 1987, compared with a 14 percent rise for all U.S. firms, according to the Census Bureau. "A whole new system of role models is being established," says Steven Stallings, president of the National Center for American Indian Enterprise Development in Mesa, Arizona. "Indians see self-employment as a viable opportunity."

In boosting reservation-based businesses, Stallings aims to create sustainable, self-reliant economies. In some areas, 92 cents of every dollar earned on a reservation is spent outside the reservation, he says. Non-Indian communities typically retain as much as 85 cents.

Stallings's center hopes to start by attracting employers to Indian country. The next step is to add retail and service businesses that will "create a revolving economy on the reservation."

This strategy is at work in Laguna, New Mexico. The Laguna Indians were hit hard in 1982, when the price of uranium plummeted and the Anaconda Mineral Company closed a mine located on their reservation. But the Lagunas have bounced back with several enterprises, including Laguna Industries, a tribal-owned manufacturing firm that employs 350 people.

Laguna Industries' clients include the Department of Defense, Raytheon, and Martin Marietta. Its flagship product is a communications shelter that U.S. forces used in the Gulf War. "It's pretty nice to see your own people getting involved in high-tech stuff," says welding supervisor Phillip Sarracino, 44.

Laguna Indians are given first priority for jobs at the plant, but several middle managers are white. Conrad Lucero, a plant group leader and former tribal governor, says that non-Indian supervisors are often retirees who lend their expertise until Indians can run things on their own.

"I have an 8-year-old daughter," says Sabin Chavez, 26, who works in the quality

TABLE 1   Indian Industries

American Indian specialty contractors had receipts of $97 million in 1987. But automotive and food-store owners may earn higher profits.

(Ten Largest Industry Groups in Receipts for Firms Owned by American Indians and Alaska Natives)

Rank	Industry Group	Firms	Receipts (in Thousands)	Receipts per Firm (in Thousands)
1	Special trade contractors	2,268	$97,400	$43
2	Miscellaneous retail	1,799	85,400	47
3	Agriculture services, forestry, and fishing	3,128	84,000	27
4	Automotive dealers and service stations	222	65,300	294
5	Food stores	301	54,300	180
6	Business services	2,532	48,600	19
7	Eating and drinking places	464	35,300	76
8	Construction	461	34,200	74
9	Trucking and warehousing	590	32,200	55
10	Personal services	1,719	26,500	15

Source: 1987 Economic Censuses, Survey of Minority-Owned Business Enterprises

TABLE 2   Indian Markets

The 1990 census showed rapid increases among American Indians who live in large metropolitan areas. Some of the increases reflect an increasing willingness to declare one's Indian heritage.

(Top Ten Metropolitan Areas, Ranked by American Indian, Eskimo, and Aleut Population in 1990; and Percent Change in That Population, 1980–90)

Rank	Metropolitan Area	1990 Population	Percent Change 1980–90
1	Los Angeles-Anaheim-Riverside, CA	87,500	5%
2	Tulsa, OK	48,200	41
3	New York-Northern New Jersey-Long Island, NY-NJ-CT	46,200	101
4	Oklahoma City, OK	45,700	82
5	San Francisco-Oakland-San Jose, CA	40,800	19
6	Phoenix, AZ	38,000	66
7	Seattle-Tacoma, WA	32,100	42
8	Minneapolis-St. Paul, MN-WI	24,000	49
9	Tucson, AZ	20,300	36
10	San Diego, CA	20,100	37

Source: 1990 census.

control division. "I'm hoping to keep this company going, so our kids can live on the reservation. It's a long shot, but we have to believe in long shots."

High morale at Laguna Industries is tempered by the risks of relying on the government. The Lagunas realize that their dependence on military contracts makes them vulnerable to cuts in the defense budget. And in August 1994, the tribe's right to bid on minority set-aside contracts will expire—partly because the business has been so successful.

"We have to be able to meet and beat our competitors on the open market," Lucero says. The Lagunas may succeed: Martin Marietta Corporation has already awarded Laguna Industries a contract based on price and not minority status, says Martin Marietta customer representative Michael King.

Laguna Industries has not solved all the tribe's problems, however. Tribal planner Nathan Tsosie estimates that unemployment runs as high as 35 percent on the reservation. Much of the housing is substandard, water shortages could impede future development, and alcoholism still tears Indian families apart. But Tsosie has an answer: "We just need to develop more. People leave the reservation to get jobs. If there were jobs here, they'd stay."

GAMBLING AND TOURISM

Indians bring some real advantages to the business world. The Lagunas show that a cohesive community can be organized into an efficient production facility. Other reservations have rich natural resources. But the biggest benefit may be "sovereignty," or the suspension of many local, state, and federal laws on Indian territory. Reservations have no sales or property tax, so cigarettes, gasoline, and other items can be sold for low prices. They can also offer activities not permitted off-reservation.

Like gambling.

"Bingo is a way for tribes to amass funds so they can get into other economic development projects," says Frank Collins, a Mescalero Apache from San Jose who specializes in development.

Bingo can be big business. One parlor on the Morongo reservation, just north of Palm Springs, California, draws 5,000 people a week and employs more than 140 people. The Morongo tribe's main objective is to develop as a major resort destination, says bingo general manager Michael Lombardi.

Lombardi won't say how much money bingo generates for the Morongos. He will say that 113 reservations allow some form of gaming, and he attributes bingo's popularity to the effects of Reagan-era cutbacks in the Bureau of Indian Affairs budget. Lombardi says then-Secretary of the Interior James Watt told Indians, "Instead of depending on the Great White Father, why don't you start your own damn business?"

Indian culture also can create unique business opportunities. On the Hopi reservation in northern Arizona, Joe and Janice Day own a small shop on Janice's ancestral property. They swap elk hooves and cottonwood sticks, useful in Indian rituals, for jewelry, and baskets to sell to tourists.

The Days would like to credit their success to their shrewd sense of customer service. But they confess that the difference between profit and loss may be their wildly popular T-shirts, which read "Don't worry, be Hopi."

Not long ago, Hopis had to leave the reservation to go to school or find work. Today, the tribe has its own junior and senior high school and an entrepreneurial spirit. But small schools and small businesses won't keep people on the reservation. The Days still make a two-hour drive to Flagstaff each week to do their banking, laundry, and shopping. "The first Hopi you can get to build a laundromat is going to be a rich man," says Joe Day.

The Days lived in Flagstaff until their children finished high school. At that point, they decided to come "home." Janice's daughter is now an accountant in San Francisco, and she loves the amenities of the big city. "But who knows?" Janice says. "She may also want to come home someday. No matter where you are, you're still going to end up coming home."

THE URGE TO GO HOME

"Going home" may also mean renewing a bond with one's Indian heritage. While the population in 19 "Indian states" grew at predictable levels during the 1980s, the Urban Institute's Jeff Passel says it soared in the non-Indian states.

For example, Passel estimated the 1990 Indian population in Arizona at 202,000 (the 1980 population of 152,700, plus the intervening 58,600 births and minus the intervening 10,300 deaths)—a figure close to the 1990 census number (203,500). But in Alabama, a non-Indian state, Passel found a huge percentage increase that he could not have predicted. Alabama's Indian population grew from 7,600 in 1980 to 16,500 in 1990, a 117 percent increase. Higher birthrates, lower death rates, and migration from other states do not explain the increase.

Passel explains the gap this way: "The people who are Indians always identify themselves as Indians. They tell the census they are Indians, and they register their newborns as Indians." These people are usually found in the Indian states. "People who are part Indian may not identify themselves as American Indians. But they don't do that consistently over time."

Today, for reasons of ethnic pride, part-Indians may tell the Census Bureau they are Indian. At the hospital, they may identify themselves as white to avoid discrimination. This is most common in non-Indian states, which Passel generally defines as having fewer than 3,000 Indians in 1950.

California ranks second only to Oklahoma in its Indian population, but its mixture of tribes is unique in the nation. Some Indian residents trace their roots to native California tribes, says Malcolm Margolin. Others came west as part of a federal relocation program in the 1950s. In California cities, Cherokees, Chippewas, and other out-of-state Indians congregate in clubs.

"What has happened is the formation of an inter-tribal ethic, a pan-Indian ethic," Margolin says. "People feel that America has a lot of problems. That cultural doubt causes them to look for their ethnic roots, for something they can draw strength from. And for Indians, it's right there. It's ready-made."

15

How Do Demographic Changes Affect Labor Force Participation of Women?

Daniel T. Lichter and Janice A. Costanzo

This article examines the major causes of the dramatic increase in women's labor force participation in the post–World War II era: declining fertility, changes in marriage patterns, rising educational attainment, and increased age of women in the labor force. A statistical distinction is made between increases in women's labor force participation that occur as a result of behavioral changes and those that occur as a result of changes of the number of women in the various demographic categories. Conclusions concerning the future of female participation in the labor force are offered.

Exercises to Guide Your Reading

1. Define and discuss the concepts of demography and demographic composition.
2. Explain the difference between the "rate effect" and the "composition effect."
3. Explain why the composition effect is stronger for black women than it is for white women.
4. Assess your plans or your mate's plans for fertility, marriage, and education in light of your plans for work.

Since World War II, U.S. labor force participation rates among women have almost doubled, reaching about 55 percent in 1985.[1] Increases in labor force activity have been pervasive for all groups, especially married women and women with young children.

Changes in the demographic composition of the female population, particularly during the past decade or so, have had great potential for altering overall participation rates.[2] For example, William Johnson and Jonathan Skinner have reported that the rise in divorce rates between 1960 and 1980 may explain up to 17 percent of the rise in labor force participation rates of women during that period.[3] Similarly, Ralph Smith has con-cluded that between 1971 and 1975, the changing demographic composition (for example, marital and family status changes) of women in the labor force accounted for 28 percent of the increase in their rates.[4] Compositional changes are likely to be small over a short time period, however, and therefore should not be expected to greatly affect overall female labor force participation rates.

By examining data covering the 15-year period between 1970 and 1985, we provide evidence on the link between changes in demographic composition and labor force participation rates among women.

Specifically, we ask: To what extent have

Reprinted by permission of *Monthly Labor Review*. November 1987. pp. 23–25.

changes in fertility rates, marital status, educational levels, and age structure accounted for growth in labor force participation rates of women since 1970?

DEMOGRAPHIC COMPOSITION

Fertility. The labor force participation rates among married women with children, particularly young children, have been steadily increasing since 1970. In 1985, nearly half of all women with children under age 18 were in the labor force, compared with less than 40 percent in 1970.[5] Moreover, the declines in fertility rates, as well as declines in family size, increasing childlessness, and delayed childbearing have freed many women to pursue employment opportunities outside the home. Completed family size, for example, decreased from 2.4 children in 1970 to 1.7 in 1984 among white women, and from 3.1 to 2.2 children among blacks.[6] Recent fertility declines are thus a potentially important demographic source of post-1970 increases in overall female labor force participation rates.

Marital Status. Substantial variation exists by marital status, with married women exhibiting labor force participation rates much lower than those of the overall female population.[7] Changes since 1970 in the marital status composition of the female population have provided a potentially significant demographic source of growth in female labor force participation. The incidence of divorce, for example, increased from about 14 per 1,000 married women in 1970 to nearly 22 per 1,000 in 1984.[8] In addition, the proportion of never-married women has risen rapidly, especially among young adults, reflecting delayed marriage. For example, the median age at first marriage among women in the United States rose from 20.6 in 1970 to 22.8 in 1984.[9]

Education. The educational upgrading of the female population has been a major facet of social change in the United States. For women age 25 or over, median years of schooling increased from 12.1 to 12.6 years between 1970 and 1980, and the percent graduating from high school grew from 52.8 to 65.8.[10] Changes in the educational composition of the female population must be included in any demographic or structural explanation of rising participation rates among the female population. Indeed, increasing educational attainment alters the relative importance of home work versus the labor market for many women. This is clearly revealed in female labor force participation rates that tend to accelerate with increasing educational attainment.

Age. Age composition is a major structural aspect of the labor force.[11] Market-related activities are clearly associated with age. The age profile of women in the labor force is curvilinear, reaching its nadir during the child-bearing years and after age 40 or so, when labor force exits begin to rise. One significant facet of labor force age structure can be linked directly to the post-World War II baby boom. That is, the baby-boom cohort of the 1950's entered the labor force in large numbers during the 1970's. As this cohort aged between 1970 and 1985, declining proportions of women were concentrated in the age categories that typically exhibit lower than average rates of participation (say, those in mid- to late 40's). The "maturing" of the baby-boom cohort thus represents another potentially significant demographic component of change for women in the labor force.

ACCOUNTING FOR CHANGE

We restrict this analysis to women ages 25–49.[12] For most women, schooling has been completed by age 25, and labor force exit rates begin to accelerate significantly after 45 or so.

The extent to which changing demographic composition accounts for the increases in labor force participation rates among women can be evaluated using standard demographic methods of decomposition or components analysis.[13] It is well known that the difference between two crude rates is attributed to differences in both status-specific rates and population composition. Differences in rates between 1970 and 1985 can thus be decomposed into parts attributed to changing propensity to participate (that is, a so-called true or rate effect) and parts attributed to changes in the distribution of women by number of children, marital status, education, and age (composition effects). The categories of population composition we consider here are provided in table 1 for blacks and nonblacks.

The results of the decomposition analysis are presented in table 2. Total labor force participation rates of women increased from 47.90 percent to 71.01 percent between March 1970 and 1985. Of the 23.11-percentage-point increase in labor force participation rates, 12.48, or about 54 percent, is at-

TABLE 2 Components of change in labor force participation rates for women, by race, 1970–85

Component	Total	Black	Nonblack[1]
1985	71.01	73.21	70.70
1970	47.90	60.21	46.47
Total effect, or change	23.11	13.00	24.23
Rate effect[2]	12.48	2.07	13.72
Composition effect[3]	10.63	10.93	10.51
Number of children under age 18	4.33	3.78	4.53
Marital status	3.00	−.18	3.05
Education	3.18	7.25	2.82
Age	.11	.08	.10

[1]Nonblack includes whites and all other racial groups, except blacks.

[2]The rate effect is the 1985–70 difference in labor force participation rates of women standardized by number of children, marital status, and age.

[3]The total composition effect is equal to the sum of the four composition effects considered here.

TABLE 1 Percent distributions of women ages 25–49, by race and selected characteristics, 1970 and 1985

	Black		Nonblack[1]	
Characteristics	1970	1985	1970	1985
Number of children under age 18:				
0	23.9	32.7	20.5	36.2
1–2	35.5	49.4	46.4	50.0
3 or more	40.6	17.9	33.1	13.8
Marital status:				
Never married	8.5	28.6	3.6	10.9
Married	67.0	41.4	89.4	72.8
Other ever-married	24.5	30.0	7.0	16.4
Years of schooling:				
Less than 12	53.0	24.2	30.3	14.2
12	34.2	42.9	48.6	43.7
More than 12	12.8	32.9	21.1	42.1
Age:				
25–32	35.5	42.8	33.3	38.9
33–41	35.3	34.6	34.2	37.1
42–49	29.2	22.6	32.5	24.0

[1]Nonblack includes whites and other racial groups, except blacks.

tributable to the changing propensity to participate. (See the "rate effect.") Simply put, a majority share of the increase over this 15-year period is attributed to changes in behavior rather than changes in demographic composition. This further implies that labor force participation rates would have increased during 1970–85, even if the demographic composition of the female population had not changed during this period. The increase in labor force participation rates for women cannot be explained away with compositional arguments.

This conclusion, however, should not be interpreted to mean that changing demographic composition or changes in the supply of women are unimportant facets of change in labor force participation rates. Indeed, 46 percent of the increase since 1970 is directly attributable to changing demographic composition. (See "composition effect," table 2.) Although past studies reveal that compositional effects are not dramatic over a short time, the effects of changing demographic composition are considerably more apparent over a longer period, such as that examined here. Moreover, when we examine the relative importance of each compositional component, data reveal that, on the one hand, changing fertility rates, as measured by number of children, account for 4.33 percentage points (or nearly 20 percent) of the overall post-1970 increase in labor force participation.[14] Marital status and education changes, on the other hand, account for smaller but roughly similar shares (about 13 percent) of the increase. Changing age composition has virtually no effect on labor force participation rates of women. As these results suggest, while not solely responsible for recent increases in labor force activity among women, changing composition nevertheless is clearly an important and too frequently ignored source of growth in labor force participation rates.

As shown in table 2, limiting the analysis to the total (or nonblack) female population also tends to mask substantial racial variations in the mix of compositional and rate effects. In contrast to nonblack women, our analysis reveals that changing composition is primarily responsible for the increase in labor force participation rates for black women, accounting for 10.93, or nearly 85 percent, of the 13.00 percentage point increase since 1970. This sizable change is mainly attributable to educational upgrading among black women. Indeed, increased education accounts for about two thirds (or 7.25/10.93) of the overall compositional effect and about 55 percent of the overall increase in labor force participation rates for black women during the 1970–85 period. The only other compositional component of any significance is the changing number of children, a demographic component that accounts for about 30 percent of the increase since 1970.

IMPLICATIONS

The period since 1970 has revealed a continuing pattern of increase in rates of female labor force participation. Rising wage rates and changing attitudes regarding work have clearly contributed to this increase.[15] Our results nevertheless suggest that demographic explanations cannot be entirely dismissed. A substantial share—almost half—of the increase has roots in ongoing patterns of demographic change, especially recent fertility declines, shifts in patterns of marriage and divorce, and educational upgrading. The changing mix of women across various population subgroups thus provides an important demographic explanation of changing female labor force participation rates, particularly for black women.

The results also imply that prospects are good for continuing high labor force participation rates for women. Demographic changes are likely to counterbalance any dampening effects of slowing wage increases or changes in family or work attitudes. Indeed, the changing demographic supply of potential female workers may account for an increasing share of future growth in labor force participation among women.[16]

ACKNOWLEDGMENT: This research was supported in part by a grant from the National Science Foundation. The helpful comments of David Shapiro and Clifford Clogg are gratefully acknowledged, as is the computational assistance of Gilbert Ko. Prithwis Das Gupta kindly provided the decomposition program used in the components analysis reported here.

FOOTNOTES

1. See William G. Bowen and T. Aldrich Finegan, *The Economics of Labor Force Participation* (Princeton, Princeton University Press, 1969); Glen G. Cain, *Married Women in the Labor Force* (Chicago, University of Chicago Press, 1966); and *Employment and Earnings* (Bureau of Labor Statistics, August 1986).
2. Elizabeth Waldman, "Labor Force Statistics from a Family Perspective," *Monthly Labor Review*, December 1983, pp. 16–20.
3. William R. Johnson and Jonathan Skinner, "Labor Supply and Marital Separation," *American Economic Review*, June 1986, pp. 455–469.
4. See Ralph E. Smith, "Sources of growth in the female labor force, 1971–75," *Monthly Labor Review*, August 1977, pp. 27–29.
5. Howard Hayghe, "Rise in Mothers' Labor Force Participation Includes Those with Young Children," *Monthly Labor Review*, February 1986, pp. 43–45.
6. National Center for Health Statistics, *Monthly Vital*

Statistics Report, Advance Report of Final Natality Statistics, 1984 (Hyattsville, MD, Public Health Service, July 18, 1986).

7. Howard Hayghe, "Working Mothers Reach Record Number in 1984," *Monthly Labor Review*, Dec. 1984, pp. 31–34.

8. National Center for Health Statistics, *Monthly Vital Statistics Report*, Advance Report of Final Divorce Statistics, 1984 (Hyattsville, MD, Public Health Service, Sept. 25, 1986).

9. National Center for Health Statistics, *Monthly Vital Statistics Report*, Advance Report of Final Marriage Statistics, 1984 (Hyattsville, MD, Public Health Service, June 3, 1987).

10. U.S. Bureau of Census, *General Social and Economic Characteristics*, United States Summary PC 80-1-C1 (U.S. Government Printing Office, 1983).

11. James P. Smith and Finis Welch, "No Time to be Young: The Economic Prospects for Large Cohorts in the United States," *Population and Development Review*, March 1981, pp. 71–83.

12. Data for this analysis are from the March 1970 and 1985 machine-readable files of the *Current Population Survey*, Bureau of Census.

13. See Prithwis Das Gupta, "A General Method of Decomposing a Difference Between Two Rates Into Several Components," *Demography*, February 1978, pp. 99–112. Methods of decomposition have a long history in demographic research. Any comparison between two crude rates is affected by differences in population composition (for example, age composition). To eliminate compositional differences, *standardized* rates are often calculated, which eliminate the confounding effects of differences by assigning a similar composition (that is, a "standard" age composition) to each population. Methods of decomposition represent a simple extension of this analytic technique by enabling us to gauge the relative effects of more than one compositional component on crude rate differences.

The general method described by Das Gupta has three primary advantages over other methods of decomposition: (1) the method can be applied to data cross-classified by any number of composi-

tional factors (for example, in the analysis presented here, we use a four-factor model); (2) results are independent of the order in which compositional factors are considered; and (3) the procedure avoids problems with the allocation and interpretation of "interaction" effects among the compositional factors. With regard to the latter point, this is accomplished by calculating the effect of one compositional factor, holding other factors constant at an average level. As a result, a "total" effect (that is, the difference in crude rates) can be uniquely partitioned into a "rate" effect (the difference between two standardized labor force participation rates, using as the "standard population" the weighted average of the 1970 and 1985 female labor force populations, aged 25–49), and "compositional" effects (in this case, one each for changing fertility, marital status, education, and age).

14. In addition to our examination of the effects of changing numbers of children, we also evaluated the effects of changes in the age composition of children. Because labor force participation rates are lowest among mothers with young children, we replicated our decomposition analysis with women separated into three categories: 0 children less than age 18; some or all less than age 6; and all children age 6–18. This analysis produced results that were similar to those reported in table 2. Changes in the age composition of children accounted for about 14 percent of the overall increase in rates for women.

15. Given the results reported here, we are unable to partition sources of the "rate" effect, but surely rising real wages and changing attitudes account for a sizeable share of this effect. See David Shapiro and Lois B. Shaw, "Growth in the Labor Force Attachment of Married Women: Accounting for Change in the 1970s," *Southern Economic Journal*, October 1983, pp. 461–473.

16. See George Masnick and Mary Jo Bane, *The Nation's Families: 1960–1990* (Cambridge, The Joint Center for Urban Studies of MIT and Harvard University, 1980). They project labor force participation rates of women to the year 1990.

16

The Spare Sex

This article identifies the extent to which women are excluded from the highest levels of private sector firms in both the United States and the United Kingdom. Reasons for the persistence of such exclusionary practices are discussed. Factors relating to women's experiences and the role played by the traditional corporate culture are assessed. The slow rate of women's progress is described, and policies to enhance the corporate status of women and minorities are recommended.

Exercises to Guide Your Reading

1. List reasons why women are not well represented at the top corporate levels.
2. Explain how excluding women from top management may weaken long-term corporate profitability.
3. Describe two or three corporate scenarios in which traditional male behaviors are likely to crowd out women's contributions.
4. Compare the policy of positive discrimination with the policy of affirmative action discussed in Readings 21 and 22.

Flick through your file of business cards. It is likely to contain three or four female names at most. You are not alone: in two years as a business journalist, the author of this article has interviewed hundreds of men and exactly two women.

Disappointing, but not surprising. Though women make up over 40% of the western workforce, the firms they work for promote very few of them far. In America and Britain alike, women hold about 2% of big-company board seats. Where women do get to run big companies, it is not by climbing the ordinary corporate ladder. The lone female chief executive of a *Fortune 500* company, Marion Sandler, of Golden West Financial, a Californian savings bank, shares the post with her husband. They bought the bank together. Katharine Graham, chief executive of The Washington Post Company until taking the chairmanship last year, inherited the firm from her father.

Talented women are not the only losers when companies fail to hire them or later refuse them promotion. Assuming that most women are potentially as good at filling executive jobs as most men (quite a big if; we come to it later), those companies are limiting their pool of available management talent by around half. Of recent graduates, 52% in America and 44% in Europe are women. The company that fails to recruit them now will find its pool of middle managers inferior to that of a wiser employer in a few years' time; likewise, which matters more, its upper management ten years later, if (as is likely) it goes on displaying the same bias further up the ladder.

Reprinted by permission of *The Economist*. March 28, 1992. pp. 17–18, 20.

DON'T BLAME BABY

Why are there so few senior women in business today? One common argument can be dismissed right away—call it the "a-few-more-years-to-go" one. It runs like this. Women started coming out of universities in substantial numbers only quite recently. In America, 1980 was the first year in which as many women graduated as men. Only in their 30s now, these women have another 15 or so years to wait before they qualify for board seats. True, but if that were all, women should be numerous among middle managers today. They are not. In 1989, according to America's Census Bureau, only 18% of American workers earning $50,000–75,000 a year were women; and above $75,000 only 12%.

The obvious reasons for that are the logistics of marriage and motherhood. Women give birth to children, and still do most of the work of bringing them up. To do a demanding job and manage family and social life simultaneously is notoriously difficult. "Top jobs are designed for people with wives," says Lucy Heller, group treasurer of Booker, a British food company.

The difficulty shows up clearly in data from the British Institute of Management. Among its members, 93% of men are married, only 58% of women. Among American executives, 90% of men have children by the age of 40, only 35% of women. For the remaining women, of course, that almost certainly means no children at all. These are depressing statistics for any ambitious girl who wants—as most still do—to combine a career with family life.

Some of the blame lies with employers. Until the 1950s, many firms refused to employ married women at any level. As recently as 1984, United Airlines lost a class-action case for sacking any air hostess who got married. Even now, many firms fear that married women will be less committed to their work than men.

They have a point. Unilever finds that whereas half of the male graduates it re-

cruits leave the firm within five years, three-quarters of the women do. One reason is that, in a sense, women have more choice about how to spend their lives than men. Men are conditioned to work; they cannot easily choose to stay at home. Women—given an adequately bread-winning partner—can. Many of them take that choice.

So far, so self-evident. But here is another way of looking at these facts: women's preoccupation with home and family is not just the cause of their failure to do well at work, but also the result of it. If women suspect they are undervalued at work, and see little hope of promotion, other ways of spending their time are bound to start looking more attractive.

A 1990 survey of women quitting large companies, carried out by Wick, a Delaware consultancy, found that only 7% wanted to

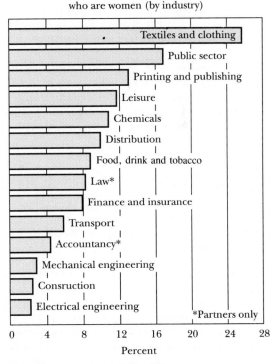

Percent of British managers who are women (by industry)

FIGURE 1. Song of the shirt.

Source: British Institute of Management.

stop working altogether. The rest planned to join other firms, to work as freelance consultants, or to start their own businesses. When BP carried out a similar exercise among graduate trainees recently, the leading reason women gave for going was not marriage or motherhood, but dissatisfaction with their career prospects. At one Johnson & Johnson unit, departing female managers complained that they had felt isolated from their male colleagues.

FELLOWS LIKE US

Could it be that this lack of esteem is justified? Given the chance, would women really be as good at running large firms as men? Most research on the way gender differences affect women's careers lies within the murky disciplines of comparative psychology and organisational behaviour. A lot of what it says is too contradictory or anecdotal (or sometimes obviously biased from the outset) to carry much weight. Yet some findings ring true.

First, people who work in large organisations have an innate tendency to hire and promote those who resemble themselves. Rosabeth Moss Kanter, a management professor now at Harvard, recognised the phenomenon in a 1977 study of "Indsco," an anonymous industrial conglomerate:

> Unlike a more communal environment, where eccentricities can be tolerated, because trust is based on deep personal knowledge, those who run the bureaucratic corporation often rely on outward manifestations to determine who is "the right sort of person."

Hence IBM's famous (but now abandoned) rules against beards and in favour of white shirts, or the WASPish whiff that surrounds J.P. Morgan bankers. Hence too, perhaps, women's difficulty in climbing the corporate ladder. "Our managers are all white, middle-aged men, and they promote in their own image," says one woman.

Because personnel policies spring right

from the heart of company cultures, it is hard for employees to question them. To criticise the kind of people a company employs is to criticise that company's whole ethos. Managers happy to defend their firm's sales strategy or cost-cutting efforts shift in their chairs when asked why they employ few women (or blacks). Men are anxious not to sound sexist, women not to sound like self-serving trouble-makers.

If looking odd in positions of power is women's first big barrier to top jobs, feeling odd in them is the second. "People come up to you at a party, and say 'Aren't you bright?' It isn't a compliment," says a female director at a London investment bank. Men are expected to be assertive. Women are not, and often do not feel happy being so.

Made to choose between being thought pushy and being actually self-effacing, women tend to choose the latter. Within mixed groups, even highly qualified women put their views less forcefully than men, and listen much more than they talk. Strident counter-examples—Margaret Thatcher is an obvious one—leap to mind just because they are so rare.

In one study, researchers taped seven uni-

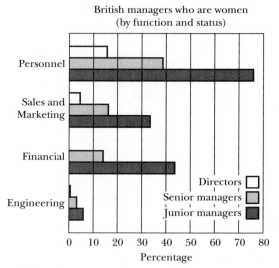

FIGURE 2. Good with people.
Source: British Institute of Management.

versity faculty meetings. With one exception, the men taking part spoke more often and at greater length than their female colleagues. Men's contributions (before someone broke in) ranged from 11 to 17 seconds in length; women's from just 3 to 10 seconds. At one academic conference, women took an average of 23 seconds to put their questions, men 53 seconds. And although they made up nearly half the audience, they contributed only a quarter of the number of questions. At INSEAD, a French management school, female students are grouped in pairs within study groups, because lone women, instructors find, seldom get a word in edgeways. Women use deferential taglines like "Don't you think?" and "Isn't it?" far more often than men do. Fine at a drinks party, not much use in the boardroom.

SLOW CHANGE

None of this is changing fast. In 1978, *Fortune*, surveying America's top public companies, found just ten women among 6,400 (five per company) highest-paid officers and directors. By 1990, among 4,000 (it studied fewer companies) the figure was up—to 19.

Surprisingly, women are doing no better within the professions such as accountancy and law than in manufacturing. These professions rely on a specific body of acquired knowledge. Women who have taken time off to have babies should find it rather easier to hold their positions on the promotion ladder. Yet none of the big law or accountancy firms has more than a handful of female partners.

Senior managers' attitudes to women's employment are changing more slowly than corporate image-makers would have you believe. Women's employment "is much like the environment—it's seen as essentially a window-dressing question," says one senior woman executive about her bosses. "If [stock market] analysts or anyone who mattered cared about it, then they would care too."

Tokenism abounds. Such female directors as there are are disproportionately likely to be found running bits of the firm without profit-and-loss responsibility—personnel or public relations, for instance—that offer little prospect of promotion to the top posts. Alternatively, they may be part-time advisers. Of the 30 female directors on the boards of Britain's biggest 100 companies, 26 are non-executives. Last June BTR, an acquisitive British conglomerate, appointed a female finance director. The chief executive quickly assured journalists that he did not believe the new appointee should be regarded "as the deputy managing director or the head of strategy."

Where firms do make genuine efforts to promote more women, it is often not because they want to, but because they have to. Talk to an American firm about its "diversity programme," and the first thing you will be assured of is that it was not legislatively inspired. That is because many are. Price Waterhouse, an accountancy group, started monitoring the progress of its female employees more closely after being sued (successfully, in the event) for failing to promote one of them to partnership. Bidders for American government contracts are vetted for the numbers of women and members of ethnic minorities they employ. Following a recent Department of Labour Report on "glass ceilings" to women's advancement, the rules for such firms are being stiffened to cover senior as well as junior levels. Stand by for lots more equal-opportunities hype.

Though feminism is hardly changing bosses' attitudes to women, rising labour costs might. On current birth rates, the number of American 15-to-24-year-olds will drop from 14.5% of the population in 1990 to 12% in 2025. Europe will experience an even steeper fall. As their choice of recruits diminishes, firms will either have to hire more women or accept lower-grade men. The last time America experienced a similar labour squeeze—in the 1950s, thanks to low birth rates during the Great Depression—women's employment opportunities improved vastly. More women got jobs, women's wages came closer to men's, and older women found it easier to get work. The same is likely to happen again.

IT CAN BE DONE

If a firm does genuinely want to use the talents of women more effectively, how should it go about it? The watershed dividing different employers' approaches is positive discrimination. Some use quota schemes. At Pitney Bowes, an American office-equipment manufacturer, 35% of all promotions must go to women, 15% to non-whites. Some companies even tie managers' pay to their fulfillment of such schemes. Baxter International, a medical-equipment manufacturer, links their bonuses to the numbers of women they promote. So too at Tenneco, a Texan manufacturer of motor components. Other companies are scrapping quotas in favour of subtler ideas.

Well-meaning as they may be, such policies can easily do more harm than good. If positive discrimination means promoting inferior women over better men, for the sake

of filling a quota, the company will suffer. Demanding jobs will start to go to people unable to fill them well. Passed over, better people will leave to join other firms. Women have done it, men will do the same. Even Baxter admits that its scheme causes some resentment among employees.

Positive discrimination can hurt the women it is designed to help. Bosses compelled to hire women to fulfil some quota are unlikely to take them seriously. "If you feel people are just there because you had to have them, then you work around them, not with them. Then they feel under-utilised, because they probably are," says Nancy Gheen, a personnel manager at Monsanto.

Like many other companies, Monsanto is trying subtler ways to employ more women and minority members. Get the environment right, and the numbers will follow, the firm hopes. One widespread technique is "sensitivity training." Monsanto employees take courses that involve lengthy discussion, for a day or so at a time, of their own attitudes to sex and race. By making people articulate their feelings, subconscious bias is brought into the open and—the firm

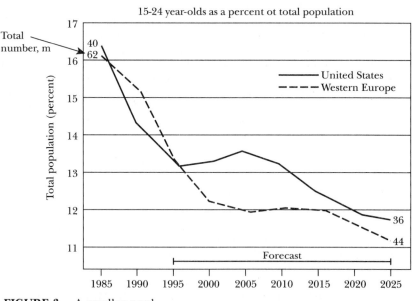

FIGURE 3. A smaller pool.
Source: United Nations.

hopes—will be reduced. US West, a telephone company, Lotus Development, a software house, and Corning, a glass-maker, all run similar courses.

ORGANISE ACCORDINGLY

Two days' worth of consciousness-raising is not going to change the universe. Even Ms. Gheen admits that "talking about feelings isn't what makes it in the business world." The real change in the way companies think about women managers will come when they change the way they think about jobs.

Most women want to have children. Raising a family requires time off, and shorter working hours, for somebody, either husband or wife. To keep good women, firms need to find ways of giving them those things, yet using them efficiently. That normally involves letting women with small children work flexible hours, not requiring them to relocate or travel at a moment's notice, or even letting them share their jobs with someone else.

In exchange, women may have to accept lower pay, or slower promotion, until they return to full-time work. Such programmes have been dubbed "mommy-tracks." The concept infuriates some feminists, who translate it into the assumption that women can only pursue slower, second-rate careers. Correct, up to a point: the truly fair solution would be for all firms to institute such arrangements for fathers too, so that couples could decide between themselves which partner is left free to pursue his or her career at the usual pace.

Papa-tracks are a long way off. But many firms are already instituting ad hoc arrangements for women. Kleinwort Benson, a London merchant bank, has discovered that even investment bankers can be mothers. "Traditionally, people said that you can't do the job part-time; you must be able to leap on the aeroplane. But gradually it's been realised that there are things people can do part-time—marketing and research. And you can't hire people of the right calibre off the street to do that job," says Lesley Knox, head of institutional fund management at the firm. In many other companies, valued women, becoming pregnant, work out similar compromises. Eventually, such arrangements may become part of accepted best practice.

Companies exist to make their shareholders money, not to engineer social change. Though mommy-tracks are to firms' ultimate advantage, since they help keep good staff, in the short term they will sometimes prove to be inconvenient and expensive. In the irritation of having to change their ways, employers should not forget to take into account the costs of turnover among employees. Part of the money spent training those who leave has gone down the drain. And back-of-the-envelope calculation of the costs of replacing a manager of ten years' standing, earning $70,000, suggests that the time it takes the new manager to get fully on top of the job is worth $25,000. If a replacement has been sought from outside, headhunters' fees, advertising and interviewing could double that.

Sisters, chief executives, your interests coincide. One day your identities might too.

CHAPTER 5

Alternative Approaches to Diversity

17

Working Women's Staunchest Allies: Supply and Demand

Gary S. Becker

This article first presents data showing that the wage gap between female and male workers has declined substantially. Reasons for this significant increase in pay equality are discussed, and the crucial role of market forces is contrasted to the distorting role of government intervention. The author concludes by contrasting the merits of policy proposals for family leave, comparable worth, and civil rights legislation.

Exercises to Guide Your Reading

1. Summarize reasons for the decline in the male-female pay gap.
2. List professions in which the number of women has markedly increased.
3. Identify structural changes underlying women's rapid entry into the paid labor force.
4. Predict this author's likely response to legislation that would increase the income tax deduction for child care expenditures.

Reprinted by permission of *Business Week*. December 2, 1991. p. 18.

Working women have plenty of problems in the workplace, as we were reminded so dramatically during the Clarence Thomas hearings. Yet those problems stand in stark contrast to women's rapid progress in occupations and earnings compared with men's since the late 1970s. The U.S. is getting much closer to granting equal pay for equal work, regardless of gender or family situation.

The proportion of married women who work has increased continuously: Now, more than 60% of married women with young children hold jobs. Women in the 1970s and '80s entered many professions at a breathtaking pace. They make up some 40% of the students in schools of law, medicine, business, architecture, and journalism, and are a small but rapidly growing share of those majoring in engineering. The percentage of male college graduates going on to law school has actually fallen since 1970, while females in the legal profession have risen from a negligible share in the early '70s to almost 25% now.

Median earnings of women working full time were comparatively stable from 1960 to 1979, at about 59% of the earnings of men—which means a gender gap of about 41%. But then, as reported in the Census Bureau's *Money Income of Households, Families and Persons*, the gap began a steady fall, dropping below 30% in 1990. I expect it to continue to fall throughout this decade.

Even 30%, however, overstates the true gap, since female full-time workers put in about 10% fewer hours a week than male full-time workers, and they have less previous job experience. The gap between men and women working the same hours and with the same experience is well under 20%.

Lame Excuse. The most important reason for women's progress is their increasing presence in the labor force, as the nature of the family has changed. Birth rates have dropped more than 35% since the late 1950s, freeing women from child care duties. Rapid expansion in the number of jobs in the service sector has let women combine child care with part-time work and flexible schedules. The exploding number of divorces after the mid-1960s forced women with dependent children to earn a living and provided a warning to married women that they should be prepared to work in the event their marriages should break up. Young women who have entered professions and other skilled occupations during the 1970s and 1980s continue to advance into more responsible positions, even if a "glass ceiling" has kept most from getting to the very top.

Not long ago, some women lost their jobs when they married. Women employees were paid much less than men, sometimes because of outright discrimination rationalized by the lame excuse that they were not the main breadwinners. The atmosphere created by civil rights legislation and the women's movement help combat such policies. These were not, however, the main forces behind their progress, since the gender gap in earnings did not begin to decline until more than a decade and a half after passage of the far-reaching Civil Rights Act of 1964. Women advanced most rapidly during the Reagan and Bush Presidencies—surely no more active in civil rights enforcement than previous Administrations. Moreover, not all minority groups advanced during the 1980s: Black men fell a little further behind white men.

Women's substantial progress during the '80s helped muffle the call for more radical legislation to aid them. There is much less support now than a decade ago for the silly system of government wage-setting figured on the basis of "comparable worth," the inevitably arbitrary judgments of statisticians and bureaucrats about what the pay should be in different occupations. Rapid entry of women into prestigious occupations has also quieted the call for quotas. Even supporters concede quotas aren't really what they have in mind.

Mothers' Helper. Instead, the drive to aid women is concentrating on other kinds of intervention in labor markets. Current favorites are mandatory, unpaid leave for parents when children are born or get sick and mandatory child care facilities at work. Bills in Congress would make child care leave available to either parent, but the example of Sweden—which has a liberal leave system—suggests that almost all would be taken by women.

Forcing business to provide leave is both inefficient and unjust. It in effect discriminates against single persons and against married women and men with no children or with grown children. It's one thing to call for a gender-neutral productivity test for pay hikes and promotions, but another to make business give preference to persons with young children. And while the present proposals are mild, everyone knows they are only a first step toward the Swedish system of requiring full pay for employees on child care leave.

The law of supply and demand, along with civil rights legislation, is steadily improving the economic position of U.S. women. Extensive intervention in labor markets to help them is unwarranted and will do more harm than good in implementing the principles of equal pay and equal employment opportunities for equal work.

18

Women as a Business Imperative

Felice N. Schwartz

This article first explains why corporate managers do not seriously consider gender issues. The next section presents criteria for determining how well a corporation is utilizing its female resources, and then the problems a corporation faces when and if it fails to develop its female employees adequately are discussed. A number of suggestions for dramatically improving the situation of working women are described in the conclusion.

Exercises to Guide Your Reading

1. Explain what the author means by a "family-friendly company."
2. Paraphrase the five levels of corporate commitment to women's development.
3. Summarize the eight costs associated with gender segregation.
4. Compare the suggestions for corporate policy advanced here with those put forward in Readings 16 and 17.

Memo to:	Peter Anderson
	President, Chairman, and
	Chief Executive Officer
	Topform Corporation
From:	Felice N. Schwartz, President,
	Catalyst
Re:	Women as a Business
	Imperative

A year ago, you asked me to analyze how Topform deals with its women and to advise you about your policies. Since then I have studied your company and talked at length with your top managers in order to arrive at a clear understanding of Topform's treatment of women.

You believe, I know, that you have made strides toward offering women equal opportunity. However, you think your efforts haven't been appreciated. The women who stand to profit most from your help don't seem grateful. You worry about the perplexingly high turnover of women within your managerial ranks, but, at the same time, you express annoyance at the messy details of modern double-gender business life, such as maternity leave and sexual harassment in the workplace. These problems seem distracting at best and, at worst, are obstacles to accomplishing your most important objectives: to make better products and to run a more profitable company.

Even though you value candor, you won't like what you're about to hear. If you are like most CEOs, you will want me to say that everything is all right, that the policies you've implemented have already made yours a family-friendly company. You will receive no such reassurances. In fact, my view is virtually the opposite: you must make a radical

Reprinted by permission of *Harvard Business Review*. March–April 1992. pp. 105–13.

change now, not take more incremental, ad hoc steps. I must challenge you, not reassure you.

It is imperative that you help women advance in your company—and not just for their sake but for the sake of Topform as well. Moreover, the atmosphere of your company, which you regard as tolerant and welcoming to all employees, is actually corrosive to women. But if you accept this challenge and make a radical change in your treatment of women, you can effect tremendous improvement in your bottom line.

You and your peers who lead the most powerful companies in the United States are missing a huge opportunity. In fact, because you fundamentally misunderstand how to manage and motivate one-half of your human resources, you tap only a fraction of their capacity. One reason you continue to ignore these problems is that a conspiracy of silence precludes discussing the matter openly. You don't voice your concerns for fear of litigation, and you are joined in this conspiracy of silence by women who don't want to be seen as different from men. You pretend that everything is all right. But you cannot fix a problem that you tacitly avoid talking about.

Your company is not alone. Women encounter unpleasant, even harsh circumstances at *most* companies in our nation, even if CEOs and managers consider themselves enlightened, thoughtful, and compassionate people. Actually, Topform is better than many other companies. But the fact that you are neither alone nor the worst offender should not console you. You still need to change.

The solution is not merely instituting some "feel good" policies. The solution is fundamental change. It is a revolution in thought and action that will have a terrific impact, an impact that can be measured in dollars and cents.

What, for example, might be the economic power of this radical policy change? Imagine for a moment that you were not considering human resources policies but were instead attending a presentation from your R&D shop about a spectacular new product. This product, which has been under development for years, is now nearing completion. If its introduction succeeds—and you believe that it will—your revenues will skyrocket. Wouldn't you react impatiently after that meeting ended, eager to get cracking? *Treating women as a business imperative is the equivalent of a unique R&D product for which there is a huge demand.* It promises to be the most important "new product launch" you and your company could implement. Making a radical change and accepting the women's imperative is the right thing to do; but, more important, it makes good economic sense.

U.S. COMPANIES: FROM ZERO TO FIVE

You asked me to evaluate Topform. As you know, I travel all over the country, visiting and discussing these issues with hundreds of top executives yearly. These site visits and discussions have given me an empirical basis for comparing your company with many others.

From your vice president of human resources, I learned that almost half of all Topform employees are women. In fact, 40% of your exempt employees and 7% of your vice presidents are female. These percentages compare favorably with national averages. But simply counting women employees, vice presidents, or board members is not an effective way to appraise corporate performance. Both of us realize that setting arbitrary numerical objectives can produce spurious accounting, which in turn produces false reassurances, while chronic underlying problems go unaddressed. Attempting to measure complicated personnel questions by using only the blunt instrument of the adding machine is a mistake. As subtle as these issues are, and as difficult as it may be to translate them into cold mathematics, it helps nonetheless to look at them critically. Consequently, I have developed a simple but effective rating system that runs from zero to five to gauge how motivated companies are to accept the women's imperative as a *business* imperative.

At the low end, *Zeros* are companies that are dead to the issue of developing women. They simply don't care. These companies make no effort to recruit, train, or promote women. Executives at Zero companies work with blinders on. They are even blasé about the law. They get sued, repeatedly in some cases, but apparently accept the costs of settling those suits as just another annoying part of doing business—their way.

Next are the companies that simply want to keep ahead of the law. They are *Ones*. They track numbers and fill out Equal Employment Opportunity Commission forms, but they don't take any initiative in leveling the playing field for women or addressing the needs of working parents, which are still, unfortunately, the needs of working women. According to one study, for instance, a third of U.S. companies have done virtually nothing that is not legally mandated to help their employees cope with family problems. By my standards, those companies are Ones.

Twos are companies that want to do what is fair and right. The Twos have formulated two or three specific policies for child care, part-time clerical jobs, or unpaid maternity leave—but those who work at the company still feel it is a man's world. Twos give little thought to women's upward mobility or to removing the obstacles to women's productivity. Deep down, the men who run these companies believe that women should not be part of the real action. They go through the motions of improving women's situations, but they have not come to terms with their deeply rooted preconceptions.

There are only a few employers who can legitimately say, "We are doing well by women," even in a limited sense, on family and work issues or leadership development. Those companies that do I call *Threes*. For example, newspaper giant Gannett, where there is a passion to develop women, is a Three. (In fact, the former publisher of Gannett's successful *USA Today*, Cathleen Black, is a woman.) The Federal National Mortgage Association, which increased the number of women employees from 4% in 1981 to 26% in 1988, is another Three. IBM, which built on Thomas Watson's respect for the individual, and Corning, which has a strategic plan for change, are both Threes.

Fours are mythical companies where one day the playing field will be leveled for everyone. No one is there yet, but some companies such as Xerox are at least trying to get there. Companies at the Four level would be truly responsive to women. These would be companies managed by men and women who have examined their own preconceptions and shaken off those vestiges of old-fashioned, outdated thinking that prevent progress.

Fives are off today's charts. The Five level is a place where the playing field itself starts off flat for both men and women. This exemplary vision includes an ideal, egalitarian environment, where the whole management structure is not a power-oriented hierarchy of ascending status at all but a jungle gym with lateral sidebars and many-leveled challenges, with help and rewards available for employees at every step. Becoming a Five will represent the ultimate achievement, and it will yield the ultimate payoff.

Right now, most companies stand at levels One or Two. Their executives ardently believe that they are "OK on women," that the policies they've adopted are appropriately enlightened. Of course, they don't think they are on the cutting edge—but, then again, they don't want to be ahead of the curve.

They are complacent—and they are in danger.

Your company, like many others, is stuck at Two.

EIGHT COSTS OF WHERE WOMEN ARE

Here is another way to view the problem. Imagine that your corporate management group takes the form of a pyramid. (Whether or not Topform's structure should be a pyramid or a different shape is an interesting question by itself but not one we will discuss at the moment.) In 1960, virtually all of the white-collar employees in your company—and in the management ranks of almost all companies in the United States—were men. Today more than a third of your managers—370 out of 1,000—are women. That represents improvement.

This improvement was almost inevitable, of course, given the changing demographics of the country. There simply are not enough capable men available today to fill all of the managerial jobs. Your human resources director can tell you that the nation's labor pool isn't growing fast enough to keep up with management demand. Family size contracted from an average of almost four children per family in the 1950s to fewer than two children per family from the mid-1970s to today. The new generation of college graduates—52% female—from which you recruit your future managers is much smaller than anticipated. This age group is actually only half the expected size based on demographic predictions that assumed the baby boom would continue.

Of course, the current downturn, as well as mergers, restructurings, and job consolidations, has had a crushing impact on the lives of those managers who have lost their jobs. This pain and despair is experienced by both men and women. We should acknowledge and sympathize with those who are suffering. However, this dismal period will end, and we must regain our competitive position in the world economy. To do so, we must mobilize our talent. Women are not part of the problem, they are part of the solution.

There are already women executives today throughout U.S. business. As a matter of fact, about 37% of your managers are women. That's progress, of a sort. But consider where most of these women are: in jobs at the bottom of your team's pyramid.

Picture the company pyramid in your mind's eye again. It is a geometric truth that if you divide any pyramid into four slices of equal height, the top slice will contain 1.5% of its volume, the next slice will contain 11%, the third slice will contain 29.5%, and the bottom layer will contain 58%.

Now note that out of 1,000 managers at Topform, 15 are in the pyramid's top slice, the corporate pinnacle where all of your other ambitious staffers set their sights. In the second slice are 110 of your managers, with 295 on the third level, and 580 on the bottom. The pyramid's bottom slice contains the entry-level management jobs where promising junior people as well as competent but unexceptional older managers are found.

When we analyze where Topform's women are, we find that their distribution is typical of the pattern for Two companies in the United States. Half of your entry-level managers on the lowest level are women. Fewer than one-quarter of the jobs in the next level up are held by women. Of the managers on the second tier, only 10% are women. And only 1 of your 15 highest ranking managers is a woman.

What is wrong with this picture? Over the last decade, you have led an effort to recruit bright, promising men and women to join Topform's management ranks, as most U.S. companies have done. You have searched for talent in the best undergraduate and business schools in the land, schools in which there are more women in attendance every year. You yourself have told me that the women at Topform are as strong in basic leadership traits like intelligence, energy, and analytical ability as the men because your standards are exacting and you expect to hire only the best people. And yet women languish after you hire them.

If women are as smart, capable, and eager to exercise their skills as men are, all of which you say you believe, then why are the highest two levels in your company almost exclusively male domains? Ignore the matter of what is right or wrong. What does that segregation, intended or not, cost you? How are you hurt?

1. You're Not Mobilizing Your Best People at the Top.

Any successful business today is only as good as its senior management team. Traditionally, the most prestigious corporations (like yours) and the top professional companies have confined their hiring to the top 10% of potential management employees. In the past, that meant selective recruiting of the highest ranked available men who could be found at elite business schools. However, today women have displaced men in these schools. Women now earn 55% of all undergraduate accounting degrees and 35% of MBAs. So if you attempt to depend solely on male graduates from the top 10% of the best schools in the country, you will drastically reduce the pool from which you draw.

2. You're Not Maintaining Quality at Every Level.

Today the marketplace offers little leeway for managerial error. The nation's leadership needs are growing rapidly both in quantity and in quality—and doing so faster than the work force itself is growing. Competition has become global and more intense. International corporations vie with one another in every sizable industry and in every market that offers promise. Products grow more sophisticated each day. Technology grows more complex. Managers have to be very, very good.

Now that a significant number of women are in management, you can concentrate on enhancing the quality of your people at every level by identifying and promoting the best women instead of benignly ignoring them after you hire them. In fact, one of the United States's greatest assets in international competition is its pool of qualified female managers. Recognition of the contribution that U.S. women can make to business success, whatever this country's current shortcomings, gives the United States a terrific advantage in competing against some of its toughest competitors like Japan. In that nation, women have barely gained token entrée into lower management circles. Japanese salarymen already seem to be working at peak capacity, which leaves little room for ratcheting up the intensity they already bring to their jobs.

Thank goodness women are available for consideration as part of the talent pool in the United States. But unless you actively draw from the entire universe of people with high potential, *including* women candidates, you will hurt your company and yourself. If you fail to draw, train, and advance women candidates, you will neither hone this national advantage, nor will you compete successfully in the United States or beyond.

3. You're Treating a Big Portion of Your Employees as Dead Weight.

There is a psychological lag between Topform's decision to employ women and your will to use them. You accept women as workers, but in your mind, they really have not entered the mainstream of business. Not only are most of the women in your managerial ranks situated at the bottom of the pyramid but they have also been shunted off to the sides. In your mind, women are ancillary. Is it possible that you still think as bosses did 30 years ago? Do you secretly think that men belong in business, while women create problems? Are you hiring, training, and advancing women only to ensure mere *adequacy*? Does adequate female managerial representation mean doing just enough to quell women's restlessness, avoid the wrath and litigation of women employees, satisfy the corporate conscience, and develop a few high performers for show? Do you pay lip service to equality between the sexes while unconsciously sabotaging that equality?

If nearly half of your managers are women who are discounted in this way, then you're dragging a very heavy anchor.

4. You're Putting a Lid on the Contribution Individual Women Can Make.

You stifle people when you make them report to less talented bosses. Many female managers, who occupy the sides and bottom of the organizational chart, are working for men who are less talented than they are. Thus their talent and vision are constrained by the limitations of the underqualified men to whom they report.

A person who works for someone less competent is stunted and thwarted by that relationship. The capable but underappreciated subordinate soon realizes that recognition for effort is not commensurate with output and that the rewards of her work are not sufficient. It is enervating to work for a boss whom one does not respect. The results are predictable: the more talented subordinate throttles down, begins to cut back, produces less, or leaves altogether.

Inequity and injustice of this kind have real fiscal costs. The company suffers from decreased productivity and inefficiency. These problems are compounded when they are systemic; for instance, when it is clear to all of the women managers in an organization that women are victimized by consistently insensitive treatment and by relegation to second-class managerial citizenship. Add to this already punishing environment the effects of inadvertent sexist behavior. To be sure, not all sexist behavior is overt, such as a pinch at the watercooler, an off-color joke that is intended to throw the woman who hears it off-guard, or much worse, pernicious sexual harassment. Some of it is tacit, unspoken, and attitudinal. Most of it is unconscious. Regardless, for many women, working means encountering a series of hurdles and tests. The problem is exacerbated at the upper levels of the company hierarchy, where negative experiences become more intense because women are fewer and more isolated.

With each step backward, women are further debilitated, and attrition among your highest potential women increases. This may, in fact, explain the relative overrepresentation of talented women entrepreneurs. Some of the best women set out to work for themselves in a supportive environment of their own creation where talent can be recognized and rewarded.

5. You're Undervaluing Promising People Who Wish to Take a Role in Family Caregiving.

Very simply, if you see commitment to your company as the inverse of employees' commitment to their families, you're creating a false and damaging dichotomy for judging employee potential. Worse, this division of commitments perpetuates the prejudice that it is not possible to combine career and family. As a consequence, business loses good people who would bring the same high standards to their work that they bring to their families—if given the choice *not* to make a choice between work and home.

It is almost second nature to think of child and elder care as "women's work," domestic issues, matters that have nothing to do with the rough-and-tumble business world. Revenues, margins, rates of return, market share—these are supposed to be the primary concerns of business. Making things and selling things are business concerns. But rearing children is a women's issue. Because women haven't been assimilated fully into business, child care isn't considered a business issue, nor is flexibility thought to be an important company priority.

No one can deny that since women have entered the nation's work force in vast numbers, there is no longer a solid family-support structure at home. Only 16% of full-time workers go home to a nonworking spouse, according to the Bureau of Labor Statistics. In two-career couples, neither parent can expect that the other will automatically tend to the needs of their children. Since high-quality, affordable day care is rare, many working parents are permanently anxious about their children. And as the population ages, these working parents are often responsible for their own elderly parents too.

But the clock will not go backward. If all of the United States's working women were to return home to cook and clean tomorrow, businesses would disintegrate. U.S. business depends on women. Companies may not use them as well as they should, but they depend on women employees no less.

The result? When companies don't offer child care and flexibility in scheduling work as matters of course, these companies suffer along with their deprived workers. And those individuals who drop out may be some of the most responsible employees, those in the company who could bring the same uncompromising standards to their performance in the workplace that they do to the rearing of their children.

6. You're Wasting Recruiting and Training Money.

On average, college-educated women postpone the birth of their first child until they are 31 years old. If a woman joins your company after her college graduation, Topform makes a decade-long commitment to her training and development. If she leaves you when her child is born—because your culture retards her career growth, or because parental-leave provisions and family support are inadequate—you fail to amortize that ten-year investment. It is worse for you, of course, if she leaves Topform to work for a competitor and puts her experience to work against you. Ironically, wherever she goes, the unhappy cycle continues because chances are good you'll replace her with another woman who may not work out at all and will in any case need training and development for years before she (or a male counterpart, for that matter) can perform on par with the original woman you lost. Then, when the replacement has a baby— which is also probable—the whole cycle begins again.

7. You're Failing to Create Beacons for the Best Women Entering the Workplace.

You know that women constitute an increasing proportion of a shrinking work force, and you believe that Topform needs all the help it can get. But do you view hiring women as a last resort? If so, that is shortsighted.

Companies that do not take pains to develop and retain able women will continue to feel the absence of women at higher levels in the future, when all talent will be scarcer. The smartest women graduating from the best schools will scout out their employment prospects, searching for the right beacons. They will conclude, reasonably enough, that companies that advance few women to the upper tiers are less attractive than those that have already demonstrated they value women. Companies that fail to develop women for leadership positions now will be forced to settle later for women who are not as qualified. Nonetheless, half of your management pyramid will be women in the future. If you attract only those women who are second tier, you will lose a competitive advantage.

8. You Could Be Capitalizing on a Tremendous Opportunity.

Women can lead your company to new profitability.

When you expand the pool from which you draw your top management, you will see greater talent at every level of the enterprise. In an information economy, an economy of ideas, an economy of knowledge, nothing is more important than the thinking skills of your people and their capacity to make smart, timely decisions. Better decisions lead to enhanced productivity, improved pricing and packaging, and more ingenious innovations. You need to attract— and win—the commitment of managers with those skills. The best way to win their commitment to Topform is to demonstrate your commitment to them. You can earn the loyalty of the women in your organization at a time when loyalty is a vanishing U.S. corporate virtue. By providing flexibility, you will retain good women through the childbearing years just as they become most useful to the company. And a solid cadre of women at the senior levels will serve as role models and mentors to junior women as they rise.

This new approach will appeal to your stockholders, more than half of whom are women, both for economic reasons and reasons of principle. Your public image will improve, which is not an insignificant issue. Today companies compete through their values as well as their products. Customers want to know what a company stands for. When a company can demonstrate that it has moved aggressively in the way in which it recruits, trains, promotes, rewards, and values women, it will not only attract the brightest women, it will speak directly to the millions of women and men who care deeply about this issue. A company's reputation for good human values is as valuable an asset as capital equipment. When your customers, clients, and employees realize that you value women as a central resource rather than inadvertently perpetuating a system that defeats them, a new, positive cycle will be born to replace the old, unhappy, expensive one.

Women are not going to go home again. The clock ticks forward, not back. So you can either force women and men who wish to participate in family life to make some very unpleasant choices, or you and your company can change. You can insist that women play by men's rules, and as a result, they will fail. Similarly, you can insist that men follow in their father's footsteps and focus their energies on careers, limiting severely their participation in their children's lives. You can require women and men to give up the dream of having children. Or you can urge those who have children to turn them over to full-time surrogate care. And some of your employees will leave Topform to work elsewhere or to start businesses of their own that give them more flexibility and career satisfaction.

Or you can do everything possible to support families while clearing away the barriers to women's—and men's—progress.

FOUR ACTIONS FOR CHANGE

The biggest obstacle to corporate change is the reluctance of leaders to see the need for it. When you accept the notion that women should be full participants in the management of your company, when you are ready to consider changing, you'll find that implementing a solution is neither difficult nor expensive. *The restraints that now hold women back can be loosened easily, and these problems will be swiftly remedied.*

There are four actions you should take to ensure that the women you employ will function as effectively as the men. The first is to acknowledge the fundamental difference between women and men, the biological fact of maternity. The second is to provide flexibility for women and men who want it. Third is to provide women who already have basic leadership traits with the special additional management skills and tools that are vital to excellent performance. The last action you can take is to improve the corporate environment by removing barriers that exist for women but not for men.

Acknowledge Maternity. End the conspiracy of silence in which leaders as well as workers pretend that they think the biological differences between the sexes do not exist. Of all women, 85% have babies. Giving birth is a uniquely female experience. These are facts. But they are facts that companies don't handle well.

We should distinguish pregnancy, childbirth, and disability from parenting. Maternity, when defined as childbearing, is predictable and finite. It is good practical policy to acknowledge this natural process and to help women as they move through it. You can manage maternity so that it takes a small fraction of current costs in productivity and attrition.

There's no denying the physical and emotional impact of pregnancy. Yet most women find pregnancy an experience of heightened energy and happy anticipation. Within the last few decades, the average woman has changed her pattern from one of leaving work at the end of the first trimester to working right up until the month, if not the week or day, of delivery. What discourages pregnant women are the attitudes of other people in the workplace. The supervisor and colleagues of the mother-to-be tend to discount her and see her condition as something negative rather than the plus it is. At best today, a pregnant woman's condition is ignored. At worst, she is forced to hide her pregnancy as long as possible and to avoid natural coping responses such as walking around at intervals during long meetings, elevating her feet when seated, or wearing comfortable clothes.

You should formulate clear, comprehensive disability and maternity-leave policies—as differentiated from a parental-leave policy—that will enable you to retain your best women. Do not require an unequivocal statement of intentions from the mother-to-be before the baby is born. Wise, self-interested companies will allow women to return to work when they are ready, when childcare arrangements are in place, and permit those women to have flexible schedules that will help them be productive. It is my belief that most women will opt to return early on part-time schedules. Thus paid maternity leave is not an issue—and a modest fraction of the expense of that forgone paid leave could be used to subsidize the part-time return of low-income women.

Finally, work coverage when the woman is on leave must be jointly planned by both the employee and her manager. Encourage frank talk. When you help women employees with maternity rather than punish them, you'll inspire their confidence and be rewarded with candor that permits you to plan accordingly. The fact that women have babies doesn't alter their commitment to a job

or the quality of their work—except when maternity goes unacknowledged, unplanned for, and unmanaged.

Provide Flexibility. Begin by accepting that parenthood is linked to business and that intact families include two parents. Note that there is no evidence that men are less nurturing than women. Just a few years ago, talk of "co-parenting" would have taxed the patience of male senior managers, so advocates of shared parental responsibility had to tackle maternity first. Now we can talk openly.

A small percentage of men *and* women are singularly career-focused, while a small number are entirely family-focused. But the vast majority of men and women want to combine family and career, and they want to switch their main focus of attention from time to time throughout their lives. Here is the main point: these men and women require flexibility in order to be productive at work and to be active, responsible parents.

Now that women are in the work force, children have a business impact. Today you must accept parenthood as a part of doing business. You can reduce its cost by consciously disregarding the traditional roles of men and women. The result will be that you, the employer, will get the best, most committed workers and that children will get the best, most committed parents. Moreover, the net return to the employer when husbands and wives share parenting will be greater. When women are forced to be primary caregivers, their productivity and their careers become stunted because they cannot come to work early or stay late. However, when parenting is shared, either parent can be home with the children and both parents are free to make a serious, sustained commitment to their employers, their careers, and their children.

Permit parents to cut back to half-time (at prorated pay) and then reenter the competition for senior management jobs, partnerships, or tenure if they choose. Let new fathers take paternity leaves in sequence with their wives. Encourage and legitimize the growing desire of men to take an active role in parenting. Since some women choose to spend five or six years with young children, don't shoot yourself in the foot by denying them reentry and the chance to move up when they return. It is crusty tradition that makes us think that the thirties are the prime career years. When these women return refreshed, guilt-free, and ready to go at full throttle, they can produce for 25 or 30 more strong years.

Let parents (and other executives) work at home. New technology—personal computers, fax machines, modems, and so on—makes working at home practical. Take advantage of the freedom this technology affords. And, finally, learn how to measure real *productivity* instead of counting hours spent in the office.

Provide Training. Helping women maximize their potential helps not only them but also your company. You recruit only the best managerial candidates, good men and women, from a pool that is both diminishing in total number and increasingly female (51% of all master's degrees, for instance, now go to women). But don't stop at simply avoiding discrimination in hiring. Recognize that women face a tougher challenge than men do after they join your male-oriented company.

Women are newcomers to the male world of business. Their socialization does not prepare them for this new world. Some men view them as temporary, uninvited guests whom they treat insensitively and accept grudgingly, if at all. Often women are penalized for lacking aggressive instincts, but, contradictorily, they are scorned for being too aggressive. So you must help your promising women with training and education that includes behavioral advice. Permit them to display the qualities that are traditionally inculcated in men: competitiveness, aggressiveness, risk-taking, and long-term, dependable commitment to a career.

Fortunately for women, the work world has become increasingly information-oriented, which means that supposedly innate feminine skills in communication and sensitivity are at a premium. But if you need managers to act authoritatively, give women permission to be as tough and aggressive as you need them to be; you'll find they respond accordingly. Watch women managers grow after they become comfortable in the workplace.

Improve the Environment. Removing the barriers that obstruct women entails first accepting the premise that women belong in the work force—and then eliminating the corrosive atmosphere that pervades most companies. The glass ceiling is not a physical barrier erected by nefarious CEOs. Rather, it is an attitudinal hurdle consisting of largely unconscious stereotypes and preconceptions. So make men aware of negative behavior. Sensitize your male managers to the new demographic realities and the practical reasons for proper conduct between the sexes at work. Eradicate sexual harassment.

Next, coach women as you do men, and accept in women the behavior that usually characterizes successful men. Assign them to line jobs that will tax and teach them. At the same time, don't feel betrayed when women plateau or drop out; instead, ask yourself whether conditions in your company forced them out. And don't worry about raising women's expectations too much by announcing your intention to change. If you don't raise expectations, women will despair that the status quo will never change.

My hope is that Topform and all U.S. companies will work to integrate the lives of their employees, permitting work and family to fit smoothly together instead of conflicting with one another. When work supplies energy to the home, and home revitalizes life on the job, each half joins to make a vibrant whole. If, on the other hand, the status quo does not change, bitterness and frustration will grow.

Can we achieve this ideal? We have come so far since the revolution began 30 years ago, when women began pouring into the work force. Further movement, accelerated movement, is not only logical but also eminently practical.

But it is not inevitable. If the status quo goes unchallenged, many more women will leave corporations and professions to become entrepreneurs. Men who remain at these corporations will be forced to work harder. They will suffer from fatigue, frustration, diminished productivity, and further estrangement from their families. The women who continue working and remain primarily responsible for home management and child care won't be able to compete for leadership positions.

Most likely, if unchallenged, the pace of change will be just fast enough to perpetuate the conspiracy of silence. In that case, we'll remain where we are now, where it is not working. Everybody knows it, but nobody is talking about it.

I believe the process of change must begin with CEOs who now cling to an image of the past that tells them women should be home rearing children. They think women's careers burn out prematurely because work is not really as important to them as it is to men. They believe there always will be enough high-performing males to replenish their ranks.

But CEOs will change because business is quintessentially realistic. Senior executives will see the many changes in the workplace that have already succeeded and the many changes that are still necessary. And they will cast aside their stereotypes and preconceptions.

The logjam impeding women's forward movement will be broken by a top-level acknowledgment that the status quo is unacceptable. As this movement accelerates, we should see more women and men break with traditional sex roles. We should see more self-determinate women. Men will grow more comfortable inside the home, and this too will have positive ramifications. Couples may be able to build partnerships that preclude feelings of exploitation and anger. Families will grow stronger.

But the best news I can offer is this prediction: your company will gain tremendous financial benefits when you accept your responsibility to women and working parents.

19

Can We Solve Black Youth Unemployment?

Harry J. Holzer

This article explores the array of social and economic forces associated with rising and persistent unemployment rates among young inner-city, African American males. Changes in the unemployment pattern for young white and black males are presented first. Three trends viewed as especially important to this position are then identified. Suggestions for public and private sector initiatives to strengthen the employment prospects for African American men are offered.

Exercises to Guide Your Reading

1. Explain the importance of distinguishing cause from effect when discussing the characteristics of unemployed black youth.
2. List the characteristics of unemployed black youth.
3. Identify and summarize the three broad trends associated with the unemployment of young black men.
4. Describe the policies for public and private sector solutions to this unemployment problem.

Two outstanding facts characterize the trends in black youth employment over the past two or three decades. The first is that wages and salaries of young blacks have risen dramatically; the second is that employment rates have fallen (and unemployment has risen) just as dramatically. The result has been a widening split within the black community between those with stable employment and relatively high earnings (otherwise known as the middle class) and those with limited employment opportunities at lower wages (the poor).

The trends in unemployment and employment for white and black men are clearly documented in Table 1. . . . We find unemployment rates rising consistently since 1969 for both groups, but much more dramatically for blacks. While some improvements in these rates begin to appear for both

by 1987, the unemployment rates of young blacks remain about two and one-half times those of young whites.

The employment-to-population ratios in the bottom part of the table present an even sharper contrast between young blacks and whites. These numbers reflect changes in labor force participation as well as employment rates. The results here show fairly stable employment ratios for young whites, which suggests that rising unemployment was mainly driven by rising participation in the labor force. The fairly severe declines for blacks reflect falling participation as well as employment. While some of the decline in participation reflects rising student enrollment rates for blacks, it is clear that this explains only a small part of the decline. There is thus an alarming rise in the number of young blacks who are neither working,

Reprinted by permission of *Challenge*. November–December 1988. pp. 43–49.

TABLE 1 Male Employment and Unemployment (Percentages)

	A. Unemployment Rates				
Ages	*1964*	*1969*	*1977*	*1981*	*1987*
		Whites			
16–17	16.1	12.5	17.6	19.9	17.9
18–19	13.4	7.8	13.0	16.4	13.7
20–24	7.4	4.6	9.3	11.6	8.4
25–54	2.8	1.5	3.9	4.8	4.5
		Blacks and Others			
16–17	25.9	24.7	38.4	40.1	39.0
18–19	23.1	19.0	35.4	36.0	31.6
20–24	12.6	8.4	21.4	24.4	20.3
25–54	6.6	2.8	7.8	10.1	9.9

	B. Employment-to-Population Ratios				
Ages	*1964*	*1969*	*1977*	*1981*	*1987*
		Whites			
16–17	36.5	42.7	44.3	41.2	40.1
18–19	57.7	41.8	65.2	61.4	60.4
20–24	79.3	78.8	80.5	76.9	79.6
25–54	94.4	95.1	91.3	90.5	90.3
		Blacks and Others			
16–17	27.6	28.4	18.9	17.9	19.3
18–19	51.8	51.1	36.9	34.5	39.1
20–24	78.1	77.3	61.2	58.0	62.1
25–54	87.8	89.7	81.7	78.6	79.2

Source: Employment and Earnings, Bureau of Labor Statistics, various issues.

nor looking for work; neither are they in school or the Armed Forces.

More evidence on this issue is presented in Table 2. For those aged 20 through 24, we see the fractions of black and white men in various categories for 1980: not employed or in school, not in the labor force, or in jail. The results are presented for those with different levels of schooling. In the bottom of the table, we find some of these numbers for those aged 35 through 44 as well.

Some of the results are quite dramatic. Employment problems for both blacks and whites worsen as education levels fall. Black nonemployment and nonparticipation rates are higher than are those of whites within each educational category, but the gaps generally widen as education levels fall. Among high school dropouts, we find one-half of the younger group of black men not working or in school; almost a quarter are not in the labor force, and about 10 percent are in jail! White dropouts are somewhat better off, especially when it comes to staying out of jail. About 30 percent of young blacks and 15 percent of young whites fall into the dropout category. For the more mature age groups, the numbers remain discouraging. In short, the prospects of those without high school degrees in our society are very bleak, especially for blacks.

TABLE 2 Labor Force Status of Young Black and White Men by Educational Attainment–1980 (Percentages)

	HS Dropouts		HS Graduates		Some College		College Graduates		All	
Ages 20–24	*W*	*B*	*W*	*B*	*W*	*B*	*W*	*B*	*W*	*B*
Percentage who are:										
Not employed or in school	28.8	50.2	14.4	28.2	18.8	27.8	7.5	18.4	7.9	20.5
Out of labor force	9.9	21.8	4.1	12.0	1.7	4.9	1.3	2.6	3.9	12.6
In jail	2.5	9.5	0.6	3.3	0.4	2.0	0.0	0.7	0.7	4.6
Ages 35–44										
Percentage who are:										
Not employed or in school	18.4	27.8	7.5	18.8	5.2	13.3	27.6	7.7	7.9	20.5
Out of labor force	9.3	15.9	3.3	9.3	2.4	6.0	1.2	4.2	3.8	10.9

Source: Finis Welch, "The Employment of Black Men," *Journal of Labor Economics*, October 1988.

Employment problems for low-income whites and especially blacks are apparent in other data as well. Some results from the 1980 census show that both labor force participation rates and wage rates rise quite consistently with family income for both whites and blacks. Again, blacks do worse at almost every income level, and many more of them are concentrated in the low-income end of the spectrum, especially since the fraction living in female-headed households is much larger for them. This tendency for participation rates to rise with higher income seems to indicate that the better market opportunities faced by those with higher incomes more than offset any disincentives that might arise from the family income being spent on these youths. The low-wage job opportunities facing young blacks from low-income families may be a large part of their employment difficulties.

Another striking characteristic is the greater tendency of young blacks to be single and living with relatives than their white counterparts, even among the unemployed. More specifically, 18 percent of white males and 11 percent of black males aged 16–24 are married; comparable rates for females are 29 percent and 16 percent respectively. While marital status and living arrangements no doubt reflect the greater employment problems of young blacks, they might also reinforce these problems by lessening the need of young blacks to pursue stable employment.

Finally, young blacks, especially in inner-city areas, have a greater tendency to be part of families on welfare and of female-headed households.

WHAT HAS HAPPENED

The past 25 years have, in many ways, been a time of great economic and social progress for the black community as a whole in the United States. The passage of equal opportunity and voting rights legislation in the mid-1960s, the beginnings of "affirmative action" requirements for contractors with the federal government, rising levels of education, and changing attitudes among both whites and blacks all contributed to the movement of young blacks into higher-paying professions and a movement toward wage and salary equality within occupations. (These trends continued into the mid-to-late 1970s but have been somewhat reversed in the 1980s. The weakening of federal enforcement of equal opportunity laws and "affirmative action" programs under the Reagan Administration may explain the recent reversal, but this question requires more study.)

If the overall earnings of the black community have risen in this time, why have black employment rates declined so dramatically at the same time? Why have poorer blacks not shared in the general progress that the black community has enjoyed?

I would argue that three broad trends that have been at work have been responsible for the lack of progress of poor blacks:

1) Various economic changes have reduced the demand for less-skilled and less-educated black men and women in our economy. Their ability to obtain jobs therefore diminished.

2) The expectations of these groups of young blacks outpaced the reality of progress for them. As a consequence, their willingness to accept as permanent low-wage (perhaps "dead-end," or menial) jobs may have declined while their abilities to obtain better ones did not rapidly improve.

3) The availability of AFDC (Aid to Families with Dependent Children), food stamps, and Medicaid rose in the 1960s and 1970s. Dependence on such transfer payments grew, as did the number of female-headed households with no employed adults. The acceptability of intermittent employment, illegitimate births, and use of drugs and/or crime rose in certain areas. All of these developments appear to have reinforced a trend toward isolation of the inner-city poor from the behavior and institutions of mainstream society, and make their escape from poverty and unemployment all the more difficult to achieve.

ECONOMIC CHANGES

Our economy has been buffeted by many long-term changes in the past few decades. The major ones include: an overall decline in economic growth and a rise in national unemployment rates; a continuing shift from manufacturing to service-industry employment; a dramatic rise in the number of women in the labor force; a dramatic rise (1960s and 1970s) and then a decline (1980s) in the number of young workers in the labor force, reflecting the entry and then the aging of "Baby-Boomers" in the workforce; and a movement of population and industry out of central-city areas toward suburban areas. Other developments (such as the OPEC oil price increases of the 1970s or the growth of imports in the 1980s) have either been reversed already or should be reversed soon.

It should not be too surprising to find that some or all of these forces had disproportionately large effects on blacks, especially those with less education and lower skill levels. The effects were also disproportionately large for both whites and blacks in certain parts of the country.

To see this more clearly, Table 3 presents overall unemployment rates for whites and blacks in 1970 and in 1980, and their ratios over the decade. These rates appear for each of the four major regions in the country, and also for fifteen of the largest metropolitan areas.

The results of Table 3 show us that unemployment in the 1970s rose for both whites and blacks, but more for blacks. For both groups, the increases were largest in the Midwest and Northeast. The industrial centers of both regions (e.g., Chicago, Cleve-

TABLE 3 Unemployment Rates, 1970 and 1980

	Whites			Blacks		
	1970	*1980*	$\frac{1980}{1970}$	*1970*	*1980*	$\frac{1980}{1970}$
United States	3.7	5.9	1.6	6.3	12.3	2.0
Regions:						
Northeast	3.3	6.1	1.9	6.0	13.3	2.2
North Central	2.9	7.0	2.4	7.8	18.1	2.3
South	2.9	4.5	1.5	5.3	9.7	1.8
West	5.4	6.2	1.2	10.3	12.1	1.2
*SMSA**						
Atlanta	2.1	3.2	1.5	3.8	9.5	2.5
Austin	2.6	3.2	1.2	3.6	6.2	1.7
Baltimore	2.4	4.7	2.0	5.4	14.1	2.6
Boston	2.9	4.6	1.6	6.5	9.2	1.4
Chicago	2.3	5.4	2.4	6.3	16.4	2.6
Cleveland	2.5	6.0	2.4	7.2	14.8	2.1
Dallas	2.3	2.1	0.9	4.7	5.8	1.2
Detroit	4.4	10.1	2.3	10.0	25.8	2.6
District of Columbia	1.9	2.7	1.4	3.9	8.2	2.1
Houston	2.1	2.5	1.2	3.9	6.0	1.5
Los Angeles	5.2	5.2	1.0	10.2	11.7	1.1
New York	3.0	5.3	1.8	5.2	12.4	2.4
Philadelphia	2.7	5.9	2.2	6.5	16.4	2.5
San Francisco	4.9	4.9	1.0	11.1	13.4	1.2
St. Louis	3.7	6.7	1.8	9.8	18.4	1.9

Source: U.S. Census of Population, 1970 and 1980.
*Standard Metropolitan Statistical Area.

land, Detroit, and Philadelphia) were among the hardest hit for both groups, while southern and western cities (e.g., Los Angeles, San Francisco, and Dallas) did well. This seems to suggest that declining manufacturing employment is a large part of the growing black employment problem. But the evidence also shows that black unemployment has risen the most where white unemployment has also risen the most, and that black unemployment has risen more rapidly than for whites almost every place. The *proportional* increases in black unemployment relative to white unemployment are not necessarily higher in the declining manufacturing areas.

We must also note that in areas such as Boston, where service industry or "high-tech" employment has grown rapidly (though this is not fully reflected in the 1980 numbers), blacks have shared in these gains. Black employment success thus seems to follow that of the overall local area quite closely, even where the local economy does not depend on manufacturing.

ROLE OF WOMEN

What else caused the unemployment rates of blacks generally to rise more than did that of whites, even in growing areas? At least part of the story seems to reflect the rapidly growing fractions of women in the labor force. Many of the women entering the labor force in the 1960s and 1970s seem to have competed with black men for lower-skill jobs in both the manufacturing and service sectors. Thus, in those metropolitan areas where women entered the labor force in the largest numbers, black male employment seems to be the lowest.

The growth of "Baby Boom" workers in the 1970s may have exacerbated these problems for young blacks, whose ability to get low-wage jobs diminished the most. But this latter factor has begun to reverse itself in the 1980s. Many economists project shortages of young workers for low-wage jobs in the 1990s, and some have already begun to appear in the late 1980s. There is at least some evidence of fast-food restaurants and other

low-wage employers paying $4.00–5.00 an hour in major metropolitan areas in order to attract workers for certain shifts. This trend seems to explain some improvements in unemployment rates for both black and white youth in the last few years.

Finally, we note the growing movement of people and jobs from central-city to suburban areas. Perhaps surprisingly, a number of studies in Chicago, Los Angeles, and other areas suggest that location of jobs within the metropolitan area *per se* is not a large part of the black employment problem, since those blacks who live near the jobs have unemployment rates almost as high as those who live further away. However, the growing segregation and isolation of poor blacks in these areas may still be a problem.

RISING EXPECTATIONS

While these economic trends have been lowering the demand for less-skilled young blacks, the expectations of these young people appear to have been growing. My own research of a few years ago indicated that unemployed young blacks sought and expected the same wages and jobs as did young whites, though clearly their ability to obtain these jobs was more limited. We have less evidence on what young blacks expected 20 or 30 years ago, though it is probable that their expectations were not as high.

Another striking fact that emerged from our study of inner-city youth was that 70 percent of unemployed black males thought they could get a job either very easily or fairly easily, despite their long spells without employment. Were they too optimistic, or were they correct in assessing low-wage job availability in which they were not very interested? If all of these young people had been willing to accept these jobs, would there have been enough for all? We don't really know with any certainty. But changing expectations of young blacks with regards to quality of jobs, and declining willingness to accept work at lower wages, appears to have played some role in the past few decades.

This leads us to the many other social

changes that have occurred among poorer blacks (and also whites) in the past few decades. Low education levels, high unemployment, and problems with the law are part of a broader picture of life for inner-city blacks who live in areas of concentrated poverty. The study of black youth employment at the National Bureau of Economic Research (NBER) a few years ago focused on black males aged 16–24 who lived in parts of three cities (Boston, Chicago, Philadelphia) that were at least 70 percent black and 30 percent below the poverty line.

In Table 4, we compare their family backgrounds with those of nationwide samples of whites and blacks. We find that only a quarter of the inner-city young blacks live in households with an adult male present; about 60 percent have no household members working or in school; almost half of the families are on welfare, and a third live in public housing (at least in 1980 they did). The NBER data also suggest that at least 15 percent of all youths in the inner-city areas participated recently in illegal activity. Given

TABLE 4 Social Characteristics and Employment Outcomes of White and Black Youth

General Characteristics	Inner-City Black Youth	All Black Youth	All White Youth
Adult male at home	28%	51%	69%
Both parents present at age 14	43	58	84
Household member working or in school	41	56	71
Family on welfare	45	25	4
Public housing	32	10	10
Employed	38	50	64
In labor force	67	74	80
Crime in past month (self-reported)	15	—	—

Sources: National Longitudinal Survey of Youth, 1979 and 1980, for All Black and White Youth Samples; and NBER Inner-city Survey for Black Youth. See papers by Viscusi, Freeman, and Lerman in Freeman and Holzer, eds. *The Black Youth Employment Crisis*, University of Chicago Press, 1986.

TABLE 5 Relationship between Social Factors and Employment/School Enrollment for Inner-City Blacks

	Percentage Employed	Percentage in School
Those with:		
Crime in past month	24%	22%
No crime in past month	26	43
Welfare families		
Age 16–18	25	76
Age 19–24	31	15
Non-welfare families		
Age 16–18	30	79
Age 19–24	50	20

Sources: National Longitudinal Survey of Youth, 1979 and 1980, for All Black and White Youth Samples; and NBER Inner-city Survey for Black Youth. See papers by Viscusi, Freeman, and Lerman in Freeman and Holzer, eds. *The Black Youth Employment Crisis*, University of Chicago Press, 1986.

the tendency toward substantial underreporting for self-reported crime rates (by as much as 50 percent in some studies), these numbers are quite dramatic. In general these results are far worse for inner-city black youth than are those for nationwide blacks or whites. Employment and labor force participation are worse for that group as well.

In Table 5, we specifically compare employment and school enrollment rates for those recently involved in crime and those not involved among inner-city black youth. We do similar comparisons between those who are part of welfare families and those who are not. As expected, we see that employment and school enrollment are lower for those involved in crime (though the employment difference is not large). The same is true for those in welfare households compared to those who are not, with especially strong differences among those aged 19 through 24. Receipt of welfare, lack of employed adults, female-headed households, and crime thus appear to be associated with high unemployment rates of young blacks in inner-city areas.

Of course, we are often not sure what is "cause" and what is "effect" here. For instance:

- Do many young people engage in crime because of weak opportunities in the regular market, or do their illegal activities lower their interest in (by providing alternative income) and ability to obtain regular jobs?
- Are so many female-headed welfare households developing because the employment problems of young black males prevent them from entering into and maintaining marriage?
- Did the growing benefit levels of AFDC encourage this process or was growing dependence merely a result of the problem?

Recent evidence suggests that AFDC may recently have had a larger direct effect on marital status than we previously thought, though questions about the magnitude of these effects remain. (On at least this last issue, one point seems quite clear: declining welfare benefits relative to inflation in the last decade have done little to help solve the employment problems of welfare mothers. Changes in the benefit program in 1981 which hurt working women on welfare also did little to help.)

We are also not sure about the exact mechanisms through which these factors work. Do young people from welfare households have worse employment records because of lower skills, lack of information and "connections" in the labor market, weak "work ethic," or fear of reduced benefit levels for their families?

An additional caveat should be added here about welfare "dependence." It is well known that many AFDC recipients are not long-term dependents. The recent discussions about the "underclass" similarly stress that only small fractions of the poor, even in inner-cities, have the characteristics of *persistent* poverty and deviant social behavior. Still, the observed fractions of inner-city black youth from these backgrounds and involved with these activities, as well as their apparent correlations with employment, remain alarming.

Some researchers have also argued that the growing social isolation of the black poor in inner-cities has weakened the institutions of that community (e.g., schools, churches) and their links with individuals. In the NBER study, the evidence clearly suggests that those from poor communities who do well in school (i.e., achieve high grades) and/or attend church regularly have better employment outcomes than those who do not. But, again, the correct interpretation of these facts (especially the latter one) is not obvious. Do those who attend church have higher skill levels, better attitudes, and motivation? Do they have better information and "connections" in the community and work force? We are not sure, though it seems plausible that "all of the above" play some role.

A few other facts seem worth noting here. When young blacks search for work, they seem to be least effective (compared to whites) when using "informal" channels (such as checking with friends and relatives) and when applying directly for jobs without referrals. This suggests that lack of information and "connections" is an important part of the problem. It also suggests that black youth make significantly worse subjective impressions on employers than do white youth. This may simply reflect the biases of employers, and their fears regarding crime, vandalism, absenteeism, and so forth from young blacks. It may also reflect the spottier work histories of many young blacks, which often become apparent as soon as they apply for work. Low skill acquisition and high turnover rates out of previous jobs seem to reproduce themselves in the future, along with lengthy periods of joblessness in between these jobs. Breaking these cycles is a major challenge for policymakers.

POLICY IMPLICATIONS

It is clear that no single reason can be given for the growing employment problems of young, inner-city blacks in recent decades. A declining number of jobs, rising expectations, and a deteriorating social environment all seem to have reinforced each other in creating this problem.

Consequently, no single policy solution exists for the problem. Both opportunities and incentives for employment must be considered. An array of approaches by governments (federal, state, and local) and private businesses or institutions must be used to combat this problem. We have some direct evidence on the uses and limitations of employment and training programs as well as welfare reform; in other areas, our comments and ideas are more speculative. The fiscal constraints imposed upon us by government budget deficits must also be kept in mind as we consider various alternatives.

It seems clear that the single most important factor determining employment opportunities for young blacks is the overall health of the economy, both aggregate and local. In areas where employment is generally diminishing, policies designed to generate or attract new and growing firms and industries might be helpful. It is much less important exactly where these firms are located in metropolitan areas than whether they exist at all.

Of course, the types of policies needed to generate such employment growth is less clear. The highly touted (by some) recent attempts of Massachusetts in attracting firms from Boston to older industrial areas (primarily involving state subsidies or funding for infrastructure, research, training, etc.) deserve closer scrutiny in this regard. Alternatively, policies to subsidize migration of low-income, unemployed people to growing areas (along with appropriate support services) might be considered.

Policies designed to improve the basic skills of young people and keep them in school also deserve high priority. Programs focusing on preschool and early-school-age children (e.g., Head Start) seem to show promising results. These efforts should help to reduce dropout rates and improve classroom performance, both of which should show results in future job market outcomes. For older students, programs emphasizing remedial education and training in the classroom seem to be the most cost effective. Summer or year-round programs that link receipt of subsidized jobs to staying in school (as in the Job Corps) show promise.

Providing close supervision and standards for performance, counseling about lo-

cal job opportunities, and successful job search procedures can complement the direct education/training effects. (Some of these latter approaches were stressed in the Supported Work demonstrations of the Manpower Development and Research Corporation several years ago. Results were somewhat more positive for welfare mothers than for low-income youths.)

A variety of states and the federal government have recently reformed welfare programs to include required or voluntary employment, training and counseling, and strengthened enforcement of child support payments by absent fathers. Though our evaluations of these different programs remain in progress (and their successes may depend not only on specific program characteristics but also on the strength of local labor markets), our preliminary results suggest that most of these programs have significant (though sometimes small) effects on employment rates for AFDC participants. To the extent that these approaches have any positive effects on employment for female heads of households, there might also be improvements in employment seen for youths residing in these households.

PRIVATE SECTOR'S ROLE

Of course, all of these approaches put the burden on governments whose fiscal commitments are already often stretched to capacity. Are there other approaches that can rely more heavily on private firms or community institutions in aiding inner-city youth employment? Our experience here is more limited, but at least a few ideas for creative new approaches seem worth mentioning.

For one thing, the links between firms, schools, and community institutions can be expanded in local areas. Firms could provide the latter with better information about what job vacancies they have, what skills they need, and how they judge prospective applicants. School placement and training activities serving low-income people and minorities might thereby be improved, and better applicants for firms might result.

Enhanced law enforcement may also be a key part of the strategy of making market employment more attractive than illegal activities. Raising perceived likelihood of arrest and conviction for these activities would probably lower their frequency of occurrence.

A possible expanded role for churches and other community agencies needs to be seriously considered as well. Can a broader range of youth be served by the networks and/or motivation from which church-going youth seem to benefit?

Finally, we note the importance of demographic changes in the youth labor market. The growing shortage of young workers, and upward pressure on wages that it should generate, may do more to enhance job opportunities for young blacks than any particular policy approach. In an environment in which the jobs exist, training and placement services are more likely to be successful than when the total availability of jobs is limited. Our hopes for improving the black youth employment situation in the coming years might therefore have some chance of being realized in this environment.

20

Occupational Apartheid

Stephen Steinberg

This article describes the origin of employment segregation as well as many of the social trends that help reproduce it. The agricultural focus of the southern economy, combined with the racism of both the North and the South, is shown to have narrowed the range of occupations open to African Americans. Affirmative action is analyzed in terms of its ability to dismantle the system of occupational segregation.

Exercises to Guide Your Reading

1. Explain and give examples of the "racial division of labor."
2. Compare the occupational structure and employment opportunities of the northern industrial economy with those of the southern agricultural economy.
3. Discuss the roles that racism and immigration have played in continuing to limit job opportunities for African Americans.
4. Illustrate the connection between affirmative action and access to the economic mainstream.

In the United States the essence of racial oppression is a racial division of labor, a system of occupational segregation that relegates most blacks to the least desirable jobs or that excludes them altogether from legitimate job markets.

The racial division of labor has its origins in slavery, when over half a million Africans were imported to provide cheap labor for the South's evolving plantation economy. During the century after slavery ended, the United States had the perfect opportunity to integrate blacks into the North's burgeoning industries. *Northern* racism prevented this outcome. Instead, the North relied exclusively on European immigrants, most of whom, like blacks, came from peasant

origins and had no previous industrial experience. In effect, a system of labor deployment evolved whereby blacks provided the necessary labor for Southern agriculture and white immigrants provided the necessary labor for Northern industry.

This regional and racial division of labor cast the mold for generations more of racial inequality and conflict. Not until the mechanization of agriculture in the decades after World War II were blacks finally liberated from their historic role as agricultural laborers in the South's feudal economy. Thus it was that in one century white planters went all the way to Africa to import black laborers, and in another century the descendants of those planters gave the descendants

Reprinted by permission of *The Nation*. December 9, 1991. pp. 744–46.

of those African slaves one-way bus tickets to Chicago and New York.

When blacks finally arrived in the North, they encountered a far less favorable structure of opportunity. Not only were these labor markets staked out by immigrant groups, who engaged in a combination of nepotism and unabashed racism, but the occupational structures themselves were changing. William Julius Wilson has argued that deindustrialization is the principal factor in the genesis of the black underclass. However, Wilson does not explain why blacks, who were never heavily represented in the industrial sector in the first place, were not absorbed into the expanding service sector. He neglects two other factors: (1) racism, which still pervades the occupational world, especially in the service sector, where the personal traits of workers play a key role in employment decisions, and (2) immigration policy, which has encouraged the influx of more than 12 million people since 1965. Thus, at the same time that we are exporting jobs, we are importing workers—at an even higher rate! In New York City, for example, there were 493,000 post-1965 immigrants employed in 1980, accounting for 17 percent of the total work force.

Nor is it the case that immigrants take only jobs that native workers spurn. Large numbers are found in such coveted job sectors as construction, hotels and restaurants, health care, and building management. It is difficult to escape the conclusion that recent immigration has had a detrimental impact on the job prospects of African-Americans and other native workers, not to speak of already settled immigrant workers. Here was another missed opportunity to upgrade the skills of marginal workers and lower racist barriers throughout the workplace.

Thus, despite the much-touted progress of the black middle class, the racial division of labor is very much intact. By some estimates, as many as half of black men of working age lack steady employment. Countless others, men and women alike, work at poverty wages, or have no job security or health benefits and are only a paycheck away from

poverty. This job crisis is the single most important factor behind the familiar tangle of problems that beset black communities.

Tragically, this nation does not have the political will to confront its racist legacy, even if that means nothing more than providing jobs at decent wages for the descendants of slaves who continue to be relegated to the fringes of the job market. Instead, a mythology has been constructed that, in ways reminiscent of slavery itself, alleges that blacks are inefficient and unproductive workers, deficient in the work habits and moral qualities that have delivered other groups from poverty. We are used to hearing this from Nathan Glazer, Thomas Sowell, Shelby Steele and others on the right, but recently even voices on the left have succumbed to gratuitous clucking about "Nihilism in Black America," to use the title of Cornel West's recent disquisition in *Dissent* (Spring 1991). What is the failure to deliver jobs to yet another generation of black youth if not nihilism on a grand scale? Jim Sleeper preaches hard work and moral discipline in New York, a city where 101,000 people recently took the civil service exam for 2,000 expected openings in the Sanitation Department. Still others on the left have declared that the problems confronting black America have less to do with race than with class, a strange message for the millions of twelfth-generation Americans still condemned to live out their lives in impoverished ghettos. By reifying "class" and shifting the focus away from "race," these would-be progressives unwittingly undermine the antiracist movement. They absolve the nation of the moral and political responsibility for making restitution for its 300-year crime, and play into the hands of those on the right who have already succeeded in removing race from the national agenda.

The pivotal issue today is affirmative action. The significance of affirmative action is that it amounts to a frontal assault on the racial division of labor. Even those who support the liberation struggle often fail to appreciate the profound impact that affirmative action has had in breaking the caste system in the occupational world. Before affirmative action, the black middle class—the one that E. Franklin Frazier lampooned in *Black Bourgeoisie*—consisted of a few businessmen and professionals anchored in the ghetto economy. It was affirmative action that opened up access to *mainstream* occupations—not just the professions and corporations but also the blue-collar and government jobs that are the staple of black employment. Despite its limitations, affirmative action has produced the first significant departure from the occupational caste system that has prevailed since slavery.

The current attack on affirmative action is reminiscent of the retrenchment at the end of the nineteenth century. America did not return to slavery, but it turned the clock back on progress made during Reconstruction. Today, it is inconceivable that there could be a return to official segregation. However, the impending evisceration of affirmative action will reinforce current patterns of occupational segregation and deepen the racial crisis. Are the American people condemned to wait until the smoldering resentments within the black community again reach an explosive climax before our political leaders take decisive action against the enduring system of occupational apartheid? What will it take to convince whites that it is in their interest, and the interest of the nation, to eliminate the vestiges of slavery?

21

A Limit to Affirmative Action?

James Blanton

This article discusses the policies of the "decadent" period of the civil rights movement, and argues that the demand for equality of outcome has replaced the demand for equality of opportunity. Likely individual emotional, psychological, and social effects of this change are identified. The situation described provides an important insight into the tensions between inclusivity, fairness, and quality.

Exercises to Guide Your Reading

1. Describe the audition policies used by symphonies.
2. Evaluate the claim that there exists a shortage of qualified African American concert musicians.
3. Discuss the causes of this shortage.
4. List possible means of eliminating this shortage. Assess the extent to which these measures are applicable to other skill areas in which there may be a shortage of qualified women, African Americans, Hispanics, Native Americans, or Asian Americans?

Virtually all of the people I have known in the musical world, including those I met during the years I spent as a professional musician, have been political liberals. As such, they are suckers for every "humane" and "compassionate" cause that comes down the pike, always available to perform at a nuclear-freeze benefit or a pro-choice rally, always ready to sign petitions and advertisements in opposition to one or another putative manifestation of war, racism, or poverty. Granted, not all have been as vulgar about their political leanings as, say, Leonard Bernstein. But if Bernstein's frenzied scrambling from one left-wing cause to another is a caricature, like all caricatures it bears an easily recognizable relationship to reality.

This may help to explain why I was so startled by the reaction of the American musical community to the news that came out of Detroit earlier this year—the news that, in the name of affirmative action, the Detroit Symphony, one of America's leading orchestras, had hired a black bass player, Richard Robinson, without the formality of an audition. What startled me was that the reaction was largely negative.

In the "real" world, such news would hardly have been news at all. The procedures of affirmative action—which is to say, race-conscious hiring goals and quotas—are

Reprinted by permission of *Commentary*. June 1989. pp. 28–32.

by now taken for granted, especially in high-profile institutions. To complain publicly about them, as I have learned since I left the music business, can be hazardous to your professional health. Yet the cries of protest from musicians over the Detroit Symphony's decision were immediate and unhesitating. Most surprisingly of all, black musicians were the first to complain, and at least one even went so far as to decline a lucrative appointment in Detroit after word of Robinson's hiring got around.

What caused so many American musicians to part company on this issue with liberal orthodoxy? When I told an older and more cynical acquaintance of my surprise, he responded with a shrug and a properly world-weary question: whose ox was being gored? He had a point. While musicians are liberals, they are also professionals, and the instinct to protect the *sancta* of one's profession from external threat is a universal one. But things are not so simple as that. Indeed, the story of the hiring of Richard Robinson, though set in the somewhat provincial world of American music, is in many ways emblematic of what might be called the decadent period of the civil-rights movement; it tells us a great deal about what we as a nation have done in the name of affirmative action, and what it has cost.

It started, like so many tales of political intrigue, with a letter.* This particular letter was written by Constance Price, a black violinist who had auditioned for the Detroit Symphony Orchestra (DSO) in 1975 after obtaining a master's degree in music from the University of Michigan. Her teacher, Jack Boesen of the Detroit Symphony, had assured her that she would get a job, and his track record gave her no reason to doubt him. Two of Boesen's older black students, Joseph Striplin and Darwyn Apple, had landed positions with major orchestras,

---

*This account is based on a four-part series of articles published in the Detroit *News* last October by Nancy Malitz, the paper's music critic.

Striplin with the Detroit and Apple with the St. Louis Symphony.

Still, it was her first professional audition, and about 30 other players were competing for the same spot. The odds were stacked heavily against Constance Price, just as they are stacked against any other instrumentalist, black or white, who wants to play with a major American symphony orchestra. Not surprisingly, she failed to get the job. Bruce Smith, a member of the Toledo Symphony and one of her fellow students at the University of Michigan, was hired instead.

Smith had auditioned four times for the Detroit Symphony before being hired. This, too, is not unusual: most people who finally land a position with a major orchestra go through several auditions before succeeding. But after her failure Price chose not to give it another shot. Instead, she took a teaching job at a local high school. She also found a new violin teacher: Mischa Mischakoff, former concertmaster of the Detroit Symphony and, earlier, of the NBC Symphony Orchestra under Arturo Toscanini. And she went back to the University of Michigan to obtain a doctorate in music and educational psychology.

Nine years later, in 1984, Constance Price finally decided to try again. Her second audition took place at the express invitation of the Detroit Symphony. Like most government-subsidized organizations, the orchestra had been under pressure to improve its record on minority hiring. Now, in 1984, it employed only one full-time black musician, Joseph Striplin, although several other blacks, including Price herself, occasionally played with the orchestra as substitutes.

Price was asked to audition as part of a program to recruit black musicians. But the competition was to be considerably stiffer this time around than it had been in 1975, with 83 candidates instead of 30. Once again Constance Price failed to make it past the preliminaries. This time, though, she sat down and wrote a letter. She sent it to Oleg Lobanov, the then-president of the Detroit Symphony. "I am writing," she began, in the interest of Detroit's black community with regard to the lack of black musicians in the DSO. Having participated in the violin auditions [and been] the recipient of a very high rating, I observed that the selection procedure did not encourage the identification and selection of qualified black applicants. It would seem that qualified black applicants who are citizens of Detroit would be valued and sought out by an orchestra serving the city whose black population is estimated at 60 percent.

Price sent copies of her letter to two of Detroit's black state legislators, Representative Morris W. Hood, Jr., and Senator David S. Holmes, Jr. Her intentions in doing so were probably not innocent; given the circumstances, circulating copies of such a letter was tantamount to lobbing a hand grenade through the front door of the Detroit Symphony's offices. Hood and Holmes, both Democratic members of Michigan's joint House-Senate General Government Appropriations subcommittee, promptly rose to the bait and demanded that the orchestra offer proof that its affirmative-action program was more than just a formal homage to the requirements of the law.

At this point, Oleg Lobanov made a tactical error. Asked by a legislator why the Detroit Symphony had not hired more black musicians, he reportedly replied that blacks "prefer to play jazz." This remark, according to Representative Shirley Johnson, another state legislator and member of the appropriations subcommittee, "caused the fuse to blow with regard to Morris Hood." Hood and Holmes spent the next four years gradually turning up the heat. "Every year on this subcommittee," Representative Johnson told the Detroit *News*, "it's the same. We get into a real heated discussion regarding the DSO and its affirmative-action programs. If it isn't Representative Hood who brings it up, it's Senator Holmes."

The orchestra, seeing the writing on the wall, finally agreed to hire another black musician by 1990 as part of a new affirmative-action plan. That was not good enough for Morris Hood. "What I want to see immediately, if not sooner," he said last July, "is another black face within the Detroit Symphony in addition to the one we already have. Two blacks in the Detroit Symphony by February 1989." Hood and Holmes also demanded that the legislature withhold half of the orchestra's appropriation until it had proved it was "maximizing its affirmative-action efforts." This threat was not to be taken lightly. Like most American orchestras, the Detroit Symphony is perpetually in the red; each year it receives $2.55 million— 8.7 percent of its budget—in appropriations from the state of Michigan.

For an orchestra to go about "maximizing its affirmative-action efforts" poses a number of dilemmas peculiar to the music business.

Blacks currently make up only 1 percent of the 4,000 musicians employed by America's leading orchestras. As of 1988, only one of the country's top orchestras, the Los Angeles Philharmonic, had as many as four blacks on its roster. The Philadelphia Orchestra had three, six orchestras had two, and four orchestras, including the New York Philharmonic, the Boston Symphony, and the Detroit Symphony, had one each. The Chicago Symphony and the Minnesota Orchestra had none.

Why? "Are you telling me we can't find qualified black musicians ... in this nation of 200 million people?" asks Morris Hood. In fact, many qualified people believe exactly that. "This is like hockey," says Joseph Striplin. "If the New York Rangers had to have ten or twelve black players, they might have a lot of trouble finding them."

The numbers leave little room for doubt. The New York Philharmonic's Musical Assistance Fund, which provides scholarships and other forms of support for minority classical musicians, recently surveyed the country's top 25 music conservatories. Out of 5,000 orchestra-bound instrumentalists, it found fewer than 100 blacks. "If you apply the standard bell curve to their probable talent," says Daniel Windham, who runs the fund, "that means 20 of them are qualified to play in a major American orchestra."

The fact that black singers are amply represented in the field of opera has led some observers to conclude that the conservatories are discriminating against incoming black instrumentalists. But though such was no doubt once the case, it is no longer so. Today's conservatories are frankly eager to enroll black musicians, singers and instrumentalists alike. The training a classical singer undergoes, however, takes less time and is far less rigorous than of an instrumentalist; some singers begin studying in earnest for major operatic careers as late as their early thirties. By contrast, a classical instrumentalist who wishes to have a serious professional career as an adult must almost always begin his training in childhood—or not at all.

Yet most American blacks, for a variety of reasons, shun classical music. They do not go to hear it (as any big-city concertgoer can tell you from experience) and they do not encourage their children to play it. To the extent that black children are urged to pursue any kind of musical career, it is usually in jazz or popular music (as Oleg Lobanov got into trouble for saying). By the time the typical young black instrumentalist discovers classical music, it is too late for him seriously to consider it as a possible career. Like it or not, this is why blacks are "underrepresented" in American conservatories and symphony orchestras, and why only one black American classical instrumentalist, the pianist André Watts, has had a major solo career. (Trumpeter Wynton Marsalis, though he also plays classical music, is primarily known as a jazz musician.) It is a problem—if it *is* a problem, and not simply a fact of life—that will not be solved by a thousand affirmative-action hiring programs.

But let us assume that qualified, or qualifiable, black candidates can be found. What then? In practice, affirmative action has come to consist of the use of color-conscious goals and quotas to increase minority representation in a given industry or academic enterprise. But a symphony orchestra that tries to apply such goals and quotas in its hiring of musicians immediately runs afoul of established audition practices instituted in the last decades—at the urging, as it happens, of black musicians themselves.

In 1969, two blacks who had previously auditioned unsuccessfully for the New York Philharmonic filed a complaint with the New York State Commission on Human Rights, charging the orchestra with discriminatory practices. The two, cellist Earl Madison and bassist Arthur Davis, asked the commission to require that they be allowed to take part in a "blind" audition, in which candidates perform behind screens in order to prevent judges from making decisions based on personal knowledge of the auditioner.

Such auditions were not standard practice in 1969, and the New York Philharmonic, arguing that "blind" auditions prevented judges from observing a musician's "physical technique" (in conductor Leonard Bernstein's words), managed to persuade the commission to turn aside Madison and Davis's request. Yet while the Philharmonic won its case, it lost the battle of the headlines. Said Whitney Young, president of the National Urban League: "It is shameful for a major cultural institution, one that gives concerts in a beautiful new hall financed by public subscription, to cling to a color bar while other fields are in the process of discarding it." In due course orchestras throughout the United States, the New York Philharmonic and the Detroit Symphony included, would adopt a blind-audition policy (it was under such a policy that Constance Price failed in 1984 to win a position), and the American Federation of Musicians would make blind auditions an industry-wide condition of union-sanctioned contracts.*

The new policy was acclaimed by the black musical community as a major step toward ridding American orchestras of discriminatory practices. Another major step

---

*In fact, the Detroit Symphony's procedure is far more "blind" even than the prevailing norm. While most American orchestras remove the screens after the preliminary auditions, the Detroit Symphony's final auditions are also blind—a policy reportedly adopted to reduce still further the likelihood of accusations of racial discrimination.

was undertaken in the 70's, when American orchestras began to develop full-scale minority-outreach programs. By today, according to the Detroit *News*, the Detroit Symphony's program actually "establishes specific racial quotas and timetables for every aspect of the DSO operation—from administrative appointments to the makeup of the chorus and the board of directors." Although several key features of this program have been jettisoned in recent months as a result of budget cuts, the Symphony has managed by means of it to develop a talent pool of local black substitute musicians who are given frequent opportunities to perform. Furthermore, it does not hold auditions for an open chair until at least one black musician has agreed to try out.

But the two initiatives designed to help black musicians are in conflict, both practical and philosophical. Thus, in 1988, thanks to the affirmative-action program, the Detroit Symphony succeeded in attracting nine black candidates out of a total field of 244. But blind auditions made it impossible to single out such candidates for special treatment once beyond the initial screening. In the event, no black players, not even the orchestra's own black substitutes, got past the preliminary auditions last year.*

According to the iron logic of affirmative action, any certified minority group that is "underrepresented" in a given industry is *ipso facto* the victim of conscious and deliberate discrimination. This was Morris Hood's explanation in 1988 for the Detroit Symphony's failure to have hired a second black player: "If, after thirteen years of pursuing it and talking about commitment, you tell me that you cannot find another black musician, I say that is totally untrue." And since black musicians had failed to make the cut at blind auditions, it followed that such au-

ditions were themselves responsible for the underrepresentation of blacks in American symphony orchestras. Pursuing this logic to its conclusion, a three-member team appointed by Michigan's Governor James J. Blanchard now recommended that the Detroit Symphony develop "new audition procedures that will ... assure ... the hiring of [minority] musicians."

At first, the orchestra remained adamant. Its music director, Gunther Herbig, told the Detroit *News* that "I am absolutely committed to the blind-audition process. It is the most just process which I [have] found anywhere in the world." Joseph Striplin said flatly that "[t]he audition issue is an area in which people in the black community are wrong. ... I know that there isn't discrimination in the auditions." But the Detroit Symphony soon learned that it was behind the times. The old ideal of color-blind equality of opportunity had long since been abandoned in favor of the newer vision of race-conscious equality of outcome. Striplin, backed by several other players, eventually came around to endorsing a "one-time-only" affirmative-action hiring program in an attempt to "prime the pump, to create role models, people whose example and influence will be felt within the black community."

February of this year arrived, and no black musician had been hired. Hood and Holmes renewed their threat. This time, they persuaded the rest of the appropriations subcommittee to go along with them. The move was well-timed—the orchestra was on tour in Europe and in no position to deal with bad publicity, much less with an attempt to cut its funding in half. One week later, the members of the Detroit Symphony voted to waive the audition requirement in their contracts to permit the agreed-upon "one-time-only" affirmative-action hire. The bass section of the orchestra unanimously recommended Richard Robinson of Detroit, who had spent the previous year playing with the orchestra as a substitute. The orchestra's state appropriation was released the next day.

---

*On the other hand, blind auditions have had an immediately beneficial effect on women: between 1973 and 1988, the number of women in the Detroit Symphony jumped from six to eighteen, and other orchestras reported comparable increases.

Initial reaction to Robinson's employment was positive. Thus, in a typical comment, Catherine French, chief executive officer of the American Symphony Orchestra League, said that "the DSO is to be applauded." In fact, the only person who seemed to have doubts was Robinson himself. From the very beginning, he appeared uncomfortable about the circumstances under which he had secured a chair in one of America's top orchestras. "I took the job," he told the Detroit *News* on the day of the announcement, "mainly to help the orchestra and the people I have come to know as friends over the last year that I have been working in Detroit as a substitute musician." A few days later he told the New York *Times*, "I would have rather auditioned like everybody else. Somehow this devalues the audition and worth of every other player."

It soon turned out, however, that Robinson was not the only black musician with misgivings. In a front-page story on the affair (March 5, 1989), the New York *Times* quoted Darwyn Apple, Jack Boesen's former student and Constance Price's old friend: "The intrusion of politics into an area where legislators are ignorant could wreak havoc with artistic integrity. This is going to discourage blacks from going to Detroit, or even applying." Michael Morgan, the black assistant conductor of the Chicago Symphony, put it even more bluntly: "Now even when a black player is hired on the merits of his playing, he will always have the stigma that it was to appease some state legislator." The *Times* also revealed that James DePriest, a highly respected black conductor who had been approached by the Detroit Symphony to replace Gunther Herbig as music director, declined the offer on account of the controversy stirred up by Hood and Holmes. "It's impossible for me to go to Detroit because of the atmosphere," said DePriest. "People mean well, but you fight for years to make race irrelevant, and now they are making race an issue."

Perhaps more suggestive than the reactions of these black musicians was the fact that so few newspaper editorials endorsed the hiring of Richard Robinson. It is hard to believe that five or ten years ago, America's opinion-makers would have failed to back the Detroit Symphony in its decision. Today they seem less certain.

Indeed, a growing number of people around the country—and not just in the music business—have begun to speak openly about some of the evolving negative effects of the policies of racial preference that have been undertaken in the name of affirmative action. Although such criticism has long been a staple of conservative or neoconservative thought, it has now also penetrated the liberal community. Within weeks of the hiring of Richard Robinson by the Detroit Symphony, for example, the New York *Times Magazine* published an article by Joseph Califano in which the Democratic activist and former Secretary of Health and Human Services recommended that his party rethink its commitment to "goals and timetables." In *Harper's*, the black academic Shelby Steele blamed affirmative-action policies for the increase of racial tension on college campuses and called for "skewing the formula for entitlement away from race and gender and back to constitutional rights." And the Supreme Court, America's most sensitive barometer of shifting public opinion, recently overturned a Richmond, Virginia, minority set-aside program as unconstitutional.

Nevertheless, although second thoughts about affirmative action are now increasingly aired in public, the policy itself is not only alive but flourishing, and (as a recent poll of *Fortune* 500 companies reveals) has become entrenched throughout the major institutions of American society. The Detroit Symphony case is thus merely a late example of affirmative action at work in an "industry" that had previously resisted it.

Moreover, while the Detroit Symphony insists that Richard Robinson's hiring was a "one-time-only" exception, there is reason to doubt that its troubles will end here. Within days of the hiring, David Holmes announced that two blacks in the Detroit Symphony were not enough, and issued a new list of what he would regard as acceptable changes in the orchestra's hiring procedures. Among these new requirements was the presence of one or two black candidates at each audition—with the total number of candidates considered at each audition to be limited to ten—and, for each black candidate, an opportunity to rehearse with the Detroit Symphony prior to auditioning.

Holmes's laundry list was denounced by other Michigan lawmakers—and ignored by Morris Hood. But black politicians in other cities have surely noted the example of Detroit, and in those cities which have "minority" majorities the pressure to step up black hiring by symphony orchestras is likely to increase as a result. The arguments will be more sophisticated in New York and Chicago, but the effect will almost certainly be the same: a gradual relaxation of the blind-audition procedure for minority candidates.

The consequences of such a relaxation are easy to predict, since similar developments have already taken place in many large corporations and graduate schools. Once blind auditions are shunted aside in favor of color-conscious selection procedures, symphony orchestras will begin competing directly against each other for a severely limited pool of talent. Such competitions will inevitably be "won" by the orchestras with the most money and prestige: New York, Philadelphia, Chicago, Cleveland, Boston, and Los Angeles. Second-rank ensembles like the Detroit Symphony will be left holding a bag long since emptied of first-rate black musicians.

Not that this will trouble the likes of David Holmes, who told the New York *Times* that the shortage of black classical musicians could be solved by training non-classical musicians to play in symphony orchestras. "Music is music," he said. "Do-re-me-fa-so-la-ti-do. I learned that in school." Although few would embrace so explicitly philistine a position, kinder, gentler versions of the "music is music" argument are already in circulation. Here is Phyllis Fleming, formerly the Detroit Symphony's education and outreach director, who now runs an all-black orchestra in Washington, D.C.:

> [A]ny major orchestra wants, first and foremost, to preserve a certain artistic tradition. That is the highest priority. And while they talk about creating programs for education and outreach, they really want to do everything they can to maintain that tradition, so it doesn't allow much room for change with regard to programming, guest artists, affirmative action, or anything else. . . . I'd rather work for an organization that is devoted to recognizing the talents of various ethnic groups at various levels. That's more important for me now than playing more Brahms and Beethoven.

Fifty years ago this April, the Daughters of the American Revolution prevented Marian Anderson, the great black contralto, from giving a recital at the racially segregated Constitution Hall in Washington, D.C. At the urging of the First Lady, Eleanor Roosevelt, Interior Secretary Harold Ickes invited Anderson to sing on the steps of the Lincoln Memorial. That performance is still remembered today as one of the great symbolic events in the history of the American civil-rights movement—though Miss Anderson, at the age of eighty-seven, continues to be somewhat reserved, even diffident, about acknowledging its larger implications. ("I wasn't trying to sway anybody into any movements or anything of that sort, you know," she told the Chicago *Tribune* recently.)

Times change, and so do the symbols that suit them. But in the case of Richard Robinson, at least the diffidence remains. Reluctant to serve as the symbol of a cause, he insists that he took his job with the Detroit Symphony not to break down the doors of prejudice but "mainly to help the orchestra." Still, Robinson symbolizes the fate of one important aspect of the civil-rights movement in 1989 just as surely as Marian Anderson symbolized it in 1939.

Everyone in a position to know agrees that Richard Robinson is a fine bass player. In the short run, it seems likely that he will retain the respect of his fellow musicians. They are, after all, good liberals. But they are also artists, and should the Detroit Symphony now begin systematically to lower its musical standards by abandoning blind auditions, it is safe to assume that in spite of Robinson's own misgivings about being hired without an audition, he will become the unwilling portent of the decline and fall of what once was a very good orchestra. That is a hard load to carry. But it is a load already carried by tens of thousands of talented middle-class blacks who have been hired in the era of mandated equality of outcome and who spend each day having to prove their worth again and again in the eyes of skeptical colleagues.

Such are some of the fruits of the decadent period of the civil-rights movement.

22

Saving Affirmative Action

James Forman, Jr.

This article summarizes the main themes of recent criticisms of affirmative action. After outlining the role of conservative court rulings, the author demonstrates how accepting the courts' negative perception of quotas is equivalent to abandoning the belief that taking account of color is a crucial element in the struggle for racial equality.

Exercises to Guide Your Reading

1. Summarize recent court rulings that narrow the scope of affirmative action.
2. Explain the goals and purposes of affirmative action.
3. Identify the assumptions of the "self-help" thesis.
4. Compare the policies of "self-help" with policies premised on the view that government has a role in remedying racial inequality.

While many observers have come to the conclusion that affirmative action is in jeopardy, little attention has been given to why this is so. Perhaps unsurprisingly in an era of an increasingly conservative judiciary and an apparent Republican stranglehold on the presidency, most explanations have focused on attacks in the courts and by conservative politicians. However, the greatest threat to affirmative action stems not from attacks by the right but from its abandonment by the left.

To be sure, the conservative assault on affirmative action ought not to be minimized. The Supreme Court, for example, has continued to chip away at affirmative action's legal foundations. By narrowly defining what constitutes an acceptable justification for an affirmative action plan, by placing heavy burdens on a government attempting to establish the necessary factual predicate for a plan, and by rigorously scrutinizing plans to make sure they target deserving beneficiaries and do not unduly burden nonbeneficiaries, the Court is continuing to narrow the scope of permissible affirmative action. These developments have been accompanied by criticisms of affirmative action in the political arena, both by conservative whites eager to tap antiblack sentiment among the white electorate and by a growing number of black conservatives concerned about the stigma suffered by the beneficiaries of affirmative action.

Criticism of affirmative action by black and white conservatives is neither new nor surprising. However, the critics have recently found an unlikely source of support. It is becoming increasingly apparent that the conservative attack on affirmative action has been accompanied and nurtured by the collapse of affirmative action's supporters, who

Reprinted by permission of *The Nation*. December 9, 1991. pp. 746, 748.

have shown an unfortunate willingness to abandon it and the vision of civil rights and government/corporate responsibility that sustains it. Perhaps the best illustration of this phenomenon, and the danger it poses, is the debate surrounding the Civil Rights Act of 1990/91.

The Civil Rights Act of 1990/91 was an attempt to expand employment discrimination protection for minorities and women, as well as to overturn a series of 1989 Supreme Court decisions limiting the scope of employment discrimination law. The bill was the main legislative priority for many civil rights organizations and liberal Democrats, just as stopping the bill was a key goal of the Bush Administration, Republican members of Congress and business groups. The principal opposition tactic, as has become well known, was to paint the bill as "quota" legislation. Opponents alleged that the bill would force employers to pay close attention to the race and gender of all job applicants, and in many cases hire minorities and women who were not as well qualified as whites under the employer's traditional method of determining merit.

Employment discrimination experts agree that antidiscrimination laws such as the Civil Rights Act encourage, and in many instances require, affirmative action. They do so by forcing employers to justify practices that disproportionately exclude minorities. If the employer is unable to prove that its practices are necessary to business, it must either abandon them or adopt affirmative action measures to insure that it hires sufficient women and minorities. In light of this reality, it is remarkable that nowhere to be found, either in the numerous press statements or in months of testimony before House and Senate committees, was a principled defense of affirmative action, of hiring with an eye to race. Also absent was any discussion of the well-documented inadequacy of many traditional measures of merit. In sum, none of the bill's supporters attempted to articulate a vision of civil rights that demands taking account of color as a critical element on the road to equality. In-

stead, the civil rights leadership abandoned the cause, explicitly denying that affirmative action was its goal.

National Urban League president John Jacob, for example, refused to defend affirmative action, noting that "another misleading critique of this bill is the suggestion that it is an affirmative action bill." Another key supporter, William Coleman, Secretary of Transportation under President Gerald Ford, indicated that "where legitimate concerns are expressed that a bill, although neutral on its face, might inadvertently coerce [affirmative action], Congress ought to inquire whether that concern has a substantial factual basis." While Coleman was arguing that this particular bill would not require affirmative action, the clear implication of his reasoning, like that of Jacob and other bill supporters, was that a bill that did require affirmative action deserved rejection.

Throughout the debate the bill's supporters adopted the rhetorical stance that this nation's employment discrimination laws, including the proposed Civil Rights Act, do not envision affirmative action in America's workplace. This was so patently false that it is hard to imagine the civil rights leadership believed it. Instead, it apparently believed that affirmative action was so politically unpalatable that it had to maintain the legislation was something that it really was not. But this bit of lobbying subterfuge had costs, the principal one being a devastating blow to the future of affirmative action. In conceding so much ideological terrain to affirmative action's opponents, supporters of racial preferences ignored the fact that these preferences place burdens on nonbeneficiaries and are a fertile source of political capital for those willing to promote racial division. The political viability of affirmative action rests on the willingness and ability of its proponents to articulate why such burdens are justifiable, even required. Such will and ability were clearly not present during the debate over the Civil Rights Act, and have yet to resurface in most black political discourse.

While there are many possible explanations for this failure of will, one that must not be ignored is that many in the black community are increasingly reluctant to endorse any program that might be perceived as placing another demand on the state in the name of black Americans. Instead, black Americans are told that success will come through self-help. Newly confirmed Supreme Court Justice Clarence Thomas has explained that no one, including the government, can "replicate my grandfather." Thomas is the most recent exponent of self-help philosophy, but he is hardly alone. In fact, the calls for self-help are echoing throughout many segments of black America, with black political dialogue increasingly abandoning claims against the state and emphasizing solving problems within our families and communities.

The current explosion of Malcolm X paraphernalia has been combined with a revisionist interpretation of Malcolm's political philosophy that portrays him as the initial proponent of the antistate, pro-self-help ideology. In the same vein, John Singleton's recent film, *Boyz N the Hood*, much acclaimed as an insightful analysis of life in the black ghetto, is centered on the proposition that a poor black child's chances of escaping the ghetto are determined by how responsibly he or she is raised. In one early scene, the film's hero lays down the ground rules of his house for his son, explaining that it is his job to "teach you how to be responsible. Your friends across the street [raised by a single mother] have nobody to show them how to do that. And you're going to see how they end up, too." Sure enough, the heroic father with the strict guidelines raises a son who is accepted at Morehouse, while the reckless single mother finds both of her sons shot dead.

The emphasis on self-help is not itself damaging, for self-help has a long history in the black community. In light of this soci-ety's historic dedication to black subordination, self-help has been a basic survival tool for some time. However, the latest version of the self-help gospel is dangerous, for it seems to carry with it a repudiation of the state's role in creating, and thus its responsibility for remedying, racial inequality.

Clarence Thomas and his grandfather deserve much credit for succeeding in the face of overwhelming odds, but this credit need not preclude recognition of the structural barriers that made and continue to make the odds for success for poor blacks (including those with caring grandparents) so long. Nor does crediting the value of studying hard and staying out of trouble preclude an understanding that affirmative measures by the government, corporate America and educational institutions have helped Thomas (and other blacks, myself included) achieve despite the long odds. Similarly, Singleton's proposition that some boys will escape the 'hood because of their family's support should not keep us from seeing that replacing the drugs and crime of South Central L.A. with jobs and education will require more than the presence of parents willing to establish ground rules for their children.

There is no doubt that black America must continue to help itself. But we must not forget that the state's historic and present-day use of public policy to further racial subordination carries with it a concomitant responsibility to combat racial inequality with the same vigor and commitment of resources that accompany other government priorities (remember Desert Storm?). Releasing the state from this obligation will insure the death of affirmative action; more important, it will leave little maneuvering room for those of us who view affirmative action as one of the first, not last, steps needed to solve the problems facing black America.

CHAPTER 6

Access, Earnings, and Education

23

Sins of Admission

Dinesh D'Souza

This article examines the effects of college admissions policies based on proportional representation. The resulting devaluation of merit criteria at Ivy League and major state universities is detailed, and the misplacement of students is described. Links between these problems and recent increases in racial tensions on college campuses are explored. The strengths of color-blind admissions policies are considered.

Exercises to Guide Your Reading

1. Define "proportional representation" in admissions policies.
2. Give examples of the devaluation of merit criteria and the misplacement of students.
3. Summarize the author's argument regarding dropout rates for minority students.
4. Compare and contrast this analysis with the analysis in Reading 24.

Reprinted by permission of *The New Republic*. February 18, 1991. pp. 30, 32–33.

When Michael Williams, head of the civil rights division of the Department of Education, sought to prevent American universities from granting minority-only scholarships, he blundered across the tripwire of affirmative action, the issue that is central to understanding racial tensions on campus and the furor over politically correct speech and the curriculum.

Nearly all American universities currently seek to achieve an ethnically diverse student body in order to prepare young people to live in an increasingly multiracial and multicultural society. Diversity is usually pursued through "proportional representation," a policy that attempts to shape each university class to approximate the proportion of blacks, Hispanics, whites, Asian Americans, and other groups in the general population. At the University of California, Berkeley, where such race balancing is official policy, an admissions report argues that proportional representation is the only just allocation of privileges for a state school in a democratic society, and moreover, "a broad diversity of backgrounds, values, and viewpoints is an integral part of a stimulating intellectual and cultural environment in which students educate one another."

The lofty goals of proportional representation are frustrated, however, by the fact that different racial groups perform very differently on academic indicators used by admissions officials, such as grades and standardized test scores. For example, on a scale of 400 to 1600, white and Asian American students on average score nearly 200 points higher than black students on the Scholastic Aptitude Test (SAT). Consequently, the only way for colleges to achieve ethnic proportionalism is to downplay or abandon merit criteria, and to accept students from typically underrepresented groups, such as blacks, Hispanics, and American Indians, over better-qualified students from among whites and Asian Americans.

At Ivy League colleges, for instance, where the median high school grade average of applicants approaches 4.0 and SAT scores are around 1300, many black, Hispanic, and American Indian students are granted admission with grade scores below 3.0 and SATs, lower than 1000. Each year state schools such as Berkeley and the University of Virginia turn away hundreds of white and Asian American applicants with straight As and impressive extracurriculars, while accepting students from underrepresented groups with poor to mediocre academic and other credentials. John Bunzel, former president of San Jose State University, argues that since the pool of qualified minority students is small, selective colleges "soon realize they have to make big academic allowances" if they are going to meet affirmative action targets.

Although universities strenuously deny the existence of quota ceilings for Asians, it is mathematically impossible to raise the percentage of students from underrepresented groups without simultaneously reducing the percentage of students from overrepresented groups. Former Berkeley chancellor Ira Heyman has admitted and apologized for his university's discriminatory treatment of Asians, and this year the Department of Education found the University of California, Los Angeles, guilty of illegal anti-Asian policies. Stanford, Brown, and Yale are among the dozen or so prestigious institutions under close scrutiny by Asian groups.

For Asian Americans, the cruel irony is that preferential admissions policies, which are set up to atone for discrimination, seem to have institutionalized and legitimized discrimination against a minority group that is itself the victim of continuing prejudice in America. Moreover, for Asians, minority quotas that were intended as instruments of inclusion have become instruments of exclusion.

The second major consequence of proportional representation is not an overall increase in the number of blacks and other preferred minorities in American universities, but rather the *misplacement* of such students throughout higher education. In other words, a student who might be qualified for admission to a community college now finds himself at the University of Wisconsin. The student whose grades and extracurriculars are good enough for Wisconsin is offered admission to Bowdoin or Berkeley. The student who meets Bowdoin's or Berkeley's more demanding standards is accepted through affirmative action to Yale or Princeton. Somewhat cynically, one Ivy League official terms this phenomenon "the Peter Principle of university admissions."

Aware of the fact that many affirmative action students are simply not competitive with their peers, many colleges offer special programs in remedial reading, composition, and basic mathematics to enable disadvantaged students to keep pace. But enrollment in such programs is generally poor; students who are already experiencing difficulties with their regular course load often do not have the time or energy to take on additional classes. Consequently, the dropout rate of affirmative action students is extremely high. Figures from the Department of Education show that blacks and Hispanics are twice as likely as whites and Asians to drop out for academic reasons. A recent study of 1980 high school graduates who entered four-year colleges found that only 26 percent of black and Hispanic students had graduated by 1986.

Even taking into account other factors for leaving college, such as financial hardship, the data leave little doubt that preferential admissions seriously exacerbate what universities euphemistically term "the retention problem." An internal report that Berkeley won't release to the public shows that, of students admitted through affirmative action who enrolled in 1982, only 22 percent of Hispanics and 18 percent of blacks had graduated by 1987. Blacks and Hispanics not admitted through preferential programs graduated at the rates of 42 and 55 percent respectively.

Although most universities do everything they can to conceal the data about preferential admissions and dropout rates, administrators will acknowledge the fact that a large number of minority students who stay in college experience severe academic difficulties. These classroom pressures, compounded by the social dislocation that many black and Hispanic students feel in the new campus environment, are at the root of the serious racial troubles on the American campus.

It is precisely these pressures that thwart the high expectations of affirmative action students, who have been repeatedly assured by college recruiters that standards have not been abridged to let them in, that they belong at the university, indeed, that they provide a special perspective that the school could not hope to obtain elsewhere. Bewildered at the realities of college life, many minority students seek support and solace from others like them, especially older students who have traveled the unfamiliar paths. Thus begins the process of minority separatism and self-segregation on campus, which is now fairly advanced and which has come as such a surprise to universities whose catalogs celebrate integration and the close interaction of diverse ethnic groups.

Distinctive minority organizations, such as Afro-American societies and Hispanic student organizations, provide needed camaraderie, but they do not provide academic assistance to disadvantaged students. Instead, they offer an attractive explanation: classroom difficulties of minorities are attributed not to insufficient academic preparation, but to the pervasive atmosphere of bigotry on campus. In particular, both the curriculum and testing systems are said to embody a white male ethos that is inaccessible to minorities.

Through the political agitation of minority organizations, many black and Hispanic students seek to recover a confident identity and sense of place on campuses where they otherwise feel alienated and even inadequate. Consequently, minority activists at several universities now have elaborate campaigns to identify and extirpate bigotry, such as racism hotlines and mandatory consciousness-raising sessions directed at white students. In addition, activists demand that "institutional racism" be remedied through greater representation of blacks and Hispanics among administrators and faculty. The logical extreme of this trend is a bill that Assemblyman Tom Hayden has introduced in the California legislature that mandates not just proportional admissions but equal pass rates for racial groups in state universities.

Both survey data and interviews with students published in *The Chronicle of Higher Education* over the past few years show that many white students who are generally sympathetic to the minority cause become weary and irritated by the extent of preferential treatment and double standards involving minority groups on campus. Indeed, racial incidents frequently suggest such embitterment; at the University of Michigan, for example, the affirmative action office has been sent a slew of posters, letters, poems—many racist—objecting specifically to special treatment for blacks and deriding the competence of minority students at the university. An increasing number of students are coming to believe what undergraduate Jake Shapiro recently told the "MacNeil/Lehrer NewsHour": "The reason why we have racial tensions at Rutgers is they have a very strong minority recruitment program, and this means that many of my friends from my hometown were not accepted even though they are more qualified."

Other students have complained that universities routinely recognize and subsidize minority separatist organizations, black and Hispanic fraternities, and even racially segregated residence quarters while they would never permit a club or fraternity to restrict membership to whites. A couple of American campuses have witnessed the disturbing rise of white student unions in bellicose resistance to perceived minority favoritism on campus.

A new generation of university leaders, weaned on the protest politics of the 1960s, such as Nannerl Keohane of Wellesley, James Freedman of Dartmouth, and Donna Shalala of the University of Wisconsin-Madison, are quite happy to attribute all opposition to resurgent bigotry. Some of this may be true, but as thoughtful university leaders and observers are now starting to recognize, administration policies may also be playing a tragic, counterproductive role. A redoubling of those policies, which is the usual response to racial tension, is not likely to solve the problem and might make it worse.

If universities wish to eliminate race as a factor in their students' decision-making, they might consider eliminating it as a factor in their own. It may be time for college leaders to consider basing affirmative action programs on socioeconomic disadvantage rather than ethnicity. This strategy would help reach those disadvantaged blacks who desperately need the education our colleges provide, but without the deleterious effects of racial head-counting. And it would set a color-blind standard of civilized behavior, which inspired the civil rights movement in the first place.

24

Why Are Droves of Unqualified, Unprepared Kids Getting into Our Top Colleges?

John Larew

This article examines the admissions policies of Ivy League colleges and finds that favoritism toward the children of alumni is common. Data supporting this conclusion are presented. The consequences of legacy preference are discussed, and the reasons for such a policy are analyzed.

Exercises to Guide Your Reading

1. Define "legacy preference."
2. Summarize arguments in defense of legacy preference.
3. Give examples of legacy preference.
4. Compare and contrast this analysis with that in Reading 23.

Growing up, she heard a hundred Harvard stories. In high school, she put the college squarely in her sights. But when judgment day came in the winter of 1988, the Harvard admissions guys were frankly unimpressed. Her academic record was solid—not special. Extracurriculars, interview, recommendations? Above average, but not by much. "Nothing really stands out," one admissions officer scribbled on her application folder. Wrote another, "Harvard not really the right place."

At the hyperselective Harvard, where high school valedictorians, National Merit Scholarship finalists, musical prodigies—11,000 ambitious kids in all—are rejected annually, this young woman didn't seem to have much of a chance. Thanks to Harvard's largest affirmative action program, she got in anyway. No, she wasn't poor, black, disabled, Hispanic, native American, or even Aleutian. She got in because her mom went to Harvard.

Folk wisdom at Harvard holds that "Mother Harvard does not coddle her young." She sure treats her grandkids right, though. For more than 40 years, an astounding one-fifth of Harvard's students have received admissions preference because their parents attended the school. Today, these overwhelmingly affluent, white children of alumni—"legacies"—are three times more likely to be accepted to Harvard than high school kids who lack that handsome lineage.

Yalies, don't feel smug: Offspring of the Old Blue are two-and-a-half times more likely to be accepted than their unconnected peers. Dartmouth this year admitted 57 percent of its legacy applicants, compared to 27 percent of nonlegacies. At the University of Pennsylvania, 66 percent of legacies were admitted last year—thanks in part to an autonomous "office of alumni admissions" that actively lobbies for alumni children before the admissions committee. "One can argue that it's an accident, but it sure doesn't look

Reprinted by permission of *The Washington Monthly*. June 1991. pp. 10–14.

like an accident," admits Yale Dean of Admissions Worth David.

If the legacies' big edge seems unfair to the tens of thousands who get turned away every year, Ivy League administrators have long defended the innocence of the legacy stat. Children of alumni are just smarter; they come from privileged backgrounds and tend to grow up in homes where parents encourage learning. That's what Harvard Dean of Admissions William Fitzsimmons told the campus newspaper, the *Harvard Crimson*, when it first reported on the legacy preference last year. Departing Harvard President Derek Bok patiently explained that the legacy preference worked only as a "tie-breaking factor" between otherwise equally qualified candidates.

Since Ivy League admissions data is a notoriously classified commodity, when Harvard officials said in previous years that alumni kids were just better, you had to take them at their word. But then federal investigators came along and pried open those top-secret files. The Harvard guys were lying.

This past fall, after two years of study, the U.S. Department of Education's Office for Civil Rights (OCR) found that, far from being more qualified or even equally qualified, the average admitted legacy at Harvard between 1981 and 1988 was significantly *less* qualified than the average admitted nonlegacy. Examining admissions office ratings on academics, extracurriculars, personal qualities, recommendations, and other categories, the OCR concluded that "with the exception of the athletic rating, [admitted] nonlegacies scored better than legacies in *all* areas of comparison."

Exceptionally high admit rates, lowered academic standards, preferential treatment ... hmmm. These sound like the cries heard in the growing fury over affirmative action for racial minorities in America's elite universities. Only no one is outraged about legacies.

- In his recent book, *Preferential Policies*, Thomas Sowell argues that doling out special treatment encourages lackluster performance by the favored and resentment from the spurned.

His far-ranging study flits from Malaysia to South Africa to American college campuses. Legacies don't merit a word.

- Dinesh D'Souza, in his celebrated jeremiad *Illiberal Education*, blames affirmative action in college admissions for declining academic standards and increasing racial tensions. Lowered standards for minority applicants, he hints, may soon destroy the university as we know it. Lowered standards for legacies? The subject doesn't come up.

- For all his polysyllabic complaints against preferential admissions, William F. Buckley Jr. (Yale '50) has never bothered to note that son Chris (Yale '75) got the benefit of a policy that more than doubled his chance of admission.

With so much silence on the subject, you'd be excused for thinking that in these enlightened times hereditary preferences are few and far between. But you'd be wrong. At most elite universities during the eighties, the legacy was by far the biggest piece of the preferential pie. At Harvard, a legacy is about twice as likely to be admitted as a black or Hispanic student. As sociologists Jerome Karabel and David Karen point out, if alumni children were admitted to Harvard at the same rate as other applicants, their numbers in the class of 1992 would have been reduced by about 200. Instead, those 200 marginally qualified legacies outnumbered all black, Mexican-American, native American, and Puerto Rican enrollees put together. If a few marginally qualified minorities are undermining Harvard's academic standards as much as conservatives charge, think about the damage all those legacies must be doing.

Mind you, colleges have the right to give the occasional preference—to bend the rules for the brilliant oboist or the world-class curler or the guy whose remarkable decency can't be measured by the SAT. (I happened to benefit from a geographical edge: It's easier to get into Harvard from West Virginia than from New England.) And until standardized tests and grade point average perfectly reflect the character, judgment, and drive of a student, tips like these aren't just nice, they're fair. Unfortunately, the extent of the legacy privilege in elite American colleges suggests something more than the occasional tie-breaking tip. Forget meritocracy. When 20 percent of Harvard's student body gets a legacy preference, aristocracy is the word that comes to mind.

A CASTE OF THOUSANDS

If complaining about minority preferences is fashionable in the world of competitive colleges, bitching about legacies is just plain gauche, suggesting an unhealthy resentment of the privileged. But the effects of the legacy trickle down. For every legacy that wins, someone—usually someone less privileged—loses. And higher education is a high-stakes game.

High school graduates earn 59 percent of the income of four-year college graduates. Between high school graduates and alumni of prestigious colleges, the disparity is far greater. A *Fortune* study of American CEOs shows the usual suspects—graduates of Yale, Princeton, and Harvard—leading the list. A recent survey of the Harvard Class of 1940 found that 43 percent were worth more than $1 million. With some understatement, the report concludes, "A picture of highly advantageous circumstances emerges here, does it not, compared with American society as a whole?"

An Ivy League diploma doesn't necessarily mean a fine education. Nor does it guarantee future success. What it *does* represent is a big head start in the rat race—a fact Harvard will be the first to tell you. When I was a freshman, a counselor at the Office of Career Services instructed a group of us to make the Harvard name stand out on our resumes: "Underline it, boldface it, put it in capital letters."

Of course, the existence of the legacy preference in this fierce career competition isn't exactly news. According to historians, it was a direct result of the influx of Jews into the Ivy League during the twenties. Until then, Harvard, Princeton, and Yale had admitted anyone who could pass their entrance exams, but suddenly Jewish kids were

outscoring the WASPs. So the schools began to use nonacademic criteria—"character," "solidity," and, eventually, lineage—to justify accepting low-scoring blue bloods over their peers. Yale implemented its legacy preference first, in 1925—spelling it out in a memo four years later: The school would admit "Yale sons of good character and reasonably good record ... regardless of the number of applicants and the superiority of outside competitors." Harvard and Princeton followed shortly thereafter.

Despite its ignoble origins, the legacy preference has only sporadically come under fire, most notably in 1978's affirmative action decision, *University of California Board of Regents* v. *Bakke*. In his concurrence, Justice Harry Blackmun observed, "It is somewhat ironic to have us so deeply disturbed over a program where race is an element of consciousness, and yet to be aware of the fact, as we are, that institutions of higher learning ... have given conceded preferences to the children of alumni."

If people are, in fact, aware of the legacy preference, why has it been spared the scrutiny given other preferential policies? One reason is public ignorance of the scope and scale of those preferences—an ignorance carefully cultivated by America's elite institutions. It's easy to maintain the fiction that your legacies get in strictly on merit as long as your admissions bureaucracy controls all access to student data. Information on Harvard's legacies became publicly available not because of any fit of disclosure by the university, but because a few civil rights types noted that the school had a suspiciously low rate of admission for Asian-Americans, who are statistically stronger than other racial groups in academics.

While the ensuing OCR inquiry found no evidence of illegal racial discrimination by Harvard, it did turn up some embarrassing information about how much weight the "legacy" label gives an otherwise flimsy file. Take these comments scrawled by admissions officers on applicant folders:

- "Double lineage who chose the right parents."
- "Dad's [deleted] connections signify lineage

of more than usual weight. That counted into the equation makes this a case which (assuming positive TRs [teacher recommendations] and Alum IV [alumnus interview]) is well worth doing."

- "Lineage is main thing."
- "Not quite strong enough to get the clean tip."
- "Classical case that would be hard to explain to dad."
- "Double lineage but lots of problems."
- "Not a great profile, but just strong enough #'s and grades to get the tip from lineage."
- "Without lineage, there would be little case. With it, we'll keep looking."

In every one of these cases, the applicant was admitted.

Of course, Harvard's not doing anything other schools aren't. The practice of playing favorites with alumni children is nearly universal among private colleges and isn't unheard of at public institutions, either. The rate of admission for Stanford's alumni children is "almost twice the general population," according to a spokesman for the admissions office. Notre Dame reserves 25 percent of each freshman class for legacies. At the University of Virginia, where native Virginians make up two-thirds of each class, alumni children are automatically treated as Virginians even if they live out of state—giving them a whopping competitive edge. The same is true of the University of California at Berkeley. At many schools, Harvard included, all legacy applications are guaranteed a read by the dean of admissions himself—a privilege nonlegacies don't get.

LITTLE WHITE ELIS

Like the Harvard deans, officials at other universities dismiss the statistical disparities by pointing to the superior environmental influences found in the homes of their alums. "I bet that, statistically, [legacy qualifications are] a little above average, but not by much," says Paul Killebrew, associate director of admissions at Dartmouth. "The admitted group [of legacies] would look exactly like the profile of the class."

James Wickenden, a former dean of admissions at Princeton who now runs a college consulting firm, suspects otherwise. Wickenden wrote of "one Ivy League university" where the average combined SAT score of the freshman class was 1,350 out of a possible 1,600, compared to 1,280 for legacies. "At most selective schools, [legacy status] doubles, even trebles the chances of admission," he says. Many colleges even place admitted legacies in a special "Not in Profile" file (along with recruited athletes and some minority students), so that when the school's SAT scores are published, alumni kids won't pull down the average.

How do those kids fare once they're enrolled? No one's telling. Harvard, for one, refuses to keep any records of how alumni children stack up academically against their nonlegacy classmates—perhaps because the last such study, in 1956, showed Harvard sons hogging the bottom of the grade curve.

If the test scores of admitted legacies are a mystery, the reason colleges accept so many is not. They're afraid the alumni parents of rejected children will stop giving to the colleges' unending fundraising campaigns. "Our survival as an institution depends on having support from alumni," says Richard Steele, director of undergraduate admissions at Duke University, "so according advantages to alumni kids is just a given."

In fact, the OCR exonerated Harvard's legacy preference precisely because legacies bring in money. (OCR cited a federal district court ruling that a state university could favor the children of out-of-state alumni because "defendants showed that the alumni provide monetary support for the university.") And there's no question that alumni provide significant support to Harvard: Last year, they raised $20 million for the scholarship fund alone.

In a letter to OCR defending his legacies, Harvard's Fitzsimmons painted a grim picture of a school where the preference did not exist—a place peeved alumni turned their backs on when their kids failed to make the cut. "Without the fundraising activities of alumni," Fitzsimmons warned darkly,

"Harvard could not maintain many of its programs, including needs-blind admissions."

Ignoring, for the moment, the question of how "needs-blind" a system is that admits one-fifth of each class on the assumption that, hey, their parents might give us money, Fitzsimmons's defense doesn't quite ring true. The "Save the Scholarship Fund" line is a variation on the principle of "Firemen First," whereby bureaucrats threatened with a budget cut insist that essential programs rather than executive perks and junkets will be the first to be slashed. Truth be told, there is just about nothing that Harvard, the richest university in the world, could do to jeopardize needs-blind admissions, provided that it placed a high enough priority on them.

But even more unclear is how closely alumni giving is related to the acceptance of alumni kids. "People whose children are denied admission are initially upset," says Wickenden, "and maybe for a year or two their interest in the university wanes. But typically they come back around when they see that what happened was best for the kids." Wickenden has put his money where his mouth is: He rejected two sons of a Princeton trustee involved in a $420 million fundraising project, not to mention the child of a board member who managed the school's $2 billion endowment, all with no apparent ill effect.

Most university administrators would be loathe to take such a chance, despite a surprising lack of evidence of the legacy/largess connection. Fitzsimmons admits Harvard knows of no empirical research to support the claim that diminishing legacies would decrease alumni contributions, relying instead on "hundreds, perhaps thousands of conversations with alumni whose sons and daughters applied."

No doubt some of Fitzsimmons's anxiety is founded: It's only natural for alumni to want their kids to have the same privileges they did. But the historical record suggests that alumni are far more tolerant than administrators realize. Admit women and blacks? *Well, we would*, said administrators

earlier this century—*but the alumni just won't have it*. Fortunately for American universities, the bulk of those alumni turned out to be less craven than administrators thought they'd be. As more blacks and women enrolled over the past two decades, the funds kept pouring in, reaching an all-time high in the eighties.

Another significant historical lesson can be drawn from the late fifties, when Harvard's selectiveness increased dramatically. As the number of applications soared, the rate of admission for legacies began declining from about 90 percent to its current 43 percent. Administration anxiety rose inversely, but Harvard's fundraising machine has somehow survived. That doesn't mean there's *no* correlation between alumni giving and the legacy preference, obviously; rather, it means that the people who would withhold their money at the loss of the legacy privilege were far outnumbered by other givers. "It takes time to get the message out," explains Fitzsimmons, "but eventually people start responding. We've had to make the case [for democratization] to alumni, and I think that they generally feel good about that."

HEIR CUT

When justice dictates that ordinary kids should have as fair a shot as the children of America's elite, couldn't Harvard and its sister institutions trouble themselves to "get the message out" again? Of course they could. But virtually no one—liberal or conservative—is pushing them to do so.

"There must be no goals or quotas for any special group or category of applicants," reads an advertisement in the right-wing *Dartmouth Review*. "Equal opportunity must be the guiding policy. Males, females, blacks, whites, Native Americans, Hispanics ... can all be given equal chance to matriculate, survive, and prosper based solely on individual performance."

Noble sentiments from the Ernest Martin Hopkins Institute, an organization of conservative Dartmouth alumni. Reading on, though, we find these "concerned alumni" aren't sacrificing *their* young to the cause. "Alumni sons and daughters," notes the ad further down, "should receive some special consideration."

Similarly, Harvard's conservative *Salient* has twice in recent years decried the treatment of Asian-Americans in admissions, but it attributes their misfortune to favoritism for blacks and Hispanics. What about legacy university favoritism—a much bigger factor? *Salient* writers have twice endorsed it.

What's most surprising is the indifference of minority activists. With the notable exception of a few vocal Asian-Americans, most have made peace with the preference for well-off whites.

Mecca Nelson, the president of Harvard's Black Students Association, leads rallies for the hiring of more minority faculty. She participated in an illegal sit-in at an administration building in support of Afro-American studies. But when it comes to the policy that Asian-American activist Arthur Hu calls "a 20-percent-white quota," Nelson says, "I don't have any really strong opinions about it. I'm not very clear on the whole legacy issue at all."

Joshua Li, former co-chair of Harvard's Asian-American Association, explains his complacency differently: "We understand that in the future Asian-American students will receive these tips as well."

At America's elite universities, you'd expect a somewhat higher standard of fairness than that—especially when money is the driving force behind the concept. And many Ivy League types *do* advocate for more just and lofty ideals. One of them, as it happens, is Derek Bok. In one of Harvard's annual reports, he warned that the modern university is slowly turning from a truth-seeking enterprise into a money-grubbing corporation—at the expense of the loyalty of its alums. "Such an institution may still evoke pride and respect because of its intellectual achievements," he said rightly. "But the feelings it engenders will not be quite the same as those produced by an institution that is prepared to forgo income, if need be, to preserve values of a nobler kind."

Forgo income to preserve values of a nobler kind—it's an excellent idea. Embrace the preferences for the poor and disadvantaged. Wean alumni from the idea of the legacy edge. And above all, stop the hypocrisy that begrudges the great unwashed a place at Harvard while happily making room for the less qualified sons and daughters of alums.

After 70 years, it won't be easy to wrest the legacy preference away from the alums. But the long-term payoff is as much a matter of message as money. When the sons and daughters of today's college kids fill out *their* applications, the legacy preference should seem not a birthright, but a long-gone relic from the Ivy League's inequitable past.

25

Minority Access: A Question of Equity

The Carnegie Foundation for the Advancement of Teaching

This article examines data on minority enrollment in undergraduate, graduate, and professional schools. Changes in the enrollment rates of European-American, African-American, Hispanic, and Asian students are compared, and explanations for the trends are offered. Issues of equality of representation and educational opportunity are discussed.

Exercises to Guide Your Reading

1. Describe differences in African-American and European-American college enrollment.
2. Summarize enrollment data (in Tables 4 and 5) for graduate and professional schools.
3. Identify the role of high schools, college admissions officers, and the federal government in helping to achieve equality of educational opportunity.
4. Compare minority enrollment on your campus with the data presented in this article. Explain any differences you find.

The issue of minority access to higher education should be of concern to all Americans. While the minority proportion of the American population is increasing, with the exception of Asian Americans—who have made impressive gains in enrollment at all levels of higher education—other minorities are still under-represented in college, and in graduate and professional schools. Because we exclude institutions located in outlying areas—Guam, Pacific Trust Territories, Virgin Islands, and Puerto Rico—and institutions that did not report the racial/ethnic status of their student body, our table totals may be smaller than those presented in some other sources.

In this issue of *Change: Trendlines*, we examine data on undergraduate, graduate, and professional school enrollment from 1976 to 1980, and from 1980 to 1984. Overall, the most serious declines have been experienced by blacks, and while Hispanics have made gains, of the major ethnic groups, they remain the least represented in higher education. While our focus is on minority enrollments, data on white students are included throughout for purposes of comparison.

UNDERGRADUATE LEVEL

Enrollments at the undergraduate level grew for all ethnic groups, except blacks, between 1976 and 1984. The number of Asian undergraduates grew by 87 percent during this period; Hispanics, by 23 percent; whites, by 6 percent; Native Americans (Pacific Islanders and Alaskan Natives are included among Native Americans), by 5 percent. The num-

Reprinted by permission of *Change*. May–June 1987. pp. 35–39.

ber of black undergraduates also rose between 1976 and 1980, but then declined precipitously. By 1984, fewer blacks were enrolled as undergraduates than in 1976, for an overall drop of 4 percent (Table 1).

While blacks were the only ethnic group to actually suffer a decrease in undergraduate enrollment over the whole eight-year period, they were not the only group to see the gains made in 1976–1980 diminished during the next four years. Whites and Native Americans also experienced declines in college enrollment from 1980 to 1984. And, although Asian and Hispanic enrollments continued to grow, they did so at a considerably lower rate (Table 1).

These trends in undergraduate enrollment look somewhat different when enrollments are expressed as a proportion of the young adult population. As Table 2 shows, the ratio of white undergraduates to the population of white 18- to 24-year-olds has remained constant from 1976 to 1984, at around 30 percent. Changes in enrollment figures for blacks and Hispanics did not track so well with changes in the young adult population of these groups. The ratio for blacks declined from 26 percent to 21 percent over these eight years, and the ratio for Hispanics declined from 23 percent to 20

percent. These declines are all the more discouraging because they come at a time when the pool of black and Hispanic high school graduates has been on the rise (Table 2).

Many observers of these trends in college enrollment have suggested that rising college costs and increasingly stiff restrictions on financial aid have played a part. These considerations may also influence whether or not students decide to enroll in college full-time. With this possibility in mind, it is interesting to note that there has been a decline in full-time college attendance among all the major ethnic groups. Although whites and blacks continue to have the highest rate of full-time enrollment, the figure for both groups declined from 70 percent in 1976 to 66 percent in 1984. The figure for Asians declined from 67 percent to 64 percent, for Native Americans, from 63 percent to 58 percent, and for Hispanics, from 59 percent to 56 percent, during the same period (Chart 1).

GRADUATE SCHOOL

Enrollment in graduate school, both for whites and for minorities, declined from 1976 to 1984. Indeed, it fell further for

TABLE 1 Undergraduate Enrollment in Higher Education by Race and Ethnicity: 1976, 1980, and 1984

	All Students	White	Total Minority	Asian*	Black	Hispanic	Native American**
Fall 1976	8,432,240	6,899,743	1,402,487	152,533	865,147	323,540	61,267
Fall 1980	9,262,820	7,465,722	1,606,192	214,989	932,055	390,440	68,708
Fall 1984	9,063,178	7,293,747	1,579,267	284,897	830,986	399,333	64,051
Percent Change							
1976–1980	9.9	8.2	14.5	40.9	7.7	20.7	12.1
1980–1984	−2.2	−2.3	−1.7	32.5	−10.8	2.3	−6.8
1976–1984	7.5	5.7	12.6	86.8	−3.9	23.4	4.5

*Includes Pacific Islanders

**Includes Alaskan Natives and American Indians

Source: U.S. Department of Education, "Fall Enrollment in Colleges and Universities," Surveys: 1976, 1980, and 1984.

TABLE 2   Population 18- to 24-Year-Olds—High School Graduates and College Enrollment: 1976, 1980, and 1984

	Total	White	Black	Hispanic
		(Numbers in Thousands)		
1976 population 18-to-24 years	26,936	23,157	3,293	1,437
High school graduates	21,006	18,484	2,131	782
Percent	78.0	79.8	64.7	54.4
Enrolled in college	8,432	6,900	865	324
Percent	31.3	29.8	26.3	22.5
1980 population 18-to-24 years	29,118	24,717	3,711	1,954
High school graduates	22,449	19,469	2,454	1,099
Percent	77.1	78.8	66.1	56.2
Enrolled in college	9,263	7,466	932	390
Percent	31.8	30.2	25.1	20.0
1984 population 18-to-24 years	28,768	23,939	3,919	2,019
High school graduates	22,465	19,028	2,808	1,122
Percent	78.1	79.5	71.7	55.6
Enrolled in college	9,063	7,294	831	399
Percent	31.5	30.5	21.2	19.8

Source: U.S. Department of Commerce, Current Population Reports, "Educational Attainment in the United States," Series P-20, Various Years.

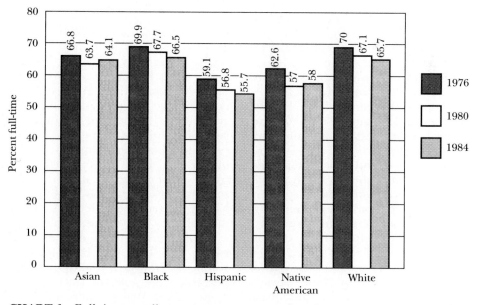

CHART 1 Full-time enrollment as a percentage of total undergraduate enrollment by race and ethnicity: Fall 1976, 1980, and 1984.

Source: U.S. Department of Education, Fall Enrollment Surveys: 1976, 1980, and 1984.

TABLE 3   Graduate Enrollment in Higher Education by Race and Ethnicity: 1976, 1980, and 1984

	All Students	White	Total Minority	Asian*	Black	Hispanic	Native American**
Fall 1976	1,079,307	905,371	107,898	18,446	65,338	20,234	3,880
Fall 1980	1,097,567	899,245	112,172	23,534	59,976	24,278	4,384
Fall 1984	1,063,995	856,061	104,680	27,318	50,717	23,144	3,501
			Percent Change				
1976–1980	1.7	−0.7	4.0	27.6	−8.2	20.0	13.0
1980–1984	−3.1	−4.8	−6.7	16.1	−15.4	−4.7	−20.1
1976–1984	−1.4	−5.4	−3.0	48.1	−22.4	14.4	−9.8

*Includes Pacific Islanders

**Includes Alaskan Natives and American Indians

Source: U.S. Department of Education, "Fall Enrollment in Colleges and Universities," Surveys: 1976, 1980, and 1984.

whites (5 percent) than for minorities as a whole (3 percent). When the minorities are separated into different ethnic groups, however, we see a pattern of gains and losses similar to what we found above for undergraduate enrollment. Again, Asians made impressive gains, increasing their enrollment in graduate school by 48 percent, and Hispanics came next, with a gain of 14 percent. The number of Native Americans enrolled in graduate school declined by 10 percent from 1976 to 1984, while blacks suffered the greatest loss, 22 percent (Table 3).

If we compare the period from 1976 to 1980 with the period from 1980 to 1984, we find another familiar pattern. For all ethnic groups, gains in the earlier period were diminished or reversed, and losses intensified. As we can see from Table 3, Asian enrollments in graduate school grew 28 percent from 1976 to 1980, but only 16 percent from 1980 to 1984. Graduate enrollments for Hispanics grew 20 percent from 1976 to 1980, but then turned around for a loss of 5 percent during the next four years. The earlier gain of 13 percent made by Native Americans was actually eradicated by a subsequent decline in graduate enrollments of 20 percent. And, while whites and blacks experienced losses in both four-year periods, their losses were greater in the later period. White graduate enrollments declined 1 percent

and then 5 percent, while black graduate enrollments declined 8 percent from 1976 to 1980 and then 15 percent from 1980 to 1984 (Table 3).

PROFESSIONAL SCHOOL

Professional school enrollments rose from 1976 to 1980 for all ethnic groups except Native Americans. In fact, it was in professional schools that Asians, Hispanics, and blacks all made their greatest gains. Asian enrollments in professional schools increased by 120 percent during these eight years; Hispanic enrollments were up 69 percent; and black enrollments in 1984 were higher than in 1976 by 16 percent. In contrast, white enrollment in professional schools rose only slightly, by 4 percent, while Native American enrollments declined dramatically, by 23 percent (Table 4).

Again, however, we find differences between 1976–1980, and 1980–1984. Asian enrollments grew at a slightly higher rate (49 percent) from 1980 to 1984 than they had from 1976 to 1980 (47 percent), but none of the other groups did as well in the later period as they had before. Hispanics, whose enrollments rose by 42 percent from 1976 to 1980, saw a smaller rise of 19 percent from 1980 to 1984. Blacks' gains of 14 percent in

TABLE 4   Enrollment in Professional Degree Programs by Race and Ethnicity: 1976, 1980, and 1984

	All Students	White	Total Minority	Asian*	Black	Hispanic	Native American**
Fall 1976	246,677	222,220	21,158	4,116	11,195	4,587	1,260
Fall 1980	275,732	246,316	26,541	6,065	12,775	6,513	1,188
Fall 1984	265,648	231,503	30,803	9,061	13,033	7,743	966
Percent Change							
1976–1980	11.8	10.8	25.4	47.4	14.1	42.0	−5.7
1980–1984	−3.7	−6.0	16.1	49.4	2.0	18.9	−18.7
1976–1984	7.7	4.2	45.6	120.1	16.4	68.8	−23.3

*Includes Pacific Islanders

**Includes Alaskan Natives and American Indians

Source: U.S. Department of Education, "Fall Enrollment in Colleges and Universities," Surveys: 1976, 1980, and 1984.

1976 to 1980 were whittled down to a gain of only 2 percent from 1980 to 1984. White professional school enrollments first grew by 11 percent, and then dropped 6 percent, while Native Americans lost 6 percent of their professional school enrollments in 1976 to 1980, and lost 19 percent from 1980 to 1984 (Table 4).

In which specific fields did students of the various ethnic groups form the largest blocks? Whites, of course, accounted for over 82 percent of the students in the four fields shown in Table 5, but predominated in veterinary medicine (about 95 percent), where few minority students (5 percent) enrolled. Although more Asians chose to study medicine and law than dentistry, they made their best showing in dentistry: In 1984, Asians accounted for 7 percent of all students enrolled in this field. The most popular profession for black and Hispanic students was law, but it was in medicine that their numbers were most visible, blacks comprising around 6 percent of all medical students, and Hispanics around 4 percent in 1984. While the actual numbers have changed considerably from 1976 to 1984, there appears to have been little change over time in the general pattern for each racial and ethnic group (Table 5).

MINORITY REPRESENTATION

The proportion of students of different ethnic groups enrolled in the undergraduate, graduate, and professional school populations are presented in Table 6. From these data, we can see that the proportion of white students at all levels of higher education dropped between 1976 and 1984, and that the proportion of minorities in the undergraduate and professional school populations rose. (Foreign students account for the differences remaining between white and minority students.)

Asian enrollments clearly grew at the highest rates during this period: The proportion of Asians in the student population rose considerably at all levels. Hispanics, however, also improved their position in the undergraduate, graduate, and professional student populations from 1976 to 1984. Native Americans maintained their position in undergraduate enrollments, but declined at the graduate and professional levels. And, although the proportion of blacks in the professional school population improved slightly, the proportion of blacks in the undergraduate and graduate school populations declined.

If we look down the columns of Table 6,

TABLE 5 Enrollment in Selected Professional Degree Programs by Race and Ethnicity: 1976, 1980, and 1984

	All Students		White		Minority		Asian*		Black		Hispanic		Native American**	
	Total	%	Total	%	Total	%	Total	%	Total	%	Total	%	Total	%
Total enrollment														
1976	246,677	100.0	222,220	90.1	21,158	8.6	4,116	1.7	11,195	4.5	4,587	1.9	1,260	0.5
1980	275,732	100.0	246,316	89.3	26,541	9.6	6,065	2.2	12,775	4.6	6,513	2.4	1,188	0.4
1984	265,648	100.0	231,503	87.1	30,803	11.6	9,061	3.4	13,033	4.9	7,743	2.9	966	0.4
Dentistry														
1976	20,101	100.0	18,032	89.7	1,793	8.9	549	2.7	822	4.1	354	1.8	68	0.3
1980	22,599	100.0	19,685	87.1	2,627	11.6	963	4.3	1,012	4.5	508	2.2	144	0.6
1984	19,952	100.0	16,513	82.8	3,005	15.1	1,346	6.7	966	4.8	623	3.1	70	0.4
Law														
1976	119,242	100.0	108,628	91.1	9,743	8.2	1,425	1.2	5,430	4.6	2,443	2.0	445	0.4
1980	118,944	100.0	107,149	90.1	11,043	9.3	1,682	1.4	5,730	4.8	2,932	2.5	699	0.6
1984	116,779	100.0	103,967	89.0	12,016	10.3	2,089	1.8	5,950	5.1	3,555	3.0	422	0.4
Medicine														
1976	57,668	100.0	50,661	87.8	6,277	10.9	1,342	2.3	3,454	6.0	1,275	2.2	206	0.4
1980	70,825	100.0	61,560	86.9	8,719	12.3	2,287	3.2	3,920	5.5	2,275	3.2	237	0.3
1984	67,692	100.0	57,226	84.5	9,974	14.7	3,517	5.2	3,884	5.7	2,344	3.5	269	0.4
Veterinary medicine														
1976	6,126	100.0	5,849	95.5	258	4.2	36	0.6	125	2.0	34	0.6	63	1.0
1980	8,100	100.0	7,720	95.3	348	4.3	73	0.9	173	2.1	84	1.0	18	0.2
1984	9,133	100.0	8,629	94.5	460	5.0	88	1.0	204	2.2	133	1.5	35	0.4
Other														
1976	43,540	100.0	39,050	89.7	3,087	7.1	764	1.8	1,364	3.1	481	1.1	478	1.1
1980	55,264	100.0	50,202	90.8	3,804	6.9	1,060	1.9	1,940	3.5	714	1.3	90	0.2
1984	52,092	100.0	45,168	86.7	5,348	10.3	2,021	3.9	2,069	4.0	1,088	2.1	170	0.3

*Includes Pacific Islanders

**Includes Alaskan Natives and American Indians

Source: U.S. Department of Education, "Fall Enrollment in Colleges and Universities," Surveys: 1976, 1980, and 1984.

TABLE 6 **Enrollment by Race and Ethnicity as a Percentage of Total Undergraduate, Graduate, and Professional Enrollments: 1976, 1980, and 1984 (Percent)**

	1976	1980	1984
White			
Undergraduate	81.8	80.6	80.5
Graduate	83.9	81.9	80.5
Professional	90.1	89.3	87.1
Minorities			
Undergraduate	16.6	17.3	17.4
Graduate	10.0	10.2	9.8
Professional	8.6	9.6	11.6
Asian*			
Undergraduate	1.8	2.3	3.1
Graduate	1.7	2.1	2.6
Professional	1.7	2.2	3.4
Black			
Undergraduate	10.3	10.1	9.2
Graduate	6.1	5.5	4.8
Professional	4.5	4.6	4.9
Hispanic			
Undergraduate	3.8	4.2	4.4
Graduate	1.9	2.2	2.2
Professional	1.9	2.4	2.9
Native American**			
Undergraduate	0.7	0.7	0.7
Graduate	0.4	0.4	0.3
Professional	0.5	0.4	0.4

*Includes Pacific Islanders

**Includes Alaskan Natives and American Indians

Source: U.S. Department of Education, "Fall Enrollment in Colleges and Universities," Surveys: 1976, 1980, and 1984.

instead of across the rows, another pattern comes into view. In 1976, we can see that white representation in the student population *went up* from the undergraduate (82 percent) to the graduate (84 percent), to the professional (90 percent) levels. In contrast, of course, minority representation went down: Minorities accounted for 17 percent of the undergraduate population in 1976, 10 percent of the graduate population, and 9 percent of the population in professional school. By 1984, a somewhat different pattern held. The proportion of whites in the professional school population was still higher than the proportion of whites at other levels, but the proportion of minorities in professional school had risen to exceed the proportion of minorities in graduate school. In 1984, this was indeed the case for each of the separate minority groups (Table 6).

CONCLUSION

It is important that a search for trends in participation at different levels of higher education by various racial/ethnic groups not lose sight of equity concerns. With the notable exception of Asians, the proportion of minorities in higher education does not reach the level of their presence in the population: According to the 1980 Census, blacks account for nearly 12 percent of the nation's population; Hispanics (may be of any race) nearly 6 percent; Asians and Pacific Islanders, 1.5 percent; and Native Americans, less than one percent. The disparity is likely to increase since population projections indicate the numbers of minorities in the American population will continue to grow.

Clearly, the task of equal educational opportunity becomes more urgent and requires greater effort than simply leaving open the door to higher learning. Colleges must be concerned that recruitment and admissions procedures bring in significant numbers of students from under-represented groups and that, once enrolled, minority students receive the support necessary to succeed academically. Further, colleges should seek out promising minority students early in their undergraduate careers and identify possible candidates for graduate and professional school. High schools, too, have a responsibility to work closely with colleges to encourage high school completion and assure adequate preparation for college-level work. And the federal role in assisting economically disadvantaged students of all racial and ethnic backgrounds must be reinforced rather than diminished. Quality and equality remain a national obligation to all students and the urgent agenda for higher education.

26

Campus Racism

Walter E. Williams

This article describes recent increases in racial and ethnic intolerance on college campuses across the United States. The role of college admissions policies in creating this environmental change is explored. Minority preparation for college is characterized, and details of the African American educational deficit are given.

Exercises to Guide Your Reading

1. Give examples of racial and ethnic differences in measures of academic preparation.
2. Define "negative-sum game," and explain why the author applies it to college affirmative action admissions policies.
3. Describe your reaction to this article.
4. Compare and contrast this article with Reading 30.

The decade of the 1980s has seen a rise in racial incidents on America's campuses. At Smith College, "NIGGERS, SPICS, AND CHINKS QUIT COMPLAINING OR GET OUT" was painted on a campus building. In a UC Berkeley building, "NIPS GO HOME" was scrawled on the wall. The University of Michigan's Ann Arbor campus radio station featured ethnic jokes aimed at blacks. *The Dartmouth Review,* an independent conservative student newspaper, published an article satirizing black language titled, "Dis Sho' Ain't No Jive, Bro." A leaflet opposing Holocaust studies and a swastika painted on a wall were found at Stanford University. At Philadelphia's Temple University, a White Student's Union was formed. Since 1986, the National Institute against Prejudice and Violence has documented racial incidents on 160 college campuses, including some of the nation's most

prestigious. In addition, more and more colleges are becoming the focal point of membership recruitment by the White Aryan Resistance, Skinheads, and the Ku Klux Klan.

Racial incidents have not been a one-sided coin. A black full professor at Dartmouth College frequently uses the term "honky" in his classroom in reference to whites. A black student at Vassar College hurled anti-Semitic insults at a Jewish student which included "dirty Jew," "stupid Jews," and "f— Jew." At the University of Pennsylvania campus, three black non-students crushed the skull of an Oriental student. On the campuses of Drexel University and the University of Pennsylvania, black non-students have been alleged to systematically seek out white students to extort and rob.

Civil-rights advocates, affirmative-action officials, and politicians see the increase in

Reprinted by permission of *National Review.* May 5, 1989. pp. 36–38.

campus racial incidents as the result of an "atmosphere" created by the Reagan Administration. Their reasoning is that by its attacks on affirmative action, the Administration created a perception of a tolerance for racism. To counteract this "atmosphere," there have been calls for more affirmative-action recruitment programs, mandated Black Studies classes as part of the college curriculum, more "cultural diversity," and more resources devoted to race relations.

Here we might explore the opposite line of causation and ask instead, what role has current campus racial policy played in the build-up of resentment and bitterness, and the consequent rise in campus racial incidents?

Affirmative action in recruitment makes the assumption, implicit or explicit, that a pool of black academic talent exists and that the paucity of blacks enrolled in the nation's colleges, medical schools, and law schools is a result of racial discrimination in admissions. Whether colleges currently engage in discriminatory policies against blacks is a matter for speculation; however, the question of just how large is the pool of black academic talent that meets standard college admissions criteria is not.

Black students score well below the national average on every measure of academic achievement. In 1983, fewer than 4,200 black college-bound high-school graduates, out of 75,400, had grade-point averages of 3.75 (B+) or better, compared to 7,858 out of 36,048 Asians, and 115,722 out of 701,345 whites. That means that 5.5 percent of black college-bound seniors earned B+ averages, compared to nearly 22 percent for Asians and 16.5 percent for whites.

Standard Achievement Test (SAT) scores tell an even more dismal story about college preparation. In 1983, across the nation, 66 out of 71,137 black college-bound seniors (less than a tenth of 1 percent) achieved 699, out of a possible 800, on the verbal portion of the SAT, and fewer than a thousand achieved scores of 600 or higher. On the

mathematics portion of the SAT, 205 blacks had scores over 699 and fewer than 1,700 achieved scores of 600 or higher.

Of the roughly 35,200 Asians taking the test, 496 scored over 699 on the verbal portion (1.4 percent) and 3,015 on the mathematics. Of the roughly 963,000 whites taking the test, 9,028 scored over 699 on the verbal (just under 1 percent) and 31,704 scored over 699 on the mathematics.

An important debate wages over just what SAT scores measure and predict, and how reliably they do so. Regardless of the outcome of the debate, the tests do say something about academic achievement in the tested material. Black performance on them has important implications concerning the availability of academically qualified black students for college recruitment.

At some of the nation's most prestigious schools, the SAT scores of the student body are as follows: at Amherst, 66 percent of the students score above 600 on the verbal and 83 percent above 600 on the mathematics; at Bryn Mawr, 70 percent above 600 on the verbal and 70 percent over 600 on the mathematics; at Haverford, 67 and 86 percent; at MIT, 72 and 97 percent. The median student SAT scores for the verbal and mathematics portions are 600 at Brown, Columbia, Cornell, Dartmouth, Duke, Georgetown, Harvard, Oberlin, Princeton, Williams, Yale, and other colleges ranked as most competitive. Student SAT scores at schools ranked very competitive, such as Franklin and Marshall, Lafayette, Brandeis, and Lehigh, range in the high 500s and low 600s.

The black scores on the SAT, compared with the SAT performance of the general student body at the most prestigious schools, suggests that even if these schools made every heroic recruitment effort, it would be impossible to find much more than a tiny handful of blacks who would match the academic characteristics of these schools' average student. In 1983, there were 570 blacks who had combined SAT verbal and mathematics scores above 1,200, compared to 60,400 whites who did. That means, given the paucity of well-qualified blacks, that less-elite schools, among the nation's more than three thousand institutions of higher learning, are quickly left drawing from the lower end of the pool of college-bound black students.

At the graduate-school level, the academic tale is even more gruesome. The Graduate Record Examination (GRE) is used as a part of the admissions process by most graduate schools. It has three parts: verbal, quantitative, and analytical. In 1983, the mean national GRE scores were 499 on the verbal, 516 on the quantitative, and 522 on the analytical. Black mean scores were well below the national means: 370 on the verbal, 363 on the quantitative, and 363 on the analytical, which translates into a 129-point deficit on the verbal, 153 on the quantitative, and 159 on the analytical. Black performance on the GRE is lower than that of any other ethnic group reported taking the test (American Indians, Mexican-Americans, Asians, Puerto Ricans, Latin Americans, and Whites).

Poor black performance on standardized tests is frequently dismissed as owing to cultural bias of the test. If the charge of cultural bias has merit in the first place, in the sense that a culture-free test could be devised, one would expect cultural bias to be exhibited most strongly on the verbal portion of the test, where there are questions of reading comprehension, language, and literature. A much better performance relative to the national mean would be expected on those parts of the test where cultural bias is minimized—i.e., mathematics and analytic reasoning. As it turns out, blacks are closer to the national norm on the verbal portion of the GRE and furthest behind on the quantitative and analytical portions.

The Asian population is more culturally distinct than other reported groups taking the GRE. However, the mean Asian score on the verbal portion of the GRE is 479, just 20 points below the national mean and 109 points higher than blacks. On the quantitative portion of the GRE, Asians' mean score is 575, outscoring the nation by 59 points. On the analytical portion, the Asian mean score is 522, identical with the national mean. Therefore, we might ask: If the examination is culturally biased, how is it that people of a culture far more alien to the American culture score close to the national mean?

Black performance on the GRE also allows us a preliminary assessment of what goes on while blacks are undergraduates. When blacks enter college as freshmen, their SAT scores as a percentage of the national norm are about 80 percent. After four years of college, those who take the GRE achieve scores that are only 71 percent of the national norm. Whatever the caveats regarding what tests measure, an unambiguous conclusion is that the achievement deficit of blacks does not diminish during four years of undergraduate training.

The fact that the black achievement deficit does not diminish demands more investigation into the possible reasons. Maybe there is nothing that can be done in the space of four or five years of college to significantly repair pre-college damage. Maybe the pattern of courses chosen by black students are not the most effective in terms of remediation. In any case, much more needs to be done to search for answers to these important questions.

Colleges and universities, under many sources of pressure, have sought to increase their enrollment of black students. If colleges adhered to rigid academic guidelines for admission, most would be frustrated in these efforts. Therefore, academic standards must be compromised. That is, colleges and universities must have one standard for admittance for whites and a lower one for blacks.

Whatever justification may be given for such a practice, it cannot help but build resentment, bitterness, and a sense of unfair play among whites, as it has already in matters of hiring, promotions, and layoffs. Official policy calling for unequal treatment by race is morally offensive whether it is applied to favor blacks or applied to favor whites.

Recently, charges have surfaced about discrimination against Asian-Americans at some of the nation's most prestigious colleges like UCLA, Harvard, Berkeley, and Brown. In 1982, Asians admitted to Harvard had a combined SAT score of 1,467, compared to a combined SAT score of 1,355 for whites. On the average, an Asian had to score over 100 points higher to be admitted than a white. At Brown, between 1983 and 1987, the Asian admittance rate declined, while Asian academic performance (SAT scores and grade-point averages) increased.

Jack Bunzel reports in *The Public Interest* (Fall 1988) that "virtually all American-Indians, Hispanics, and blacks who apply to Berkeley, and meet the minimum UC requirements, are admitted [though it is possible to meet those requirements with a GPA of 2.78]. . . . white or Asian students are rarely accepted by Berkeley without a GPA of at least 3.7 or 3.8." According to Bunzel, for an Asian to have a 50 percent chance of admission to Berkeley, he needs to have an Academic Index score of 7,000, while a score of 4,800 is enough for a black.

The other side of the admittance issue is the graduation issue. According to Bunzel, UC Berkeley figures show that 66 percent of white students and 61 percent of Asian students graduate within five years. Only 41 percent of Hispanics and 27 percent of blacks graduate in five years. These facts show that affirmative-action programs in college recruitment do not come close to being even a zero-sum game where blacks benefit at the expense of Asians. It is more like a negative-sum game, where everybody is worse off. In other words, Berkeley's affirmative-action program leads to the rejection of Asian and white students with a higher probability of graduation in favor of black and Hispanic students with a significantly lower probability of graduation. Thus, white and Asian students are being sacrificed to the benefit of no one.

This kind of affirmative action is not only inept social policy, it produces personal tragedy. Bunzel relates a story told by Donald H. Werner, headmaster of Westminster School:

UC Berkeley made decisions on two of its stu-

dents this past year, both Californians. Student A was ranked in the top third of his class, student B in the bottom third. Student A had College Board scores totaling 1,290; student B's scores totaled 890. Student A had a good record of citizenship; student B was expelled last winter for breaking a series of major school rules. Student A was white; student B was black. Berkeley refused student A and accepted student B.

The use of dual standards by college administrators, in an effort to produce "diversity" in the student body, is widespread. Whatever noble goals foster dual standards, one of their side-effects is that of producing racial animosity and resentment. It is easy to understand, though not to justify, how individuals who may never have harbored feelings of racial resentment can come to resent blacks, Hispanics, and other "protected" groups.

Blacks have difficult experiences on campus: high chances of being on academic probation and feelings of alienation from the larger community, which may be manifested in self-segregation, and dropping out of college. Today, there is little evidence of acts of official college racial discrimination against blacks. The bulk of black problems stem from poor academic preparation for college. Continually focusing on affirmative-action programs at the college level, while ignoring the massive educational fraud taking place at the primary and secondary schools blacks attend, means that campus problems will exist in perpetuity. It means most blacks will always need special admission privileges.

Today, many major cities have black mayors, large black representation on the city councils, and many black teachers and principals; in some large cities the superintendent of schools is black. That means blacks have many more policy choices than they had in the past. In the name of future generations of blacks, it is high time that responsible black people stop worrying about what whites are doing to blacks and begin to focus on what blacks are doing to blacks.

27

Barriers in the Path of the Non-College-Bound

Anne C. Lewis

This article explains how economic and social conditions can contribute to the high school dropout rate. The potential for vocational training to counter these forces is assessed. The leadership role of the federal government in this situation is evaluated, and new directions for educational policy are suggested.

Exercises to Guide Your Reading

1. Give examples of choice in schools.
2. List the characteristics of "at-risk youth."
3. Discuss the strengths of programs that provide alternatives to the academic diploma.
4. Evaluate reasons for and against dropping out of high school.

In two months the Reagan Administration will celebrate the fifth anniversary of the release of its report on education reform, *A Nation at Risk*. Undoubtedly, the Administration will claim that in those five years much has been accomplished to promote choice in education, a major goal of Secretary of Education William Bennett. Magnet schools and home study are flourishing, and states are experimenting with broader choices within the public schools. Indeed, the word *choice* no longer scares educators.

During this same interval, however, local, state, and congressional leaders have become increasingly concerned with choices of another kind: the decisions of young people, primarily those from minority and/or low-income backgrounds, to drop out of school, start families too early, and act as if their futures were stunted and without hope. Most of us view these choices as bad ones.

Some members of the current Adminis-

tration contend that schools should not waste their time and resources on young people who insist on making such unwise decisions. Yet those who have taken the time to analyze the situation of at-risk youth might not draw such stark distinctions between right and wrong choices. In some ways, the decisions that these young people are making are very logical ones, given the obstacles that confront them. Furthermore, the dilemmas facing many young people today are linked to the choices that federal officials have made—an issue one can safely predict will not be covered in the April report on education reform.

For the first time, however, we now have a national report that *does* address problems unique to the 50% of young Americans who do not attend college and to the large percentage of American youths who do not complete high school. *The Forgotten Half*, the interim report of Youth and America's Fu-

Reprinted by permission of *Phi Delta Kappan*. February 1988. pp. 396–97.

ture: The William T. Grant Foundation Commission on Work, Family and Citizenship, released in January, cautions against stereotyping the non-college-bound as a largely dysfunctional group. The report starkly describes the economic realities that have made the hurdles higher than ever before for young people trying to enter the workforce.

The report makes one thing clear: Washington decision makers should be concerned about the rapidly changing—and, too often, deteriorating—employment futures awaiting these young people. While the commission does not condone the unfortunate choices that many young Americans make, it tries to understand why these young people do not try harder to succeed. Consider the future as they see it:

- Young people are strongly encouraged to finish high school, but young male graduates between 20 and 24 years of age who were working in 1986 earned 28% less in constant dollars than they would have earned in 1973. In the same period, the percentage of family income devoted to housing has increased astronomically.
- Even with a high school diploma, today's young people are much less likely than their counterparts in the 1970s to find full-time jobs. Between 1974 and 1986 the percentage of non-college-bound high school graduates who were working full-time one to two years after graduation fell from 73% to 49%.
- In the past, many young people held manufacturing jobs, which guaranteed them good wages, benefits, and security. Between 1979 and 1985 the number of manufacturing jobs in the U.S. declined by 1.7 million. Manufacturing jobs have been replaced by jobs in retail trade and services. But it takes two retail jobs to equal the wages of one manufacturing job. High-wage employment for males under 20 fell from 57% in 1968 to 36% in 1986. In 1974, 46% of all the jobs held by black males between the ages of 20 and 24 were in blue-collar, craft, and operative occupations at wages sufficient to support a family. By 1986, only 25% of black males between the ages of 20 and 24 held such jobs.
- Less than 44% of young male workers earned

enough in 1985 to support a family of three above the poverty line of $8,737; earnings of minority males averaged much lower (Hispanics, $7,760; blacks, $5,299).
- Marriage rates of young people are down considerably—by 46% overall among 20- to 24-year-olds since 1974 and by 62% among blacks in that age group. Although the rate of out-of-wedlock births among blacks has been decreasing, the percentages still remain high. William Wilson, a sociologist at the University of Chicago and a member of the Grant Foundation's commission, points out that the high rate of out-of-wedlock births among blacks is related more to the lack of wage-earning black males than to any other factor.

Understanding these figures may give educators at the local level some perspective on their failures and successes—and perhaps enough gumption to challenge narrowly conceived notions about what constitutes effective schooling. The Grant Foundation's commission notes that alternative programs can motivate young people to prepare for the world of work as well as or better than exclusively academic programs. Alternative programs can foster problem solving and the cooperative work styles that employers say they want.

The purpose of such programs is not to avoid learning basic skills but to help youngsters reinforce them in ways that seem relevant to their needs. Lauren Resnick of the University of Pittsburgh, in a keynote address to education researchers last year, and Sue Berryman, director of the Research Center on Education and Employment at Teachers College, Columbia University, have made the same point: much of what the current education reforms seek to accomplish runs counter to the realities of the workplace. For example, the emphases on individual competitiveness, on "pure thought" without the use of tools, on learning "rules" of thought, and on learning general and theoretical principles all contrast sharply with what young people will face on the job.

Berryman goes even further. She argues

that young people who opt for vocational training have a good sense of self and of their career possibilities. Yet the disdain of federal officials toward vocational education couldn't be more obvious; their proposals have ranged from cutting federal funding for vocational education in half to wiping it out entirely.

The ripple effect of such an attitude—though kept from becoming a tide by the continued support of the Congress for vocational education—discourages state and local leaders from considering the value of second-chance programs. Hands-on, practical learning is provided by vocational education, mentoring programs, apprenticeships, and alternative schools that combine work and service experiences with classroom learning. Such programs should receive as much support as the test-driven academic programs that currently monopolize the attention of policy makers.

Local and state educators should begin to educate their communities. Schools may not be able to solve the problems of the economy (other than by increasing national productivity through greater success with students), but educators can help communities better understand the difficulties faced by the non-college-bound. These young people need more programs among which to choose to help them make better transitions from school to work. Educators, parents, business leaders, and social service agencies need to analyze the short- and long-term needs of young people and adjust their resources to the realities of the workplace.

The federal government needs to reconsider its choices, too. During the past seven years, certain programs that have proved their worth in helping young people have suffered huge cuts. The Grant Foundation's commission points out that special nutrition programs for poor mothers and their infants are serving less than half of those who are eligible; that Head Start reaches only 19% of eligible children; that Chapter 1 [the federal program that authorizes Head Start]

serves only about half of the students who are eligible.

Research efforts at the federal level are turned almost exclusively toward achieving higher academic standards, improving testing programs, and serving other interests of the college-bound. Research in vocational education has been given to a consortium of universities with few ties to the vocational community. This could be a plus, if new perspectives enable us to provide a better connection between classroom instruction and workplace realities. But if the change is merely a way to diminish further the role of vocational training, the choice will not turn out to be a good one for non-college-bound young people.

The policies of the current Administration represent another choice with disastrous consequences for many young people. The decided lack of interest in enforcing civil rights or in pursuing efforts to improve sex equity have contributed to conditions that are creating a two-tiered society. For example, blacks with a high school diploma are substantially more likely to be unemployed than whites who dropped out of school. In 1986 the unemployment rate for black *graduates* was 27%, while the unemployment rate for white *dropouts* was 20.7%.

The percentage of black high school graduates going on to college declined from 32% in 1975 to 27% in 1985. Researchers at the Educational Testing Service studied black college students and white college students with comparable economic and social backgrounds and standardized test scores; they found that the black students received lower college grades than their white counterparts.

The poverty rate among young white families doubled between 1973 and 1975, rising from 11.7% to 24.7%. In that same time period, the poverty rate among young black families rose from 42.9% to 62.1%.

Research, more investment in successful programs, and new efforts to reduce discrimination against minorities are not among the choices being made by the Administration. In the past few years, our national leadership has chosen to virtually ignore the specific needs of half of the students in our schools, thereby fooling the public—and perhaps itself—into believing that there is one best system of education for all.

Many students are smart enough not to buy that idea. Their choices may be limited, and too many of those choices may be negative. But we should give them some credit for being able to estimate the height of the barriers they face.

CHAPTER 7

Discrimination in Education

28

The Classroom Climate for Women

Bernice R. Sandler

This article summarizes the results of several studies that show that the experiences of women in college are less positive and less growth-enhancing than are those of male students. Findings indicate that females are often singled out for different treatment or ignored. Faculty behaviors that have a negative impact on female students are discussed. Reasons for the disparities between female and male students are examined.

Exercises to Guide Your Reading

1. List faculty behaviors that denigrate female students.
2. Identify social factors that contribute to the situation facing women students.
3. Give examples of institutional arrangements that may reinforce negative signals to female college students.
4. Discuss the implications of this study for other students who are "different" and on the career choices of women.

Reprinted by permission of *USA Today*. July 1988. pp. 50–53 (reprinted in *The American Woman: 1987–1988*).

The obvious barriers that for so many years stood between women and equal educational opportunity are largely gone. Today, female students can enter academic institutions and fields of study of which their mothers and grandmothers could only dream. Yet, like society as a whole, the academic world is still infected with attitudes that can militate against achievements by women. Thus, although women may now attend most of the same colleges and universities that men do, and be taught in the same class by the same faculty, the female student's classroom experiences are likely to be less positive than her male peer's.

The problem is that although most faculty want—and, indeed, try—to be fair, faculty of both sexes tend to treat female students quite differently from male students. In a variety of subtle ways (often so subtle that neither the professor nor the student notices that anything untoward has occurred), faculty behavior can convey to every student in the room the implication that women are not as worthwhile as men and that they are not expected to participate as fully as men in class, in college, or in life.

These findings were reported in 1982, when the first comprehensive report on the classroom climate for women students was published by the Project on the Status and Education of Women (PSEW) at the Association of American Colleges. Based on a review of the literature, as well as campus and individual reports, the paper, entitled *The Classroom Climate: A Chilly One for Women?* by Roberta Hall and the present author, identified over 30 ways in which faculty treated female students differently from male students. Following the publication of the report, some campuses began to pay attention to this issue by disseminating the paper to their faculty, conducting seminars and workshops, and undertaking related research. Nevertheless, both formal and informal information relayed to PSEW indicate that this remains a major problem across the country.

Some of the behaviors observed in the study are so small that they might be considered trivial. They do not happen in every class, nor do they happen all the time, and as isolated incidents, they may have little effect. But when they occur repeatedly, their cumulative effect can damage women's self-confidence, inhibit their learning and classroom participation, and lower their academic and career aspirations. (See, for example, El-Khawas, 1980).

The behaviors fall into two categories: ways in which female students are singled out and treated differently, and ways in which they are ignored. Some examples:

- Professors tend to make more eye contact with men than with women, so that male students are more likely to feel recognized and encouraged to participate in class.
- Professors are more likely to nod and gesture, and, in general, to pay attention when male students are talking. When women talk, faculty are less likely to be attentive; they may shuffle papers or look at their watches.
- Professors interrupt female students more than male students, thus communicating, at least in part, that what women have to say is less important than what men have to say. Moreover, when a male student is interrupted, the purpose is generally to expand on what the student is saying. Faculty interruptions of a female student, however, often consist of remarks unrelated to what the student has been saying—such as comments on her appearance—that have the effect of bringing her discussion to a halt.
- Female students are not called upon as frequently as male students, even when the women are clearly eager to participate in classroom discussion, again suggesting that what men have to say is more important than what women have to say.
- Male students are called by name more often than female students, as if men had more individual identity than women.
- Women are more likely to be asked questions that require factual answers (e.g., "*When* did the revolution occur?"), while men are more likely to be asked higher-order questions (e.g., "*Why* did the revolution occur?"). Such behavior may subtly communicate a presumption that women are less capable of independent analysis than men.
- Male students are "coached" more than female students by faculty probing for a more

elaborate answer (such as, "What do you mean by that?"). This gives male students an advantage, since probing not only encourages students to speak and develop their ideas, but also implies that they know the answer if they will just explain it more fully.

• Faculty are more likely to respond extensively to men's comments than to women's comments. Women's comments are more likely to be ignored or to receive an ambiguous "uh-huh." Often, when a point made by a female student elicits no response, the same point made subsequently by a male student elicits a positive response from the professor, who gives the male student approval and credit for the point as if it had not been raised previously. Thus, men receive much more reinforcement than women for intellectual participation.

Why should these behaviors occur? Many certainly have their origins in patterns and attitudes established long before students and faculty reach the college classroom. A major underlying reason is that throughout our society, what women do tends to be seen as less valuable than what men do.

Numerous experiments have demonstrated that devaluation of women occurs. (See, for example, Paludi and Bauer, 1983; Paludi and Strayer, 1985). A typical experiment involves two groups of people. Each group is presented with several items, such as articles, works of art or résumés, and asked to evaluate them. The items shown to each group are identical, but those items ascribed to women for one group are ascribed to men for the other. The results of these experiments are remarkably consistent: if people believe a woman was the creator, they will rank the item lower than if they believe it was created by a man. Both men and women devalue those items ascribed to females. Studies of how people view success shows a similar pattern: both men and women tend to attribute males' successes to talent, females' successes to luck. (See, for example, Erkut, 1979.)

Thus, female students can be just as well prepared, just as articulate, and just as willing to participate in discussion as their male peers, and still receive considerably less attention and less reinforcement from faculty than do male students. No wonder women students generally participate less in class than men!

The subtle behaviors described above are by no means the only factors that chill the classroom climate for women. Faculty remarks that overtly disparage women are still surprisingly prevalent. PSEW staff continually receive reports of such remarks. So is sexual harassment, which is experienced by 20 to 30 percent of all female students. The campus surveys in PSEW's files confirm these figures. The relatively small percentage of women on most faculties means that female students typically have fewer role models, less opportunity to benefit from mentoring, and less opportunity for informal talk with faculty (male faculty are more likely to engage in those conversations with male students). And there is a widespread lack of structural support for women's concerns: on many campuses there is no women's center at all; on many others the centers are inadequately funded. There are too few programs for reentry students (among whom women substantially predominate); there are still too few women's studies courses, and those that exist too often receive only limited support, if not denigration. All of these factors communicate to female students that although they have been allowed inside the gates, women are still outsiders in the academic world.

NOTES

El-Khawas, Elaine H. *Differences in Academic Development During College.* Men and Women Learning Together: A Study of College Students in the Late 1970s. Providence, Rhode Island: Brown University, Office of the Provost, April 1980.

Erkut, Sumru. *Expectancy, Attribution, and Academic Achievement: Exploring Implications of Sex-Role Orientation.* Working Paper No. 27. Wellesley, Massachusetts: Wellesley College Center for Research on Women, 1979.

Paludi, Michele A. and William Bauer. "Goldberg Revisited: What's in an Author's Name." *Sex Roles,* 9, No. 3 (1983): 387–90.

———— and Lisa A. Strayer. "What's in an Author's Name? Differential Evaluations of Performance as a Function of Author's Name." *Sex Roles,* 12, Nos. 3–4 (1985): 353–61.

29

Are Girls Shortchanged in School?

Rita Kramer

This article responds to the report of the American Association of University Women (AAUW) that charges that females face sexual discrimination in education. The author argues that this report is flawed by both weak data and poor methodology. The critique concludes with an examination of policies calling for increased remediation for female students.

Exercises to Guide Your Reading

1. Identify weaknesses in the data used in the AAUW report.
2. Illustrate flaws in the argument that textbooks are gender biased.
3. Discuss the relative impact of biology, personal development, and culture on the differential successes of boys and girls in math and science.
4. Evaluate the claim that policies to overcome gender bias are "anti-intellectual."

In America today, more girls graduate from high school than boys and more of them go on to college, where they make up 55 percent of the total enrollment. Yet according to a report recently released by the American Association of University Women (AAUW), "girls are invisible" in classrooms which "day in, day out, deliver the message that women's lives count for less than men's."

This report, *How Schools Shortchange Girls*, has been enthusiastically greeted by the media. With almost no attempt to evaluate the evidence on which it purports to be based, front-page articles in most of the nation's leading newspapers have simply passed on the report's conclusions: that standardized tests are biased against girls; that curricula and textbooks ignore or stereotype women; that teachers demonstrate bias by paying less attention to girls; and that because of discrimination girls lag behind boys in math and science and tend not to pursue careers in those fields.

All these charges are either false or misleading. And no wonder, since *How Schools Shortchange Girls* is based on a body of research some of which is outdated, much of which is trivial (unpublished doctoral dissertations and obscure publications), and some of which was done under the auspices of the organization issuing the report—a little like quoting yourself as an authority for your own opinions. The report ignores any published evidence—of which there is quite a bit—that does not support its conclusions and overlooks any inconvenient facts that contradict or even tend to modify those conclusions or suggest explanations other than bias for any statistical discrepancy in favor of boys (though not when the numbers favor girls).

Reprinted by permission of *Commentary*. June 1992. pp. 48–49.

Take, for example, the charge that the Scholastic Aptitude Test (SAT) is biased against girls. True, girls do somewhat less well than boys on the SAT, which is used to help determine admission to college; it is also true that girls get higher grades in college than boys. Since the SAT thus "underpredicts" the performance of girls in college, it must, says the AAUW report, be biased against them. But this could just as well be turned around and used as evidence that boys are the victims of grading bias. After all, scholars not quoted in the report have pointed out that girls tend to take more courses in which grading is easier (art, music, literature), and which involve the verbal skills in which girls do better, than the tougher math and science courses more boys tend to take.

The charge that textbooks are biased against women is even more bizarre. Thus, a quantitative analysis of the content of three leading high-school texts in American history carried out at the Center for the Study of Social and Political Change at Smith College (and not cited by the AAUW report) found that women are portrayed more favorably than men; that there are proportionately more pictures of women, largely in untraditional roles; that even minor achievements by women are given extensive treatment compared to the achievements of men; that women are never represented unflatteringly, although men may be; that most accounts of historical events such as wars are considered primarily in terms of the contributions made by women (and minorities).

Students who read nothing but these textbooks (and that means most students in American high schools) wind up knowing more about minor female characters in the American past than about men who have had a significant influence on world and national affairs. The 1987 National Assessment of Educational Progress test of history and literature found that more high-school students could identify Harriet Tubman than Winston Churchill or Joseph Stalin and more knew that the Seneca Falls Declaration

concerned women's rights than when Lincoln was President. In *American Voices*, a new Scott, Foresman entry into the lucrative textbook market, the index entries under "Women" and "Women's" are more than twice as long as those under World War I and World War II together.

As for the observation that teachers pay more attention to boys, this is one of those ambiguous findings that the authors of the AAUW report automatically ascribe to bias. It has long been common knowledge that boys are more aggressive and harder to control in the traditional classroom. Calling on them more frequently may be a strategy for keeping them in line, focusing them on the academic task at hand. But even so, there is no evidence to indicate that this kind of attention translates into their learning more, earning better grades, or getting into college more easily (which, as we have seen, they do not).

Nor is there any evidence that, as the AAUW report charges, girls "are systematically discouraged from" and "are being steered away from" science, mathematics, and technology. The report—ignoring the possibility that biological, developmental, or cultural factors may well have something to do with the relative disinclination of girls to study these subjects—once again simply assumes that bias is at work. Accordingly, it suggests special programs for girls in math and science.

But encouraging girls to go into previously avoided fields, and then to work hard at excelling in them, is not exactly what the authors of the AAUW report have in mind here. We get some notion of what they do have in mind from a talk given by one of them, Dr. Peggy McIntosh, an associate director at the Wellesley College Center for Research on Women, to teachers in Brookline, Massachusetts, in the fall of 1990.

McIntosh begins by describing a little girl who is unable to solve the problems on a worksheet that asks her to add a series of three numbers such as 1 + 3 + 5. McIntosh objects to the assignment as an example of "the right/wrong, win/lose/kill or be killed system" that defines learning as mastery—"vertical thinking," as she calls it.

Vertical thinking involves "competition, exact thinking, decisiveness, being able to make an argument that will persuade others or to turn in the perfect paper." To avoid such evils, McIntosh recommends revising the assignment in terms of "lateral thinking," which instead of asking, "How am I doing?" asks, "What is it to be alive?" One way of doing this is just to give the child the answers. Another is to let the children solve all problems in a group. (Incidentally, McIntosh's program for curricular innovation involves putting "not just math, but biology and chemistry off the right/wrong axis.")

The AAUW report, then, reflects the increasingly widespread attitude in American life that sees everything in terms of bias and group entitlements and ignores all the subtle and complex aspects of human nature that differentiate individuals—including women—from one another. As usual, the bottom line is a call for remedial legislation—in this case for a reactivation of the Women's Educational Equity Act Program (WEEAP).

It was under WEEAP that federal funding was made available in 1974 for the development of "nonsexist" textbooks and other curricular materials. But since the Department of Education's publication in 1983 of the report of the National Committee on Excellence in Education, A *Nation at Risk*, programs for school reform have concentrated on issues other than gender bias—most notably on why American children of both sexes do so poorly on all measures of academic ability compared to children in other countries, whom they manage to outdo only on measures of self-esteem. Under the present Secretary, Lamar Alexander, the focus of the Department of Education is on raising academic standards throughout the system from kindergarten to college. Along the way, requests for continued funding for WEEAP have been dropped.

It is this process that the AAUW seeks to reverse by persuading us that the problem with our schools is gender bias rather than a bias against academic achievement. But sharing this latter bias to the full, the AAUW report could not be expected to fight it. And indeed, accepting its shoddy analysis and carrying out the predictably anti-intellectual recommendations that follow from it would only make our schools worse—for girls and boys alike.

30

Race and the Schooling of Black Americans

Claude M. Steele

This article discusses the educational crisis confronting black Americans. A portrait of the differential successes of minority and dominant-race students is offered, and the effects of the persistent devaluation of blacks in American life are described. Reasons for the successes of programs that counter these messages are analyzed.

Exercises to Guide Your Reading

1. Illustrate the widening achievement and educational gap between black and white students.
2. List factors associated with social disadvantage and the achievement deficit of black students; explain the inadequacy of explanations rooted in the social disadvantage perspective.
3. Give examples of the devaluation of black students.
4. Compare and contrast "wise" and "unwise" schooling.

My former university offered minority students a faculty mentor to help shepherd them into college life. As soon as I learned of the program, I volunteered to be a mentor, but by then the school year was nearly over. Undaunted, the program's eager staff matched me with a student on their waiting list—an appealing nineteen-year-old black woman from Detroit, the same age as my daughter. We met finally in a campus lunch spot just about two weeks before the close of her freshman year. I realized quickly that I was too late. I have heard that the best way to diagnose someone's depression is to note how depressed you feel when you leave the person. When our lunch was over, I felt as gray as the snowbanks that often lined the path back to my office. My lunchtime companion was a statistic brought to life, a living

example of one of the most disturbing facts of racial life in America today: the failure of so many black Americans to thrive in school. Before I could lift a hand to help this student, she had decided to do what 70 percent of all black Americans at four-year colleges do at some point in their academic careers—drop out.

I sense a certain caving-in of hope in America that problems of race can be solved. Since the sixties, when race relations held promise for the dawning of a new era, the issue has become one whose persistence causes "problem fatigue"—resignation to an unwanted condition of life.

This fatigue, I suspect, deadens us to the deepening crisis in the education of black Americans. One can enter any desegregated

Reprinted by permission of *The Atlantic Monthly*. April 1992. pp. 68, 70, 72, 74–78.

school in America, from grammar school to high school to graduate or professional school, and meet a persistent reality: blacks and whites in largely separate worlds. And if one asks a few questions or looks at a few records, another reality emerges: these worlds are not equal, either in the education taking place there or in the achievement of the students who occupy them.

As a social scientist, I know that the crisis has enough possible causes to give anyone problem fatigue. But at a personal level, perhaps because of my experience as a black in American schools, or perhaps just as the hunch of a myopic psychologist, I have long suspected a particular culprit—a culprit that can undermine black achievement as effectively as a lock on a schoolhouse door. The culprit I see is *stigma*, the endemic devaluation many blacks face in our society and schools. This status is its own condition of life, different from class, money, culture. It is capable, in the words of the late sociologist Erving Goffman, of "breaking the claim" that one's human attributes have on people. I believe that its connection to school achievement among black Americans has been vastly underappreciated.

This is a troublesome argument, touching as it does on a still unhealed part of American race relations. But it leads us to a heartening principle: if blacks are made less racially vulnerable in school, they can overcome even substantial obstacles. Before the good news, though, I must at least sketch in the bad: the worsening crisis in the education of black Americans.

Despite their socioeconomic disadvantages as a group, blacks begin school with test scores that are fairly close to the test scores of whites their age. The longer they stay in school, however, the more they fall behind; for example, by the sixth grade blacks in many school districts are two full grade levels behind whites in achievement. This pattern holds true in the middle class nearly as much as in the lower class. The record does not improve in high school. In 1980, for example, 25,500 minority students, largely black and Hispanic, entered high school in Chicago. Four years later only 9,500 graduated, and of those only 2,000 could read at grade level. The situation in other cities is comparable.

Even for blacks who make it to college, the problem doesn't go away. As I noted, 70 percent of all black students who enroll in four-year colleges drop out at some point, as compared with 45 percent of whites. At any given time nearly as many black males are incarcerated as are in college in this country. And the grades of black college students average half a letter below those of their white classmates. At one prestigious university I recently studied, only 18 percent of the graduating black students had grade averages of B or above, as compared with 64 percent of the whites. This pattern is the rule, not the exception, in even the most elite American colleges. Tragically, low grades can render a degree essentially "terminal" in the sense that they preclude further schooling.

Blacks in graduate and professional schools face a similarly worsening or stagnating fate. For example, from 1977 to 1990, though the number of Ph.D.s awarded to other minorities increased and the number awarded to whites stayed roughly the same, the number awarded to American blacks dropped from 1,116 to 828. And blacks needed more time to get those degrees.

Standing ready is a familiar set of explanations. First is societal disadvantage. Black Americans have had, and continue to have, more than their share: a history of slavery, segregation, and job ceilings; continued lack of economic opportunity; poor schools; and the related problems of broken families, drug-infested communities, and social isolation. Any of these factors—alone, in combination, or through accumulated effects—can undermine school achievement. Some analysts point also to black American culture, suggesting that, hampered by disadvantage, it doesn't sustain the values and expectations critical to education, or that it fosters learning orientations ill suited to school achievement, or that it even "opposes" mainstream achievement. These are the chestnuts, and I had always thought them adequate. Then several facts emerged that just didn't seem to fit.

For one thing, the achievement deficits occur even when black students suffer no major financial disadvantage—among middle-class students on wealthy college campuses and in graduate school among black students receiving substantial financial aid. For another thing, survey after survey shows that even poor black Americans value education highly, often more than whites. Also, as I will demonstrate, several programs have improved black school achievement without addressing culturally specific learning orientations or doing something to remedy socioeconomic disadvantage.

Neither is the problem fully explained, as one might assume, by deficits in skill or preparation which blacks might suffer because of background disadvantages. I first doubted that such a connection existed when I saw flunk-out rates for black and white students at a large, prestigious university. Two observations surprised me. First, for both blacks and whites the level of preparation, as measured by Scholastic Aptitude Test scores, didn't make much difference in who flunked out; low scorers (with combined verbal and quantitative SATs of 800) were no more likely to flunk out than high scorers (with combined SATs of 1,200 to 1,500). The second observation was racial: whereas only two percent to 11 percent of the whites flunked out, 18 percent to 33 percent of the blacks flunked out, even at the highest levels of preparation (combined SATs of 1,400). Dinesh D'Souza has argued recently that college affirmative-action programs cause failure and high dropout rates among black students by recruiting them to levels of college work for which they are inadequately prepared. That was clearly not the case at this school; black students flunked out in large numbers even with preparation well above average.

And, sadly, this proved the rule, not the exception. From elementary school to graduate school, something depresses black achievement *at every level of preparation, even the highest.* Generally, of course, the better prepared achieve better than the less prepared, and this is about as true for blacks as for whites. But given any level of school preparation (as measured by tests and earlier grades), blacks somehow achieve less in subsequent schooling than whites (that is, have poorer grades, have lower graduation rates, and take longer to graduate), no matter how strong that preparation is. Put differently, the same achievement level requires better preparation for blacks than for whites—far better: among students with a C+ average at the university I just described, the mean American College Testing Program (ACT) score for blacks was at the 98th percentile, while for whites it was at only the 34th percentile. This pattern has been documented so broadly across so many regions of the country, and by so many investigations (literally hundreds), that it is virtually a social law in this society—as well as a racial tragedy.

Clearly, something is missing from our understanding of black underachievement. Disadvantage contributes, yet blacks underachieve even when they have ample resources, strongly value education, and are prepared better than adequately in terms of knowledge and skills. Something else has to be involved. That something else could be of just modest importance—a barrier that simply adds its effect to that of other disadvantages—or it could be pivotal, such that were it corrected, other disadvantages would lose their effect.

That something else, I believe, has to do with the process of identifying with school. I offer a personal example:

I remember conducting experiments with my research adviser early in graduate school and awaiting the results with only modest interest. I struggled to meet deadlines. The research enterprise—the core of what one does as a social psychologist—just wasn't *me* yet. I was in school for other reasons—I wanted an advanced degree, I was vaguely ambitious for intellectual work, and being in graduate school made my parents proud of me. But as time passed, I began to like the work. I also began to grasp the value system that gave it meaning, and the faculty treated me as if they thought I might even be able to do it. Gradually I began to think of myself as a social psychologist. With this change in self-concept came a new account-ability; my self-esteem was affected now by what I did as a social psychologist, some-thing that hadn't been true before. This added a new motivation to my work; self-respect, not just parental respect, was on the line. I noticed changes in myself. I worked without deadlines. I bored friends with ap-plications of arcane theory to their daily lives. I went to conventions. I lived and died over how experiments came out.

Before this transition one might have said that I was handicapped by my black work-ing-class background and lack of motivation. After the transition the same observer might say that even though my background was working-class, I had special advantages: achievement-oriented parents, a small and attentive college. But these facts alone would miss the importance of the identification process I had experienced: the change in self-definition and in the activities on which I based my self-esteem. They would also miss a simple condition necessary for me to make this identification: treatment as a valued per-son with good prospects.

I believe that the "something else" at the root of black achievement problems is the failure of American schooling to meet this simple condition for many of its black stu-dents. Doing well in school requires a belief that school achievement can be a promising basis of self-esteem, and that belief needs constant reaffirmation even for advantaged students. Tragically, I believe, the lives of black Americans are still haunted by a spec-ter that threatens this belief and the identi-fication that derives from it at every level of schooling.

THE SPECTER OF STIGMA
AND RACIAL VULNERABILITY

I have a good friend, the mother of three, who spends considerable time in the public school classrooms of Seattle, where she lives. In her son's third-grade room, managed by a teacher of unimpeachable good will and competence, she noticed over many visits that the extraordinary art work of a small black boy named Jerome was ignored—or, more accurately perhaps, its significance was ignored. As genuine art talent has a way of doing—even in the third grade—his stood out. Yet the teacher seemed hardly to notice. Moreover, Jerome's reputation, as it was passed along from one grade to the next, included only the slightest mention of his talent. Now, of course, being ignored like this could happen to anyone—such is the overload in our public schools. But my friend couldn't help wondering how the school would have responded to this talent had the artist been one of her own, middle-class white children.

Terms like "prejudice" and "racism" often miss the full scope of racial devalua-tion in our society, implying as they do that racial devaluation comes primarily from the strongly prejudiced, not from "good peo-ple" like Jerome's teacher. But the preva-lence of racists—deplorable though racism is—misses the full extent of Jerome's bur-den, perhaps even the most profound part.

He faces a devaluation that grows out of our images of society and the way those im-ages catalogue people. The catalogue need never be taught. It is implied by all we see around us: the kinds of people revered in advertising (consider the unrelenting racial advocacy of Ralph Lauren ads) and movies (black women are rarely seen as romantic partners, for example); media discussions of whether a black can be President; invitation lists to junior high school birthday parties; school curricula; literary and musical can-ons. These details create an image of society in which black Americans simply do not fare well. When I was a kid, we captured it with the saying "If you're white you're right, if you're yellow you're mellow, if you're brown stick around, but if you're black get back."

In ways that require no fueling from strong prejudice or stereotypes, these images expand the devaluation of black Americans. They act as mental standards against which information about blacks is evaluated: that which fits these images we accept; that which contradicts them we suspect. Had Jerome had a reading problem, which fits these images, it might have been accepted as characteristic more readily than his extraordinary art work, which contradicts them.

These images do something else as well, something especially pernicious in the classroom. They set up a jeopardy of double devaluation for blacks, a jeopardy that does not apply to whites. Like anyone, blacks risk devaluation for a particular incompetence, such as a failed test or a flubbed pronunciation. But they further risk that such performances will confirm the broader, racial inferiority they are suspected of. Thus, from the first grade through graduate school, blacks have the extra fear that in the eyes of those around them their full humanity could fall with a poor answer or a mistaken stroke of the pen.

Moreover, because these images are conditioned in all of us, collectively held, they can spawn racial devaluation in all of us, not just in the strongly prejudiced. They can do this even in blacks themselves: a majority of black children recently tested said they like and prefer to play with white rather than black dolls—almost fifty years after Kenneth and Mamie Clark, conducting similar experiments, documented identical findings and so paved the way for *Brown v. Topeka Board of Education.* Thus Jerome's devaluation can come from a circle of people in his world far greater than the expressly prejudiced—a circle that apparently includes his teacher.

In ways often too subtle to be conscious but sometimes overt, I believe, blacks remain devalued in American schools, where, for example, a recent national survey shows that through high school they are still more than twice as likely as white children to re-

ceive corporal punishment, be suspended from school, or be labeled mentally retarded.

Tragically, such devaluation can seem inescapable. Sooner or later it forces on its victims two painful realizations. The first is that society is preconditioned to see the worst in them. Black students quickly learn that acceptance, if it is to be won at all, will be hard-won. The second is that even if a black student achieves exoneration in one setting—with the teacher and fellow students in one classroom, or at one level of schooling, for example—this approval will have to be rewon in the next classroom, at the next level of schooling. Of course, individual characteristics that enhance one's value in society—skills, class status, appearance, and success—can diminish the racial devaluation one faces. And sometimes the effort to prove oneself fuels achievement. But few from any group could hope to sustain so daunting and everlasting a struggle. Thus, I am afraid, too many black students are left hopeless and deeply vulnerable in America's classrooms.

"DISIDENTIFYING" WITH SCHOOL

I believe that in significant part the crisis in black Americans' education stems from the power of this vulnerability to undercut identification with schooling, either before it happens or after it has bloomed.

Jerome is an example of the first kind. At precisely the time when he would need to see school as a viable source of self-esteem, his teachers fail to appreciate his best work. The devalued status of his race devalues him and his work in the classroom. Unable to entrust his sense of himself to this place, he resists measuring himself against its values and goals. He languishes there, held by the law, perhaps even by his parents, but not allowing achievement to affect his view of himself. This psychic alienation—the act of not caring—makes him less vulnerable to the specter of devaluation that haunts him. Bruce Hare, an educational researcher, has documented this process among fifth-grade boys in several schools in Champaign, Illinois. He found that although the black boys had considerably lower achievement-test scores than their white classmates, their overall self-esteem was just as high. This stunning imperviousness to poor academic performance was accomplished, he found, by their deemphasizing school achievement as a basis of self-esteem and giving preference to peer-group relations—a domain in which their esteem prospects were better. They went where they had to go to feel good about themselves.

But recall the young student whose mentor I was. She had already identified with school, and wanted to be a doctor. How can racial vulnerability break so developed an achievement identity? To see, let us follow her steps onto campus: Her recruitment and admission stress her minority status perhaps more strongly than it has been stressed at any other time in her life. She is offered academic and social support services, further implying that she is "at risk" (even though, contrary to common belief, the vast majority of black college students are admitted with qualifications well above the threshold for whites). Once on campus, she enters a socially circumscribed world in which blacks— still largely separate from whites—have lower status; this is reinforced by a sidelining of minority material and interests in the curriculum and in university life. And she can sense that everywhere in this new world her skin color places her under suspicion of intellectual inferiority. All of this gives her the double vulnerability I spoke of: she risks confirming a particular incompetence, at chemistry or a foreign language, for example; but she also risks confirming the racial inferiority she is suspected of—a judgment that can feel as close at hand as a mispronounced word or an ungrammatical sentence. In reaction, usually to some modest setback, she withdraws, hiding her troubles from instructors, counselors, even other students. Quickly, I believe, a psychic defense takes over. She *disidentifies* with achievement; she changes her self-conception, her outlook

and values, so that achievement is no longer so important to her self-esteem. She may continue to feel pressure to stay in school— from her parents, even from the potential advantages of a college degree. But now she is psychologically insulated from her academic life, like a disinterested visitor. Cool, unperturbed. But, like a pain-killing drug, disidentification undoes her future as it relieves her vulnerability.

The prevalence of this syndrome among black college students has been documented extensively, especially on predominantly white campuses. Summarizing this work, Jacqueline Fleming, a psychologist, writes, "The fact that black students must matriculate in an atmosphere that feels hostile arouses defensive reactions that interfere with intellectual performance. . . . They display academic demotivation and think less of their abilities. They profess losses of energy." Among a sample of blacks on one predominantly white campus, Richard Nisbett and Andrew Reaves, both psychologists, and I found that attitudes related to disidentification were more strongly predictive of grades than even academic preparation (that is, SATs and high school grades).

To make matters worse, once disidentification occurs in a school, it can spread like the common cold. Blacks who identify and try to achieve embarrass the strategy by valuing the very thing the strategy denies the value of. Thus pressure to make it a group norm can evolve quickly and become fierce. Defectors are called "oreos" or "incognegroes." One's identity as an authentic black is held hostage, made incompatible with school identification. For black students, then, pressure to disidentify with school can come from the already demoralized as well as from racial vulnerability in the setting.

Stigmatization of the sort suffered by black Americans is probably also a barrier to the school achievement of other groups in our society, such as lower-class whites, Hispanics, and women in male-dominated fields. For example, at a large midwestern university I studied, women match men's achievement in the liberal arts, where they suffer no marked stigma, but underachieve compared with men (get lower grades than men with the same ACT scores) in engineering and premedical programs, where they, like blacks across the board, are more vulnerable to suspicions of inferiority.

"WISE" SCHOOLING

> When they approach me they see ... everything and anything except me.... [this] invisibility ... occurs because of a peculiar disposition of the eyes....
> —Ralph Ellison, *Invisible Man*

Erving Goffman, borrowing from gays of the 1950s, used the term "wise" to describe people who don't themselves bear the stigma of a given group but who are accepted by the group. These are people in whose eyes the full humanity of the stigmatized is visible, people in whose eyes they feel less vulnerable. If racial vulnerability undermines black school achievement, as I have argued, then this achievement should improve significantly if schooling is made "wise"—that is, made to see value and promise in black students and to act accordingly.

And yet, although racial vulnerability at school may undermine black achievement, so many other factors seem to contribute—from the debilitations of poverty to the alleged dysfunctions of black American culture—that one might expect "wiseness" in the classroom to be of little help. Fortunately, we have considerable evidence to the contrary. Wise schooling may indeed be the missing key to the schoolhouse door.

In the mid-seventies black students in Philip Uri Treisman's early calculus courses at the University of California at Berkeley consistently fell to the bottom of every class. To help, Treisman developed the Mathematics Workshop Program, which, in a surprisingly short time, reversed their fortunes, causing them to outperform their white and Asian counterparts. And although it is only a freshman program, black students who take it graduate at a rate comparable to the Berkeley average. Its central technique is group study of calculus concepts. But it is also wise; it does things that allay the racial vulnerabilities of these students. Stressing their potential to learn, it recruits them to a challenging "honors" workshop tied to their first calculus course. Building on their skills, the workshop gives difficult work, often beyond course content, to students with even modest preparation (some of their math SATs dip to the 300s). Working together, students soon understand that everyone knows something and nobody knows everything, and learning is speeded through shared understanding. The wisdom of these tactics is their subtext message: "You are valued in this program because of your academic potential—regardless of your current skill level. You have no more to fear than the next person, and since the work is difficult, success is a credit to your ability, and a setback is a reflection only of the challenge." The black students' double vulnerability around failure—the fear that they lack ability, and the dread that they will be devalued—is thus reduced. They can relax and achieve. The movie *Stand and Deliver* depicts Jaime Escalante using the same techniques of assurance and challenge to inspire advanced calculus performance in East Los Angeles Chicano high schoolers. And, explaining Xavier University's extraordinary success in producing black medical students, a spokesman said recently, "What doesn't work is saying, 'You need remedial work.' What does work is saying, 'You may be somewhat behind at this time but you're a talented person. We're going to help you advance at an accelerated rate.'"

The work of James Comer, a child psychiatrist at Yale, suggests that wiseness can minimize even the barriers of poverty. Over a fifteen-year period he transformed the two worst elementary schools in New Haven, Connecticut, into the third and fifth best in the city's thirty-three-school system without any change in the type of students—largely poor and black. His guiding belief is that learning requires a strongly accepting relationship between teacher and student. "After all," he notes, "what is the difference between scribble and a letter of the alphabet to a child? The only reason the letter is meaningful, and worth learning and remembering, is because a *meaningful* other wants him or her to learn and remember it." To build these relationships Comer focuses on the overall school climate, shaping it not so much to transmit specific skills, or to achieve order per se, or even to improve achievement, as to establish a valuing and optimistic atmosphere in which a child can—to use his term—"identify" with learning. Responsibility for this lies with a team of ten to fifteen members, headed by the principal and made up of teachers, parents, school staff, and childdevelopment experts (for example, psychologists or special-education teachers). The team develops a plan of specifics: teacher training, parent workshops, coordination of information about students. But at base I believe it tries to ensure that the students—vulnerable on so many counts—get treated essentially like middle-class students, with conviction about their value and promise. As this happens, their vulnerability diminishes, and with it the companion defenses of disidentification and misconduct. They achieve, and apparently identify, as their achievement gains persist into high school. Comer's genius, I believe, is to have recognized the importance of these vulnerabilities as barriers to *intellectual* development, and the corollary that schools hoping to educate such students must learn first how to make them feel valued.

These are not isolated successes. Comparable results were observed, for example, in a Comer-type program in Maryland's Prince Georges County, in the Stanford economist Henry Levin's accelerated-schools program, and in Harlem's Central Park East Elementary School, under the principalship of Deborah Meier. And research involving hundreds of programs and schools points to the same conclusion: black achievement is consistently linked to conditions of schooling that reduce racial vulnerability. These include relatively harmonious race relations among students; a commitment by teachers and schools to seeing minority-group members achieve; the instructional goal that students at all levels of preparation achieve; desegregation at the classroom as well as the school level; and a de-emphasis on ability tracking.

That erasing stigma improves black achievement is perhaps the strongest evidence that stigma is what depresses it in the first place. This is no happy realization. But it lets in a ray of hope: whatever other factors also depress black achievement—poverty, social isolation, poor preparation—they may be substantially overcome in a schooling atmosphere that reduces racial and other vulnerabilities, not through unrelenting niceness or ferocious regimentation but by wiseness, by *seeing* value and acting on it.

WHAT MAKES SCHOOLING UNWISE

But if wise schooling is so attainable, why is racial vulnerability the rule, not the exception, in American schooling?

One factor is the basic assimilationist offer that schools make to blacks: You can be valued and rewarded in school (and society), the schools say to these students, but you must first master the culture and ways of the American mainstream, and since that mainstream (as it is represented) is essentially white, this means you must give up many particulars of being black—styles of speech and appearance, value priorities, preferences—at least in mainstream settings. This is asking a lot. But it has been the "color-blind" offer to every immigrant and minority group in our nation's history, the core of the melting-pot ideal, and so I think it strikes most of us as fair. Yet non-immigrant minorities like blacks and Native Americans have always been here, and thus are entitled, more than new immigrants, to participate in the defining images of the society projected in school. More important, their exclusion from these images denies their contributive history and presence in society. Thus, whereas immigrants can tilt toward assimilation in pursuit of the opportunities for which they came, American blacks may find it harder to assimilate. For them, the offer of acceptance in return for assimilation carries a primal insult: it asks them to join in something that has made them invisible.

Now, I must be clear. This is not a criticism of Western civilization. My concern is an omission of image-work. In his incisive essay "What America Would Be Like Without Blacks," Ralph Ellison showed black influence on American speech and language, the themes of our finest literature, and our most defining ideals of personal freedom and democracy. In *The World They Made Together*, Mechal Sobel described how African and European influences shaped the early American South in everything from housing design and land use to religious expression. The fact is that blacks are not outside the American mainstream but, in Ellison's words, have always been "one of its major tributaries." Yet if one relied on what is taught in America's schools, one would never know this. There blacks have fallen victim to a collective self-deception, a society's allowing itself to assimilate like mad from its constituent groups while representing itself to itself as if the assimilation had never happened, as if progress and good were almost exclusively Western and white. A prime influence of American society on world culture is the music of black Americans, shaping art forms from rock-and-roll to modern dance. Yet in American schools, from kindergarten through graduate school, these essentially black influences have barely peripheral status, are largely outside the canon. Thus it is not what is taught but what is *not* taught, what teachers and professors have never learned the value of, that reinforces a fundamental unwiseness in American schooling, and keeps black disidentification on full boil.

Deep in the psyche of American educators is a presumption that black students need academic remediation, or extra time with elemental curricula to overcome background deficits. This orientation guides many efforts to close the achievement gap—from grammar school tutoring to college academic-support programs—but I fear it can be unwise. Bruno Bettelheim and Karen Zelan's article "Why Children Don't Like to Read" comes to mind: apparently to satisfy the changing sensibilities of local school boards over this century, many books that children like were dropped from school reading lists; when children's reading scores also dropped, the approved texts were replaced by simpler books; and when reading scores dropped again, these were replaced by even simpler books, until eventually the children could hardly read at all, not because the material was too difficult but because they were bored stiff. So it goes, I suspect, with a great many of these remediation efforts. Moreover, because so many such programs target blacks primarily, they virtually equate black identity with substandard intellectual status, amplifying racial vulnerability. They can even undermine students' ability to gain confidence from their achievement, by sharing credit for their successes while implying that their failures stem from inadequacies beyond the reach of remediation.

The psychologist Lisa Brown and I recently uncovered evidence of just how damaging this orientation may be. At a large, prestigious university we found that whereas the grades of black graduates of the 1950s improved during the students' college years until they virtually matched the school average, those of blacks who graduated in the 1980s (we chose only those with above-average entry credentials, to correct for more-liberal admissions policies in that decade) worsened, ending up considerably below the school average. The 1950s graduates faced outward discrimination in everything from housing to the classroom, whereas the 1980s graduates were supported by a phalanx of help programs. Many things may contribute to this pattern. The Jackie Robinson, "pioneer" spirit of the 1950s blacks surely helped them endure. And in a pre-affirmative-action era, they may have been seen as intellectually more deserving. But one cannot ignore the distinctive fate of 1980s blacks: a remedial orientation put their abilities under suspicion, deflected their ambitions, distanced them from their successes, and painted them with their failures. Black students on today's campuses may experience far less overt prejudice than their 1950s counterparts but, ironically, may be more racially vulnerable.

THE ELEMENTS OF WISENESS

For too many black students school is simply the place where, more concertedly, persistently, and authoritatively than anywhere else in society, they learn how little valued they are.

Clearly, no simple recipe can fix this, but I believe we now understand the basics of a corrective approach. Schooling must focus more on reducing the vulnerabilities that block identification with achievement. I believe that four conditions, like the legs of a stool, are fundamental.

- If what is meaningful and important to a teacher is to become meaningful and important to a student, the student must feel valued by the teacher for his or her potential and as a person. Among the more fortunate in society, this relationship is often taken for granted. But it is precisely the relationship that race can still undermine in American society. As Comer, Escalante, and Treisman have shown, when one's students bear race and class vulnerabilities, building this relationship is the first order of business—at all levels of schooling. No tactic of instruction, no matter how ingenious, can succeed without it.
- The challenge and the promise of personal fulfillment, not remediation (under whatever guise), should guide the education of these students. Their present skills should be taken into account, and they should be moved along at a pace that is demanding but doesn't defeat them. Their ambitions should never be scaled down but should instead be guided to inspiring goals even when extraordinary dedication

is called for. Frustration will be less crippling than alienation. Here psychology is everything: remediation defeats, challenge strengthens—affirming their potential, crediting them with their achievements, inspiring them.

But the first condition, I believe, cannot work without the second, and vice versa. A valuing teacher-student relationship goes nowhere without challenge, and challenge will always be resisted outside a valuing relationship. (Again, I must be careful about something: in criticizing remediation I am not opposing affirmative-action recruitment in the schools. The success of this policy, like that of school integration before it, depends, I believe, on the tactics of implementation. Where students are valued and challenged, they generally succeed.)

- Racial integration is a generally useful element in this design, if not a necessity. Segregation, whatever its purpose, draws out group differences and makes people feel more vulnerable when they inevitably cross group lines to compete in the larger society. This vulnerability, I fear, can override confidence gained in segregated schooling unless that confidence is based on strongly competitive skills and knowledge—something that segregated schooling, plagued by shortages of resources and access, has difficulty producing.
- The particulars of black life and culture—art, literature, political and social perspective, music—must be presented in the mainstream curriculum of American schooling, not consigned to special days, weeks, or even months of the year, or to special-topic courses and programs aimed essentially at blacks. Such channeling carries the disturbing message that the material is not of general value. And this does two terrible things: it wastes the power of this material to alter our images of the American mainstream—continuing to frustrate black identification with it—and it excuses in whites and others a huge ignorance of their own society. The true test of democracy, Ralph Ellison has said, "is ... the inclusion—not assimilation—of the black man."

Finally, if I might be allowed a word specifically to black parents, one issue is even more immediate: our children may drop out of school before the first committee meets to accelerate the curriculum. Thus, although we, along with all Americans, must strive constantly for wise schooling, I believe we cannot wait for it. We cannot yet forget our essentially heroic challenge: to foster in our children a sense of hope and entitlement to mainstream American life and schooling, even when it devalues them.

31

American Indians in Higher Education: A History of Cultural Conflict

Bobby Wright and William G. Tierney

This article presents the history of the college education of Native Americans. The role played by cultural differences in determining Anglo-American and Native American experiences in higher education is discussed, and the involvement of the federal government in shaping education programs is described. The current status of American Indians in higher education is reported. Proposals for improving their educational attainment are advanced.

Exercises to Guide Your Reading

1. Summarize the colonial experiments in American Indian higher education.
2. Describe the switch from higher education to vocational training as the focus for Indian education.
3. Give examples of the differences between tribal colleges and mainstream campuses for Native Americans.
4. Determine which factors account for the greater successes of the tribal colleges.

Caleb Cheeshateaumuck, an Algonquian Indian from Martha's Vineyard, graduated from Harvard College, class of 1665. An outstanding scholar, Caleb could read, write, and speak Latin and Greek as well as English—not to mention his own native language. Although fully able to meet Harvard's rigorous academic demands, the young native scholar did not escape the dangers associated with life in an alien environment. He died within months of his college degree, victim of a foreign disease to which he had no immunity.

Caleb was among the first in a long line of American Indians who have attended colleges and universities during the past three centuries. He represents, too, the challenge and the triumph, as well as the failure and tragedy, that characterize the history of American Indian higher education. These conflicting outcomes reflect the clash of cultures, the confrontation of lifestyles, that has ensued on college campuses since colonial days. Euro-Americans have persistently sought to remold Native Americans in the image of the white man—to "civilize" and

Reprinted by permission of *Change*. March–April 1991. pp. 11–14, 17–18.

assimilate the "savages"—but native peoples have steadfastly struggled to preserve their cultural integrity. The college campus has historically provided a stage for this cross-cultural drama.

Within a decade of the first European settlement in America, plans for an Indian college were already underway. The earliest colonial efforts to provide Indians with higher education were designed to Christianize and "civilize" the Indians, thus saving them from the folly of their "heathenish" and "savage" ways. The hope was that educated Indians, as schoolmasters and preachers, would become missionary agents among their own brethren.

In 1617, King James I launched the initial design, when he enjoined the Anglican clergymen to collect charitable funds for "the erecting of some churches and schools for ye education of ye children of these [Virginia] Barbarians." The following year, the English set aside 1,000 acres at Henrico, Virginia, for construction of a "college for Children of the Infidels." However, the Virginia natives resisted such cultural intrusions. Their rebellion in 1622, an attempt to rid their lands of the English forever, was only partially and temporarily successful, but it abruptly ended the scheme for an Indian college in Virginia.

In New England, the 1650 charter of Harvard College heralded the next educational design. It provided for the "education of the English and Indian youth of this country in knowledge." Charitable contributions from England supported the construction of the Indian College building on Harvard's campus, completed in 1656. During the four decades of its existence, although it had a capacity for 20 students, the structure housed no more than six Indian scholars—Caleb Cheeshateaumuck among them. Most of that time, the "Indian college" housed English students and the college printing press.

In Virginia, the native rebellion of 1622 had ended the initial plans for an Indian college. Seven decades later, the 1693 charter of the College of William and Mary reaffirmed the English desire to educate and "civilize" the Indians. It established William and Mary, in part, so "that the Christian faith may be propagated amongst the Western Indians." Robert Boyle, an English scientist and philanthropist, inspired this divine mission when he willed a bequest for unspecified charitable and pious uses. The president of William and Mary obtained the lion's share of this charity, which he used to build the Brafferton building in 1723, purportedly to house resident native scholars. No Indian students were in residence for two decades following its completion, however, and only five or six attended during the life of the Brafferton school. Following feeble efforts and insignificant results, the American Revolution stopped the flow of missionary funds

TABLE 1

Control/Level of Institution	1976	1978	1980	1982	1984
Public	67,757	68,460	74,244	76,959	71,642
Four-year	28,445	27,197	29,062	30,857	29,568
Two-year	39,312	41,263	45,182	46,102	42,074
Private	8,610	9,425	9,679	8,957	11,030
Four-year	6,765	7,807	7,867	7,166	7,913
Two-year	1,845	1,618	1,812	1,791	3,117

Source: U.S. Department of Health, Education, and Welfare, Office for Civil Rights, *Racial, Ethnic and Sex Enrollment Data from Institutions of Higher Education*, 1976, 1978, and U.S. Department of Education, Center for Education Statistics, Higher Education General Information Survey, various years.

TABLE 2

Number of Indian students taking SAT test, 1976[1]	2,632
Number of Indian students taking SAT test, 1989	18,005
Mean Indian SAT score, 1989	812
Mean U.S. SAT score, 1989	903
Number of Indian students in higher education, 1986–87[1]	89,000
Tribal college enrollment, 1981 (FTE)[2]	1,689
Tribal college enrollment, 1989 (FTE)	4,400

Sources:

[1]Quality Education for Minorities Project, *Education That Works: An Action Plan for the Education of Minorities* (Report Summary), Massachusetts Institute of Technology, January 1990.

[2]American Indian Higher Education (1989), cited in *Black Issues in Higher Education* (December 7, 1989).

from England, and William and Mary has since ignored the pious mission on which it was founded.

In the mid-18th century, Eleazar Wheelock, a Congregational minister, passionately engaged in the academic training of Indian youth. Wheelock founded Dartmouth College, chartered in 1769, for "the education & instruction of Youth of the Indian tribes in this Land in reading, wrighting [sic] and all parts of Learning which shall appear necessary and expedient for civilizing and Christianizing children of pagans . . . and also of English Youth." He built the College with charity collected by Samson Occum, Wheelock's most successful convert and a noted Indian scholar, who solicited a substantial endowment for native education. Nonetheless, by the time he established Dartmouth, Wheelock's interest in Indian schooling waned in favor of the education of "English youth." As a result, the College became increasingly inaccessible to potential Native American converts. While a total of 58 Indians attended from 1769 to 1893, Dartmouth produced only three Indian graduates in the 18th century and eight in the 19th.

The College of New Jersey (now Princeton University), although not specifically professing an Indian mission, admitted at least three Indian students. The first, a Delaware youth, attended the College in 1751 under the sponsorship of the Society in Scotland for the Propagation of Christian Knowledge, benefactors also of Dartmouth's Indian program. Although reportedly proficient in his learning and "much beloved by his classmates and the other scholars," the unfortunate young Delaware died of consumption a year later. Jacob Woolley, one of Wheelock's first students, enrolled in 1759, though he was expelled before completing his degree. Finally, Shawuskukhkung—also known by his English name, Bartholomew Scott Calvin—attended the College in 1773. During his second year of residence, however, the charitable funds from Great Britain that supported his attendance ceased, as a consequence of the Revolutionary War, forcing Calvin to abandon his studies.

TRIBAL RESISTANCE

The colonial experiments in Indian higher education proved, for the most part, unsuccessful. Targeted tribal groups resisted missionary efforts and tenaciously clung to their traditional life ways. Among those who succumbed to education, their physical inability to survive the alien environment compounded the failure. Hugh Jones, an 18th-century historian of Virginia, admitted that, at the College of William and Mary

> hitherto but little good has been done, though abundance of money has been laid out. . . . [An] abundance of them used to die . . . Those of them that have escaped well, and been taught to read and write, have for the most part returned to their home, some with and some without baptism, where they follow their own savage customs and heathenish rites.

The general Indian sentiment is illustrated by the Six Nations' response to the treaty commissioners from Maryland and Virginia, who in 1744 invited the Indians to send their sons to the College of William and Mary. "We must let you know," the Iroquois leaders responded,

> we love our Children too well to send them so great a Way, and the Indians are not inclined to give their Children learning. We allow it to be good, and we thank you for your Invitation; but our customs differing from yours, you will be so good as to excuse us.

The colonial era ended and, with the birth of the new nation, Indian education increasingly became a matter of federal policy. Influenced by the limited results of the colonial educational missions, George Washington voiced a shift in policy from an emphasis on higher learning to vocational training for American Indians. "I am fully of the opinion," he concluded,

> that this mode of education which has hitherto been pursued with respect to these young Indians who have been sent to our colleges is not such as can be productive of any good to their nations. It is perhaps productive of evil. Humanity and good policy must make it the wish of every good citizen of the United States that husbandry, and consequently, civilization, should be introduced among the Indians.

This educational philosophy unfolded in the 19th century and dominated until the 20th, even in the midst of tribal efforts to gain a foothold in higher education.

TRIBAL SUPPORT

While some tribes violently resisted attempts to "civilize" them through education, other Indian groups eagerly embraced higher learning. At the same time that Dartmouth was educating 12 members of the Five Civilized Tribes, the Cherokees and the Choctaws organized a system of higher education that had more than 200 schools, and sent numerous graduates to eastern colleges. The 1830 Treaty of Dancing Rabbit Creek set aside $10,000 for the education of Choctaw youth. The first official use of the funds provided under this treaty occurred in 1841, when the tribe authorized the education of Indian boys at Ohio University, Jefferson College, and Indiana University. The 1843 Report of the Commissioner of Indian Affairs mentioned the education of 20 Choctaw boys, 10 at Asbury University, and 10 at Lafayette College.

Choctaw graduates from tribally operated boarding schools were selected on the basis of their promise and allowed to continue their education until they had completed graduate and professional study at colleges in the states. Several members of the Five Civilized Tribes entered Dartmouth in 1838, and, in 1854, Joseph Folsom, a Choctaw, received a degree. In all, 12 Choctaw and Cherokee students received support to attend Dartmouth from the "Scottish Fund"— the legacy of their predecessor, Samson Occum. Ironically, the Choctaw academic system, responsible for a literacy rate exceeding that of their white neighbors, collapsed when the federal government became involved in the late 1800s.

The first university in which Indians were to play a significant role was proposed in 1862. As was the case at Harvard, however, the Ottawa Indian University was more a dream than a reality. The Ottawas never received the promised university, as they were removed by the federal government to Oklahoma in 1873.

Bacon College, founded by the Baptists in 1880, also received Indian support, which came in the form of a land grant from the Creek tribe. Dedicated to training of Indian clergy, the college opened to three students. By the end of its fifth year, 56 students had enrolled. Bacon College still operates today with a strong (but not exclusive) commitment to educate American Indians.

EDUCATION AS ASSIMILATION

Indians who attended universities and colleges during the 17th, 18th, and 19th centuries, for the most part, studied the same subjects as did the white students. However, as the federal government began to dominate Indian education in the late 19th century, significantly reducing the role of missionary groups, private individuals, and the states, the result was a continual de-emphasis on higher learning. Instead, the role of higher education changed to vocational training.

In 1870 Congress appropriated $100,000 for the operation of federal industrial schools. The first off-reservation boarding school was established at Carlisle, Pennsylvania, in 1879. The boarding school, exemplified at Carlisle, dominated the federal approach to Indian education for half a century. Its methods included the removal of the students from their homes and tribal influences, strict military discipline, infusion of the Protestant work ethic, as well as an emphasis on the agricultural, industrial, and domestic arts—*not* higher academic study.

Most importantly, these institutions were designed to remake their Indian charges in the image of the white man. Luther Standing Bear, a Sioux, attended Carlisle in 1879. He recalled the psychological assaults he and others encountered during the educational process.

> I remember when we children were on our way to Carlisle School, thinking that we were on our way to meet death at the hands of the white people, the older boys sang brave songs, so that we would meet death according to the code of the Lakota. Our first resentment was in having our hair cut. It has ever been the custom of Lakota men to wear long hair, and old tribal members still wear the hair in this manner. On first hearing the rule, some of the older boys talked of resisting, but realizing the uselessness of doing so, submitted. But for days after being shorn we felt strange and uncomfortable.... The fact is that we were to be transformed.

Fueled by a large congressional appropriation in 1882, 25 boarding schools opened by the turn of the century—among them, Santa Fe Indian School, which became the Institute of American Indian Arts, a two-year postsecondary school, and Haskell Institute (now Haskell Indian Junior College) in Lawrence, Kansas. These institutes, like the normal schools of the 19th century, were not true colleges. Their standards of training, at best, approximated only those of a good manual-training high school. The range of occupational futures envisioned for Indian students was limited to farmer, mechanic, and housewife.

By the turn of the century, only a few talented Indian youth went on for further training at American colleges and universities. Ohiyesa, a Sioux, was among them. Adopting the notion that "the Sioux should accept civilization before it was too late," Charles A. Eastman (his English name) graduated from Dartmouth College in 1887, and three years later received a degree in medicine at Boston University. Eastman was keenly aware that his academic success depended on his acceptance of American civilization and the rejection of his own traditional culture. "I renounced finally my bow and arrow for the spade and the pen," he wrote in his memoirs. "I took off my soft moccasins and put on the heavy and clumsy but durable shoes. Every day of my life I put into use every English word that I knew, and for the first time permitted myself to think and act as a white man."

Ohiyesa's accomplishments were rare in the 19th and early 20th centuries. The education of Native Americans—although still preserving the centuries-old purpose of civilizing the "savages"—seldom exceeded the high school level. The impact of this neglect on Indian educational attainment is reflected in enrollment figures. As late as 1932, only 385 Indians were enrolled in college and only 52 college graduates could be identified. At that time, too, American Indian scholarships were being offered at only five colleges and universities.

FEDERAL EFFORTS

Not until the New Deal era of the 1930s, a period of reform in federal Indian policy, did Indian higher education receive government support. The Indian Reorganization Act of 1934, among other sweeping reforms, authorized $250,000 in loans for college expenses. By 1935, the Commissioner of Indian Affairs reported 515 Indians in college. Although the loan program was discontinued in 1952, the Bureau of Indian Affairs had established the higher education scholarship grant program in 1948, allocating $9,390 among 50 students. Indian veterans returning from World War II and eligible for GI Bill educational benefits added to the growing number of college students. According to estimates, some 2,000 Native Americans were enrolled in some form of postsecondary education during the last half of the 1950s. The enrollment grew to about 7,000 by 1965. Sixty-six Indians graduated from four-year institutions in 1961, and by 1968 this figure had almost tripled. Still, in 1966, only one percent of the Indian population was enrolled in college.

During the 1970s, a series of federal task force and U.S. General Accounting Office reports called attention to the academic, financial, social, and cultural problems that Indian students encountered in pursuing a college education. These reports fell on attentive Congressional ears. By 1979 the Bureau of Indian Affairs Higher Education Program was financing approximately 14,600 undergraduates and 700 graduate students. Of these, 1,639 received college degrees and 434 earned graduate degrees. In addition, federal legislation, including the Indian Self-Determination and Education Assistance Act of 1975 and the Tribally Controlled Community College Assistance Act of 1978, spawned striking new developments in Indian higher education.

Perhaps the most dramatic policy change reflected in the new legislation was the shift to Indian control of education. For the first time, Indian people—who had thus far been subjected to paternalistic and assimilationist policies—began to take control of their own affairs. Higher education was among the targets of the new Self-Determination programs, best illustrated by the development of tribally controlled community colleges.

TRIBAL COLLEGES

Tribal colleges evolved for the most part during the 1970s in response to the unsuccessful experience of Indian students on mainstream campuses. Today, there are 24 tribally controlled colleges in 11 western and midwestern states—from California to Michigan, and from Arizona to the Dakotas. These institutions serve about 10,000 American Indians and have a full-time equivalent enrollment of about 4,500 students.

Because Indian students most often live in economically poor communities, tuition is low and local tax dollars do not offer much assistance. Congress has authorized up to $6,000 per student, but, in reality, the amount released to the colleges decreased throughout the Reagan era so that by 1989 the amount generated for each student was only $1,900. Tribal leaders point out how odd it is that those students who are most at-risk receive the least assistance. One would think that if the government was serious about increasing opportunities for Indian youth, then colleges would be provided the funds necessary to aid those youth. Such has not been the case.

CURRENT DEMOGRAPHICS

By all accounts the Native American population of the United States is growing at a fast pace and becoming increasingly youthful. Current estimates place the total population of American Indians in the United States at slightly less than two million. Between 1970 and 1980, Indians between the ages of 18 and 24 increased from 96,000 to 234,000. The average age of this population is 16.

Although Native Americans live throughout the United States, over half live in the southwest. California, Oklahoma, Arizona, and New Mexico account for slightly less than 50 percent of the total Indian population. Native Americans are equally split between those who live in rural and urban areas. Los Angeles, Tulsa, Oklahoma City,

Phoenix, and Albuquerque have the largest numbers of urban Indians. The largest reservations in the United States are the Navajo Reservation in what is now New Mexico and Arizona and the Pine Ridge Reservation in the present state of South Dakota.

American Indians are among the most economically disadvantaged groups in the United States. The unemployment rate for American Indians who live on reservations often approaches 80 percent, with the median family income hovering around $15,000. The percentage of Native Americans who live below the poverty line is three times the national average. About 50 percent of the Native American population over 30 years old has not completed high school.

Given the propensity for Native American students to leave one institution prior to an academic year's completion, valid estimates of how many high school graduates actually participate in a freshman year at a postsecondary institution are difficult to determine. A student, for example, may graduate from high school and decide to attend a particular college and he or she may leave relatively soon thereafter; a few months later the student may re-enroll at another institution. Meanwhile, the previous college may not even be aware the student has left. Consequently, a valid national percentage of Native American high school graduates who are college freshmen is unknown.

We do know that in 1980 there were 141,000 high school graduates, and 85,798 students were enrolled in postsecondary education. The general lesson to be learned here is that less than 60 percent of Native American high school students complete the 12th grade, and that less than 40 percent of those students go on to college. More simply, if 100 Indian students enter the 9th grade, only 60 will graduate from high school. Of these graduates, a mere 20 will enter academe, and only about three of these will receive a four-year degree.

Not surprisingly, more than half of those students who go on to college will enter a two-year institution, and over 70,000 of the students will attend public institutions. The proportion of American Indian students who enroll full-time is around 50 percent, and Native American women outnumber their male counterparts on college campuses by about 20 percent.

THE TASK AHEAD

What does this information tell us about American Indian participation in postsecondary education? The composite population of Native Americans is economically poorer, experiences more unemployment, and is less formally educated than the rest of the nation. A greater percentage of the population lives in rural areas, where access to postsecondary institutions is more limited. Although a majority of the population lives in the southwest, they attend postsecondary institutions throughout the country.

They have a population that is increasingly youthful, yet only three out of 100 9th-graders will eventually receive a baccalaureate. Those four-year institutions that have the largest percentage of Indian students are either in economically depressed states of the country such as Montana and South Dakota, and those colleges that have the highest proportion of Indian students—tribal colleges—receive only a fraction of what they should receive from the federal government to carry out their tasks.

This overview highlights the problems and challenges that American Indians have faced regarding higher education. One certainty is that the federal government must renew its support for at-risk college students. Society can no longer afford excluding populations simply because they are different from the mainstream or prefer to remain within their own cultural contexts. All evidence suggests that Indian students and their families want equal educational opportunities. They seek better guidance in high school, more culturally relevant academic programming and counseling, and more role models on campus. Indian students do not want to be excluded from a university's doors because they cannot afford the education, and they do not want to be lost on a campus that doesn't value and accommodate their differences.

Many of the same challenges that confronted Caleb Cheeshateaumuck at Harvard face Indian college students today. A Native American senior recently reflected on her four years at school and the dysfunction between the world of higher education and the world from which she had come. "When I was a child I was taught certain things," she recalled, "don't stand up to your elders, don't question authority, life is precious, the earth is precious, take it slowly, enjoy it. And then you go to college and you learn all these other things, and it never fits."

Now, more than three centuries after Caleb Cheeshateaumuck confronted the alien environment of Harvard, the time is long overdue for cultural conflict and assimilationist efforts to end. American Indians must have opportunities to enter the higher education arena on their own terms—to encounter challenge without tragedy and triumph without co-optation. Only then can higher education begin a celebration of diversity in earnest.

32

Latino Youths at a Crossroads

Luis Duany and Karen Pittman

The authors list a number of educational policies that they believe will enhance Latino academic achievement, including: improved education in Latino communities; programs for working with the parents of Latino students; closer ties between schools and employers; and improvements in Latino postsecondary enrollments. The benefits of these policies are described.

Exercises to Guide Your Reading

1. Give two examples of recommended policies from each of the seven categories of proposed actions.
2. Describe the educational environment facing Latino youth.
3. Analyze problems unique to young Latinas (Latin American women).
4. Compare and contrast the proposals for improving education in this article with those found in Readings 30 and 33.

This nation's Latino youth are at a crossroads. Their relatively low educational attainment and achievement stand as barriers to their economic security. The action steps recommended here must be accompanied by increased school-readiness efforts, including expansion of Head Start; comprehensive early childhood development programs; and developmentally appropriate child care. And like all children, Latinos must have the basics in life—decent health and nutrition, safe neighborhoods, adequate family income, and supports for families facing severe stress.

1. Improve the quality of education received by Latino youths. This nation should embark immediately on an all-out effort to overhaul schools serving Latino students to:

• Educate all students with challenging, rigorous core curricula that will prepare them for postsecondary education or decent jobs; remove unnecessary obstacles, such as tracking and grouping, that discourage preparation for higher education.
• Ensure that Latinos have access to the very best teachers—Latinos and others—who know their subject matter, have mastered a wide range of instructional techniques, and believe all youngsters can learn.
• Eliminate funding inequities and assure that Latinos have access to resources equal to those available in predominantly white schools.
• Reduce the number of Latino students held back. Latino students fall behind early and stay behind until they drop out. Responsibility must be on schools to ensure that all students are on track and fully prepared to succeed in academic work by the fourth grade.
• Increase multicultural curricula and build a multicultural school environment. Too often, multicultural curricula are artificial add-ons rather than truly integrated programs that change the school environment to welcome

Reprinted by permission of *The Education Digest*. January 1991. pp. 7–11.

and respect students and families of different cultures. If Latino students and parents are to feel a part of schools, schools must reflect at least part of their culture and daily life.

- Increase support services, including guidance counselors sensitive to Latino culture, strengthened in-school systems for monitoring student progress, and sustained individual contact with adults. According to the Hispanic Policy Development Project, Latino youths almost unanimously identify "someone caring" as the most important factor in academic success. Such relationships are important because parents and relatives of so many Latino students have little educational experience.

2. Help parents help their children to achieve. There are many ways that schools, community organizations, and employers can help parents to help their children do well in school:

- Provide more free or affordable literacy programs for Latino parents. These programs should respond to parents' needs for literacy training and continuing education in both Spanish and English.
- Develop aggressive parent education programs to teach parents how schools work and how to help their children achieve. Programs should focus on relating the importance of schooling to future opportunities, explaining changes in the economy and what students must do to prepare. Bilingual workshops can address topics such as drugs, discipline, and relating to a new culture. Latino parents should be informed about the higher education system, with an emphasis on access and financing. These discussions should be held early so parents are aware of the educational and career options available to their children.
- Increase the use of schools for community activities, such as adult education, after-school care, health and social services, and recreation, so that parents have nonthreatening reasons to go to the school. Announcements of these activities should be posted in neighborhood stores and other frequented spots in the community and made on local radio and in Spanish and English newspapers.
- Establish closer working relationships between schools and Latino religious and community organizations for offering classes for

students and parents, advocating changes that reflect parents' concerns, helping parents understand the educational system, and interpreting their children's placement and progress in that system.

- Develop outreach approaches to parents who are either non-English speaking or have low literacy skills in either language. Schools' traditional reliance on written communication has to be supplemented with phone calls, community meetings, and home visits. Latino community organizations should be used to relay and interpret information.
- Employ more bilingual and Latino adults in schools so that Latino parents feel welcome and understood. Ideally, this should occur on all levels, from the principal down. In practice, however, many schools may have to start by increasing the number of Latino classroom aides and community volunteers.
- Create more opportunities for parents to volunteer in schools to use their expertise and contribute to multicultural curricula. To help form parent networks, businesses can allow parents time off with pay to participate in school projects.

3. Increase the relevance of school to work. Young Latinos must see the relevance of school for future employment and earnings. Students have to understand and believe that rewards received through part-time or full-time work in low-wage jobs are substantially less than those they could receive with a high school or college diploma. These future-oriented lessons will have to be balanced with opportunities for part-time and summer employment that provide both income and career-relevant experience. Among the programs and policies that could improve school retention, postsecondary enrollment, and school-to-work transition for Latinos are:

- Earlier introduction to work and higher education through community service programs, career exploration activities, and college/secondary school partnerships sponsored and coordinated by schools, community organizations, or businesses.
- Increased availability of part-time jobs that do not interfere with school schedules. Young Latinos who need employment should be as-

sisted in finding jobs on weekends and in summer rather than during evening hours. Perhaps subminimum wages need to be subsidized to reach minimum wage levels so youths are encouraged to keep their work hours at levels that would allow them to continue school.

- Clear employment-related incentives for staying in school and making progress. Among other efforts, school/business partnerships should guarantee summer jobs contingent on school progress or full-time jobs with higher pay after high school graduation.
- Work-study programs for students with strong vocational preferences or a pressing need to work. Tension between school and work can be eased with formal work-study programs that link classroom learning with on-the-job experience.
- Apprenticeship programs for students with high school diplomas, combining on-the-job training with continued academic skills building, and educational incentive programs for employed students without high school diplomas who want to get equivalency certificates or attend college part time while working. These and other skills-building programs are especially important for Latinos because of the large proportion who either are dropouts or have no postsecondary education.

4. Reduce early dropouts. Special efforts can reduce the high incidence of *early* dropping out that takes place among Latinos:

- Elementary to middle grades transition programs. Integrated counseling, tutoring, and early work exposure programs are needed to keep students in school and progressing through middle grades.
- Effective programs that address the special educational, counseling, and employment needs of overage students and students who already have left school. These programs are critical, given the high proportion of Latinos who leave school before tenth grade or never enter high school.
- Efforts to foster true bilingualism among Latino students, including intensive English-as-a-second-language classes. Classroom materials in Spanish should be provided in conjunction with Spanish-speaking tutors. Value must be placed on fluency in Spanish as well as English.

5. Meet the needs of Latinas. Early efforts that target the special needs of Latinas (females) are particularly critical. Latinas head a significant proportion (23 percent) of all Latino households and 44 percent of Puerto Rican households. The high school dropout rates of Latinas, coupled with their relatively high birth rates, make their needs worthy of special and sustained attention.

With only 27 percent of young Latina mothers who began childbearing in their teens completing high school, this group must be targeted for dropout recovery and parent-involvement programs that focus on developing adult literacy by helping young mothers respond to their children's needs. Programs encouraging postsecondary education and job training efforts—while remaining sensitive to the importance of family life—must reach out to Latinas as well as Latino males.

Latina youths and their parents have to be reached during the late elementary and middle school years with concrete information about the cost of leaving school and early parenthood and about the increased importance of high school and postsecondary education for young women, even when they plan to marry and begin families. Research suggests that, even more than black and white teen mothers, young Latinas leave school *before* pregnancy.

Latina youths, especially when they or their parents were born outside the U.S., often are straddling two cultures with very different expectations for childbirth and attainment of secondary and postsecondary education. These young women, more than Latino males or their non-Latino peers, need school and parental support for continued education and timely information and access to family planning services.

PAYING FOR COLLEGE

6. Improve postsecondary enrollment. To increase the numbers of Latino youths who benefit from postsecondary education, strong new emphasis must be given to:

- Guaranteeing payment of college costs. The trend toward providing loans rather than grants for college costs should be reversed. Additionally, state and federal governments should explore ways to relieve the burden of student debt on low-income youths by canceling all or part of student loans in return for public service, by extending loan deferment periods, and by linking repayment to postcollege income.
- Aggressive postsecondary outreach and federally funded programs to counsel and place Latino students in postsecondary institutions, particularly four-year colleges.
- Expansion of programs to support students in postsecondary schools. Given the extreme retention problems faced by Latinos in college, these programs must be expanded and include academic, financial, and personal supports. Especially important are programs that encourage transfers from two-year to four-year institutions.
- Efforts to prepare teachers for Latino students. More Latinos should be encouraged and helped to enter teaching. All teachers should receive education that enables them to be effective educators, fosters multicultural appreciation, and demonstrates that *all* children can learn.

7. Assess responsibilities. Finally, businesses, schools, community organizations, and parents all need to assess their responsibilities to help improve the achievement of Latino youths. They must require accountability of federally supported education programs in terms of student outcomes. For this to happen, these sectors need better understanding of Latino diversity in the U.S. Such information must come from the federal government, through improved collection and distribution of data on Latinos. To further underscore the importance of achievement among Latino youths, a Task Force on Hispanic Education should be appointed within the federal Domestic Policy Council.

TOO GREAT A RISK

The problems of Latino youths in this country cannot be ignored. Representing a significant portion of the population in the next century, Latinos must be capable of participating fully in society to ensure this nation's long-term security. We cannot afford to sacrifice the Puerto Rican, Cuban-American, Mexican-American, Central and South American, and other Latino youths. The risk is too great—for Latino youths and for the country.

33

Rich Schools, Poor Schools

Arthur E. Wise and Tamar Gendler

This article describes the wide range of educational programming that is directly related to differences in school district funding. The successes of and challenges to major reform efforts aimed at equalizing school district funding are discussed. The issue of local control is analyzed in the context of constitutional guarantees of equal opportunity.

Exercises to Guide Your Reading

1. Give examples of educational discrepancies between rich and poor school districts; infer the likely racial and ethnic impact of such discrepancies.
2. Explain the legal arguments used in lawsuits concerning financial equity.
3. Summarize the arguments opposing school finance reform.
4. Evaluate the claim that local control justifies spending inequality among school districts.

America continues to wonder why children from more advantaged families do better in school than children who grow up in poverty. Certainly, part of the discrepancy results from what an advantaged family is able to offer its children—adequate nutrition, a stable home, collections of books, trips to museums. But part of the discrepancy results from the schools that the nation provides. While children from advantaged families are more likely to attend clean, well-appointed schools staffed by adequate numbers of qualified teachers and supplied with up-to-date books and technological aids, children from disadvantaged families are more likely to attend class in dilapidated school buildings staffed by less-than-fully qualified teachers, supplied with outdated textbooks, and few, if any, technological aids.

In many places across the nation, these discrepancies are especially stark. Consider these facts which come from recent school finance lawsuits: While some Texas districts spend over $8,000 a year per student, Elizario Independent School District is so poor that it offers no foreign languages, no prekindergarten program, no college preparatory program, and virtually no extracurricular activities. Elizario is not alone; each year, the 150,000 students living in the state's poorest districts receive educations costing half that of their 150,000 wealthiest counterparts. This inequity does not result from lack of effort by any of the residents of the poorer districts; the taxpayers supporting the 150,000 students at the bottom face tax rates double those of taxpayers at the top. Elizario's tax rate of $1.07 (per $100 of property value) is some 35 cents above the state average.

In New Jersey, where Moorestown provides over 200 microcomputers for its 2,400

Reprinted by permission of *The Education Digest*. December 1989. pp. 3–5.

students (a ratio of 1:11), East Orange High School, with a population of 2,000, has only 46 (a ratio of 1:43). East Orange is a poor district, with average assessed valuation per pupil of $40,675, 21 percent of the state average. To compensate, the city's school tax effort has been above the state average every year for the past 10, as high as 144 percent. Still, the district spends less than $3,000 per pupil per year, has no elementary art classrooms, a gym that serves as a school library, and "science areas" consisting of a sink, a shelf, and some storage space.

Why should the students in poor districts in Texas receive an education that costs half as much as students' in wealthier districts—even though the taxpayers pay proportionally twice as much? Why should the future computer programmer in East Orange share her computer with 42 classmates while her counterpart in Moorestown shares hers with 10? Because her community's property wealth—the assessed valuation of each house—is a fifth of most cities?

INEQUALITY GROWS

Throughout the 1970s, prodded by actual or threatened lawsuits, many states passed laws aimed at reducing the vast discrepancies in funding among districts. But soon thereafter, inflation, fiscal constraints, politics, and self-interest took their tolls. By the end of the decade, many of the reforms that had been instituted had been rendered nearly ineffectual, and during the 1980s, while the world focused on excellence, inequality in finance grew.

In states where watchfulness continued, the results of school finance legislation were dramatic. In New Mexico, the intent of the 1974 equalization legislation "'to equalize financial opportunity at the highest possible revenue level and to guarantee each New Mexico public school student access to programs and services appropriate to his educational needs regardless of geographic or local economic conditions,' has been realized." California, which 12 years ago was

chastised by its supreme court in *Serrano* v. *Priest*, has equalized finances so that students now receive nearly an equal share of the state resources to develop their individual abilities.

Despite these successes, the realization of how rapidly the effects of reform can be eroded has been sobering. New lawsuits have had to be brought in states where the issue seemed resolved a decade ago. In 1988 alone, three major decisions mandating school finance reform have been handed down in Montana (*Helena* v. *Montana*), Texas (*Edgewood* v. *Kirby*), and New Jersey (*Abbot* v. *Burke*). Each uses one or both of two basic arguments: that denying equal educational opportunity violates the state's constitutional obligation to provide a thorough and efficient education for all children, or that since education is a fundamental right, denying equal educational opportunity violates children's rights to equal protection under the law.

In the 1973 *San Antonio* v. *Rodriguez* case before the U.S. Supreme Court, Texas had argued that the inequities in funding across school districts were an unfortunate byproduct of the compelling interest in local control of schools. In *Edgewood*, the defense offered a similar argument, but the court found that "Local control of school district operations in Texas has diminished dramatically in recent years, and today most of the meaningful incidents of the education process are determined and controlled by state statute and/or State Board of Education rule, including such matters as curriculum, course content, textbooks, hours of instruction, pupil-teacher ratios, training of teachers, administrators, and board members, teacher testing, and review of personnel decisions and policies." The state regulates not only administrative procedures but also basic features of the curriculum.

Clearly, local districts have lost much of their historical control over the content of their educational offerings. In fact, "the only element of local control that remains undiminished is the power of wealthy districts to fund education at virtually any level they choose, as contrasted with the property-poor districts who enjoy no such local control. . . ."

The myth that local control justifies vast discrepancies in spending among districts is thus discredited in two ways. First, the possibility of meaningful local control is in fact enhanced by a funding system that insures equalized opportunity for districts to fund educational programs, for it allows all districts, not just those with large tax bases, to exercise options in financing their schools. But Texas has demonstrated that it does not even truly value local control; a state that regulates and standardizes as Texas does can hardly claim that its commitment to local control compellingly outweighs the need to abide by the constitutional guarantees of equal opportunity and the right of all students to an efficient education.

Throughout the history of school finance reform, opponents of change have offered three arguments. In states without an explicit education clause, they have tried to show that education is not a fundamental right and is therefore not subject to the close scrutiny implied by the equal protection clause. In states such as New Jersey that have a "thorough and efficient" clause, and in states such as Montana that accept education as a fundamental right, the defense has relied on two other major arguments: that local control outweighs the rights of districts to equal funding, and that financial input has no effect on the quality of the education a district is able to offer.

The issue of local control has already been discussed in the context of Texas. But many states in the pursuit of excellence since 1980 have aggressively tried to improve and control local schools through regulation; some have even gone so far as to enact takeover legislation through which they would govern local school systems from the capital. By their actions, states have shown that standardized tests, statewide curricula, uniform textbooks, and consistent teacher evaluation all outrank local control.

PART III

HOUSEHOLDS, HABITATS, AND HEALTH

The readings in Part III discuss the economic status of families, children, housing, and wellness, since these aspects of social life strongly influence and are influenced by economic conditions. As these subjects are not often covered in economics textbooks, it will be useful to make the connections to economic theory explicit. Before beginning, it is helpful to recall that oftentimes economic discussions have omitted the unpaid labor performed within households from the consideration of economic topics. One effect of this is that the economics of the family, and the corresponding economic status of women and children, have been obscured, since activities within households have special consequences for women and children.*

In recent years, economists using the traditional tools of the theory of individual choice have discussed household arrangements (who does what in the home has been referred to as the "sexual division of labor"), childbearing, and divorce. Several of the readings in Part III embody the perspective of the "new home economics," which argues that freely made individual choices are the principal causes of the economic status of women and children, and that it would thus be inappropriate to try to alter their life conditions through government intervention.

This position is criticized by both liberal and radical economists, who find common ground in their opposition to the view that "free choice" is the cause of the economic vulnerability experienced by mothers/women and their dependent children. Some liberal observers point out that societal expectations and cultural norms play a very large role in shaping both the choices and the options of young women. If this is the case, then in what sense are the decisions that conform to these pressures "free"? From this perspective, analyses that depend on the utility-maximizing framework to explain the status of women and children in families are not much more than defenses of the status quo, since they take the existing sexual division of labor and distribution of power as given. Thus liberal and radical analyses of the family, children, housing, behavior, and health tend to stress institutional structures and history rather than free choice.

Important differences do, however, separate the radical and liberal positions. Perhaps most significant is the radical interpretation of particular social arrangements. For example, a liberal analysis might present a very accurate portrait of the indignities facing poor women and their children as they attempt to navigate the welfare maze. Some solutions for making the system more humane would

*For an excellent historical, multicultural examination of these topics see Teresa Amolt and Julie Matthaei, *Race, Gender, and Work: A Multicultural Economic History of Women* (Boston: Southend Press), 1993.

follow. Radicals, however, might argue that these indignities serve positive functions for the system as a whole. In this view, dehumanizing and demonizing "the poor" prevents people from recognizing the extent to which exploitation and oppression are shared experiences and expressions of particular social arrangements. The media, popular culture, and political rhetoric all conjure up images of lazy, freeloading, sexually active women as the typical poor person on welfare. These symbols, and the emotions that they elicit, help maintain divisions within the population. Employed workers, both male and female, can easily blame "welfare cheats" for high taxes, rising crime rates, and a variety of other social ills. These images also perform a disciplinary function, since no one wants to live this kind of life. Moreover, the threat of unemployment becomes even more ominous when it is coupled with the scorn and derision heaped upon the poor. Consequently, radicals argue that the economic status of families and children, persistent racial and ethnic segregation, and "underclass" behavior, as well as the day-to-day consequences of a for-profit health care system, are inextricably linked to the underlying dynamics of class exploitation based on surplus labor. Once this connection is made, it is possible to see that the social divisions associated with gender, race, and class yield handsome benefits for the capitalist system.

As you read the articles that follow, be alert to the way in which they extend the three contenting positions in economics. The conservative/free market interpretation, in which all social outcomes are seen as the result of freely made choices, is consistently applied to the issues raised in Part III. The logical policy conclusion follows—do nothing, or laissez faire. The liberal/imperfectionist view, in which structural problems are believed to prevent individuals from acting in their own best interests, is developed in a number of the readings. The logical conclusion is that governments need to change individual circumstances. And several of the readings advance the radical/exploitation argument that seemingly irrational behaviors or apparently benevolent institutions actually reinforce existing patterns of power and wealth. Here the policy connection is less obvious. One thing is clear, however: radicals believe that it is very important for grass-roots social activists to strive continually to illuminate the hidden messages in our culture that disguise exploitation, racism, and sexism, since this is a first step to seeing the injustices of the capitalist system.

The four articles in Chapter 8 turn our attention to the economic aspects of family life. We begin here because data on household income are frequently used to assess the economic welfare of different groups. It is important to know what is happening to households since these units approximate what we personally know as the family. Reading 34 presents a sweeping statistical portrait of the economic forces shaping the life opportunities of newly formed American families. The author argues that the increasing pressures on young families stem from eroding economic advantages of family formation. Reading 35 offers similar information but to a different end. Here the author's purpose is to support the adoption of government policies that will help two-earner families deal with the many pressures they face as they juggle the competing demands of work and children. Reading 36 summarizes the debate over the economic impact of divorce. Reading 37 discusses the ways in which stereotypical and bigoted views about African Americans have shaped both the "theories" about black families as well as social policies toward them. This discussion will help us understand the many ways that family life is dependent upon economic and political forces.

Chapter 9 explores economic relationships that affect children. Of principal concern are provisions for day care. This issue has become increasingly important as a result of the large numbers of women with preschool children who now work full-time. Providing safe, emotionally stable, and mentally stimulating environments for children is of vital concern to parents, teachers, taxpayers, and policy makers. The economic analyses of the problems associated with day care reflect the broader social division on the question of government involvement in the market. Conservatives argue from the laissez-faire premise that markets do a very good job of meeting individual demands. Consequently, in the conservative vision there is no need for government regulation of the child care industry since such regulations would make child care more expensive and less responsive to individual tastes and preferences. Conservatives do believe that it would be appropriate for the government to use the tax code to help shape the relative costs and benefits of staying at home with the children. Liberal economists, on the other hand, tend to favor a global approach that integrates tax policies and regulations to increase the supply of "good" day care while ensuring the ability of working mothers to pay for it. A related set of policies concerns the relationship between child support payments and Aid to Families with Dependent Children (AFDC). Here the argument focuses on the incentives and disincentives that can affect the work effort of mothers with young children.

Chapter 10 presents a portrait of racial and ethnic segregation in the United States. Its connection to textbook discussions of housing choice, urban economics, and monetary policy is not difficult to explain. In economic textbooks, the choice of residential location is typically viewed as a simple matter of exercising tastes and preferences, given income and prices. The articles in this chapter raise questions about the applicability of such models, since the behavior of real estate agents, banks, and others involved in housing transactions may be quite tainted by elements of racism and sexism. (To review the evidence it may be helpful to reread Reading 4.) Thus, the observed result that most people live in neighborhoods that defy the description "integrated" may not reflect choice but rather direct discrimination. Compounding the problems associated with discrimination in housing markets are the profound structural changes in the U.S. economy that have moved high-paying, manufacturing jobs from city centers to outlying suburban areas. As a result, there may be a severe mismatch between the location of entry-level jobs and the location of low-income housing. Over the last two decades, several proposals for revitalizing urban areas have been proposed, and the readings in this chapter evaluate these competing policy recommendations. Finally, the role of the nation's central bank in implementing macroeconomic policy is discussed as this relates to the rise and decline of various regions. The neutrality of monetary policy is questioned, and the role of grass-roots organizations in generating the flow of funds needed for urban renewal is discussed.

The articles in Chapter 11 relate most directly to the frequently unstated assumptions of textbook economics that generally present the role of rational choice in the formation of economic outcomes, but almost never discuss the social contexts within which such rational behavior may be exercised. These readings offer a basis from which we may begin to understand how circumstance may enlarge or contract the areas of our lives in which we are free to choose.

A comparison of the labor market behavior of various ethnic minorities is the starting point of the chapter in Reading 45. Here we discover how the label "underclass" actually hides many diverse patterns of economic behavior. Reading 46 presents a philosophical reflection on the quality of life in contemporary urban America that considers the relationship between fundamental human aspirations for bettering one's life and the overwhelmingly negative experiences of the urban core. Will the interaction between these cultural and political forces constrain people's ability to recognize and act in their own self-interest? Thomas H. Kean, former governor of New Jersey, approaches the problem differently in Reading 47, stressing the role of individual responsibility in both shaping and escaping life in our urban ghettos. This argument sharply counterpoises earlier discussions and suggests that existing opportunities in the cities are adequate, but that the problem is getting poor people to use the available resources to their best advantage. The interconnection of gender, poverty, and ethnicity is captured dramatically in Reading 48. Here we encounter a "real-life" situation in which one woman's rational choices appear to have been reduced to killing herself and her children. In describing this situation, the author argues that the reproduction of poverty does much to sustain both the economic and moral self-satisfaction of the middle class. In Reading 49, the chapter concludes with a discussion of "self-help" in African American communities to highlight the divergence between the cultural portrayals of minority Americans and the reality of their lives. Taken together, these readings provide a rich background for discussions of such economic topics as the labor supply decision, the causes and effects of poverty, and the role of direct government intervention.

In Chapter 12 the "health care crisis" is disaggregated by race, ethnicity, sex, and age. The interaction of these variables yields new insights into U.S. policy debates on health care reform. The chapter begins in Reading 50 with an argument that calls into question conventional wisdom by asking, "what health-care crisis?" Readings 51 and 53, from the *Journal of the American Medical Association*, reveal the negative impact that race and ethnic origin have on well-being. Practicing physicians operating fully within the existing health care system find strong evidence that poverty itself causes disease! Reading 52 shows how sexual biases in medical testing, drug marketing, and perhaps even in medical practice place women at greater risk than men. Reading 54 discusses the problems that may arise out of paying for an elder's health care, even when this person has lived a productive, high-income life. The last article in the chapter, Reading 55, compares and contrasts methods that society may use for paying for health care. As in earlier chapters, these readings provide a vantage point for viewing the standard economic treatment of health care. Macroeconomic outcomes associated with income distribution (by race, sex, ethnicity, and age) may well interact with microeconomic behaviors (of consumer choice, labor market activities, and educational attainment) to make health care an issue that cannot be solved with a "one-size-fits-all" policy approach.

CHAPTER 8

Families

34

Vanishing Dreams of America's Young Families

Marian Wright Edelman

This article analyzes the changing economic circumstances of families headed by Americans aged twenty-five to twenty-nine. Data reveal deteriorating standards of living for these families regardless of marital status, race, ethnicity, or level of education. The author identifies the likely short- and long-term consequences of these trends as well as the ways that young adults have changed their behavior in response to these circumstances. Recommendations include a three-pronged policy that offers "a fair start, a healthy start, and a head start."

Exercises to Guide Your Reading

1. List the economic changes that have adversely affected young American families.
2. Distinguish between the short- and long-term effects of increased poverty among young families.
3. Predict the impact of these changes on at least three aspects of the U.S. economy over the next twenty years.
4. Describe and defend the author's recommended policies. Then describe and *criticize* the policies.

Reprinted by permission of *Challenge*. May–June 1992. pp. 13–19.

Americans from all walk of life are profoundly anxious—troubled by what they see around them today and even more by what they see ahead. This anxiety, not only about their own futures but also about the nation's future, is manifested in countless ways: in paralyzing economic insecurity; in an emerging politics of rejection, frustration, and rage; in a growing polarization of our society by race and by class; and in an erosion of the sense of responsibility to help the weakest and poorest among us.

But this anxiety about the future is *most* vivid when we watch our own chilren grow up and try to venture out on their own—struggling to get established as adults in a new job, a new marriage, a new home or a new family.

It's true that young families always have faced an uphill struggle starting out in life. But today's young families have been so battered by economic and social changes over the past two decades that the struggle has taken on a more desparate and often futile quality.

And as parents of my generation watch many of their adult children founder—failing to find steady, decent-paying jobs, unable to support families, shut out of the housing market, and often forced to move back home—they know that something has gone terribly wrong. Often they don't know precisely what has happened or why. But they do understand that these young adults and their children may never enjoy the same opportunities or achieve the same standard of living or security that our generation found a couple of decades ago.

TWO GENERATIONS IN TROUBLE

Young families with children—those headed by persons under the age of thirty—have been devastated since 1973 by a cycle of falling incomes, increasing family disintegration, and rising poverty. In the process, the foundations for America's young families have been so thoroughly undermined that two complete generations of Americans—today's young parents and their small children—are not in great jeopardy. Figure 1 captures the poverty rates of those two jeopardized generations.

Young families are the crucible for America's future and America's dream. Most children spend at least part of their lives—their youngest and most developmentally vulner-

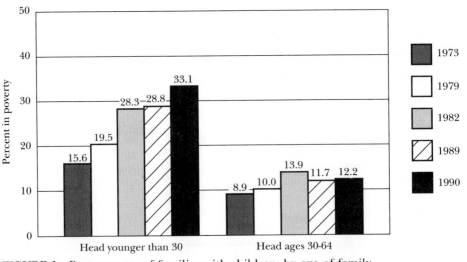

FIGURE 1 Poverty rates of families with children, by age of family head, 1973, 1979, 1982, 1990.

able months and years—in young families. How we treat these families therefore goes a long way toward defining what our nation as a whole will be like twenty, fifty, or even seventy-five years from now.

What has happened to America's young families with children is unprecedented and almost unimaginable.

Adjusted for inflation, the median income of young families with children plunged by one-third between 1973 and 1990 (Table 1). This median income includes income from all sources, and the drop occurred despite the fact that many families sent a second earner into the workforce. As a result, poverty among these young families more than doubled, and by 1990 a shocking 40 percent or four in ten children in young families were poor.

The past two decades have been difficult for many other Americans as well. But older families with children have lost only a little economic ground since 1973, and families without children have enjoyed substantial income gains. By far the greatest share of the nation's economic pain has been focused on the weakest and most vulnerable among us—young families with children.

This is *not* a story about the current recession, although the recession surely is having a crushing impact on young families. Even comparing 1973 to 1989—two good economic years at the end of sustained periods of growth—the median income of young families with children dropped by one-fourth. Then just the first few months of the recession in 1990 sent young families' incomes plummeting to new depths.

This also is not a story about teenagers. While America's teen pregnancy problem remains tragic and demands an urgent response, only 3 percent of the young families with children we are discussing are headed by teenagers. More than 70 percent are headed by someone aged twenty-five to twenty-nine. The plight of America's young families is overwhelmingly the plight of young adults who are both old enough and eager to assume the responsibilities of parenthood and adulthood, but for whom the road is blocked.

Finally and most importantly, this is *not* simply a story about someone else's children, about minority children or children in single-parent families or children whose parents dropped out of high school.

ALL YOUNG FAMILIES AFFECTED

Huge income losses have affected virtually every group of young families with children: white, black, and Latino; married-couple and single-parent; and those headed by high

TABLE 1 Median Incomes of Families with Children by Age of Family Head, 1973–1990 (in 1990 Dollars)*

	1973	1979	1982	1989	1990	Change 1973–1990
All families with children	36,882	36,180	31,819	35,425	34,400	−6.7%
Family head younger than 30	27,765	25,204	20,378	20,665	18,844	−32.1%
Family head age 30–64	41,068	39,978	35,293	39,525	38,451	−6.4%
Young families' median income as a share of older families' income	68%	63%	58%	52%	49%	

Note: The money incomes of families for all years prior to 1990 were converted into 1990 dollars via use of the Consumer Price Index for All Urban Consumers (CPI-U). The U.S. Bureau of Labor Statistics has generated an alternative price index for the years preceding 1983 that conforms to the current method of measuring changes in housing costs. This index is known as the CPI-UXI. Use of this price index would reduce the estimated 1973 real income by about 7 percent, thus lowering the estimated decline in the median income of young families between 1973 and 1990 from 32 percent to approximately 25 percent. None of the comparisons of median income between various groups of families are affected by these changes.

school graduates as well as dropouts. Only young families with children headed by college graduates experienced slight income gains between 1973 and 1990.

In other words, the tragedy facing young families with children has now reached virtually *all* of our young families. One in four *white* children in young families is now poor. One in five children in young *married-couple* families is now poor. And one in three children in families headed by a young *high school graduate* is now poor. Nearly three-fourths of the increase in poverty among young families since 1973 has occurred outside the nation's central cities. And poverty has grown most rapidly among young families with only one child (Figure 2).

There is no refuge from the economic and social shifts that have battered young families with children. We can pretend that they won't reach our children and our grandchildren. We can pretend that those who play by the rules will be O.K.

We can pretend, but that will not change the reality—the reality that young families have lost a third of their median income, that two in five American children in young families live in poverty, and that these facts have devastating consequences.

Those consequences include more hunger, more homelessness, more low birth-weight births, more infant deaths, and more child disability. They also mean more substance abuse, more crime, more violence, more school failure, more teen pregnancy, more racial tension, more envy, more despair, and more cynicism—a long-term economic and social disaster for young families and for the country. In virtually every critical area of child development and healthy maturation, family poverty creates huge roadblocks to individual accomplishment, future economic self-sufficiency, and national progress.

Plummeting incomes and soaring poverty and growing gaps based on age and education and race mean more of all these problems, yet many of our leaders seem not to understand why they are occurring. But there is not really a puzzle, when we recognize that the nation has marginalized and pauperized much of two generations of Americans—young parents and young children.

Young families not only lost income in huge amounts, but as the permanence and quality of their jobs deteriorated, they lost fringe benefits like health insurance as well. In the decade of the 1980s the proportion of *employed* heads of young families with children whose employers made health insurance available by paying all or part of the

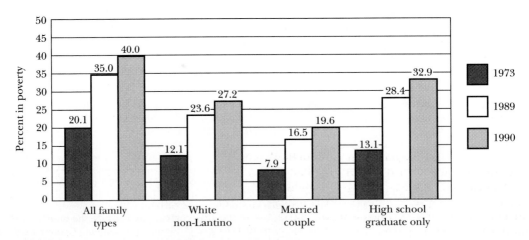

FIGURE 2 Poverty rates of children in young families, by characteristics of the family head, 1973, 1989, 1990.

cost dropped by one-fifth. And employers cut back on coverage for dependent spouses and children even more than for workers.

Fewer and fewer young pregnant women have been getting adequate prenatal care because they are poorer and less likely to have adequate insurance or any insurance. And our falling vaccination rates and renewed epidemics of measles and other wholly preventable diseases among preschoolers are being driven by plunging incomes in young families, eroding health insurance coverage, and unraveling government programs.

Falling incomes also have devastated young families in an increasingly expensive housing market. One-third fewer young families with children were homeowners in 1991 than in 1980. Young renter families increasingly are paying astronomical shares of their meager incomes for rent. More and more are doubling up or becoming homeless—in some surveys three-fourths of the homeless parents in this country are under age thirty.

Young families are not only suffering from the hunger, housing, health, and other problems that their plummeting incomes have caused. They are suffering as well because they are falling further and further behind the rest of the society—imperiling their attachment to the core work force and to mainstream values and threatening their potential to reacquire the American dream in the decades to come.

In 1973 the income of older families with children was not quite one-and-a-half times that of young families with children. By 1990 it was more than double that of the young families.

COMBINATION OF CAUSES

There is no single cause of young families' plight. Instead, they have been pummelled by a combination of profound changes in the American economy; the government's inadequate response to families in trouble; and changes in the composition of young families themselves.

Much of the increase in their poverty is due to economic shifts and to changing government policies that have made it more difficult for young families to obtain adequate incomes. These changes have hurt all young families with children, regardless of their family structure, race or ethnicity, or educational attainment.

Unlike members of earlier generations, young workers today no longer can be confident of finding stable jobs with decent wages, even if they get a high school diploma or spend a couple of years in college. Since 1973, slower growth in U.S. productivity and declines in blue collar employment made some drop in inflation-adjusted median earnings for young workers inevitable. By last year the average wages of *all* nonsupervisory workers (of all ages) in the private sector fell to their lowest level since the Eisenhower Administration.

But the losses have been focused disproportionately on young workers. The median annual earnings of heads of young families with children fell a staggering 44 percent from 1973 to 1990. In other words, in the span of less than a generation this nation nearly *halved* the earnings of young household heads with children (Table 2).

These dramatic earnings losses occurred across-the-board. For example, young white families with children were hit as hard as young Latino families: the median earnings of both groups fell by two-fifths. College graduates as well as high school graduates and dropouts lost big chunks of income. But the drop in median earnings for high school dropouts and for young black family heads has been particularly devastating–in each case more than two-thirds.

The erosion in pay levels (due in part to the declining value of the minimum wage) combined with the growth of temporary or part-time and part-year jobs to put a triple whammy on young workers: far lower annual earnings; less secure employment; and less access to health insurance and other employer-provided benefits.

The huge drop in earnings among America's young workers has not received much attention. In part it has been obscured by

TABLE 2 **Median Annual Earnings of Heads of Young Families with Children, 1973 and 1990 (in 1990 Dollars)**

	1973	1990	% Change 1973–1990
All heads of young families with children	22,981	12,832	−44
Married couple	25,907	17,500	−33
Male-headed	18,547	14,000	−25
Female-headed	2,073	1,878	−9
White, non-Latino	25,024	15,000	−40
Black, non-Latino	13,860	4,030	−71
Latino	15,924	9,000	−44
Other, non-Latino	17,664	12,000	−32
High school dropout	15,014	4,500	−70
High school graduate	23,817	14,000	−41
Some college	26,496	18,000	−32
College graduate	31,795	25,721	−19

the almost Herculean work effort of young parents. Many young married-couple families have tried to compensate for lower wages by sending a second worker into the work force. These second earners have softened (but not eliminated) the economic blow. But the growing number of young parents working longer hours or coping with two jobs has placed young families with children under tremendous stress and generated new offsetting costs, especially for child care. Many families, moreover, have two jobs that together provide less security and less support and less access to health care than one good job did a generation ago. This two-earner strategy is totally unavailable, moreover, to the growing number of single-parent families.

ECONOMIC SHIFTS AND FAMILY CHANGES

Today's young families with children look considerably different from those in the early 1970s. They are more likely to be mi-

nority families or single-parent families. Both groups are more likely to be paid low wages and to be poor than other families. So poverty among young families and children as a whole also rises.

The growth in young female-headed families with children is in part a reflection of changing values. But the economic hardships associated with falling earnings and persistent joblessness among young adults have contributed significantly to falling marriage rates and the increasing rates of out-of-wedlock childbearing. And the fastest growth in out-of-wedlock childbearing has occurred among women in their twenties, not among teenagers, a growth driven in significant part by the earnings free-fall for young adults.

The capacity to support a family has a powerful impact on the marriage decisions of young people. More than two centuries ago Benjamin Franklin wrote: "The number of marriages ... is greater in proportion to the ease and convenience of supporting a family. When families can be easily supported, more persons marry, and earlier in life."

Increases in poverty among young families with children are *not* the result of young Americans having more children. Indeed, young adults have responded to a tightening economic vise by postponing childbearing and choosing to have fewer children. But these attempts to adapt their behavior have been overwhelmed by the far more rapid pace of economic decline and social disintegration they have encountered.

As a result of these economic and social changes, in 1990 a child in a family headed by a parent under age 30 was:

- twice as likely to be poor as a comparable child in 1973;
- if living with both parents, two and a half times as likely to be poor as in 1973;
- nearly three times more likely to have been born out-of-wedlock than his counterpart two decades ago;
- one-third less likely to be living in a home owned by her family than just a decade ago; and

- three times more likely to see his family pay more than one-half its income for rent.

But despite the devastating suffering these numbers suggest, children in young families have been given less and less government help over the last two decades. They were getting less to begin with—government programs are particularly stingy when it comes to helping younger adults and young children. And in the 1970s and especially the 1980s young families saw programs that might help them cut rather than strengthened and reconfigured to adapt to new realities. As a result, government programs were less than half as effective in pulling young families out of poverty in 1990 as in 1979.

HARD HIT MINORITY FAMILIES

The changes of the last two decades have had a very profound impact on minority young families, especially those that are black. As Table 2 shows, the median earnings of the heads of young black families with children fell 71 *percent* from 1973 to 1990 (from $13,860 to $4,030 in 1990 dollars). Their total family incomes from all sources fell 48 percent. The *median* income of these young black families is now below the federal poverty line for a family of three. In 1973 it was nearly double that poverty line. *Two out of three* children in young black families now are poor.

This crisis for young black families is contributing mightily to the tearing apart of the black community. This society cannot year after year increase the poverty and isolation and hopelessness of black mothers and fathers and children—it can't keep turning the screws tighter and tighter—without appalling consequences. We see those consequences in the emergency rooms and unemployment lines and prisons and homeless shelters and neonatal intensive care wards and morgues of our cities and our suburbs and rural towns. We see it in the omnipresent violence that destroys so many black lives and leaves blacks and whites alike so

fearful. More blacks die from firearms each year in this country than died in the century's worth of despicable lynchings that followed the Civil War. More black men die from firearms every six weeks in Detroit than died in the 1967 Detroit "riot." More black and Hispanic men die from firearms in Los Angeles every two weeks than died in the 1965 Watts "riot." [*Editor's note:* This speech was given two weeks before the most recent outbreak of violence in Los Angeles.]

Frankly, though, I would be skeptical that this nation would attack this cataclysm for young black families were it not for the fact that young *white* families are only a step or two behind in the scope of their economic depression and family disintegration. Perhaps the most important story told in this report is the impact of two decades of this Depression for the young on three types of families we often assume are insulated from hard times:

- From 1973 to 1990 the poverty rate for children living in young *white* families more than doubled to *27 percent.*
- From 1973 to 1990 the poverty rate for children in young *married-couple* families went up two-and-a-half times—to *20 percent.*
- And the child poverty rate in young families headed by *high school graduates* went up even faster, to *33 percent.*

In other words, a generation ago white or married-couple young families or those headed by high school graduates were fairly well insulated from poverty. The damage of the last two decades has cut so broadly and deeply that now one in four white children in young families, one in five children in married-couple young families, and one in three children in families headed by young high school graduates is poor.

PRIVATE AND PUBLIC RESPONSE

What response do we see to these problems from private and public leadership? Precious little.

Too much of the business community is wholly untroubled by stripping away from millions of Americans the minimum family-supporting wages, fringe benefits, and job security that could help make our families strong again. The Administration has no higher domestic priority than cutting capital gains taxes for the rich. The Congress and the Administration together persist in keeping defense spending above the levels of the average year in the Cold War—impoverishing our society and the world by arming ourselves not only against real external threats but against weapons-justifying fantasies, while letting the internal enemies of poverty, disintegration, violence, and hopelessness rage unabated. The Congress can't mount the political will to get Head Start—a program universally conceded to be effective and cost-effective—to more than one in three eligible children or to pass the refundable children's tax credit that experts from all parts of the political spectrum think is a minimum first step to tax equity and family economic security.

Finally, far too many of the nation's Governors and state and national legislators have responded to budget crunches and political turmoil by scapegoating the poor—trying to bolster their political fortunes by pummeling the welfare recipients whose assistance gobbles up a grand total of 2 to 3 percent of state budgets.

In hard times in the past our society usually has had escape valves—an inherent balance that gave to the powerless help from one institution when others turned their backs—from the federal government when the states were at their worst, from the courts when Congress and the executive were unresponsive. Now we seem to be in an awful time when every institution is competing to pander to the powerful and further penalize the poor.

A FAIR START

In response to the economic plight of America's young families, Congress and the President must take three immediate steps in 1992 to ensure that every child has a *fair* start, a *healthy* start, and a *head* start.

A *fair start* means renewed and sustained economic growth and enough jobs at decent wages to restore the pact our nation used to have with young families—that personal sacrifice and hard work will be rewarded with family-supporting jobs. A fair start also means enactment of a refundable children's tax credit to bolster the incomes of families with children, as proposed in recent months in various forms and amounts by the National Commission on Children and key members of Congress from both parties. Such a credit would reduce federal income taxes for middle- and low-income families and help the lowest income families that have no tax liability through a tax refund.

While creating no new bureaucracies, a refundable children's credit would target tax relief and economic support precisely to the group—families with children—that has been hardest hit by declining incomes and rising poverty rates since 1973. The Administration's alternative proposal—to expand the personal exemption for children—is extremely regressive. It gives $310 to a family with two children if their income exceeds about $100,000; $280 if it is over $50,000; $150 if income is between $15,000 and $50,000; and zero if it is under about $15,000.

Finally, a fair start means creation of a child support insurance system to give all single parents the chance to lift their families out of poverty through work, ensuring that all children who are not living with both parents receive a minimally adequate child support payment from the absent parent or the government when it fails to collect from the absent parent.

What we *don't* need in this time of great crisis for young families with children is a negative approach rooted in welfare-bashing and welfare cuts that ends up hurting children. Families on welfare are the victims of the recession, not the cause of it. They are victims of budget deficits, not the cause of them. But nearly one-fourth of all young families with children are forced to rely upon Aid to Families with Dependent Children (AFDC) to meet their basic needs, and they are extremely vulnerable to misguided attacks on this essential safety net for children.

Our political leaders know these truths. Yet during an election year too many cannot resist the temptation to direct the public's frustration and anger toward the poorest of poor Americans—those families and children who rely upon welfare for basic income support.

There *are* ways we can and must improve welfare. For example, we agree with the Administration that welfare parents often don't have enough financial incentive to work because current welfare rules strip them of virtually all of their earnings when they do work. That is why we opposed the repeal of earnings incentives by President Reagan and the Congress in 1981, and why we think they should be restored now for all welfare families, not just those in a few demonstration counties.

But most of the welfare "reforms" now underway in states are little more than crass attempts to slash state budgets without regard to their impact on families with children. Reducing or stopping benefits to newborns when they are the second or third child in a family, as now proposed by several states, is punitive, pointless, and immoral. Only political leaders who are hopelessly out of touch with the realities of poor families' lives could think that an extra $2.50 per day in welfare benefits would cause teen parents to have a second child, or that reducing the added benefit to $1.25/day (as the Governor of Wisconsin and the President now propose for that state) constitutes any serious effort at welfare reform. All they will succeed in doing is taking desperately needed food, clothing, and shelter from infants.

It's time for the President, Congress, and more of our Governors to be honest with the American people about the problems facing our economy, our poor families, and our children.

The problem is *not* large numbers of welfare parents trying to "beat the system" by having more children or moving to another state to get higher benefits. The problem is

a set of short-sighted, budget-driven welfare rules that make it virtually impossible for parents to work their way gradually off the welfare rolls and a dearth of stable, family-supporting jobs that would allow them to make it on their own.

In many ways, the welfare problem is the same problem facing all young families with children—the result of sharply falling wages, too few job opportunities for those with little education or training, and too little investment in the skills and supports poor parents need to make it in today's economy. And serious solutions begin with a fair start, a healthy start, and a head start for our young families.

A HEALTHY START, A HEAD START

A *healthy start* means a national health plan to assure insurance coverage for all Americans. Children and pregnant women need basic health care *now*, however. As an immediate step, the President and Congress must extend Medicaid coverage to every low-income child and pregnant woman. And to ensure that this insurance provides real access to essential health services, not merely theoretical coverage, children need universal access to vaccines and increased funding for community health centers, and other public health activities.

A *head start* means full funding of Head Start. A first step in bolstering the productivity of our next generation of workers lies in adequate investments in quality child care and early childhood development. Every dollar invested in good early childhood development programs saves $5.97 in later special education, welfare, crime, and other costs. Yet Head Start still reaches only one in three eligible preschool children.

As recommended by prominent business groups, educators, and a broad range of study commissions that have examined the educational problems of disadvantaged children and youths, the President and Congress should ensure every child a Head Start by 1995 by enacting immediately S.911, the

School Readiness Act, and accelerating the funding increases it provides.

A head start also means passing family preservation legislation that will strengthen and preserve families in crisis so that they can better protect, nurture and support their own children. So many of these young parents want to be better parents, and with intensive family preservation services they can get the help they need.

These are essential first steps. To reach them and go beyond them, we're going to have to make the President and Congress come to recognize that child and family poverty and insecurity are a national disaster that requires our addressing them with a pittance of the zeal and shared commitment we now apply to digging out after a devastating hurricane or earthquake or confronting a crisis abroad.

35

The New American Family

Lester C. Thurow

This article begins by comparing the earnings and employment of men and women over the last several decades. The author argues that two incomes are necessary to sustain a comfortable, middle-class standard of living. Policies to help ease the burdens on two-worker families are offered.

Exercises to Guide Your Reading

1. List the services needed by the "new American family," and explain why they are needed.
2. Define the term "assortative."
3. Identify the factors responsible for closing the pay gap between men and women.
4. Identify and discuss the economic aspects of the social trends associated with the rise in two-earner families.

Some conservative and religious groups are trying to turn the clock back to the days when women stayed at home and men earned enough for the entire family. But those days are gone. Women's earnings today play an increasingly important role in determining whether families can afford to maintain a typical American lifestyle. In many cases, a working husband and a working wife are a must for economic survival. Groups who wish to preserve the traditional family unit would be better advised to work toward programs that reduce the strain on working parents and make dual incomes possible.

During much of the twentieth century, female earnings were not a substantial factor in the income of husband-wife families. Many women stayed home, and there was an enormous gap between male wages and wages for women who did work. From the 1930s (when figures were first available) through most of the 1970s, the earnings of full-time female workers were only 56 to 59 percent of male earnings. Such disparity persisted despite enormous increases in the number of women in the labor force and the introduction of affirmative-action programs in the 1960s. Yet by the late 1970s the earnings gap had begun to close, and by 1985 (the most recent year for which we have data) female earnings had risen to 65 percent of those of males.

Female unemployment rates were also consistently above those for males until recently. In the 1970s, unemployment rates for women over the age of 20 exceeded unemployment rates for adult men by 1.5 percent. By 1986, the two rates had reached parity, and thus far in 1987 adult female unemployment is running slightly below that of males.

Reprinted by permission of *Technology Review*. August–September 1987. pp. 26–27.

Higher earnings opportunities for women are also opening up. The number of women earning more than $50,000 per year more than tripled in the last 10 years, climbing from 91,000 women in 1975 to 341,000 in 1985 (in constant 1985 dollars). Such incomes, of course, are still exceedingly rare for women; those earning more than $50,000 make up only 1 percent of all U.S. working women.

Unfortunately, female salaries are rising in proportion to male salaries not because women are doing better but because men are doing worse. Between 1975 and 1985 (after correcting for inflation), median male earnings fell 8 percent for all men and 5 percent for those who work full-time year-round. In contrast, median female earnings rose 18 percent for all women and 4 percent for those who work full-time year-round. These advances in real female earnings were actually much slower than those achieved in the previous decade when male wages were rising rapidly.

The reasons for falling male earnings are easy to find. The industries hurt most by foreign competition—autos, machine tools, steel—were precisely the industries that provided the most high-earnings jobs for men, especially men who did not go to college. With the decline of these industries, men were left with fewer good-income jobs. In the jobs they did retain, they were often forced to accept "give backs"—lower wages to keep their jobs.

That foreign competition emerged for our best jobs should come as no surprise. Those plotting foreign industrial policies were not interested in capturing the low-income service jobs traditionally held by women. Foreign ministries such as Japan's Ministry of International Trade and Industry were interested in the high-wage industries traditionally populated by men.

Furthermore, most of the growth in the American economy in the last 10 years has occurred in the service and white-collar occupations that are traditionally large employers of women. As a result, female employment opportunities are growing much faster than male employment opportunities. These female jobs are still low-paid, but with the disappearance of many high-earnings male jobs, they look better than they used to.

DINKS SET THE EXAMPLE

Along with the shifting trend in male and female salaries come dramatic changes in the work patterns of the American family. Of the 87 million households in the United States in 1984, 50 million were traditional intact husband-wife families. Of the 40 million husband-wife households with earnings (the rest were mostly retired), 28 million—or 70 percent—reported earnings by both husband and wife. These families had median incomes of $31,000—$22,000 earned by the husband and $9,000 earned by the wife. While the dominant pattern today is a full-time year-round husband worker and a part-time or part-year wife worker, this pattern is rapidly shifting toward a lifestyle in which both husband and wife work full-time year-round. In 1984, 11 million families had two full-time workers, and these families had a median income of $39,000; $24,000 earned by the husband and $15,000 earned by the wife.

Such statistics signal a fact of life. If a family wants the average American lifestyle, it has to have a working husband and a working wife. Only 11 percent of working men will earn $39,000 or more on their own. Only 1 percent of working women will earn $39,000 or more on their own. Without an intact husband-wife working family, few families have any chance of maintaining a middle-income lifestyle. In 1984, the average household income for those not in husband-wife families was only $12,000. Meanwhile, two-parent families are having fewer children. Families with a dual income and no kids (DINKS) increasingly set the economic pattern that others try to emulate.

Ironically, the increasing participation of women in the workplace is causing the incomes of those families earning the highest salaries to grow much faster than the income of the average American family. Economically, American mating is highly assortative. If one looks at the husband-wife group where both are year-round, full-time workers, a husband earning $6,000 to $7,000 per year (essentially a minimum-wage male) is most likely to be married to a female earning $6,000 to $7,000 per year. The middle-income male earning $20,000 to $25,000 per year is most likely to be married to women making $10,000 to $15,000—a middle-income female. The probability that a middle-income male will be married to a female making more than $25,000 is only 9 percent. In contrast, a man earning more than $75,000 per year is most likely to be married to a woman making over $25,000 per year. Furthermore, almost none of the working wives of such high-earning males earn less than $10,000 per year.

Given these economic trends, families with an at-home wife will increasingly find that they cannot afford the material standard of living enjoyed by those around them. Thus those who embrace the traditional two-parent family will have to embrace the working wife. She is now part of the prototypical American family.

Programs such as day care, affirmative action, and government-funded allowances for children are not threats to the new traditional family. They are services urgently needed to sustain it. And for families in which men earn low wages, they are essential. Yet the United States is one of the few industrialized nations that does not require or encourage companies to provide day care for their employees. Nor does the United States, unlike Canada, France, and the Scandinavian countries—provide monthly allowances to both rich and poor families depending upon the number of children they have.

These are surprising blind spots for a nation that makes as much noise about the virtues of the family as the United States does. Rather than focusing on putting the working wife back in the home, we would be better advised to support today's American family by promoting day care, subsidies for families with children, and affirmative action.

36

At Issue: Do Men Experience a Huge Rise in Their Standard of Living After Divorce?

Lenore J. Weitzman and Jed H. Abraham

These two brief readings offer competing assessments of the financial impact of divorce on women's standard of living. Weitzman argues that judges in no-fault divorce cases incorrectly assume that women who have been full-time home-makers are economically equal to husbands who have been continuously employed. Thus, women and children are bound to suffer when court-ordered alimony and child support payments are based on this reasoning. Abraham, in contrast, argues that Weitzman's conclusions are biased by her selective use of data. Thus, he cites the emotional and financial upheavals of the divorce itself as the principal source of changes in the standard of living.

Exercises to Guide Your Reading

1. Defend the position with which you disagree.
2. Criticize the position with which you agree.
3. Explain the impact of marriage on female and male economic opportunities.
4. Compare and contrast the remedies offered by the authors. Evaluate both positions in light of the "backlash" identified in Reading 65.

Yes, says Lenore J. Weitzman, sociologist and author of *The Divorce Revolution* (1985).

No-fault [divorce's] standards for alimony and property awards have shaped radically different futures for divorced men on the one hand, and for divorced women and their children on the other. Women, and the minor children in their households, typically experience a sharp decline in their standard of living after divorce. Men, in contrast, are usually much better off and have a higher standard of living as a result of divorce. . . .

Since a woman's ability to support herself is likely to be impaired during marriage, es-pecially if she is a full-time homemaker and mother, she may not be "equal to" her former husband at the point of divorce. Rules that treat her as if she is equal simply serve to deprive her of the financial support she needs. . . .

In fact, it is marriage itself that typically creates the different structural opportunities that men and women face at divorce. While most married women give priority to their family roles, most married men give priority to their careers. Even if both of them are in the labor force, it is more likely that she will forgo further education and train-

Reprinted by permission of *Editorial Research Reports*. October 26, 1990. p. 629.

ing while he gains additional education and on-the-job experience. As a result her earning capacity is likely to be impaired while his is enhanced. . . .

If the divorce rules do not give her a share of his enhanced earning capacity (through alimony and child support awards), and if divorce rules expect her to enter the labor market as she is, with few skills, outdated experience, no seniority, and no time for retraining, and if she continues to have the major burden of caring for young children after divorce, it is easy to understand why [she] is likely to be much worse off than her former husband. . . .

[Our] research shows that on the average, divorced women and the minor children in their households experience a 73 percent decline in their standard of living in the first year after divorce. Their former husbands, in contrast, experience a 42 percent rise in their standard of living.

The divorced man generally finds himself much better off financially after divorce because his work and income continue uninterrupted. The courts do not typically require him to share his salary with his former wife, nor do they typically require him to contribute equally to support their children. He is therefore left with a much larger proportion of his income and a higher standard of living than he had during marriage. . . .

Mothers of young children . . . experience great hardships as a result of the new rules. Courts award inadequate amounts of child support which leave the primary custodial parent, who is the mother in 90 percent of the divorce cases, with the major burden of supporting the children after divorce. Yet even these minimal child support awards go unpaid. Enforcement is lax and less than half of the fathers fully comply with court orders to pay child support.

No, says Jed H. Abraham, an attorney and an executive member of the Child Custody Committee of the American Bar Association's Section of Family Law.

Because society generally rewards wom-
en's work outside the home less well than men's work outside the home, it may be expected that women will not fare as well as men after divorce. It should not even be surprising to find that in the first few years after divorce, due to the costs and stresses generated by the breakup of the marital home, ex-husbands as well as ex-wives fare less well than their married counterparts. [Lenore J.] Weitzman's result—that in the first year after divorce women experience a 73 percent decline in their standard of living, whereas men experience a 42 percent rise in their standard of living—confounds these expectations by a wide margin. And, indeed, an analysis of [her result's] derivation will cast considerable doubt on its dependability. . . .

[The] pool of information from which Weitzman derives her standard of living figures is not a random sample. . . . The final sample was essentially self-selected. Self-selected interviewees often have ulterior motives for agreeing to be interviewed. . . . [M]any interviewees shared (or were infected with) the reforming spirit of Weitzman and her colleagues. . . . It is fair to suspect that not all of their enthusiastic responses were unbiased.

The data Weitzman collected from her interviewees included information "about income, occupation, and employment as well as property ownership and value." She does not report detailed expense ("needs") information. In any case, in computing the standards of living—the income/needs ratios—of the men and women in her sample, she does not use their personal needs data. She does not use real expense data at all. . . . There are many problems with Weitzman's methodology. . . .

Central to the thrust of Weitzman's economic argument are the children who remain with the custodial parent, usually the mother. . . . Weitzman's solution to a custodial mother's low income/needs ratio is to increase her income by imposing large, additional alimony and child support obligations upon her ex-husband. An alternate method would be to reduce the custodial mother's needs. This could be accomplished by instituting some form of joint custody arrangement between the parents. . . .

Contemporary divorce law generates social costs because it sunders an economically efficient household unit into two inefficient and antagonistic halves. An antidote will not be found in amendments which tax still more the financial and spiritual resources of both parties and harden the remnants of the post-divorce family into implacable adversaries. It will not be found between the covers of *The Divorce Revolution*.

37

The Politics of Family in America

Jewell Handy Gresham

This article presents a history of the political uses of theories about African American families. Beginning with the racist arguments deployed in defense of slavery, the author analyzes the common themes and policy conclusions of many accepted portraits of African American families. Sources as diverse as Census Bureau reports, television news specials, and presidential addresses illustrate the extent to which dominant cultural images deny the central role of families in African American life.

Exercises to Guide Your Reading

1. Give examples of the misuse of data on African Americans.
2. Explain the link between racism and sexism.
3. List public events and/or statements consistent with racist views of African Americans.
4. Define and give examples of scapegoating and projection.

> The past is not dead. It's not even past.
> –William Faulkner

In April 1844, Secretary of State John Calhoun, the pre-eminent Southern philosopher of States' rights, directed a letter to the British ambassador in Washington attesting that where blacks and whites existed in the same society, slavery was the natural result. Wherever the states changed that providential relationship, the blacks invariably degenerated "into vice and pauperism accompanied by the bodily and mental afflictions incident thereto—deafness, blindness, insanity, and idiocy." In the slave states, in contrast, the blacks improved greatly "in number, comfort, intelligence, and morals."

To prove his point, Calhoun supplied statistics from the 1840 census. The data showed a shocking rate of black insanity in New England: one out of every fourteen in Maine, every twenty-eight in New Hampshire, every forty-three in Massachusetts, etc. The overall figure for the North was almost ten times the rate in the South, where only one "lunatic" for every 1,309 blacks was shown in Virginia, one in 2,447 in South Carolina, etc.

At the time Calhoun wrote that letter, one of the country's leading newspapers had just broken the scandal of the plot by President Tyler's Administration to annex Texas as slave territory—a potential constitutional crisis certain to inflame the bitter North-South conflict. In that context, Calhoun's statistics were intended less for the British than for Congress, to which he forwarded copies.

Reprinted by permission of *The Nation*. July 24–31, 1989. pp. 116–20, 122.

There was only one flaw in his argument: The figures were false. Dr. Edward Jarvis of Massachusetts General Hospital, a leading specialist in the incidence of insanity, immediately challenged them. Joined by the prestigious American Statistical Association [A.S.A.], Jarvis conducted an exhaustive study of every town and county in the free states in which black insanity had been reported by the Census Bureau. In case after case, the number of "insane" blacks proved larger than the state's total black population!

The A.S.A.'s comprehensive study—forwarded to former President John Quincy Adams in the House of Representatives—concluded that "it would have been far better to have no census at all, than such a one as has been published" and urged Congress either to correct the data or "discard or disown" it "as the good of the country . . . and as justice and humanity shall demand." But when Adams, as recorded in his diary, confronted Calhoun at the State Department, the latter "answered like a true slavemonger. . . . He writhed like a trodden rattlesnake on the exposure of his false report to the House . . . and finally said that where there were so many errors they balanced one another, and led to the same conclusion as if they were all correct." The A.S.A. report—blocked by the Speaker and the proslavery majority in the House—never reached the floor.

While these developments unfolded, Southern slaves were of course in no position to challenge the claims in which their welfare was critical. Nor did the free blacks of New York City under the leadership of the distinguished black physician/abolitionist James McCune Smith stand a chance of having their memorial to Congress protesting the "calumnies against free people of color" recognized. For those who held political power, it was imperative that blacks simply not exist except as objects, and the truth or falsity of what was said was beside the point. What mattered, then as now, was not the *facts* but only that the semblance of "substance" be provided for a time sufficient to confuse the issue and carry the day.

"THE NEED TO SEGREGATE OR QUARANTINE A RACE"

After the Civil War, the Calhoun view of the inherent degeneracy of blacks, which held that they could not survive outside slavery, was tenaciously clung to by the outnumbered whites of Mississippi. In 1865 the *Meridian Clarion* asserted with unconcealed satisfaction that the black race was doomed: "A hundred years is a long time to one man; but to a nation or a race, it is but a limited period. Well, in that time the negro will be dead."

In due course, Mississippi produced figures to prove it: The 1866 state census showed a more than 12 percent decline in the black population. Unfortunately for the prophets, however, this data was as accurate as Calhoun's: The 1870 Federal census showed an *increase* of more than 7,000, which turned out to be an undercount of between 50,000 and 75,000, corrected in the 1880 Federal figures.

Nonetheless, in the 1880s, the Reverend C. K. Marshall, the most prominent preacher in the state, predicted that "by January, 1920 . . . except for a few old people [who] will linger as the Cherokees do on their reservation . . . the colored population of the south will scarcely be counted."

With the passage of more years without apparent visible diminution in black ranks, however, white theories of a built-in biological solution to the black "problem" obviously had to be augmented. In *The Plantation Negro as Freeman* (1889), the historian Philip A. Bruce used the black family as a device for attacking all blacks. Bruce, the scion of a former Virginia slaveowner, simply advanced Calhoun's thesis: With the end of slavery, the loss of white "supervision" led to a severe and menacing deterioration in blacks' social and moral condition. The black family as such did not exist, he announced; black children, accordingly, were born into a state of moral degeneracy.

Bruce viciously castigated black women. Alluding to the alleged propensity of black men to rape white women, he asserted that they found "something strangely alluring and seductive ... in the appearance of a white woman" because of the "wantonness of the women of his own race." The "fact" that black women failed to complain of being raped by men of their race counted as "strong proof of the sexual laxness of plantation women as a class."

Herbert Gutman called Bruce's work perhaps the most important connecting link between the "popular" views of African-American degeneracy in the 1880s and the supportive pseudoscientific works of the ensuing decades before World War I. These latter writings rested heavily on the pseudoscientific data of Social Darwinism—the doctrine of survival of the fittest. The historian George Frederickson explains the relevance of such theories in his book *The Black Image in the White Mind*:

> If the blacks were a degenerating race with no future, the problem ceased to be one of how to prepare them for citizenship or even how to make them more productive and useful members of the community. The new prognosis pointed rather to the need to segregate or quarantine a race liable to be a source of contamination and social danger to the white community, as it sank ever deeper into the slough of disease, vice, and criminality.

THE DEVICE UPDATED

It was against these brutally repressive rationalizations still undergirding the Southern apartheid system after World War II that the civil rights revolution of the 1950s and 1960s erupted. And it was at the climactic stages of that struggle that Labor Department official Daniel Patrick Moynihan conceived, in December 1964, his supposedly secret "internal memorandum" on the black family.

Whether Moynihan knew his history or not, his report served the time-tested purpose: Whenever the system is in crisis (or shows signs of becoming transformed); whenever blacks get restless (or show strength); whenever whites in significant

numbers show signs of coming together with blacks to confront their mutual problems (or enemies), the trick is to shift the focus from the real struggle for political and economic empowerment to black "crime," degeneracy, pathology and—in Moynihan's innovative twist—the "deterioration" of the black family (previously defined as nonexistent!).

Moynihan's report was subtitled "The Case for National Action." But just how much serious "action" it intended was made plain in the author's next "internal memo"— this time to Richard Nixon—counseling "benign neglect."

In the light of subsequent events it is interesting to discover in *Pat*, the Senator's biography, that it was presidential assistant Bill Moyers who, in May 1965, first brought the black family report, until then ignored, to Lyndon Johnson's attention and arranged for the President to deliver a major policy speech based on it.

Curiously, the Moyers-arranged speech bypassed all agencies of the government set up to aid the passage of the President's civil rights agenda. It was delivered at the graduation exercises of Howard University before an overwhelmingly black audience of thousands of students, parents, friends and dignitaries. Apparently few observers among the editors, journalists and scholars present found what Johnson did reprehensible. Howard was one of the colleges that had sent a sizable contingent of students into the revolutionary *nonviolent* Southern struggle which at that moment was galvanizing, inspiring and, in a thousand unforeseeable ways, transforming the nation. Before the young people whom he should have congratulated for the extraordinary example of sacrifice and heroism they were setting, the President emphasized the "historical" degenerate state of the families from which they came!

True, words of noble intent were there (as they were in Moynihan's original), and they heartened many. But so were the declarations of black degeneracy that reinforced the racism of many more and signaled the open-door policy for what was to come. Through the summer, however, the "secret" Moynihan report continued to be leaked to selected journalists. Then came the event that cemented its impact. Ten days after the August passage of the Voting Rights Act of 1965, Watts exploded—and in a mad scramble for instant wisdom, journalists turned to the black family report and drew on its conclusions as explanations for the violent civil disorders.

What did it explain? What were the causes of Watts and the succeeding ghetto rebellions? Not, as the Kerner commission concluded in 1967, the division of America into two societies, separate and unequal. Not historical white racism, Depression-level unemployment and the intolerable conditions of the ghetto that cut short the dreams and lives of millions of black men, women and children. Not at all. "Ours is a society," offered Moynihan, "which presumes male leadership in private and public affairs.... A subculture such as that of the Negro American, in which this is not the pattern, is placed at a distinct disadvantage." To overcome that disadvantage, he said, the malaise of the black family, characterized by the unnatural dominance of a "black matriarchy," had to be cured.

In contrast, Moynihan wrote: *"The white family has achieved a high degree of stability and is maintaining that stability."* (Emphasis added.) Against the backdrop of the next twenty-five years, this declaration would be hilarious were it not for the fact that, for untold millions of *white* working women—divorced, single and joint providers—the idealized patriarchal structure held up as an icon had always been a myth! Indeed, even as Moynihan wrote the words, the modern women's movement for equal rights and a sense of selfhood, submerged under the centuries-old domination of that very model, was being forged in the crucible of the civil rights struggle.

Those who found the Moynihan report useful were presumably unaware that the archetypal sexism on which it rests is inextricable from its racism. At any rate, the report signaled, at the very height of the civil rights

movement, that Northern whites would pick up where the South was forced to leave off in blocking the long black struggle for parity with whites in American life.

LINE OF DESCENT

On January 25, 1986, Bill Moyers, Moynihan's original booster, invoked the full power of a prime-time, two-hour CBS Special Report to beam the old theme into millions of homes. The title: *The Vanishing Black Family—Crisis in Black America* (shades of the old Mississippi *Meridian Clarion!*). The East Texan, in sympathetic "liberal" guise, took cameras into a Newark, New Jersey, housing project for an "intimate" portrait of black teen-age welfare mothers, sexually irresponsible if not criminal youth, a smiling black male "superstud," and pervasive pathology all around. Moyers's report was directed not at the cause of the plight of the people whose confidences he elicited. Viewers were shown, rather, a pathology in black America so overwhelming and irredeemable as to leave the panel of blacks brought in at the end to "discuss" the subject helpless to dissipate the impact of the carefully selected imagery.

The result, whatever sympathy toward individual victims white viewers might have felt, and whatever responsibilities some might acknowledge that America has for its racist "past," could only be: First, to utterly terrify most as to the very nature of their fellow black citizens by reinforcing, with "liberal" authority, the most archetypal of racist myths, fears and stereotypes—a picture of "jungle" immorality and degeneracy inarticulateness and sloth so rife that the onlookers could actually forget the terrible national corruption, wholesale public and private immorality, and other massive problems about them, in horrified fascination with the doings of these Others. And second, to make the situation seem so hopeless that "realistically" there is nothing to be done about it anyway. Racism is no longer the problem, self-destructiveness is. And if that is so, why continue to throw good taxpayer dollars after bad? In the words of the older black woman selected by Moyers to deliver the clincher at the end: "If Martin Luther King were alive, he would not be talking about the things I think he was talking about—labor and all that. He would be talking about the black family."

It is hard to believe that it was simply bad taste that led CBS to choose the very week of the first national celebration of King's birthday to televise his fellow Southerner's broadside. African-Americans had hardly had a moment to savor the honor to the martyred black minister before their psyches were so powerfully assaulted.

The extent of the commonplace manner in which deep-seated black response is blocked out from the larger society may be seen in several postscripts to the broadcast beginning when the National Black Leadership Roundtable [N.B.L.R.], comprising the chief executive officers of more than 300 national black organizations, directed a detailed letter to CBS to protest the "untimely and indeed . . . suspect" airing of an "unbalanced, unfair and frequently salacious" documentary.

The N.B.L.R. challenged the implication "that the *only* legitimate and sanctioned family form is nuclear and patriarchal," and observed:

> One was left with the impression that black families generally do not have fathers in the home, but there was no serious examination of the reasons for the absence of the father within some black families. The unconscionable high levels of unemployment, underemployment, imprisonment, drug addiction and mortality among black men—effects of an economy which does not fully respond to the employment needs of all Americans—all play a role. . . . Single-parent families then, are not, as implied . . . the result of "immorality" or promiscuity, but rather are adaptive responses to economic and social forces.

Two months later CBS vice president of public affairs broadcasts Eric Ober, speaking for Moyers, replied. He refused to meet with Walter Fauntroy, N.B.L.R. president, or

"any member of your group." And to the N.B.L.R. query as to what "experts" had been consulted within the black community, he replied that the "experts we consulted were primarily officials of *the Department of the Census.*" (Emphasis added.) Little did he know the history.

The reinforcing white response was predictable. In early 1987, the Columbia University Graduate School of Journalism gave its highest award in broadcast journalism—the Alfred I. DuPont—Columbia University Gold Baton for the "program judged to have made the greatest contribution to the public's understanding of an important issue"—to CBS News for the Moyers Special Report on "the disintegration of black family life."

Moyers's contribution lies not only in his restoration to primacy of old images through the power of television but in his encouragement of the willingness, indeed the eagerness, of large numbers of white Americans to have all that he portrayed be true at any cost so that the victims might deserve their fate. Such is the depth of the entrenched white desire to avoid facing the society's culpability for creating and maintaining the two ever more unequal "societies" the Kerner report asked us to face up to a generation before.

RESTRAINING THE "DARKER IMPULSES"

In such a climate, it is not surprising that politicians like "centrist" Democrat Charles Robb, L.B.J.'s son-in-law and former Virginia Governor, now Senator, promptly picked up Moyers's cue. Once upon a time, black people were the victims of white racism, Robb conceded in his keynote speech to a conference on the Johnson presidency. But that time has passed. "It's time to shift the primary focus from racism, the traditional enemy from without, to self-defeating patterns of behavior, the new enemy within."

Approval by establishment opinion makers was swift to follow. A *New York Times* editorial endorsed Robb's brand of "hard truth," and journalists flung the name of the messenger into the public arena as a worthy candidate for President.

In such a climate, the level of public tolerance of the intolerable increased. Even years before, there had been little reaction when, at a speech in New Orleans to the International Association of Chiefs of Police, President Reagan had drawn "applause and some whoops of approval" for remarks that included the following:

> It has occurred to me that the root causes of our ... growth of government and the decay of the economy ... can be traced to many of the same sources of the crime problem.... Many of the social thinkers of the 1950s and '60s who discussed crime only in the context of disadvantaged childhoods and poverty-stricken neighborhoods were the same people who thought that massive government spending could wipe away our social ills. The underlying premise in both cases was a belief that there was nothing permanent or absolute about any man's nature—that he was a product of his material environment, and that by changing that environment ... we could ... usher in a great new era. The solution to the crime problem will not be found in the social worker's files, the psychiatrist's notes or the bureaucrat's budget.... Only our deep moral values and strong institutions can hold back that jungle and restrain the darker impulses of human nature.

Most black people knew immediately of which "jungle" and whose "darker impulses" Reagan was speaking, and that his words represented a not-so-subtle invitation to white-against-black terror.

Reagan's position was a *theological* one in the American Calvinist tradition, a division of the world into good and evil, with a scapegoat selected to serve as "sacrificial animal upon whose back the burden of unwanted evils is ritualistically loaded," in Kenneth Burke's definition. Through such projections, the culture thus expiates its sins and receives absolution.

The Reagan rhetoric directed to the assembled police officers was a direct corollary of his theological labeling of the Soviet Union as an "evil empire" (a remark now implicitly withdrawn in the case of the Russians, but not that of African-Americans!). It indicates how high is the level of responsibility for nationwide police practices of treating black Americans as if they are foreign enemies and, with sickening regularity, eliminating many. And it also indicates the treatment of a variety of foreign "enemies"—now mostly desperately struggling Third World countries—on the basis of a "moral" stance rooted in the myths of a fatalistically corrupt domestic system.

It is on this level that the politics of family—which is to say the politics of power and domination—threatens not only domestic but world social, political and economic order.

It is likewise on this level that the political manipulation of the intermingled race/sex/religion syndrome of the society is irrevocably wedded to violence; in its ultimate form, militaristic. For the identities of those who create the monsters in the mind (Toni Morrison calls the creations "grinning apes in the head") require ever vigilant attention to finding and confronting replicas in the external world.

It is this system of macho ethics that was successfully drawn upon in George Bush's march to the White House. True to tradition, the ultimate scapegoat tapped was a black male, the rapist Willie Horton (whether real or fancied does not traditionally matter), projected before millions via television and print.

Those who make use of such a repugnant and dangerous tactic—among them South Carolina's Lee Atwater, now chair of the Republican National Committee, and Texan James Baker 3d—know these traditions well. And they know further that it is not possible for the image of a black man accused of rape to be flashed before black Americans by white men independent of the psychic association for blacks with lynchings. After the election, *The New York Times* not only contributed the verdict to history that the Bush campaign was "tough and effective," this preeminent sheet augmented that judgment with strident editorial criticism of black students at Howard for their successful protest action when Lee Atwater was suddenly named to the University's Board of Trustees.

While white perception of black criminality is readily evoked, white awareness of black anger or anguish has been not only historically avoided but, on the deepest psychic levels, guarded against. Existentially, the concept of black people as vulnerable human beings who sustain pain and love and hatreds and fears and joy and sorrows and degradations and triumphs is not yet permitted in the national consciousness. Hence the constant need of the dominant society, in age after age, to reinforce linguistic and ritualistic symbols that deny black humanity.

Historically, white terror is the sustaining principle of the system. Whether overtly applied or covertly threatened, not only has this basic device of subjugation never been nationally rejected, it has, on the contrary, always been sanctioned.

THE FAMILY
AS UNIFYING PRINCIPLE

A few weeks after his election, George Bush addressed the Republican Governors Association in Alabama where, some months before, several black legislators had been arrested for trying to remove the Confederate Flag from above the State Capitol, presided over by Republican Governor Guy Hunt. The theme of the conference—"Century of the States"—resurrected overtones of Calhoun's old brand of States' rights. To this audience, a smiling Bush announced that building more prisons was a major domestic priority of his Administration (on education, he emphasized that the initiative would be left up to the states).

Only a few weeks later a smiling Bush assured a black gathering celebrating the birthday of Martin Luther King, Jr., that he is committed to the fulfillment of King's dream of America, just as they are. That King's dream does not include the construction of prisons is immaterial. In the prevailing political realm, language does not matter: Symbols are all.

However, the renewed focus on the black family has introduced a sleeper. For the very technology of communication which carries the message of black pathology to white people conveys to blacks the unmistakable message that once again the dominant culture needs the assurance that black pathology prevails. Clearly, we must bestir ourselves to face the threat. Ironically, we have been handed a mighty weapon. To millions of ordinary human beings the family is not a symbol to be manipulated by opportunistic politicians but the essential nurturing unit from which they draw their being. For African-Americans (and for hundreds of millions of others), it is the institution around which our historical memories cling. Through the extended family of mothers, fathers, sisters and brothers, uncles and aunts, cousins and unsung numbers of others who simply "mothered" parentless children, black people "got over."

It is unbelievable that on the eve of the twenty-first century those who are still fashioning the political formula for WHO and WHAT make a family remain overwhelmingly male!

But it is women who give birth, and children who represent the one essential entity which must exist if the family does. It is simply inconceivable that women, that society, can any longer allow men to retain almost exclusive domain over the vital process of defining the human family.

The concept of "family" can and should be a unifying, rather than divisive, principle. Given the weight of U.S. history that we uniquely bear, black women should step forth collectively not only as blacks but as women, in the name of our lost children throughout history—including most urgently the present generation. One of the first steps is to confront, in all their ramifications, the racist/sexist myths historically concocted by opportunistic, ruthless or naïve white males in the interests of white-over-black and male-over-female dominance.

Never again should the future of black children—or children anywhere in the world—be left in such hands!

CHAPTER 9

Children

38

Liberals, Conservatives, and the Family

Jessica Gress-Wright

This article contrasts competing approaches to helping families with children. On the one hand are liberal proposals for expanded government programs, while on the other are conservative calls for a return to traditional household arrangements. The differences between these approaches and their likely effects are captured in the author's description of the debate over day care.

Exercises to Guide Your Reading

1. Identify supporters of the Act for Better Child Care.
2. Describe the major differences between home-based day care and center-based day care.
3. Give examples of the structural economic pressures facing families.
4. Predict the effects that the Act for Better Child Care will have on (a) home-based day care; (b) church-sponsored day care; and (c) the relative costs and benefits of staying at home with one's children.

Reprinted by permission of *Commentary*. April 1992. pp. 43–46.

In her new book, *When the Bough Breaks*, Sylvia Ann Hewlett recites the dreary litany of economic and social stress on the American family. Since 1973, real wages have fallen and the median family income has been barely maintained by a surge of mothers into the workforce. At the same time, the costs of housing, transportation, and college education have all risen much faster than inflation, while, to compound the injury, the tax burden on families has increased.

The consequences have not been far to seek. Today, parents spend 40 percent less time with their children than a generation ago, and one quarter of all children under the age of six are poor. The divorce and illegitimacy rates have risen so far that, by one estimate, a white child born in the early 80's will have only a 30-percent chance to live to age seventeen with both biological parents at home, and a black child, a 6-percent chance. Nor is this all. The child suicide rate has tripled, scores for basic-skills tests used by large corporations to recruit new workers have fallen dramatically, juvenile crime continues to rise, the high-school dropout rate, once falling, has begun to climb again. Today no neighborhoods are exempt from the social and economic fallout of the past twenty years.

Politicians have hardly been indifferent to the family's cries of distress. Quite the reverse: as the *National Journal* cleverly put it a few months before the 1988 presidential election, "Mom's at work, the kids are at day care, Grandma's in the nursing home, and the checkbook's on empty. These are the problems of the New Family, and Congress is tuning in."

Conservatives and Republicans, of course, had long decried the wreckage of American family life, brought about, as they saw it, by the social policies of the 60's and 70's; indeed, the prospect of undoing some of the damage had been one of the main appeals of the Reagan candidacy in 1980, and "strengthening the family" continued to serve, at least rhetorically, as a catchword of the Right. What was new in the late 1980's was the addition to these ranks of a number of left-wing Democrats who dominated what the (London) *Economist* has called the "iron triangle" of American policy making: "that coalition of special interests, Congressmen, and civil servants" which for 25 years had pushed government as the solution to our family problems. In the stressed parents of the New Family, these Democrats saw a golden opportunity. If they could wrest the moral banner of "strengthening the family" from the conservatives' grasp, they could garner a huge pool of new voters while still promoting the familiar agenda of big government.

The chosen vehicle was not tax breaks, child allowances, or divorce reform, but child care.

In 1987, the Act for Better Child Care (ABC), the centerpiece of the Democratic bid to seize the initiative in national family policy, was introduced by Representative Dale Kildee (D.-Mich.) and Senator Christopher Dodd (D.-Conn.). It was "designed to improve the safety and quality of child care throughout the country and to help low- and moderate-income working parents pay for such care." ABC meant to address what Ellen Galinsky, then president of the National Association for the Education of Young Children (NAEYC), called the "trilemma of child care: availability, affordability, and quality."

ABC was supported by a broad coalition of unions, feminists, advocacy organizations, and policy elites, each of whom had a financial and ideological stake in the bill's passage. Thus, the teachers associated with NAEYC, desperate for higher pay, were relying on ABC to restrict competition from low-wage family day-care providers and church-based day-care centers, as well as to provide the subsidies which would make higher salaries possible. Unions hoped to recruit badly needed new members from the ranks of the subsidized teachers. Feminists wanted to enable women to stay in the workforce. The Children's Defense Fund (CDF) wanted to recover the influence and patronage it had lost under Reagan. And "the liberal developmental intelligentsia" (in Jay Belsky's wry self-characterization) wanted a chance to apply its expertise in child-rearing on a national scale.

Last, there was an important element of political revenge. The day-care lobby had never forgiven Richard Nixon for reneging on his promise to support the 1972 Child and Family Services Act. (He vetoed it, under pressure from the Right, on the grounds that it would promote, in George Will's phrase, the "sovietization of the American family.") ABC was the chance to strike back.

ABC's provisions reflected the interests and prejudices of those who wrote the bill and campaigned for its passage. Given that provenance, it soon became evident, not surprisingly, that ABC would not, in fact, improve the availability, affordability, and quality of child care *for ordinary parents.* "Availability" and "affordability" were carrots, vote-getters; in fact, the amount proposed—$2.5 billion for one year, only 70 percent of which could be used for subsidies—was derisory compared to the $75–100 billion it would cost to implement ABC's promises nationwide.

Under the provisions of the bill, moreover, the state would have to go after all providers who broke licensing rules, which meant that upward of 90 percent of all *current* day care in America would be ineligible for subsidy. This was the stick of "quality," and its enforcement would deprive parents of most forms of family day care—in which, typically, a young mother or an empty nester takes in a few children from the neighborhood. The irony was that parents have always preferred this sort of arrangement, for the good reason that it is the *only* kind of paid child care which has seemed able to solve the trilemma of availability, affordability, and quality, and to offer the advantages of convenience and flexibility to boot.

ABC had other problems, some of them inherent. For constitutional reasons, any government program which subsidized day care directly could not support sectarian activity. The wrangles over what this meant for church-based day care, which accounts for about 30 percent of all center-based care, went on for months. Finally, by using government funds to establish an infrastructure and subsidize paid care, ABC made it less attractive to stay home with children and thereby discriminated against precisely the sort of families who had the most to offer their children. ABC would expand the numbers of families needing help, while reducing the numbers of families able to do without it.

Despite a tremendous publicity campaign, ABC's passage was stormier than expected. Instead of a quick victory in time for the 1988 election, getting a child-care bill through Congress turned into a protracted three-year fight which would end by challenging the political foundations of the Democratic party.

The bill introduced in 1987 was passed, in two different versions, by the House and the Senate in 1988, only to die amid partisan acrimony and a filibuster led by Senator Orrin Hatch (R.-Utah). In an effort to overcome conservative opposition, ABC was reintroduced in January 1989 not by Dodd and Kildee but by Dodd and a newly-coopted Hatch. It was bolstered by the Great American Family Tour, a massive media blitz led by Representative Pat Schroeder (D.-Colo.) and a national survey placed in women's magazines designed to prove that parents wanted government-sponsored child care. Once again, however, ABC failed. This time, significantly, it was betrayed from within.

The defectors were two influentially placed Democrats, Representative George Miller (Calif.), of the House Select Committee on Children, Youth, and Families, and Representative Tom Downey (N.Y.), acting chairman of the House Ways and Means Subcommittee on Human Resources. Downey and Miller saw the writing on the wall when the newly-elected George Bush threatened to veto ABC. They set up their own rival: a bill combining an earned-income tax credit, which would put funds directly in the hands of poor working parents, and an earmarked child-care entitlement added to the

Title XX Social Services Bloc Grants given to states. Both provisions directly repudiated the political agenda of ABC, which was to channel funds and the power of choice away from parents and to the day-care lobby.

ABC and its competitor were fought over through the summer, but ultimately both died in conference. The day-care lobby had been shafted by its own side.

Predictably, the lobby, headed by Marian Wright Edelman of the Children's Defense Fund, the "patron saint of bureaucratic child care," reacted with rage. The CDF had elected Congressman Miller its man-of-the-year just a few months earlier, out of gratitude for his support of ABC and his status as one of Edelman's most veteran allies. When the bill died, Edelman leaked a private memo excoriating Miller and Downey for their betrayal of the cause. Miller retaliated by calling her "hysterical"; Downey refused to take her telephone calls.

But Edelman was undaunted. When ABC was introduced for the third time early in 1990, she led dozens of minority "child-care victims" onto the House floor in an attempt to embarrass Congress into passing the twice-resurrected bill. Downey was indifferent. "There is," he said, "a paternalism among liberals about how people should live their lives. That's what I find most disturbing."

ABC's supporters among those liberals were not prepared to cede. Throughout 1990, amid squabbles over political philosophy and political turf, ABC and rival bills were patched and stitched and amended and patched again, until no one could be sure what would emerge from Congress. In the end, a package was passed consisting of a watered-down ABC, funded at $2.5 billion for five years (instead of $2.5 billion for the first year, as in the original bill), and a big $18.3 billion tax-relief package directed at low-income working parents. Ron Haskins, chief minority staffer on the House Ways and Means Committee, called it a major defeat for the day-care lobby. But Representative Gus Hawkins (D.-Calif.), a leading supporter of ABC, said that while the funding was inadequate, "it was a beachhead we may be able to use in the future." NAEYC was jubilant.

The reality, in other words, was ambiguous. The tax-relief portion of the bill, which would target direct aid to working parents with children, was a major gain for an emerging conservative/neoliberal coalition. It addressed the real causes of the "child-care crisis"—economic pressure on families—in a way which rewarded positive values like work and marriage. On the other hand, the ABC portion of the bill *was* a beachhead. It established (limited) federal regulation of day care, as well as the essentials of an infrastructure, something the lobbyists sought above all else; and it set no limits on future authorizations. The day-care lobby retained a toehold from which to fight.

Still, by failing to push through a truly massive new program, the lobby had lost the first round in a trial of strength which it itself had sought. Worse, the fight, instead of ensuring a quick and easy victory through Republican defections, as planned, had instead split the Democrats and humiliated the activists. The iron triangle of policy elites inside and outside government had been bent, and had been seen to be bent.

Thus was the 1987–90 effort to use child care to spearhead a revanche of the Great Society thwarted by new political realities. Nor was the emerging coalition between (some) Democrats and Republicans limited to child-care legislation. Terms like "new paradigm" and "new consensus" had been first applied to welfare reform and workfare proposals in 1987, as intellectuals and politicians once in the forefront of the social revolutions of the 60's began to realize that Ozzie and Harriet may have had more to offer—and big government less—than they once believed. Thus, a Left-liberal like Alan Wolfe, who had in the past looked to the Marxist transformation of society, could now be found gently defending the family and civil society in his book, *Whose Keeper?*, while an old child-care stalwart like Edward Zigler of Yale could be seen advocating child allowances and parental choice as an alternative to the intrusive provisions of ABC.

Two separate and radically divergent reports, which came out only twelve months apart, showed how quickly the new consensus took shape. In the summer of 1990, the National Research Council (NRC) issued *Who Cares for America's Children? Child-Care Policy for the 1990's.* The NRC report was a typical product of the iron triangle. It acknowledged that parents prefer informal family day care to center care. It accepted that center care in particular was beset by recurring problems of too high costs, too little flexibility and convenience, too many difficulties in meeting the needs of infants, older schoolchildren, and the handicapped, too many sick children, too low wages, and too high turnover. It also warned that, for centers to help those children to whom they *were* suited, they had to offer consistent and loving care provided by an ample staff of highly trained and personally devoted teachers. Yet it confessed that in order to ensure such care, centers would have to pay teachers more while charging parents less.

Having described a form of child care which clearly had little to offer anybody except social-service agencies in search of compensatory care for neglected ghetto children and a few relatively affluent parents in search of a nice nursery school for their preschoolers, the NRC panel glibly concluded that the government, ideally, ought to sponsor day care as the solution to the ills of America's parents and children.

The NRC's one sensible recommendation was parental leave to care for infants, a policy which has had unexpectedly benign effects in Scandinavia (where paid leave ranges from six months to eighteen months in duration). Its recommendations for older children were simply silly. In the absence of even enough money to subsidize center care of reasonable, much less superior, quality, the NRC proposed that the government enact regulations which would forbid parents to use "bad" care, regardless of cost or convenience. Worse, it had the gall to name in-formal family day care—cheap, flexible, good, and preferred by parents—as one of the kinds of bad care that should be denied subsidy. It also recommended that the government encourage more parents to work, so that the problem for which it had no solution could grow rather than shrink! In short, the NRC was an object lesson in the construction of a perfect policy cul-de-sac.

The very next summer, in 1991, the National Commission on Children, chaired by Senator John D. Rockefeller IV (D.-W.Va.), released its own report. Significantly titled *Beyond Rhetoric: A New American Agenda for Children and Families*, it appeared to be worlds away from the NRC report. The commission's members came from across the policy spectrum, from Marian Wright Edelman of the Children's Defense Fund on the Left to Allan Carlson of the Rockford Institute on the Right. The report claimed that its recommendations (with the important exception of national health insurance) were, amazingly, adopted unanimously.

A "populist" answer to the iron-triangle thinking of the NRC, the Rockefeller report got things right from the beginning. It correctly identified the basic problem as structural changes in the family exacerbated by economic stagnation; the proper object of policy as the child; and the proper solution as the restoration of the intact nuclear family and an ethics of parental responsibility. It talked hard talk about crime, teenage pregnancy, divorce, and the importance of parents.

That being said, many of the Rockefeller report's recommendations were as dreamy as anything the iron triangle ever thought up. They were populist, to be sure, but in the wrong way. Were day-care teachers, social workers, and schoolteachers paid too little? The answer was vapid: "They will be paid more when we value them more." Were American families felled by crushing hospital bills? The answer was simple: enact national health insurance. The liberals on the commission had clearly not read the economic literature on care-giving (especially the meticulous work of Victor Fuchs on the structural forces depressing day-care wages), nor had they, evidently, heard the news from Scandinavia and Eastern Europe that political will is no match for economic reality.

There was a further problem. Despite its sensible support for a $1,000 tax credit for each child, the liberal majority on the Rockefeller commission did not really come out in favor of making it easier for parents to choose to care for their own children. It recommended more funding of the 1990 child-care programs, effectively subsidizing working parents at the expense of a greater tax burden on stay-at-home parents.

Most seriously of all, some of the Rockefeller provisions would, despite the pro-family rhetoric, discourage marriage and work. Under the influence of Marian Wright Edelman, for example, the commission proposed that the government pay single mothers who could not collect support from the child's father. What it did not mention was that such a proposal would amount to a back-door welfare increase of nearly 40 percent for an unmarried welfare mother of two, who would receive a $2,870-to-$4,500 annual rise in income as opposed to the $2,550 a poor working two-parent family with two children would get from the earned-income tax credit and child credit combined.

In short, if the Rockefeller report understood the problem, when it came to concrete solutions it fell back on too many of the same old impracticalities and misguided incentives. It is not hard to see why. As Professor William Galston put it,

For decades, the revolution in the American family evoked a polarized reaction: liberals talked about structural economic pressures facing families and avoided issues of personal conduct, and conservatives did just the reverse. Liberals habitually reached for bureaucratic responses, even when they were counterproductive, and conservatives reflexively rejected government programs even when they would work.

The new consensus had finally asked the right questions, then, about what was wrong with the family, and had even come to the right conclusions about the policy goal. For the first time in 30 years, members of the Democratic policy elite had broken silence on the consequences of the reckless social experiments of the 60's and 70's, and joined with conservatives and Republicans to forge, in Galston's words, "a non-bureaucratic, choice-based public activism" free of the "frequently cumbersome and intrusive institutions of the welfare state."

But the struggle to define this new public activism has only begun, and (as the example of the Rockefeller report suggests) many are the battles to be fought—especially over the exact role of government—before anything like a functioning policy can be put in place. Already there are signs that the intra-party Democratic revolt may be in danger, as the current recession encourages dreams of a return to government handouts. One can only hope that in the ensuing debate, everyone concerned remembers that the *proper* role of government is not to hinder but to support, wherever possible, the restoration of the functioning family.

39

New Start for Head Start

Douglas J. Besharov

This article summarizes the results of research on the effectiveness of various approaches to enriching the preschool experiences of disadvantaged children. The long- and short-term benefits of the Head Start program are contrasted to the long-term benefits of other programs. Suggestions for improving the long-term effects of Head Start are offered.

Exercises to Guide Your Reading

1. Identify the strengths and weaknesses of the Head Start program.
2. Explain how various social problems may undercut the effectiveness of Head Start.
3. Describe the major features of the "two-generation" approach to interventions for at-risk children.
4. Discuss the need for programs like those described, and evaluate the extent to which limited funding undermines program successes. Compare your conclusions to the conclusions of Reading 33.

Head Start, the federal government's early childhood development program for low-income children, is one of the nation's most popular antipoverty programs. In 1980, President Carter praised it as "a program that works"; President Reagan included Head Start in the "safety net"; and President Bush has almost doubled its funding.

Politicians of both parties are now calling for further increases in the number of children served. Last year, under the leadership of Senator Edward Kennedy, the Senate Committee on Labor and Human Resources voted to make Head Start an "entitlement" for all poor children, and President Bush recently proposed a $600 million increase that would give almost all eligible children at least one year of Head Start. In a January 31 debate among candidates for the Demo-cratic presidential nomination, several of the contenders indicated that they would go farther than the president had in his January budget message. "He offered $500 [sic] million [to fund Head Start]," Governor Bill Clinton said. "I'd offer $5 billion in the first year." Clinton also said he would design incentives for states to put additional funds into preschool programs. Senator Harkin indicated that he would expand the program beyond Bush's proposal and include three-year-olds at a cost of another "$2 to $3 billion." Senator Bob Kerrey added that he thought all of the Democratic candidates "support fully funding Head Start," a clear criticism of the president's more limited approach.

Ironically, this latest support for further expansions comes just as a growing number

Reprinted by permission of *The American Enterprise*. March–April 1992. pp. 52–59.

of experts are concluding that to be effective against deep-seated patterns of intergenerational family poverty, the array of Head Start services needs to be enriched before the number of children it serves is increased. The experts have a clear agenda for reform: to reach disadvantaged children much earlier with more-intensive developmental and health services; to help low-income parents nurture and teach their own children; and to encourage unemployed parents to work or continue their education. Small-scale demonstration projects have been started to test these ideas, but they do not go far enough. Unfortunately, given the costs of a new approach involving parents and children, it may be easier for politicians to continue to expand the number of children served by existing Head Start programs and to support limited demonstration projects than to change Head Start's fundamental character. The critical point, however, is that involving parents as well as children in a new approach will do more to improve children's futures because it will also give their parents a chance for a new start in life.

MIXED RESEARCH FINDINGS

The public believes that Head Start "works," but the professional view of the program is decidedly more mixed. Among knowledgeable observers, there is a growing consensus that the program is not nearly as effective as it could be.

Head Start began in 1965 as a six-week experiment in using child development services to help fight the original War on Poverty. It quickly became a year-round, though not full-year, program. It now serves about 600,000 children, most of whom are four years old, at an annual cost of almost $2 billion.

Head Start's impact on the immediate well-being of disadvantaged children is unambiguously impressive. "Children's health is improved through the program; immunization rates are better; participants have a better diet, better dental health, better ac-

cess to health and social services; their self-esteem and cognitive abilities are improved; parents are educated and become involved as both volunteers and employees," according to Milton Kotelchuck and Julius B. Richmond, writing in the journal of the American Academy of Pediatrics.

These are important gains, but Head Start's popularity is based on the widespread impression that it permanently lifts poor children out of poverty by improving their learning ability and school performance. Unfortunately, the evidence on this score is disappointing.

Claims that Head Start works stem largely from widely publicized research conducted at the Perry Preschool Project of Ypsilanti, Michigan. In the early 1960s, researchers began tracking 123 three- and four-year-old children enrolled in this program for two and a half hours a day, five days a week (for either one or two years). The program was reinforced by teacher visits to the home.

Following the children through their teen years, the Ypsilanti researchers found that children who had this preschool experience fared much better than those in a control group of children who had not. On a test of functional competency in adult education courses, those who had gone through the program were over 50 percent more likely to score at or above the national average than those in the control group. What is more important, compared to the control group, employment and postsecondary education rates were almost double, the high school graduation rate was almost one-third higher, teenage pregnancy rates were almost half, and arrest rates were 40 percent lower. A small number of other research projects have also been conducted. They report similar, though not as spectacular, success.

Lost in the publicity surrounding this research, however, is the fact that it is based almost entirely on non-Head Start programs. Neither the Perry Preschool nor most of the other carefully evaluated preschool programs were part of Head Start. The evaluated preschools were invariably better funded and (unlike Head Start) had more professionals on the staff. Head Start is a distinctly low-budget operation, spending, for example, about 60 percent less per child than did the Perry Preschool. And even though Head Start programs have a commitment to parent involvement, the Perry Preschool and many other research-oriented programs tended to spend much more time working with parents. Indeed, the final report of the Cornell Consortium for Longitudinal Studies, one of the other major research projects on the subject, specifically warned that "caution must be exercised in making generalizations [about its findings] to Head Start."

When researchers study actual Head Start programs, the findings are less impressive. The most complete review of past Head Start research was conducted for the Department of Health and Human Services (HHS) in 1985. After reviewing the results of 210 Head Start research projects, the study found that the educational and social gains registered by Head Start children disappeared within two years. The study reported that "one year after Head Start, the differences between Head Start and non-Head Start children on achievement and school readiness tests continued to be in the educationally meaningful range, but the two groups scored at about the same level on intelligence tests. By the end of the second year, there were no educationally meaningful differences."

The report did find a tendency for Head Start graduates to be "less likely to fail a grade in school or to be assigned to special education classes than children who did not attend. However, this finding is based on very few studies."

This conclusion reinforces the results of a 1969 Westinghouse study that found few long-term gains from Head Start participation. That study was widely criticized on methodological grounds, and its weaknesses allowed Head Start's supporters to overlook its critical findings. Initially, some Head Start advocates also tried to discredit the 1985 HHS study by criticizing its methodology, but the inability of research studies to detect long-term gains among Head Start students undercuts this argument. Moreover, in private even its staunchest advocates acknowledge that Head Start has serious shortcomings that often prevent it from making a lasting impact on disadvantaged children.

These mixed findings from a handful of studies—there has been surprisingly little research—do not mean that Head Start funding should be cut. With the poverty rate for children continuing at unacceptably high levels, Head Start's short-term benefits alone justify its continuation. These ambiguous research findings, however, do signal a need to modify the program to reflect what has been learned in the past quarter-century.

UNREASONABLE EXPECTATIONS

Social and academic advances do not come automatically with a child's enrollment in a preschool program, no matter how good the program is. Even the much-touted Perry Preschool had what can only be described as mixed success in breaking deep-seated patterns of poverty and welfare dependency. The high school graduation rate of enrollees was almost one-third higher, but 33 percent of the program group still failed to graduate. Teenage pregnancy rates were almost half, but there were still 64 pregnancies per 100 girls. And AFDC (Aid to Families with Dependent Children) rates were more than one-third lower, but 18 percent of the 19-year-olds were already on welfare.

Head Start, like all preschool programs, can do only so much to help children caught in a web of social and familial dysfunction. It is unrealistic to expect the Head Start experience—about four hours a day for about eight months of one year—to overcome such powerful negative experiences as inadequate nutrition, parental drug abuse, domestic or neighborhood violence, and a host of other psychological or physical degradations. As the blue-ribbon Advisory Panel for the Head Start Evaluation Design Project warned: "Policymakers and the general public should not be oversold that early education and intervention programs such as

Head Start, even when implemented in a high-quality fashion, are some kind of panacea that succeed [sic] even in the absence of appropriate ongoing child and family support."

Moreover, Head Start is serving an increasingly troubled part of the poverty population. Twenty-six years ago when Head Start was established, there were not as many working mothers, so it tended to serve the full spectrum of poor families. But over the years, as more mothers with preschoolers have entered the labor force and therefore need full-time child care, Head Start's part-time nature has made it an unrealistic option for relatively well-functioning parents. In 1972, one-third of all Head Start programs operated full-day; today the proportion is 15 percent. Many Head Start programs have, in effect, become child-care ghettos for poor mothers who collect AFDC rather than work. About 68 percent of all Head Start children are now on AFDC, a figure that has climbed steadily over the years.

Parental substance abuse has become a particularly serious problem for Head Start programs. "One out of every five preschool children is affected in some way by substance abuse," according to a Head Start Bureau handbook for grantees. The Central Vermont Head Start/Family Foundations program reported that one-third to two-thirds of its families had substance abuse problems in the home, 40 percent of its mothers had their first child when they were teenagers, and 32 percent of the parents had no high school diploma or General Equivalency Diploma.

These social problems undercut Head Start's effectiveness. A recent Congressional Research Service [CRS] report described the "concern of Head Start administrators and program directors that the number of families with serious problems has increased in recent years and that these problems limit families in fully participating in Head Start." (Some programs reported that drug trafficking activities in some areas prevent teachers from making home visits.) The CRS survey

of Head Start programs found that substance abuse was the most serious problem facing families. Child abuse was second.

The powerful social and individual forces that combine to keep families in persistent poverty require broader, more intense intervention.

TWO-GENERATION PROGRAMS

Even though the intergenerational transmission of poverty has long been understood, most early childhood education programs have operated with the assumption that they could break deep-seated patterns of family poverty by working with the child alone, to give that child a "head start" in life. Now, many of those who work with disadvantaged children have concluded that to counteract these intergenerational forces, they must focus on the child and the parent.

"In the old days, we used to say, 'Give us children for a few hours a day, and we will save them.' Now we know that we have to work within the entire family context," says Wade Horn, the Commissioner of HHS's Administration for Children, Youth and Families. Anne Mitchell, of the Bank Street College of Education, put it this way: "Perhaps the most complete intervention we could design for at-risk young children and their families would be a comprehensive package that combines full-day, year-round early childhood programs (that are in the best senses both custodial and educational) with parent education/family support programs that have a strong employment training component."

The revised approach is called "two-generation programs," and it has three interrelated elements. The first is reaching disadvantaged children much earlier with more-intensive developmental services. Head Start and other early childhood education programs tend to focus on three- and four-year-olds, but by then, damage may already have been done.

From its earliest days, Head Start has attempted to reach younger children. In 1967, for example, the first Parent and Child Centers were established to provide instruction in the home on infant care and child development to parents of children under three and to refer parents to other forms of assistance. (In 1990, funding for these centers was doubled, and there are now 100 centers.)

Innovators are now experimenting with ways to involve two- and even one-year-olds in a richer and more diverse set of developmental activities, combined with counseling and education services for parents. One of the best known of these efforts is the independently funded Beethoven Project, located in Chicago's Robert Taylor Homes, which began serving families with children from birth through five years in 1986. The project, whose official title is the Center for Successful Child Development, provides counseling and education services for parents as well as developmental child care for infants and toddlers.

In 1988, Congress established the Comprehensive Child Development Program (CCDP), a five-year demonstration project loosely modeled on the Beethoven Project. Pregnant women and mothers with a child under the age of one were accepted into the program for up to five years. There are now 24 demonstration projects at various universities, health agencies, public schools, social service agencies, private agencies, and Head Start centers that, over the course of the demonstration, will serve a total of about 2,500 families.

The second element of two-generation programs is helping low-income parents to nurture and teach their own children. There is only so much that a child development program can do in the few hours that it has with a child. Early childhood educators are increasingly recognizing that they can leverage far more change in the lives of children if they can help parents become more effective nurturers and teachers. This is the concept underlying the project Even Start Family Literacy Programs, the Department of Education's literacy program for parents with children ages one through seven.

Funded in 1989, there are now 119 Even Start centers, with at least one in every state. As Even Start parents become literate, they are encouraged to support their children's learning.

Many local Head Start programs now provide instruction for parents in infant and child care, health care, and nutrition. Some also provide a range of more general support services for disadvantaged young parents who must deal with substance abuse, family health, mental health, domestic violence, housing, transportation, and legal problems. To assist these efforts, in 1991 the Head Start Bureau funded 32 substance abuse projects in local centers and 11 Family Support Projects for such problems as teenage pregnancy, homelessness, and family violence. The president's recent proposal contains funds for adult literacy programs for all Head Start centers.

Third, two-generation programs encourage unemployed parents to work or continue their education. Being a good parent requires a healthy degree of self-respect; without it, apprehension or depression can be so paralyzing that parents cannot care for themselves, let alone their children. And these days, with so many middle-class mothers working, self-respect—especially for single mothers—means being economically self-sufficient, or at least partially so.

To help single mothers who have poor job-related skills and little work experience, Head Start programs are providing, or arranging for, various self-sufficiency services, including literacy classes, employment counseling, job readiness services, and job training. Some Head Start programs are encouraging mothers to obtain work and job training under the Job Opportunities and Basic Skills (JOBS) program by providing full-day care. (Roughly half of all Head Start parents are eligible for this.)

Demonstration projects testing various approaches are also under way. Project New Chance, a 16-city research and demonstration project, seeks to increase the self-sufficiency of young mothers. Managed by the Manpower Demonstration Research Corporation and funded by private foundations and the Department of Labor, it provides young mothers (ages 16 to 22) with education, employment, and parenting skills programs, family planning and health services (including pediatric care), as well as on-site developmental child care. (The average age of the children in the 2,200 families being served is 18 months.)

The Head Start Bureau has also funded a number of demonstrations aimed at increasing the self-sufficiency of parents. The Comprehensive Child Development Programs assist parents and family members with prenatal care and referrals for education, vocational training, employment counseling, housing, and income support. Education is given in infant and child development, nutrition, health care, and parenting.

As part of a group of grants aimed at broadening the scope of services offered by Head Start, the Head Start Bureau created Family Service Centers, three-year projects that focus on the problems of substance abuse, unemployment, and illiteracy. In addition to providing literacy classes and referrals and support for substance-abuse treatment, many Centers provide actual job training to parents of Head Start children. Such training is often coordinated with the Job Training Partnership Act (JTPA) or Job

Opportunities and Basic Skills (JOBS) training programs. Other centers provide only classes in job-searching skills or employment referral services.

A PROJECT NEW START?

The impetus for two-generation programming comes from local service providers, child advocacy groups, and federal administrators who see first-hand the inability of current Head Start services to break patterns of deep-seated poverty. No one knows, however, whether these kinds of parent-oriented services will work any more effectively than the basic Head Start model. To find out, we will need a long-term effort to develop and test alternative program designs—a nationwide demonstration whose scope and status would be equal to the original Head Start project—a "Project New Start," if you will.

Such a demonstration would be expensive and difficult to mount, but ignoring Head Start's problems—and failing to pursue the promise of two-generation programs—would be unfair to the disadvantaged children and families Head Start is meant to serve. They deserve the best program we can deliver.

40

The Day-Care Reform Juggernaut

Ron Haskins and Hank Brown

This article questions the need for increased government involvement in the child care system. The authors argue that the most significant economic problem associated with day care is the absence of adequate tax exemptions for minor dependents. Restoring the tax deduction for children to the level of prior decades is seen as the best way to solve the child care problem.

Exercises to Guide Your Reading

1. List the authors' objections to the Act for Better Child Care.
2. Discuss the pro's and con's of increased federal regulation of the day care system.
3. Identify the "interest groups" that would be produced by the proposed regulations.
4. Compare and contrast this analysis with that in Reading 34.

One of the hottest issues now on the Washington social policy agenda is day care. There is a near-consensus that something should be done; the danger is that conservatives and moderates will be seduced into supporting a liberal initiative that is a guaranteed disaster.

Day care is a problem for many mothers, in part because of social changes that have seen more single, full-, and part-time working mothers than ever before. These make such traditional solutions as having relatives or friends watch the kids more difficult. But the "child-care crisis" is in fact part of a far larger problem: raising children is expensive, whether you use day care or not. Those who focus their efforts on day care at the expense of other needs of children and parents are pushing a very particular horse.

Stripped of rhetoric, "child care," as enshrined in the Democrats' Act for Better Child Care (ABC), boils down to the familiar liberal approach to social problems: intervene directly in the market, put lots of restrictions on the type of service and who can provide it (thus greatly increasing the cost to the point where many families can no longer afford the service), then dole out federal cash in subsidies so that millions of families become dependent on the government. As Aaron Wildavsky notes, Democrats use spending to create constituents.

Now, many conservative constituents argue that day care is intrinsically inferior to home care. But Congress is not that receptive to the arguments of social conservatives. It will take the position that it should not engage in social engineering, "forcing" women out of the job market. But the "child-care" initiatives are also social engineering,

Reprinted by permission of *National Review.* March 10, 1989. pp. 40–41.

for they assume 1) that day care per se is the main problem, 2) that the Federal Government is better equipped than parents to determine the appropriate type and cost of day care, and 3) that the best type happens to be professional day care—the most expensive kind.

It's not too late to avoid the creation of yet another entitlement, if we can shift the ground from rhetoric to facts. Last year, Congress heard a thousand anecdotes about families that could not find the kind of care they wanted; of course, Congress can find an anecdote to support any point of view on any social problem. But if there is a supply *crisis*, prices should be going up. Survey data make it plain that prices have risen quite modestly in the past decade, about 8 percent. For most families, day care is at most a nagging problem, not a crisis.

Another false claim about cost, one slavishly repeated in the media, is the statement that day care currently costs $3,000 a year per child, more in many populous areas. In fact, national surveys show that the average American family with a working mother spends about $1,400 per year on care. Even if the families that get free care from relatives (the grandmothers the regulators are so eager to replace with expensive professionals) are eliminated from the calculations, and if only families with a mother who works full-time are included, the average expenditure is still only about $2,100 per year.

To be fair, this is still a considerable expense for some families. Sandra Hofferth, an analyst at the Urban Institute in Washington, D.C., estimates that single, black mothers with earnings below the poverty line pay an astounding 26 percent of their earnings for child care: the national average is about 10 percent.

But the truth is, these figures are so high because Congress goes in for disguised social engineering in the matter of child care—through the tax code. By allowing the personal income-tax exemption, and the deductions for dependents to be virtually wiped out by inflation, we have instituted de facto fiscal discrimination against *everyone* with

TABLE 1. Personal Exemptions for a Family of Four in 1987 Dollars

1912	45,977
1931	32,090
1940	22,764
1945	11,321
1984	4,376
1987	7,600

children, whether the mother is single or married, working or at home.

In his budget, President Bush has begun to restore these deductions, at least for the poorest families; we can let them keep their money so that they can raise their children the way they think best. That's a genuine solution to what is the real problem, namely, the tax on children.

Is there, then, any remaining reason to regulate day care? Fiery, anecdotal congressional testimony tells us that unregulated care isn't safe. But the biggest study ever to address the safety of unregulated care was conducted in 1981 by Abt Research Associates and Stanford Research Associates. Based on a comparison of nearly eight hundred regulated and unregulated day-care homes in Philadelphia, San Antonio, and Los Angeles, the authors were "consistently impressed" by the quality of care and concluded that it was "stable, warm, and stimulating," that it "cater[ed] successfully to the developmentally appropriate needs of the children in care," and that parents who used unregulated care were highly satisfied.

So regulation addresses a problem that has been wildly exaggerated. But it goes on to create its own problem—increased costs. Virtually everyone agrees that imposing regulatory requirements, whether directly or through the states, will bring dramatic cost increases. Researchers at the University of North Carolina recently estimated that standards such as those sure to result from federal regulation will nearly double the cost of care. This is a surprisingly frank assessment, given the researchers' strong support for federal regulation: many families will not be able to bear the additional costs and will therefore need government assistance.

But in an era of $150-billion budget deficits, that government assistance just won't be forthcoming in the required amounts. Currently, about four million children, under age five and with working mothers, receive paid care, at an average cost of $42 per week. The North Carolina study estimated that the cost of "quality" care would average about $100 per week; if this increase is applied only to those four million children, the added cost is $12 billion, on top of the nearly $7 billion the government already spends on day care. With the S&L and nuclear clean-up crises, the government can't pick up that bill.

So who will? Everyone with children in day care will pay more, but poor families will pay a much higher proportion of their incomes. Sandra Hofferth's poor urban mothers will have to pay *more* than 26 percent of their incomes, increasing an already substantial disincentive to work. In other words, the proposed regulations hit the neediest hardest.

Given the dubious benefits and costs of regulation, why are so many so intent on establishing federal regulations? No doubt, some are convinced that their actions will increase children's well being. But there are other reasons, having more to do with the self-interest of those advocating regulation and subsidies than with children's safety.

Costs jump dramatically when regulations are imposed because day-care facilities must then hire more workers—and those workers must be more like teachers than nannies because they must meet bureaucratic standards of quality (presumably ensuring quality day care the way we've ensured quality education). Thus, "child-care specialists" will be influential in the provision of day care; they're sure to guard the entitlement program better than grandmothers. New special interest group number one.

And regulation doesn't work without enforcement; with at least 1.5 million day-care homes and forty thousand centers to be reg-

ulated, we can expect a lot of oversight—and further costs, and a burgeoning, "necessary," bureaucracy. New special interest group number two.

In addition, the increased costs make government subsidies necessary. As government creates those subsidies through legislation such as the ABC bill, it creates yet another large block of voters with an interest in maintaining yet another federal program and the politicians who support it. And mothers are very hard to attack as a special interest group. Number three.

Though ABC failed last year, liberals did make surreptitious progress toward their day-care objectives under the guise of welfare reform. Strong regulatory provisions were a part of the welfare bill until a few days before final enactment; conflicts between Democrats from various House committees allowed Ways and Means Republicans to mute the call for federal regulation. But one significant provision still crept in: welfare mothers who find work and so escape welfare now get one year of both day care and health insurance, so that losing these benefits will not be a disincentive to work. This creates an inequity Congress is sure to try to fix: surely a woman who worked to stay off welfare, even though she was as deserving as another who did not, should be entitled to that same free year?

When this refrain, along with the others we've mentioned, is heard in Congress this month, moderates and conservatives, led by President Bush, should insist that major new grant money for day care, all-encompassing federal day-care regulation, and other broad disruptions of the market are unacceptable. If Congress then passes such measures, a presidential veto could almost certainly be sustained.

Those of us concerned about the real problem should also support the President's initiative: to increase the deduction for dependent children, at least for low-income families. This addresses many of the issues on the national social policy agenda: 1) it's better than raising the minimum wage because it focuses benefits on low-income families without increasing the cost of labor and thus throwing out of work the very people it intends to help; 2) it's better than heavy-handed regulation of the day-care market because it allows families rather than bureaucrats to control day-care expenditures (in terms both of how much to spend and what sort of program in which to place children) while simultaneously not discriminating against low-income working families that choose to raise their children at home; 3) it's better than day-care subsidies or vouchers because all the money spent on the "program" goes directly to benefit those who need it—none is wasted on handling by bureaucrats; and 4) it's better than an expanded welfare program because it makes work more attractive by effectively increasing wages.

Most important of all, the Bush initiative obviates the need for federal day-care regulation by leaving responsibility and control in the hands of those who best know the needs of children and working mothers: the mothers, and fathers, themselves. By so doing, it avoids one of the greatest hoaxes of modern social legislation: that families can safely yield yet another responsibility to big government.

41

A Fresh Start on Welfare Reform

Barbara R. Bergmann

This article advocates welfare reform based on the principle of parental responsibility. The author identifies the major weaknesses of the current child support
payment system and then describes an experimental Wisconsin program. The
potential problems and the impact of the new system are addressed. The author
concludes that with these recommended changes in child support, the welfare
rolls would be significantly reduced, fewer children would live in poverty, and
more women would be gainfully employed.

Exercises to Guide Your Reading

1. List data on the current average child support awards, and compare them to
the actual child support payments made.
2. Identify major innovative features of the Wisconsin experiment.
3. Summarize the weaknesses of the current child support system.
4. Evaluate Bergmann's proposal in light of arguments about the economic situation of American families presented in Chapter 8.

There is good news on the welfare reform
front. The frustrating, two-decade-long
search for welfare reform may be coming to
a successful conclusion. At last, a reform is
in the works that will reduce poverty among
single mothers, get them into the mainstream, and eventually reduce the burden
on the taxpayers. The key idea, in Senator
Daniel Patrick Moynihan's words, is "parental responsibility."

Parental responsibility translates into two
prescriptions: (1) Biological parents who live
apart from their children will have to contribute a share of whatever incomes they
have for child-support payments; (2) Single
parents with custody of their children will
be put in the position of wanting and being
able to take substantial jobs to support

themselves and to share in providing the
support of their offspring.

Under a parental responsibility system,
beefed-up, reliable child-support payments
would take the place of traditional welfare
payments. But there is more going on here
than the substitution of one pot of dollars
for another. There are crucial differences
between welfare and child support. One obvious difference is that all welfare payments
come from the taxpayers, while child-support payments come mostly from the absent
parent.

A second difference is that welfare payments are lowered or lost when a single
mother works. Child-support payments can
be administered so as to continue when she
works, whatever her earnings. So child sup-

Reprinted by permission of *Challenge*. November–December 1987. pp. 44–50.

port would not deter work, as welfare does. An income consisting of the mother's wages *plus* the father's child-support payments would put many single mothers above the poverty line.

There are, of course, legitimate and serious questions about the "parental responsibility" agenda. Don't most AFDC (Aid to Families with Dependent Children) children have fathers who are poor or are teenagers, or whose identity or whereabouts is unknown? Are there jobs for single mothers? What kind of jobs will they be? How about the right of a mother to stay home with her kids? Those backing the new system believe they have good answers for all of those questions.

Senator Moynihan's new bill takes us several valuable steps in the direction of a parental responsibility reform. But the action is by no means confined to the nation's capital, or to those states where welfare mothers are being helped to get jobs. The real frontier is in the Wisconsin state capital, Madison, at the University of Wisconsin's Institute for Research on Poverty. A talented, energetic, and pragmatic group from the Institute, led by Professor Irwin Garfinkel, is teaming up with the forward-looking elements in the Wisconsin state government to mount a tryout for some key elements of the new system.

A NEW DEAL ON CHILD SUPPORT

The centerpiece of the parental responsibility system is a radically new child-support regime, with new ways of deciding what child-support payments should be, collecting the payments, and getting them delivered to the parent taking care of the child. The system envisaged by the Wisconsin group de-emphasizes the role of court proceedings, judges, and lawyers. Instead it relies on what is essentially a tax-and-transfer system run by administrators. It promises to collect and transmit payments from the absent parent to the custodial parent in a timely and reliable way.

For those cases where, for whatever reason, payments collected by the state from the absent parent are less than a guaranteed amount set by statute, the state would make up the difference. Thus, the new system would provide the child of a single parent a guarantee of a minimum child-support payment, which will not be lost if the single parent works. The minimum payment for a child's expenses guaranteed by the state would cover the cases where the father of the child had low income or could not be found.

Under the new system, employers would withhold child-support payments from the paychecks of all parents—fathers or mothers—who live apart from their children. Withholding child support from paychecks would be as routine and nonstigmatized as the withholding of federal and state income taxes. Employers would forward the money to the state, and the parent bringing up the child would get a monthly child-support check from the state. By contrast, under current practice in most states, the absent parent is expected to make payments on his or her own initiative directly to the parent with the child. Withholding only starts after delinquency, and most often not even then.

In place of a case-by-case determination of what the child-support payment should be, the Wisconsin idea is to levy for child support a uniform percentage of the absent parent's income. An absent parent of one child would pay 17 percent of pretax income, with the percentage rising in cases involving more children (see Table 1). The minimum payment to be received by a one-child family has been set at $3,000 per year.

Currently in most states, a judge sets child-support payments at some fixed amount, and it requires a court proceeding to get that changed. But payments can be due for 18 years or longer, and inflation erodes the purchasing power of fixed awards. The Wisconsin group's idea is that absent parents should pay a percentage of their current income. So the support obligation in terms of

TABLE 1. Child Support System Under Trial in Wisconsin

Number of Children	Assessment for Child Support on Pre-Tax Income of Absent Parent	Minimum Child Support Guaranteed by State*
1	17%	$3,000
2	25	3,500
3	29	4,000
4	31	4,500
5 or more	34	5,000

*The minima will be escalated by the Consumer Price Index.

dollars would grow as earnings of the absent parent grow, either because of inflation or because of individual advancement.

The amount of child support awarded under the Wisconsin group's formula does not depend on the income of the custodial parent getting the payment, only on the income of the parent making the payment. If a custodial parent's earnings rise, perhaps because she has worked more hours or taken a better job, the child-support payment does not go down.

For those custodial parents who can only expect to get jobs with relatively low wages, the "zero taxation" on child support as earnings rise provides the motivation to get a job and stay employed. The custodial parent may receive both wages and child support. Under the current welfare system, women who find jobs with even modest paychecks lose welfare money, so getting a low-wage job is pointless. Under the guaranteed-child-support system, even a low-wage job will be advantageous, because no child support will be lost.

In a small minority of cases, the Wisconsin formula would require that a man or woman with a modest income send substantial payments to a relatively affluent ex-spouse who has custody of the child. A carpenter making $25,000 whose child was in the custody of his ex-wife, a lawyer making $40,000, would have to send her $354 a

month. In an even more extreme example, a practical nurse earning $14,000 with a child in the custody of her ex-husband, a physician making $80,000, would be called on to make payments of $198 a month. In the vast majority of cases, however, child-support payments would flow from the household with the higher per-capita income to the household with the lower per-capita income.

The principle behind such a system is that anyone who parents a child, whatever his or her earning capacity, should share in the support of that child. When both parents live together with the child they both contribute to the upkeep of the child, in terms of cash and in terms of services. A parent living apart should continue to make contributions, as that parent would were the family together. Nevertheless, where the custodial parent is at the high end of the income scale, many people would feel that the Wisconsin formula should be altered to call for smaller payments on the part of the absent parent.

The Poverty Institute group led by Garfinkel is working with the state welfare agency and the state legislature to enact and put into practice a step-by-step approach to the new system. In Wisconsin the reforms will apply to all new divorces, separations, and out-of-wedlock births, not merely to the cases of those children who would otherwise be on AFDC. It will apply at all income levels, regardless of whether the parents had a long or a short relationship, in wedlock or outside it. Remarriage of either parent will not affect the child-support obligation. It will help women and children who are not on welfare remain off the rolls, and it will produce financial help for middle-income divorced women and their children.

Senator Moynihan's bill would establish some of the essential features of the Wisconsin group's system in all states, but it allows states to develop their own formulas. The courts would have to follow the state-developed formula on the size of awards in each case unless evidence were presented that the formula produced inappropriate results in a particular case. Moynihan's bill would also establish automatic wage withholding from an absent parent's salary as soon as an award is established.

PRESENT SYSTEM FAILS

The Wisconsin group's ideas on child-support reform seem radical. Is the system so broken that it needs so much fixing? A look at the current situation suggests that the answer is yes. Child support is now in the orbit of an archaic, overloaded, and haphazardly run judicial system, which does a horrendously poor job of setting payments and enforcing collection regularly. Many single mothers are forced to go on welfare, and the majority of single mothers get little or no help from the fathers of their children.

Judges in divorce cases have had considerable discretion as to whether to make a child-support award and as to the amount to be paid. The wide latitude given to judges has meant that many awards have been far below any reasonable standard. Some judges have seen fit to make awards that were almost jokes—$7 per week per child is one example.

In 1985, the average award in force was $2,220 per year, about $1,250 per child. That works out to $3.45 per child per day, certainly less than half of the amount an employed mother—with daycare fees to pay—would have to spend to keep a child fed, clothed, housed, and cared for, even at a poverty-level standard of living. After accounting for inflation, child-support awards in force in 1985 were actually smaller than those in force in 1978.

Low as awards were, actual collections were smaller still. Of the $10.9 billion due in child-support payments for 1985, only $7.2 billion was received. This is hardly surprising in a culture where payment delinquency is a way of life. Many of us fail to make payments we owe for our cars, our department store bills, our credit card purchases. The merchants to whom we owe money understand that collection is far from

automatic. They send us computerized bills reminding us to pay. When we miss payments they add on interest penalties, and send us letters containing threats that our credit ratings will suffer or our possessions will be seized. By contrast, parents owing child support have been expected to remind themselves faithfully to sit down and write a check each week or each month without the assistance of any of these reminders, penalties, or threats.

Where the father has been delinquent, the mother has had to hire an attorney to try to get the court system to compel him to pay. Being short of funds, she may not be able to do that. At best, she has to wait months for a court hearing of the case. Postponements, nonappearances, excuses, promises to do better string the process out. A father, brought in for a hearing before a judge after months or even years of delinquency, may make partial restitution and promises of regular payment. However, it is not unusual for him to make a payment or two, but thereafter cease paying anything, starting the whole cycle again.

After one or two experiences with the expense, aggravation, and trouble of hauling a delinquent before a judge, and with the uselessness of doing so, many mothers simply give up on the process. Where the mother and father live in different states the problems are compounded. A new child-support system that was national in scope would cut through this morass.

CAN FATHERS PAY?

The failure to obtain child support from many absent fathers has been rationalized on two grounds. One argument commonly given is that the fathers who pay little or no child support are themselves poor and are simply unable to pay anything. Another is that the fathers of many children are unknown. It is, of course, true that some fathers are nonemployed teenagers, others are disabled, and still others have dropped out of sight. However, researchers have found that in a majority of cases, fathers could pay.

Absent fathers who are divorced (the majority of absent fathers) are not on average poorer than other men. Their average income is about equal to the average income of all male wage earners. A study of divorced couples by Martha Hill of the University of Michigan showed that only in 10 percent of the cases where the mother was in poverty was the father also in poverty. Only 2.2 percent of ex-husbands would have become poor if they had been forced to share their incomes with their ex-wives and children so as to equalize living standards in the two households. Looking at the fathers of children on AFDC, a number of studies done in the 1979–80 period placed their average income at about $11,000.

Robert Lerman's recent study found that about 70 percent of black unwed fathers aged 19 to 26 lived above the poverty line, as did 80 percent of young, white unwed fathers.... Of those above the poverty line, 42 percent paid no child support whatever. Better enforcement procedures would certainly garner more support for these young men's children. Among young unwed fathers who are poor, about a quarter do pay modest amounts, and others might do so too.

The difficulty of deciding whether a man is or is not the father of a certain child has also been exaggerated. Advances in genetics have produced tests of paternity whose probability of error are less than one in a billion. These scientific advances should make elaborate judicial proceedings unnecessary. But the formal establishment of paternity is still conducted in an archaic court setting, with lawyers, a judge, and all the time-consuming and expensive trappings of a trial. As a result, social welfare agencies make little effort to establish legal paternity in cases where the father of a baby is a teenager. However, most teenage fathers will in a few years be prime-age workers, and almost all of them will have incomes out of which some support could be paid.

Senator Moynihan's bill will encourage states to collect fathers' Social Security numbers in all births. It will penalize states by denying them federal funds if they lag in establishing formal paternity. These incentives may lead to a streamlining of procedures for establishing paternity.

PUNITIVE TO POOR BLACKS?

As time goes on, fewer fathers live with and support their children. This is true in all population groups, but is most advanced among blacks. Of all white families with children in 1984, 17 percent were maintained by single mothers. Among black families with children, 56 percent were maintained by single women.

The problem of race compounds the effects of marital instability. Past and present discrimination against blacks in schooling and employment makes their opportunities more constricted than those of white Americans. Black fathers are more likely to be unemployed than white fathers, and if employed are more likely to have an unstable job at low wages. Men without good jobs are less likely to get or remain married. Black mothers face both race and sex discrimination in employment.

Given all this, it is no wonder that black women are more likely than white women to find the pathetically low standard of living that welfare provides to be the best choice among the set of undesirable alternatives open to them. Going on welfare has been the only way that some black women have of becoming mothers and sustaining the lives of their children. Hispanic women also suffer disproportionately from these problems.

Replacing welfare by child support, even with the government guarantee feature, might reduce the flow of dollars from the government to the black community. Many who are left of center take the view that a move to "parental responsibility" would be oppressive to blacks. They have long argued that it is unjust and useless to pursue black men for child support payments and to push black mothers to leave off full-time mothering. They believe that until we can eradicate both racism and the effects of our racist past, welfare payments for impoverished black mothers and children are the least we can do. And the more generous the payments are, the better.

Whatever the ethical merits of that argument, it is unlikely that we could raise welfare benefits enough to get single mothers and their children—white as well as black—up to a decent standard of living. Only a paycheck for the single parent could do that. Currently, one state out of the fifty pays enough in benefits to put welfare families above the poverty line. Some states pay half that amount. Besides, the commonsense view that steeply higher welfare benefits would encourage more reliance on welfare is popular and not necessarily incorrect.

MORE WORK FOR MOTHERS?

The proponents of "parental responsibility" actively advocate jobs for single mothers. The level of child support they would guarantee is about two-thirds the level of current welfare benefits. It is intended as help with the expenses of children, not as the sole long-term support of a mother and children. Only by working a job would the single mother

have a decent standard. Would the mothers now on welfare want to work?

The change in incentives that occurs when child support becomes assured is illustrated in Figure 1. Even where the mother must give up a dollar of welfare for each dollar of child support she receives, the introduction of reliable child support—that will not be lost when she earns—improves her opportunities. It puts her in the position of receiving income from two sources, wages and child support. If welfare is abolished, the incentive to get a job is increased still further.

But pushing mothers to get jobs runs into opposition from some old-fashioned liberals who are attached to the idea that the best place for mothers is home full-time with their children. Accordingly, they are lukewarm at best to child-support reform, and favor more generous welfare benefits and welfare rules that would allow and encourage mothers to stay home and yet live more comfortably. These liberals ignore the changes in the economic position of women and in the attitudes toward mothers' employment. Prior to the 1970s, it might have been persuasively argued that being home with her children was the normal place for a good and caring mother. Forcing a mother to abandon the full-time care of her children

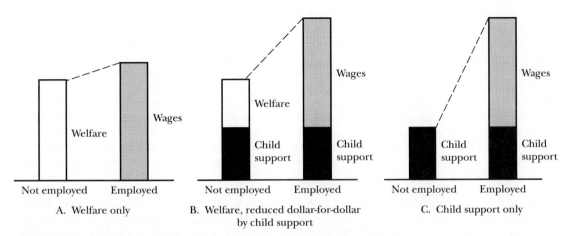

FIGURE 1. Income on and off the job under various support systems.

because she was poor and lacking a man's support would have been considered cruel.

Now, however, the full-time mother is the exception rather than the rule. More than half of the mothers with children less than a year old are in the labor force. The housewife-like position of the welfare mother no longer conforms to majority practice, even of mothers with husbands. The choice that so many mothers have made to take employment undermines the assumption that husbandless mothers can and should choose to devote themselves full-time to motherhood and homemaking, at public expense. The classic liberal position on welfare is neither wise nor politically feasible any longer, and does no service to the women and children involved.

Many conservatives are devoted to the tenet that "a woman's place is in the home," which would imply that husbandless mothers ought to be helped to stay home. However, conservatives dislike encouraging people to be dependent on the government, and dislike taxing the well-off to finance welfare. Further, conservatives tend to think badly of the behavior that got single mothers into their present fix—having out-of-wedlock pregnancies or failing to keep a husband happy.

So conservatives have come down on the side of work as the solution to the welfare problem. The more punitively inclined conservatives favor forcing welfare clients to "work off their benefits." The more sensible are thinking in terms of a modest work guarantee. In a notable *New Republic* article (July 7, 1986), Mickey Kaus advocated abolishing welfare, but guaranteeing anybody a job paying less than the minimum wage. Some version of this latter idea might have a great deal of merit. If a guarantee of a minimum-wage job (perhaps for all parents) were combined with child-support reform, it could keep children out of poverty in times of high unemployment.

Most discussions of welfare have failed to highlight the special need of single parents for jobs that are well-paying, since these parents are helping to support children. If most single parents were white men, good jobs would be open to them, and almost all of them would already be self-supporting, and above the poverty line. Both affirmative action and training for jobs that women have not traditionally held are needed to get single mothers into relatively well-paying jobs, to which few of them now have access.

Senator Moynihan's bill includes a Job Opportunities and Basic Skills (JOBS) Program to be run by the states. It would include remedial education, on-the-job training, help in job search, and community work experience.

ARE JOBS AVAILABLE?

When the suggestion is made that single mothers now on welfare (close to 4 million of them) would be better off in jobs, the objection is sometimes posed that jobs are not there for them to have. Those who argue in this way seem to be implying that most of the welfare mothers would be unable to get jobs, or would be displacing others, and so reforming welfare would simply increase the number of unemployed people by 4 million.

This objection does not take account of the fact that, historically, the labor force has grown continuously, and that except in unusual times, new entrants have been absorbed. As new supplies of labor become available, the economy adapts, and the number of jobs grows. The growth of jobs is not perfectly synchronized with the growth of the labor force, and there are periods of economic ill health when the growth of jobs ceases. But over the longer term the labor force and employment grow at roughly the same rate. In the decade of the 1970s, the labor force grew by 23 million, of whom 13 million were women, and the number of jobs grew about proportionately. There is no reason to believe that the entry into the job market of single mothers coming off welfare would pose any problems of absorption not posed by the growth of the labor force from other sources.

Naturally, the absorption into the labor force of single mothers currently on welfare will be eased if economic policy can successfully keep unemployment rates low. Low unemployment rates and healthy economic growth are desirable for this reason, and for many other reasons as well. However, the idea that we cannot reform welfare until we have a special guarantee that jobs are available for welfare mothers is erroneous. One might as well say that no new young people should be allowed to come into the labor force until new jobs have been earmarked for them.

There is a sense, however, in which the unemployment problem of single parents is more acute than that of other people. The consequences of a spell of unemployment are more severe for a single parent than for a spouse in a two-earner couple, or for a single person with no child to support. This suggests that the unemployment insurance system ought to be more generous to single parents in terms of size and duration of benefits.

A somewhat liberalized version of unemployment insurance could be made available to single parents. Like the regular unemployment insurance, it would be limited in duration, but would be available to single parents just entering the labor market. Adequate child support, plus their earnings, supplemented by unemployment insurance, would keep a high percentage of single parents out of poverty.

OTHER PARTS OF THE PACKAGE

There are two additional programs for single parents that should be part of the "parental responsibility" welfare-reform package—child care and health care. Single mothers need to have their children taken care of while they are looking for jobs, and while they are at work, and in many cases their paychecks could not stretch to pay for adequate care. Nor should they have to make do without the assurance of health care for themselves and their children.

Conservatives have been strongly resistant to government-sponsored day care, both because of their general opposition to most government programs, and because they have not wanted to facilitate mothers' jobs. They have opposed most extensions of government health programs. But they will have to choose between meaningful welfare reform and these traditional positions.

Senator Moynihan's bill would give some federal assistance to the states providing such benefits for nine months after welfare recipients get jobs. However, this is clearly inadequate, and would in short order leave large numbers of children at the low end of the scale, especially those with physical and behavioral problems, worse off than they are now.

A far better alternative would be to provide all children of single parents with day care at federal expense. How could the cost be justified? Single parents are bringing up a significant portion of the next generation of Americans in a situation that is socially and financially difficult. They will become more active in supporting themselves when the incentives are improved. But they need help from the rest of us in these respects, and nothing but direct government aid will give it to them.

Senator Kennedy has introduced a bill that would mandate employers to provide health care benefits for all workers. That would especially benefit less skilled women workers, whose employers have excluded them from health benefits. The alternative would be for the government to continue to pick up the bill, as it should do in any case for the unemployed.

ENDING THE POVERTY OF SINGLE PARENTS AND THEIR CHILDREN

We will never be able to solve the problem of supporting single mothers and their children just by tinkering with the present welfare system. The "parental responsibility" welfare reform will encourage single mothers to seek employment as other women do. It has the potential to raise the standard of living of single parents and their children, and at the same time reduce their dependence on public funds. It will create less spite toward single mothers than the present system and stigmatize them less. Larger and more regular child-support payments from fathers, subsidized child care and medical care for employed single parents, and better access to jobs with male-level wages are the cure for the welfare problem.

Single motherhood is not a passing phenomenon in our communities and in our economy. It will not be reduced in the foreseeable future by the preaching of good behavior. The children of single mothers are an increasing proportion of all of our children. At long last, we have proposals for a set of policies that would allow single mothers and their children to live in the mainstream of American life. If Moynihan and the Wisconsin vanguard can bring that off, they will have done something very fine indeed.

CHAPTER 10

Community

42

Segregation Forever?

Dan Gillmor and Stephen K. Doig

This article discusses the extent of residential racial segregation. The ratios of "racial isolation" for various metropolitan areas are presented, and urban counties are ranked on a "dissimilarity index." Historical trends in segregation are identified.

Exercises to Guide Your Reading

1. Define the following terms: rate of racial isolation; dissimilarity index; and white flight.
2. Summarize the study's findings.
3. List the causes of residential segregation.
4. Compare and discuss trends in integration in cities in the North and in the South and Southwest.

More than 25 years have passed since the Civil Rights Act of 1964 outlawed racial discrimination in housing. Yet data from the 1990 census show that black-white segregation is still a fact of life in America.

A study conducted last year by the Knight-Ridder newspaper chain compares levels of racial segregation in the 1980 and 1990 censuses. It shows that a decade of seeming progress for blacks in many economic and

Reprinted by permission of *American Demographics*. January 1992. pp. 48–51.

social areas has barely weakened residential segregation at the neighborhood level. In fact, black-white integration in the nation's 50 largest metropolitan areas has improved only slightly. Some cities fared much better than others, but several showed clear signs of increasing black segregation. The overall numbers are anything but a cause for celebration.

"For the foreseeable future, segregation is a way of life in residential living," says Benjamin Hooks, executive director of the National Association for the Advancement of Colored People. "There will be no dramatic change quickly, although there are some positive seeds being planted."

Several measures show that metropolitan Detroit regressed the most during the decade. Detroit does have pockets of integration today where none existed a generation ago, but the overall numbers show that large cities like Detroit are still divided by suburbanization and white flight. Some middle-class blacks have joined the exodus to the suburbs, but in most places this has only occurred in limited numbers.

The influx of Hispanics and Asians has dramatically altered the demographic composition of Florida, the Southwest, and parts of the West Coast. The study found apparent improvements during the 1980s in those areas because Asians moved into white areas while Hispanics (usually white) moved into black areas. But there was little evidence of any major change in black-white conditions.

"Americans don't have a common racial experience," says Gary Orfield of Harvard University. The study shows a "mixture of demographic change, suburban expansion, and black-Hispanic transition."

RACIAL ISOLATION

The Knight-Ridder study looked at two key measures of residential segregation for all census block groups. The first measure was "racial isolation." A person is racially isolated if at least 90 percent of the residents of her block group are of her racial group.

Thus, black Americans live in racial isolation if they live in block groups in which at least 90 percent of residents are also black. White residents of 90 percent white neighborhoods are also considered racially isolated.

The study's second measure ranks the most heavily populated urban counties according to a "dissimilarity index." This measure is a number between 0 and 100 that shows how well a county's black and white populations mix at the neighborhood level. A score of 0 means that every block group in the county has the same black-white ratio as does the county as a whole. A score of 100 means that every block group is either all black or all white.

Neither measure provides much evidence of social advancement during the 1980s. Thirty percent of black Americans live in virtually all-black neighborhoods, down from 34 percent in 1980. The number of blacks who live in racial isolation was 9.1 million in both censuses. And much of the remainder of the black population lives in neighborhoods that are still overwhelmingly black, although they did not reach the 90 percent level.

At least two of every three white Americans still live in essentially all-white neighborhoods. That level was down from nearly 75 percent in 1980, however, mainly due to integration of Asians into white neighborhoods.

Forty-four of the 50 largest metro areas did show some gains in integration during the 1980s. Most of these metros also progressed during the 1970s. In only two states (Michigan and Illinois) plus the District of Columbia do a majority of black residents live in racial isolation.

Racial isolation describes the majority of the black and white population in 7 of the nation's 50 largest metro areas: Chicago, Cleveland, Detroit, Memphis, St. Louis, Baltimore, and Philadelphia. Most of these are northern and industrial cities that have seen an epidemic of white flight to the suburbs. Chicago led the most isolated list for blacks, with 71 percent of the metro area's black population living in almost all-black neigh-

TABLE 1. Black Isolation (25 of the Top 50 Largest Metropolitan Areas, Ranked in Descending Order of Black Isolation, Percent of Blacks in Isolation in 1990, and Percentage Point Change in Isolation, 1980–90)

	Percent of Blacks in Isolation, Metro 1990	Percentage Point Change in Isolation, 1980–90
Chicago, IL	71%	−9.1
Cleveland, OH	67	0.4
Detroit, MI	61	4.0
Memphis, TN-AR-MS	58	−0.6
St. Louis, MO-IL	54	−3.3
Baltimore, MD	53	−5.4
Philadelphia, PA-NJ	53	0.1
Buffalo, NY	48	2.6
New Orleans, LA	47	−3.2
Kansas City, MO-KS	44	−6.0
Atlanta, GA	43	−6.1
Milwaukee, WI	42	−7.0
Newark, NJ	41	−2.6
Indianapolis, IN	39	−6.0
Washington, DC-MD-VA	37	−9.3
Cincinnati, OH-KY-IN	34	0.5
Fort Lauderdale-Hollywood-Pompano Beach, FL	34	−29.6
Miami-Hialeah, FL	3?	−8.3
Orlando, FL	32	−22.4
Charlotte-Gastonia-Rock Hill, NC-SC	32	−0.9
Pittsburgh, PA	32	−2.4
New York, NY	31	3.0
Nashville, TN	30	−4.6
Houston, TX	30	−19.5
Tampa-St. Petersburg-Clearwater, FL	30	−11.0
Average for 50 metros	37	−6.7

Note: "Isolation" is defined as living in a block group that is at least 90 percent of the same race. The percentage point change columns show change since 1980: for example, Chicago's 71 percent black isolation has dropped 9.1 points since 1980, when it was 80 percent. These are metropolitan areas, not the central city. Thus, Washington, D.C., shows relatively low isolation as a metro, even though within D.C., 69 percent of blacks are living in block groups that are more than 90 percent black.

Source: Authors' calculations of 1980 and 1990 censuses.

borhoods. But even that was an improvement from 80 percent in 1980.

The most segregated major metropolitan area for blacks and whites is probably Cleveland. More than two of every three blacks in the Cleveland area live in racially isolated enclaves, along with four of every five whites.

THE MOST SEGREGATED

Racial divisions are starkly obvious in the neighborhoods of downtown Detroit. Nowhere in America has white flight had such a powerful effect on the center city. The metro area is a seven-county region of south-east Michigan, and it barely grew in population during the past decade. But suburban sprawl took over vast new areas during the 1980s, and almost all of the inhabitants in the new suburbs are white. Meanwhile, the city of Detroit has lost about half of its population since 1950.

The top 50 metro areas have an average black isolation score of 37 percent. In 15 areas, the score was 37 percent or higher. And in 4 of those areas, black isolation increased. In Detroit, it rose 4 percentage points, to 61 percent, by far the largest increase. Wayne County, Michigan, where Detroit is located, lost more than 200,000 whites during the decade.

Wayne County's dissimilarity index of 86 was the highest among urban counties with significant black populations. Second place went to Cook County (Chicago), followed by Cuyahoga County (Cleveland), Philadelphia County, and Erie County (Buffalo). Wayne County was one of only two such counties that showed an increase in dissimilarity; the other was Fulton County (Atlanta).

Detroit-area leaders are troubled by the 1990 numbers. "What you see is a white population continually seeking to escape from living in neighborhoods with a black population, and that's shameful," says Arthur Johnson, president of the Detroit NAACP.

The Detroit metro area showed significant racial progress only in Oakland County, which contains some of Detroit's most affluent suburbs. Isolation dropped there for both blacks and whites, thanks to an influx of middle-class blacks into several Oakland County cities near Detroit. But the other major county in metro Detroit, Macomb, remains almost entirely white.

MIAMI'S MORE INTEGRATED

The south Florida counties of Dade (Miami) and Broward (Fort Lauderdale) are just a two-hour flight from Detroit. But in key respects, they are in another world. The major component of demographic change along this part of Florida's east coast is population growth, driven primarily by a vast influx of Latin immigrants. This is an entirely different demographic equation. It has resulted in real racial progress, despite a decade of often strident politics and several widely publicized racial confrontations.

One-third of Dade County's blacks were living in racial isolation in 1990, down from 41 percent in 1980. The percentage for whites dropped even more dramatically, from 75 percent to 49 percent during the period. In Broward County, black isolation dropped from 64 percent to 34 percent, and white isolation dropped from 92 percent to 73 percent.

"We're still far from an integrated community," says Toni Eisner, chairwoman of the Dade County Equal Opportunity Board. "But it's good that we're not going backward."

Some sociologists argue that the decreases in black isolation in Dade County and other areas of the nation, particularly in the Southwest and along the West Coast, don't necessarily mean progress in black-white integration. The influx of low-income Hispanics and Asian immigrants has made a huge difference in places like Miami and Los Angeles. In many instances, white isolation has declined because of increases in the presence of Asians. In other areas, poor Hispanics, who are mostly white, have moved into what were predominantly black neighborhoods. This shift reduces racial isolation by creating a different problem: a multicultural ghetto.

Some areas may appear integrated as one ethnic group gradually displaces another. An example is northeast Dade County, an area that was predominantly white in 1980. By 1990, many of its neighborhoods were more than one-third black, and few doubt that the area will have a black majority in the next few years.

This shift may also be happening in Southfield, Michigan, a suburb of Detroit that appears statistically well integrated. The city's leaders believe that, without planning, their town may be in transition to a mostly black population within the next genera-

Segregated states as measured by racial isolation

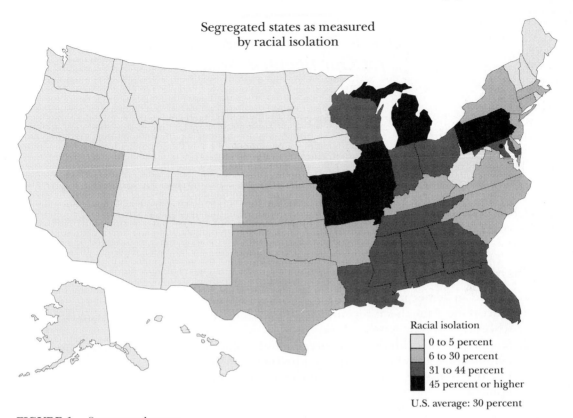

FIGURE 1. Segregated states.

Note: Isolation is defined as living in a block group that is at least 90 percent of the same race.

Source: Authors' calculations of 1990 census.

tion. They are working to ensure that their reputation for racial diversity does not revert to a reality of de facto segregation.

The causes of residential segregation are well understood, but that does not make them easy to correct. Many suburban real estate agents continue to steer black clients away from white neighborhoods, despite local and federal fair housing laws.

Another factor is money. Blacks tend to be poorer, so many of them cannot afford a home even in suburbs that would welcome them. But money does not explain away segregation. If it did, poor whites and poor blacks would live in the same neighborhoods. They don't.

More than 20 years ago, in the wake of race riots that tore enormous social and political holes in the nation's inner cities, the Kerner Commission concluded that America's alleged melting pot was growing cold. The commission warned that the United States was moving toward two nations, one black and the other white, that were separate and unequal. Our new study shows that in 1990, little real progress has been made.

"We've known for some time how intractable the residential segregation phenomenon is," says Bill Tidwell, director of research at the National Urban League. "Now we know that those historical patterns haven't been broken."

43

Enterprise Zones Are No Solution
for Our Blighted Areas

Sar A. Levitan and Elizabeth I. Miller

The authors identify the principle obstacles to urban economic development and then evaluate the impact of enterprise zone designation on inner-city poverty and unemployment. Then the impact of tax incentives and reduced regulation are compared to direct assistance to determine the most effective means to stimulate urban economic life.

Exercises to Guide Your Reading

1. Define an "enterprise zone."
2. Discuss the claim that direct intervention in the inner cities will distort market forces.
3. Summarize the differences between the legislation supported by the Bush administration and that supported by Dan Rostenkowski.
4. List the elements of effective policies to encourage urban economic development.

Even in the best of times, poverty and high unemployment remain the rule for blighted areas. To help these areas, the Bush administration has advocated the designation of distressed neighborhoods as enterprise zones. Once designated as an enterprise zone, they would be entitled to special tax reductions and relief from regulation. The underlying rationale for enterprise zones is that a reduction of taxes, regulation, and other "government imposed barriers" will result in an infusion of capital into depressed neighborhoods. This, in turn, will lead to more business operations and an overall net gain in investment and jobs. Empirical evidence is lacking, however, that reducing federal taxes and relaxing regulations will alleviate the problems of inner cities.

Taxes play at best a secondary role in business investment decisions. Other factors—including the availability of a skilled labor force, proximity to transportation and markets, local amenities, and the physical security of the sites—play a far more important role when businesses consider expansion, relocation, or starting a new venture. High unemployment, poverty, and crime weigh against investing in blighted areas, as do dilapidated infrastructures and inferior services and amenities. Modest tax incentives and deregulation alone do not provide adequate inducements to offset the deterrents of locating in a blighted area.

Reprinted by permission of *Challenge.* May–June 1992. pp. 4–8.

Many believe an infusion of small businesses is needed to vitalize blighted areas. The Bush administration argues that a reduction in government financial and regulatory barriers, as proposed in enterprise zones, will encourage small businesses and entrepreneurs to start new businesses in zones. Tax incentives and deregulation, however, would have at best a nominal impact in increasing the number of startup businesses. Entrepreneurs do not decide to start businesses because of marginal tax relief. In addition, most small firms would be unable to utilize the tax credits offered in proposed enterprise zone legislation, because few businesses in their early years have the tax liabilities needed to take advantage of tax breaks.

Two policy options for administering aid to designated areas are tax expenditures and direct subsidies. Advocates of unfettered free markets argue that policies based on direct assistance have failed because their reliance on subsidies fosters a dependence on government handouts. This, they assert, stifles free enterprise and interferes with market forces. They contend that tax breaks, in contrast, encourage free enterprise and business growth. The distinction free market advocates draw between direct subsidies and tax exemptions is not persuasive; both policies distort free-market operations. Enterprise zones are subsections of larger economic markets, yet tax breaks and deregulation apply only to the zones. Enterprise zone theory is premised on government intervention in the market to favor a designated area. It follows that the subsidies accompanying designation may diminish the competitive capabilities of firms outside the boundaries of the zone, which may be equally depressed. Due to government intervention, these firms will have a distinct disadvantage compared to their zone competitors.

Compared with direct subsidies, revenue foregone through the tax code is normally an ineffective mechanism for revitalizing blighted areas. Tax expenditures proposed in enterprise zone legislation have few strings attached to their use. There is no guarantee that the income produced by the tax expenditures will benefit the zone or its residents. A company can choose to pocket profits generated by the tax credits rather than reinvest in the zone or hire zone residents. Direct government grants or subsidized loans usually provide safeguards, requiring subsidies be used for their intended purposes.

PENDING LEGISLATION

In March 1992, Congress passed enterprise zone legislation—it was included in the Democratic tax package, but President Bush vetoed the bill. The two major bills presently before the Congress, sponsored by the Bush administration and the chairman of the House Ways and Means Committee, Dan Rostenkowski, offer only tax cuts. Although the bills differ in their choice of allowable tax expenditures, the main recipients of tax subsidies in both bills are investors, not residents or local proprietors (see Table [1]). Rostenkowski's bill rewards employers for hiring zone residents while the administration's bill offers a nominal subsidy to employees. The remaining assistance goes to investors.

The major difference between the two bills is the cap Rostenkowski places on the amount of tax incentives available to businesses and investors in a given year. The provision is intended to preclude the escalation of program costs. Without the cap, the unforeseen costs that arose from tax-free industrial development bonds may be repeated. Before they were restricted, tax-free industrial development bonds accounted for significant revenue loss to the federal government without commensurate returns. Also, in the absence of a cap on capital gains, investors may develop the area, displacing the old residents with new buildings.

The administration opposes placing a cap on the dollars spent for the program because a cap would require the government to allocate tax subsidies to businesses. Ac-

TABLE 1. Comparison of the Administration and Rostenkowski Bills

Provisions	Administration (HR23)	Rostenkowski (HR11)
Job credit for employer	None	10 percent of wages and health insurance paid to zone residents
Refundable tax credit to employees	5 percent of qualified wages; annual maximum of $525 per worker	None
Stock deduction	Stock deductions for ordinary losses	Deductions of worthless stock
Capital gains	Permanent exclusion	Deferral of capital gains
Financing of child care facilities	None	60-month amortization and rehabilitation credits

cording to the administration, this would entail the appointment of a local "zone czar" charged with earmarking subsidies for individual businesses. The administration conveniently ignores the fact that by selecting a limited number of areas to receive federal assistance, the administrator charged with designating zones implicitly becomes a zone czar.

Many assumptions, some arbitrary, have to be made in order to estimate the costs of the proposed legislation. Given the size and caps of the Rostenkowski bill, a ball park estimate by the Congressional Joint Taxation Committee has placed its costs over four years at $2 billion:

- $200 million, 1st year;
- $400 million, 2nd year;
- $600 million, 3rd year;
- $800 million, the 4th year.

Because the administration's bill allows fifty zones, twice the number authorized in Rostenkowski's bill, its cost would be at least doubled. The administration, however, imposes no caps on the generous incentives it offers. Its costs will remain uncertain, but could initially deplete the Treasury by significantly larger amounts than that estimated for the Rostenkowski bill. Depending on the zones that are designated, the level and type of investment in the zones, and the number of employees hired, just to name a few variables, the administration's bill could cost ten times the projected amount of the Rostenkowski bill. It is unlikely, however, that an enterprise zone program will be limited to fifty zones, further increasing its costs.

Aside from the magnitude and type of incentives a viable enterprise zone initiative would offer, the designation process of the zones is likely to preclude a successful program. Placing limits on the number of areas receiving federal aid creates political problems. Every member of Congress will insist that his or her district or state receive a fair share of the federal funds appropriated for enterprise zones. Past federal programs that were geographically targeted, including the Area Redevelopment Act (ARA) and Model Cities, were expanded to include a much larger number of areas than originally intended. The designer of ARA envisioned it would help a few dozen areas. By the time the bill was signed into law, one of every five counties qualified, and a year later over 1000 counties were included in the ARA program. Originally designed for three cities, the model cities program ballooned to encompass over 120 cities. Expansion of the ARA and model cities programs was a political necessity to secure congressional passage, but it diminished the ability of these programs to achieve their goals by spreading their resources too thinly.

Enterprise zone legislation may face the same fate. Besides the administration bill that authorizes fifty zones, two other bills have been introduced in the current Congress; one authorizes 100 zones in rural areas, and the other calls for twelve zones on Indian reservations. Although the needs of impoverished rural areas and Indian reservations are not in question, these bills indicate the likelihood that an enterprise zone program, if enacted, would repeat the experience of earlier federal legislation addressed to aid depressed areas. The original rationale for an enterprise zone initiative was to target assistance to truly blighted areas, but history shows that in a political arena, achieving this goal is difficult if not impossible.

If Congress succeeds in limiting the number of areas eligible for designation, federal officials will have to choose among qualified areas because pending legislation does not establish rigorous criteria for designation. The selection of zones will offer difficult decisions for officials. If they choose areas with potential for redevelopment, then the most needy and poorest areas will be bypassed by the program because they are the least likely to succeed. If they decide to assist the most blighted areas, they would need to limit sharply the number of eligible zones since these communities require relatively large investments. Focusing on the needs of the most blighted areas would diminish potential support for the program because success would be hard to demonstrate and more viable areas would resent spending a disproportionate share of the program's resources

on the poorest areas. In either case, areas in extreme distress would be hard put to take advantage of the proposed enterprise zone benefits, casting doubt on the viability of the program.

In line with the 1990 deficit reduction legislation, an enterprise zone initiative would entail either an equal cut in other discretionary domestic programs or a tax increase. Although neither alternative is palatable to the administration or Congress, proponents of the legislation have failed to face up to this conundrum. Scarce funds from established and proven social programs should not be used to experiment with an initiative grounded in supply-side economics. Given other domestic priorities, the pending enterprise zone proposals should not be placed at the top of the administration or congressional wish list.

STATE EXPERIENCE

While Congress has debated enterprise zone legislation during the last decade, thirty-seven states and the District of Columbia have enacted enterprise zone programs designed to combat the blight of inner city and rural areas. Pending federal legislation relies on tax breaks, but state governments have taken a multifaceted approach to enterprise zone programs. The diversity of economic development tools utilized by state enterprise zones has resulted in more varied assistance packages, but the total resources allocated for state programs are meager. Despite state differences, tentative results fail to demonstrate enterprise zones' ability to revitalize blighted areas.

The experience of state enterprise zone programs reinforces the view that politics creates obstacles to limiting the number of zones. Illinois state legislators were unable or unwilling to deny zone benefits to most areas that applied for designation. Beginning with a generous forty-eight zones, the state has since qualified twice that number. Kentucky and New Jersey used other "innovative" means to expand eligibility. They enlarged their zones' physical boundaries to include relatively affluent areas. This, of course, detracts from the original purpose of helping depressed communities.

In designating enterprise zones, several states used a zone's potential for growth as a controlling factor for designation. Indiana and New Jersey favored areas with a strong potential for becoming economically viable. Their policies promised a high probability of "success" because they excluded the most needy areas. In contrast, Michigan selected an extremely depressed area, and tax incentives alone failed.

State experiences indicate that few small businesses are able to take advantage of most tax concessions. Only sales tax exemptions were found to be useful to small businesses. Because small businesses normally receive their initial capital from friends and family, tax concessions on nonexistent stock and capital gains were inconsequential to them. In addition, most small businesses could not use tax credits unless they were refundable. This presents strong doubts whether small businesses have been able to take advantage of state programs. Because small businesses may not be able to partake in the incentives, they may be placed at a competitive disadvantage with the larger, established firms able to obtain the subsidies.

The employment and training of zone residents, particularly the disadvantaged, were not a prime consideration when states designed and implemented enterprise zone policies. For example, 40 percent of businesses operating in New Jersey's zones and unable qualify for zone benefits claimed that to operate profitably they could not meet the state's requirement of hiring 25 percent of their work force from zone residents. The surveyed firms indicated that a better trained work force would improve business conditions in zones. In the absence of educational and basic skills training programs, state zone policies have been of little help to the long-term unemployed and unskilled, who should be prime targets for assistance. Enterprise zone policies created few net jobs or businesses. The majority of the new businesses

that moved into state enterprise zones were either relocating firms or businesses that would have started without government incentives. The jobs they created would have existed without the subsidies but might have been situated outside the zone. Zones' gains were other areas' losses.

The limited tax resources of the states were a serious impediment to successful enterprise zone programs. Excluding unemployment insurance payroll taxes, state taxes account at most for five percent of total business expenses, which sharply limits the tax credits states can offer. Whatever the value of states as laboratories for social experimentation, their zone policies and programs strongly indicate that states are ill equipped to revitalize blighted areas.

EMPOWERMENT: A VISION BASED ON FAITH

Conceptually, enterprise zone legislation is an attractive policy. The proposed programs appear to offer an innovative and targeted strategy for revitalizing depressed areas. The administration has described enterprise zones as offering "empowerment," a buzzword currently in vogue with fiscal conservatives wishing to help the poor. Using a free-market approach, advocates claim their goal is to bestow power on the poor and enable them to forge their destinies. The rhetoric surrounding enterprise zones distorts reality and tends to obfuscate the needs of blighted area residents along with the real costs of their rehabilitation. Empowerment cannot be achieved on the cheap and is not a substitute for direct help.

The overall effectiveness of a federal enterprise zone program is problematic. Pending bills do not address the principal cause of distress—the idleness or waste of blighted area residents. "Empowering" zone residents requires that they become economically self-sufficient. For this to happen, residents need to be able to compete effectively in the labor market. Tax expenditures will not accomplish this, nor will they provide the mechanisms needed to "empower" zone residents. Many residents lack the basic skills needed for most jobs. Only when residents are empowered with a good education and salable skills will residents be able to raise themselves out of poverty. Educating and training people requires direct expenditures. None of the bills addresses this issue. For these reasons, the proposed assistance is not likely to succeed in combating urban or rural economic depression.

The initial advocates of enterprise zones argued (and some still do) that the program will be costless; the resulting investments will more than compensate the government for lost tax revenue. The same people, however, also promised that the 1981 tax cuts would raise federal revenue and reduce the national deficit. Because business start-ups and employment have not significantly increased in state zones and are unlikely to do so in federal zones, there is little reason to believe federal enterprise zones will increase net federal revenue.

The most a federal enterprise zone program can hope for is a zero-sum game as investments are transferred from nonzone areas to zones. Redistribution of investment could have a detrimental effect on neighboring areas, except when a business leaves a full employment area, which is a rarity these days. Most blighted areas are surrounded by neighborhoods whose economies may be only marginally better or even worse than that of the zones. Directing investment away from contiguous areas may further destabilize their economies.

In the real world, an effective enterprise zone program will require direct expenditures. Stuart M. Butler of the Heritage Foundation, a staunch advocate of enterprise zones, has argued that an attractive tax and regulatory climate is only one precondition for economic development. Testifying before a House Ways and Means subcommittee he stated, "Other ingredients are required if economic development is to occur. Action needs to be taken . . . to tackle the staggering increase in drug use and crime within the inner cities. . . ." These "other ingredients"

will not come free and without them, tax incentives alone will fall far short of inducing business to expand or relocate in enterprise zones. State experiences have shown that improvements in physical appearance, service, and infrastructure are extremely important to revive an area.

Reliance on the private sector to correct the ills of blighted areas is based on a wish lacking empirical support. It is not the responsibility of the private sector to improve the physical and human infrastructures of decayed areas. In fact, the private sector abandoned these areas for more attractive and safer environments in the suburbs or outside the United States, which exacerbated the deterioration of inner cities and impoverished rural areas. Tax reductions and relaxed regulations in and of themselves will not bring businesses back to depressed communities. And tax expenditures are not without their costs. Cuts in taxes will lead to lost government revenue on top of unprecedented deficits. The shortfall will be met either by a reduction in services provided by the government or by raising revenues. In either case, the community pays for the tax cuts.

Past attempts to aid depressed areas at both the state and federal levels have demonstrated the complexity of the problems blighted areas face. If the federal government were serious about combating blight, it would need to address economic deprivation wherever it exists as well as its causes. The deep-seated problems of inner cities and impoverished rural areas cannot be easily alleviated, although it can be argued that every little bit helps. As currently proposed, however, the alleviation of deprivation in one area is likely to come at the expense of contiguous areas. Robbing Peter to pay Paul has been tried before, but it is hardly a model for a new initiative.

Should Congress decide to spare a few billion dollars to aid residents of depressed communities, it should consider investing the funds in rehabilitating depressed communities with direct investments in human and physical infrastructures. Existing antipoverty programs are examples of human resource programs able to help people in blighted areas. A judicious expansion of these efforts and the creation of jobs for the poor wherever chronic high unemployment persists are likely to prove a more effective approach to attacking the deep-seated problem of inner city and rural poverty than experimenting with unproven and doubtful programs.

Assisting the residents entails improving their education and skill levels. Once the residents are able to compete effectively for employment, it will not be necessary to bring job opportunities to their back yards. Equipped with the necessary skills, they will be able to travel outside the zone to earn a living. Improvements in amenities and infrastructure should address, at a minimum, transportation facilities, police protection, and the educational and training system. This is the most effective strategy to empower the residents of blighted communities.

44

Redlining Cities: How Banks Color Community Development

Peter Dreier

This article links discrimination by banks in home mortgage and commercial lending, a practice known as "redlining," to the deterioration of the inner cities. The discussion reveals the connection between the recent crisis in the financial sector and urban decay. Community action and government policies to counter redlining are described, as is the resistance of the banking industry to antidiscrimination measures. Strategies for overcoming redlining are discussed.

Exercises to Guide Your Reading

1. Define "redlining," and give examples of how it hurts minority neighborhoods.
2. Describe legislation designed to promote bank lending in urban communities.
3. List responses of the banking industry at the national, state, and local levels to disclosures about its discriminatory practices.
4. Summarize the successful strategies to combat redlining used in Boston, and relate them to the ongoing changes in the structure of the financial sector.

Headline-grabbing crises in the American banking and financial system vie with lurid coverage of urban decline as staples of our domestic news. The general public essentially perceives these as two separate areas of crisis. But they are interconnected, as this examination of the banking practice known as "redlining" reveals.

The health of America's cities depends on both public and private investment. The 1980s witnessed a decline in federal funds for cities and community development, forcing local governments and community organizations to seek private financing (developers, corporations, banks, and foundations) for community development projects. At the same time, government deregulation of the banking industry led to an orgy of speculation that destabilized both the industry and urban neighborhoods.

The savings-and-loan scandal, as well as the collapse and merger of many commercial banks, have recently put the arcane and complex topic of banking industry reform on the front pages and on the national agenda. Often lost in the crossfire between different sectors of the industry, government regulators, the Bush Administration,

Reprinted by permission of *Challenge*. November–December 1991. pp. 15–23.

and Congress is the question of how banks serve (or don't serve) the poor and the urban neighborhoods in which they live.

An examination of "redlining"—the practice of discriminating against poor and minority neighborhoods in the provisions of bank lending and consumer services—illustrates this in sharp relief. Also, a review of grassroots activism across the country to pressure banks to invest in poor and working class areas, particularly urban minority neighborhoods, highlights the potential and pitfalls of community organizing around redlining during a period of dramatic change in both the nation's banking system and federal policy toward cities.

URBAN FISCAL CRISIS AND REDLINING

Redlining emerged as a community organizing and political issue in older American cities in the late 1960s and early 1970s, when the ghetto revolts had subsided. Restructuring of both the global and national economies was changing the face of these cities, which were losing their manufacturing industries—and the jobs and tax base that those created. Cities were also experiencing a decline in overall population size, despite increases in their minority populations. White middle-class residents were fleeing to the suburbs in the wake of market forces (including the movement of jobs to these areas) and government policy (especially in federal transportation, defense, and housing). Widening economic disparity between suburbs and cities evolved, along with deepening fiscal crises in the nation's older cities.

Most pundits viewed these changes as a kind of natural law—the inevitable rise and fall of older cities. But in Baltimore, Boston, Chicago, Cleveland, New York, and elsewhere, neighborhood residents and small business owners began to discern a red pen in the invisible hand of the market—especially in the pattern of bank lending decisions. Banks were refusing to make home and business loans to certain neighbor-hoods, creating a self-fulfilling prophecy of neglect and deterioration. Moreover, these decisions were often based on subjective perceptions—bankers' views of certain neighborhoods as risky—rather than on objective reality. Stable working-class families, for example, were rejected for home improvement loans, despite their ability to pay. Small businesses were unable to obtain loans to start or expand their operation despite evidence of consumer demand for their products and services. Renters seeking mortgages to purchase a home were turned down, even though they had the downpayment and income to qualify.

Local activists concluded that their neighborhoods were experiencing systematic disinvestment, not isolated lending decisions by individual loan officers. These activists undertook local efforts to convince banks to revise their perceptions and lending practices. Some were simply education campaigns to change how bankers—often suburban residents with stereotyped images of city neighborhoods—viewed these areas. Other efforts involved organizing consumer boycotts—"greenlining" campaigns of neighborhood banks that refused to reinvest local depositors' money in their own backyards. Most of these local efforts ended in frustration, although some neighborhood groups achieved small victories, including agreements between banks and community organizations to provide loans or maintain branches in their neighborhoods.

Eventually, activists from across the country, working on similar issues, discovered each other and recognized their common agendas. From these localized efforts grew a national movement—part and parcel of the burgeoning neighborhood activism of the 1970s—to address the problem of bank redlining.

BANK PERFORMANCE AS A LOCAL ISSUE

In response to this emerging "neighborhood movement," Congress (with the support of the Carter administration after 1976) sponsored a number of initiatives to promote community self-help efforts. These included two key pieces of legislation—the Home Mortgage Disclosure Act (HMDA) of 1975 and the Community Reinvestment Act (CRA) of 1977—designed to combat banks' redlining practices. HMDA required regulated lenders (thrifts, commercial banks and credit unions) to disclose the location, by census tract, of their home mortgages and home improvement loans. The CRA imposed an "affirmative" responsibility on lenders to meet the legitimate credit needs of all residents of their service areas from which they draw their deposits.

In combination, HMDA and CRA provided tools to pressure banks to invest in low-income and minority neighborhoods. HMDA provided the data needed to systematically analyze the banks' lending patterns (for housing, but not commercial loans). With this information in hand, community groups could use the CRA to challenge banks' applications to federal regulators to open or close branches, acquire or merge with other banks, or engage in other businesses, on the grounds that they have demonstrated geographic and racial biases in lending and have failed to meet community credit needs.

Over the years, federal bank regulators (Federal Reserve Board, Federal Deposit Insurance Corporation, Office of the Comptroller of the Currency, and the Federal Home Loan Bank Board, now replaced by the Office of Thrift Supervision) have not proven to be proactive in terms of enforcing the CRA. More than 90 percent of all regulated lenders have received either "outstanding" or "satisfactory" CRA ratings. In rating bank performance, the regulators have not undertaken their own analyses using the HMDA data. Until 1989, no major bank application was denied on CRA grounds.

It was thus left to community groups and some local governments to enforce the CRA. If community groups made a persuasive case and mobilized politically, they could pressure banks to make agreements to change their business practices, under the threat of embarrassment and potential denial of their applications. Using an array of community organizing strategies, neighborhood groups and coalitions wrested concessions from individual banks and consortia of banks, typically by negotiating "community reinvestment agreements." Since regulators were usually not parties to these compacts, they did not feel obligated to enforce them. These agreements usually called for banks to retain or expand branch operations, create programs to expand home mortgages or home improvement loans, and make loans to community development corporations (CDCs). Some agreements addressed small business lending, multifamily housing loans, or local hiring issues.

During most of the 1980s, redlining controversies remained predominantly local issues—brushfire battles in a protracted war between community activists and lenders. Grassroots community groups became increasingly adept at challenging bank applications on the grounds of poor CRA performance.

Banks differed in their resistance to making concessions to community groups, but the banking industry generally accepted the CRA as a cost of doing business and remaining legitimate. CRA agreements became the banks' way to demonstrate their social responsibility. Banks hired consultants (occasionally former activists) to help them win over community groups, craft agreements, and ballyhoo their accomplishments.

There is no single list or repository of the many CRA agreements crafted since 1977. The Center for Community Change (CCC), a Washington, D.C.–based organization, estimates that the CRA agreements have catalyzed over $10 billion in bank lending and services over the years.

REDLINING REFORM TIED TO S&L BAILOUT

In May of 1988 the Atlanta *Journal and Constitution* published a high-profile series, "The Color of Money," describing the redlining practices of that city's major banks. The series, written by reporter William Dedman, won a Pulitzer Prize and received national attention in newsweeklies and other media. Later that year, the Detroit *Free Press* published a comparable series on bank redlining practices in the Motor City. Both papers hired academic experts to analyze the HMDA data, while reporters used interviews and anecdotes to highlight the human and social side of redlining.

Growing grassroots organizing and media attention to the redlining issue drew some vocal members of Congress into the issue, most notably Rep. Joseph Kennedy (D-Mass.), who represented Boston, where a protracted CRA controversy was unfolding. Working with various public interest groups with considerable CRA experience, Kennedy sponsored legislation requiring financial institutions to disclose additional information and to put teeth into CRA enforcement.

Kennedy's initiative would not have gained much momentum except that he and activists linked the CRA issue to the unfolding savings-and-loan bailout crisis. A decade of federal deregulation had created a climate for S&Ls to engage in speculation and fraud. By 1989, the public was beginning to become aware of the consequences. S&Ls were failing at a record pace, leaving taxpayers to bail out their government-insured depositors to the tune of $300 billion. (Today, the size of this taxpayer bailout continues to grow.)

As Congress debated the merits and the magnitude of the bailout, and as the national media banner-headlined the issue (including the activities of the "Keating Five," U.S. Senators alleged to have done favors for Arizona S&L owner Charles Keating, a major campaign contributor), CRA crusaders saw an opportunity to demand a *quid-pro-quo*. This effort was led by the Financial Democracy Campaign, a coalition of community and consumer groups, unions, and public figures such as Rev. Jesse Jackson, Jim Hightower, and Boston Mayor Ray Flynn. The key players in the coalition included the Association of Community Organizations for Re-

form Now (ACORN), Public Citizen (a Nader group), and the Center for Community Change, drawing on the network of local groups across the country—which had mushroomed to include church-based, civil rights and fair housing groups, neighborhood associations, community-action (anti-poverty) agencies, and community development organizations. Against enormous odds they successfully tied CRA reforms to the S&L bail-out legislation, in the Financial Institutions Reform, Recovery, and Enforcement Act (FIRREA) of August 1989. The sweeping bill incorporated several of Kennedy's proposals, including revising the CRA rating system, requiring disclosure of CRA ratings and evaluations, and expanding information required by HMDA to include the race, income, and gender of all mortgage applicants and borrowers by census tract.

At the same time, the growing attention to redlining issues began to resonate with regulators.

FEDERAL REGULATORS BEEF UP CRA

The Senate Banking Committee held hearings in April 1988 to review the effectiveness of regulators in enforcing CRA. In early 1989, the Federal Reserve Board began discussing a new CRA policy statement, that was adopted later that year. The new statement specified the kinds of practices on which banks would be evaluated, correcting the vague standards often criticized by lenders and community activists alike. The statement also encouraged banks to meet CRA responsibilities on an ongoing basis, rather than waiting until an application is pending to correct any deficiencies.

At the same time—perhaps to demonstrate to Congress that it took CRA seriously—in the first decision of its kind, the Federal Reserve Board denied (by a 4–2 vote) a bid by a bank-holding company to acquire another bank based on its failure to meet its CRA responsibilities. The Fed's ruling rebuked Continental Illinois (which sought to acquire a small Arizona bank) for its "important deficiencies" in upholding CRA, including "a misunderstanding on the part of the bank staff and management of the requirements of CRA," specifically citing the bank's ongoing failure to make serious efforts to ascertain community credit needs in the Chicago area. Continental's application to purchase the Arizona bank was initially challenged by the Amalgamated Clothing and Textile Workers Union, which criticized the bank's decision to terminate its retail banking services. The challenge triggered an investigation of Continental's lending record, about which—in the changing political climate—the Fed decided to make an example.

The fact that the bank was one of the nation's largest sent shockwaves through the banking industry. It also established the important precedent that the Fed would examine a bank's past performance—not simply promises to improve—in evaluating its CRA track record. This forced banks to look at the CRA more closely. Until then, most banks viewed CRA as similar to corporate philanthropy—good public relations—and relegated low-level executives to tend to it. In the new climate of increasing bank mergers and interstate banking—and thus growing opportunity for grassroots challenges to banks' expansion plans—the CRA became a more serious concern.

The banking industry engineered a two-pronged response. Across the country, banks began to participate in meetings to learn more about CRA as well as to hire additional staff to develop CRA programs and meet with community groups. At the same time, industry lobbyists in Washington began to attack CRA and HMDA. Stung by the successful efforts to strengthen these bills as part of the S&L bailout bill in 1989, they filed legislation to gut both provisions as part of President Bush's bank restructuring proposals in 1991. Community activists, unions, clergy groups, consumer advocates, and big-city mayors mounted a counteroffensive during the summer, and successfully derailed the anti-CRA amendments for the

time being, but the industry is not likely to give up. In fact, in his farewell address to bankers (October 7, 1991), outgoing FDIC Chairman L. William Seidman said that laws requiring banks to invest in their local communities were "no longer required, or affordable."

BOSTON: ONE CITY'S TELLING EXPERIENCE

From late 1988 to mid-1990, while redlining was grabbing attention at the national level, it emerged as a major issue in Boston. A protracted struggle over lending discrimination—engaging the banks, community groups, and Mayor Raymond Flynn and his administration—dominated the headlines during that entire period.

Boston had already experienced a redlining controversy in the late 1960s and early 1970s. Back then, twenty-two banks created the Boston Banks Urban Renewal Group (BBURG) to channel federally insured mortgages into Boston neighborhoods. But unscrupulous lenders and brokers engaged in widespread redlining, blockbusting, and steering, and transformed the racial composition of several neighborhoods almost overnight. U.S. Senate hearings in Boston in 1971 brought these practices to light, helping to pave the way for the federal Community Reinvestment Act in 1977 and, two years later, the first state CRA in Massachusetts.

During the late 1970s and through most of 1980s, as Boston's economy experienced a dramatic turnaround, redlining almost disappeared as a public issue. The city's role as a high-tech, medical industry, and higher education center led to significant public and private investment both in Boston's downtown and its outlying suburbs. The city's changing downtown skyline, along with its spiraling housing prices, reflected this new prosperity. By 1984, Boston had the lowest unemployment rate, as well as the highest housing prices, of any major American city. But the economic boom ignored the city's low-income and working-class neighborhoods, particularly its minority areas. This disparity helped fuel political sentiment that led the sixteen-year Mayor Kevin White to step down in 1983. Populist City Councillor Ray Flynn pledged to "share the prosperity" of Boston's downtown with its working-class neighborhoods, and won the fiercely contested election.

Under Flynn, the city government carried out a "linkage" policy requiring downtown commercial developers to contribute funds (over $30 million in the administration's first seven years) to a neighborhood housing fund; expanded city support for neighborhood-based nonprofit housing developers, utilizing long-dormant city-owned land and vacant buildings to build housing for poor and working class people; and strengthened the city's tenants' rights laws to protect renters from skyrocketing rent increases and conversion of affordable apartments to high-priced condominiums.

Still, city housing officials and housing developers noticed that many developers, as well as many working-class homebuyers, were finding it difficult to obtain financing from local banks. Lenders seemed to have more confidence in (and made lending easier for) speculative market-rate condos in the suburbs than affordable housing in Boston's neighborhoods—even though the delinquency rate was much higher for the upscale housing. (Many of the banks and S&Ls that financed these speculative investments—including the Bank of New England, the region's largest bank—soon collapsed, requiring massive taxpayer-funded bailouts.) Banking services in minority and low-income areas (branches, hours, ATMs) were inadequate, forcing community residents to turn to usurious check-cashing stores and private mortgage corporations. Community housing groups pointed out that bank mortgage products and underwriting criteria did not meet the needs of their local neighborhoods' households. For example, the typical Boston renter already paid 40 percent of his/her income for housing, but lenders limited buyers to spending 28 percent of income to purchase a home.

SYSTEMATIC STUDIES OF LENDING PRACTICES

Mayor Flynn asked the Boston Redevelopment Authority (BRA)—the city's planning agency—to undertake a systematic analysis of lending practices in Boston's neighborhoods. In January 1989, the BRA hired Charles Finn, a University of Minnesota economist, to do this study. Because Finn had worked on similar studies in Atlanta and Detroit—and the release of his findings had created controversy in both cities—the act of hiring Finn itself made Boston's banks nervous.

Shortly after the BRA proposed hiring Finn, the *Boston Globe* published the preliminary results of a study by the Federal Reserve Bank of Boston showing significant disparities on the basis of race and geography in bank mortgage lending in Boston's neighborhoods. The Federal Reserve Bank complained that the study (which had apparently been leaked to the *Globe*) was only an early draft, but—from the banks' perspective—the damage had been done: The redlining controversy was squarely at the center of public debate in Boston.

The response of the banking industry to these events went through several stages. At first, industry spokespersons engaged in damage control—denying that "redlining" was a problem, trying to discredit Finn's credibility as a researcher, and hoping that the issue would disappear. Then, acknowledging lending disparities *did* exist between black and white neighborhoods, the banks argued that the disparities were due to differences in the demand for mortgages, or to housing market discrimination, but not to racial bias by banks. Next, when it became clear that the controversy would not go away, the banks took steps to review past practices and find solutions. Through the Massachusetts Bankers Association (MBA), the banks began meeting among themselves, with government officials, and with community activists.

In addition, the MBA and the Federal Reserve Bank sponsored a series of well-attended public forums to discuss the issues and possible remedies. Meanwhile, community activists brought their concerns to the boardrooms. The Community Investment Coalition (CIC)—composed of several community development corporations, the hotel workers union, a Roxbury-based community group, and the Massachusetts Homebuyers Union, an advocacy group organized by the Massachusetts Affordable Housing Alliance (MAHA)—was formed to represent community advocates. They protested and picketed bank offices and the homes of bank officials; a few even were arrested. They invited bank officials to community meetings—and wound up meeting face-to-face with the heads of the major banks at public meetings and private negotiations.

Mayor Flynn and city officials met regularly with bankers and neighborhood activists. They prodded the banks to develop an industrywide plan and to work closely with city programs and neighborhood-based CDCs and consumer groups in developing their solutions.

While the MBA was devising its own response, the Flynn Administration and the CIC each developed a detailed proposal for a comprehensive community reinvestment plan. To work out its own plan, the MBA established several committees, each with bankers, city and state officials, and community activists. When the MBA eventually unveiled its statewide plan, it contained many elements of both the Mayor's and CIC's proposals. Mayor Flynn also enacted a "linked deposit" policy. Under this plan, the city would regularly examine the banks' track records on home mortgages, affordable housing development, hiring practices, neighborhood branches, small business loans, and participation in city-sponsored housing and neighborhood improvement programs. These evaluations would be made

public, to inform consumers and local organizations about their banks. City funds would be invested only in those banks that demonstrated their commitment to the city's neighborhoods. (About a dozen cities now have some kind of linked-deposit policies.)

Around the same time, Congressman Joe Kennedy brought the U.S. House of Representatives Banking Subcommittee (including chairman Rep. Henry Gonzalez) to Boston to hold hearings at the Federal Reserve Bank on the redlining issue—including Rep. Kennedy's proposed legislation to strengthen the federal CRA.

Meanwhile, MAHA sponsored a bill in the state legislature to toughen the state's CRA, linking it to a proposed interstate banking law supported by most Massachusetts banks. (Both eventually passed.) MAHA also kept the heat on by challenging (on CRA grounds) the applications of two major Boston banks that sought approval to open new branches—one in Japan and another in a predominantly white Boston neighborhood.

FINDINGS OF OFFICIAL STUDIES

The Federal Reserve Bank and the Boston Redevelopment Authority released the official versions of their studies in August and December 1991, respectively. These long-awaited reports each generated front page news for several days and heightened the pressure to reach a solution. Both studies, using HMDA and other data, found significant disparities in mortgage lending between predominantly white and predominantly black neighborhoods.

The final Federal Reserve Bank report, written by two bank economists and a Wellesley College professor, looking at data for 1982–87, was an aggregate analysis of all bank mortgage lending in Boston. It did not break down its findings by individual banks. It also went to great lengths to avoid attributing disparity to bank practices alone, or to suggest that it was due to conscious policy. The study found that:

housing and mortgage credit markets are functioning in a way that hurts black neighborhoods in the city of Boston. One indication is that the ratio of mortgage loans to the potentially mortgageable housing stock is substantially lower in predominantly black neighborhoods than in white neighborhoods. This pattern persists even after taking into account economic and other non-racial characteristics that could be responsible for differences between neighborhoods.

Adjusting for such factors, the study showed that white neighborhoods still had 24 percent more mortgage loans than black neighborhoods.

The imprimatur of the Federal Reserve Bank of Boston was important in providing credibility to the statements of community activists and city officials. In fact, BRA officials waited to release the Finn report until after the Fed had published its study. They wanted to use Finn's study for its maximum leverage, when negotiations were stalled and a new burst of media attention could break the logjam.

Finn's study for the BRA, covering 1981–1987, was much more hard-hitting. It compared neighborhoods with similar income profiles and discovered that commercial banks and S&Ls provided more than *three* times the number of mortgages in white neighborhoods than in similar minority neighborhoods. This wider disparity than the Fed study was due to differences in method: Finn eliminated federal and state government-insured loans (which require no bank risk and are disproportionately located in minority areas), and used a slightly different definition of minority neighborhoods. To demonstrate that there was no lack of consumer demand in these neglected neighborhoods, Finn showed that in the absence of lending by government-regulated lenders, other financing sources—private mortgage companies, credit unions, and individual sellers—provided mortgages. In perhaps the most controversial section of the report, Finn listed the lending ratios (comparing mortgage lending in white and minority neighborhoods) for each bank and

S&L. Finn also noted that while Boston's banks were disinvesting from minority areas, they were fueling the 1980s wave of speculative condominium conversions in working-class white neighborhoods, leading to gentrification and displacement. He also noted that while Boston-based banks had increased the number of branches in the metropolitan area, the number located in Boston's minority neighborhoods had declined significantly.

COMMUNITY REINVESTMENT PLAN

The reports, protests, the linked-deposit policy, and the numerous meetings turned out to be catalysts for action. In January 1990—in the midst of rising racial turmoil triggered by the Carol Stuart murder case—bankers, community activists, black clergy and developers, and city and state government officials announced a $400 million community reinvestment plan at a press conference in Mayor Flynn's office.

The banks agreed to provide $200 million in financing and investment for subsidized housing projects and another $60 million for minority small business enterprises. They also agreed to provide over $30 million in below-market mortgages for working-class homebuyers using flexible underwriting standards (such as 5 percent downpayment). Banks and government agencies agreed to cosponsored "homebuying fairs" to encourage consumers to take advantage of the new products. Banks also pledged to expand their hours and services, and to add seven new branches in minority neighborhoods. They also agreed to cash government checks (welfare, Social Security) for noncustomers—a long-held grievance demanded by antipoverty agencies, so they would no longer have to rely on rip-off check-cashing stores.

To implement the plan, the MBA created three new institutions—a consumer advisory council, a Housing Investment Corporation (to pool bank financing for subsidized housing projects), and a minority enterprise corporation (to handle commercial ventures and provide technical assistance). Bankers, community activists, and government officials served on the boards of each organization.

Despite delays in carrying out some of their promises, the banks have made progress in changing the ways they do business in low-income and minority neighborhoods in Boston. A year later, the city's analysis of bank lending patterns showed a more equal distribution of mortgages in black and white neighborhoods. Five new bank branches had already been opened or sited; Boston is one of the few cities where banks are actually expanding their branches in minority areas.

LESSONS FROM THE BOSTON EXPERIENCE

1. Recognizing the Importance of Allies. Certainly the militancy of the activists—their willingness to engage in direct action, get arrested, mobilize neighborhood residents—played a crucial role in the eventual success. But their strength and legitimacy was enhanced significantly by the support of key allies, particularly Mayor Flynn and Rep. Kennedy.

The CIC was a fragile coalition at best. It had no full-time staff, relying primarily on volunteer leaders and the part-time work of MAHA staff. Only the hotel workers' union had a large membership that could be mobilized for public meetings and protests. This weakness was illustrated by the poor turnout at a public "accountability" meeting in Roxbury attended by several top-level bankers but only a handful of community residents. Within CIC, there were serious disagreements over strategy and tactics, as well as over how much to emphasize the racial (as opposed to class) issues involved in pitting banks against neighborhood groups. CIC members also differed over how much to trust the "good faith" of the bankers as well as how closely to work with city officials,

whom some CIC members believed would steal the credit for any successful agreement, depriving the community group of a hard-won victory.

The CIC's credibility was enhanced by the fact that it had no competition. None of the major mainstream groups in the black community—churches, the NAACP, fraternal associations, business groups—joined the CIC or even participated in the debate. In some cities, but not Boston, these groups have been part of community reinvestment struggles.

In most cities engaged in this controversy, banks seek to engage the moderate voices within the black community to undermine the more militant activists. Boston's banks made a half-hearted effort to adopt this strategy, but without much success. The only moderate voice to play this part was a lone black minister who sought to play a mediating role between the banks and the CIC.

In reviewing the factors responsible for the $400 million community reinvestment agreement, *The Boston Globe* highlighted "Mayor Flynn's stubborn insistence on below-market mortgage rates" as well as "the (Flynn) administration's effort to direct public opinion against the bankers, and the documented inequities in lending practices." Moreover, Flynn became a chief ally of national groups fighting the S&L bailout and pushing for stronger CRA reform.

As a member of the House Banking Committee, Kennedy played a key role in several ways. By holding Congressional hearings in Boston during the local redlining controversy, Kennedy kept the pressure on banks. When the CIC released its recommendations, Kennedy said he endorsed them and later published an op-ed column in the *Globe* criticizing the banks.

The leak of the preliminary Fed study to the *Globe* made the Federal Reserve Bank of Boston (FRBB) an unwitting ally. Once put in this position, FRBB President Richard Syron sought to play a neutral, mediating role—for example, by sponsoring a series of forums during the summer of 1989 that brought the bankers, community activists, and government officials together and kept the issue in the news.

2. Optimizing the Role of the Media. Throughout this period, Boston's news media gave thorough—almost daily—coverage to the redlining controversy. The public forums, the direct action by community groups, several meetings between Mayor Flynn and the top bankers, the Congressional hearings, the CRA challenges, and the various proposals by industry, city and community groups all became grist for the journalists' mills. This media attention encouraged the bank industry to resolve their public relations crisis.

City officials and community activists utilized the competition between Boston's two major dailies, *The Globe* and *The Herald,* to keep the story in the news. Stories about the controversy in the national press—industry publications as well as *The New York Times*—encouraged Boston reporters and embarrassed local bankers by putting them in the national spotlight. The neighborhood weeklies also gave the story top billing.

The CIC collected information on the top bank officials—their salaries, the location and value of their homes, their institutional ties with other business, social, and civic groups. Some of this information found its way into newspaper columns, contrasting the lifestyles of the bankers with the needs of community residents in neighborhoods redlined by lenders.

Both major Boston dailies wrote frequent editorials, chiding the banks for redlining practices, prodding them to improve, calling on Congress and the state legislature to strengthen their CRA laws and enforcement. Editorial cartoonists for both papers also commented on the redlining controversy. Dan Wasserman of *The Globe* drew a cartoon welcoming to Boston South African leader Nelson Mandela, applauding him as a hero in the fight against racism, but warning him: "Just don't bother applying for a mortgage."

3. Understanding the Banking Industry. Community activists and city officials took advantage of the strengths and weaknesses of Boston's banking industry—particularly the need of top bank officials, and certain banks, for legitimacy in the eyes of the public, regulators, and their industry peers.

But despite the months of debate and controversy, the negotiation process was made easier by the fact that government officials, community activists, and leading bankers—chairmen and presidents, not simply community affairs officers—were already involved in a number of common public-private partnership ventures, such as the Boston Housing Partnership and Boston Neighborhood Housing Services. There were often serious differences of opinion, but the discussions never broke down entirely.

Boston's banking industry is highly concentrated. In 1989, the five largest banks—Bank of Boston, Bank of New England, Shawmut, State Street, and BayBanks—accounted for more than 42 percent of the deposits in the state's three hundred and thirty-four commercial banks and thrifts. The activists and city officials focused their efforts on these large institutions, recognizing that any significant remedy would require their cooperation. But the activists and city officials also used the divisions within the banking industry to their advantage.

The banking industry sought to address the controversy collectively through the MBA. However, each of the larger banks recognized that it would be a target of controversy and, on occasion, sought to act independently, particularly when it believed it could create a competitive advantage in terms of good publicity.

The community activists and city officials knew that top bank executives differed over whether and how to solve the problem on an industrywide or individual bank basis, to meet with community activists, and to accede to their demands. During various points in the negotiations, the activists and city officials used this information to embarrass specific bankers, identifying their recalcitrance as the key roadblock to an agreement. For example, when the Bank of Boston, on its own, announced a special mortgage program, activists picketed the announcement, claiming the program was inadequate and demanding an industrywide solution. The activists also used the willingness of some top bankers to admit wrongdoing and meet with activists as leverage to pressure more reluctant bankers to do the same.

Similarly, once the small Bank of Commerce, the city's only black-owned bank, agreed to make below-market fixed-rate mortgages, the larger banks could no longer argue that such a program was unprofitable and unrealistic.

4. Setting a Positive Agenda. During the negotiations, both CIC and the Flynn administration put constructive, detailed proposals on the table. They could not be portrayed simply as criticizing bank practices, because they offered banks a positive way to remedy the problems they identified. Although the Flynn Administration and community activists offered separate plans, the city officials and CIC worked together in developing these recommendations. They differed in some specifics and in magnitude, but they were parallel in terms of the categories of remedies. Both plans suggested a detailed, working knowledge of bank programs and policies, utilizing the experience of CDC staff, city officials, antipoverty agencies, and others.

When the MBA first outlined its proposed CRA program at a public meeting in September 1989, it essentially adopted the framework recommended by the Flynn Administration and CIC, differing only in the level of funds it proposed to commit. As a result, the next few months involved negotiations over details and funding levels, not the overall design of an agreement.

Throughout the controversy, both community activists and city officials repeated that what they wanted was investment, not charity. They emphasized that banks could make a profit by doing business in low-income and minority neighborhoods. They wanted any agreement to be a replicable ongoing program, not one-time "conscience" money.

5. Relying on Consumer-Oriented Legislation. A key ingredient in reaching a successful resolution in Boston was the federal and state Community Reinvestment Acts (CRA) and Home Mortgage Disclosure Act (HMDA). These laws gave the public access to the information to reveal the banks' lending patterns; it also gave the city government and community groups the clout to bring banks, concerned about federal regulators, to the negotiating table.

These laws made possible the public reports sponsored by the Flynn administration and the Federal Reserve Bank, the community groups' CRA challenges, the city's linked-deposit policy, and other key components of the Boston effort. The ongoing public debate over the federal CRA—and the prominent role played by several Massachusetts Congressmen and Mayor Flynn (through his leadership in the U.S. Conference of Mayors)—helped keep the local issue alive while reminding the local players of the wider importance of their actions.

CONCERNS FOR THE IMMEDIATE FUTURE

The 1990s will witness the most significant transformation, consolidation, and shakeout of the industry in a generation. The number of failed banks and S&Ls will continue to grow, while major banks merge with each other as well as gobble up smaller institutions. The pace of interstate and regional banking will quicken. Nonfinancial institutions will seek to engage in banking. Banks increasingly will be seeking approvals from federal and state regulators. At the same time, they will be seeking to change the laws governing the banking industry.

In this environment, community activists and their allies will have an unprecedented opportunity to use existing tools, and create new tools, to make the financial industry more accountable and responsive to community and consumer needs. They can seek to strengthen both CRA and HMDA as well as expand other consumer protection laws in order to bring greater democracy to the nation's banking industry. Obviously, the banking industry has enormous clout in Congress and among state legislatures, but the industry itself is quite fragmented, with each sector speaking with a different voice and a different self-interest.

By the end of the decade, the nation's banking industry will look very different from what it is now. Whether it will be more responsive to inner cities, communities of color, and working class people remains to be seen. Much depends on the ability of the community reinvestment movement to take advantage of this political opportunity.

The CRA and HMDA have not put an end to bank redlining in America's cities. Recent studies in a number of cities—including Atlanta, Baltimore, Boston, Chicago, Cleveland, Dallas, Detroit, Hartford, Memphis, Milwaukee, New York, Oakland, Philadelphia, Rochester, San Antonio, Trenton, and Washington, D.C.—demonstrate that banks continue to discriminate in their lending practices and branch locations. A new national survey by the Federal Reserve, scheduled for release in October 1991, reveals that minorities are two to four times as likely to be rejected for bank mortgages as whites with comparable incomes. But these laws have provided community groups and progressive local governments leverage to push banks to invest in inner cities, to hold state and federal regulators accountable, and to unveil the symbiotic ties between the industry and its regulators. Equally important, these laws help expose to public scrutiny the inner workings and logic of bank decision-making, stripping away much mythology about the efficiency and rationality of the private sector.

Obviously, community reinvestment policies cannot, on their own, solve the fundamental problems facing America's cities. But they do help raise the larger issues of how the flow of private capital—including banks—can be influenced by political pressure and government action.

CHAPTER 11

Culture and Behavior

45

Results from a Chicago Project Lead Social Scientists to a Rethinking of the Urban Underclass

Chris Raymond

This article first describes the resurgence of scholarly interest in competing theories about the causes of persistent poverty. The traditional liberal and conservative views are summarized, and the results of current research are presented. Differences among Chicago's poor are discussed, and the implications of this study for the interpretation of the causes of poverty are delineated. Suggestions for improving the economic status of the urban poor are offered.

Exercises to Guide Your Reading

1. Identify the study's findings that confirm the role of employer racism in black unemployment.
2. State the study's findings regarding the willingness of different groups to work for various hourly wages.
3. Consider the argument in Reading 19 about the pay expectations of unemployed black youth in light of this study.
4. In Reading 2, Loury discusses the problems associated with social isolation. Use the results of this study to evaluate Loury's thesis.

Reprinted by permission of *The Chronicle of Higher Education*. October 30, 1991. pp. 42–44.

Some social scientists have uncovered what they call new and surprising information about the interactions between ethnicity, race, and class. In the process, they have developed new insights into why some disadvantaged groups in Chicago are more likely than others to fall into the state of chronic poverty and welfare dependency that has come to be known as the underclass.

The findings, detailed at a meeting at the University of Chicago here this month, come at a time when scholars, policy makers, and the public are paying increasing attention to the underclass and, in particular, to the plight of young, black men who seem to bear disproportionately the brunt of economic and social problems.

At a conference in May, for example, scholars cited depressing statistics on rates of illiteracy, impoverishment, and imprisonment among black men in America, leading some to call them an "endangered species." The conference was sponsored by the 21st Century Commission, a bipartisan group of politicians and academics organized last year in response to a report by the National Research Council that said decades of economic progress among blacks had come to an end.

ANOTHER LOOK AT A 1960's THESIS

Given such concerns, some of the scholars meeting here called for some reassessment of a thesis many had long rejected.

In the 1960's, the anthropologist Oscar Lewis introduced the notion of the "culture of poverty," arguing that the poor become so dispirited by their circumstances that they develop a fatalistic outlook, which is transmitted from generation to generation.

Critics of the thesis say it blames the victims of poverty for their impoverishment.

Those critics suggest an alternative view: that persistent poverty arises primarily from changes in the structure of the economy and racial discrimination, which constrain opportunities for blacks. The constrained circumstances in turn elicit methods of coping that can be mistaken for a "culture" of poverty, according to this view.

Scholars suggest that the Chicago poverty project discussed here addresses the dispute in a way that pays more attention to the role of cultural variations among the poor, without resurrecting the notion of an autonomous culture of poverty.

"Those who endorse liberal ideology have tended to emphasize social-structural factors, including race," said William Julius Wilson, who directed the Chicago research, the Urban Poverty and Family Life Project. Conservative researchers, he said, "tend to stress the importance of group differences in values, attitudes, and human-capital traits in explaining the experiences and behavior of the disadvantaged."

Based on the new research, said Mr. Wilson, it is clear that no one factor is a sufficient explanation. "We need a broader vision of the processes that affect a poor person's chances in life," he said.

The project's researchers collected data from 1985 until 1989. This month's conference was the first complete presentation of the researchers' findings and analyses.

In the project, researchers surveyed 2,490 inner-city residents—1,177 blacks, 458 Puerto Ricans, 474 Mexicans, and 381 whites—about their work and family experiences, use of welfare, networks of friends and acquaintances, and marriage and childbearing. The researchers followed up with extensive re-interviews of 167 of the participants.

Ethnographers conducted extensive field work in nine Chicago neighborhoods. Researchers also interviewed 187 employers in companies near inner-city communities and compiled historical and census data about each area's changing economy.

In one analysis, Marta Tienda, a professor of sociology at the University of Chicago, and Haya Stier, an assistant professor of sociology at the University of Haifa in Israel, found that plant shutdowns and automation, often cited as "structural" reasons for joblessness, accounted for only one in five job losses that Chicago parents experienced in the 1980's. Quitting, being fired, and promotions accounted for the other lost jobs. However, more blacks than Latinos said that, because of their race, they had more difficulty finding new jobs.

Repeatedly, the researchers said, the comparisons between certain groups—in particular, blacks and Mexican immigrants—confounded conventional wisdom. Mexicans, as a whole, were the least educated of all the groups studied and had the poorest English-speaking skills—but they were the most likely to hold jobs. Even without a high-school diploma, more than 9 of 10 Mexican respondents had jobs, compared with about one-half of the blacks, 8 of 10 whites, and 7 of 10 Puerto Ricans, reported Robert Aponte, a research associate at Michigan State University.

Yet when interviewers asked people how high a wage they expected in deciding to take a job, blacks said they would accept less than $6 an hour, while Mexicans cited $6.20 and whites, $9. Those findings, said Ronald Mincy, a research associate at the Urban Institute in Washington, contradict the theory that "blacks don't work because they want high wages."

MEXICANS' VIEWS OF WELFARE

At the same time, Mexicans take a much dimmer view of welfare than do blacks, found Martha Van Haitsma, a researcher with the Urban Poverty and Family Life Project. She reported that 63 percent of the Mexicans, but only 22 percent of the blacks, said that people go on welfare because they don't want to work, rather than because jobs are unavailable.

Research by Ms. Van Haitsma and Richard Taub suggests why more Mexicans than blacks have jobs. Compared with Mexican immigrants, blacks are much more likely to live in the very poorest neighborhoods.

In contrast, Mexican immigrants tend not to live in the poorest areas and thus are more likely to be around other employed people.

They also are likely to have close ties to others who preceded them to this country. Those ties are a source of recommendations to employers who rely more on personal characteristics than on formal credentials in hiring workers, argued Ms. Haitsma. Mexican immigrants are also more likely than blacks to have access to an automobile to get to work, and to have more than one adult in the household to share child-care duties.

Furthermore, the Mexican "culture of honor" stresses the importance of marriage and the husband's being the breadwinner, said Mr. Taub, a professor of social sciences at the University of Chicago. And because Mexicans compare their admittedly poor-paying, "dead end" jobs here to their even worse circumstances back home, they tend to have a stronger work ethic than do blacks, who compare their situation with that of whites in the mainstream, he and others argued.

STRONGER WORK ETHIC SEEN

Employers who responded to the survey said they preferred to hire Mexicans—or any other immigrants—over blacks, because they thought immigrants had a stronger work ethic. In contrast, many employers viewed black men as unreliable workers.

The differences in rates of employment and other socioeconomic measures among Mexicans, blacks, and whites suggest, said Mr. Wilson, who is also a professor of sociology at the University of Chicago, that both culture and changes in economic structure are needed to explain black poverty.

"Inner-city black men grow bitter about and resent their employment prospects and often express these feelings in their harsh, often dehumanizing, low-wage work settings," he said.

Those feelings, he said, coupled with erratic work histories in jobs that employers expect to show high rates of turnover, "create the widely shared perception that blacks are undesirable workers."

That perception reinforces discrimination, "not only because employers are turning more to the expanding immigrant and female labor force, but also because the number of jobs that require contact with the public continues to climb," Mr. Wilson argued.

Although Mr. Wilson's project was sparked by concerns about the underclass, what sets it apart from much contemporary poverty research is its direct and extensive comparison of blacks with poor whites, Mexicans, Puerto Ricans, and other ethnic groups, other scholars say.

Furthermore, most recent ethnographic studies of poverty have been limited to interviews with a small handful of subjects, at least in part because of controversy over the culture-of-poverty thesis.

"Bill Wilson has made poverty research respectable again," says Herbert Gans, a professor of sociology at Columbia University. Also, he adds, the incorporation of ethnographic research into the study is already having positive reverberations on foundation officers who formerly looked askance at qualitative methods, he says.

Said Mr. Wilson: "There has been a tendency in our field not to discuss issues that are unflattering. But you don't let ideology get in your way of the interpretation of the facts."

Mr. Wilson, an avowed liberal and one of the most outspoken and eloquent scholarly critics of conservative notions of a culture of poverty, argued forcefully in his 1987 book *The Truly Disadvantaged* that changes in the structure of the urban economy and of neighborhoods, rather than cultural factors, best accounted for the rise of chronic poverty among blacks. In the last year or so, he says he has had to alter his views to take cultural factors into account.

"For a long time," observed Mr. Taub of Chicago, "it's been difficult even to talk about these things. There are cultural differences. Some is baggage people bring with them, some is baggage they learn from dealing with their situation."

In telephone interviews, other scholars familiar with the urban-poverty research said

that they were not yet ready to embrace explanations that might seem to revive a culture-of-poverty view. Yet they agreed that culture and structure play important, if complexly related, roles in influencing economic status.

"MANY GRAINS OF SALT"

David E. Hayes-Bautista, a professor of medicine and director of the Chicano Studies Research Center at the University of California at Los Angeles, has been studying Latino groups in California, and his results, he said, raise "many grains of salt" about the cultural thesis.

"Oscar Lewis portrayed the culture of poverty as people who are dispirited and alienated, yet that is not so of Latinos in California," said Mr. Hayes-Bautista.

He found that among Anglos, American-born Latinos, and immigrant Latinos, the last group has the strongest work ethic, but the highest rate of poverty in the state. Latinos have the "right" cultural values, not a culture of poverty, he added, "but it's not paying off."

Mr. Gans, a long-standing critic of the term "underclass," thought that the Chicago researchers erred in comparing black Americans to Mexican and other immigrant groups. "Immigrants are always more energetic," he said, while blacks are shunted to the lowest rung on the economic and social ladder because of their race.

Nonetheless, any effective social policy has to take into account both economic structure and cultural attitudes, scholars here said.

As he has argued before, Mr. Wilson said that the best hope for the inner city was a revitalized economy. But he said that more immediate steps could be taken to address the findings of the current research: setting up neighborhood job-information centers, developing forms of shared transportation to distant jobs, and improving access to child care.

Mr. Taub, cognizant of the "culture of

honor" among African Americans, which stresses autonomy and personal respect, suggested that programs be set up to train and recruit black men into entrepreneurial jobs or those, like long-distance truck-driving, that provide freedom from supervision.

Based on her research, Kathryn Neckermann, a research associate with the Chicago poverty project, suggested that educators instill in children raised in blue-collar families the attitudes, language skills, and behaviors needed to succeed in white-collar occupations.

Lawrence M. Mead, a professor of politics at New York University, concurred: "The problem seems to be not that people don't want to work, but that they do but think it's not possible."

46

Nihilism in Black America: A Danger that Corrodes from Within

Cornel West

This article first summarizes liberal and conservative views of policies to help African Americans, and then identifies the shortcomings of each position. Psychological depression, feelings of personal worthlessness, and social despair are linked to economic deprivation and political powerlessness. Current problems associated with the shattering of black civil society are traced to corporate market institutions and the commodification of black life. Suggestions for change are advanced.

Exercises to Guide Your Reading

1. List the author's reasons for the tendency of liberals to overlook culture and values, and of conservatives to misconstrue problems associated with culture and values.
2. Explain the difference between African Americans as "agents" and as "victims."
3. Describe the crisis in black leadership, and evaluate its effects.
4. Discuss the ways that corporate market institutions adversely affect black communities.

Recent discussions about the plight of African Americans—especially those at the bottom of the social ladder—tend to divide into two camps. On the one hand, there are those who highlight the *structural* constraints on the life chances of black people. This viewpoint involves a subtle historical and sociological analysis of slavery, Jim Crowism, job and residential discrimination, skewed unemployment rates, inadequate health care, and poor education. On the other hand, there are those who stress the *behavioral* impediments on black upward mobility. This focuses on the waning of the Protestant ethic—hard work, deferred gratification, frugality, and responsibility—in much of black America.

Those in the first camp—the liberal structuralists—call for full employment, health, education, and child-care programs, and broad affirmative action practices. In short, a new, more sober version of the best of the New Deal and the Great Society: more government money, better bureaucrats, and an active citizenry. Those in the second camp—the conservative behaviorists—promote self-help programs, black business expansion, and nonpreferential job practices. They sup-

Reprinted by permission of *Dissent.* Spring 1991. pp. 221–26.

port vigorous "free market" strategies that depend on fundamental changes in how black people act and live. To put it bluntly, their projects rest largely upon a cultural revival of the Protestant ethic in black America.

Unfortunately, these two camps have nearly suffocated the crucial debate that should be taking place about the prospects for black America. This debate must go far beyond the liberal and conservative positions in three fundamental ways. First, we must acknowledge that structures and behavior are inseparable, that institutions and values go hand in hand. How people act and live are shaped—though in no way dictated or determined—by the larger circumstances in which they find themselves. These circumstances can be changed, their limits attenuated, by positive actions to elevate living conditions.

Second, we should reject the idea that structures are primarily economic and political creatures—an idea that sees culture as an ephemeral set of behavioral attitudes and values. Culture is quite as structural as the economy or politics; it is rooted in institutions like families, schools, churches, synagogues, mosques, and communication industries (television, radio, video, music). Similarly, the economy and politics are not only influenced by values but also promote particular cultural ideals of the good life and good society.

Third, and most important, we must delve into the depths where neither liberals nor conservatives dare to tread, namely, into the murky waters of despair and dread that now flood the streets of black America. To talk about the depressing statistics of unemployment, infant mortality, incarceration, teenage pregnancy, and violent crime is one thing. But to face up to the monumental eclipse of hope, the unprecedented collapse of meaning, the incredible disregard for human (especially black) life and property in much of black America is something else.

The liberal/conservative discussion conceals the most basic issue now facing black America: *the nihilistic threat to its very existence.* This threat is not simply a matter of relative economic deprivation and political powerlessness—though economic well-being and political clout are requisites for meaningful black progress. It is primarily a question of speaking to the profound sense of psychological depression, personal worthlessness, and social despair so widespread in black America.

The liberal structuralists fail to grapple with this threat for two reasons. First, their focus on structural constraints relates almost exclusively to the economy and politics. They show no understanding of the structural character of culture. Why? Because they tend to view people in egoistic and rationalist terms according to which they are motivated primarily by self-interest and self-preservation. Needless to say, this is partly true about most of us. Yet, people, especially degraded and oppressed people, are also hungry for identity, meaning, and self-worth.

The second reason liberal structuralists overlook the nihilistic threat is a sheer failure of nerve. They hesitate to talk honestly about culture, the realm of meanings and values, because to do so may seem to lend itself too readily to conservative conclusions in the narrow way Americans discuss race. If there is a hidden taboo among liberals it is to resist talking about values *too much* because it takes the focus away from structures, especially the positive role of government. But this failure leaves the existential and psychological realities of black people in the lurch. In this way, liberal structuralists neglect the battered identities rampant in black America.

As for the conservative behaviorists, they not only misconstrue the nihilistic threat but inadvertently contribute to it. This is a serious charge, and it rests upon three claims. First, conservative behaviorists talk about values and attitudes as if political and economic structures hardly exist. They rarely, if ever, examine the innumerable cases in which black people do act on the Protestant ethic and still remain at the bottom of the social ladder. Instead, they highlight the few instances in which blacks ascend to the top, as if such success is available to all blacks, regardless of circumstances. Such a vulgar rendition of Horatio Alger in blackface may serve as a source of inspiration to some—a kind of model for those already on the right track. But it cannot serve as a substitute for serious historical and social analysis of the predicaments of and prospects for all black people, especially the grossly disadvantaged ones.

Second, conservative behaviorists discuss black culture as if acknowledging one's obvious victimization by white supremacist practices (compounded by sexism and class condition) is taboo. They tell black people to see themselves as agents, not victims. And on the surface, this is comforting advice, a nice cliché for downtrodden people. But inspirational slogans cannot substitute for substantive historical and social analysis While black people have never been simply victims, wallowing in self-pity and begging for white giveaways, they have been—and are—*victimized*. Therefore, to call on black people to be agents makes sense only if we also examine the dynamics of this victimization against which their agency will, in part, be exercised. What is particularly naive and peculiarly vicious about the conservative behavioral outlook is that it tends to deny the lingering effect of black history— a history inseparable from though not reducible to victimization. In this way, crucial and indispensable themes of self-help and personal responsibility are wrenched out of historical context and contemporary circumstances—as if it is all a matter of personal will.

This ahistorical perspective contributes to the nihilistic threat within black America in that it can be used to justify right-wing cutbacks for poor people struggling for decent housing, child care, health care, and education. And, as I pointed out earlier, while liberals are deficient in important ways, they are right on target in their critique of conservative government cutbacks for services to the poor. These ghastly cutbacks are one cause of the nihilist threat to black America.

The proper starting point for the crucial debate about the prospects for black America is the nihilism that increasingly pervades black communities. *Nihilism is to be understood here not as a philosophic doctrine that there are no rational grounds for legitimate standards or authority; it is, far more, the lived experience of coping with a life of horrifying meaninglessness, hopelessness, and (most important) lovelessness.* This usually results in a numbing detachment from others and a self-destructive disposition toward the world. Life without meaning, hope, and love breeds a cold-hearted, mean-spirited outlook that destroys both the individual and others.

Nihilism is not new in black America. The first African encounter with the New World was an encounter with a distinctive form of the Absurd. The initial black struggle against degradation and devaluation in the enslaved circumstances of the New World was, in part, a struggle against nihilism. In fact, the major enemy of black survival in America has been and is neither oppression nor exploitation but rather the nihilistic threat—that is, loss of hope and absence of meaning. For as long as hope remains and meaning is preserved, the possibility of overcoming oppression stays alive. The self-fulfilling prophecy of the nihilistic threat is that without hope there can be no future, that without meaning there can be no struggle.

The genius of our black foremothers and forefathers was to create powerful buffers to ward off the nihilistic threat, to equip black folk with cultural armor to beat back the demons of hopelessness, meaninglessness, and lovelessness. These buffers consisted of cultural structures of meaning and feeling that created and sustained communities; this armor constituted ways of life and struggle that embodied values of service and sacrifice, love and care, discipline and excellence. In other words, traditions for black surviving and thriving under usually adverse New World conditions were major barriers against the nihilistic threat. These traditions consist primarily of black religious and civic institutions that sustained familial and communal networks of support. If cultures are, in part, what human beings create (out of antecedent fragments of other cultures) in order to convince themselves not to commit suicide, then black foremothers and forefathers are to be applauded. In fact, until the early seventies black Americans had the lowest suicide rate in the United States. But now young black people lead the nation in suicides.

What has changed? What went wrong? The bitter irony of integration? The cumulative effects of a genocidal conspiracy? The virtual collapse of rising expectations after the optimistic sixties? None of us fully understands why the nihilistic threat is more powerful now than ever before. I believe that the commodification of black life and the crisis of black leadership are two basic reasons. The recent shattering of black civil society—black families, neighborhoods, schools, churches, mosques—leaves more and more black people vulnerable to the nihilistic threat. This shattering spawns a deracinated and denuded people with little sense of self or existential moorings.

Black people have always been in America's wilderness in search of a promised land. Yet many black folk now reside in a jungle with a cutthroat morality devoid of any faith in deliverance or hope for freedom. Contrary to the superficial claims of conservative behaviorists, these jungles are not primarily the result of pathological behavior. Rather, this behavior is the tragic response of a people bereft of resources in confronting the workings of U.S. capitalist society. This does not mean that individual black people are not responsible for their actions—black murderers and rapists should go to jail. But it does mean that the nihilistic threat contributes to criminal behavior—a threat that feeds on poverty *and* shattered cultural institutions. The nihilistic threat is now more powerful than even before because the armor to ward against it is weaker.

But why this shattering of black civil society, this weakening of black cultural institutions in asphalt jungles? *Corporate market institutions* have contributed greatly to this situation. By corporate market institutions I mean that complex set of interlocking enterprises that have a disproportionate amount of capital, power, and influence on how our society is run and on how our culture is shaped. Needless to say, the primary motivation of these institutions is to make profits, and their basic strategy is to convince the public to consume. These institutions have helped create a seductive way of life, a culture of consumption that capitalizes on every opportunity to make money. Market calculations and cost-benefit analyses hold sway in almost every sphere of U.S. society.

The common denominator of these calculations and analyses is usually the provision, expansion, and intensification of *pleasure*. Pleasure is a multivalent term; it means different things to many people. In our way of life it involves comfort, convenience, and sexual stimulation. This mentality pays little heed to the past, and views the future as no more than a repetition of a hedonistic-driven present. This market morality stigmatizes others as objects for personal pleasure or bodily stimulation. On this view, traditional morality is not undermined by radical feminists, cultural radicals in the sixties, or libertarians, as alleged by conservative behaviorists. Rather, corporate market institutions have greatly contributed to undermining traditional morality in order to stay in business and make a profit. This is especially evident in the culture industries—television, radio, video, music—in which gestures of foreplay and orgiastic pleasure flood the marketplace.

Like all Americans, African Americans are influenced greatly by the images of comfort, convenience, machismo, femininity, violence, and sexual stimulation that bombard consumers. These seductive images contribute to the predominance of the market-inspired way of life over all others—and thereby edge out nonmarket values—love, care, service to others—handed down by preceding generations. The predominance of this way of life among those living in poverty-ridden conditions, with a limited capacity to ward off self-contempt and self-hatred, results in the possible triumph of the nihilistic threat in black America.

A major contemporary strategy for holding the nihilistic threat at bay is to attack directly the sense of worthlessness and self-loathing in black America. This *angst* resembles a kind of collective clinical depression in significant pockets of black America. The eclipse of hope and collapse of meaning in much of black America is linked to the structural dynamics of corporate market institutions that affect all Americans. Under these circumstances black existential *angst* derives from the lived experience of ontological wounds and emotional scars inflicted by white supremacist beliefs and images permeating U.S. society and culture. These wounds and scars attack black intelligence, black ability, black beauty, and black character daily in subtle and not-so-subtle ways.

The accumulated effect of these wounds and scars produces a deep-seated anger, a boiling sense of rage, and a passionate pessimism regarding America's will to justice. Under conditions of slavery and Jim Crow segregation, this anger, rage, and pessimism remained relatively muted because of a well-justified fear of brutal white retaliation. The major breakthroughs of the sixties—more psychically than politically—swept this fear away. Sadly, the combination of the market way of life, poverty-ridden conditions, black existential *angst*, and the lessening of fear toward white authorities has directed most of the anger, rage, and despair toward fellow black citizens, especially black women. Only recently has this nihilistic threat—and its ugly inhumane outlook and actions—surfaced in the larger American society. And it surely reveals one of the many instances of cultural decay in a declining empire.

What is to be done about this nihilistic threat? Is there really any hope, given our shattered civil society, market-driven corporate enterprises, and white supremacism? If one begins with the threat of concrete nihilism, then one must talk about some kind of *politics of conversion*. New models of collective black leadership must promote a version of this politics. Like alcoholism and drug addiction, nihilism is a disease of the soul. It can never be completely cured and there is always the possibility of relapse. But there is always a chance for conversion—a chance for people to believe that there is hope for the future and a meaning to struggle. This chance rests neither on an agreement about what justice consists of nor an analysis of how racism, sexism, or class subordination operate. Such arguments and analyses are indispensable. But a politics of conversion requires more. Nihilism is not overcome by arguments or analyses; it is tamed by love and care. Any disease of the soul must be conquered by a turning of one's soul. This turning is done by one's own affirmation of one's worth—an affirmation fueled by the concern of others. This is why a love ethic must be at the center of a politics of conversion.

This love ethic has nothing to do with sentimental feelings or tribal connections. Rather it is a last attempt at generating a sense of agency among a downtrodden people. The best exemplar of this love ethic is depicted on a number of levels in Toni Morrison's novel *Beloved*. Self-love and love of others are both modes toward increasing self-valuation and encouraging political resistance in one's community. These modes of valuation and resistance are rooted in a subversive memory—the best of one's past without romantic nostalgia—and guided by a universal love ethic. For my purposes here, *Beloved* can be construed as bringing together the loving yet critical affirmation of black humanity found in the best of black nationalist movements, the perennial hope against hope for transracial coalition in progressive movements, and the painful struggle for self-affirming sanity in a history in which the nihilistic threat *seems* insurmountable.

The politics of conversion proceeds principally on the local level—in those institutions in civil society still vital enough to promote self-worth and self-affirmation. It surfaces on the state and national levels only when grass-roots democratic organizations put forward a collective leadership that has earned the love and respect of and, most important, that has proved itself *accountable* to these organizations. This collective leadership must exemplify moral integrity, character, and democratic statesmanship within itself and within its organizations.

Like liberal structuralists, the advocates of a politics of conversion never lose sight of the structural conditions that shape the sufferings and lives of people. Yet, unlike liberal structuralism, the politics of conversion meets the nihilistic threat head-on. Like conservative behaviorism, the politics of conversion openly confronts the self-destructive and inhumane actions of black people. Unlike conservative behaviorists, the politics of conversion situates (not exonerates) these actions within inhumane circumstances. The politics of conversion shuns the limelight—a limelight that solicits status seekers and ingratiates egomaniacs. Instead, it stays on the ground among the toiling everyday people, ushering forth humble freedom fighters—both followers and leaders—who have the audacity to take the nihilistic threat by the neck and turn back its deadly assaults.

The nihilistic threat to black America is inseparable from a crisis in black leadership. This crisis is threefold. First, at the national level, the courageous yet problematic example of Jesse Jackson looms large. On the one hand, his presidential campaigns based on a progressive multiracial coalition were *the* major left-liberal response to Reagan's conservative policies. For the first time since the last days of Martin Luther King, Jr.— with the grand exception of Harold Washington—the nearly *de facto* segregation in U.S. progressive politics was confronted and surmounted. On the other hand, Jackson's televisual style resists grass-roots organizing and, most important, democratic accountability. His brilliance, energy, and charisma sustain his public visibility—but at the expense of programmatic follow-through. We are approaching the moment in which this style exhausts its progressive potential.

Other national nonelectoral black lead-

ers—like Benjamin Hooks of the NAACP and John Jacobs of the National Urban League—rightly highlight the traditional problems of racial discrimination, racial violence, and slow racial progress. Yet their preoccupation with race—the mandate from their organizations—downplays the crucial class, environmental, and patriarchal determinants of black life chances. Black politicians—especially new victors like Mayor David Dinkins of New York City and Governor Douglas Wilder of Virginia—are part of a larger, lethargic electoral system riddled with decreasing revenues, loss of public confidence, self-perpetuating mediocrity, and pervasive corruption. Like most American elected officials, few black politicians can sidestep these seductive traps. So black leadership at the national level tends to lack a moral vision that can organize (not just periodically energize), subtle analyses that enlighten (not simply intermittently awaken), and exemplary practices that uplift (not merely convey status that awes) black people.

Second, this relative failure creates vacuums to be filled by bold and defiant black nationalist figures with even narrower visions, one-note racial analyses, and sensationalist practices. Louis Farrakhan, Al Sharpton, and others vigorously attempt to be protest leaders in this myopic mode—a mode often, though not always, reeking of immoral xenophobia. This kind of black leadership is not only symptomatic of black alienation and desperation in a country more and more indifferent or hostile to the quality of life among black working and poor people; it also reinforces the fragmentation of U.S. progressive efforts that could reverse this deplorable plight. In this way, black nationalist leaders often inadvertently contribute to the very impasse they are trying to overcome: inadequate social attention and action to change the plight of America's "invisible people," especially disadvantaged black people.

Third, this crisis of black leadership contributes to political cynicism among black people; it encourages the idea that we cannot really make a difference in changing our society. This cynicism—already promoted by the larger political culture—dampens the fire of engaged *local* activists who have made a difference, yet who also have little interest in being in the national limelight. Rather they engage in protracted grass-roots organizing in principled coalitions that bring power and pressure to bear on specific issues.

Without such activists there can be no progressive politics. Yet state, regional, and national networks are also required for an effective progressive politics. That is why local-based collective (and especially multigen-

dered) models of black leadership are needed. These models must shun the idea of one black national leader; they also should put a premium on critical dialogue and democratic accountability in black organizations.

Work must get done. Decisions must be made. But charismatic presence is no legitimate substitute for collective responsibility. Only a charisma of humility and accountability is worthy of a leadership grounded in a genuine democratic struggle for greater freedom and equality. This indeed may be the best—and last—hope to hold back the nihilistic threat to black America.

47

Rescuing the Urban Poor

Thomas H. Kean

The author, former governor of New Jersey, argues that government programs contribute substantially to persistent black poverty. Disincentives to marry, work, and maintain neighborhood quality are traced to Aid to Families with Dependent Children, the federal tax code, and subsidized housing programs. Particular attention is paid to the way that inner-city schools contribute to these problems. Recommendations for improving schools, families, and housing are put forward.

Exercises to Guide Your Reading

1. Summarize the disincentive effects of government antipoverty programs.
2. Describe policies that would have positive incentive effects.
3. Discuss the role of education in the civil rights movement and in black economic advancement.
4. Identify the main points of difference between this article and Reading 46.

Like many white children growing up in the 1930's and the 1940's, I was insulated from much of the prejudice and oppression that black Americans had to endure. Still, even as a child, I knew something was wrong. My father was a Congressman, so I was brought up in Washington, D.C. Schools were separate. We couldn't even go to the movies with a black friend. As it was explained to me in class by a white teacher, the "coloreds" had their own theaters.

I remember my father's anger when he was turned away from a restaurant near the Capitol because he was with a black constituent. I was angry too. From that anger grew a sense of purpose. I marched with Dr. Martin Luther King, Jr., and, as a student at Columbia University, helped open the first northern chapter of the Southern Christian Leadership Conference, on 125th Street in Harlem.

I thought of those days in July, 1986, as I sat next to Coretta Scott King at the unveiling of the Statue of Liberty. I thought of the irony of this country offering freedom, hope, and opportunity to Europe's poor while denying it to our own of African descent.

When history books are written a century from now, the civil rights movement will be viewed as one of the most significant periods of social change in human history. The civil rights movement forced *all* Americans, of every color and nationality, to face that contradiction. The civil rights movement fought for power—power at the voting booth, power in the schoolyard, and power in the American economy.

Twenty years later, much has changed. Nevertheless, if you walk the streets and alleys of our major cities, you hear the same call—the call for empowerment.

For a large number of black Americans,

Reprinted by permission of *USA Today*. November 1987. pp. 72–75.

the picture of a prosperous and comfortable America is no more real than the image of the "Bill Cosby Show" flickering from old TV sets. These poor black Americans belong to a distinct community—a community of poverty, despair, and deprivation; a community in which over 60% of the children live in single-parent households headed by women; a community in which unemployment is two and sometimes three times the national average; a community in which, every single day, over 40 teenagers give birth to their third child. This is the community of poverty in America. Sadly, it seems more permanent today than it did 20 or 30 years ago.

What went wrong? Why has the dream been deferred for so many? Why, when civil rights were gained for all, did not economic rights for all follow? The answers to these questions are complex. However, no matter how we look at it, we have to admit that part of the blame must lay at the doorstep of government.

During the past 20 years, a collection of programs designed to end poverty for all instead have fostered it for too many. Remember the war on poverty? Well, poverty won. As Hosea Williams put it, "The war on poverty lost because by the time it trickled down to the poor, all we got was scraps from the table."

The numbers are appalling and frightening. One-third of black Americans live below the poverty line. Half of all convicted felons are black, even though blacks account for only 12% of the population. Black unemployment, 6.7% in 1970, is stuck at 15% today. What happened?

ENCOURAGING DEPENDENCY

The same government that ensured civil rights for black Americans too often inadvertently encouraged dependency in return. Our welfare system, for example, encouraged people not to work and provided no rewards to those who got a job. We created

financial incentives for our children to have children. Our criminal justice system told the drug pusher and gang leader that the risks are worth it; there are few incentives for obeying the law. Our housing policy prevents urban residents from owning their own homes.

We have created a community of poverty in our inner cities which isolates our poorest people from the rest of our society and sustains them in their dire poverty without providing the incentives to break free. Consider teenage pregnancy. If you are a young woman and you have a child, but no means to support it, you may receive Aid to Families with Dependent Children (AFDC). You know that money will come through from the government every month, rain or shine, which can be used to help feed your children.

Of course, few 14-year-old girls wake up each morning and decide to get pregnant so they can get AFDC payments. In fact, most recent studies indicate getting pregnant is seen as a badge of maturity and sophistication in the ghettos, rather than a calculated economic decision. Nevertheless, AFDC becomes an umbilical cord for those women and their children from the mainstream into the ghetto society. It permits the single-parent society to continue.

AFDC operates like the deduction for the business lunch. No businessman goes into an overpriced restaurant in order to run up a big deduction. Without the deduction, however, businessmen would quickly do without expensive lunches and switch to a cheaper way of spending their lunch hours.

AFDC doesn't pull existing families apart, but it makes it possible for families to never form. Moreover, the new family mutation—a pregnant young mother with several children and no father—is a recipe for more of the same.

Just how debilitating this is can be seen when you look at relationships between black family income and white family income. While black two-parent families are closing the gap with whites (their income is now 78% of whites), the gap between whites and single-female black families is growing. The black female-headed family now represents a greater number of poor Americans—19.3%, up from 7.3% in 1959. Unless we change the cycle of poverty begetting poverty—and provide incentives for families to remain together—we will face a vastly increased number of poor people, more desperate and hopeless with each generation.

AFDC isn't the only example of perverse incentives in operation. The relationship between the Federal tax code and the availability of government aid discourages many from obtaining employment.

There are people today who live below the poverty line, yet pay, in effect, the highest marginal tax rates in the country. Let's say a poor black woman who now draws AFDC payments, food stamps, and other aid decides she wants to give her family a better shot by earning money through a full-time job. She will find that, between paying income taxes and losing benefits, she will lose between 80 cents and $1.50 for every extra $1.00 she could earn. Why bother?

Not that everyone sits down at night wearing a green eye-shade and a pocket calculator, but often in our inner cities, it becomes apparent quickly that it is easier to do nothing and "get over" than struggle and get by.

Or consider our housing policy. A great many inner-city residents live in housing that was built or subsidized by the Federal government. Until quite recently, these tenants had no way to buy their residence and with it a sense of responsibility and permanence. Is it any wonder that subsidized housing is so often run-down and unkempt?

There are some in my party who look at all this and say government is hurting urban America. These people believe government ought to just get out of the anti-poverty business.

There are others who blame the victim. After all, the urban poor are poor because of their own weaknesses. Those people are wrong. Just because poverty still exists

doesn't mean that government should throw up its hands and go home. Nor does it mean that the poor will always be with us. In fact, some programs—Head Start, for example—have enjoyed great success.

I believe that government can make a difference. Government can create a climate so that our urban poor can help themselves and beat poverty. Not only can government do this, Republican government can do this—and do it better than the Democrats can.

I will admit that, for a good number of years, the Democrats had better ideas and solutions to fighting poverty in America. After 1932, they were more attentive to the needs of urban Americans than the Republican Party was. However, those days ended sometime during the 1970's. Democratic thinking became first baroque, then rococo. Unable to provide new ideas or plans, they returned time and again to old ideas, turning stale politically and intellectually. Their old ideas perpetuated the cycle of dependency and poverty.

At the same time, Democrats began taking blacks for granted, arrogantly assuming that they could call on the black vote in November, but forget about those voters the rest of the year. In election after election, black voters would give 90% of their support to Democratic candidates.

What have black Americans to show for this unalloyed loyalty?—government programs that perpetuate poverty, rather than end it, and a paucity of blacks in high elective office. There are no black senators, no black governors, and, with the notable exception of Rep. William Gray (D.-Pa.), no black leaders in Congressional leadership.

I will concede that the Republicans, the party of Lincoln and the party that freed blacks from slavery, has not done enough lately to woo black voters, but we are beginning to. Sixty percent of the black New Jerseyans who voted for governor in 1985 supported me. In Louisiana, a white Republican Congressman, Bob Livingston, wins reelection routinely with 75% of the black vote in a district where one-third of the voters are black. The 1986 Republican nominee for governor of Michigan was black.

NEW IDEAS

We are starting to show that black voters will respond to Republican candidates with new ideas that respond to their needs. What are those ideas? Urban enterprise zones, tenant ownership of public housing, reform of the tax code so that poor Americans don't have to pay taxes—these ideas were all conceived and developed within the Republican Party. These are the kind of ideas that can break the cycle of dependency in our inner cities and give urban Americans the opportunity to get a job, raise a family, and finally put an end to poverty in America.

In no area is the need for new ideas more pressing than in education, particularly in meeting the problems of our urban schools. Historically, education has been the catalyst for the liberation of black Americans.

The most enduring work of the Freedman's Bureau was the development of a common education system for former slaves. The NAACP and the National Urban League were born in the service of education to meet black needs. Most of the landmark civil rights cases dealt with constitutional issues around the use or misuse of public education—especially *Brown v. Board of Education* in 1954.

It was the struggle in the schools which gave Dr. King commitment for the Montgomery Movement in 1955. It was from the schools that the strategy of economic boycott was born in 1959. It was in the schools that the Federal government finally stood for justice at Little Rock, Alabama, and the University of Mississippi, and it was in the schools that the Student Nonviolent Coordinating Committee was born and black voter registration launched. John Jacob, president of the Urban League, put it simply and directly: "Black survival is directly linked with education."

Today, however, urban schools are no longer the seedbeds of social change. Instead, they are mere warehouses of unfulfilled human potential. In our urban schools—particularly schools in which the majority of students are black—we see a pattern of rules and regulations, dogma and doctrine that perpetuate powerlessness.

Consider for a moment the problem of disruptive students. Perhaps no other criterion separates good schools from bad schools than the treatment of unruly students. In good schools, students know what is expected and what will happen if their behavior deviates. In bad schools, no clear or explicit signals exist.

If the teacher doesn't want profanity, fights, or sarcasm, the teacher says to the student, "If you won't disrupt, then I won't demand too much of you. You'll be able to get by with minimum effort." By making these truces, we set the wrong tone. We lose the incentives for good behavior and hard work.

Consider the issue of academic standards. The urban schools in my state are filled with children who perform substantially below their grade level. That's what the academics say—what they mean is that these children simply can not even read or write.

Yet, for years, our response has been to simply pass these children from grade to grade, regardless of performance, until the child drops out. That child soon finds himself or herself condemned to low-paying, dead-end jobs for the rest of his or her life.

A black friend of mine in the city runs a string of grocery stores. He desperately needs people to work the cash registers. The neighborhood kids want the jobs very badly. Sometimes, they wait in line for hours to be interviewed. My friend asks these kids a simple question: "If a product is three for $1.00, how much does one item cost?" The kids look at the floor. They can't answer. It breaks my friend's heart. These are kids he wants to help, but he can't. Instead, they are back on the street, with drugs and crime their only alternatives.

What kind of message do we send when we promote and even graduate our children regardless of whether they have mastered even the minimum skills required of their grade? The message is simple. We say to our youngsters, you can't succeed. You are powerless. No matter if you study or not, you graduate. Your actions have no consequences. Is it any wonder that, years later, these human beings are on the street? Is it any wonder they can not get a job?

Finally, consider our treatment of urban schools as institutions. In my state, as in many others, we give extra money to schools for compensatory education. Yet, the system is biased so that the more children in remedial classes, the more money a school gets. We reward failure and penalize success. Under that system, schools will never let students out of special classes, because they would lose money.

As budgets get larger and student performance declines, support for education deteriorates. People forget that when you spend money on the education of a child, it is so much cheaper than spending money on prisons or spending money on welfare programs.

What we must do is really simple. We must restructure incentives to reward achievement for both the schools and students.

Take the problem of disruptive students. Urban schools must have clear-cut codes of conduct, and they must create alternative education programs for students who consistently violate those codes. The rules must be clear: if students misbehave, they will be removed from the classroom; if the disruptive behavior continues, the student will be suspended.

With a good alternative education program—one that usually costs no more than regular education—we can meet the needs of the disruptive student and maintain classroom discipline. However, the message must be clear—if you interrupt the learning of other students, you leave the classroom and perhaps the school.

We can no longer pass our students from grade to grade with scant concern for their ability to even read or write. We must put in place rigorous tests in basic skills. All high school students must pass these tests before they are given a diploma. No longer can we pass our problems on to employers and colleges. No longer can we let our children suffer for our mistakes.

Basic skills tests will be controversial. In my state, some educators have talked of failure rates as high as 70%. These people say that urban children simply can not learn to read and write and do arithmetic.

That is nonsense. I know our children have the ability to learn. The question is, do our schools have the capacity to teach? If they do not, that is our failure, not our children's.

Convincing students that their behavior does have consequences is vitally important. What is equally important is changing the incentives facing our schools themselves.

Federal and state governments should restructure their formulas for compensatory education. No longer should schools with the largest classes receive the most money. Instead, let's give the extra money to schools that get children out of special classes and back with their classmates.

I believe that all children have a right in this democracy to a good education. A handful of school districts in New Jersey—mostly urban schools with black majorities—repeatedly have failed to meet minimum state standards. Students in those schools are being denied what is a constitutional right in my state to a thorough and efficient education.

In June, 1986, I announced a change of policy regarding those schools. If those schools continue to fail and if, by every piece of evidence, they are not educating children, then the state of New Jersey will take over. We will replace the school boards, superintendents, and other key administrators.

We are telling our urban school districts that no longer will we turn our backs and tolerate mediocrity. We no longer are going to blame our children. We are going to fix the schools.

By doing so, we will prove that the development of the poorest black or Hispanic student is just as important as the education of the middle-class student in the suburbs. We will prove that institutional actions, just like individual actions, do indeed have consequences.

BREAKING THE BACK OF POVERTY

We need nothing less than a national assault on the problems plaguing our urban schools. We can no longer tolerate a situation where an entire community of children is deprived of the basic skills needed to hold a job. We must recognize that, when we fail in education, our failure is our children.

It's not going to be easy. It will take the cooperation of everyone—the Federal government, states and the cities.

I believe the Republican Party will take the lead in this area, but I call on the leadership of both great political parties to make education a priority. If we fail here, we fail everywhere. We must not fail. We will never break the back of poverty unless we provide a decent education to every child in our cities.

Black Americans can not let government off the hook. Black Americans should not let government play "Big Daddy." We must not let government tell urban dwellers that it simply can't do anything about poverty in America.

James Baldwin, the great black writer, once wrote, "Not everything that is faced can be changed, but nothing can be changed until it is faced." Government and the entire urban community together must face the fundamental issue of the 1980's: how to empower the urban Americans—not paralyze them.

I am a historian, and to me the history of black Americans is a story of human possibility. Black America has produced some of the greatest leaders in history—people like W.E.B. Dubois, Booker T. Washington, Benjamin Banneker, Jackie Robinson, Martin Luther King, Jr., and Whitney Young.

What is amazing about each of these people is that they came out of an atmosphere of hardship and oppression. From poor schools and sometimes broken families came some of the people richest in intelligence, integrity, and ideas in human history.

That says something. If these black Americans can contribute so very much, think of what all black Americans can contribute with an equal chance as the rest of us—with good schools and solid family.

It hasn't happened yet. This is a country that has put a man on the moon, found a cure for polio, and forged technology that boggles the mind. Still, we have yet to find a way to empower urban Americans to become a competitive force in American life.

We have yet to fulfill Whitney Young's dream of a "society in which each human being is free to flourish and develop to the maximum of their God-given potential." When that day arrives, and it must, I can guarantee you that the Statue of Liberty will smile a little wider.

Whenever I think of the potential in Americans, I think of the gifted scholar, singer, and actor from my home state—Paul Robeson. I remember a song he used to sing called "The House I Live In." In the song, Robeson asked, "What is America to me?" He spoke of many things, including a certain special word—"Democracy." He reminded us of the words of Lincoln, of Jefferson and Payne, of Washington and Douglass, and the task that still remains. To Robeson, America was "The right to speak my mind out, and the air of feeling free."

He concluded, "The town I live in, the street, the house, the room, the pavement of the city or a garden all in bloom: the church, the school, the clubhouse, the million lights I see, but especially the people, that's America to me." America is all these things, but today, America still is all those things to only some people.

The promise of America will never be fulfilled until we throw open our doors and let urban Americans share in the power and opportunity we all enjoy, until those who are strong demand inclusion of the weak, until those who have power demand inclusion of the powerless, and until those who are rich feel an obligation to the poor. That time is coming. I believe it. I feel it.

On his deathbed, W.E.B. Dubois wrote: "The only possible death is to lose belief in life simply because the Great End comes slowly, because the time is long." Black power in this country has been a long time coming, but I am one American who believes that the Great End is within our grasp.

48

The Poverty Industry: Do Government and Charities Create the Poor?

Theresa Funiciello

The author describes the situation that may confront single women with children when they lose the economic support of their husbands. The step-by-step process of entering the welfare system and its impact on all aspects of daily life are detailed. The economic consequences of male abandonment are compared to those of widowhood. Policies for improving the situations of single women with children are discussed, with special attention paid to the comparison between income security and services.

Exercises to Guide Your Reading

1. Summarize the likely results of the principal wage earner's abandonment of his/her family.
2. Give reasons for the expansion of services to the poor.
3. Define "income security," and give examples of programs designed to increase it.
4. Analyze the author's answer to the question: "Do government and charities create the poor?"

Firefighters returning from a false alarm in Queens, New York, one beautiful October day in 1989 were gazing into the sky when they passed an apartment complex. Ten stories up, a body was dangling from the window. Hector Faberlle and his coworkers yelled up front to get the rig turned around. Just as it arrived back at the building, a little girl, naked, hit the ground. Faberlle ran to resuscitate her as two other firefighters dashed into the building.

According to Faberlle, "We tried to stabilize her. Just as she was breathing on her own, I heard people screaming. I looked up and saw another small child spinning down." Witnesses said a woman had seemed to dangle him before she let go of him. Hussein, age three, fell on his seven-year-old sister. "After that we couldn't get a pulse from her and blood was spilling from her mouth."

Ameenah Abdus-Salaam, a 32-year-old black middle-class Muslim housewife, was trying to send all five of her children back to Allah, through their apartment window. Her daughter Zainab was pronounced dead at the hospital. Hussein survived and a year later is still in rehabilitation. Just as Ms. Abdus-Salaam was about to toss out her one-year-old, firefighters burst in. As they were overtaking her, she urged the children to go quickly, as if they would go on their own. All were naked. According to one news re-

Reprinted by permission of *Ms. Magazine*. November–December 1990. pp. 33–34, 36–38, 40.

port, she said, "We came into this world with nothing and that's how we're going to leave." Three children and their mother, who intended to jump when she completed the task, were rescued.

Ms. Abdus-Salaam was charged with murder, attempted murder, first- and second-degree assault, reckless endangerment, and endangering the welfare of a child. Neighbors said the mother was loving and the children were always polite and clean, as if that rendered the occurrence more mysterious. And then Ameenah Abdus-Salaam and her children vanished from our collective memory.

When I was young I could not possibly have understood or forgiven (as if it were mine to forgive) the acts of Ameenah Abdus-Salaam on October 5, 1989. Some of that youth I spent as a Muslim—drapes for clothes, virtually nonstop prayers, my two feet of hair cordoned with a bolt of white cloth bound so tightly I could never forget it was there. I took this religion as seriously as those that preceded it, starting with Catholicism (I went to *that* church every day until I was 18). My religion was as solid as a rock mountain pervious only to centuries of dripping water. (Latent feminism finally crept up on me.)

In Islam, everything is ritualized, from sex to eating. That's how I know what Ameenah Abdus-Salaam was doing calmly while she held Hussein out of the window before letting go. She was praying.

In form and function, as in other patriarchal religions, Muslim women are buried alive in contradictions. They are equal; no, superior; no, inferior—to men, to snakes, to witches. Make no mistake: an Islamic woman without a man, especially a woman with children, isn't remotely like a fish without a bicycle.

This woman had five children, aged one to eight years, and was recently separated from her husband. She had trouble making her last month's rent. She surely feared a descent into poverty and probably homelessness. (As of this writing she is not granting interviews.) Ahead lay the streets. Welfare. Welfare hotels. Drugs, prostitution,

guns, knives, gambling, drunkenness, and all manner of spiritual death. But for a woman with the option of deliverance, it wasn't inevitable.

Some years after shedding my Muslim garb, I had a baby and ended up homeless and on welfare myself. Not long after, I organized a welfare rights center, where we (the mothers trapped in this system) tried, among other things, to sort out the differences between "us" and "them" (mothers not on welfare). One subject was the stereotype of child abuse. It was something each of us understood at some terribly private gut level, but never articulated outside our circle; even then, we were cautious.

My own revelation came when my daughter was about a year old. At one point, she was sick and cried almost nonstop for a week. I was experiencing severe sleep deprivation coupled with the trauma of being unable to comfort her. For one horrible moment, I felt like hurling her against the wall. Fortunately, my mother came by unexpectedly and held the baby for a couple of hours, giving me time to gather composure. My daughter's fever broke and we both survived. But ever since, I have understood child abuse. And any parent who claims not to understand it in that context, ain't hardly trying.

I had been very close to where Ameenah Abdus-Salaam was. On another level, our circumstances were very different. A homeless mother of five (I had only one) has virtually no chance of being taken in by friends or family for more than a night or two. A homeless mother of four or more has only a 16 percent chance of keeping her children together. If she stays in an abandoned building with them and gets caught, they'll be taken away for "neglect." Still, there are commonalities shared by women of all races and religions, from rural to urban poverty. The merciless anxiety, the humiliation of being shuttled back and forth like herded animals, the stress of keeping kids in school, are constant. Only the details vary.

In New York City, if she were able to keep them together, at some point they would approach an Emergency Assistance Unit (EAU), which is obligated to shelter them in some way. This would mean waiting for hours, sometimes even days, on plastic chairs or the bare floor. If the family didn't eat pork, they'd eat nothing, since baloney sandwiches are about all they'd get for several meals. Some nights they might be moved (often after midnight) to a roach, lice, and rat infested welfare hotel for a few hours. In the morning the family would be shuttled back to wait again.

If they were lucky, after some days they would finally be placed in a welfare hotel or "transitional" shelter. These often provide less space per family member than that required for jail cells. Because the family was large, they wouldn't even get apartment referrals from city workers until after they'd been in this hell for months. (One rural homeless mother told me her family was placed in a motel with bars instead of windows and not one store or school within walking distance. She was at the mercy of a barely functional shuttle system for the homeless.)

At first, many mothers try to continue taking children to their previous schools. In New York City, this usually means traveling with them (other babies in tow) to another borough in the morning and returning for them in the afternoon. When one child is too sick to travel, none go to school. After a while, the mother might try to place the children in a school closer to the shelter. Legal, yes. Easy, no. If the mother does accomplish this, other kids in the new school will soon realize her children are "untouchables." School life will become anathema to her kids. They'll begin to adopt the coping mechanisms of other homeless kids who *will* associate with them.

Night brings scant respite. Police sirens. Gunshots from outside or down the hall. Families fighting. Too many people and too few beds, often with neither sheets nor blankets, much less pillows. The mattresses have long since burst like pastry puffs. Bedbugs pinch.

Those of us who are lucky have a little stove in the room. I'll never forget the first time I used one in a welfare hotel. I had just added eggs to the frying pan when swarms of roaches scrambled out of the lit burner in every direction—including into the frying pan. It was days before I could bring myself to try it again. All the things most people take for granted become little horrors.

If the Abdus-Salaam family emerged from the "temporary" shelter intact and were placed in an apartment, the world would think their problems solved. But now they would be a welfare family. Overnight she would switch from homeless victim to society's victimizer. Her living conditions would not improve nor her stress diminish, but she would join the larger class of poor women—despised abusers of the system—welfare mothers. To have come this far would have been a heroic feat, but what would be said of her is that she's a drain on national resources, has too many children she shouldn't have had if she couldn't afford to, and she doesn't "work."

On welfare, the chances of having enough money to live in a remotely decent neighborhood and pay for basic human needs are laughable—even in New York, where welfare benefits are "high." On the day when the Abdus-Salaam family almost came to total halt, the *maximum* monthly grant in New York City for a mother and five children was $814.20—or *less than three fifths of the federal poverty threshold for the same size family*. The *average* New York grant for six was $655 per month. (In January 1990 there was a slight, almost negligible increase in aggregate benefits.) Assuming the family received the maximum, the rent allotment would have been $349. Assuming the absurd—that they could find habitable housing for that price in New York or most any other U.S. city—they would be left with $465.20, or about $2.50 per person, per day, for most of their food. (Food stamps would provide less than two weeks of nutritionally adequate food for the month.) That same $2.50 must cover some of their medical expenses, and *all* their utilities, toothpaste, toilet paper, furniture, soap, baby bottles, diapers, laundry, transportation, kitchen utensils, and clothing. If Ms. Abdus-Salaam lived in South Dakota, she'd have had just about $1.88 for all those things. If she were a single mother living in California aged 25 or less, she'd have a 98 percent chance of landing on welfare. In New York, if she took one subway ride in search of an elusive job, she'd use up over 90 percent of her daily ration. If she's menstruating and needs to buy a box of sanitary napkins, she'd have to dip into her children's share. Like millions of women, she has at her disposal only one commodity guaranteed to produce sufficient income to keep her family together: her body. For some women that's unthinkable; for example, to a devout Muslim, even survival does not justify such a damning act. Yet to kill herself—only herself—would be to act irresponsibly to her children. Had *Mr.* Abdus-Salaam died instead of leaving the family, everything would have been different.

Ameenah would have been the recipient of sympathy and support. As a widow with minor children, she would become a Social Security recipient instead of a welfare mother. (The maximum family benefit for survivor families on Social Security in 1989—$1,898.90 per month—could be enough to continue living modestly where she was. While this sum is hardly lavish, the family would remain above poverty.) No social policy experts would go nuts because she didn't have a "job." In fact, she would be thought a good mother for taking care of her children full-time, "at least while they're small." If and when she did get a paying job, she could earn thousands of dollars without a reduction in her Social Security check. (On welfare, a job would be taxed at 100 percent. Outside of minimal work-related expenses, for the most part her welfare check would be reduced one dollar for every dollar she was paid.) The message: the needs and rights of women and children are determined by the nature of their prior relationship to a man; the only difference between "survivor" families and "welfare" families is the imprimatur of the father. How did such a cruel policy come to be?

Whose Welfare?

The Social Security Act of 1935 was the legislative blast-off point. From the start it had the aim of protecting men—and only incidentally their families—from the vagaries of the marketplace. It insured most citizens, but *not* mothers separated from living husbands. The elderly—men, by more than two to one because of their labor-force participation rates back then—were designated beneficiaries of old age insurance. It was also this bill that created unemployment insurance, intended primarily to cover males temporarily disjointed from the waged labor market. Widows (the *good* single mothers/wives) and their children were to receive survivors' benefits. (Early on, if the father divorced his wife two minutes before he died, she was not eligible for "his" Social Security benefits.) Children with living but absent fathers were almost left out, but Frances Perkins and others fought to cover them through what came to be called Aid to Dependent Children (ADC). ADC kids were presumed to live with their mothers, as in fact almost all did. But *no sum of money was designated for the women*; Perkins lost that one. It wasn't until the 1950s that the caretaker parent (mother) was added to the beneficiary unit, and ADC was changed to AFDC, or Aid to *Families* with Dependent Children.

AFDC is the program most frequently thought of today as "welfare"; 94 percent of its recipients are single mothers and their children. Conservatives, especially during the Reagan era, argued recipients opted out of the job market in favor of plentiful dollars on the dole, offered by Lyndon Johnson's Great Society legacy. In fact, for most of the post 1960s, the purchasing power of cash assistance to poor families plummeted, though aggregate social spending soared. The Great Society was a culprit—but for different reasons than those given by Reaganites. *It emphasized a service strategy to the near exclusion of income security*—with the long-term effect of eroding the income security of millions of people, thousands of whom became homeless. The conceptual framework that supported this disaster held into the 1990s, long after the nation had surrendered in the War on Poverty.

War (Games) on Poverty

The foundation for the Great Society was laid in the Kennedy administration. Income maintenance had been ruled out; it was thought to breed a degenerative social disease—dependency. (There was no rigorous examination of this notion, although income maintenance was really the same as Social Security payments to survivor families, and "dependency" didn't destroy *them*.)

President Johnson declared War on Poverty not only because he felt the political necessity to carry on where Kennedy left off, but because big spending programs aimed at reducing the effects of poverty had been his turf as far back as the New Deal. He liked programs that doled out contracts across the country. Although income maintenance strategy was discussed during (and after) his administration, he too rejected it. But he did appoint an investigatory Commission on Income Maintenance Programs, which continued into the Nixon administration. Barbara Jordan, then a Texas state senator, was one of the few commission members not from the business community; still, even dominated by such stalwart capitalists as IBM's Thomas Watson and the Rand Corporation's Henry Rowen, the commission ultimately endorsed the "creation of a universal income supplement program . . . to all members of the population in need."

Why did Johnson reject income redistribution? The decline in the industrial base had limited certain jobs, and Democratic reform movements had put a stranglehold on party machines accustomed to wielding power through the jobs *they* controlled. Johnson's War on Poverty must have seemed an excellent chance to rebuild the party machine. So services emerged with regularity, each new "need" defined by the helping industry and by elected officials shagging dollars or votes. (When it works to their advantage, Republicans have shown they can also use service money to control allegiances. But

---

A LITTLE PERSPECTIVE

Compare. The total federal share of AFDC payments in 1987 was $8.8 billion dollars, covering approximately 11 million people, mostly women and children, nationwide. *AFDC represents less than one percent of the federal budget annually. National defense consumes 27 percent* and in most years increases faster than the pace of inflation. The total federal share of AFDC is just over one percent of the projected cost of bailing out the savings and loans and other financial institutions; it's less than Bush's proposal for the "war on drugs" this year.

Put in social policy perspective, the "non-profit" human service sector (not counting hospitals and institutions of higher learning) in New York City alone in 1982 received $10.6 billion dollars. The largest single source of revenue for that sector was government contracts. The money and power was concentrated: only 21 percent of all New York "non-profit" human service agencies accounted for 90 percent of the expenditures. Had just 10 percent of that money been given directly to poor families, welfare benefits would have doubled in New York (where one out of every 11 recipients in the country lives). And there is every reason to believe that more jobs would have been created than lost, especially in poor neighborhoods, since that's where poor people spend their money.   —T.F.

---

generally, Republican conservatives, while railing about "big government," hand out their patronage through the military. Government spending is rarely about social remedies *or* defense; it's a contemporary form of patronage.)

The Great Society programs were the perfect vehicle for distributing patronage on a grand scale: Community Action, Vista, Model Cities. The service (plus economic development) strategy was to achieve a marriage of otherwise feuding factions: mayors, poor people (who at first had cause for optimism), civil rights leaders, liberals, and the press. Were it not for the Vietnam war, Johnson had every reason to believe reelection in the bag. His programs were shoring up a deteriorating political machine while providing the rhetorical posture for an end to poverty.

Among the War on Poverty designers was Kennedy administration holdover Richard Boone, who repeatedly urged citizen participation in the Office of Economic Opportunity (OEO) programs, believing institutional change possible only with the "maximum feasible participation" of community (poor) people. Community Action Agencies (CAAs) were hatched to do the job.

But with the exception of a few highly publicized locations, input by poor people was nonexistent. In *Betrayal of the Poor*, Stephen Rose wrote that no poor people or neighborhood representatives were involved in any of the 20 cities, although—*after* programs were designed and money budgeted—some members of groups to be served appeared on the agencies' boards of directors. In *The Great Society's Poor Law*, Sar Levitan concurred, noting that "affluent citizens who happened to live in a 'target area' could represent the poor. The law could therefore be observed without having a single low-income person on the CAA board."

CAAs genuinely committed to citizen participation were either swiftly defunded or never got out of the planning stages. Participation of poor people never took place; only the appearance of it occurred.

The mirage of participation had value, though. The impact of the civil rights, women's, and welfare rights movements was felt strongly through the 1970s, so that it was politically uncouth for advantaged parties to act in the absence of input from the disadvantaged. By manipulating the input, the social welfare establishment could appear to address poverty with the imprimatur of poor people (most commonly, women on welfare). The resulting aura of equality made it easier to get and maintain government and private foundation grants. The pretense of poor people's participation thus legitimized the social welfare institutions. The Great Society *did* offer a guaranteed income—to the social welfare establishment. By the 1980s, genuflecting to "participation" was dispensed with altogether.

Meanwhile, various other legislative events also displaced income needs in favor of "service." The 1962 and 1967 Amendments to Social Security Law set the stage. First, the federal government moved to increase the states' revenue share for family services from 50 to 75 percent. Second, states were allowed to contract these services out to *nongovernmental agencies* (previously, local welfare departments were the sole service providers using federal dollars).

Those states that previously and systematically had denied welfare benefits to millions of needy families (especially black families) were now eager to qualify for the windfall revenue sharing. But first they had to find people categorically eligible for welfare. Furthermore, in order to capture services dollars from the feds, states would actually have to pay the families welfare benefits (which were also federally subsidized, but not so liberally). Not to worry. Cash assistance levels were set *by* the states, so it was (1) possible to find families eligible for welfare (to get the federal funding for services) and (2) set AFDC *levels so low that families would stay poor.*

The welfare rolls climbed so fast the phenomenon was characterized as an "explosion." This legislated windfall to states (combined with the War on Poverty strategy of delivering megabucks to state and local governments for "services" to the poor) set off a spending spree—that was peaking just when purchasing power of cash assistance began to decline.

The decrease was coupled with an increase in rhetoric about "dependency" and the necessity for women to "work." Never mind that the jobs didn't (and still don't) exist that would pay enough to lift them out of poverty. Never mind that single parenting under any circumstances *is* "work," and even harder work in poverty.

The Birth of an Industry

What became the professionalization of being human took off, bloating under government contracts. For every poverty problem, a self-perpetuating profession proposed to ameliorate the situation without altering the poverty. In *The Politics of a Guaranteed Income*, published in 1973, Daniel Patrick Moynihan noted the "astonishing consistency" with which middle-class professionals "improved" the condition of lower-class groups by devising schemes that would first improve their *own* condition. It doesn't take a genius to figure out that paying the administrators of a homeless shelter two or three thousand dollars a month for each family instead of providing a permanent apartment is ludicrous. Yet the most massive growth in AFDC spending in the 1980s has been for just that purpose. Furthermore, to keep the "service" engine stoked, every manner of failure has been ascribed to the families themselves. Laziness. Cheating. Dependency. The families lack resources to defend themselves, though the "helping" institutions always have government and/or foundation funds to lobby (ostensibly on the families' behalf) for *more* funding.

What has happened over the last quarter century *has* been an income redistribution scheme, the most disturbing one this country has ever seen: a redistribution from poor women and children to middle-class professionals—with men at the top calling the shots.

This has been done not only with government tax dollars but also with private charitable (and tax deductible) dollars. The United Way. The American Red Cross. The Children's Aid Society. The independent federations of Protestant, Jewish, and Catholic charities. Hands Across America.... Each year, the New York *Times* begs its readers daily, from Thanksgiving to February, for its "Neediest Cases Fund." For nearly a century the *Times* has reported that all the money goes to the poor through eight social service agencies who distribute it, with no funds spent on "administration or fundraising." This is a wild exaggeration from the venerable newspaper; most of the money pays workers' salaries in the agencies, and has for years. Not to mention that the male directors of several of these already obese

agencies are paid salaries in excess of $100,000 annually. Not bad for social work.

The "Workfare" Myth

In the great welfare reform debates of the late 1980s, social welfare professionals fell all over each other running after more funding (for themselves) through the jobs, training, and child care provisions of the so-called welfare reform bill, ironically presided over by Moynihan. Forgotten were the words of the President's Commission on Income Maintenance two decades earlier: "Services cannot be a substitute for adequate incomes; they cannot pay rent or buy food for a poor family." (The few surviving organizations of poor women put guaranteed income at the top of their lists, but they are rarely listened to. After all, they have no money.)

What stalled the "reform" debates for months was the issue of how much money would be allocated for those running the "reform" programs, and a turf war over whether the programs would be run by welfare departments or contracted out to private charities. (Everybody knew getting the women to "work" didn't mean getting them out of poverty.) Welfare rolls dipped slightly and briefly, but are now on the rise again nationwide. And the number and percent of single-parent female families living in profound poverty continues to climb. The relentless theme, from both the right and the left, still is to get those "nonworking" mothers to work.

In fact, the key to the tragedy of U.S. welfare policies is the notion of work—specifically, the unpaid and uncounted labor of women outside the waged labor market. About the only time the word labor is applied to women outside the wage system is in reference to the birthing process.

If any woman reading this were penniless today and went to apply for welfare to feed her children, she would not receive her first welfare check for about a month. Not because the welfare is prohibited from giving her money sooner, but because they are allowed to take 30 days to determine the obvious: that she is poor. The 30-day deadline might come and go with no relief. Or destructive policies plus bureaucratic bungling might prevent a check from ever coming. If she did make it onto the rolls, she might—like at least one million needy U.S. citizens every year—be cut off despite being still legally entitled to welfare. This process has been given the name "churning" by the welfare department, as needy people are routinely cut off and sometimes put back on months later.

One ghastly result of such U.S. social policy is that far more children die from poverty than slip away at the hands of mothers like Ameenah Abdus-Salaam. Twelve times as many poor children die in fires than do nonpoor children. Eight times as many die of disease, according to a study done by the state of Maine—where, by the way, 98 percent of the population is white. Thirty times as many low birth weight babies die as do normal weight babies. In 1987, one in two homeless mothers in New York reported *losing* weight during pregnancy. Even at the bottom, luck plays a role: whose kid is hit by a stray bullet, whose kitchen stove explodes because it was used nonstop as the only source of heat in a frozen apartment, whose infant dies of pneumonia. Poverty is the number one killer of children in the U.S.A. Murder by malfeasance.

Children are poor because their mothers are poor.

Ameenah Abdus-Salaam's tragic acts may not be so mysterious, after all. The miracle is that more women, facing similar anguish, don't do the same.

On September 19, 1990, I attended a court hearing. Ameenah Abdus-Salaam's male attorney had pleaded her "not responsible by reason of mental disease or defect." Two court-appointed psychiatrists agreed, and recommended she be released—no longer a danger to herself or anyone else. District Attorney John Santucci's office refused to accept the recommendation until another psychiatrist, of the D.A.'s choosing, can evaluate her. The case could drag on indefinitely. The male judge has consistently refused to set bail. Ameenah herself was not "produced" for the proceedings. All four walls of the courtroom are of elaborately carved wood. Above the judge's throne, in raised gold letters, gleam the words *In God We Trust*. However misguided it may seem to outsiders, that was the one thing Ameenah Abdus-Salaam intended to do.

49

Self-Help—A Black Tradition

Dorothy Height

This article presents historical examples which counter recent negative portrayals of African American families. The experiences of black Americans under slavery, Jim Crow, and the recent civil rights movement illustrate the deep commitment of blacks to self-help. Contemporary self-help programs are described.

Exercises to Guide Your Reading

1. Describe the traditional black extended family.
2. List the major self-help organizations founded by African Americans.
3. Identify social and economic factors contributing to the history of dual-worker black families.
4. Compare and contrast the approach to improvements in the black community advanced in this reading with those offered in Readings 46 and 47.

It is our task to make plain to ourselves the great story of our rise in America from "less than dust" to the heights of sound achievement.... The situation we face must be defined, reflected and evaluated.
—Mary McLeod Bethune, 1937

Recent negative portrayals of the black family have made it painfully clear to most African-Americans that although much has changed in the national life, much remains the same. The incessant emphasis on the dysfunctioning of black people is simply one more attempt to show that African-Americans do not really fit into the society—that we are "overdependent" and predominantly welfare-oriented. Quite overlooked in this equation is the fact that most black Americans are, on the contrary, overwhelmingly among the *working* poor.

Equally overlooked when the disingenuous topic of the supposed lack of black "self-help" is conjured up, is a fundamental truth: that the major energies of black people in America historically have had to be directed to attaining the most elementary human freedoms (such as owning one's own body and the fruits thereof) that our white sisters and brothers take for granted. The civil rights movement of the 1950s and 1960s was perhaps the most extraordinary example of a mass "self-help" movement in American history: self-help mounted under grave conditions to throw off the yoke of American apartheid. Yet it was not a new event so much as the continuation of an old tradition. Since the end of the slave era black people have had to provide services for one another in every conceivable way: feeding and clothing the destitute; tending the sick; caring for orphaned children and the aged; establishing insurance companies, burial so-

Reprinted by permission of *The Nation.* July 24–31, 1989. pp. 136–38.

cieties, travelers' accommodations when hotels were segregated—the list goes on.

In 1909, almost fifty years before the modern civil rights movement emerged, the National Association for the Advancement of Colored People (preceded by the Du Bois–organized Niagara Movement) was founded following the lynching of a black man in Springfield, Illinois. Its first major undertaking was the fight against the hundreds of such atrocities then occurring annually. The Urban League was founded the next year to advance economic self-help.

Eighteen years earlier, a fearless journalist named Ida B. Wells began a crusade against lynching, by lecturing, organizing and compiling the first documentation of the social, political and economic facts behind the atrocities. In 1895, the National Association of Colored Women's Clubs was formed to bring to bear the collective strength of women in ameliorating the desperate conditions in which our people lived.

What is clear to us in the current era of ever mounting disparagement of the black family—and the internalizing by our young people of the negativism thrust upon them daily—is that we need a movement that will retrieve and build upon the value system of the traditional extended family, the strong sense of kinship ties that goes back to the days of the trans-Atlantic slave trade, when it was up to us either to forge ties of mutual support or perish as a people. Those unbreakable bonds sent people searching for one another after the forced separations of slavery. They are still evident in our custom of calling one another brother and sister—and mother, aunt and uncle—even when there is no blood relationship. There's an entire history behind these interactions that is precious to our sense of self-worth and identity as a people. Those who attempt to supplant our conception of ourselves with their own are either ignorant of this proud history or, worse, bent on concealing or eradicating it.

The history of self-help among blacks offers models that will be useful in the search for innovative approaches to current prob-

lems. For instance, I recall that in 1939, when I worked in the Harlem Y.W.C.A., the Florence Crittendon Homes took in unmarried white mothers, but there was not a bed in the city for unwed black mothers. The only help available to them was in the limited facilities the Y.W.C.A. could provide. To supplement these we found some black women who belonged to an organization called Club Caroline and who were able to acquire a small house to shelter unwed mothers. Their example was followed by black women's clubs all over the country, whose members formed a national network of assistance, keeping registers of people who were willing to take in a young mother. Economic realities today make it impossible for black people to set up enough small homes to accommodate the large numbers of single mothers, drug addicts, the jobless and homeless, and the thousands of unclaimed black infants languishing in hospitals and foster homes.

Nevertheless, we can learn something from the methods used by the traditional black extended family in which adults possessed the authority to look out for the young, whether or not they were blood relatives. We may not be able to restore entirely the old concept of the extended family, given the present complex (and chaotic) social, political and economic conditions in the large urban centers. But enough of it survives to draw upon in encouraging more caring communities in which neighbors look around them to see what's happening and set up networks for alerting others to impending threats. It is important for our young people to know that our past holds valuable traditions. Black sociologists have not been alone in pointing out that instead of constantly focusing on the problems of black families, their white counterparts should examine its historic strengths: the respect for older people, the communal nurturing of children, the ability to feed an entire family on next to nothing, the unceasing toil of parents (often assisted by the community) to send their children through college, the black entrepreneurs who built up businesses to serve our needs after others refused to. In short, our endless coping skills.

We have always stressed the work ethic. We have never been a lazy people; hard work has killed a great number of us. A. Philip Randolph, president of the Brotherhood of Sleeping Car Porters, used to say that what black folk needed was not more work but more pay for the work that they do, and they could manage the rest. It is only recently in the cities, where higher skills are required and the quality of education has deteriorated, that unemployment and the grimmest kind of poverty have become constants and whole generations are growing up in neighborhoods where few people have jobs.

Some social analysts are correct when they say that public policies had a great deal to do with producing this state of affairs, but they refuse to acknowledge the impact of racial discrimination on education and employment. They define a "family" as a social/economic/political unit with a man at its head, and they continue to insist on this definition even at a time when divorce rates and serial marriages, resulting in merged families and increasing numbers of female-headed households, reveal how archaic it is.

For black people, this definition has never applied. Black traditions of the extended family grew out of the primary need to survive, an urgency that for the most part made gender differentials largely irrelevant. So did the grim economic realities that traditionally necessitated that both black men and women work in order to earn a decent living for their families—or, for that matter, to make their way at all. That throughout history many black women have had to accomplish these things without male partners consistently at our sides is much more the result of the racism that limits—and frequently destroys—black males than of "immorality" (as white scholars could discern, if they ever deigned to do research in this area).

Blacks have never said to a child, "Unless you have a mother, father, sister, brother, you don't have a family." I think that the wrongheaded emphasis on the nuclear family has led to the demoralization of young people, both white and black. Because of it, a child who is not part of a nuclear family— or whose family does not behave in the manner of the model—may well say, "I'm nobody."

THE N.C.N.W. AND THE BLACK "FAMILY CELEBRATIONS"

For fifty-four years the National Council of Negro Women [N.C.N.W.]—composed of civic, church, educational, labor, community and professional organizations uniting 4 million members—has carried on the tradition of black self-help. We at the N.C.N.W., following in the footsteps of our founder, the indefatigable educator Mary McLeod Bethune, have focused attention on the concerns of black women and their families. On behalf of young black people, the N.C.N.W. has taken counteractions aimed at restoring or bolstering collective self-esteem in order to lift the morale of the people in coping with the problems they face, whether related to drugs, education, teen-age pregnancy, employability, health problems or whatever they might be.

In recent years we at the N.C.N.W. have built on the special tradition of black "family celebrations" to bring people together. In 1986 we sponsored the first Black Family Reunion Celebration, held on the Washington Mall with almost 200,000 people in attendance. In 1987 three others followed, in Washington, Los Angeles and Detroit. In 1988 a coming-together was celebrated in Philadelphia and again on the Washington Mall in what had become a national movement.

So far, nearly 2 million African-Americans have flocked to the black family celebrations, a turnout that attests to the hunger of our people to hear something other than the constant negativism that is directed our way, to gain strength and inspiration from one another and, in many cases, to secure advice or help from someone we can trust. We have used these occasions to stress black history and the tradition of helping one another, qualified by our awareness that we now live in a society and world that is vastly different from the simpler times in which our sense of community—whatever threatened us—was intact.

In these celebrations, the N.C.N.W. stresses what we consider to be genuine family values. Coretta Scott King shared what it has meant to be a single mother for all the years since her husband's assassination. She spoke not as the wife of a martyred leader but as the mother of children whom she had to bring up alone. We regularly have Masons come to talk about their early history and how they have contributed to the building of their communities. We have celebrities galore, but we also have young people rapping about teen-age pregnancy, drugs or whatever is their most urgent concern. And we also provide allied services. In Washington, when the D.C. Drugmobile was brought to the Mall, the lines before it were as long as those before the black film festival. The impact of our offerings has been felt in the public schools, where teachers report that in the week following the reunion celebration, children flock to school eager to make reports on their activities. All because we have a children's pavilion with black history puppets and African and African-American storytelling.

The N.C.N.W. also offers health checks. At the very first celebration, 20,000 people were tested for cholesterol levels and untold numbers for high blood pressure. Many had never had checkups of any kind before. And children waited patiently in line to get their teeth examined at facilities provided by the Howard University College of Dentistry.

Long lines also formed before our education booths. A young woman taxi driver told me recently that until she and her husband attended the Black Family Reunion Celebration she did not know that someone could earn a high-school diploma without going back to the classroom. Subsequently,

they decided that they were too young to be included in the numbers of unskilled blacks predicted for the year 2000. Both took extra jobs and were studying for the General Education Development test.

I was sobered by the realization that this young woman might have lived near an adult education center and never dreamed that it was meant for her. The N.C.N.W. is helping people understand that they can be active on their own behalf. At the Family Celebration in Atlanta we disseminated information from the Summer Youth Employment Training Program about jobs that were going begging for lack of applicants. When the young people in attendance discovered that the opportunities were not limited to those with special qualifications, they promptly got on the telephone to call their friends. As a result, there were applicants for almost all the jobs before the celebration ended.

There are many such stories growing out of our reunions. Of course, some may say the victories are small compared with the breadth of the problem. But activities in which a million people participate cannot be taken lightly. We at the N.C.N.W. and other black self-help organizations have no intention of spending our time lamenting the inadequacies of a society that has failed to develop the means to make every member aware that he or she belongs. The N.C.N.W. has a wide range of programs to serve African-American women and their families in the United States and an international division to assist women and their families in African countries. Currently, we are working to make a difference in all of the critical areas of human suffering enumerated here. Our first priority, as exemplified by our Black Family Reunion Celebrations, is to make clear that ours is a caring community and to inspire others, particularly our young, to press on in various ways, both to advance themselves and to further the larger struggle of our people.

One lesson is plain as we proceed: that public officials can establish all kinds of public programs thought up by people removed from the problems, and most will not work because the people for whom the programs are intended have been permitted no input in defining the problems as they actually know them to be, or in recommending the solutions. Skilled black professionals (and sensitive others) trusted by the community because they have contributed to its well-being can play a vital role in contributing to the formulation of wiser public policies—if only we can get decision-makers to listen.

CHAPTER 12

Health

50

What Health-Care Crisis?

Fred Barnes

In this article the author challenges conventional wisdom by arguing that the U.S. health care system does not need significant reform. Pointing to both the quality and quantity of its health care, the author concludes that the U.S. system is the best in the world. In his view the major problem is that the key players in the health care policy debates have confused issues of health *insurance* with those of health *care*.

Exercises to Guide Your Reading

1. Summarize the evidence supporting the author's view.
2. Distinguish between "health" and the "health care system."
3. Illustrate the relationship between behavioral and health problems.
4. Develop criteria for evaluating the author's argument.

Bill and Hillary Clinton have contributed heavily to a national myth. Mrs. Clinton, as boss of the administration task force plotting to overhaul America's health-care system, refers routinely to "the health-care crisis." Her husband uses the same phrase ("Our government will never again be fully solvent until we tackle the health-care crisis," Clinton declared in his State of the Union address on February 17). And he goes

Reprinted by permission of *The American Spectator*. May 1993. pp. 20–23.

one step further. "A lot of Americans don't have health insurance," he told a group of schoolkids February 20 during a nationally televised children's town meeting at the White House. "You know that, don't you? A lot of Americans don't have health care."

The press also trumpets the crisis theme. *Parade*, the popular Sunday supplement, emblazoned its February 28 cover with this headline: "THE GROWING CRISIS IN HEALTH CARE." The result is that the American people, despite their personal experience, now believe there actually is a health-care crisis. Most opinion polls show roughly three-quarters of Americans are satisfied with the availability and quality of the health care they receive. Yet, in most polls, 60 to 70 percent feel the health-care system is failing and needs significant, if not radical, reform.

There is no health-care crisis. It's a myth. If millions of seriously ill Americans were being denied medical care, that *would* be a crisis. But that's not happening. Everyone gets health care in this country—the poor, the uninsured, everyone. No, our health-care system isn't perfect. There isn't enough primary care—regular doctor's visits—for many Americans. Emergency rooms are often swamped. The way hospitals and doctors are financed is sometimes bizarre. Health care may (or may not) be too costly. But it's the best health-care system in the world—not arguably the best, but the best. Its shortcomings can be remedied by tinkering, or at least by less-than-comprehensive changes. An overhaul of the sort Hillary Clinton envisions is not only unnecessary, it's certain to reduce, not expand, the amount of health care Americans receive (price controls always lead to less of the controlled commodity). Then we really will have a health-care crisis.

You don't have to take my word that there's no crisis now and that health care here is the world's best. There's solid evidence. Let's examine four key aspects of the health-care debate: access, false measures of quality health care, true measures, and how America's system compares with those of other industrialized democracies (Canada, Germany, Japan, Great Britain).

ACCESS

Will someone please tell Bill Clinton that having no health insurance is not the same as having no health care? The uninsured get health care, only less of it than the insured. Being uninsured means "one is more likely to use emergency-room care and less likely to use office, clinic, or regular inpatient care," said Richard Darman, President Bush's budget director, in congressional testimony in 1991. "This is not to suggest that this is desirable. It is not." But it *is* high-quality health care.

Doctors in emergency rooms are specialists. In fact, they have a professional organization, the American College of Emergency Physicians. Its motto is: "Our specialty is devoted to treating everyone in need, no questions asked." Turning away patients isn't an option. Federal law (section 9121 of the Consolidated Omnibus Budget Reconciliation Act of 1985) requires medical screening of everyone requesting care at a hospital emergency room. If treatment is needed, it must be provided. What this adds up to is "universal access" to health care in America, as one head of a hospital board told me.

It's no secret how much health care the uninsured get. The American Hospital Association estimated in 1991 that hospitals provide $10 billion in uncompensated care annually. Another study found that the 16.6 percent of the nonelderly population who are uninsured—36.3 million people—accounted for 11 percent of the nation's personal health-care expenditures in 1988. They had 37 percent fewer sessions with doctors and 69 percent fewer days in the hospital. There's a reason the uninsured get less health care, beyond the fact most work in low-paying jobs without health insurance. The uninsured tend to be young, thus healthy. According to a new poll by Frederick/Schneiders, 39 percent are 18–29 years of age and another 25 percent are 30–39. By the way, the elderly (65 and up), who require more medical care, are covered. Ninety-nine percent are eligible for Medicare.

To make sure we really have universal access, I checked on how victims of the most recent epidemic, AIDS, are treated. These are the folks doctors are supposed to be leery of dealing with.

What if a penniless AIDS patient shows up at, say, the Whitman-Walker Clinic in Washington, D.C.? That patient, even if indigent, gets treatment. When the time comes (T-cell count below 500), the patient is started on AZT, which costs about $5,000 a year. Later, the patient gets expensive, experimental drugs: DDI, DDC, D-4T. The drugs are paid for mostly by federal funds. There's also doctor care, painkillers, laboratory work. To prevent infections or complications, the patient is treated with prophylaxis.

A friend of mine volunteered to help an indigent, bedridden AIDS patient. He was amazed at the level of care. "It was an endless supply of extremely sophisticated drugs, an elaborate IV system [to feed the patient], and eventually a five-day-a-week home help nurse," my friend said. "Sometimes we had so much medicine, we had to throw it away. There was never a sense we'd be left in the lurch." The patient had no insurance. He lived with a boyfriend, but the boyfriend was not required to pay for any of the care. The federal and city governments—the taxpayers—footed the bill. The American Medical Association says "lifetime medical care" for a single AIDS patient costs $102,000.

FALSE TESTS

Judging by the two most common measures of health, life expectancy at birth and the infant mortality rate, health care in the United States is not the best or even among the best. In 1990, life expectancy in America was 72 years for males, 78.8 for women. This put the U.S. behind Canada, France, Germany, Italy, Japan, and Great Britain, among others. On infant mortality, the U.S. fared still worse, ranking nineteenth in 1989 with a rate of 9.7. (The infant mortality rate is the number of deaths of children under one year of age, divided by the number of births in a given year, multiplied by 1,000.) Finland, Spain, Ireland, East Germany, and Italy finished higher.

What's wrong with these measures? Just this: they're a reflection of health, not the health-care system. Life expectancy is determined by much more than the quality of a nation's health care. Social factors affect life expectancy, and this is where the U.S. runs into trouble. "Exacerbated social problems . . . adversely affect U.S. health outcomes," noted three Department of Health and Human Services officials in the fall 1992 issue of *Health Care Financing Review.* "The 20,000 annual U.S. homicides result in per capita homicide rates 10 times those of Great Britain and 4 times those of Canada. There are 100 assaults reported by U.S. emergency rooms for every homicide. About 25 percent of spinal cord injuries result from assaults." And so on. The incidence of AIDS is even more telling. Through June 1992, there were 230,179 reported AIDS cases here, two-thirds of whom have died. Japan, where life expectancy is four years longer for men than in the U.S. and three years longer for women, has had fewer than 300 AIDS cases. Once social factors have played out, the U.S. ranks at the top in life expectancy. At age 80, when most people are highly dependent on the health-care system, Americans have the longest life expectancy (7.1 years for men, 9.0 for women) in the world.

The infant mortality rate (IMR) is also "reflective of health and socioeconomic status and not just health care," wrote four Urban Institute scholars in the summer 1992 issue of *Health Care Financing Review.* And there are measurement problems. Many countries make no effort to save very-low-birth-weight infants. They aren't recorded as "live born" and aren't counted in infant mortality statistics. In contrast, American hospitals make heroic efforts in neonatal intensive care, saving some infants, losing others, and driving up the IMR. "The more resources a country's health-care system places on saving high-risk newborns, the more likely its registration will report a higher IMR," according to the Urban Institute scholars.

Social factors probably have a bigger impact. A poverty rate twice Canada's and Germany's, a rash of drug-exposed babies, a high incidence of unmarried teenage pregnancy—all lead to low-birth-weight infants and affect the IMR. "Infant mortality rates of babies born to unmarried mothers are about two times higher than the rates of babies born to married mothers," the scholars write. The point is not that America's high IMR is excusable, but that it's grown to abnormal levels in large part because of factors unrelated to the quality of health care.

Not only that. The entire medical system bears the brunt of social and behavioral problems that are far worse in the U.S. than in other industrialized democracies. "We have a large number of people who indulge in high-risk behavior," says Leroy L. Schwartz, M.D., of Health Policy International, a non-profit research group in Princeton, New Jersey. Behavioral problems become health problems: AIDS, drug abuse, assaults and violence, sexually transmitted diseases, etc. "The problem is not the health-care system," says Dr. Schwartz. "The problem is the people. Every year the pool of pathology in this country is getting bigger and bigger. We think we can take care of everything by calling it a health problem." But we can't.

REAL TESTS

While primary and preventive care are important, the best measure of a health-care system is how well it treats the seriously ill. What if you've got an enlarged prostate? Your chances of survival are better if you're treated here. The U.S. death rate from prostate trouble is one-seventh the rate in Sweden, one-fourth that in Great Britain, one-third that in Germany. Sweden, Great Britain, and Germany may have higher incidences of prostate illness, but not high enough to account for the wide disparity in death rates.

An ulcer of the stomach or intestine? The death rate per 100,000 persons is 2.7 in the U.S., compared to 2.8 in the Netherlands, 3.1 in Canada, 4.9 in Germany, 7.6 in Sweden, and 8 in Great Britain. A hernia or intestinal obstruction? The American death rate is 1.7. It's 2 in Canada, 2.7 in Germany, 3 in the Netherlands, 3.1 in Great Britain, and 3.2 in Sweden. Can these be attributed solely to varying incidences of ulcers and obstructions? Nope.

I could go on, and I will. The overall death rate from cancer is slightly higher in America than in Sweden or Germany, but lower than in Canada, the Netherlands, and Great Britain. But for specific cancers, the U.S. has the lowest death rate: stomach cancer, cervical cancer, uterine cancer. Only Sweden has a lower death rate from breast cancer. The U.S. also has the second lowest death rate from heart attack. No matter what the disease—epilepsy, hypertension, stroke, bronchitis—the U.S. compares well. For a country with a heterogeneous population and large pockets of pathology, this is remarkable. Life expectancy for American males at 65 is 14.7 years, only a tad less than Canada (15), Sweden (14.9), and Switzerland (14.9), more homogeneous countries with fewer social problems. (I'm grateful to Dr. Schwartz for all these figures.)

Another measure that's important is the proliferation of new technology. "Major medical technology has had a profound impact on modern medicine and promises even greater impact in the future," wrote Dale A. Rublee, an expert in cross-national health policy comparisons for the AMA's Center for Health Policy Research, in *Health Affairs*. He compared the availability of six technologies—open-heart surgery, cardiac catheterization, organ transplantation, radiation therapy, extracorporeal shock wave lithotripsy, and magnetic resonance imaging—in the U.S., Canada, and Germany in

1987. "Canada and Germany were selected because their overall health-care resources are fairly comparable to the United States," Rublee wrote. The U.S. came out ahead in every category, way ahead in several. In MRI's, the U.S. had 3.69 per one million people, Germany 0.94, Canada 0.46. For open-heart surgery, the U.S. had 3.26, Canada 1.23, Germany 0.74. For radiation therapy, the U.S. had 3.97, Germany 3.13, Canada 0.54. Small wonder that, as Rublee put it, "American physicians, with a universe of modern technology at their fingertips, are the envy of the world's physicians."

RIVAL SYSTEMS

Canadian politicians get special health-care privileges, moving to the head of waiting lists or getting treatment at the elite National Defence Medical Centre. But that wasn't sufficient for Robert Bourassa, the premier of Quebec. He came to the National Cancer Institute in Bethesda, Maryland, for diagnosis, then returned to the U.S. for surgery, all at his own expense.

The Canadian health-care system has many nice attributes, but speedy treatment isn't one of them. Ian R. Munro, M.D., a Canadian doctor who emigrated to the U.S., wrote in *Reader's Digest* last September of a young boy in Canada who needed open-heart surgery to free the blood flow to his lungs. He was put on a waiting list. He got a surgery date only after news reports embarrassed health officials. After waiting two months, he died four hours before surgery. This was an extreme case, but waiting is common in the Canadian system, in which the government pays all costs, including set fees for private doctors. A study by the Fraser Institute in 1992 found that 250,000 people are awaiting medical care at any given time. "It is not uncommon for patients to wait months or even years for treatments such as cataract operations, hip replacements, tonsillectomies, gallbladder surgery, hysterectomies, heart operations, and major oral surgery," according to Edmund F. Haislmaier,

the Heritage Foundation's health-care expert. Canada has other problems: health costs are rising faster than in the U.S., hospital beds and surgical rooms are dwindling, and doctors are fleeing (8,263 were practicing in the U.S. in 1990).

The Japanese model isn't any better. When Louis Sullivan, M.D., President Bush's secretary of health and human services, visited Japan, he was surprised to find medical care matched that of the U.S.—the U.S. of the 1950s. Japan has universal access and emphasizes primary care at clinics, financed mostly through quasi-public insurance companies. The problem is price controls. "Providers seek to maximize their revenue by seeing more patients," wrote Naoki Ikegami, professor of health at Keio University in Tokyo. "This dilutes the services provided."

Patients receive assembly-line treatment. "In outpatient care, a clinic physician sees an average of 49 patients per day [and] 13 percent see more than 100," Ikegami said. For the elderly, a survey found, the average number of doctor's visits for a six-month period was 17.3 (3.6 here) and the length of visits was 12 minutes (30 in the U.S.). Like Canada's queues, this is an extraordinarily inefficient way to dispense care. Patients return repeatedly to get the same care that in the U.S. is given in a single visit.

Japanese doctors also prescribe and sell drugs. Not surprisingly, they sell plenty. Thirty percent of the country's health expenditures are for drugs (7 percent in the U.S.). In Japan, wrote Ikegami, "no real incentives exist to maintain quality." The one exception is specialists at Japan's teaching hospitals. To avoid queues, patients pay bribes of $1,000 to $3,000 to be admitted to a private room and treated by a senior specialist.

Germany also has strict fees for doctors, with predictable results. Annual doctor's visits per capita are 11.5 (5.3 here), a figure exceeded only by Japan (12.9). In other words, price controls are as inefficient in Germany as in Japan. Hospitals face perverse incentives, too. The government pays a fixed rate per day, regardless of the patient's illness or length of stay. So hospitals pad their billings by keeping patients for unnecessarily long recuperations, which compensates for the losses they incur taking care of critically ill patients.

Then there's Great Britain, home of the National Health Service [NHS]. Officials take great pride in having reduced the number of patients waiting more than two years for medical attention. In 1986, the number was 90,000; in 1991, 50,000. In April 1992, it was down to 1,600. Sounds great, but there's a catch. The number of patients waiting six months or less grew by 10 percent. The overall drop in waiting lists was only three percent. And this was achieved, a survey by the National Association of Health Authorities and Trusts found, chiefly because of a 13 percent hike in NHS spending in 1991, not increased efficiency. The good news in Great Britain is that private insurance is allowed and 6.6 million Brits have it. Insurance firms encourage beneficiaries to have an operation or other treatment in a private hospital. Sure, the company pays, but it knows that once a patient has experienced care in a private hospital, he'll never go back to the socialized medicine of NHS. And he'll keep buying health insurance. Private hospitals, anxious to fill empty beds, have their own come-on. At Christmas, they offer discount prices for operations.

In truth, the U.S. has little but painful lessons to learn from the health-care experience of other countries. There's practically nothing to emulate. On the contrary, foreign health officials, Germans especially, now look at the incentives in the American medical system as a way to remedy problems in their health-care systems. Hillary Clinton and health policy wonks should stop apologizing for our system.

They won't. The existence of a few health-care problems, chiefly the lack of proper primary care for several million Americans, allows them to declare a crisis and go on wartime footing. Liberals love this. Hillary's task force meets in private, keeps the names of its members secret, obsesses over leaks, spurns the advice of outsiders (doctors, Republicans). The program that emerges is sure to dwarf the problem. If enacted, it will make the problem worse. This is a common phenomenon in Washington. Some people never learn.

In 1991, an American official addressed Russian health experts in Moscow. He bemoaned that many Americans get care at emergency rooms and occasionally wait six or eight hours. To the American's shock, the Russians erupted in laughter. In Russia, with twice as many doctors per capita as the U.S., a wait of six to eight hours represented unusually fast service.

51

Medical Apartheid: An American Perspective

Durado D. Brooks, David R. Smith, and Ron J. Anderson

The authors describe the similarities between the U.S. and the South African systems of health care. For both societies, the failure to provide adequate hospital services or preventive care combines with the harsh environmental conditions of poverty to produce parallel social consequences. Community-Oriented Primary Care is presented as a viable alternative to the current situation.

Exercises to Guide Your Reading

1. Give examples of similar health care problems (both rural and urban) in the United States and South Africa.
2. Describe the individual and social costs of the existing two-tiered system of medical care in the United States and South Africa.
3. Summarize the Community-Oriented Primary Care model, and compare it to the existing system for delivering health care.
4. Discuss and evaluate the authors' proposals for improving health care for African American and Latino populations.

The Republic of South Africa has been the target of international protests, boycotts, and derision based on the treatment accorded their black majority population. Many of the most strident demands for change have come from the United States. While it is clear that the South African system must be dramatically restructured, it should also be noted that the plight of America's black and brown citizens is in dire need of attention. This is particularly evident in the area of health care.

Most Western nations treat health care as a public good, similar to education for the young. The United States and the Republic of South Africa share the dubious distinction of being the only industrialized countries that continue to view health care as a privilege. This failure to ensure access to basic health care services for all citizens results in substantial economic and human losses for these countries.

The medical care system of presentday South Africa has been recently described by Nightingale et al.[1] The segregated nature of this system is not surprising, but the similarities to health care provision in the United States are startling. The health care systems of both nations are characterized by inadequate (or totally absent) care for large segments of their population, gross inequities in the allocation of health care resources, and poorly coordinated and economically inefficient bureaucracies.

While apartheid in South Africa is strictly along racial lines, the segregation in our

Reprinted by permission of *Journal of the American Medical Association.* November 20, 1991. pp. 2746–49.

country occurs primarily as a function of socioeconomic status. However, since ethnic minorities comprise a disproportionate share of our country's poor, these groups remain the primary victims of oppression. African Americans and Americans of Hispanic descent are more likely to be uninsured and less likely to have access to health care than the non-Hispanic white population.[2] Among hospitalized patients, lack of insurance has been correlated with significantly fewer expensive diagnostic studies and an increased risk of in-hospital death.[3]

Despite dissimilarity in the structure and process of apartheid between the United States and South Africa, the manifestations are the same. The wide disparity in socioeconomic status, preventable disease incidence, and life expectancy between white citizens and people of color in both nations bear witness to the myriad inequities of the current social and health care systems.

SYSTEMS OF CARE

Nightingale et al.[1] describe a South African medical system in which a large number of narrowly focused agencies have been established to address different aspects of health care. The result is a multiplicity of competing authorities that add layers of bureaucratic lethargy and costs, and prevent the efficient provision of health care services. This is analogous to the factionalism present in most metropolitan areas of the United States. In Dallas County, Texas, a variety of city, county, and private agencies provide limited services on varying days at inconsistent locations. Areas of overlap and, more important, major gaps in services abound. Well babies may be seen at one location, but immunizations must be obtained at a different site, while ill children must travel to different clinics or the county hospital. Sites for comprehensive health care services are almost nonexistent. Collaborative attempts to create such comprehensive networks are often met with resistance due to the self-interests of involved agencies, without regard for the needs of the service population.

Through the apartheid laws, the South African government has rigidly divided the nation's population into racially defined groups (white, Asian, colored, and black). On this scale, socioeconomic level and standard of living decline dramatically as cutaneous melanin level rises. Dr. Nightingale places much of the blame for the poor health status of South Africa's blacks on the living conditions, which relegate the black population to periurban "townships" and rural "homelands." Defined as "separate and rigidly segregated communities," these areas are typified by miserable housing, poor sanitation, and inadequate or nonexistent health care. Who can read this description and fail to recognize the haunting similarity to America's inner cities, the *colonias* of south Texas, or our Native American reservations?

Financial and nonfinancial barriers to health care have been built into and reinforced in America's metropolitan areas. Long ago, medicine abandoned urban neighborhoods and completed a process of involution. Primary care and other medical services were pulled from the community, and coalesced at inaccessible "medical centers." These barriers have created and propagated growing segments of our populace that can be aptly described as *Les Miserables*—people constantly searching for ways to get over, around, or through these very real barriers.

South African hospitals that serve the disenfranchised majority population are overcrowded and overwhelmed by the sheer numbers of people needing assistance. Many of these institutions face the additional burdens of outdated equipment and facilities, limited staff, and grossly inadequate budgets.[4]

In many areas of the United States, public hospitals constitute the only health care alternative for the impoverished. Parkland Memorial Hospital in Dallas, Tex, is the primary provider of medical services for the economically disadvantaged of Dallas County. This 940-bed facility has been recognized as one of America's premier medical institutions.[5] Despite this national reputation for excellence, Parkland fights a daily battle for continued economic viability. Like similar public institutions throughout the nation, our service population is overwhelmingly poor and minority. Many of the inequities described in the South African medical system are mirrored in the medical environment in Dallas and in the indigent health care arena across the United States.

Parkland's occupancy rate generally exceeds functional capacity, requiring diversion of ambulances away from our emergency department. Due to the volume of patients needing Parkland's care, medical admissions were diverted to other facilities for a total of 93 days in 1990. Fortunately, diversion of trauma patients has not yet been necessary. However, the 30% increase in trauma volume last year (due largely to drug- and gang-related violence) is threatening to overwhelm this system and thereby diminish resources dedicated to the care of victims of automobile accidents, industrial mishaps, and other trauma.

In addition to the nearly 150,000 patients treated in the emergency department each year, Parkland's outpatient clinics see 1500 scheduled patients every day. While patients with appointments are seen in a timely fashion, an additional 300 patients a day are processed through our walk-in ambulatory care clinic. Waiting times for the ambulatory care clinic average 7 to 8 hours. Due to the lack of accessible primary care services for Dallas' poor, this is the only available site of treatment for many patients. Although many view this as "free care," the burden imposed on the working poor by the loss of a day's wages makes this anything but free. In addition, the long waits cause approximately one of every nine of these nonscheduled patients to leave prior to receiving care. These patients often return later in a more advanced stage of their illness, necessitating more intensive (and expensive) treatment, or hospitalization. Public hospitals across our nation serve a similar "safety net" function, straining their already limited resources.

Conditions are more tenuous for the residents of rural areas in South Africa and the United States. Medical facilities are primitive or nonexistent for South Africa's homelands, and a similar situation is developing in our nation. More than 20% of Texas' 254 counties have no acute care hospital, and 119 counties do not have hospital obstetrical or newborn services.[6] While only 8% of U.S. births occur in Texas, we account for fully one third of all out-of-hospital births nationally (and these births are disproportionately among minority women). This may contribute to infant mortality rates in some rural counties that are seven times greater than the national average.[6]

While the options for care in rural America are diminishing for many, barriers to service for the poor have always been severe (particularly for the poor of color). Without a rural equivalent of public safety net hospitals and their house-staff providers, even those minority patients with Medicaid coverage often cannot find a private physician to provide their care. Recently, in Denton County, Texas (a wealthy county with 33 obstetrician-gynecologists), a patient who had Medicaid coverage was unable to find a physician willing to accept her for pregnancy care (Klein D. "Children at Risk." New York, NY: Public Television, WNET; aired on PBS, November 1, 1991).

PREVENTABLE DISEASE

A number of other parallels between the health care systems of South Africa and metropolitan areas in the United States are evident. These regions share strikingly high rates of black infant mortality, and a greater prevalence of diseases such as tuberculosis, pneumonia, and measles. These diseases have been all but eliminated among South Africa's white minority population through improved education, nutrition, sanitation, and immunization programs. Similarly, U.S. blacks die at much higher rates than whites from preventable diseases. Blacks and Hispanics suffer disproportionately higher complications from diabetes and hypertension, and African-American men in Harlem have a shorter life span than men in many impoverished Third World nations.[7-9]

Precise quantitative comparisons of morbidity and mortality rates in the United States and the Republic of South Africa are difficult due to woeful inadequacies in South African data. This is particularly true for data regarding their black population.[10] However, available information exemplifies the shared health care problems of the nonwhite populations of both nations.

Infant mortality has been viewed as a sensitive indicator of the health status of a population, reflecting adequacy of medical care and social systems. Adverse social circumstances have been strongly associated with increased levels of infant mortality.[11] Despite its position as one of the world's wealthiest nations, the infant mortality rate in the United States remains distressingly high compared with that of other industrialized nations. The U.S. rate of 10 infants lost for each 100,000 births (20th in the world)[12] is a national disgrace.

Even in states such as Texas that have achieved infant mortality rates lower than the national average, there remain danger zones. Analogous to "drowning in a river only 3 feet deep," there are communities in the very shadow of America's finest medical institutions where infant mortality rates rival those of Third World nations.

Accurate figures for black infant mortality for the entire Republic of South Africa are not available, and existing records demonstrate tremendous geographical variation. Black infant mortality rates as high as 282 per 1000 births have been documented in rural homelands,[13] and a national mortality rate for black infants is estimated to be between 94 and 124 deaths per 1000 live births.[14] This is in stark comparison with the nationwide average of 13.5 deaths per 1000 births among white South Africans.[15] Data from selected urban areas in South Africa demonstrate the potential benefits of improving access to health care services (even substandard services). While the ratio of black-to-white infant deaths remains approximately 3:1, black infant death rates as low as 27 per 1000 births have been achieved.[15,16] This rate is actually superior

to current black infant mortality rates of up to 38 per 1000 births in some large standard statistical communities of Dallas County (D. Bacchi, unpublished data, 1990).

Hypertension is prevalent in the black and white populations of both nations. Complications of hypertension such as end-stage renal disease (ESRD) can be prevented through early detection and adequate treatment. Studies of patients with ESRD in two urban areas of South Africa found hypertension to be responsible for 32% and 33% of kidney failure among blacks, but only 10% of the disease in whites.[17,18] In a similar fashion, 42.5% of black patients with ESRD in the United States have hypertension as the primary cause of their renal disease, while hypertension accounts for only 17.4% of ESRD in the U.S. white population.[19] Other investigators have calculated the risk of ESRD from hypertension in Jefferson City, Ala, to be nearly 18 times higher in blacks than in whites.[20]

Measles is yet another preventable disease that takes a heavy toll on the impoverished of both nations. Nonwhite children in South Africa continue to experience significant morbidity and mortality from this disease, while it has been largely eliminated among the white minority.[21,22] Poverty-related factors such as overcrowding, poor sanitation, and malnutrition are clearly related to the spread of this disease, but the failure to ensure immunization of infants and children is the primary reason for the persistence of this scourge.

Along with Los Angeles, Calif., Dallas will long be remembered in our nation's conscience as the center of America's 1990 measles epidemic. Although the disease occurred primarily in ethnic minorities and the poor, the entire Dallas community was affected. The financial costs of more than 2500 cases of measles and the tragedy of young lives lost to this totally preventable disease will haunt us for years to come. The failure to provide a $3 immunization in some cases resulted in thousands of dollars in hospital expenses, while 12 young people paid the ultimate price—death.

OPPORTUNITIES FOR CHANGE

Testimony to the similarity of health care issues in the United States and the Republic of South Africa is also provided by perusal of recent medical literature. Access to care, health care financing, national health insurance, and related topics are frequently recurring themes in the major journals of both nations. It is encouraging to find many of South Africa's physicians and medical institutions at the forefront of the anti-apartheid movement. Organizations including the Progressive Primary Health Care Network and the National Medical and Dental Association have worked aggressively against apartheid and toward a health care plan for postapartheid South Africa.[1,23] In addition, the Medical Association of South Africa (the country's largest physician organization) has called for the abolition of apartheid and the establishment of a social and health care system free of racial and economic discrimination.[24]

The changes proposed to improve the health status of black South Africans are similar to those that are necessary to remedy the situation of the impoverished of Dallas and throughout the United States. The fragmented, categorical system that currently attempts to serve underprivileged citizens should be replaced. This system is inefficient—it creates barriers for patients, resulting in costly delays and duplication of effort. What is needed is ready access to comprehensive primary care services, lack of which has been clearly correlated with morbidity and excess deaths.[7,25,26] Community education and health promotion activities are desperately needed. Any meaningful long-term solution must also include measures to increase the number of minorities pursuing careers in health-related fields.

Dallas County is making strong efforts to improve the deplorable local situation through Parkland Hospital's Division of Community-Oriented Primary Care (COPC). In this model of care, the health status and needs of a defined community are assessed, and a health care plan is designed and implemented based on these identified needs. The COPC approach combines epidemiology, individual patient care, and general public health concerns. The COPC model has been favorably reviewed by the Institute of Medicine.[27] These concepts have been applied in a number of settings in the United States with varying degrees of success.[27,28] Ironically, the basic philosophy and structure of COPC originated in South Africa more than 40 years ago. Working with the native community in Polela, South Africa, Sidney L. Kark, MD, and his associates organized one of the first successful COPC models.[29] Many of the current efforts in COPC have their genesis in the work of Dr. Kark.

With the support of Dallas' citizens and local government, Parkland Hospital's division of COPC is establishing a network of health centers conveniently located in economically deprived neighborhoods. Emphasizing preventive medicine and promoting healthy lifestyles, these centers provide a full spectrum of health care services at accessible locations. Providers are on call 24 hours a day, available to answer questions from worried parents, refill prescriptions, and decrease costly, unnecessary emergency department visits. Care is also provided in nontraditional settings, reaching those in need in homeless shelters, churches, and schools. Evening and weekend office hours ensure access for the working poor (for whom losing a day's wages due to a visit to a physician may have catastrophic consequences). The system is designed to give these disenfranchised citizens something they have never had—a family physician.

Community education programs are an integral part of COPC. These programs are designed to make at-risk populations aware of early signs of disease, the importance of routine preventive care, and the benefits of reducing risk factors for many diseases. The community is empowered by such knowledge, and citizens are encouraged to take a much more active role in their own health care.

The physicians, nurses, and other health

care providers of COPC are of diverse ethnic and societal backgrounds, matched with the populations that they serve. In addition to providing medical care, these providers are encouraged to take an active role in community affairs, and serve as role models for the communities' youth.

The effectiveness of this program is measured by an assessment of baseline health attributes of the target population, and the formation of specific health outcome goals and objectives. Attainment of these objectives will benefit the entire community, and provide direct benefit to health center staff through an incentive program based on these outcomes (a unique aspect of Parkland's COPC model).

The value of such comprehensive care was demonstrated during Dallas' recent measles epidemic. Certain standard statistical communities served by COPC in collaboration with the Dallas County Health Department experienced 60% fewer measles cases than projected for these high-risk areas (Dallas County Health Department, unpublished data, 1990).

This process of assessing the health status, risk factors, and beliefs of a community, then designing interventions based on this profile is undergoing a much needed resurgence in South Africa. Projects such as the Mamre Community Health Project[30] and a recently initiated door-to-door study of cardiovascular risk factors among urban blacks[31] are using techniques pioneered by Dr. Kark 40 years ago.

SOCIETAL IMPLICATIONS

Programs like COPC can change the face of indigent health care provision in South Africa and the United States and we should encourage the development of more such innovations. However, it must be realized that health care does not exist in a vacuum. Nightingale observes that "health specific effects are superimposed on the more general consequences of apartheid," and elsewhere states, "even if apartheid policies ended to-

morrow, their effects on health would persist for years."[1] Society must appreciate the interrelatedness of health, decent housing, education, and economic opportunity. Recent work has shown that, in addition to commonly recognized hazards (diabetes, hypertension, lack of accessible care), poverty functions as an independent risk factor for premature death in African Americans.[32] Poverty and lack of health insurance have also been postulated to be the greatest impediments to health care for Hispanics.[9]

It must be emphasized that there are clear differences in the discriminatory policies in force in South Africa and those functioning in the United States. The Republic of South Africa is a nation in which all social, economic, and political institutions have developed within an all-pervasive racist ideology. Apartheid in South Africa is a legally sanctioned (and in many instances, legally required) policy. Laws such as the Group Areas Act and the various land acts proscribe where one may live and work and who may own property. The recent repeal of these laws will no doubt lead to a gradual improvement in the economic station of some South African blacks; however, this improvement will be years in the making. Meanwhile, apartheid laws and policies continue to disallow any meaningful political participation by the black majority, and severely limit the influence of the Asian and colored populations.

Conversely, in the United States, most legal obstacles to nonwhite progress have been dismantled over the past 40 years, and legislation has been advanced to ensure equal protection under the law for all citizens. This has allowed significant gains in many aspects of life for America's ethnic minorities. Unfortunately, the removal of legal barriers alone is not sufficient to reverse the devastating effects that centuries of discriminatory policies have had on income and educational attainment. Due to these historical inequities, the majority of American's black and brown populations continue to lag far behind the white majority with regard to economic achievement and stability. Though legally sanctioned discrimination based on race has declined, educational and economic realities have imposed and maintained de facto apartheid for a substantial portion of America's minority citizenry.

CONCLUSION

It is clear that South Africa's system of apartheid has entered a terminal phase. As the persecuted majority prepares to reclaim the land of their ancestors, plans for a post-apartheid South Africa are under way. Similarly, our nation must anticipate and prepare for its future.

Those who view America's impoverished and disenfranchised populations solely as a burden on society are failing to recognize economic realities. Over the next 10 years, blacks, Hispanics, and other minorities will make up a large share of the expansion of the U.S. labor force, while white males will constitute only 15% of new entrants to the job market.[33] America cannot maintain its lead position in the international marketplace with a poorly educated, unhealthy work force. It therefore serves the self-interest of today's affluent and middle-class citizens to provide adequate health care and opportunities for educational and economic advancement for our nation's underclass. We must deal with hopelessness and helplessness and the conditions that spawn unhealthy behaviors through policies that encourage inclusiveness and social justice. Only through such empowering processes can we hope to eliminate this functional apartheid from America's medical and social system.

REFERENCES

1. Nightingale E.O., Hannibal M.A., Geiger J., Hartmann L., Lawrence R., Spurlock J. Apartheid medicine: health and human rights in South Africa. *JAMA* [*Journal of the American Medical Association*]. 1990; 264:2097–2107.

2. Trevino F.M., Moyer M.E., Valdez R.B., Stroup-Benham A.S. Health insurance coverage and utilization of health services by Mexican Americans, mainland Puerto Ricans, and Cuban Americans. *JAMA.* 1991; 265:233–237.

3. Hadley J., Steinberg E.P., Feder J. Comparison of uninsured and privately insured hospital patients. *JAMA.* 1991; 265:374–379.

4. Abkiewicz S.R., Ahmed A.S., Alli M.A., et al. Conditions at Baragwanath Hospital. *S. Afr. Med. J.* 1987; 72:361.

5. Dietrich H.J., Biddle V.H. *The Best in Medicine: How and Where to Find the Best Health Care Available.* New York, NY: Harmony Books; 1990:18.

6. Texas Hospital Association. *Women and Children First: A Plan for Improving Texas' Maternal and Child Health Outcomes in the 1990s.* Austin, Tex: Texas Hospital Association; 1991:14.

7. Schwartz E., Kofie V.Y., Rivo M., Tuckson R.V. Black/white comparisons of deaths preventable by medical intervention: United States and the District of Columbia, 1980–1986. *Int. J. Epidemiol.* 1990; 19:591–598.

8. McCord C., Freeman H.P. Excess mortality in Harlem. *N. Engl. J. Med.* 1990; 322:173–177.

9. Council on Scientific Affairs, American Medical Association. Hispanic health in the United States. *JAMA.* 1991; 265:248–252.

10. Botha J.L., Bradshaw D. African vital statistics: a black hole? *S. Afr. Med. J.* 1985; 67:977–981.

11. Molteno C.D., Kibel M.A. Postneonatal mortality in the Matroosberg Divisional Council Area of the Cape Western Health Region. *S. Afr. Med. J.* 1989; 75:575–578.

12. Children's Defense Fund. *The State of America's Children.* Washington, DC: Children's Defense Fund; 1991:60.

13. Knutzen V., Bourne D. The reproductive efficiency of the Xhosa. *S. Afr. Med. J.* 1977; 51:392–394.

14. Yach D. Infant mortality rates in urban areas of South Africa, 1981–1985. *S. Afr. Med. J.* 1988; 73:232–234.

15. Rip M.R., Bourne D.E. The spatial distribution of infant mortality rates in South Africa, 1982. *S. Afr. Med. J.* 1988; 73:224–226.

16. Wyndham C.H. Mortality rates of black infants in Soweto compared with other regions of South Africa. *S. Afr. Med. J.* 1986; 70:281–282.

17. Seedat Y.K., Naicker S., Rawat R., Parsoo I. Racial differences in the causes of end-stage

renal failure in Natal. *S. Afr. Med. J.* 1984; 65:956–958.

18. Gold C.H., Isaacson C., Levin J. The pathological basis of end-stage renal disease in blacks. *S. Afr. Med. J.* 1982; 61:263–265.

19. Eggers P.W., Connerton R., McMullan M. The Medicare experience with end-stage renal disease: trends in incidence, prevalence, and survival. *Health Care Financing Rev.* Spring 1984; 5(3):69–88.

20. Rostand S.G., Kirk K.A., Rutsky E.A., Pate B.A. Racial differences in the incidence of treatment for end-stage renal disease. *N. Engl. J. Med.* 1982; 306:1276–1279.

21. Bourne B.E., Rip M.R., Woods D. Characteristics of infant mortality in the RSA, 1929–1983. *S. Afr. Med. J.* 1988; 73:230–232.

22. Kettles A.N. Differences in trends of measles notifications by age and race in the western Cape, 1982–1986. *S. Afr. Med. J.* 1987; 72:317–320.

23. Mji D., Vallabhjee K.N. Health in post-apartheid South Africa. *S. Afr. Med. J.* 1990; 78:122–123.

24. Policy statement on discrimination in medical practice. *S. Afr. Med. J.* 1989; 75:560. Editorial.

25. Dana M.R., Tielsch J.M., Enger C., Joyce E., Santoli J.M., Taylor H.R. Visual impairment in a rural Appalachian community. *JAMA.* 1990; 264:2400–2405.

26. Council on Ethical and Judicial Affairs, American Medical Association. Black-white disparities in health care. *JAMA.* 1989; 263:2344–2346.

27. Connor E., Mullan F., eds. *Community Oriented Primary Care: New Directions for Health Services Delivery.* Washington, DC: Institute of Medicine, National Academy Press; 1983.

28. Nutting P.A., Wood M., Conner E.M. Community-oriented primary care in the United States. *JAMA.* 1985; 253:1763–1766.

29. Kark S.L. *The Practice of Community-Oriented Primary Health Care.* New York, NY: Appleton-Century-Crofts; 1981.

30. Klopper J.M.L., Tibbit L. The Mamre Community Health Project. *S. Afr. Med. J.* 1988; 74:319–320.

31. Heart disease study launched in western Cape. *S. Afr. Med. J.* 1990; 77:12.

32. Otten M.W., Teutsch S.M., Williamson D.F., Marks J.S. The effect of known risk factors on the excess mortality of black adults in the United States. *JAMA.* 1990; 263:845–850.

33. *Workforce 2000, Work and Workers for the 21st Century: Executive Summary.* Washington, DC: Hudson Institute Inc; 1989:89–95.

52

Women and Health Care: Unneeded Risks

Leonard Abramson

This article shows how gender biases permeate many aspects of the U.S. medical system. The roles of drug researchers, doctors, and federal officials are examined. The consequences of biased practices are discussed.

Exercises to Guide Your Reading

1. List the racial and gender differences that may be medically important.
2. Give examples of gender bias in medical practice and research.
3. Critique research practices that exclude women and minorities.
4. Evaluate arguments in defense of racially and sexually biased medical practices.

Women are spending more on health care than men and consume about 60% of the prescription drugs used in the U.S. each year. Yet, medical researchers treat them with little concern, gearing many of their studies exclusively to males. Often, a physician prescribing for a woman is flying blind—extrapolating from test results based solely on the experience of men.

Arguing that using women in test populations would distort the data because of hormonal changes during the menstrual cycle, many researchers opt to study men. This can lead to faulty conclusions, however. Half the population has menstrual cycles, and they will get better care if it is known how their bodies react to medication.

Heart disease is the number-one killer of women. About 250,000 die from heart ailments each year, about six times the number that are killed by breast cancer. One of every two will fall prey to some sort of heart problem in her life; by contrast, one of every nine will get breast cancer.

The news of a 1988 study of 22,071 volunteers produced banner headlines announcing that small amounts of aspirin on a regular basis can reduce the chances of a heart attack. That good news about aspirin referred only to men—none of the test participants was a woman.

When a woman asks her doctor if she should take a daily aspirin to cut the risk of heart attack, an honest physician must answer, "I don't know." Some doctors, intuitively, say young women don't need aspirin because their naturally high estrogen levels protect them against heart disease. That advice may be sound or foolhardy. The physician isn't sure because no one has studied aspirin's effect on female hearts.

The aspirin study is the rule, not the exception. Research assessing the links between smoking and cataracts examined the medical history of 838 men, but not a single woman. Similarly, not one female was among the 12,866 subjects of a study exploring the relationship between heart disease and high

Reprinted by permission of *USA Today*. September 1992. pp. 87–89.

cholesterol as well as lack of exercise and smoking. Another linking job stress and high blood pressure also excluded women.

Females also get short shrift because such problems as contraception, breast cancer, and postpartum depression don't receive the attention of male ailments. Just three of 2,000 National Institutes of Health (NIH) researchers specialize in obstetrics and gynecology. The NIH spent 10 times as much on AIDS research as on breast cancer in 1989, even though breast cancer killed eight times as many Americans as AIDS in the past decade.

The NIH finally may be seeing the light, scheduling a late 1992 launching of a $500,000,000 study of the major causes of sickness and death in older women—cancer, heart disease, osteoporosis, and stroke. Moreover, it has created the Office of Research on Women's Health to ensure that females are represented appropriately in Federally financed studies.

Clinical trials required before the Food and Drug Administration (FDA) approves new drugs often are limited to men—leaving doctors to guess how they will affect women. Rep. Henry Waxman (D.-Calif.), who chaired Congressional hearings on medical research, came away convinced the exclusion of females is dangerous. "Drugs are developed with incomplete data on metabolic differences between men and women. Diseases are studied without an understanding of the effects of hormones," he noted.

Complaints about research techniques are not just philosophical bleating about equality. The medical dangers are real. For example, the menstrual cycle affects some antidepressant drugs, and most physicians believe medication must be administered differently at various points in the cycle. "Doctors just aren't getting the kind of guidance they need when they try to prescribe for women," Rep. Patricia Schroeder (D.-Colo.) points out.

Women are not the only patients at risk because medical research heavily is biased toward middle-aged white men. Senior citizens, who consume a disproportionately large amount of medication and are major users of the health care system, systematically are excluded from many clinical studies. They also tend to ignore the very real physiological differences between the various ethnic groups.

In an egalitarian society, it may be uncomfortable to talk about gender- or race-based differences, but facts are facts. Metabolic rates vary among ethnic groups, as do drug absorption rates. Jews have Tay-Sachs disease; blacks have sickle cell anemia. Differences must be acknowledged.

Although there is growing recognition of the research gap in both the scientific community and the government, remedies have been slow. The NIH, in particular, deserves low grades for failing to implement its policy of including women as research subjects. Despite the pledge to eliminate "men only" studies, the organization's grant application booklet has not been updated to reflect the new rules. A revised application form was issued in March, 1992—more than four years after the new policy was set forth. The NIH's Division of Research Grants has told its staff that the inclusion of women should not be a "factor of scientific merit" in the initial evaluation of grant applications.

A General Accounting Office (GAO) review of NIH grant applications shows that 20% had no information about the sex of the study group; one-third indicated they would study both sexes, but did not state in what proportions, and a number of applicants proposed all-male studies—without any rationale for excluding females.

In fact, the NIH scientific review group approved an all-male study of coronary heart disease. It said the exclusion of women was appropriate because heart ailments disproportionately affect men—an astonishing judgment since almost as many females as males die from heart disease each year.

NIH deputy director William Raub conceded the failure. "The word didn't get to everyone it should have reached. Those who received the word about the policy don't seem to understand it, and most distressing of all . . . some of those who received this policy and understand it have demonstrated some arrogance or indifference with respect to it," he told Congress after hearing the GAO report. The NIH has vowed to do better, and director Bernadine P. Healy is pushing for more inclusion of women in future studies.

FDA officials warn that drug companies may stop making new products if excessively stringent rules require that test populations include women or the elderly. Pharmaceutical industry officials claim that forcing them to include women, the elderly, or other specific groups would boost costs and cause delays in getting new treatments to market. Some have complained that clinical tests might be "subgrouped to death."

Expanding test populations will cost money. Research that includes both men and women must be larger than a one-sex study to have the same statistical validity. In effect, the researcher must conduct two parallel studies because test subjects should be as similar as possible to ensure that the only variable is the tested treatment itself. In this case, good economics produces faulty research.

Females also must be alert to doctors who are less aggressive when treating ill women. A study team at the Cedars-Sinai Medical Center in Los Angeles concluded that women have to be much sicker than men before physicians recommend heart bypass surgery. As a result, female patients, older and sicker, were more likely than males to die during the post-operative period.

The researchers indicated that women were far more likely to have suffered a heart attack or other sign of coronary disease before being recommended for bypass surgery. Men frequently had bypass surgery following abnormal stress tests, even though there had not been any clinical symptoms of disease. "For women's symptoms to be acted on, they have to be significantly sicker. They have to prove there is something going on," Dr. Steven Kahn of Cedars-Sinai told *The New York Times*.

The Cedars-Sinai study suggests that physicians are lulled into complacency because coronary disease tends to strike women later in life than it does men. Estrogen, which is produced in the ovaries until menopause, appears to provide females with a natural protection against heart attacks.

A perception that heart attacks are a man's problem seems to have reduced the vigilance of both doctors and their female patients. Yet, after menopause, women develop heart ailments at the same rate as their male counterparts.

Men start to die from coronary ailments in their 40s. Women's hearts tend to give out in their late 50s or early 60s. Each year, about 250,000 of each sex die from heart disease, but death rates are dropping more rapidly for men.

Most physicians resent suggestions they treat women with less concern than men. They say it is often harder to diagnose heart ailments in women. Men are more likely to have heart attacks as a first symptom of coronary disease. For women, the first sign of trouble often is chest pain that is easy to mistake for other problems.

The Cedars-Sinai study is just one of several inquiries that suggest women have a harder time getting treatment for heart disease. It seems likely that doctors' attitudes are part of the reason.

One study revealed that only four percent of women with abnormal stress tests were referred for angiograms in an effort to find blockages in coronary arteries. Forty percent of men with similar results were told to have the procedure.

Boston-area medical research institutions produced some dismaying results when they gathered 13 male doctors to review videotapes of a man and a woman complaining about chest pains. Both patients were 40 years old, smoked, and said they had high-stress jobs.

Two-thirds of the internists urged additional tests and evaluation for the male patient, but only one-third thought the female should have further tests. All the doctors said the man should stop smoking, but not one thought the woman should quit. Two of the 13 felt she was a candidate for psychiatry.

CANCER, C-SECTIONS, AND OTHER WORRIES

Women often are the victims of lax care, conflicting research, and unreliable testing, even when dealing with medical matters peculiar to females. Cancer is probably the single most frightening word for many Americans. For most women, breast cancer is the most dreaded malignancy. It kills 40,000 Americans each year, and the treatment is physically and emotionally traumatic.

The best chance of cure and of avoiding mastectomy to remove the cancerous breast is early detection—through self-examination and mammogram—and prompt treatment. It is estimated that one-fifth of breast

Average-size lump found by getting regular mammograms

Average-size lump found by first mammogram

Average-size lump found by woman practicing regular breast self-examination (BSE)

Average-size lump found by woman practicing occasional BSE

Average-size lump found by woman untrained in BSE

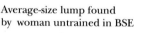

FIGURE 2.   Size of tumors found by mammography and breast self-exam.
Source: The Breast Health Program of New York

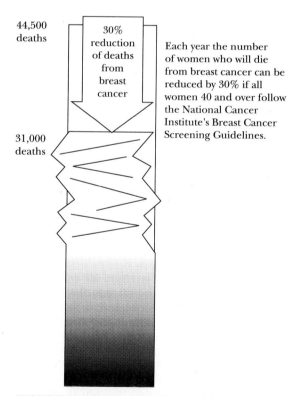

44,500 deaths

30% reduction of deaths from breast cancer

Each year the number of women who will die from breast cancer can be reduced by 30% if all women 40 and over follow the National Cancer Institute's Breast Cancer Screening Guidelines.

31,000 deaths

FIGURE 1.   Cancer screening could save 13,500 women's lives.
1 - Estimated deaths for 1991
2 - Projected reductions
Source: The National Cancer Institute, 1991

cancer deaths could be prevented by a timely mammogram. Nevertheless, too few doctors follow American Cancer Society (ACS) guidelines urging regular mammograms beginning at age 40. Only 37% heed the recommendations for mammogram X-rays every one to two years after age 40 and once a year upon reaching 50, according to a 1989 survey by the Society.

A 1988 poll by the Roper Organization for *U.S. News and World Report* showed that 46% of women above the age of 45 never had received a mammogram. Of these, 56% said their physicians never suggested it. Expense—the procedure can cost as much as $200—was cited by more than one-quarter as a reason for forgoing the exam.

A study released by the Physician Insurers Association of America in July, 1990, revealed a disturbing tendency for doctors to minimize patients' discoveries of breast lumps. It noted that, in 69% of malpractice cases which resulted in payment to the patient, the physician delayed action after the patient discovered a breast lump. In more

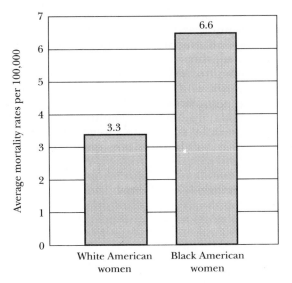

FIGURE 3. The likelihood of black American women dying from cervical cancer.

Source: Cancer Statistics Review, 1973–88, The National Cancer Institute

than half the cases, the doctors said their own physical findings were at odds with the patients'. Doctors guilty of malpractice hardly are representative of the profession, but that study shows one more reason for women to be vigilant.

Women—indeed, all patients—also experience medical uncertainty due to variabilities in laboratory standards. Pap smear tests to detect cervical cancer have caused unneeded trauma because of enormous sampling error and a very high number of "false positive" results.

In one scandalous 1990 incident, New York City's Department of Health acknowledged it had a year's backlog of 2,000 unanalyzed Pap smears. How many women have missed out on a timely treatment because their test results figuratively were lost in the mail?

While doctors are slow to recommend heart bypass surgery for women, they seem far too eager to deliver babies by Caesarean section. The C-section rate nearly has quintupled, from 5.5% in 1960 to nearly 25%— an increase without any plausible medical

explanation. In 1987, there were 934,000 C-sections performed in the U.S. A study by the Public Citizens Health Research Group estimates about half the C-sections were unnecessary and half of these could have been avoided by vaginal deliveries for women who had a Caesarean simply because they had one before.

The Public Citizens data suggests some C-sections are motivated by money. The report cited C-section rates in private for-profit hospitals of nearly 25% in 1987, compared to 15% for public hospitals and military facilities. Self-paying patients were far less likely than those with insurance to have Caesareans.

The incidence of this procedure varies widely among individual doctors. In Maryland, for example, some physicians reported that better than half their deliveries were by C-section. Of 484 Maryland doctors delivering more than 20 babies in 1987, 172 reported performing C-sections over 30% of the time and 43 had rates that exceeded 40%. At the other extreme, 12 physicians performed C-sections less than 10% of the time.

Such wide variances can not be explained by facts. The frequency with which doctors diagnosed dystocia or hard labor seems to explain much of the variation. Clearly, "hard labor" is in the eye of the beholder.

Hysterectomies also are performed with greater frequency than many experts think necessary. Studies show wide regional variations that are hard to explain. Fewer than five of 1,000 women have hysterectomies in the Northeast, but eight of 1,000 in the South undergo the procedure.

Medicine is not perfect. Some practitioners think it is as much art as science. Diagnosis can be tricky, and the same symptoms may mean different things in different people—the physician truly needs to know his or her patient.

Nonetheless, saving money is a poor reason for designing medical research that excludes half the population. When thousands of women die because doctors did not treat them quickly enough or poorly designed research provided incomplete information, there is something woefully wrong. Unnecessary surgery—whether C-sections or avoidable mastectomies—should not be tolerated. It adds billions of dollars to the nation's health care costs and causes unneeded pain and suffering.

There is a growing realization that much of our medical research is flawed. It would be unforgivable if women's health care continued to suffer because we failed to act.

Quality measurements of medical care can reduce unnecessary surgery and procedures. Along with annual certification using quantitative measurements for care, they also can save more than 20% from the nation's health care bill.

Oscar Wilde once said that "Success is a science. If you have the conditions, you get the results." We know how to get the results for women. It is our duty to create the conditions.

53

Hispanic Health in the United States

Council on Scientific Affairs

The authors identify and describe the conditions that predispose Hispanic Americans to a disproportionate share of illness and poor health. The impact of low income and lack of health insurance is analyzed. Cultural and language differences, along with the process of acculturation, are discussed.

Exercises to Guide Your Reading

1. Describe the major demographic differences between Hispanic and non-Hispanic populations.
2. Illustrate the relevance of demographic characteristics for health status.
3. Summarize the problems Hispanics face when they attempt to utilize the health care system.
4. Compare the health care status of the three major subgroups of Hispanics.

Poverty, lack of education, and access barriers to health care predispose many American minorities to disproportionate mortality and morbidity. Hispanics are the fastest growing minority in the United States. Since 1980, the Hispanic population has increased 34%, while the non-Hispanic population has increased only 7%. In March 1988, there were 19.4 million Hispanics in the United States.[1,2] By 2000, Hispanics will number an estimated 31 million, the largest minority group in the United States.[3]

Certain factors contributing to morbidity and mortality features are endemic among Hispanics, particularly when examined by subgroup. In addition, cultural norms, poor knowledge of English, and socioeconomic status affect Hispanics' use of health care. Compared with non-Hispanics, Hispanic families are more than 2½ times as likely to live below the poverty level.[1] Poverty and lack of health insurance contribute to the Hispanic health care challenge of today. This report examines these concerns and suggests ways for the American Medical Association to educate physicians about the health needs of this growing population.

BACKGROUND

Demographics

The Hispanic population has diverse national origins and cultures. The literature divides Hispanics into five subgroups: Mexican American, Puerto Rican, Cuban American, Central or South American, and "other" Hispanics.

Persons of Hispanic descent may have recently moved to the United States or their families may have lived here for centuries. Hispanics may be bilingual, speak only English, speak only Spanish, or speak a little of

Reprinted by permission of *Journal of the American Medical Association*. January 9, 1991. pp. 248–52.

both. When Spanish is spoken, Hispanics often use different idioms among subgroups, which makes communication confusing among the different groups. In addition, cultural values, education, and family income vary by subgroup. Most of the literature focuses on Mexican Americans, Puerto Ricans, and Cubans. Scant data exist on Central or South Americans and other Hispanic subgroups.

Of the 19.4 million Hispanics in the United States, 62.3% are of Mexican origin, 12.7% are Puerto Rican, 5.3% are Cuban, 11.5% are Central or South American, and 8.1% are of other Hispanic origin. Subgroups tend to concentrate in different geographic areas, with Mexicans in California and Texas, Puerto Ricans in New York, and Cubans in Florida. Chicago has the most diverse cultural groupings, with proportions similar to the national divisions.[1,2] . . . Table 1 further breaks down the Hispanic population by state.[4]

High birthrates and immigration account for the rapid Hispanic population growth in the United States. Compared with the fertility rate of the general population (65 of 1000 births), Hispanics have a higher fertility rate (97 of 1000 births), give birth to children at younger ages, and have more children.[3] Since the median age of Hispanics is 25 years and males and females are proportionally distributed, the high birthrate is expected to continue.

As of 1988, about half of all Hispanics completed 12 years of schooling. However, more than twice as many non-Hispanics as Hispanics finished 4 or more years of college. Less education predisposes Hispanics to high unemployment rates and poverty. Lack of education may also limit Hispanic understanding and use of the US health system.

Employment rates differ slightly between Hispanics and non-Hispanics, but proportionally many more Hispanics (8.5%) are unemployed compared with non-Hispanics (5.8%). For Hispanics, the 1988 mean income was $25,736, in contrast to $37,388 for non-Hispanics. Compared with non-Hispanics, Hispanics are more than $2\frac{1}{2}$ times as likely to live below the poverty level. Of the subgroups, Cuban Americans have the highest incomes, while Puerto Ricans have the lowest. Nearly 40% of Puerto Ricans live below the poverty level, in contrast to about 14% of Cubans (Figure 1).[1]

Despite their lower incomes, Hispanics spend proportionally more of their disposable income on health care. Yet as a group, Hispanics are more likely than the general population to be uninsured. Cuban Americans, with the most education and highest incomes, are the most likely to have private

TABLE 1.   States with the Largest Hispanic Populations, 1988*

State	State's Hispanic Population, in Thousands	State's Total Population of Hispanics, %	State's Hispanic Population as Share of US Hispanic Population, %
California	6762	24.3	33.7
Texas	4313	25.8	21.5
New York	1982	11.2	9.9
Florida	1586	12.7	7.9
Illinois	855	7.5	4.3
Arizona	725	20.8	3.6
New Jersey	638	8.4	3.2
New Mexico	549	36.7	2.7
Colorado	421	13.0	2.1

*Data from the US Bureau of the Census.[4]

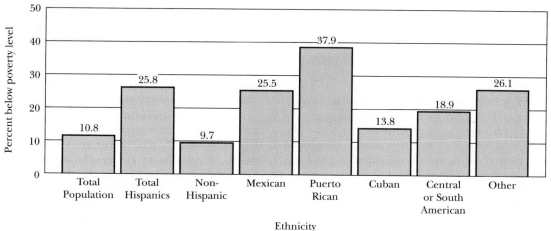

FIGURE 1. Percent of families below the poverty level in 1987.
Data from the US Bureau of the Census.[1]

health insurance (74%). Puerto Ricans, with the lowest incomes and highest unemployment rates, are most likely to have Medicaid coverage (32%). Although more Mexican Americans than Puerto Ricans are employed, they are the most likely to be uninsured (30%) (Figure 2).[5,6] Mexican Americans who work tend to have jobs with no insurance benefits and/or they cannot afford insurance premiums for their large families.[4]

Use of Health Care

Use of health care by Hispanics is affected by perceived health care needs, insurance status, income, culture, language, and other factors that are beyond the scope of this report. Based on data from the National Health Interview Survey, Mexican Americans, who have the least insurance, visit physicians least often. Puerto Ricans have the highest physician visit rates, suggesting that

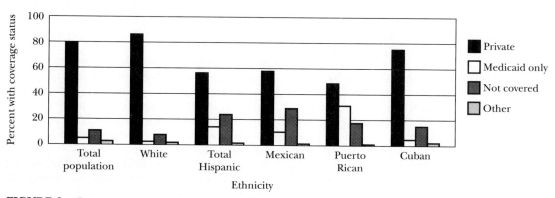

FIGURE 2. Insurance status of persons younger than 65 years in the Standard Metropolitan Statistical Area in 1978 and 1980.
Data from Trevino and Moss.[6]

persons on Medicaid have greater access to care than other poor, uninsured groups and that they tend to have more severe illnesses than those who are employed and insured.[6,7]

Preliminary data from the Hispanic Health and Nutrition Examination Survey (HHANES) of the National Center for Health Statistics, conducted in 1982 to 1984, confirm these trends. Compared with whites, about half as many Hispanics have a regular source of health care.[8] Thirty-nine percent of Puerto Ricans had a physical examination within a year, compared with 34% for Cubans and 25% for Mexican Americans.[3] Excluding Cubans, only about 60% of Hispanics initiate prenatal care in the first trimester, compared with 80% of whites. Hispanics are three times as likely as non-Hispanics to receive no prenatal care. Among the subgroups, Puerto Ricans received prenatal care later and less often.[3] Variation in Medicaid coverage may exist because of concentrations of Hispanics of different national subgroups in states with high Medicaid eligibility requirements.

Compared with whites, twice as many Hispanics report using the emergency department as a source of primary care. Digestive disorders and physical impairment constitute the most frequent presenting problems vs other potentially more serious conditions, such as circulatory and respiratory difficulties.[9] In addition, Hispanics are more apt to enter hospitals via emergency departments. Compared with whites, Hispanics have longer and more expensive hospital stays.[10]

Health care use is also governed by access to comprehensive and preventive health care. Overall, Hispanics are less likely to have private insurance than either whites or blacks.[11] Working Hispanics are more likely to be underemployed, employed part-time, or have jobs with no insurance benefits. Jobs that do offer insurance may impose high co-payments for employees, which Hispanics often cannot afford to pay because of their large families. This lack of insurance restricts Hispanic access to adequate health care.[11,12] As an urban and poor minority,

Hispanics receive the most health care from large, public hospitals that have rotating staffs, particularly for patients on Medicaid or other public funding.[13] In such settings, patients rarely experience continuity of health care. Hispanics who have no insurance or have public funding find themselves seeking care from institutions that focus on tertiary rather than primary care.

Low incomes and lack of health insurance restrict Hispanic access to primary health care more than any other variables.[11] Expanding Medicaid coverage to include everyone below the federal poverty level and mandating that employers offer health insurance for reasonable premiums would help Hispanics who have little or no insurance coverage.

In addition, Hispanics face cultural and language barriers. Although Hispanics constitute 7.9% of the US population, less than 5% of all US physicians and students in medical schools are Hispanic.[14] Differences in culture and language from that of most health care workers contribute to a lack of use of preventive care by Hispanics. For example, Hispanic patients who speak English are more likely to have a regular source of medical care compared with those who speak only Spanish.[15] Because Hispanics, blacks, and other minorities are underrepresented in medical schools, the American Medical Association has encouraged the recruitment and retention of these students.[16,17]

Furthermore, patients who are poor and do not speak English well or at all and who feel estranged from the complicated US health care system encounter complex obstacles to accessing preventive care. Acculturation, or the adaptation of persons from one culture to another, influences Hispanic use of health care. A recent study of Mexican Americans showed that less acculturated persons had significantly lower likelihoods of outpatient care for physical or emotional problems. Even when controlling for need, the less acculturated patients with Medicaid used inpatient services four times less than the more acculturated patients with Medicaid.[18] Other research supports the hypothesis that Hispanics need services but are reluctant to use them because of barriers related to culture and language. When researchers manipulated variables by minimizing cultural and language obstacles, Hispanic use of the health services at that facility increased.[19]

At times, Hispanic patients may be more likely to perceive their illnesses according to folk practices. Folk-defined illnesses or culture-bound syndromes have intrigued researchers over the years, and as a result they may be more of an artifact in the literature than a prevalent cultural influence. Hispanic patients may describe their illnesses according to their cultural understanding. For example, patients may complain of a fright sickness known as *susto* or a fighting attack called *ataque*. Often these complaints have biologic bases that need careful and sensitive medical exploration to accurately diagnose and treat the illness.[20-22]

Controversy exists among Hispanic health experts concerning the frequency with which folk healers, or *curanderos*, are used. Anderson et al[23] note that while up to 20% of Hispanics may regularly use home remedies, the use of folk healers may be infrequent. Pedro Poma, MD, believes this practice varies considerably among the cultural subgroups and that the practice is fairly widespread in some subsets (oral communication, April 1990).

When communicating with a Hispanic patient, health care providers are often, either directly or indirectly, communicating with the patient's family. Most Hispanic families emphasize interdependence, affiliation, and cooperation. Important decisions are made by entire families, not individuals.[3] Thus, Hispanic patients may discuss the physician's diagnosis and treatment recommendations with their families before deciding to follow them.

HISPANIC HEALTH STATUS

Mortality

Accurate estimates of Hispanic death rates are impossible to determine because, until 1988, the national model death certificates did not contain Hispanic identifiers.[3] Although some states incorporated Hispanic origin on their death certificates, such reporting is not uniform and lacks precision. For example, funeral directors completing death certificates may indicate ethnic origin by observation rather than by inquiry with family.[24] The standardized collection of consistent vital statistics on Hispanics by designated state agencies would provide more accurate data.

Nevertheless, researchers have attempted to study Hispanic mortality rates by examining surnames on death certificates and by reviewing 1979 to 1981 mortality data tapes from the National Center for Health Statistics, which classified deaths by age, sex, cause of death, and place of birth.[3,25,26] Overall, Hispanics die of the major national killers: heart disease, cancer, and stroke.[3] Compared with the general population, Hispanics suffer from excess incidence of cancer of the stomach, esophagus, pancreas, and cervix.[27] Death due to stomach cancer is twice as high for Hispanics as for whites.[3,27,28] Hispanic women suffer from cervical cancer twice as often as white women,[3,27,29] but their 5-year survival rates slightly exceed those of whites.[30]

Alcoholism and cirrhosis are prevalent among Hispanics, particularly Mexican Americans and Puerto Ricans.[3,31,32] Mexican-born men have a 40% higher risk of death due to cirrhosis than white men. A review of autopsies from the University of Southern California Medical Center between 1918 and 1970 revealed that 52% of all deaths of Mexican-American men aged 30 to 60 years were due to alcoholism, compared with 24% for white men.[31] In addition to alcoholism, Hispanics share a disproportionate number of deaths due to narcotic addictions.[3]

Violent deaths account for high mortality rates among male adolescents and young adults of Mexican-American, Puerto Rican, and Cuban origin.[25,26] All three Hispanic male subgroups exceed white male deaths due to homicide. Puerto Rican males have higher death rates due to homicide than black males. Cuban and Puerto Rican males

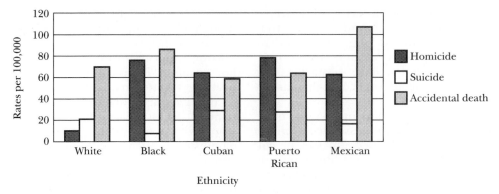

FIGURE 3.   Male age-adjusted homicide, suicide, and accident death rates in the United States from 1979 to 1981. Solid bars indicate death by homicide; hatched bars, suicide; and dotted bars, accidents. Data from Rosenwaike.[25]

surpass white males for suicides. Accidents occur most frequently among Mexican-American males and least often among Cubans (Figure 3).[25]

Morbidity

Of the three major subgroups, Puerto Ricans report the worst health status. In 1979 to 1980, more Puerto Ricans reported chronic health problems as a limitation of their major activities than blacks, Mexican Americans, and Cubans. At the same time, compared with whites and other Hispanic subgroups, Puerto Ricans had the highest incidence of acute medical conditions.[6, 20]

Compared with whites, Hispanics have three times the risk of diabetes.[12, 33] Obesity and diet are largely correlated with diabetes in Hispanics. The HHANES study revealed that 26.1% of Puerto Ricans, 23.9% of Mexican Americans, and 15.8% of Cubans aged 45 to 74 years have diabetes.[31] In addition, approximately 30% of males and 39% of females of Mexican-American descent are overweight, as are 29% of males and 34% of females of Cuban descent and 25% of males and 37% of females of Puerto Rican backgrounds.[34] Mexican-American women suffer from gallstones twice as frequently as white women. In addition, Mexican Americans

have a higher incidence of gallbladder cancer than whites.[12, 35]

Not only do more Mexican Americans have diabetes than whites, but their disease is also of greater metabolic severity and places them at higher risk for complications. For example, Mexican Americans suffer a higher prevalence of diabetic retinopathy. In addition, the incidence of diabetes-related end-stage renal disease has been reported to be six times that of whites.[35] Given the Mexican-American propensity for obesity and diabetes, it is not surprising that this group also tends to have higher levels of cholesterol and triglycerides than whites.[36, 37] Despite these potential risks, the incidence of cardiovascular mortality is not greater for Mexican Americans than whites.[3, 35, 37]

In general, Hispanics who are poor exhibit a higher risk for unrecognized and untreated hypertension.[3, 37–39] Also, hypertension is more prevalent among Hispanics than whites.[3, 12, 37] Data from the HHANES study indicated that almost half of the Puerto Ricans surveyed with hypertension did not know they had it.[40] Cigarette smoking among Hispanics contributes to their risk for cardiovascular disease. According to data from the HHANES study, 43.6% of adult Mexican-American men smoked compared with 41.8% of Cuban men, and 41.3% of Puerto

Rican men.[41] A San Francisco (Calif) study revealed that men who are less acculturated have higher smoking rates and women who are more acculturated smoke more than their less culturally adapted counterparts.[42] Researchers link smoking with the nearly doubling of lung cancer rates among Hispanic men and women from 1970 to 1980.[31]

In addition to an increased risk for lung cancer, the incidence for tuberculosis is 4.3 times greater for Hispanics than whites.[43] From 1980 to 1987, New York City experienced a marked increase in tuberculosis cases, especially among 30- to 39-year-old Hispanics. Researchers suggest this increase relates to latent tuberculosis infection, which is activated by the human immunodeficiency virus (HIV) among Hispanics in that city.[43]

Although Hispanics constitute only 7.9% of the US population, they account for 14% of reported acquired immunodeficiency syndrome (AIDS) cases, nearly 21% of AIDS cases among women, and 22% of all pediatric AIDS cases.[3,44] Hispanics are at greater risk for HIV infection, not because of their race and culture, but because of underlying factors such as living in high-prevalence areas and exposure to intravenous drug use.[44] Most of the Hispanic AIDS cases in the Northeast are among intravenous drug users. Heterosexual transmission of HIV from intravenous drug users to their sexual partners is more prevalent among Hispanics because of cultural restrictions against the use of condoms[45] (Navarro M. AIDS and Hispanic people: a threat ignored. *The New York Times*. December 29, 1989: 1, 4). The 1987–1988 National Center for Health Statistics Survey indicates that Hispanics know less about HIV and AIDS than non-Hispanics.[46] An Oregon survey of Hispanic outpatients revealed that only 50% thought condoms could help prevent transmission of HIV.[47] Because certain groups are at greater risk for HIV infection through drug use and because cultural differences may affect the understanding of HIV transmission, the American Medical Association suggests that AIDS prevention education programs be tailored

to subgroups (such as Mexican Americans and Puerto Ricans) considering their cultural and language differences.[48]

Perhaps related to cultural restrictions on the use of condoms and the cultural importance of motherhood and child rearing, Mexican-American females tend to have high rates of teenaged pregnancies and high-parity births. According to 1983 and 1984 data from 23 states, 31% of Mexican-American females and 30% of Puerto Rican females aged 15 to 19 years have given birth.[3] Despite the young ages at the time of pregnancy and the lack of prenatal care, Hispanic females, especially Mexican Americans, have lower rates of premature deliveries and low birth weight.[3,49,50] Among the subgroups, Puerto Ricans have the highest birthrates for unmarried young women and the highest infant mortality attributed to low birth weight. Puerto Rican poverty and its effect on access to health care contribute to this group's lack of prenatal care and concomitant infant mortality.[12,51] As Hispanic women become more acculturated, the risk of giving birth to low birth weight babies increases.[50] In addition, increased acculturation is associated with decreased breast-feeding of infants. These trends, combined with the fact that Hispanics are three times more likely than non-Hispanics to receive *no* prenatal care, contribute to the morbidity of urban, poor Hispanic mothers and infants.[3]

SUMMARY

Hispanics are the fastest growing minority in the United States. As a heterogeneous group, Hispanics are multicultural and can be monolingual or bilingual. They are divided into five subgroups: Mexican American, Puerto Rican, Cuban, Central and South American, and other Hispanics. Poverty, little education, lack of insurance, and high unemployment rates pose barriers to health care for Hispanics.

Poverty and lack of health insurance are the greatest impediments to health care for Hispanics. Use of health care services by Hispanics is affected by perceived health needs, socioeconomic status, insurance, language, and culture. Many Hispanics who work cannot afford insurance premiums. Those without insurance who report health needs avoid the health system until they are ill. The literature suggests that as Hispanics adjust to the US health system, both culturally and linguistically, they will use health services more often and more beneficially.

The literature also suggests that as Hispanics become more acculturated, their health status worsens. Hispanics increase their use of tobacco and consume a less healthy diet as they adapt to the US culture. As Hispanics live longer in the United States, their morbidity and mortality rates for certain diseases increase. Hispanics suffer a disproportionate share of AIDS cases, and males are more likely to die of violence. Diabetes, hypertension, tuberculosis, certain cancers, and alcoholism rates are higher for Hispanics than for whites.

By working with Hispanic health organizations on health promotion and disease prevention through community advertisement and education and by increased recruitment and retention of Hispanic medical students, the medical system can help Hispanics become more involved with their own health care. In addition, Spanish-language preventive health literature can help the less acculturated understand and use the health system appropriately. Finally, medical research geared toward decreasing the disproportionate rates of mortality and morbidity among Hispanics will contribute to the greater well-being of all Hispanics and to the knowledge and skill of all health providers.

REFERENCES

1. US Bureau of the Census. *The Hispanic Population in the United States: March, 1988*. Washington, DC: US Dept of Commerce; 1988. Current Population Reports series P-20, No. 438.
2. Arnold C.B. From the editor's desk. *Stat. Bull.* 1988; 69:1.
3. *Delivering Preventive Health Care to Hispanics: A Manual for Providers*. Washington, DC: The National Coalition of Hispanic Health and Human Services Organizations; 1988.
4. US Bureau of the Census. Washington, DC: US Dept of Commerce; 1989. Current Population Report series P-20, No. 444.
5. Lipton B., Katz M. Understanding the Hispanic market. *Med. Market Media*. 1989; 24:9, 10, 12, 18.
6. Trevino F.M., Moss A.J. Health insurance coverage and physician visits among Hispanic and non-Hispanic people. In: *Health—United States, 1983*. Washington, DC: Public Health Service; 1983:45–48. US Dept of Health and Human Services publication PHS 84-1232.
7. Trevino F.M., Moss A.J. *Health Indicators for Hispanic, Black, and White Americans*. Washington, DC: Public Health Service; 1984. US Dept. of Health and Human Services publication PHS 84-1576. National Center for Health Survey series 10, No. 148.
8. The Robert Wood Johnson Foundation. Access to health care in the United States: results of a 1986 survey. *Spec. Rep.* 1987; 2:3–11.
9. White-Means S.I., Thornton M.C., Yeo J.S. Sociodemographic and health factors influencing black and Hispanic use of the hospital emergency room. *J. Natl. Med. Assoc.* 1989; 81:72–80.
10. Munoz E. Care for the Hispanic poor: a growing segment of American society. *JAMA [Journal of the American Medical Association]* 1988; 260:2711–2712.
11. Andersen R.M., Giachello A.L., Aday L.U. Access of Hispanics to health care and cuts in services: a state-of-the-art overview. *Public Health Rep.* 1986; 101:238–252.
12. Secretary's Task Force on Black and Minority Health. *Hispanic Health Issues, VIII*. Washington, DC: US Dept of Health and Human Services; 1986.
13. Secretary's Task Force on Black and Minority Health. *Crosscutting Issues in Minority Health, II*. Washington, DC: US Dept of Health and Human Services; 1985.
14. Poma P.A. The Hispanic health challenge. *J. Natl. Med. Assoc.* 1988; 80:1275–1277.
15. Hu D.J., Covell R.M. Health care usage by Hispanic outpatients as function of primary language. *West. J. Med.* 1986; 144:490–493.
16. Jonas H.S., Etzel S.I., Barzanski B. Undergraduate medical education. *JAMA*. 1989; 262:1011–1019.

17. American Medical Association Board of Trustees. *Minority Students and Faculty in US Medical Schools*. Chicago, Ill: American Medical Association; 1989: 41. Report F, A-89.

18. Wells K.B., Golding J.M., Hough R.L., et al. Acculturation and the probability of use of health services by Mexican Americans. *Health Serv. Res.* 1989; 24:237–257.

19. Trevino F.M., Bruhn, J.G., Bunce H. Utilization of community mental health services in a Texas-Mexico border city. *Soc. Sci. Med.* 1979; 13A:331–334.

20. *Crosscultural Medicine: Clinical and Cultural Dimensions in Health Care Delivery to Hispanic Patients*. Chicago, Ill: Crosscultural Pathways and the Hispanic Health Alliance; 1990.

21. Trotter R.T. Folk medicine in the Southwest: myths and medical facts. *Folk Med.* 1985; 78:167–179.

22. DeLaCancela V., Guarnaccia P.J., Carrillo E. Psychosocial distress among Latinos: a critical analysis of *ataques de nervios*. *Humanity Soc.* 1986; 10:431–447.

23. Anderson R.M., Lewis S.Z., Giachello A.L., Chiu G. Access to medical care among the Hispanic population of the southwestern United States. *J. Health Soc. Behav.* 1981; 22:78–79.

24. Trevino F.M. Vital and health statistics for the US Hispanic population. *Am. J. Public Health*. 1982; 72:979–981.

25. Rosenwaike I. Mortality differentials among persons born in Cuba, Mexico, and Puerto Rico residing in the United States, 1979–1981. *Am. J. Public Health*. 1987; 77:603–606.

26. Shai D., Rosenwaike I. Violent deaths among Mexican-, Puerto Rican- and Cuban-born migrants in the United States. *Soc. Sci. Med.* 1988; 26:269–276.

27. Secretary's Task Force on Black and Minority Health. *Cancer, III*. Washington, DC: US Dept. of Health and Human Services; 1986.

28. Public Health Service. *Cancer and Minorities: Closing the Gap*. Washington, DC: Dept. of Health and Human Services; 1987.

29. DeLaRosa M. Health care needs of Hispanic Americans and the responsiveness of the health care system. *Health Soc. Work*. 1989; 14: 104–113.

30. Freeman H.P. Cancer in the socioeconomically disadvantaged. *CA*. 1989; 39:266–287.

31. Hispanic health risks. Maxwell B., Jacobson M. In: *Marketing Disease to Hispanics*. Washington, DC: Center for Science in the Public Interest; 1989:7–26.

32. Schinke S.P., Moncher M.S., Palleja J., et al. Hispanic youth, substance abuse, and stress: implications for prevention research. *Int. J. Addict*. 1988; 23:809–826.

33. Public Health Service. *Diabetes and Minorities: Closing the Gap*. Washington, DC: Dept of Health and Human Services; 1987.

34. Centers for Disease Control. Prevalence of overweight for Hispanics—United States, 1982–1984. *MMWR*. 1989; 38:838–843.

35. Diehl A.K., Stern M.P. Special health problems of Mexican-Americans: obesity, gallbladder disease, diabetes mellitus, and cardiovascular disease. *Adv. Intern. Med.* 1989; 34:73–96.

36. Vega W.A., Sallis J.F., Patterson T.L., et al. Predictors of dietary change in Mexican-American families participating in a health behavior change program. *Am. J. Prev. Med.* 1988; 4:194–199.

37. Secretary's Task Force on Black and Minority Health. *Cardiovascular and Cerebrovascular Disease, IV*. Washington, DC: US Dept of Health and Human Services; 1986.

38. Barrios E., Iler E., Mulloy L., et al. Hypertension in the Hispanic and black population in New York City. *J. Natl. Med. Assoc.* 1987; 79:749–752.

39. Kumanyika S., Savage D.D., Ramirez A.G., et al. Beliefs about high blood pressure prevention in a survey of blacks and Hispanics. *Am. J. Prev. Med.* 1989; 5:21–26.

40. Munoz E., Lecca P.J., Goldstein J.D. *A Profile of Puerto Rican Health in the United States: Data From the Hispanic Health and Nutrition Examination Survey, 1982–1984*. New York, NY: Long Island Jewish Medical Center; 1988.

41. Escobedo L.G., Remington P.L. Birth cohort analysis of prevalence of cigarette smoking among Hispanics in the United States. *JAMA*. 1989; 261:66–69.

42. Marin G., Perez-Stable E.J., Marin B.V. Cigarette smoking among San Francisco Hispanics: the role of acculturation and gender. *Am. J. Public Health*. 1989; 79:196–198.

43. Rieder H.L., Cauthen G.M., Kelly G.D., et al. Tuberculosis in the United States. *JAMA*. 1989; 262:385–389.

44. Centers for Disease Control. Acquired immunodeficiency syndrome (AIDS) among blacks and Hispanics—United States. *MMWR*. 1986; 35:655–666.

45. Schilling R.F., Schinke S.P., Nichols S.E., et al. Developing strategies for AIDS prevention research with black and Hispanic drug users. *Public Health Rep.* 1989; 104:2–11.

46. National Center for Health Statistics. AIDS knowledge and attitudes in the black and Hispanic populations. *Public Health Rep.* 1989; 104:403–404.

47. Hu D.J., Keller R., Fleming D. Communicating AIDS information to Hispanics: the importance of language and media preference. *Am. J. Prev. Med.* 1989; 5:196–200.

48. American Medical Association Council on Scientific Affairs. *Reducing Transmission of Human Immunodeficiency Virus (HIV) Among and Through Intravenous Drug Abusers.* Chicago, Ill: American Medical Association; 1988. Report C, A-88.

49. Poma P.A. Pregnancy in Hispanic women. *J. Natl. Med. Assoc.* 1987; 79:929–935.

50. Scribner R., Dwyer J.H. Acculturation and low birthweight among Latinos in the Hispanic HANES. *Am. J. Public Health.* 1989; 79:1263–1267.

51. Secretary's Task Force on Black and Minority Health. *Infant Mortality and Low Birthweight, VI.* Washington, DC: US Dept of Health and Human Services; 1986.

54

Pleading Poverty

Donald Korn

The author discusses the ways that families attempt to cope with the enormous costs of long-term care for the elderly. Strategies for dealing with tax problems, emotional distress, and asset loss are described.

Exercises to Guide Your Reading

1. List reasons for and against giving one's assets to one's children.
2. Identify some health care problems unique to the elderly.
3. Compare the health care problems discussed in this article to those facing women and minority groups.
4. Evaluate the benefits and costs of Medicare.

A long stay in a nursing home can substantially drain assets, to say nothing of the children's inheritance. Costs average $30,000 a year nationally, but climb to as high as $60,000 in the Northeast.

Medicaid pays the bill for the indigent, but to qualify, a person must have nothing more than a house, car, household effects, term life insurance policies and a few thousand dollars in cash. Many elderly people, facing long-term nursing home bills, seek to qualify for Medicaid by giving away their assets.

The notion of purposely impoverishing oneself to go on public assistance sounds unAmerican, if not downright illegal. Increasingly, however, the elderly are doing just that. Parents give their assets to their children. Then, after a waiting period (usually 30 months), they qualify for Medicaid.

In real life, of course, it's not so simple. The emotional stress of giving it all away can be severe. "It's very demeaning to lose your independence," says Lloyd LeVine, a North-

brook, Ill., financial planner, "especially at an age when you know you won't be able to earn it back." Yet the loss of personal control is a necessity in order to qualify as a Medicaid poverty case.

By giving away almost everything they own, parents place their futures in their children's hands. "Sure, middle-aged children may promise to turn over the CD [certificates of deposit] interest to parents," says Indianapolis financial planner Gary Pittsford. "But what happens if a child dies and a son-in-law or daughter-in-law inherits? What happens in case of a divorce?" Bad business deals, lost jobs and many other circumstances can endanger assets transferred from parent to child.

Tax rules can bite, too. Consider the case of Dr. E, sandwiched between his 80-something widowed mother, who already has had two strokes, and his two children in private colleges.

He and his siblings don't want their mother's $300,000 estate diminished by a long

Reprinted by permission of *Financial World*. July 23, 1991. pp. 62–63.

nursing home stay. "If she gives us the CDs," he says, "we'll owe income tax at a much higher rate than hers. If she gives us the house, we'll lose her $125,000 capital gains exemption [available to sellers over age 55] and we'll owe much more in taxes when we sell it." The house, it's true, can stay in his mother's name, but the state may place a "Medicaid lien" on it after her death.

An alternative to simply turning assets over to the children is to put them in an irrevocable (cannot be materially altered) trust. Technically, the assets no longer belong to the elderly person, who then qualifies for Medicaid. The income from the trust goes to a beneficiary, who may pass them along to the elderly person. "I think some Medicaid trusts are form over substance," says LeVine. "I'm afraid they may be pierced."

The situation is bad enough for a widow or widower trying to hold onto assets, but it's even rougher for a married couple. According to Medicaid rules, all assets owned by either spouse are spousal assets. "That applies," says Boston attorney Harley Gordon, "even if one spouse inherited money, or brought money to a second marriage. Not even a prenuptial agreement overrides the Medicaid rules."

Suppose that when Sandra Rich marries Tom Paltry, a prenuptial agreement states that her $300,000 will remain beyond his reach. But Medicare says the $300,000 is a marital asset. For one spouse to qualify for Medicaid, the other can hold no more than half of all marital assets.

Adding insult to injury, there are state-imposed caps that take precedence. So if Tom gets sick and goes into a nursing home, Medicaid won't pay if Sandra is over her state's limit—$66,480 worth of assets excluding her home. (In some states, the limit is as low as $13,296. Both maximum and minimum allowances are indexed for inflation.)

Many of these problems can be avoided by planning ahead. You can buy a long-term care (LTC) insurance policy designed to pay a fixed benefit while the insured person is in a nursing home. A policy that pays $80 per day will provide around $29,000 per year. LTC policies have only been around for a few years and there have been many reports of abuses, including high agent commissions and policy restrictions. However, the industry is maturing and several first-rate insurers now offer coverage. "I particularly like the policies offered by American Express Life Assurance Co.," says Pittsford. *Consumer Reports* recently gave top marks to policies sold by Atlantic & Pacific, an insurance company reportedly facing financial strain, and the Prudential policies sold through the American Association of Retired Persons. A good LTC policy should pay if the insured person can't perform certain "activities of daily living" such as dressing and using the bathroom. Severe memory loss, for instance, from Alzheimer's disease, also should qualify a person for benefits.

LTC policies should provide for care in any type of nursing home, paying benefits for at least three years. You may be willing to pay extra for an inflation clause that will automatically increase the daily benefit.

LTC policies can be expensive, especially when bought by an elderly person. If an individual is in his 60s or 70s, the policy can cost $2,000 or more per year. Double that for a married couple. Moreover, a 65-year-old may pay $40,000 in premiums over 20 years and never collect a penny if he doesn't go into a nursing home.

An alternative is a life insurance policy that has a special rider enabling the insured to tap a death benefit early, in case of catastrophic illness or long-term nursing home care. Say an individual is covered by a $250,000 life insurance policy with such a rider. If he's in a nursing home, the policy may permit him to withdraw up to $2,000 per month. After two years, for example, he will have drawn down $48,000 worth of "living benefits." Now he has an insurance policy that will pay $202,000 at his death.

Some companies, such as First Penn-Pacific and Lincoln National Life, charge 5% to 15% extra for this privilege. Prudential includes the rider with most of its life insurance policies, at no charge, but living benefits are limited to terminal illnesses and to nursing home stays that are expected to be lifelong. Life insurance is more expensive than LTC insurance, but you know that someone will collect, as long as you keep paying the premiums.

Be sure to check an LTC rider to see if the coverage is broad enough. To buy either LTC insurance or life insurance with an LTC rider, the insured must be in good health.

On the other hand, an insured elderly person may already have a permanent life policy that he has owned for years. Over that time, substantial cash value has built up. Now, rather than cash in the policy, he may be able to use tax-free policy loans to meet living expenses and, if necessary, pay nursing home bills.

To Gordon, author of *How to Protect Your Life Savings from Catastrophic Illness and Nursing Homes*, LTC insurance can be an excellent stopgap. "If you can qualify for and afford a good policy, buy it," he says. "That will buy you time." If an individual needs to go to a nursing home, the LTC policy may pay for three years of care. If it looks like a lengthy stay, assets can be given away. (At this point, loss of independence won't be as strong a factor.) Then, by the time the LTC policy has paid out its benefits, 30 months

will be up and you can rely on Medicaid to pay ongoing nursing home bills. "In a lot of cases," says Gordon, "Medicaid won't be needed because not everybody lives longer than three years in a nursing home."

Gordon doesn't recommend applying for Medicaid before entering a nursing home. "Many nursing homes don't welcome Medicaid patients because the reimbursement rates are so low," he says. "Keep some money in your own name. Not only will you preserve independence, you'll be able to enter an excellent nursing home as a private-pay patient." Don't let parents enter a nursing home that's exclusively private-pay, if they intend to apply for Medicaid later. Some good nursing homes accept both types of patients, charging private patients perhaps twice what they receive from Medicaid. "I'm not aware of any situations in which care was downgraded when a patient switched from private pay to Medicaid," says Gordon.

So Medicaid isn't the end of the world. But it shouldn't be the beginning of the planning process. Your goal should be to keep your parents independent and self-supporting, as long as possible. When all else fails, consider Medicaid qualification. Intentional impoverishment should be a last resort, not the first one.

55

Paying for Health

Sir Douglas Black

The author compares the perspectives of accountants, managers, and physicians with the perspective of health economists to determine the proper role of each in health care policy formation. The impact of different ways of organizing a health care system on global health budgets is analyzed. The role of physicians and economists in shaping allocations of health care resources within that budget are addressed.

Exercises to Guide Your Reading

1. Identify the specific expertise and point of view associated with accountants, managers, physicians, and economists in the health care system.
2. Distinguish between factors affecting individual health and those affecting population health.
3. Give examples of the strengths and weaknesses of the three types of health care systems that the author outlines.
4. Evaluate the author's argument regarding the role of physicians in allocating health care dollars.

In many countries, the cost of health is a matter of increasing concern, not simply to health professionals and managers, but also to politicians and the media. Advances in medical knowledge and skills, whether they come from stepwise increments in knowledge, or from the uncommon "breakthroughs" so dear to the media, are making possible realistic prevention or treatment for a widening range of diseases. For these particular diseases, modern medicine is highly effective; but it is also more sophisticated, and thus more expensive, generating costs which have to be set against the economic benefits which flow from successful treatment. And there are still very many diseases, notably tumors, arthropathies, and arterial diseases which are often not amenable to radical treatment, and which cause high mortality and even greater morbidity. The very success of medicine in younger age-groups adds to the burden imposed on services by the more vulnerable elderly; and in many countries this accentuates an underlying demographic trend towards an increased proportion of elderly people in the population. Concern over the economic consequences of these developments has enlisted the interest of professional economists, and there is now a flourishing disci-

Reprinted by permission of *Journal of Medical Ethics.* September 1991. pp. 117–23.

pline of health economics. It is important to distinguish the contribution of a health economist from those of an accountant, of a manager, and of a health professional. An accountant is expert in financial costs, but not in the assessment of benefits, particularly those which are difficult to translate into money values, such as increased perception of well-being or release from anxiety. A manager is concerned with process, whether it be of systems or of staff; and not with outputs which he is ill-qualified to assess, but which are nevertheless of prime concern to the patients for whom the service is designed. A health professional practices the art of the possible within the scope and limitations of his expertise. But the health economist has to take a view which is in some ways broader than any of these, taking in not just the costs of process, but also the values of outcomes. And he has in some sense to be a trustee for tomorrow's patients, in face of the seemingly inexhaustible demands made by patients of today, often most stridently not by patients themselves but by their self-appointed proxies. His is not of course a self-standing, free-range discipline—he depends on the accountant for an assessment of costs; on the manager for maintaining a system which will provide the information needed for economic analysis; and on the health professional for an analysis of available options and for categorization of disease states and their likely outcomes. As someone who is primarily a physician, I am conscious of my rashness in entering the domain of the health economist; but I have always looked on health economists as natural allies of clinical doctors and nurses, so I look on my incursion as one into friendly territory.

And of course in this paper I can cover only a small part of that territory. I limit myself to three main themes—the determinants of health, some of which rather happily turn out to be "free goods"; the share of national resources which it is reasonable to devote to "health," and the criteria for making choices within the (necessarily limited) resources available for health.

DETERMINANTS OF INDIVIDUAL HEALTH

The first down-payment on our health is made some nine months before we first see the light, and whatever element of choice there may be in it, it is certainly not our own. That payment, vicariously made, gives us a quantum of health capital which is a major determinant of the health experience which we may subsequently enjoy. Our health capital at fertilization may already be reduced by the seeds of future specific "heritable diseases," or by a multifactorial genetic endowment which threatens our life-span through a variety of handicaps such as an increased liability to raised blood pressure or to a form of diabetes. Nor of course is the womb the safe haven of popular belief—many a pregnancy ends spontaneously in abortion or stillbirth, not always due to intrinsic non-viability of the fetus, but sometimes occurring in women who are to all appearances healthy as well as in women with specific disorders such as renal failure. Some congenital malformations and some forms of mental subnormality can be related to prenatal influences which pertain to the intra-uterine environment rather than to genetic endowment (1). Particularly before we are born, the distribution of responsibility for good or bad health between the seed and the soil is often a matter of speculation; and also of little pragmatic consequence, beyond the provision of the best antenatal care and appropriate clinical genetic advice, which are of course important in their own right.

Our state of dependency persists after birth into infancy, and in diminishing degree into childhood and adolescence. The environment in which we grow up, and which to a large extent now shapes our lives, is partly natural (and no species has a greater range of habitat), and partly societal (parents, siblings and peer groups, schooling and social class). Accidents, infection and sadly in many parts of the world undernutrition and malnutrition, are the main threats to physical development. Mental development requires appropriate stimulation as well as native intellectual capacity. Many of the things which influence our physical and mental development are beyond our control; but as we become mature, or at least more mature, we begin to have perceptions of autonomy. In the matter of health, we appear to have choices in such matters as what we eat, whether we smoke or drink, and what risks we customarily accept. The choice may not be as autonomous as it is perceived to be by the chooser—there must be an element of social determinism (family circumstances, peer group influence), perhaps even inbuilt cravings for food or mood-changing agents. But unless we are completely deterministic in our outlook, we must, after all allowance has been made for what is beyond our control, accept that we are capable of making at least some of the relevant choices, and by the same token accept the moral responsibility of doing so.

The main theme of this paper relates to populations or societies, and not directly to individuals. Why then should I choose to preface it with an outline picture of the influences on individual health? Most obviously, because any population is an aggregation of individuals. But also, to give at the outset an indication of the complexity of the issues involved, so as to give a ground for deprecating simple solutions; and to affirm that societal provision, important though it is, is not enough—we also share in the determination of our own health.

DETERMINANTS OF HEALTH IN POPULATIONS

From the time of Hippocrates, it has been known that health is affected by "airs, waters and places," influences which will potentially affect all those exposed to them. However, the effect of such general agents on particular people will be greatly modified by individual susceptibility, and this too has been known at least from the time of Pythagoras—not everyone who eats broad beans will suffer from favism. There is thus a dynamic interaction between factors to which the whole *population* is exposed, and important characteristics of the *individual*, which may be constitutional (for example, compromised immune system), behavioral (so-called "life-style"), or societal (social/occupational status).

The reality of life in primitive societies is probably closer to the picture of Thomas Hobbes ("the life of man, solitary, poor, nasty, brutish and short"), than to Rousseau's "noble savage." Sadly enough, the scourges of war, pestilence and famine are still with us in many parts of the world; but for our present purpose, an historical perspective seems more appropriate than a geographical one. There has been registration of deaths in England and Wales since 1838; and before that there are records of population from which changes in mortality can be inferred. Thomas McKeown (1) has made these records the basis of an influential analysis of the factors which may have contributed to the steady increase in life-expectancy which has taken place from around 1700 onwards. For the earlier period before "causes of death" were attributed, he ascribes the improvement mainly to improved living conditions, and a better diet, and also—surprisingly—to decline in the practice of infanticide in poor families (Disraeli is said to have believed that infanticide "was hardly less prevalent in England than on the banks of the Ganges"). The decline in mortality is better documented over the past century and a half—the death-rate fell from 23.3 (men) and 20.7 (women) per thousand in 1871–5 down to 12.0 (men) and 11.4 (women) in 1983 (2). As with the earlier period, McKeown ascribes the greatest effect to improved standards of living, particularly better nutrition giving increased resistance to infection; and also to improvements in sanitation and hygiene, which would also help to reduce infective illness. By comparison with these social and environmental changes, McKeown attaches less importance to advances in clinical medicine, dramatic though these have been; he points out, in particular, that these have only become significant long after the decline in mortality has become well established. He does not deny the importance of a high standard of medical practice in relieving suffering, and in "curing" acute episodes of illness, especially those due to infection. But at the population level, he sees the social factors as paramount. When we were studying the great and growing differences in "health" between "non-manual" and "manual" workers (3), my colleagues and I came to a similar conclusion, that any disparity in access to medical care was not so important in causing disadvantage to manual workers as was a constellation of factors associated with social deprivation—such things as poor and crowded housing, which favor infection; poor nutrition, the diet being unbalanced rather than insufficient; greater risk of accident in the home, at work, or in travel; and an unwise life-style, with smoking one important variable between the "classes." Important as these social factors are, they are not the whole story. In the past decade, since McKeown wrote, it has become apparent that there has been a greater fall in mortality in those diseases for which there is effective prevention or treatment than in those diseases for which such measures are not yet available. No great surprise there, but what has become clear is that this effect is of sufficient magnitude to show up in statistics of mortality, and not simply as anecdotal evidence (4).

Let me conclude this section on the determinants of health by giving the good news which I promised in the introduction, that some important determinants of health are "free goods," in the sense that they carry no "accountable" costs. For the individual, there is—for weal or woe—his genetic endowment. And as a member of his group, he enjoys the sun, when it shines; and the air which he breathes—for even in the UK, fiscal enterprise has gone no further than metering the water he drinks or bathes in. There is also a health bonus to be enjoyed by those who are congenially employed in a free society.

DETERMINATION OF THE GLOBAL HEALTH BUDGET

Health care in a modern society costs much money, and employs many people. Moreover, its claims on national resources have to be judged in comparison with those of housing, education, and social security, which in themselves can make important contributions to peoples' health. There is an "open-endedness" about possible claims for resources for health, which is perhaps more easily recognized by those who have to meet them than by those who make them. Respect must go to politicians who have the candour to say that not all claims can be met, particularly if they say so while in office, and not in the comparative freedom of being in opposition. Possibly to the disadvantage of his own political future, Dr. David Owen said in 1976: "All the evidence there is, both na-

FIGURE 1. Mortality of males in Finland over the period 1969–81, from diseases "amenable" to treatment (———) and from diseases "non-amenable" to treatment (– – –). The points from each year are expressed as a percentage of the 1969 figure, which was 47 per 100,000 population for "amenable" diseases, and 222 per 100,000 population for "non-amenable" diseases.

tional and international, suggests that if need is not infinite, it is certainly so large relative to the resources which society is able to provide now and in the foreseeable future that we can never hope to meet it completely" (5).

But recognition of the problem, though necessary, is only the first step towards trying to solve it. Attempts to do so are of three general types:

1 The "free market" or "laissez-faire" approach, in which people make their own arrangements with "providers" for health care. This makes access to health care part of the "reward system" of society, by virtue of which those who "do well" financially are privileged to enjoy more expensive health care.
2 An insurance-based system, in which people in good health make a regular contribution, sometimes supplemented by their employer, towards future costs of health care. Examples are the Lloyd George health insurance scheme in Britain, and "Blue Cross" in the USA.
3 A "national" system, in which resources are derived from general taxation, and entitlement is universal in the sense that every citizen can obtain primary care from a "general practitioner" or "family doctor."

Although directly employed by a university, I did my clinical work in the National Health Service (NHS) for many years, and had previously practised in the insurance-based system which ran from 1911 to 1948. Before 1948, the State benefit was limited to employed persons, and excluded their wives and children, as well as the largely self-employed "middle classes." Having witnessed the partial removal of the financial hardship caused by illness, I have an admitted bias towards the national system.

It should be noted that these three systems can co-exist in the same country, and generally do. For example, in Britain although the NHS predominates, there is a minor insurance component in its finance; and there is also an appreciable private sector. Conversely, in the USA, with its predominantly private system, partly insurance-based, there is much state-financed provision of health care for "veterans" and the "indigent."

Controversy on the relative merits of a free-market system, based on "enterprise" and "liberty," and a state system based on "fairness" and "equality," sometimes lacks the grace of "fraternity," the third ideal of revolutionary France. A free-market system is blamed for its lack of comprehensiveness, a state system for "bureaucracy and waste." The accusation of "waste" often made in the USA but echoed in Britain itself is at least susceptible of objective analysis. *Per capita* health costs in the USA are three times those in Britain, and the administrative component of these costs is comparably higher; there may also be a component of unnecessary procedures, carried out for fear of litigation, or simply for gain.

Since there is a trend for more affluent countries to spend more on health, a more realistic comparison of health expenditure should perhaps be made with countries in Europe with comparable "gross domestic product" (GDP) to that in Britain. Table 1 shows the proportion of GDP devoted to health in seven European countries, including Britain. The comparison does not suggest conspicuous waste in the British system.

If the bold question were to be asked, not why we spend so much on health, but rather why in comparison with other comparable

TABLE 1. **European Countries with Comparable *Per capita* GDP: Percentage of GDP Devoted to Health Care (1986 Figures)**

	Percentage
France	8.5
Netherlands	8.3
Austria	8.0
Italy	6.7
Belgium	7.1
Finland	7.5
Britain	6.2

Note The comparable percentage for the USA is 11.1, for Canada 8.5, and for Greece 3.9.

countries do we spend so little, I can suggest a number of reasons. The most important of these is our success or good fortune in having preserved a nation-wide system of primary care, based on universal right of access to general practitioners, who are increasingly being trained to a high standard, and who commonly know both patients and their families. They are thus in a position to modify public expectations of what medicine can (or cannot) do; and to control access to expensive, and it may be unnecessary diagnostic and therapeutic procedures in the hospital sector. More directly economic factors include the relative efficiency of using an established system of raising revenue by general taxation, in comparison with a network of insurance or similar agencies; and the opportunity given by a national system to governments of exercising fiscal control. This opportunity has not been neglected, and must have contributed to our relatively low place in the league of health expenditure; more specifically, it has allowed successive governments, as monopoly employers, to protect health service workers from the moral dangers of excessive affluence.

I believe, in short, that we have a system of health care which is not only economical, but also effective in terms both of general availability, and of contributing to health statistics which compare well with those of countries which spend substantially more on health care. As professionals, doctors play their part by avoiding waste in what they do; but the major decisions on the global health budget are inescapably political. Once the size of the national cake, and the proportion of it which can be devoted to health, have been decided, doctors can and must play a larger role in the choices within the health budget. Some elements of decisions on allocations within the health budget remain preponderantly political in a broad sense, for example the proportion of resources to be given to acute services, and the balance between care in institutions and in the community; but even in these medical advice should form a part of the decision-making process.

ALLOCATION WITHIN THE GLOBAL HEALTH BUDGET

When it comes to choices within a fixed budget, a guiding concept is that of "opportunity cost." Simply stated, this says that if you spend a pound in one way, you cannot then spend it in another, thus foregoing the second, perhaps equally or more desirable, "opportunity," and thus incurring whatever "cost," in the shape of loss of benefit, failure to take that opportunity entails. This may seem simple, even simplistic; but in applying the notion to health services, Alan Williams (6) exposes difficulties:

> The golden rule is that only when we are satisfied that the *most* valuable thing that we are *not* doing, is less valuable than the *least* valuable thing that we *are* doing, can we be sure that we are being efficient in the pursuit of welfare. I guess we have a long way to go yet.

That too may seem simple; but embedded in it is the need for a judgement of the relative value of different options. As already mentioned, the size of the global health budget, and even certain major allocations within it, are matters primarily for *political* judgement, informed where appropriate by medical advice, but not dictated by it. But for those decisions which are substantially influenced by what is currently possible in clinical terms—the "state of the clinical art"—I would contend that *professional* judgement becomes inescapable, and even paramount over managerial aspirations and the clamour of pressure groups. By saying "professional," I do not mean "just doctors," but the array of professions concerned with providing services, and also economists with an interest in health matters.

How do I justify this emphasis on the *professional and economic*, in contrast to the *managerial and actuarial* input to decision-making in situations where there is a material clinical component? I take my stand on the great and increasing complexity of the medical database, which requires *informed* interpretation; on the need to assess outcomes as well as process, both of which require a professional input; but most of all, on the nature of the service which constitutes the main, if not the sole, justification of any health care system. For illustration of these matters, I would like to turn to the care of patients with renal failure, for which at one time I shared responsibility with colleagues who taught me so much.

Importance of the "State of the Art"

My illustration of the importance of the medical database is in a sense "historical," showing how the options for treating end-stage renal failure have changed over the years, and with them the economic dimension of what is possible. For convenience, I have set out in Table 2 the availability and cost of successive options. (Renal failure has many causes, some of which are reversible; but when these have been ruled out, and the glomerular filtration rate has fallen from its

TABLE 2. End-Stage Renal Failure: Development and Cost of Options

Option	Availability Date	Approximate Cost
Transplant (identical twins)	1958	(£6,000)
Intermittent haemodialysis hospital	1960	£14,500
Intermittent haemodialysis home	1965	£9,500
Low-protein high-calorie diet	1963	(Palliative measure)
Cadaver transplant	1965	(£6,000) £1,500
CAPD	1980	£8,000

Notes "Availability date" is an estimate of the date at which the option became generally available in the UK. "Cost" is annual maintenance cost, except for the "one-off" cost of transplant, which is shown in parenthesis. CAPD is Continuous Ambulatory Peritoneal Dialysis. Before 1950 there was no effective way of avoiding death, given irreversible end-stage renal failure.

normal level of about 120 ml/min to 5 ml/min or less, end-stage renal failure is reached; and before the "fifties" death in uraemic coma was inevitable.) Consideration of costs in isolation would show that a renal transplant, with manageable initial cost, and "low" maintenance cost for immunosuppressive agents, is the "best buy"—and in general it gives better "quality of life" than a regime of repeated dialysis. But it is limited in application by the availability of suitable kidneys, and also by the need not just for surgeons trained in transplantation but also for competent dialysis before and after operation, and during episodes of rejection. Again, a crude financial comparison of "hospital" and "home" dialysis, much to the advantage of the latter, neglects two important considerations. Patients who need hospital dialysis are commonly the most severely affected, with complications which in themselves require expensive treatment; and there is the considerable "social cost" to patient and family of repeated dialyses at home. It is easy for politicians, goaded on by pressure groups, to say—as indeed they did say in the USA—that every patient in end-stage renal failure has an entitlement to treatment. But the confident statement of such an objective is not invariably followed by provision of the means needed to achieve it. The extent to which it can be achieved clearly involves professional judgement and dedication, as well as managerial skills and political will.

Importance of Outcome

A favourable outcome has two main components—*survival*, which is necessary, but not all-sufficient; and *well-being*, or "quality of life," which is of course much harder to assess, but nevertheless of great importance. One possible, relatively "hard," measure of outcome is the capacity for employment; and some years ago I applied this in an attempt to assess the "value" of different methods of treating renal failure (7). From past experience with the various methods, the likelihood or "probability" (p) of different states of fitness can be ascertained; more arbitrarily or subjectively, an estimate of the worthwhileness or "utility" (u) of the various degrees of fitness for work can be made. For each method of treatment, the "value" is estimated by summing the products of "p" and "u" for the various possible outcomes. Table 3 shows some results obtained in this way, and once again the assessment is incomplete—it looks as if there is little to choose between home dialysis and transplant—but that misses out both the burden to the family of home dialysis, and the greater well-being, on average, of those who have had a successful transplant.

A more general attempt to combine survival and well-being in a single measure of outcome is represented by the QALY approach—QALY being an acronym for "Quality Adjusted Life Years" (8). The QALY of a procedure (which might be an operation, a course of medication, or even a change of diet) is an estimate of the number of years which it should add to the life of a patient, adjusted by an estimate of the quality of the additional life to be enjoyed. This is certainly an important correction—for example, the frequency and duration of survival of patients who have sustained a stroke may both be increased by treatment, but the quality of the life so prolonged may be low.

This is allowed for in the QALY matrix—for example, a patient who could not get out of bed and was also suffering severe pain or other distress would contribute a negative value to the assessment of the procedure under investigation, and likewise a patient who was irreversibly unconscious. Although the QALY approach has the great merit of taking account of "state of health" and not just "mere life," there are some drawbacks. The estimate of additional years of life must be the mean of variable individual experiences, within each of which it cannot be easy to distinguish between survival which is part of the natural history of the disease and survival which is directly due to the procedure. This estimate of survival is then "adjusted" by a subjective estimate of "quality of life," drawn from a quite small panel of health workers and convalescent patients. Since older patients have inherently reduced expectancy of life, there may be bias against them; but it may be noted that this does not prevent hip replacement from outdistancing both renal transplants and coronary bypass surgery in the "QALY stakes." It may not be surprising that QALYs are popular with paediatricians and orthopaedic surgeons, less esteemed by nephrologists and geriatricians. It may also be that the simplicity of a single index may be deceptive; and that the complexity of "quality of life" may

TABLE 3.   Terminal Renal Failure: Fitness for Work after Different Methods of Treatment

Method of Treatment	FT	PT	Unemp (Probability of Outcome)	Unfit	Σ pu
		Degree of Employment			
Dialysis (Hospital)	0.34	0.25	0.21	0.20	0.54
(Home)	0.64	0.16	0.14	0.06	0.74
Transplant (Live-donor)	0.75	0.10	0.10	0.05	0.77
(Cadaver)	0.66	0.12	0.13	0.09	0.71
Estimated utility	0.90	0.60	0.30	0.10	

In this table the horizontal rows give, for each method of treatment, the *probability* (p) of the outcome specified at the top of the corresponding column. The final row gives an estimate of the *utility* (u) of each of the outcomes. The final column (Σ pu) gives an overall estimate of the relative "value" of the method described at the start of the corresponding Σ row. In the heading, FT = full-time, PT = part-time, Unemp = fit for some work, but unemployed.

necessitate a multi-factorial assessment, such as that provided, for example, by the Nottingham Health Profile (9). However, if agreement could be reached on the weighting to be accorded to each of the thirteen components of that profile, that too is reducible to a single index—but the "if" in that clause is a large one.

Nature of Health Care

My strongest ground of concern for what I see as an unjustified encroachment of managers and accountants on areas which are more properly and suitably the responsibility of professionals trained and experienced in the provision of health care, whether for individuals or for communities, lies in the nature of the service to be provided. Procedures and attitudes which may be appropriate for managing a chain-store are unlikely to be appropriate in a health service. The "hard sell" can of course have applied to it a veneer of "public relations," but that still leaves it far removed from what is needed for health care, which is deeply personal, sometimes painfully so; and which demands a conjunction of human sympathy and professional skill which cannot be replaced either by a purely cash transaction, or by dictate from a manager (or politician) on high.

Let me summarize in a few words what I have been trying to say. The determinants of health are many and complex, even if some of them are economically "free." The large economic decisions—how much for "welfare," and within that how much for "health"—are inescapably political, even if the expenditure on "health" is hidden in the web of private care. But when it comes to the assessment of priorities *within* the health budget, present trends to transfer decisions from health professionals to managers and accountants are not only harmful to patients, but also massively wasteful. This can be simply shown by looking at health costs in the USA, where commerce rules.

REFERENCES

1. McKeown T. *The role of medicine: dream, mirage, or nemesis.* Oxford: Blackwell, 1979.
2. Goldacre M.J., Vessey M.P. Health and sickness in the community. In: Weatherall D.J., Ledingham J.G.G., Warrell D.A., eds. *Oxford textbook of medicine* (2nd ed.). Oxford: Oxford Medical Publications, 1987:**3.**10–**3.**17.
3. Townsend P., Davidson N. *Inequalities in health: the Black report.* Harmondsworth: Penguin Books, 1982.
4. Black D. *Invitation to medicine.* Oxford: Blackwell, 1987.
5. Owen D. *In sickness and in health: the politics of medicine.* London: Quartet Books, 1976.
6. Williams A. Efficiency and welfare. In: Black D., Thomas G.P., eds. *Providing for the health services.* London: Croom Helm, 1978:25–32.
7. Black D. Medical decisions. *Scottish medical journal* 1978; 25:91–98.
8. Williams A. The value of QALYs. *Health and social services journal* 1985; Jul 18:"Centre 8":3.
9. Hunt S.M., McKenna S.P., McEwen J., Williams P., Papp E. The Nottingham health profile: subjective health status and medical consultations. *Social science and medicine* 1981; 15(**A**):221–229.

EVALUATING FAIRNESS, ELIMINATING INEQUALITY

The reading in Part IV offer various perspectives on policies aimed at improving the economic conditions confronting women and people of color. To illustrate the sources and effects of the profound disagreements separating the various policies, we have developed an extended analogy in which economists and the economy are discussed in terms of the connected processes of medical diagnosis, prescription, and treatment. Indeed, it is not difficult to visualize the economy as a patient with a set of symptoms that are to be diagnosed by three doctors. Of course, once each doctor has offered a medical (expert) opinion, each offers a different treatment regime.

When Dr. Letitbe takes the patient's history, he notes that the patient is worried about social and economic inequality. These worries manifest themselves as widespread pain. Upon examination, Dr. Letitbe finds no evidence to warrant medical or surgical intervention. Although inequality was present, thereby confirming that the patient was not delusional, the sources of the inequality were found to be natural economic processes. Any attempt to change these processes would result in a situation in which "the cure is worse than the disease."

Dr. Letitbe reassures the patient by explaining that in market economies, income and economic rewards flow to individuals based on the value of their contributions to total output, or their productivity. Since individuals are not endowed with equal, talents, skills, or intelligence, there will of course be income inequality. Even individuals with equal talents, skills, and intelligence will have different preferences for education and employment, so choices made about schooling and occupations will lead to different incomes too. Dr. Letitbe says, "Don't worry, be happy," and proceeds to explain that previous doctoring is responsible for most of the patient's painful symptoms. The patient is asked to stop following the advice of other doctors, because, in the view of Dr. Letitbe, when medication is prescribed or surgery performed to reduce inequality, patients actually become sicker! All such interventions interfere with the proper functioning of vital economic organs. Incentives are reduced, productivity falls, and the entire system becomes sluggish. Dr. Letitbe explains that the best course of action is to do nothing. If the patient is truly and deeply bothered by the persistence of inequality, a psychiatrist might help. The problems that the patient reports are all in the head—there is nothing wrong with the body economic.

A second doctor is then called in to take the patient's history. Dr. Tinkeredge is shocked to learn how long the patient has been suffering. She is even more upset when she hears how localized the pain is. Dr. Tinkeredge runs some tests, and checks the production and circulation systems. The examination and tests reveal that dozens of imperfections are interrupting the body's otherwise normal functioning: plaque in the arteries, discriminatory neural activity, and sticky cells are jointly impeding circulation. Insufficient nutrients are available to maintain full utilization of the system's productive capacity. As production slows, circulation is adversely affected. In the face of inadequate aggregate nutrition, some organs are forced to consume less than others. The patient's growth has become very unbalanced, with standards of living varying dramatically across the body. The homeostatic relationship between production and consumption intensifies a negative cycle of decline.

Dr. Tinkeredge explains to the patient that although most of the problem is rooted in production, the best way to treat the symptoms is to focus on circulation. Tinkeredge would begin by trying to raise the volume of income-generating circulation, since an insufficient level of circulation restricts the ability to synthesize needed nutrients and thus complicates matters by creating an additional problem of excess capacity. In addition, the doctor recommends a drastic shift in diet away from mergers and industrial deregulation. Dr. Tinkeredge calls in a team of experts to re-regulate production in an attempt to patch internal damage to the productive structure. Additional experts are brought in to stimulate circulation and neural activity. With Dr. Tinkeredge at the helm, all aspects of recovery will be managed by experts who will, on a daily basis, fine-tune all phases of the stimulatory medical package. In a jointly issued report, the team predicts accelerating growth as equality increases.

Doctor number three arrives next. Dr. Overhaul's examination reveals that economic problems related to race and gender inequality are symptoms of a deadly systemic problem. Widespread, persistent, and continuous exploitation induces in the patient violent cycles of binge eating, followed by periods of nausea leading to vomiting, and if unchecked, eventual starvation. In the eating phase, many cells—especially those that are female and of different colors—are called into action. More and more calories are necessary to fuel the cells. Surpluses are eroded, and the patient's nutritional reserves are depleted. Once this happens, needed productive resources are hoarded by the class of organs that, by virtue of pregiven and inherited property rights, has a monopoly on these resources. As a result of hoarding, the elements necessary for production are withdrawn from use. Thus the patient becomes weaker and weaker. In this weakened state, the patient contracts two serious long-term viruses. Now, in addition to exploitation, racism and sexism will further distort production. At the same time, consumption continues to respond to the excess demands of dominant organs, and the market system meets even their most frivolous tastes and preferences.

Dr. Overhaul is worried: will it be possible to cure these diseases without losing the patient? Is it possible that so many adaptations to these symptoms have occurred that eliminating exploitation while combating racism and sexism may actually cause heart failure? Dr. Overhaul offers a progressive treatment in which activist medication to counteract the complicating viruses is prescribed. These medications will help build alliances of and bridges between the isolated, marginalized, and oppressed cells. As coalitions grow stronger, the viruses will grow weaker, and it will finally be possible to perform radical surgery to reconstruct the patient's social relations. Only after this surgery will the patient be able to live a satisfying, meaningful life based on production for human fulfillment with equality for all.

Each doctor, like economists operating within different paradigms, literally "sees" different processes in action in the economy and wider society. As a result, each offers different diagnoses, and these in turn determine the treatments (or policies) that are advocated. For each doctor in the analogy, both the causes and effects of inequality based on race, gender, and ethnicity are different. A similar situation prevails in economics, and as a result, each school of economists offers a different prescription for economic ills. The readings in Part IV highlight these differences.

Economists frequently begin their discussions of the economic status of diverse groups by comparing their incomes and earnings with virtually all studies finding that women and minorities earn less than white males. This starting point has several effects. First, the focus on earnings means that material, financial measures play a central role in discussions of economic and social well-being. Reading 56 challenges this emphasis on monetary measures of welfare. Second, the observation that women, minorities, and men tend to have quite different earning levels leads most mainstream economists to focus on the attributes of individuals to explain these differences. Reading 57 wrestles with the commonly held view that attributes of the poor are the principle reasons for their low socioeconomic achievements. The authors of this piece present the history of this position to show that a policy emphasis on the poor, rather than on the availability of jobs that pay enough to lift people out of poverty, is mistaken. Reading 58 puts forward a coordinated set of economic policies that are intended to counteract the declining economic status of urban Americans. Reading 59 advocates the controversial policy of paying reparations to African Americans to compensate for the consequences of their exploitation during and after the slave era, and Reading 60 mounts a spirited defense of "supply side" economics, which argues that accentuating the rewards to wealthiest Americans is the surest way to prosperity.

Next we turn to problems facing women in the work force. In Reading 61 we find the argument that gender-based differences in income are the primary problem facing women, which justifies interventions to make the wage-setting process fairer. The author of Reading 62 compares government interventions in labor markets to other interventions that alter the distribution of income, and questions the logic of opposing government interventions in labor markets while generally ignoring the income-changing effects of other interventionist policies. Reading 63 reflects on the many successes of government policies aimed at reducing race-linked poverty. Keep the medical analogy developed earlier in mind so that you can match policy proposals, evaluations, and critiques to the competing schools of economic analysis.

The articles in Chapter 14 link analyses of social diversity to the prevalent

cultural understandings of race, ethnicity, and gender in an attempt to illuminate the claim that equality is an important goal of economic and social policy.
Here you will encounter arguments that have been made in different ways and
in different contexts throughout this volume. Now, though, the discussions give
voice to the frequently dismissed position that the fate of particular individuals
can not be understood apart from the social whole. These readings underscore
the point that our community ties, our family relationships, and indeed our
racial, ethnic, and gendered identities are inextricably tied to our histories, economic lives, and cultural practices. Reading 64 discusses the strengths and weaknesses of multicultural curricula to reveal the crucial role education play in
shaping ideology about race, gender, ethnicity and class. Reading 65 investigates
the validity of recent reports which conclude that women's life status is deteriorating to highlight the strength of conventional sexist attitudes. Reading 66
critiques the currently fashionable "blame the victim" analyses of black poverty
and offers an alternative explanation rooted in an analysis of U.S. corporate and
foreign policy choices. Reading 67 summarizes of the Bishop's letter on the U.S.
economy and then articulates the types of policies needed to promote the cause
of economic justice. In this view, it is impossible to promote a genuine equality
without simultaneously taking into account the complexity of racial, sexual, and
cultural relations in our society. By recognizing this reality, we can work together
to create communities in which acceptance of and respect for diversity permits
all of us to realize our emotional and material pleasures through the contradictory relationships that connect us to each other.

CHAPTER 13

Economics, Policies, and Justice

56

What's So Bad About Being Poor?

Charles Murray

This article asks us to reconsider the meaning of poverty by suggesting that simple measures of money income are inadequate. Instead, the possibility that the extent of the choices one has in arranging one's life may be more important for personal happiness. Since concern for the economic status of minorities and women often begins with the fact of their insufficient earnings, this article raises the possibility that if these groups do face economic problems, such problems may have more to do with the constraints imposed by well-intended reformers than with the material dimensions of a life organized by one's free choices.

Exercises to Guide Your Reading

1. Summarize the author's definition of poverty.
2. Give examples that illustrate his thesis.
3. Identify the strengths and weaknesses of this argument.
4. Defend the author's argument about poverty. Critique the author's argument about poverty.

One of the great barriers to a discussion of poverty and social policy in the 1980s is that so few people who talk about poverty have ever been poor. The diminishing supply of the formerly poor in policy-making and policy-influencing positions is a side effect of progress. The number of poor households dropped dramatically from the beginning of World War II through the end of the 1960s. Despite this happy cause, however, it is a troubling phenomenon. From the beginning of American history through at least the 1950s, the new generation moving into positions of influence in politics, business, journalism, and academia was bound to include a large admixture of people who had grown up dirt-poor. People who had grown up in more privileged surroundings did not have to speculate about what being poor was like; someone sitting beside them, or at the head of the table, was likely to be able to tell them. It was easy to acknowledge then, as it is not now, that there is nothing so terrible about poverty *per se*. Poverty is not equivalent to destitution. Being poor does not necessarily mean being malnourished or ill-clothed. It does not automatically mean joylessness or despair. To be poor is not necessarily to be without dignity; it is not necessarily to be unhappy. When large numbers of people who were running the country had once been poor themselves, poverty could be kept in perspective.

Today, how many graduates of the Kennedy School of Government or of the Harvard Business School have ever been really poor? How many have ever had close friends who were? How many even have parents who were once poor? For those who have never been poor and never even known any people who were once poor, it is difficult to treat poverty as something other than a mystery. It is even more difficult to be detached about the importance of poverty, because to do so smacks of a "let them eat cake" mentality. By the same token, however, it is important that we who have never been poor be able to think about the relationship of poverty to social policy in a much more straightforward way than the nation's intellectuals and policy-makers have done for the past few decades. To that end, I propose a thought experiment based on the premise that tomorrow you had to be poor. I do not mean "low-income" by Western standards of affluence, but functioning near the subsistence level, as a very large proportion of the world's population still does.

In constructing this thought experiment, the first requirement is to divorce yourself from certain reflexive assumptions. Do not think what it would be like to be poor while living in a community of rich people. I do not (yet) want to commingle the notions of absolute poverty and relative poverty, so you should imagine a community in which everyone else is as poor as you are, indeed, a world in which the existence of wealth is so far removed from daily life that it is not real.

The second requirement is to avoid constructing an imaginary person. The point is not to try to imagine yourself in the shoes of "a poor person" but to imagine what *you*, with your particular personality, experiences, strengths, and limitations (including your middle-class upbringing and values), would do if you were suddenly thrust into this position.

To do all this in the American context is difficult. Any scenario is filled with extraneous factors. So let me suggest one that I used as a way of passing the time when I was a researcher driving on the back roads of rural Thailand many years ago. What if, I would muse, I had to live for the rest of my life in the next village I came to (perhaps a nuclear war would have broken out, thereby keeping me indefinitely in Thailand; any rationalization would do)?

In some ways, the prospect was grim. I had never been charmed by sleeping under mosquito netting nor by bathing with a few buckets of cloudy well water. When circumstances permitted, I liked to end a day's work in a village by driving back to an air-conditioned hotel and a cold beer. But if I had no choice . . .

As it happens, Thailand has an attractive

peasant culture. Survival itself is not a problem. The weather is always warm, so the requirements for clothes, fuel, and shelter are minimal. Village food is ample, if monotonous. But I would nonetheless be extremely poor, with an effective purchasing power of a few hundred dollars a year. The house I would live in would probably consist of a porch and one or two small, unlit, unfurnished rooms. The walls might be of wood, more probably of woven bamboo or leaf mats. I would have (in those years) no electricity and no running water. Perhaps I would have a bicycle or a transistor radio. Probably the nearest physician would be many kilometers away. In sum: If the criterion for measuring poverty is material goods, it would be difficult to find a community in deepest Appalachia or a neighborhood in the most depressed parts of South Chicago that even approaches the absolute material poverty of the average Thai village in which I would have to make my life.

On the other hand, as I thought about spending the next fifty years in a Thai village, I found myself wondering precisely what I would lack (compared to my present life) that would cause me great pain. The more I thought about the question, the less likely it seemed that I would be unhappy.

Since I lacked any useful trade, maybe I could swap the Jeep for a few *rai* of land and become a farmer. Learning how to farm well enough to survive would occupy my time and attention for several years. After that, I might try to become an affluent farmer. One of the assets I would bring from my Western upbringing and schooling would be a haphazardly acquired understanding of cash crops, markets, and entrepreneurial possibilities, and perhaps I could parlay that, along with hard work, into some income and more land. It also was clear to me that I probably would enjoy this "career." I am not saying I would *choose* it, but rather that I could find satisfaction in learning how to be a competent rice farmer, even though it was not for me the most desired of all possible careers.

What about my personal life? Thais are among the world's most handsome and charming people, and it was easy to imagine falling in love with a woman from the village, marrying her, and having a family with her. I could also anticipate the pleasure of watching my children grow up, probably at closer hand than I would in the United States. The children would not get the same education they would in the States, but I would have it within my power to see that they would be educated. A grade school is near every village. The priests in the local *wat* could teach them Buddhism. I could also become teacher to my children. A few basic textbooks in mathematics, science, and history; Plato and Shakespeare and the Bible; a dozen other well-chosen classics—all these could be acquired even in up-country Thailand. My children could reach adulthood literate, thoughtful, and civilized.

My children would do well in other ways too. They would grow up in a "positive peer culture," as the experts say. Their Thai friends in the village would all be raised by their parents to be considerate, hard-working, pious, and honest—that's the way Thai villagers raise their children. My children would face few of the corrupting influences to be found in an American city.

Other personal pleasures? I knew I would find it easy to make friends, and that some would become close. I would have other good times, too—celebrations on special occasions, but more often informal gatherings and jokes and conversation. If I read less, I would also read better. I would have great personal freedom as long as my behavior did not actively interfere with the lives of my neighbors (the tolerance for eccentric behavior in a Thai village is remarkably high). What about the physical condition of poverty? After a few months, I suspect that I would hardly notice.

You may conclude that this thought experiment is a transparent setup. First I ask what it would be like to be poor, then I proceed to outline a near-idyllic environment in which to be poor. I assume that I have a legacy of education experiences that would help me spend my time getting steadily less poor. And then I announce that poverty isn't so bad after all. But the point of the thought experiment is not to suggest that all kinds of poverty are tolerable, and even less that all peasant societies are pleasant places to live. When poverty means the inability to get enough food or shelter, it is every bit as bad as usually portrayed. When poverty means being forced to remain in that condition, with no way of improving one's situation, it is as bad as portrayed. When poverty is conjoined with oppression, be it a caste system or a hacienda system or a people's republic, it is as bad as portrayed. *My thought experiment is not a paean to peasant life, but a paean to communities of free people.* If poverty is defined in terms of money, everybody in the Thai village is poor. If poverty is defined as being unable to live a modest but decent existence, hardly anyone there is poor.

Does this thought experiment fail when it is transported to the United States? Imagine the same Thai village set down intact on the outskirts of Los Angeles. Surely its inhabitants must be miserable, living in their huts and watching the rest of the world live in splendor.

At this point in the argument, however, we need no longer think in terms of thought experiments. This situation is one that has been faced by hundreds of thousands of immigrants to the United States, whether they came from Europe at the end of World War II or from Vietnam in the mid 1970s. Lawyers found themselves working as janitors, professors found themselves working on assembly lines. Sometimes they worked their way up and out, but many had to remain janitors and factory workers, because they came here too late in life to retool their foreign-trained skills. But their children did not have to remain so, and they have not. A reading of their histories, in literature or in the oral testimony of their children, corroborates this pattern. Was a Latvian attorney forced to flee his country "happy" to have to work as a janitor? No. Was he prevented

by his situation—specifically, by his poverty—from successfully pursuing happiness? Emphatically, no.

Let us continue the thought experiment nonetheless, with a slightly different twist. This time, you are given a choice. One choice is to be poor in rural Thailand, as I have described it, with just enough food and shelter and a few hundred dollars a year in cash: a little beyond bare subsistence, but not much. Or you may live in the United States, receive a free apartment, free food, free medical care, and a cash grant, the package coming to a total that puts you well above the poverty line. There is, however, a catch: you are *required* to live in a particular apartment, and this apartment is located in a public-housing project in one of the burned-out areas of the South Bronx. A condition of receiving the rest of the package is that you continue to live, and raise your children, in the South Bronx (you do not have the option of spending all of your waking hours in Manhattan, just as the village thought experiment did not give you the option of taking vacations in Bangkok). You still have all the assets you took to the Thai village—once again, it is essential that you imagine not what it is like for an Alabama sharecropper to be transplanted to the South Bronx, but what it would be like *for you.*

In some ways, you would have much more access to distractions. Unlike the situation in the Thai village, you would have television you could watch all day, taking you vicariously into other worlds. And, for that matter, it would be much easier to get books than in a Thai village, and you would have much more money with which to buy them. You could, over time, fix up your apartment so that within its walls you would have an environment that looked and felt very like an apartment you could have elsewhere.

There is only one problem: You would have a terrible time once you opened your door to the outside world. How, for example, are you going to raise your children in the South Bronx so that they grow up to be the adults you want them to be? (No, you don't have the option of sending them to live elsewhere.) How are you going to take a walk in the park in the evening? There are many good people in the South Bronx with whom you could become friends, just as in the village. But how are you to find them? And once they are found, how are you to create a functioning, mutually reinforcing community?

I suggest that as you think of answers to those questions, you will find that, if you are to have much chance to be happy, the South Bronx needs to be changed in a way that the village did not—that, unlike the village as it stood, the South Bronx as it stands does not "work" as an environment for pursuing happiness. Let us ignore for the moment how these changes in environment could be brought about, by what combination of government's doing things and refraining from doing things. The fact is that hardly any of those changes involve greater income for you personally, but rather changes in the surrounding environment. There is a question that crystallizes the roles of personal *v.* environmental poverty in this situation: How much money would it take to persuade you to move self and family to this public-housing project in the South Bronx?

The purpose of the first two versions of the thought experiment was to suggest a different perspective on one's own priorities regarding the pursuit of happiness, and by extension to suggest that perhaps public policy ought to reflect a different set of priorities as well. It is easy in this case, however, to assume that what one wants for oneself is not applicable to others. Thus, for example, it could be said that the only reason the thought experiments work (if you grant even that much) is that the central character starts out with enormous advantages of knowledge and values—which in themselves reflect the advantages of having grown up with plenty of material resources.

To explore that possibility, I ask you to bear with me for one more thought experiment on this general topic, one I have found to be a touchstone. This time, the question is not what kinds of material resources you

(with your fully developed set of advantages) need for your pursuit of happiness, but what a small child, without any developed assets at all, needs for his pursuit of happiness—specifically, what your own child needs.

Imagine that you are the parent of a small child, living in contemporary America, and in some way you are able to know that tomorrow you and your spouse will die and your child will be made an orphan. You do not have the option of sending the child to live with a friend or relative. You must select from among other and far-from-perfect choices. The choices, I assure you, are not veiled representations of anything else; the experiment is set up not to be realistic, but to evoke something about how you think.

Suppose first this choice: You may put your child with an extremely poor couple according to the official definition of "poor"—which is to say, poverty that is measured exclusively in money. This couple has so little money that your child's clothes will often be secondhand and there will be not even small luxuries to brighten his life. Life will be a struggle, often a painful one. But you also know that the parents work hard, will make sure your child goes to school and studies, and will teach your child that integrity and responsibility are primary values. Or you may put your child with parents who will be as affectionate to your child as the first couple but who have never worked, are indifferent to your child's education, think that integrity and responsibility (when they think of them at all) are meaningless words—but who have and will always have plenty of food and good clothes and amenities, provided by others.

Which couple do you choose? The answer is obvious to me and I imagine to most readers: the first couple, of course. But if you are among those who choose the first couple, stop and consider what the answer means. This is *your own child* you are talking about, whom you would never let go hungry even if providing for your child meant going hungry yourself. And yet you are choosing years of privation for that same child. Why?

Perhaps I set up the thought experiment

too starkly. Let us repeat it, adding some ambiguity. This time, the first choice is again the poor-but-virtuous couple. But the second couple is rich. They are, we shall say, the heirs to a great fortune. They will not beat your child or in any other way maltreat him. We may even assume affection on their part, as we will with the other couples. But, once again, they have never worked and never will, are indifferent to your child's education, and think that integrity and responsibility (when they think of them at all) are meaningless words. They do, however, possess millions of dollars, more than enough to last for the life of your child and of your child's children. Now, in whose care do you place your child? The poor couple or the rich one?

This time, it seems likely that some people will choose the rich couple—or more accurately, it is possible to think of ways in which the decision might be tipped in that direction. For example, a wealthy person who is indifferent to a child's education might nonetheless ship the child off to an expensive boarding school at the earliest possible age. In that case, it is conceivable that the wealthy ne'er-do-wells are preferable to the poor-but-virtuous couple, *if* they end up providing the values of the poor family through the surrogate parenting of the boarding school—dubious, but conceivable. One may imagine other ways in which the money might be used to compensate for the inadequacies of the parents. But failing those very chancy possibilities, I suggest that a great many parents on all sides of political fences would knowingly choose hunger and rags for their child rather than wealth.

Again, the question is: Why? What catastrophes are going to befall the child placed in the wealthy home? What is the awful fate? Would it be so terrible if he grew up to be thoughtlessly rich? The child will live a life of luxury and have enough money to buy himself out of almost any problem that might arise. Why not leave it at that? Or let me put the question positively: In deciding where to send the child, what is one trying to achieve by these calculations and predic-

tions and hunches? What is the good that one is trying to achieve? What is the criterion of success?

One may attach a variety of descriptors to the answer. Perhaps you want the child to become a reflective, responsible adult. To value honesty and integrity. To be able to identify sources of lasting satisfaction. Ultimately, if I keep pushing the question (Why is honesty good? Why is being reflective good?), you will give the answer that permits no follow-up: You want your child to be happy. You are trying to choose the guardians who will best enable your child to pursue happiness. And, forced to a choice, material resources come very low on your list of priorities.

So far, I have limited the discussion to a narrow point: in deciding how to enhance the ability of people to pursue happiness, solutions that increase material resources beyond subsistence *independently of other considerations* are bound to fail. Money *per se* is not very important. It quickly becomes trivial. Depending on other non-monetary conditions, poor people can have a rich assortment of ways of pursuing happiness, or affluent people can have very few.

The thought experiments were stratagems intended not to convince you of any particular policy implications, but rather to induce you to entertain this possibility: When a policy trade-off involves (for example) imposing material hardship in return for some other policy good, *it is possible* (I ask no more than that for the time being) that imposing the material hardship is the right choice. For example, regarding the "orphaned child" scenario: *If* a policy leads to a society in which there are more of the first kind of parents and fewer of the second, the sacrifices in material resources available to the children involved might conceivably be worth it.

The discussion, with its steady use of the concept of "near-subsistence" as "enough material resources to pursue happiness," has also been intended to point up how little our concept of poverty has to do with subsistence. Thus, for example, if one simply looks at the end result of how people live, a natural observation concerning contemporary America might be that we have large numbers of people who are living at a subsistence or sub-subsistence level. But I have been using "subsistence" in its original sense: enough food to be adequately nourished, plus the most basic shelter and clothing. The traditional Salvation Army shelter provides subsistence, for example. In Western countries, and perhaps especially the United States, two problems tend to confuse the issue. One is that we have forgotten what subsistence means, so that an apartment with cockroaches, broken windows, and graffiti on the walls may be thought of as barely "subsistence level," even if it also has running water, electricity, heat, a television, and a pile of discarded fast-food cartons in the corner. It might be an awful place to live (for the reasons that the South Bronx can be an awful place to live), but it bears very little resemblance to what "subsistence" means to most of the world. Secondly, we tend to confuse the way in which some poor people *use* their resources (which indeed can often leave them in a near-subsistence state) with the raw purchasing power of the resources at their disposal. Take, for example, the

apartment I just described and move a middle-class person with middle-class habits and knowledge into it, given exactly the same resources. Within days it would be still shabby but a different place. All of which is precisely the point of the thought experiments about Thailand and the South Bronx: money has very little to do with living a poverty-stricken life. Similarly, "a subsistence income" has very little to do with what Americans think of as poverty.

That being the case, I am arguing that the job of designing good public policy must be reconstrued. We do not have the option of saying, "First we will provide for the material base, then worry about the other necessary conditions for pursuing happiness." These conditions interact. The ways in which people go about achieving safety, self-respect, and self-fulfillment in their lives are inextricably bound up with each other and with the way in which people go about providing for their material well-being. We do not have the option of doing one good thing at a time.

In discussing the conditions for pursuing happiness I have put material resources first only because that is where they have stood in the political debate. I am suggesting that properly they should be put last.

57

Why "Workfare" Fails

Sarah K. Gideonse and William R. Meyers

This article discusses the various paths the U.S. government has followed in its attempts to help the poor. This historical approach to aid policies allows the authors to identify common assumptions about poverty and poor people that have shaped the responses to poverty. The authors argue that policies that embody these assumptions will not succeed in lifting many out of poverty.

Exercises to Guide Your Reading

1. List the reasons why traditional poverty policies are likely to fail.
2. Identify the authors' suggestions for more successful antipoverty policies.
3. Identify the "micro" and "macro" aspects of this argument.
4. If you find yourself in agreement with the article, list the points you would make if you were to criticize this point of view. Or, if you find yourself in disagreement with the article, list the points you would make if you were to justify this point of view.

Government programs for the poor periodically come under energetic attack from policymakers and the public for failing to reduce the number of people receiving welfare and other income subsidies. Critics argue that the dole undermines the family breadwinner's incentive to work, besides costing too much. Occasionally, criticism of welfare leads to policy changes.

Such a change occurred in the 1960s, in reaction to a precipitous increase in the welfare rolls. The mechanization of agriculture, urban migration, and unionization had led to a shortage of unskilled jobs, and relief had become more generous and less restrictive. Congress in the Lyndon Johnson era began to enact a series of welfare amendments instituting work requirements for employable welfare recipients. The most im-

portant change was the incorporation of the Work Incentive Program (WIN) into Aid to Families with Dependent Children (AFDC) in 1967.

Until the passage of the WIN amendments, AFDC allowances permitted mothers without husbands to remain at home with their children. But WIN required employable recipients—including mothers of school-age children and all able-bodied fathers—to register for social and job services as a condition of income support. Congress authorized WIN programs to offer help in finding jobs; to fund education, job training, and public service jobs; and to support these efforts with counseling and daycare. Participants were supposed to accept legitimate job offers. The legislation also included a work incentive: Instead of reducing a fami-

Reprinted by permission of *Challenge*. January–February 1988. pp. 44–49.

ly's relief check by one dollar for each dollar earned, the first $30 of earned income a month plus one-third of additional wages was disregarded.

After 1971, Congress required state programs to give priority for services to the most job-ready WIN enrollees: fathers and volunteering mothers whose motivation to succeed was considered high. Although WIN resembled conventional manpower programs in the types of services provided, it was distinguished by its requirement of mandatory participation.

The number of families on relief stabilized in the 1970s, but WIN failed to diminish that number substantially. It also failed to increase the proportion of welfare mothers working and the proportion of cases closed because clients found work. So, despite WIN, sharp criticism of welfare programs has continued.

"WORKFARE" PROPOSALS

Reagan's election in 1980 heralded renewed efforts to reduce government subsidies to poor families. The new administration sought to end WIN and to replace it with "workfare," a generic name for programs that require adult welfare recipients to work off their grants in public jobs. Critics call workfare the modern equivalent of the workhouse, but workfare advocates hope that an aversion to working in menial jobs without pay will deter the poor from going on relief. In their view, "The prospect of sweeping streets and cleaning buildings for a welfare grant will deter Betsy Smith from having the illegitimate child that drops her out of school and onto welfare." Workfare also means that the poor will earn their relief checks and no longer get what many feel is a free ride at the expense of those who work hard to make a living.

The 1981 Omnibus Reconciliation Act (OBRA) permitted states to mount workfare programs and gave states greater leeway in designing other WIN programs to meet local market conditions. OBRA also restricted welfare eligibility and benefits. The WIN budget was reduced from $365 million in 1979 to $110 million in 1986, and Congress reluctantly ended WIN in June 1987.

The Reagan Administration then wanted to replace WIN with a program called Greater Opportunities for Work (GROW), which would require adult welfare recipients, including mothers with young children, to engage in education and job training. The Administration introduced legislation allowing states to set up experimental welfare programs that could modify existing rules of nearly 100 programs. States could, for example, set their own eligibility and benefit levels for AFDC; combine benefits from various programs into one cash payment; and establish stiff work requirements that exempt only the disabled and mothers of children under three years old. These provisions responded to a complaint that access to a combination of welfare and in-kind subsidies such as food stamps, housing, and Medicaid allows poor families to be better off on welfare than if they were working.

It is more than just conservatives obsessed with ridding the country of "welfare queens" who want to change the welfare system. Governors, legislators, welfare administrators, and private groups are all calling for welfare reform. Governors want to reduce burdensome welfare costs as federal grants to states decline. Equally important, they want to promote the prosperity of their states. The existence of a large number of unproductive and unskilled people, at a time when a smaller youth cohort has created labor shortages, threatens to undermine economic recovery. Reformers have for some time wanted to make income support more equitable and more generous and are willing to accept stiffer work requirements as part of a fairer program. There is also widespread alarm about creating a permanent underclass with no tradition of self-support or skills to find and keep jobs.

In 1987, the National Governors' Association passed a resolution recommending that people on welfare be required to sign a contract to find jobs if they can. In return the governors want the federal government to pay for education, training, daycare, and transportation to get them ready for work. The governors also advocate paid public jobs for those who cannot find employment in the private sector. The governors want to continue daycare and Medicaid coverage for a year after a mother goes to work.

The governors' proposals derive from their experience with work programs authorized under OBRA in 1981. The best known of these are in the booming economies of Massachusetts and California, where expanded WIN programs linking welfare benefits with work or training have increased the numbers of welfare recipients going to work. California and Massachusetts legislators have backed these efforts with significant funding: Massachusetts budgeted quadruple the amount of its federal WIN allocation in 1985, and California appropriated over $100 million for childcare services alone. Ohio, West Virginia, Illinois, and New York are among the other states experimenting with work programs for welfare recipients.

The media call these efforts "workfare." But workfare as traditionally defined—unpaid work in exchange for relief—is an option most states exercise only when welfare recipients fail to obtain paid jobs after receiving training and job placement services. Even then, states have not required recipients to participate in long-term workfare programs.

Congressional committees worked with a governors' task force in developing a comprehensive welfare reform bill. In April 1987, the House Ways and Means Subcommittee on Public Assistance approved a bill authorizing a Family Support Program to replace AFDC. The program's centerpiece is a packet of mandatory work, education, and training programs, similar to the governors' proposal but less generous because of budget constraints and conservative opposition. Able-bodied parents with children under three years of age must participate if training and daycare are available, and states

that have enough funds may require participation by parents with children as young as age one. The bill requires states to earmark resources to help long-term welfare recipients and those likely to become so, such as teen-age parents. The federal government would pay part of the costs of daycare for six months and of Medicaid for nine months for recipients who manage to work themselves off the welfare rolls. In computing welfare benefits for the working poor, states will be able to ignore the first $100 of earned income per month and 25 percent of additional income.

The bill also requires all states by the end of the decade to extend benefits to two-parent families whose principal wage earner is unemployed (since 1962 an option for states that half chose to reject) and to set a minimum benefit level equal to 15 percent of a state's median family income. Other committees acting on this bill are softening some of the work requirements.

After lengthy hearings, Senator Daniel Patrick Moynihan (D-N.Y.), chair of the Senate Finance Subcommittee on Social Security and Family Policy, proposed the Family Security Act of 1987 to replace AFDC. The bill, which includes work and training provisions similar to the House bill, conceives of welfare only as a supplement or last resort after child-support payments and mothers' wages are found inadequate to support a family. This bill costs half of what the House version does because it does not increase welfare benefits. The White House has refused to endorse either the Senate or House bill, but some compromise may eventuate.

WORK PROGRAMS: A RECORD OF FAILURE

Should these reform proposals become law, is it likely that they will succeed in taking people off welfare and putting them in the workforce? We think it unlikely. These proposals represent approaches that have always failed to increase significantly the ability of indigent families to become self-supporting. Policies to combat indigence continually seem to be selected from a limited pre-existing repertoire of government responses, some of which date from the end of feudalism. In their major thrust, the new proposals, touted as a significant shift in welfare policy, are hard to distinguish from WIN and AFDC, except in details. Moynihan's proposal resembles ideas championed by Russell Long and other Senate conservatives in the early 1970s. Let's look at the record for clues about why programs like WIN always lose.

Government responses to indigence since the 14th century have had common features. They are based on a belief that defects in the poor themselves prevent them from succeeding in the economic system. In this country, the welfare explosion of the 1960s led to a characteristically American interpretation of these defects, conditioned by traditional beliefs in individual responsibility and the importance of work. Generally, our society has viewed the values, character, and accomplishments of the poor as flawed. In the 1960s, for example, a favorite explanation was psychological instability. A continuing explanation for welfare dependence is a "culture of poverty" that passes on maladaptive behavior to each new generation. The least accusatory defect attributed to the poor is their lack of the skills and attitudes needed for success in the workplace. Even when society views the personal defects of the poor as caused by factors beyond the individual's control, such as racial discrimination, society still expects the poor to take responsibility for their own improvement.

Since the Depression of the 1930s, some federal programs in America have provided income for "deserving" families without an able-bodied breadwinner, but more often they have aimed at remedying personal defects that prevent poor people from meeting society's expectations. To this end they have provided temporary social services, tried to upgrade work skills, and offered economic and psychological incentives to work. On the assumption that welfare dependence often results from laziness and irresponsibility,

welfare agencies have also promoted work through coercion: refusing relief, requiring work for relief, paying low benefits, and treating the poor in a demeaning way.

Other common features in governmental responses to indigence throughout history deserve mention. These responses have benefited employers by maintaining the supply of low-wage labor and have tried to minimize the burden on taxpayers by keeping down welfare costs. Government responses have also had the specific intent of buttressing the work ethic and promoting paternal responsibility for family support. Some examples will illustrate these functions.

The Elizabethan Poor Laws of 17th-century England were among the earliest government regulations of the poor. Local administrators of the laws could restrict eligibility for relief as employers' labor needs expanded. Residency requirements to obtain relief prevented the unemployed from migrating to other localities with better paying or more desirable jobs. Only when widespread joblessness threatened civil disorder in the 18th century did the government act to subsidize wages under the Speenhamland Plan. But the plan undermined the quality of work effort. Because workers received subsidies regardless of their level of performance and were unlikely to increase their earnings, the plan effectively reduced the workers' motivation to satisfy their employers. (Much later, this was a problem with CETA.) By 1834 Parliament supplanted it with revised poor laws that gave the able-bodied poor a choice between the public workhouse and jobs at existing wages.

During the 1940s and 1950s in the United States, states administered the federal AFDC program in ways designed to keep welfare rolls small and to ensure the availability of workers for low-wage or temporary work. Because the federal government contributes only a portion of total relief costs (currently about 55 percent), states and localities have always had an interest in reducing caseload size to keep down costs. Many welfare agencies refused able-bodied persons relief, or provided them with relief inadequate for survival, and cut them off from relief when local jobs were available. This pattern was particularly common in the South.

One response by federal policymakers to the welfare explosion in the 1960s was legislation requiring mandatory training and work for adult recipients. A Community Work and Training Program (CWT) for fathers was a precursor of WIN. Used mainly for "work relief" (people work in exchange for relief, like workfare) rather than job training, CWT often focused on improving work habits (such as showing up on time and following orders) rather than on improving job skills.

Manpower programs—including the Comprehensive Employment and Training Act (CETA) of the 1970s, WIN, and more recently the Job Training Partnership Act (JTPA) and state "workfare" programs—have focused on improving the education, job skills, habits, and attitudes of the disadvantaged to make it worthwhile for employers to hire them at prevailing wages. Some programs are designed to upgrade basic literacy and computational skills; others also provide occupational training as a restaurant worker, daycare worker, or nurse's aide, for example. They subsidize on-the-job training or short-term work, such as summer youth employment, to provide experience in the workplace. They also provide training in how to look for a job. Except for nonexempt welfare recipients, participation in these programs has been voluntary.

Occasionally manpower programs work to increase the number of jobs available to low-income workers: "job development" consists of identifying unlisted job openings and convincing employers to interview clients. Public service jobs, such as in WPA and CETA, may be created but are temporary and invoked as a last resort.

These programs, which aim to put the poor in the workplace rather than on the relief rolls, have not noticeably reduced poverty or helped people obtain decent unsubsidized jobs that afford some security. It is unlikely that the measures have increased significantly the proportions of welfare recipients who would have gone to work without the programs. The figures tell the story: the percentage of American families in poverty has increased from 11.4 percent in 1978 to 14 percent in 1985. That year, a family of four with cash income under $10,989 fell below the federal government's official poverty line. According to a Census Bureau Report, in 1986 14.5 million families received noncash benefits such as Medicaid, food stamps, reduced-price school lunches, and subsidized housing, and another 5 million were apparently eligible but did not receive such assistance.

WHY WIN LOSES

Why do work requirements fail to reduce the percentage of families needing income assistance? There are several basic reasons:

• They aim at the mismatch between worker characteristics and employers' requirements, rather than at the wage structure of the labor market itself: most jobs available to welfare recipients pay too little to move a family above the poverty line. Welfare recipients, even if they receive government-supported job training, often lack the formal education, specialized skills, and extensive job experience needed for better paying jobs. A job at the minimum wage of $3.35 an hour pays $134 for a 40-hour week and $6,968 for a 52-week year, well below the federal poverty line for a family of four. And the proportion of low-wage jobs continues to increase; according to Barry Bluestone and Bennett Harrison, between 1979 and 1985, 44 percent of new jobs paid less than $7,400 a year in 1986 dollars (*New York Times*, February 1, 1987, sec. 3, p. 3). Appropriate jobs are often not available where the unemployed live, such as inner-city ghettos, parts of Appalachia, and industrial communities such as Gary, Indiana. In periods of high unemployment, blue-collar jobs become scarce everywhere. Discrimination exists; in recruiting new workers, employers use race, class, and sex as ways of estimating likely job performance.

• At least until the Job Training Partnership Act—the manpower program that replaced CETA in 1982—most manpower programs did not emphasize training in marketable skills, because they wanted to stretch their funds over the largest number of people. Also, less explicit objectives, such as income support, work experience, and riot prevention took precedence over job training. Much of the funds were used for temporary public-service jobs, and participants have been largely unsuccessful in finding well-paid private-sector jobs afterward. After its early years, WIN also shifted away from an initial emphasis on education and training. The Talmadge Amendments, passed in 1971, required that local programs spend the bulk of their funds on placing the more employable enrollees in private-sector jobs, on-the-job training, and public-service jobs.

• Welfare recipients often lack the literacy and computational skills needed to benefit from job training, if indeed they are found eligible for such training. In selecting participants, manpower programs favor the most employable and those who can be made job-ready in a short time—in the case of the Job Training Partnership Act, usually under 12 weeks. WIN was required by law to give service priority to the parent with the greater work history, usually the father. A program's job placement rates affect continued program funding by the state and federal government, and job developers had difficulty finding jobs for illiterate and inexperienced participants. Moreover, programs look more efficient when participants can enter employment after short-term training. Yet recipients with less education and experience (for whom getting jobs is a bigger hurdle) need manpower services most. The hardcore unemployed will need public assistance for years unless they are trained and helped to get a decent job.

• Congress has been unwilling to appropriate enough money to provide training and services for most of the needy. WIN rarely served more than a third of those required to enroll. JTPA can reach only a small proportion of those needing job training. Yet without jobs, job training, and ancillary services such as daycare, a work requirement cannot be enforced. Rehabilitation takes more time and money than our government has been willing to invest.

• Congress has not confronted the disincentives to working built into programs for low-income families. If families earn enough money to become disqualified for welfare, they also become ineligible for other subsidies and in-kind benefits such as food stamps, Medicaid, and public housing. Welfare policy does not permit families to develop equity and savings as a cushion for life without income supports, because welfare agencies take such assets into account in determining eligibility and level of income subsidy (see Stack in For Further Reading). Families of unemployed men lose all benefits when fathers work 100 hours a month, regardless of income. Available jobs often do not pay a decent wage, workers are frequently laid off, and few jobs offer medical insurance. So if welfare recipients go to work full-time, they often end up with a lower standard of living and even less security.

The kinds of jobs available to welfare recipients discourage working and make being on welfare more acceptable. People in insecure, poorly paid, and demeaning jobs that offer little intrinsic satisfaction reduce their work effort. Welfare recipients who do obtain good jobs may fail because their sex, race, ethnicity, or class makes them socially unacceptable to established workers. Social acceptance is a prerequisite for the informal on-the-job guidance by co-workers that is so necessary for job success (see Doeringer and Piore in For Further Reading). Participation in the underground economy becomes increasingly appealing, particularly for urban youth.

• Finally, we have not reached consensus about whether mothers of preschoolers should be required to leave their children in the care of others to go to work. In WIN's early days, social workers often excused mothers who did not volunteer for the program. Amendments to WIN in 1972 formally excused mothers of preschool children. And while congressional ambivalence about expecting mothers to work has lessened, an amendment to the pending House bill, that excuses mothers with children under 15 years of age from work unless childcare is guaranteed, passed the Education and Labor Committee with little opposition. The practical difficulties of finding and funding daycare continue to undermine efforts to put mothers to work.

Moreover, we have been unwilling to impose sanctions on welfare recipients who fail to meet work obligations. One reason is our concern about the consequences for the family's children; another is the difficulty of taking away something that has already been given.

PROGNOSIS FOR CURRENT PROPOSALS

Given this history, what is the prognosis for current plans such as the governors' initiatives to get the poor back to work? Continued failure seems likely because of four factors:

(1) *Inability of the economy to generate enough adequately paying jobs is most important.* The proposed reforms do not address the problems of the private-sector labor market. And public-service employment has a poor record; it provides some income, but for most it does not lead either to employment in the private sector or to higher wages.

(2) *Disincentives to work.* The governors' proposal described earlier does address in part some of the disincentives. The governors want to continue Medicaid and daycare for a year after a welfare recipient takes a job. However, although one year is probably not enough, Congress is unlikely to support even that. Under Republican pressure, the House bill reduced that time and delayed the implementation of the provisions. Many jobs available to welfare recipients do not provide health benefits, and the cost of daycare, where available, can leave little to live on. Because government funds to subsidize daycare are scarce, two-parent families are usually excluded and only those parents making the lowest wages qualify.

The bill before the House substantially increases the "income disregard" feature of WIN. Unfortunately, this provision may serve as a disincentive to work. Recipients may work only enough to supplement income, not enough to leave welfare. Research shows that incentives such as disregards for wages and work expenses are most effective when welfare grants are low and work is necessary for family survival. Other disincentives related to the characteristics of available jobs remain; these jobs tend to be short-term, low-paid, and lacking in health benefits and opportunity for advancement.

(3) *Cost.* The governors' proposals recognized that effective welfare reform will be expensive. But the House bill's initial authorization was reduced in order to obtain enough committee support, and the Senate bill authorizes even less. These bills would allow only a modest increase in the proportion of parents already in training and work programs. Even so, the administration and its congressional supporters oppose many of the bills' provisions, charging that the real price will be far higher than projected.

(4) *Creaming: training those most likely to succeed anyway.* Advocates want programs to be successful. Therefore they tend to train those of the poor most likely to succeed rather than the hard-core, long-term unemployed, who are so hard to help. Legislators are becoming aware of this problem. A bill introduced by Senator Edward M. Kennedy (D-Mass.) in 1987 gave states bonuses if they succeeded in training long-term welfare recipients and in finding them jobs. The House welfare reform bill gives priority to long-term welfare recipients or those likely to become so.

Still, the rhetoric has suggested little understanding of how much remedial education will be necessary, and how expensive that will be, before job training and placement of the majority of adult welfare recipients can be attempted. For example, California's Social Services Department, in testing volunteers for their experimental "workfare" program (Greater Avenues for Independence or GAIN), has discovered that 70 percent will need some remedial education in reading and arithmetic and to qualify for even the most menial jobs; a third will require at least six months of such education. So clients will stay on welfare rolls longer and require expensive remediation. New York City's program has been overwhelmed by needs for social services, education, and training. Program administrators will find important constraints to carrying out the federal and state policymakers' goal of moving all able-bodied adults from welfare to the workplace. Such has been the experience of other programs serving the poor.

Financial disincentives to working have been little recognized, and creaming has been inadequately addressed. The enormous cost of an effective program has gone unrecognized. Most important, the root cause, the structure of the labor market— that is, the scarcity of decent, adequately paying jobs for the poor—has been ignored. If a breadwinner for a family of four earns little better than the minimum wage, the family is still below the poverty level. Unless very expensive training is undertaken to raise greatly the productivity of the disadvantaged and hence the wages they can command, poverty cannot be noticeably reduced.

58

A Marshall Plan for America: A Land of Diverse People Living and Working Together

John E. Jacob

The author argues that political, technological, economic, and demographic trends pose fundamental challenges to the future of America. To overcome barriers of racism and diversity, he recommends building interracial and inter-ethnic coalitions around shared concerns over poverty, injustice, jobs, and affordable housing. The severity of the social and economic problems in urban centers leads the author to advocate "Operation Urban Storm," a modern-day "Marshall Plan for America," as the only possible way to reverse the decay of the central cities.

Exercises to Guide Your Reading

1. List the differences in the challenges confronting civil rights activists in the 1960s and the 1990s.
2. Explain the author's claim that "America's future in this new, changing world will depend on its ability to develop the human resources of all of its diverse people."
3. List and explain the principle features of the proposed "Marshall Plan for America."
4. Evaluate the claim that the policies adopted by Reagan and Bush—"disastrous strategies that fail to address America's social and economic problems"—were based on three myths: that America "is a color-blind society"; that "the free market can solve social problems"; and that "government can only play a limited role."

We come to Atlanta this week to continue our journey on the road to "Making a Difference in the '90s." For the 1990s are a critical decade for African Americans and indeed for all Americans—a decade that will decide whether America maintains its leadership role or whether it sinks to second-class status ... whether African Americans progress toward parity, or whether we fall further behind.

We enter this critical decade after years of stalled progress ... battling to preserve our limited gains ... facing urban decline ... racial tensions ... economic recession.

But ours has always been an uphill struggle. Never more so than now.

Reprinted by permission of *Vital Speeches of the Day* (speech given July 1, 1991). November 1, 1991. pp. 58–62.

For today's world is an often confusing place. It is changing at an incredibly fast pace.

We are in a revolutionary new era in which America faces great challenges that will affect the future of African Americans and of all our people.

I'll just touch briefly on four of the revolutions that are sweeping the world today, and some of the challenges they pose.

The first is political—the global trend toward democracy and inclusion.

It is symbolized by the collapse of communism, the weakening of apartheid, and the cries of self-determination now being heard in places as far apart as Kurdistan and Kashmir.

We are challenged to harness that drive toward democratic ideals . . . to channel it to positive changes that respect the dignity and potential of all people.

The second is technological—as new scientific developments sweep away old ways of doing things.

It's a trend symbolized by "smart bombs" and high definition television . . . the application of high technology to weapons of destruction and to consumer goods alike.

We are challenged to direct the development of technological change so that it becomes the vehicle to make life better, and not the vehicle to destroy life.

Technology drives a third revolution—the economic revolution.

It is symbolized by empty factory buildings in the inner city and shining new office towers in the suburbs . . . by highly trained professionals working for big corporations and by despairing, jobless men on street corners . . . by shrinking job opportunities in major American industries and "Made in Japan" stickers on the cars and appliances we buy.

We are challenged to take part in that economic revolution . . . to help our young people get the education and the skills to hold productive jobs . . . and to implement public policies that enable every citizen to be productive.

Finally, there is the demographic revolution.

That is symbolized by the wave of new immigrants pouring into the industrial nations . . . by the rising tide of African American majorities in our major cities . . . and by a national work force that is growing slower, and is more dependent on women and minorities.

We are challenged to meet the needs of a more diverse society by developing an appreciation for other cultures and by building bridges that cross racial and ethnic lines.

Four revolutions that will shape our lives.

And four sets of challenges that will drive our personal and citizenship responsibilities.

Those of us who grew up in the civil rights struggle must come to terms with this revolutionary new era.

For the issues have changed and the challenges are in many ways much more difficult.

In the 1960s, we could mount a drive for national civil rights laws to protect constitutional rights that had been illegally denied to African Americans.

But in the 1990s white resentment is fanned by demagogic shouts of "quotas" . . . and we find ourselves debating the merits of a civil rights bill that turns on legal definitions of "business necessity" and "disparate impact."

In the 1960s, we were fighting for the right to vote. In the 1990s, African American elected officials preside over crumbling cities without the resources to meet the needs of their people.

In the 1960s we had identifiable villains like Bull Connor and the Klan.

In the 1990s, even violent racists don't do as much damage as the crack dealer on the corner or the child with a handgun and no conscience.

In the 1960s we had to deal with employers who refused to hire African Americans except to sweep up.

In the 1990s, we have to deal with employers who say they can't get people with the skills to do demanding jobs, and with glass ceilings that keep minorities and women out of positions of corporate power.

But one thing remains constant—in the 1990s, as in the 1960s, African Americans are disproportionately poor and are victimized by discrimination and by unequal opportunity.

That has to change. Not simply for reasons of morality and fairness.

But also because America's future in this new, changing world will depend on its ability to develop the human resources of all of its diverse people.

Diversity will be the burning issue of the 1990s—and beyond.

Demographers say that by mid-century whites will no longer be a majority of the population. It's already happened in the state of California and in cities like New York, where no single group is in the majority.

Today, thirty-two million Americans are black. Twenty-five million are Hispanic. Seven-and-a-half million are Asian.

Those totals mask even more extensive diversity—African Americans from the Caribbean and from Africa . . . Hispanic Americans from every country in the Hemisphere . . . Asian Americans who include fifth-generation Americans and new arrivals from places as different as Cambodia and Sri Lanka.

Will America use that wonderful mosaic of difference to create a truly pluralistic society?

Will it remove the barriers to African Americans and other minorities?

America's future depends on positive answers. But the sad fact is that America is really unprepared for diversity.

Too many Americans are intimidated by differences and hung up on stereotypes.

A few months ago, a nationwide survey by the University of Chicago's National Opinion Research Center found what we all know and have been saying for years—that Americans are victims of racist thinking that negatively stereotypes all minorities.

The survey found that three out of four white Americans stigmatize blacks as lazy, violent, unintelligent people who prefer welfare to work.

To a lesser extent, they held similar negative stereotypes about Hispanics and Asians.

The disease of racism threatens to poison America's destiny as a pluralistic, multicultural democracy.

We must remember that America's history is stained with the evils committed against minorities and newcomers.

This is the land where African Americans won our constitutional rights and other minorities secured freedoms unknown in their homelands.

But it is also the land where blacks were enslaved, oppressed, lynched, and brutalized. The land of wholesale slaughter of Native Americans . . . of anti-Irish riots . . . of quotas that kept Jews from schools and jobs . . . of detention camps for Japanese Americans.

And this is also the land where each wave of newcomers learned that the fastest way to become a real American was to absorb the racism of the majority.

People who faced discrimination themselves quickly learned to keep blacks out of their unions, out of their neighborhoods, and out of their schools.

We need to confront that painful history, because there are signs today that the past may repeat itself.

There's evidence of racial stereotyping among many of today's new minorities—and some African Americans hold negative stereotypes about other groups.

That's important for everyone to understand—and to do something about.

So let me repeat—there's evidence of racial stereotyping among many of today's new minorities—and some African Americans hold negative stereotypes about other groups.

That's sure to make a lot of white supremacists very happy.

But it's not in anyone else's interest. And it is something that could crack the

American mosaic and endanger America's future.

America has to come to terms with diversity. It needs to protect minority rights ... end discrimination ... provide education and training opportunities for a diverse workforce ... and stop stereotyping people.

But African Americans will also have to adjust to the new ethnic realities.

We've become used to seeing race relations in terms of black and white. But race relations in the 1990s and into the 21st century will be more complex.

We need to encourage inter-group cooperation. And we need to guard against divide-and-conquer tactics that encourage inter-group frictions.

That won't be as easy as it sounds.

There is a danger that the diversity issue will be manipulated to concentrate on the concerns of emerging new minorities to the exclusion of blacks.

And we've already seen the way cultural misperceptions have bred conflict.

In many cities there is friction between African Americans and Arab or Korean storekeepers.

In cities like Miami, African Americans confront a power structure that is not white, but Hispanic.

In cities like Washington D.C., Hispanic immigrants confront a power structure that is black.

In many cities, African American mayors, police chiefs, and school superintendents are in a strange situation for us—being resented by other minorities as the holders of power ... the Establishment.

So it's a mistake to think that we can achieve unity simply because we share the nonwhite or minority label.

But it's also a mistake to think we can go it alone in a diverse society.

If history is any guide, White America will pick and choose among its minorities.

Some will be accepted grudgingly and allowed in the door.

Others—and especially African Americans—will be confined to the cellar.

We can't allow that to happen.

We'll need to build inter-racial and inter-ethnic coalitions around concerns we share and issues that can unite.

Issues like: poverty ... injustice ... jobs ... training opportunities ... access to quality education and health care ... affordable housing.

And those coalitions have to be based on the question: is it good for America?

Not just: is it good for African Americans? But: is it good for America?

If the answer is "yes," African Americans will benefit disproportionately since we are disproportionately burdened by poverty and the social problems that poverty breeds.

And if the answer is "yes," we can attract the support to move our country forward and solve many of its problems.

Re-assessing our relations with other minorities is part of the necessary process of adjusting to a society that is being transformed.

We need to address old paradigms and adjust them to this new era. New occasions teach new truths, and there is nothing wrong with questioning positions of an era gone by.

That doesn't mean hopping on the bandwagon of fashionable new trends. Rather, it means carefully re-examining positions in the light of changing circumstances.

Let me briefly mention just three of many issues that may require some new thinking.

One is enterprise zones.

Many of us have questioned their effectiveness, and correctly suggest they are not and cannot be the answer to black unemployment problems.

But the African American economy has been in permanent Depression and anything legal that might improve it should be tried.

In the absence of a federal commitment to national job creation programs, we can support an enterprise zone program that includes expanded job opportunities for people living in poverty neighborhoods.

School choice is another issue that bears re-examination.

There is no way we can support a voucher

system that includes private schools, because that would destroy public schools.

But we can take another look at public school choice programs as one of many school reforms.

Not the choice programs now being thrown together with a slogan and a prayer. But choice programs with strict controls that guarantee parent information processes ... eliminate tracking ... and prepare all children for high academic achievement.

A final issue that needs rethinking is political representation.

Right now congressional district lines are being redrawn by state legislatures.

With the help of technical experts from the Republican Party, some districts are being reshaped to rope in as many African American voters as possible.

Some think that's a great idea—creating all-black districts to ensure election of black representatives.

But we have to ask if this isn't a new form of political apartheid—assuring some safe congressional seats for blacks at the cost of losing influence with legislators from adjoining districts.

Is it better for African Americans to be 80 percent of the voters in one district or to be 25 percent of the voters in many districts?

Does racial redistricting maximize our participation or does it dilute our potential strength?

The answers may differ in different areas and states.

But strategies that made sense when we just got the vote may not be the best strategies for leveraging our influence on issues that require broad legislative coalitions.

And political strategies based on racial polarization may not be the best strategies at a time when predominately white cities like Seattle and Denver and Los Angeles elect African American mayors.

The new era we are entering is going to mean rethinking those and other issues and positions—and that can often be a painful process.

But we are not the only ones who need to address old paradigms.

Our national leaders need to re-examine the disastrous strategies that fail to address America's social and economic problems.

Those strategies are based on three myths:

One, we are a color-blind society.

Two, the free market can solve social problems.

Three, government can only play a limited role.

For over a decade, those myths deepened racial and class divisions, devastated the cities, and weakened America's competitiveness.

It's time to scrap them.

And the place to begin is with the myth about being a color-blind society.

America is a color-blind society only in its blindness to the needs and the aspirations of African Americans.

People don't like to think about race ... about discrimination ... about injustice. They'd rather pretend it's been taken care of.

But it's our job to make them think about it—and it's our job to make them do something about it.

Because racism is alive and well in these United States.

The consensus on civil rights has been replaced by racial fears and stereotypes. The consensus against discrimination has been replaced by winking at it and hoping the issue will disappear.

It won't. That's why Congress has to pass a civil rights bill that effectively reverses Supreme Court decisions that encourage job discrimination.

Those decisions—and others that restrict basic civil liberties and limit constitutional rights—tell us that the Supreme Court no longer stands by our side. It is now on our back. It is removing gains of the past and building new barriers to our future.

While I am gratified that the President has nominated an African American to the seat held by Justice Marshall, it is clear that Clarence Thomas is no Thurgood Marshall.

I share the alarm caused by the addition of yet another Justice likely to overturn *Roe v. Wade* and affirmative action rulings.

But I would hope that Judge Thomas' life experiences will lead him to closer identification with those in America who are today victimized by poverty and discrimination.

And I would hope that he sees the irony in opposing affirmative action while at the same time being an affirmative action appointee.

Yes, he has the qualifications for the job of Supreme Court justice. So do literally hundreds of other people.

But there are only nine positions—and only one was vacant. So additional criteria were applied—criteria like racial and ethnic diversity ... life experiences ... experience in government ... and political considerations.

Judge Thomas' nomination should tell the Administration and Judge Thomas himself, that affirmative action and merit are not mutually exclusive.

Without affirmative action, merit will always be equated with whiteness. And without strong anti-discrimination laws, African Americans, women, and other minorities will continue to be economically vulnerable.

That is why we so strongly urge the Senate to pass a strong civil rights bill, and why we urge the President to sign it.

He should finally reject the advice of hard-liners like Chief of Staff John Sununu and White House Counsel Boyden Gray, and the political consultants who see the phony quota issue as next year's Willie Horton.

Americans should not be confused by legalistic haggling over technicalities ... by false quota charges ... or by thinking that a bill that benefits white women and all minorities is a "black" bill.

The Civil Rights Act of 1991 is about discrimination.

Quotas aren't the problem. Discrimination is.

Let's be clear about that. I repeat:

The Civil Rights Act of 1991 isn't about quotas. It's about discrimination.

It's about not hiring qualified blacks ... refusing to promote qualified Hispanics ... discriminating against qualified women.

African American organizations carried the load for the Civil Rights Act even though we'd rather be fighting on other battlegrounds—on priorities like more jobs, better schools, and more and better training opportunities.

But this is a fight that was forced upon us by an extremist Supreme Court and by an Administration that made race a partisan political issue.

The struggle over the civil rights bill is a struggle for the soul of America ... about the kind of people we are and the kind of country we want to become ... about replacing the myth of a color-blind society with the reality of a diverse, equal opportunity society.

Let's look at Myth Number Two—the free market can solve our social problems.

It can help—a strong free enterprise economy that creates jobs and opportunities is necessary but insufficient.

Without socially directed investments and government programs, cities continue to deteriorate, poverty remains largely intact, and social divisions deepen.

That's the story of the booming eighties, when America became an experimental laboratory for free market theories. While the free market flourished and industries restructured to become more profitable, government trashed poor people's programs to end so-called dependency. Civil rights enforcement was de-emphasized. College grants and training opportunities were cut.

How did that experiment work here in Atlanta, a city that grew and flourished during the boom?

A new book titled "The Closing Door: Conservative Policy and Black Opportunity" tells the story.

New jobs were created. Lots of them. But they were in the white suburbs and went to newcomers from outside the city. Metro area wealth increased. Inner city poverty got worse.

Here's the authors' conclusion, and I quote:

The Atlanta experience shows that it is essential to confront the issue of racial discrimination directly, as the color line remained an extremely powerful force in distributing opportunity and destroying aspirations.

It's the same story for the whole nation—the gap between white and black, rich and poor, got wider, and the free market alone can't close that gap.

Closing the gap takes partnerships between the private sector, the voluntary sector, and an activist government that opens doors instead of closing them.

That brings us to the third myth that has dominated our national life for over a decade—the myth that government has a limited role in solving social and economic problems.

That one is hard to understand.

We're in the midst of a recession that's hurting everybody—black and white; a recession that's thrown almost two million people out of work over the past year.

Cities are closing fire stations and libraries, laying off teachers, shutting down child care centers and drug clinics.

All this comes on top of a decade of growing black poverty and urban decay.

The President's response is to give speeches beating up on the Great Society and to keep calling for a thousand points of light—as if government was the electric company.

But whatever its shortcomings, the Great Society worked.

No one—not even the President of the United States—should be confused about that.

In only five years, the Great Society brought about history's biggest reduction in poverty.

Medicare ... Medicaid ... Head Start ... the Job Corps ... the civil rights laws. All Great Society programs. All proof that government can and does and should make a difference.

Voluntarism is important. Everyone should be involved in helping people in need. The Urban League, its programs, and its volunteers are America's brightest points of light.

The voluntary sector is doing what it can—and it's doing a lot.

But it's cynical to say that voluntarism is the answer.

Voluntarism can ameliorate some of the worst effects of our social problems. But those problems are massive—and only government has the power and the resources to solve them.

And voluntarism cannot even be effective in softening the inequities of our society when nonprofit agencies are denied resources to manage those volunteers and to implement necessary programs.

Nor can voluntarism solve the deep structural problems that condemn millions of Americans to poverty and hardship.

A strategy of voluntarism can be more helpful if community-based organizations are used as intermediaries, delivering programs backed by government and the private sector.

Those points of light need to be hooked up to the powerful generator of a national domestic policy aimed at getting to the root causes of poverty and unequal opportunities.

Today, we have no such domestic policy.

Listen to this quotation from someone who knows: Quote:

The White House is the epicenter of national policy. There are problems of poverty, despair, and economic decline in many people's neighborhoods which the President has both a moral and a political obligation to combat.

End of quote. A moral and a political obligation!

That wasn't said by John Jacob. It wasn't Ben Hooks. It wasn't Jesse Jackson. And it wasn't Maynard Jackson.

That quote comes from Jack Kemp, the President's Secretary of Housing and Urban Development.

We're not buying into all of Secretary Kemp's program, which is burdened by the free market myth.

But we do buy into the view that government has a moral and a political obligation to combat America's economic and social problems.

Government can't just be a cheerleader for volunteers. It's got to be a quarterback, calling the plays and setting the game plan for deep changes in our society.

The President plays a pretty good game of quarterbacking international policy. But he needs to get back into the game of domestic policy.

And in the Persian Gulf crisis, he has a good model for developing a domestic game plan.

Why did America win the Gulf War in 100 hours?

The answer is clear. We developed clear objectives ... assembled overwhelming resources to achieve those objectives ... and let General Colin Powell coordinate a unified air, sea, and land campaign.

Why is America losing the war in the cities?

Again, the answer is clear. It lacks clear objectives. It cuts off resources. Its programs are uncoordinated and often contradictory.

How can America win in the cities?

Once more, the answer is clear: The way we won in the Gulf. By mounting an Operation Urban Storm the way we mounted Operation Desert Storm.

Develop clear objectives to end poverty and renew urban America.

Commit the necessary resources and target them to develop the enormous human resources of our youth and the people on the margins of our society.

Coordinate that massive effort through coalitions of government, the private sector, and the voluntary sector, with clear, accountable lines of authority.

The Urban League has developed a domestic policy game plan that can win the war in the cities.

We have called for an Urban Marshall Plan ... a Marshall Plan for America ... a ten year, $50 billion annual investment in our people and in our infrastructure.

Since we issued our call, others have jumped on the Marshall Plan bandwagon.

There have been proposals for a Marshall Plan for eastern Europe. A Marshall Plan for the Gulf. Gorbachev wants the West to fund a Marshall Plan for the Soviet Union.

The original Marshall Plan worked. It put western Europe back on its feet after World War Two. That's why everyone wants a Marshall Plan for their country or their region.

But there's only one place where a Marshall Plan makes sense.

And that's right here at home—rebuilding our cities, bringing poor people into the economic mainstream, investing in making America competitive again.

Our Marshall Plan for America isn't only for African Americans, but for all Americans.

And we developed it because of the hard realities staring us in the face.

We looked at the nation and the world. We saw the political, technological, economic, and demographic revolutions transforming a global society.

We saw the irreversible trends gathering force: the cries for participation, the shift to knowledge work, the faster economic growth of our countries, the growing diversity of our society and our workforce.

And we put that all together and concluded that unless America invests in its future and in its people, its people will have no future.

We'll have a once-proud democratic society split between haves and have-nots; between those with decent jobs and those with no jobs, between a smaller white population and a larger minority population. All fighting over the crumbs from a smaller economic pie.

That's the handwriting on the wall of the future and it's why we proposed a Marshall Plan for America—to rewrite that future by rebuilding the physical infrastructure essential to economic growth and by rebuilding the human infrastructure essential to economic competitiveness.

In the year-and-a-half since we offered our Marshall Plan for America, some Congressional representatives have expressed interest, but the Administration has been silent.

It did come up with a transportation and

highway improvement program that will cost over $120 billion over five years.

But that program doesn't include the core of the Urban Marshall Plan infrastructure proposal—targeted recruitment and training of the disadvantaged.

Without that, it's just another pork barrel program instead of a unified plan to bring the economy to a higher level of productivity.

So tonight, we renew our call for a Marshall Plan for America.

We tell our nation once more—and it cannot be repeated often enough—that unless America invests in the future of all of its people, it will lose its world leadership role and all Americans will lose their standard of living.

I don't expect the Administration to see the light and become an overnight convert to the Marshall Plan idea.

But I do expect growing numbers of Americans—of all races and classes—to come to understand that our plan is in the national interest.

It's not a black plan or a special interest plan, but an American plan—a plan for a strong, economically competitive, powerful and democratic 21st century America.

The Urban Marshall Plan should be the catalyst for the long overdue national debate about our future.

For the United States is moving into a new century without a strategic plan ... without a clear idea of where we want to be in ten or twenty or thirty years.

We've been busy celebrating our military power, waving the flag, and shouting that we're Number One. So busy, we haven't noticed our declining economic power and the social tensions that could bring us down.

A Marshall Plan for America would change all that.

It would mobilize the country behind a positive program to ensure America's greatness ... behind a vision of a future America that is truly an open, pluralistic, integrated society.

Our America needs to recapture the vision of itself that has inspired people around the world for over two centuries.

It is a vision of a diverse people living together in harmony and respect with liberty and justice for all.

That's the vision that separates the United States from all other nations in the world.

And that American vision of freedom and democracy and opportunity still inspires the world's people.

It is a vision that drives the hopes of little black children in Atlanta ... a vision dear to people in faraway lands struggling to be free ... a vision that flourishes in the minds and hearts of people of all races and all cultures.

It is a strong vision. It has to be, to have survived the contradictions of its birth in a slave society.

It is a vision that has been tarnished by injustice and violated by unfairness.

It is a vision that has been abused by racism ... tattered by exploitation ... trampled by discrimination.

But as much as we are disappointed and saddened by the way that noble vision has been violated more often than it's been followed, we are not disappointed in the vision itself.

Much as we are frustrated at the way that vision has been applied to others more than to ourselves, we are not frustrated at the vision itself.

And much as we deplore the failure of Americans to revive and cherish that unique vision, we do not deplore the vision itself.

Rather, we are inspired by it ... by the vision of a land of diverse peoples living and working together in equality, in harmony, in mutual respect.

That vision may be old in years but it is young in its meaning for a nation struggling to achieve equality for all ... a people grappling with the terrors of racism ... a land of diverse peoples entering an unknown future.

And it is a vision to which we of the Urban League movement hold fast.

For ours is a struggle to help our society fulfill its vision, even as it often drifts away from the best of its heritage.

We of the Urban League live daily with the shattered violations of the American vision—with the children victimized by drug gangs and bad schools, with the adults who don't have work, don't have food, don't have hope.

But we carry on, with faith in the vision articulated by the Founding Fathers, who gathered together at birth a nation based on the revolutionary principle that:

> We, the People of the United States create a government to "establish justice, . . . promote the general welfare, and secure the blessings of liberty to ourselves and our posterity."

We carry on with faith in that vision as articulated by Dr. Martin Luther King, Jr., who dreamed:

> that one day on the red hills of Georgia the sons of former slaves and the sons of former slave owners will be able to sit down together at the table of brotherhood.

And we labor in pursuit of that same vision, as defined by the late, great, Whitney M. Young, Jr., when he said:

> We seek not to weaken America but to strengthen it; not to divide America but to unify it; not to decry America, but to purify it; not to separate America but to become part of it.
>
> This is our land. Here we have risen from slavery to freedom and here will we rise from poverty to prosperity.
>
> This is our land.
>
> Here we shall overcome.

This then, is our vision of an America that is just and fair . . . an America in which we shall prosper . . . an America that is and always will be, our land.

Here, we shall overcome.

That is what we of the Urban League are about.

That is why we have come to Atlanta this week.

That is what this Conference is all about.

Let this Conference begin!

59

Reparations for Black Americans

Charles Krauthammer

The author begins by assessing the effects of legislation aimed at improving racial equality. Policies of preferential treatment are said to miss the mark, since they have been expanded to include millions of people who have no claim to a heritage stamped by the experience of slavery. The author advocates reparations for African Americans as a once-and-for-all solution to the economic claims of the descendants of those economically, politically, and socially damaged by America's slave system.

Exercises to Guide Your Reading

1. List the characteristics of affirmative action that the author sees as negative.
2. Define the term "reparations," and give examples of the uses of reparations.
3. Explain the strengths and weaknesses of a policy of reparations.
4. Compare and contrast the arguments for reparations with the arguments for affirmative action.

"Nobody's asking for reparations. I'm asking you to give us the crumbs from the table," said Craig Washington, one of five black Congressmen from the South on the floor of the House. What crumbs? More and stronger affirmative action as mandated by the Civil Rights Act of 1990.

George Bush, an aristocrat who hates to deny crumbs to anyone, vetoed the bill anyway, on the ground that it encouraged racial quotas. But the bill was more than just bad legislation. It was a sign of intellectual bankruptcy in our thinking about race. As race relations worsen, as ethnic divisions harden, as an ex-Nazi pulls nearly as many votes in Louisiana as did the 1988 Democratic presidential candidate, the country has run out of ideas.

Take the Civil Rights Act of 1990. It makes it easier for minorities to sue the boss if the employee roster does not meet some statistical measure of racial balance. A nightmare for employers, a bonanza for lawyers, a crumb for blacks. How many, after all, would be helped by such legislation, and at what cost?

There is no denying that affirmative action has started some blacks on the ladder of advancement and thus helped create a black middle class. There is equally no denying that because it violates the rights of some people purely on the grounds of race, it has exacerbated racial resentments.

But as Shelby Steele argues, preferential treatment for blacks has an even more pernicious cost; it creates corrosive doubt in the

Reprinted by permission of *Time*. December 31, 1990. p. 18.

eyes of both whites and blacks about the worth of any black achievement. However much people may deny it, no one can see a black professor or doctor without having the thought run through his mind: Did he make it on his own or did he get through on a quota? These doubts gratuitously reinforce in both blacks and whites a presumption of racial inferiority.

Moreover, the idea that affirmative action is just a temporary remedy is a fraud. With every new civil rights act, like the one just attempted and soon to be reintroduced in the 102nd Congress, ethnic quotas and race consciousness become more deeply woven into American life. The current uproar over race-based college scholarships reminds us just how divisive the issue can be.

What is to be done? Representative Washington has it exactly backward. Forget the crumbs, demand reparations. It is time for a historic compromise: a monetary reparation to blacks for centuries of oppression in return for the total abolition of all programs of racial preference. A one-time cash payment in return for a new era of irrevocable color blindness.

Why reparations? First, because they are targeted precisely at those who deserve them. By now affirmative action has grown to include preferential treatment for Hispanics, women, the handicapped, and an ever-expanding list of favored groups. This is absurd. By what moral standard should, say, a Marielito, already once rescued by America, enjoy a preference over, say, an Italian-American vet or an Irish cop? A Richmond ordinance struck down two years ago by the Supreme Court assigned 30% of city subcontracts to firms owned by minorities, defined as "Blacks, Spanish-speaking [citizens], Orientals, Indians, Eskimos or Aleuts." Richmond, capital of the Confederacy, is not known for its mistreatment of Eskimos. Yet under the law, Richmond would have had to prefer an Alaskan Eskimo to a local white in city contracting.

Let us be plain. Richmond's sin—America's sin—was against blacks. There is no wrong in American history to compare with slavery. Affirmative action distorts the issue by favoring equally all "disadvantaged groups." Some of those groups are disadvantaged, some not. Black America is the only one that for generations was officially singled out for discrimination and worse. Why blur the issue?

Reparations focus the issue most sharply. They acknowledge the crime. They attempt restitution. They seek to repay some of "the bondman's 250 years of unrequited toil." They offer the wronged some tangible means to elevate their condition.

For that very real purpose, reparations should be more than merely symbolic. Say, $100,000 for every family of four. That would cost the country a lot—about 50% more than the cost of our S&L sins—but hardly, for a $6 trillion economy, a bankrupting sum. (A 10-year 75¢ gas tax, for example, would pay the whole bill.) Recession may not be the best time to start such a transfer, but America will come out of recession.

The savings to the country will be substantial: an end to endless litigation, to the inefficiencies of allocation by group (rather than merit), to the distortion of the American principle of individualism, to the resentments aroused by a system of group preferences. The fact is, we already have a system of racial compensation. It is called affirmative action. That system is not only inherently unjust but socially demoralizing and inexcusably clumsy. Far better an honest focused substitute: real, hard, one-time compensation.

But is not cash-for-suffering demeaning? Perhaps. But we have found no better way to compensate for great crimes. Germans know that the millions they have dispersed to Holocaust survivors cannot begin to compensate for the murder of an entire civilization. Yet for irremediable national crimes, reparations are as dignified a form of redress as one can devise.

Racial preferences, on the other hand, are a demeaning form of racial tutelage. Better the dignity of a debt repaid, however impersonally, than the warm glow of condescension that permeates affirmative action.

It is time to reclaim the notion of color blindness before it is too late. A one-time reparation to blacks would help real people in a real way. It would honor our obligation to right ancient wrongs. And it would allow us all a new start. America could then rededicate itself to Martin Luther King Jr.'s proposition that Americans be judged by the content of their character, not by the color of their skin.

60

Wealth and Poverty Revisited

George Gilder

The author contends that "history has confirmed all these claims" that "tax cuts and deregulation" are the means to deal with America's economic problems. Liberal tax-and-spend policies are blamed for the increase in crime, single-parent families, poverty, and illiteracy, since such policies undercut the patriarchy that is "an indispensable bulwark of civilization." The article concludes with a moral defense of capitalism as the only economic system that forces workers and businesses to meet the needs of others.

Exercises to Guide Your Reading

1. Explain the difference between the income effect and the substitution effect of tax cuts.
2. Give examples of how tax cuts foster productivity growth and equality.
3. Illustrate the relationship between consumption and production, and explain its role in the author's argument.
4. Summarize the evidence the author presents to support the view that "capitalism at last demonstrated conclusively its superiority as an economic system."

Wealth and Poverty began its career as a modest tract, to be called "The Pursuit of Poverty," sharing a total advance of $8,000 with *Visible Man*, which sold some 800 copies in the first year and achieved poverty for me. Nonetheless, when first published in late 1980, *Wealth and Poverty* leapt toward the top of best-seller lists in much of the civilized world. It was seen as the Bible of the incoming administration of Ronald Reagan and, indeed, Reagan himself had read early drafts of the final chapters and written enthusiastically to the author. Beginning with the erudite campaign director William Casey, the cerebral budgeteer David Stockman, and the visionary adviser Jack Kemp, several top Reagan aides helped edit the book before publication.

On release, however, interest was chiefly confined to Washington. At Basic Books in New York, editor Midge Decter had had to work hard to win a first printing of some 5,000 copies. Basic's publicity chief refused to send copies to Stockman to distribute to the cabinet at its introductory press conference. The Basic man explained: "They won't review the book. We'll wait for the *New York Times*."

The explosion of demand for this supply-side tract surprised nearly everyone except myself, who like most authors had imagined best-seller performance for all his books, including *Visible Man*. From *People* magazine to "60 Minutes," I found myself racing through the gauntlets of sudden celebrity, dwarfed by huge screens above me blaring

Reprinted by permission of *The American Spectator*. July 1993. pp. 32–37.

my face at massive audiences, blandished by intent presidents, vice presidents, and cabinet leaders with yellow pads at the ready, and beset by ardent journalists and photographers from Washington, Paris, Rome, and Seoul.

As a celebrity, however, I had many limitations, including a genuine disdain for television journalists: all the feminist women with their frizzy hair, designer jogging suits, and impeccable *Kultursmog*, and the endlessly conformist young men, with their bland, obligatory little touches of rebellion, such as dirty running shoes with their coats and ties, and all determined to become rich by promoting socialism (without even knowing it). Within a few months, they understandably stopped calling on me, and I found to my surprise that I rather missed them.

The whirl now moved on to Diana, Madonna, Michael Kinsley, and other more durable luminaries who could smile at a camera or undress before it (yet another promotion strategy entirely overlooked by Basic Books as they awaited the verdict of Roger Starr at the *Times*). I moved on to smile at microchips. I soon discovered that, amid all the uproar, the central theme of my work had not been grasped even by some of my closest intellectual allies in the conservative movement. Indeed, the central theme was missed by nearly all reviewers. This failure was so widespread that I was forced to conclude that it was mostly my fault. To rectify the situation, I published an explanatory essay in 1982 in *The American Spectator*, which in 1979–80 had issued two key chapters of *Wealth and Poverty* before its publication.

Most critics focused on the policy implications of the book. On the surface, the book makes many claims and prophecies for the efficacy and justice of tax cuts and deregulation. Although the left continues to demur, history has confirmed all these claims, and conservatives have generally accepted them.

Today, in both the Academy and Congress, some of the more besotted Keynesians still assert that the impact of broad tax-rate reductions may be adverse for the economy because the income effect (people have more money, so they need to work less) overcomes the substitution effect (work pays more relative to leisure, so they work more).

For example, Alice Rivlin, the estimable chief economist at Clinton's Office of Management and Budget, has long maintained that high tax rates spur workers to new frenzies of effort while low tax rates lure them into leisure. The chairman of Clinton's Council of Economic Advisers, Laura Tyson, is so benighted that across all the desolate wastes of socialism she can see "no evidence" that high taxes retard growth. She previously seemed well in over her head as the fourth-ranking economist at her own Berkeley Roundtable on International Economics [BRIE]. But now, through the magic of quotas, this lame leftist has raced ahead of fellow BRIE stalwarts John Zysman, Stephen Cohen, and Michael Borrus, all far more widely and impressively published than Tyson and all having qualified themselves equally well for the administration by getting every tax, trade, and technology issue wrong for fifteen years.

Clinton cannot even tell a glum demonstrator or litigator from a potential marine, or a tax from an investment, but he sure can tell a man from a woman. Clinton's crude treatment of women as an interest group to be bought off like the Trial Lawyers by putting a series of leftist and pro-lesbian females on display reveals his real contempt for women. I predict that the single most baffling disappointment of Clinton's career will be his failure to win a majority of females in 1996 after reducing his administration to a comic auxiliary of the Women's Political Caucus in pursuit of their votes. Women may vote differently from men, but they are no more eager to see themselves or their husbands pay ever more taxes in an ever-shrinking private economy.

In the real world outside the administration, responsible analysts now accept the supply-side case. As Martin Feldstein recently wrote in the *Wall Street Journal*. "Statistical evidence has convinced the overwhelming majority of the economic profession that individuals respond very substantially to the incentives created by tax rules." Extending the definition of "work" to all productive economic activity, it can be seen that in general the lower the tax rates, the more real "work" is done, and the healthier the economy. As I show in *Wealth and Poverty*, work in the form of tax finagles or in the form of uncapitalized and thus inefficient manual labor may thrive in a high-tax economy. But effective work—expanding productivity and growth—requires lower marginal tax rates: lower rates on additional earnings and capital gains.

In this debate, Paul Craig Roberts first made the crucial point and I expanded on it. While one individual might work less because a tax cut brings him more income, most individuals cannot work less. If most individuals worked less, national income would decline. People in general would have less income, and by the income effect would have to work more. Thus the income effect on one worker (or investor) cancels itself out with many workers (and investors).

The substitution effect necessarily prevails, and people work more (and supply other factors of production more abundantly) when they are taxed less onerously on their additional efforts and inputs. That is why Arthur Laffer's famous curve is right. Contrary to widespread political claims to the contrary, U.S. revenues rose steadily at every government level following implementation of the 1980s tax cuts. The total government deficit had declined nearly 50 percent as a share of GNP until new taxes were levied and sweeping regulations imposed by the federal government and thirty-five states during the late 1980s and early 1990s. As has been demonstrated repeatedly throughout history, lower tax rates bring more revenues and high tax rates eventually destroy an economy.

By the 1990s, contrary to the claims of the current administration, the U.S. at all levels of government was back near world leadership in taxes. Although nations with nationalized health care show nominally higher tax burdens, the U.S.—with its government regulated, insured, and subsidized health-care system and its acute problems of AIDS and inner-city violence—spends some 50 percent more per capita on health care. Exclusive of health-care levies, U.S. producers now face tax rates as onerous as any in the industrialized world outside Scandinavia. U.S. taxes on capital are near the world's highest. In general the lowest tax rates are found in the "newly industrialized countries" of Asia that now lead the world both in economic growth and in growth of government revenues. The low-tax arguments of *Wealth and Poverty* are more relevant than ever today, as more and more of our industrial rivals discover the magic of supply-side economics.

As I explore more deeply in *Recapturing the Spirit of Enterprise* (ICS Press, 1992), the tax-rate reductions in the 1980s not only enhanced productivity; they also fostered equality. While the existing rich thrived in the inflationary, high-tax environment of the late 1970s and early 1980s, the move to lower tax and inflation rates after 1982 reversed this concentration of financial power. High taxes, after all, do not stop you from being rich; they stop you from getting rich and challenging existing wealth. After the Reagan tax cuts went into effect, for example, some 60 percent of the previous incumbents fell out of the Forbes 400 Richest Americans list, displaced by insurgent new wealth.

The huge surge of inequality constantly bewailed in the media actually happened in the late 1970s, when, by the measure of the Congressional Budget Office and the Federal Reserve Board, some 62 percent of income gains went to the wealthiest one percent of the population. Between 1980 and 1989, however, that number dropped to 38 percent for the top percentile. After 1983, when the Reagan tax cuts unleashed America's entrepreneurs, the top percentile's share of income gains plummeted all the way to 20 percent.

The same pattern of radically increasing equality that occurred in incomes can be also found in the distribution of wealth. The largest increases in real wealth in the 1980s accrued to mostly middle-class holders of corporate and public-employee pension plans. In the red by hundreds of billions of dollars in 1980, these funds gained some $2 trillion in real worth during the rest of the decade. At the same time, as Jude Wanniski points out, the creation of more than 20 million new jobs was crucial in wiping out a $4 trillion deficit in the Social Security system. Media estimates of maldistributed wealth that focus on stock and real estate gains by the rich but fail to measure this some $6 trillion of gains in real middle-class net worth are like a topographical survey of the American continent that leaves out the Rocky Mountains.

Meanwhile, an explosion of small-business creation and expansion allowed more income mobility than in any previous era, with a Treasury study showing that during the 1980s earners in the bottom fifth were more likely to reach the top fifth than to stay at the bottom.

On one point, however, *Wealth and Poverty* made a serious error. In several chapters, I cited the so-called personal savings rate—a Keynesian residual computed by subtracting consumption spending from national income—as a suitable measure of the amount of personal savings available for productive investment. Thus, I opened myself to the charge that the low personal savings rates during the Reagan administration revealed a key flaw in the supply-side case.

The fact is that the measured personal savings rate has virtually nothing to do with the ability to invest. By that measure, the Soviet Union during its final years or the U.S. during the Great Depression could have been world-beating investors. Investment depends not on the avoidance of consumption but on the growth of assets or entrepreneurial ideas that can serve as collateral for loans or issues of equity.

This thesis was powerfully expounded by Jude Wanniski's associate, David Goldman of Polyconomics, in a recent essay called "The New Jersey School of Supply-Side Economics" (a comedown from the school that once grandly explained "The Way the World Works," but let it pass). Goldman's paper showed that "the savings rate does not determine the level of investment; in practice the elasticity of capital with respect to opportunity is unlimited. At any given time, the market can draw upon a nearly inexhaustible fund of uncollateralized assets to transform into capital." During the 1980s, the U.S. achieved an immense buildup of some $37 trillion of such collateral, spearheaded by new assets and new technologies that resulted in a tripling of stock market values and fueled the high rates of growth during that period.

The immense growth of real private savings during the 1980s is indicated by a rise from $160 million to over $1 trillion in the excess of corporate equity over corporate debt. Even much of the debt, such as junk bonds, was in fact a form of high-risk equity disguised for tax purposes as interest-paying securities. Since *Wealth and Poverty* repeatedly repudiated such demand-side jargon as the personal savings rate, it was ironic that this slip into the Keynesian idiom occasioned what seemed the most telling critique of the supply-side arguments.

Supply-siders reject the very notion that consumer demand is a significant force in economic growth. With a false dichotomy between so-called final purchases (mostly performed by individuals as consumers) and intermediate spending (mostly performed by individuals in their roles in businesses), the usual demand-side models suggest that consumer spending comprises close to 70 percent of the economy. As Mark Skousen has shown, the correct measure is close to one-third. But in general, consumers still cannot buy or save anything without producing first. Personal savings is just a spurious residual of the already spurious Keynesian measure of consumer demand.

As *Wealth and Poverty* maintained, all purchasing power and savings are the result of past, present, or projected production and of entrepreneurial risk-taking on unique technologies and business ideas. Being unique, these investments entail uninsurable risk and must be complemented by a flow of capital gains and other sources of new investment. Average personal savings rates are irrelevant to this process. The real lesson of the "savings" critique of supply-side economics and of *Wealth and Poverty* is that in order to depict the real forces of growth, we must eschew the entire demand-side model of the economy and all the conceptual baggage it contains.

The 1980s, in general, fully vindicated *Wealth and Poverty's* social and economic arguments. This was the era when leftist dreams all collapsed in travesty. The mock-heroic youth of the 1960s emerged from schools sure that their nation was evil and owed them a living for their moral superiority, and capable of making no contribution to society except passing on their crippling creeds to future generations. The 1980s taught them the unwanted lesson that Marxist slogans, a sense of grievance, and a rhetoric of rights and "demands" are economically useless. Disdainful of science, enterprise, and other practical learning, they moved into law, teaching, and politics. Incapable of performing any useful task for a business, they thronged into the environmental movement. There they could harass businesses from a moral pinnacle without submitting to the humbling discipline of serving customers. They crowded onto the pulpits of the media and the academy in such numbers that a reporter or a professor often made less money than a garbage man. Seething at such obvious inequities of capitalism, they castigated the prosperous for "greed" and "workaholism."

Wealth and Poverty predicted the death of socialism. The 1980s were the decade when socialism died and left nothing but a bristling carcass of weapons pointed toward the West. It was the decade when tax rates were cut in fifty-five nations, following our success, and revenues dropped in nearly all nations that raised their rates. It was the era when capitalism at last demonstrated conclusively its superiority as an economic system. It was the era when U.S. economic growth rates, long lagging behind the rest of the world, surged ahead of Europe, Africa, and Latin America, and nearly caught up with Japan's for the first time since the early 1950s.

The 1980s also saw the longest peacetime expansion on record, with the highest rates of investment in capital equipment and the highest sustained rates of manufacturing productivity growth of any postwar recovery. During the 1980s, the U.S. increased its share of global manufacturing output, global exports, and global production. Contrary to thousands of reports to the contrary, U.S. balance sheets mostly improved, with debt as a share of assets dropping drastically for both businesses and households, as equity, net-savings, and real-estate values rose far more rapidly than indebtedness. Even government debt, as a share of GNP or in relation to real national assets, remained under control by historic and international standards.

After the tax rate reductions urged by *Wealth and Poverty* took effect in 1983 and 1984, total revenues at all levels of government rose some 9 percent a year in real terms, far faster than during the high-tax 1970s. During the 1980s recovery, industrial output rose nearly 40 percent, personal income 20 percent, and all segments of American society benefited from the creation of 22 million new jobs at rising real wages. Black employment rose 30.3 percent and Hispanic employment nearly 50 percent. Unlike previous decades of growth, moreover, the American expansion of the 1980s came in the face of declining growth in Europe and Japan. Rather than being pulled ahead by faster development abroad as in previous decades of growth, the U.S. in the 1980s led the world economy. The greatest U.S. triumph was the computer revolution, entirely a product of relentless discipline and entrepreneurial genius in capitalist nations. Computer industry revenues more than quadrupled; unit sales rose by a factor of hundreds; and computer cost-effectiveness rose ten-thousand-fold. At the end of the decade, U.S. companies still held some two-thirds of the world market, and in critical software and leading-edge microchips their market share was above 70 percent and growing. In particular, the U.S. led in using personal computers, with well over half of the world's 100 million PCs located in the U.S. in 1990. The U.S. still commands three times as much computer power per capita as the Japanese or Europeans.

This development, which impelled most of the world's economic growth during the decade, was also disastrous for the left. The left has always pinned its hopes on politics. The converging technologies of computers and telecommunications are radically reducing the power of politicians. An ever-increasing share of world wealth assumed the mobile form of information technologies which, unlike the massive industrial systems of the past, are difficult to measure, capture, or tax. The computer age is an age of mind—elusive, and hard to control. This ascent of mind, predicted in *Wealth and Poverty*, is devaluing all the entrenchments of material resources and geography within the ken and command of politicians. As Mikhail Gorbachev himself has observed, the computer revolution was critical to the crisis of Communism: "We were among the last to understand that in an age of information science the most valuable asset is knowledge, springing from human imagination and creativity. We will be paying for our mistake for many years to come."

The entire left suffered a similar discomfiture. Nonetheless, under the slack domestic leadership of President George Bush, who joined Congress in simultaneously increasing taxes, spending, and regulation, the direction of policy was reversed from a decade before. The morale of liberalism suddenly began to recover.

Under the Clinton administration—with its strange notion of taxing and tariffing the nation into prosperity—this liberal recovery is likely to be short-lived. Although the left may never believe it, demand-side economics is dead. In an increasingly competitive global economy, a government can no more

raise its revenues simply by raising its taxes than a company can raise its income simply by raising its prices. Like a company, a government must constantly lower its prices and improve its services to expand its markets (its tax base). In the 1990s, the U.S. needed further rounds of tax-rate reductions, deregulations, and simplifications in order to lower its deficit.

In spite of a period of economic malaise, however, the U.S. economy commands tremendous strengths. The world-leading technologies financed by venture capital and junk bonds during the 1980s laid the foundation for strong economic expansion through the rest of the century. In the absence of a siege of protectionism, based on the obtuse notion that a trade balance is desirable in an age of global capital markets, the U.S. economy could double in real terms by early in the next century.

Why then are so many people properly worried about the future of our economy? It is not just the threat of still more taxes, spending, and regulation. An equal danger remains the one spelled out in the poverty theme of *Wealth and Poverty*. By the critical indices of marital stability, which is what mostly matters, the eighties brought tragedy to millions of American families and their children. Contrary to all the claims of the left, female-headed families are usually a disaster, incapable of disciplining boys or of escaping poverty. Poverty alone, however, is not the key problem. Census figures showed that the poorest Americans spent some two times more money than they reported as income. Their plight was one not chiefly of money but of morale brought on by the erosion of the moral codes of civilized society. America's cities discovered that patriarchy is not some optional outdated feature of human life but an indispensable bulwark of civilization itself. If men do not rule as husbands and providers for their families, they rule the streets in gangs and terrorize the society with their violence.

Although not economic in nature, this persistent problem of family breakdown cast a pall of failure on all the economic triumphs of the 1980s. Both sought and desired by the left as a form of liberation, family breakdown accounted for most of the crime, drug, racial, and other "poverty" problems widely blamed on Reagan policy. Without paternal discipline and role models, teenage boys run amok in nearly all societies.

Most of all, family dissolution was crucial in the single greatest propaganda triumph of the left since the Great Depression: the homeless who haunt all the proud towers of eighties prosperity. Like the Great Depression, which was caused by massive tax and tariff hikes, the homeless problem is a harvest of misguided government: economically favoring divorce and illegitimacy over marriage, deinstitutionalizing the mentally ill, rescinding vagrancy laws, stifling cheap housing with regulations, codes, and controls, and creating a short-order welfare system for millions of disgruntled Americans unable to fill out the forms for AFDC but nonetheless fully able to figure out how to qualify as homeless.

In the morbid feedback loops of liberalism, the answer to such problems is always more government subsidies for homelessness and family breakdown, and thus more propaganda for the enemies of America. As the most gullible of Americans, many intellectuals blamed the homeless on the capitalist successes of the 1980s.

American intellectuals prefer socialist regimes where intellectuals seem to rule, rather than an America where power and status accrue chiefly to the providers of useful goods and services. Typical were the rabble of mindworkers who gathered in Rio at the Environmental Summit of 1992 and leapt to their feet to give a standing ovation to Fidel Castro. Many intellectuals prefer a so-called "society of poets," where most people live in fear and famine (Communist Cuba or Nicaragua), to a society where capitalists surpass intellectuals in income and status.

The 1980s thus gave new impetus to the arguments of *Wealth and Poverty*. But the key theme holding it all together was the moral

sources of capitalism, and it was this idea that was generally missed or misconstrued. From William F. Buckley, who debated me on "Firing Line," to Ayn Rand who devoted part of her last speech to denouncing me, to Irving Kristol and Michael Novak, some of my most trusted mentors firmly spurned my idea of a profound affinity between the altruistic themes of the Judeo-Christian tradition and the practical imperatives of supply-side capitalism. Capitalism, as most of my critics insisted, is morally neutral; it accommodates moral behavior and imparts freedoms that are important to moral choices. But in itself capitalism is no more or less moral than any other economic order. Capitalism is a mechanism for accommodating individual tastes and demands. The moral character of those tastes and demands is irrelevant to the system. Capitalism is no more or less moral than an automobile; the moral issue is where and how you drive it.

Ayn Rand, whom I regard to be one of the titans of the history of capitalism and freedom, did uphold the higher morality of the system. But she declared that capitalism is moral not because it fosters the humble service of others, as I contended, but precisely because it rejects humility and service—what Rand considered the craven altruism of Christianity and socialism. In other words, capitalism in Rand's view is moral because it is selfish; it exalts the autonomous individual in his quest for heroic stature and achievement.

I agreed with Rand's stress on heroic achievement as the central force of capitalist success. Thus I was gratified to note that the heroic achievers who shine in her novels—from John Galt to Howard Roark and Ragnar Daneskjold—often found themselves upholding a selfishness that seemed as mystically intense and transcendent and as heroically sacrificial as an artist's vision of Jesus on the Cross. No matter how much Rand professed her selfishness, her characters—and her own career—refuted her.

Nonetheless, Rand's identification of socialism with Christianity, as wrong as I believe it to be, sprang from a long and addled infatuation of leading clerics with the worst excesses of the welfare state. She was right about the death-wish socialism of many establishment churches. But she was profoundly wrong in believing that capitalism could prevail by defying all the highest moral traditions and ideals of the world's great religions.

Rand's work had the key virtue of casting the issues in stark relief. My other critics reduced them to a tautological muddle of a self-interest so elastic that it could accommodate nearly any activity at all, from launching a computer revolution to taking an overdose of sleeping pills. On the left and on the right, my critics were confounded by the demand-side fallacy: the false assumption that capitalism is primarily driven by consumer demand. By this standard, anything that excites the desire of consumers to spend is a positive force in economic growth. Since prostitution, divorce, drug addiction, pornography, adultery, fornication, homosexuality, and other forces of social dissolution all increase the purchase of market goods, as opposed to goods provided in the home, all may be said to enhance the rise of the GNP. Thus conservatives and socialists can sometimes come together on social issues. To the extent that both believe the engine of economic growth is driven by greed, they can see permissiveness as favorable to growth under capitalism.

All these views of capitalism are false. Demand, whether avaricious or just, is impotent to impel growth without disciplined, creative, and essentially moral producers of new value. All effective demand ultimately derives from supply; a society's income cannot exceed its output. The output of valuable goods depends not on lechery, exploitation, and license but on varying mixtures of thrift, sacrifice, altruism, creativity, discipline, trust, and faith. To the extent that immorality debauches the moral capital of the society—to the extent that it distracts workers and entrepreneurs from the long-term effort to create new value—these sources of demand actually undermine economic growth.

By a supply-side standard, immorality diverts, obsesses, and depraves the men and women who must forgo immediate returns, sacrifice immediate pleasures, master difficult disciplines, and respond to the needs and desires of others if they are to create successful businesses. I do not say that there are no greedy capitalists, only that the inner dynamic of capitalism is orientation toward the needs of others. Capitalism has been incomparably the most productive economic system in the history of the world because it best evokes the effort and creativity—the moral quality and productive energy—of workers and businessmen who put the needs of others before their own gratifications.

This moral dynamic at the heart of the system drives entrepreneurs constantly to reinvest their profits. Entrepreneurs do not consume their wealth; they recycle it by giving it to other people in productive ways. This means that the very people who have proven their ability to create wealth control the process of future wealth creation. In the form of investments, they endow other entrepreneurs who are judged best able to prevail in the competitions in service that impel the progress of the capitalist economy. All this economic activity is other-directed, as David Riesman observed in the early 1950s. Indeed, it is the altruistic mandate of business and religion that makes them both so offensive to self-centered intellectuals who believe that the self-expression of art and liberated sexuality is the highest form of human activity. Greed is a form of waste that undermines capitalist growth rather than fuels it.

Real greed and selfishness most often cause people to seek short-term comfort and security first. They turn to the state for the benefits that they lacked the moral discipline to earn on their own by serving others. Greed, as I write in *Wealth and Poverty*, leads as by an invisible hand to an ever-growing welfare state—not to wealth and capitalism, but to poverty and socialism. This is the argument I made in my 1982 *American Spectator* article, which I've included in the third chapter of the new edition of *Wealth and Poverty*, and it's an argument that remains critical to the future of all free economies.

61

Pay Equity—Surprising Answers to Hard Questions

Barbara Bergmann

This author advocates government intervention to achieve pay parity between jobs that are typically male and those that are typically female. Measures of comparable worth, based on widely accepted rankings of skill, would make markets operate as if there were no legacy sex discrimination to distort the payment of female occupations. This would correct for the fact that the market generally undervalues female human capital. The disemployment and inflation effects of such policies are estimated, and the conclusion is advanced that fairness can be achieved at a low cost.

Exercises to Guide Your Reading

1. Summarize the job evaluation process discussed in this article.
2. Give examples of typical male jobs and typical female jobs that have similar skill ratings.
3. Identify the key advantages and disadvantages of using a program like comparable worth to achieve pay equity between male and female workers.
4. Either justify or criticize, on economics grounds, the continued existence of pay disparities between male and female workers.

The campaign for "pay equity" or "comparable worth"—that employers should raise wage rates in the occupations dominated by women—will surely accelerate, especially if the Democrats take the White House in 1988. The pay equity campaign raises a host of questions, even for those of us who think that the market's verdict on wages has been skewed by widespread discrimination. How can we compare men's and women's jobs, and do it in a way that makes economic sense? Where will the money come from for the extra pay for the women? Won't the raises in women's pay cut employers' demand for women workers, forcing women into unemployment?

With good reason, economists shy away from tinkering with the verdict of a free marketplace. But discrimination exerts a powerful influence on the wages the market sets. An engineered rise in the pay of the typically female occupations can serve as a healthy corrective to the influence of employers who discriminate on the demand side of the labor market.

If we look closely at the way pay equity realignments are actually being implemented, we see that the methodology makes

Reprinted by permission of *Challenge*. May–June 1987. pp. 45–51.

sense in economic terms. The comparison of men's and women's jobs turns out to be a straightforward application of the human capital principles that would rule in a discrimination-free market. Pay equity adjustments can be financed in a relatively painless and inflation-free way. Finally, there is considerable warrant for believing that pay equity wage adjustments do not bring with them seriously damaging side effects for women or for the economy generally.

HOW JOBS ARE COMPARED

Table 1 gives an example of the way men's and women's jobs are compared for purposes of pay equity adjustment. A firm of professional personnel consultants performed these evaluations for the government of the state of Washington. They rated the jobs of state employees on four "compensable factors": knowledge and skills, mental demands, accountability, and work conditions. The consultants judged the truck driver's job to be devoid of any skill requirements not found in the general population. They rated a secretarial job to be modestly ahead of an auto mechanic's job in terms of knowledge and skill required. With respect to mental demands, the secretary's job was judged to be about on a par with the mechanic's. The consultants found that the registered nurse's job required higher skill, knowledge, and mental ability than the civil engineer's.

Both the truck driver and the mechanic were awarded points under the heading of working conditions, because of the moderate lifting requirements and occasional danger of injury on their jobs. The nurse got more points on the work conditions factor than any of the other occupations listed in the table—not surprising, since she deals with excrement, blood, patients who may be violent, and dead bodies.

The last column of Table 1 gives the 1985 salaries paid to the employees of Washington State in those job titles. The state claims to have set the salaries in each occupation

at market rates. For the traditionally male occupations, there is a good correlation between market-set salaries and the scores arrived at in the study. This suggests that, for men at least, the study did a good job of measuring worker characteristics that the market values.

JOB EVALUATIONS MEASURE HUMAN CAPITAL REQUIRED

It is no accident that the job evaluation scores of the male jobs in Table 1 are well correlated with their market-based salaries, since the scores are designed to include measures of human capital. The pay equity job evaluations focus on the duties of the job, and by implication on the qualities the worker must bring to the job to perform those duties successfully.

The compensable factor "knowledge and skills" is highly correlated with length and intensity of education and training. The compensable factor "mental demands" measures the problem-solving abilities needed for the job. These may require inborn talent, a form of human capital that the market also pays for, perhaps enhanced by education. Jobs with high "accountability" scores require that workers have the experience and education, but also qualities of mind and character, that fit them to make well-considered independent judgments.

The compensable factor "work conditions" adds points for work taking place out-of-doors, and work that is physically heavy, or carries some chance for injury. This factor recognizes that the market awards extra pay for a job that workers would otherwise shun. Designers of job evaluation schemes try to follow the market's weighting of the various compensable factors, and as a result they give the "work conditions" factor only a modest weight, just as the market does.

While the job evaluation scores correlate well with male salaries, the salaries the state has set for the two female jobs in Table 1 are obviously way out of line with their scores. Secretaries employed by the state are

TABLE 1. Evaluations of Six Job Titles from the Comparable Worth Study Done for the Employees of the State of Washington

	Knowledge and Skills	Mental Demands	Accountability	Work Conditions	Total Points	Salary as of 1/85
Delivery truck driver	No previous exp. required. Brief on-the-job learning period required. (61)	Standardized work routines. Recall rather than analysis required. (10)	Duties routine, work closely controlled. (13)	Moderate lifting, some danger. Conditions occasionally undesirable. (13)	97	$382
Auto mechanic	Mechanical skill required. (106)	Similar procedures and methods, analysis of recurring nature. (26)	Methods clearly defined, work frequently reviewed. (30)	Moderate lifting, some danger. Conditions occasionally undesirable. (13)	175	465
Secretary (grade III)	Activities require vocational competence and/or adeptness. Capability in dealing with others required. (122)	Similar procedures and methods, analysis of recurring nature. (35)	Methods clearly defined, work frequently reviewed. Actions influence results. (40)	Job at a desk. Little lifting, danger minimal. (0)	197	306
Civil engineer	Comprehension of complex principles and practices. Capability in dealing with others required. (160)	Varying or complex procedures. Routine analysis. (53)	Activities generally defined, review after the fact. Actions influence results. (61)	Moderate lifting, some danger. Conditions occasionally undesirable. (13)	287	513
Registered nurse	Comprehension of complex principles and practices. Requires capability to persuade and motivate. (184)	Varying or complex procedures. Nonroutine analysis. (70)	Activities generally defined, review after the fact. Actions influence results. (70)	Moderate lifting, some danger. Disagreeable conditions much of the time. (17)	341	411
Senior computer systems analyst	Comprehension of complex principles and practices. Capability in dealing with others required. (212)	Varying or complex procedures. Nonroutine analysis. (80)	Activities generally defined, review after the fact. Actions influence results. Moderate fiscal impact. (80)	Job at a desk. Little lifting, danger minimal. (0)	372	553

Source: Characterization of job requirements is taken from "State of Washington, Comparable Worth Study, September 1974," prepared by Norman D. Willis in consultation with Ann O. Worcester (Norman D. Willis & Associates, Management Consultants). Salaries and point scores are from an unpublished tabulation made for the author by Helen Remick, Director, Office of Affirmative Action, University of Washington.

paid less than delivery truck drivers. Nurses are paid less than auto mechanics. The market—and the state of Washington—has paid for women's knowledge, skill, ingenuity, and sufferance of difficult working conditions at a rate lower than it has paid for the same characteristics in men. The market's verdict is conditioned by discrimination, and that is what pay equity tries to set right. Pay equity is an attempt to approximate the result of a free market in which discrimination is absent.

The original slogan of the pay equity movement, "equal pay for jobs of comparable worth," carried with it the erroneous suggestion that a job should be evaluated by looking at the benefit the employer gets from the services the worker in the job performs. This would have made little sense.

Sometimes a function vital to a business, such as tending the furnace that runs an entire factory, can be performed by an untrained, unskilled employee. Such an employee might be given a modest premium for being extra careful and alert. But there would be no valid reason to pay the particular employee singled out to do such a vital job a great deal more than would be paid to any other worker in the shop with the same low skills. Pay equity job evaluations have avoided the fallacious "worth to the employer" idea. Instead they are in harmony with the orthodox idea that in a nondiscriminatory market, each occupation's wages would over the long run depend mainly on the human capital required to perform that occupation.

TECHNIQUE NOT NEW

The job evaluation techniques used in pay equity are not new. These techniques were invented and developed for business firms, which have used them as an aid to setting pay scales for many decades. A large employer will have a great variety of job titles, many of them unique to that establishment, for which no market information is available. So in practice, some method of assigning wages other than by reference to the market must be adopted. For such firms, the only alternative to a systematic internal job evaluation scheme would be a set of wage rates based largely on internal politicking.

There is, however, a crucial difference between pay equity job evaluations and the job evaluation methods currently practiced in most business establishments. The essence of pay equity is that the women's and men's jobs are rated by the same system. In pay equity, the wage in a predominantly female job is set equal to the wage of a predominantly male job that has the same job evaluation score. By contrast, job evaluation systems used by business usually avoid comparing the male and female jobs directly. If they did compare them, firms would be paying women far higher salaries than would be necessary to hire them, far higher salaries than a discriminatory market assigns them. For obvious reasons, most firms prefer not to.

To avoid doing that, an employer will generally split the jobs into a number of groups or clusters. Some of the clusters will consist mostly of jobs that women hold, and some will be made up mostly of jobs that men hold. Each cluster will be sex-segregated to a high degree. Each cluster will be evaluated and assigned wages separately. Different nomenclature, grading methods, and point systems will be used for each cluster to give the impression that the evaluations of the jobs in one cluster have no relation at all to the evaluations of jobs in any other cluster.

For each cluster of jobs, the employer will pick a job whose market wage is easily determined because the duties are fairly standard from one employer to another. For these jobs, which are designated as "key jobs," the employer will pay market wages. Then the employer will set the pay of any job in relation to the key job in its cluster. The pay of a job will be higher or lower than that of the key job, depending on the job's score in the evaluation.

This use of clusters and key jobs is illustrated in Figure 1. Secretary is the key job

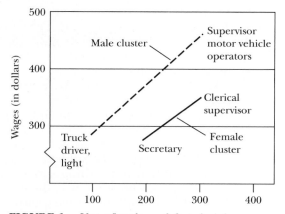

FIGURE 1. Use of male and female job clusters to avoid paying male-level wage scales to women.

Note: The figure illustrates the usual implementation of job evaluation results within a single establishment. Wages are from unpublished Bureau of Labor Statistics tabulations for 1985. Points are derived from Washington State job evaluations.

for the women and light-truck driver is the key job for the men. A female office supervisor will be in the same cluster as the secretary, and the male supervisor of motor vehicle operators will be in the same cluster as the male light-truck driver. Because they are in different clusters, the male supervisor will get a weekly salary $100 or so more than the female supervisor. Yet their jobs, if rated by the same system, would have a similar score.

The use of the key job system preserves the benefits to the employer of job evaluation schemes—it offers an objective process for assigning wage levels to a large number of jobs. At the same time, the employer avoids paying female occupations the same wages as male occupations with the same value point score.

Sometimes the desired differential between male and female occupational wages is achieved by superimposing some distinguishing label on some of the job titles, such as "management" or "exempt." This label is then used to justify paying certain workers (mostly men) more than other workers with the same job evaluation point score, but whose jobs are not given the label.

Job evaluation schemes that are cleansed of such dodges give a good approximation to the wages a well-working, nondiscriminatory job market would pay. Economists, who have long extolled the rationality of business decisions, should not be surprised that business firms, in adopting job evaluation, made implicit use of human capital reasoning before economists invented it. Pay equity negates only one aspect of business rationality—the desire to reap the benefit to be derived from confining women workers to traditionally female jobs at low wages.

WHO WILL PAY FOR PAY EQUITY?

Raising women's wages in accordance with job evaluations throughout the economy might erase about one-third of the gap between men's and women's wage rates. (Much of the remainder of the gap is due to discriminatory exclusion of women from some higher-skilled jobs and better-paying firms, and would have to be attacked through affirmative action.) Pay equity adjustments that closed one-third of the gap might add $2–3 billion a week to women's pay checks, or between $100 and $150 billion a year. These figures appear large. But they need to be put into the perspective of the nation's wage bill, and the changes it undergoes each year.

To close one-third of the pay gap in the whole economy in a single year, on the assumption that the dollar amount of men's paychecks would remain unchanged while women's pay advanced, would have required in 1982 that some $117 billion be added to women's paychecks. This would have increased women's pay by 22 percent. Such a sum would have amounted to 6 percent of the entire wage bill and 5 percent of total national income in that year.

However, there would be relatively little strain in transferring such sums if pay equity raises for women were phased in over a period of a few years. The funds to make the pay equity adjustments could come out of the regular increases in the money compensation for workers which normally occur each year. Looking back over the 1982–84 period, worker compensation rates per hour increased by 8.1 percent in 1982, 4.3 percent in 1983, 4.7 percent in 1984. That adds up, with compounding, to 18 percent over a three-year period.

Those 18 percent increases were spread fairly evenly between male and female workers. Male workers got their money wage rates increased by about 18 percent, and female workers got their pay increased by about the same 18 percent, meaning that the percentage gap between the sexes changed very little.

Suppose, instead, that for that limited period of three years, 6 percent (out of the 18 percent) had been concentrated on raising the wage scales of women workers (see Table 2). That probably would have been about sufficient to finance pay equity adjustments for women throughout the economy. The remainder of the pay increase money would have been available to spread evenly between male salaries and the newly beefed-up women's salaries. An 18 percent across-the-board increase in money wage rates *that actually occurred* could have been converted into

a 35 percent increase for women and an 11 percent increase for men.

How much would male workers have suffered if a third of their pay increases had been diverted to women over a three-year period? Men's real wages would have been at a virtual standstill for that period (to be exact, they would have declined one-third of a percent per year). That would have meant a standstill in living standards for single males and for the relatively affluent male earners who maintain nonearning spouses. Two-earner couples, who are now in the majority in the economically active age groups, would have been affected relatively little. Their incomes would have advanced about 6 percent in real terms over the three years, just as they did in the absence of pay equity adjustments. Single or divorced women, who have high poverty rates, would have experienced substantial rises in real income. That sounds like a redistribution of income that many would endorse as just and socially desirable. Along with the gains to women, a great many poor children would have their living standards raised.

But does the money for pay equity have to come from funds that would otherwise go

TABLE 2.   How to Pay for Pay Equity ($ in Billions)

Across-the-Board Distribution of Increases (No Progress in Closing the Gap)	Men	Women	Both Sexes
Original wage bill (in 1982)	$1,325	$541	$1,866
18 percent increase (1982–4)	238	97	335
Final wage bill	1,563	638	2,201

Concentrating Part of the Increase on Women (Closing about a Third of the Gap)	Men	Women	Both Sexes
Original wage bill	$1,325	$541	$1,866
Pay equity increase of 22 percent for women	0	117	117
Amended wage bill	(1,325)	(658)	(1,983)
11 percent increase on amended wage bill	146	72	218
Total wage increase	146	189	335
Final wage bill	1,471	730	2,201

Note: Original wage bill based on national income and Current Population Reports data for 1982; wages by sex based on Bureau of Labor Statistics data for 1982–84, as reported in the *Economic Report of the President, Transmitted to the Congress, February 1985*, table B-41, p. 279.

to increase the salaries of men? Might not some or all of it come out of profits? A look at the way national income is shared out shows that it would be unrealistic to expect to get all or even a large part of the pay equity adjustment money out of the share of national incomes going to profits. Corporate profits and proprietors' incomes are 11 percent of income, while the pay equity adjustment is in the neighborhood of 5 percent. A pay equity process that cut profit shares in half is unlikely, even if it were considered wise.

While profits might absorb some fraction of the costs, one would expect that those firms that had to make big adjustments, and felt unable to keep increases to the male workers low enough to make up for them, would avoid infringements on their profits by raising prices. The resulting addition to the rate of inflation above what it would otherwise be would not be large—perhaps an addition of 1 or 2 percent.

EFFECTS ON EMPLOYERS

An establishment that has realigned its wages will have a wage structure very different from that of most other establishments—at least while the pay equity movement is in its infancy. It may simply have raised the wages in its female jobs, and kept its wages for male jobs in line with those in other establishments. In this case, it will have a considerably larger wage bill than they, which might well handicap a private employer in a competitive industry.

The more realistic alternative is to give the female job titles larger increases than the male job titles. If, at the same time, other establishments were giving males and females equal percentage increases, then the establishment making the pay equity adjustment is going to find itself with wages in traditionally male jobs that are lower than those in other firms.

Establishments that realign their wage structures by letting male wages lag behind wages in other establishments may experi-

ence a loss of labor in traditionally male jobs, and an inability to recruit able men to fill them. While some may see this as a drawback to pay equity, properly regarded it is an advantage. In fact, this is a case of pay equity strengthening the motive for employers to practice affirmative action. Such a situation should push the firm to recruit women as trainees for its traditionally male jobs.

DISPLACEMENT EFFECTS

Opponents of pay equity have argued that raising the price of women's labor in the stereotypically female occupations can be expected to shrink the amount of labor that employers will wish to employ in such occupations. Some employers might want to replace their women workers with men if they are forced to pay wages high enough to attract men. Because affirmative action has so far been slow, the absorption into typically male occupations of those women workers who might be displaced can by no means be guaranteed.

The interesting question is not whether there will be displacement effects, but how large they will be. In thinking about this issue, we can look at the experience of countries that have made large relative adjustments in women's pay relative to men's. The experiment has been tried in Australia on quite a significant scale. There, the custom has been for administrative boards to set minimum wages for a wide range of occupations, and the minima they set apparently do influence the wages employers actually pay. In the late 1970s, the minimum pay boards decided to get rid of about half of the gap between men's and women's pay on average, and women's pay rose by 30 percent. Two economists, Robert Gregory and Ronald Duncan, made a study of the effects on women's employment of these substantial upward pay adjustments. They concluded that the disemployment of women must have been quite small. Pay adjustments for women in Great Britain seem to have

had the same result—little or no extra unemployment for women workers.

Gregory and Duncan's explanation of the
low rate of displacement is that men's and
women's occupations complement each
other in the productive process. At least in
the short and medium run, employers find
it difficult to reorganize the productive process in a way that would allow them to cut
down on the employment of some occupational groups but not others. Nor does there
appear to be much replacement of women
by men in the traditional women's jobs.
Ironically, the pervasiveness of sex segregation, the fixed ideas of employers about who
should do which job, and the reluctance of
men in most circumstances to enter occupations perceived as being appropriate to
women appear to have protected women's
jobs, even as their wage rates rose substantially. Whether this low disemployment effect will hold up in the longer run remains
to be seen.

Progress in opening typically male jobs to
women would reduce the disemployment effects of pay equity. But whatever the net disemployment effects of the pay equity adjustments do turn out to be, they must be considered as a trade-off for the higher wages
women would get while employed. Higher
unemployment rates for women would
translate into longer spells of unemployment for those women who found themselves out of a job. It is important to realize,
however, that those employed at higher
wages, thanks to pay equity adjustments, and
those banished to the unemployment office
for longer stays are not two distinct groups,
one gaining and the other losing. In actual-
ity, there is a considerable circulation of individuals into and out of jobs. The woman
who becomes unemployed and has to spend
an extra week out of a job because of pay
equity reforms might well find that at the
end of her spell of unemployment, her new
job has higher pay. The research done so far
implies that the gains to women from higher
pay while employed would swamp the losses
due to higher unemployment rates. It suggests, in fact, that the latter would hardly be
noticeable.

GENTLE PERSUASION

The originators of the pay equity movement
were two lawyers, Winn Newman and Ruth
Weyand. They got the idea that employers
who paid low wages in typically female occupations could be sued under the Civil
Rights Act for practicing "sex-based discrimination in pay." Federal judges, however, appear hostile to the legal theory that an employer who pays market wages could be
ruled to be discriminating.

However, pay equity adjustments are
going forward apart from lawsuits. State and
local governments have come under political or union pressure to make pay equity
wage realignments. Legislative bodies have
commissioned job evaluation studies, and
proceeded to appropriate funds to raise the
pay in the female job titles. Political pressure to do this will probably continue even
if lawsuits fail through judicial hostility to
the pay equity concept. Legislation has been
introduced to study the wage levels of federal employees, with the purpose of justifying a realignment.

If wages are realigned for a significant
proportion of employees in the public sector, there will be an effect, through the labor
market, on private employers, even if they
are legally immune from forced realignment. If private employers fail to raise wages
in the women's occupations, they will lose
the best women workers to the public sector,
which is sizeable enough to absorb a considerable proportion of them. In all likelihood
there would be some upward readjustment
of wages in female occupations by private
employers to avoid this.

In the past, unions have not been interested in using any of their bargaining leverage to negotiate raises in pay for women
workers that would advance women relative
to men. The pay equity campaign of the
American Federation of State, County, and
Municipal Employees (AFSCME) represents
a break in union traditions of acquiescence
to inferior pay for women. Under the spur
of declining union membership, other
unions may follow AFSCME's lead.

Opponents of pay equity adjustments enjoy frightening the business community with the nightmare of a large and stupidly run federal agency, which would fix by administrative fiat the wage rate for every job in every business in the country. Such an inclusive approach would be expensive, unwieldy, and unnecessarily intrusive.

However, it would be useful for the federal government to issue a set of well-publicized pay "guidelines," which could be used by women workers to pressure their employers and their unions. The Labor Department might set up minimum wage recommendations for the largest of the typically female occupations—typist, secretary, retail sales clerk, child-care worker, teacher, social worker, librarian, nurse. Another approach would be for the Equal Employment Opportunity Commission (EEOC) or the Labor Department to evaluate a group of common male and female occupations, and recommend wage ratios for them. For example, the recommendation might be that an employer pay secretaries x percent more than that employer pays truck drivers. The observance of such minima or ratios might be required of government contractors, along with currently required affirmative action plans.

These guidelines or minima would at the very least change peoples' attitudes on what wages were fair. Even without an enforcement mechanism, they might well have an appreciable effect.

THE PUSH BEHIND PAY EQUITY

The real impetus behind the pay equity campaign is the growing belief among women and among men that the present lineup of wage rates is unfair. It is plain to see that women are far behind men of equivalent education, skill, and intelligence in terms of pay.

Economists have long derided St. Thomas Aquinas' idea of "the just price." But what people think is right and decent does influence their economic actions. This is especially true in matters of personnel administration, where a sense of grievance and unfairness can reduce productivity.

Many of the women in the typical female occupations are single mothers, single-handedly supporting children at or close to the poverty line. The increased fairness and the diminishment of poverty are good reasons for pushing pay equity. Realigning wages of male and female occupations according to a human capital scheme is not likely to do a lot of economic harm. On the contrary, it can move us toward a more rationally run and efficient labor market than we have now.

62

How Is Affirmative Action Like Crop Subsidies?

Gary S. Becker

This article compares affirmative action programs with other government programs of economic favoritism. The author points out that there are many markets in the U.S. where the government intervenes to establish prices (and quantities) that are different than those that would be established by the free play of supply and demand. Despite the functional similarity between, for example, agricultural price supports and affirmative action, many more people argue fervently about the latter. The conclusion questions the economic reasons behind such an intense debate.

Exercises to Guide Your Reading

1. Define "affirmative action."
2. Give examples of government programs that are similar to affirmative action.
3. Use simple supply-and-demand graphs to predict how a specific labor market would respond to the implementation of a vigorous affirmative action policy.
4. On what basis could you support the outcome predicted in (3) above? On what basis could you criticize the outcome predicted in (3)?

Many conservative intellectuals are passionately opposed to quotas and other parts of affirmative-action programs, while liberals just as fervently advocate them. Yet the depth of emotion on this issue seems misplaced when affirmative action is recognized for what it is: a federal regulation that probably causes less harm than many other programs but does hurt some individuals, as it caters to minorities with political clout.

I don't like group quotas and other aspects of affirmative-action programs, but I am puzzled by the handwringing and anger of those who are opposed, especially some intellectuals. Although no one has even rough estimates of the social costs and benefits of these programs, I strongly suspect that certain other subsidies and regulations do more damage. Examples include tax and other breaks to the housing industry, the declines in labor-force participation of elderly persons induced by the tax on Social Security benefits, and higher consumer prices due to quotas on imported cars, textiles, computer chips, and, until recently, steel.

Opposition to affirmative-action programs may be strong because their effects can be so visible: for example, when such programs are used to admit students with weak records to law schools, medical schools, and premier universities or to help promote minority members into high-level jobs, while

Reprinted by permission of *Business Week*. April 27, 1992. p. 18.

people who are more qualified are passed over. The harm from most other programs is indirect or hidden from view.

Ethical Appeals. Some opponents argue that affirmative-action regulations are worse than other government programs because the criteria are inborn characteristics: race, gender, national origin, and the like. But other programs that have nothing to do with inherited characteristics often in reality help only a small group. For example, hardly anyone not brought up on a farm ever becomes a commercial farmer. Thus, subsidies to agriculture are in a sense unavailable to people who grow up in cities.

Supporters of affirmative action deny that it is the result simply of political power. They argue that justice demands compensation for the horrors of past discrimination. Opponents argue just as strongly that quotas violate our culture's principle of equal treatment for equal skills, and they reject the notion that the present generation can be held responsible for discrimination in the past.

Both sides in this debate make valid points, but arguments about benefits are usually couched in terms of moral and ethical justifications, partly to gain the support of other voters. When was the last time you heard anyone defend a government program simply on the grounds that the person wanted to have the benefits? Although Republican opposition to quotas has helped the party make political inroads at the national level among white male blue-collar workers who traditionally voted for Democrats, clearly affirmative-action programs would not be politically viable if they had the support only of those blacks, women, and others who benefit.

Shadow of Doubt. Most other government programs could not have been implemented without support from persons not much affected by them one way or the other. Surely, management and employees at Chrysler Corp. did not have enough clout by themselves to get the large federal bailout a decade ago. Alone, the small number of sugar growers in the U.S. would not have had much chance of getting the restrictive quotas on sugar imports that have been in effect for the past 70 years. This need to inflate self-interest into a broader moral and ethical point is why no business executive pleads for government subsidies by explaining that otherwise he might lose his job or have to take a big cut in pay. Instead, he complains about unfair competition from abroad or frightens voters with tales of defense vulnerabilities or the loss of jobs and stockholder equity if help is not forthcoming.

Opponents make much of how affirmative action detracts from the achievements of the most qualified members of minority groups. These able people suffer psychologically from skepticism about whether they deserve their success. Stephen L. Carter, a black professor at Yale Law School, in his book *Reflections of an Affirmative Action Baby*, poignantly describes his experiences with this attitude.

Of course, the doubt cast on the qualifications of successful minority members is unfortunate. But every government program hurts someone—often even some members of the groups that benefit. Studies have documented, for example, that programs involving acreage restrictions on agricultural crops benefit rich farmers sometimes at the expense of poor farmers, who do not get their fair share of the allotments.

Recognizing that affirmative-action programs are government regulations with a complicated incidence of costs and benefits does not resolve the dispute over whether or not they are desirable. But it may help focus the debate on the real question: Do they cause as much harm or do as much good as other government programs that generate very little debate?

63

The Great Society Didn't Fail

Margaret Burnham

This article critically evaluates the Great Society and the War on Poverty programs to show why it is important to distinguish between policies that failed due to poor design and those that failed due to underfunding or government abandonment. Following this, the author argues that the lack of jobs with adequate pay, coupled with racism, destines African Americans (more than other Americans) to lives on the economic margin. Conclusions concerning the desirability of full employment policies are discussed.

Exercises to Guide Your Reading

1. Describe the main features of the War on Poverty and the Great Society.
2. Identify the programs from the War on Poverty and the Great Society that were targeted for elimination during the 1980s.
3. Discuss the politically stabilizing effects of these programs.
4. Compare and contrast the social costs and social benefits of these programs.

The Great Society did not fail. It was abandoned. . . . Johnson's early emphasis on poverty, civil rights, and medical care led many critics to assimilate the Great Society to the goals of traditional, New Deal liberalism, and then to cite its failure in order to prove the obsolescence of the liberal tradition.
      —Richard N. Goodwin
Kennedy-Johnson speechwriter who coined the term "the Great Society," in Remembering America: A Voice From the Sixties, *1988*

At the time the extraordinary progression of events now called the civil rights movement was initiated in 1955 by Rosa Parks's defiant refusal to yield her seat on a segregated Montgomery, Alabama, bus, U.S. society was organized on the basis of a racial apartheid system in Southern states and a corollary order of racially discriminatory barriers in most of the Northern ones.

Despite decades of heroic effort in the courts (culminating in a few isolated triumphs) by such organizations as the National Association for the Advancement of Colored People, most of the race-based discriminatory laws were still in place when Parks took her stand. Not, in short, until the black Southern nonviolent uprising of the 1950s and 1960s—followed by riots in the great Northern ghettos—were measures taken by the Federal government to render null and void all laws securing racially oppressive patterns of behavior in American life.

If the United States can stand before the world today with legalized apartheid within its borders eradicated, that fact is the legacy of the thousands who fought the battle in the South, and the blacks and whites across

Reprinted by permission of *The Nation.* July 24–31, 1989. pp. 122–24.

the country who fought with or supported them. Many people died in that struggle, which former Attorney General Ramsey Clark has rightly called "the noblest quest of the American people in our times."

The entire idea of a Great Society was a response to this people's movement, just as Richard Nixon's programs—the Comprehensive Employment Training Administration [CETA] and the like—reflected the Northern insurrections. Had nothing else come out of the body of legislation enacted under the rubric of John Kennedy's War on Poverty and Lyndon Johnson's Great Society, it would still not be possible to call any era that heralded the end of legalized apartheid in the United States a failure. How telling that few of the most vocal critics of the 1960s choose to laud it.

Attention having been duly paid here, the caveat must immediately follow that if anyone proceeds today under the impression that the term "Great Society" ever referred to a massive program of measures designed fundamentally to address the domestic problems of race and poverty, that person should be promptly told the reality. No such agenda ever existed. As historic as the attempt was, only bits and pieces of innovative programs were enacted—Head Start and the Job Corps, for example—representing a piecemeal rather than a systematic approach.

Even so, the resulting benefit for tens of thousands of human beings historically deprived of entry to social, political and economic channels giving promise of a better life was significant, as were the benefits to the stability of the society. Even if the amelioration effected still left the black masses (and others of the poor) far from redeemed, it also left them less inclined to abandon hope that the mythic American promises extended to black people too.

What the Great Society affirmed was the responsibility of the Federal government to take measures necessary to bring into the social and economic mainstream any segment of the people historically excluded. In the context of the struggle marking the era, this meant specifically—though not exclusively—black people.

An ostensible commitment to this goal was evidenced by the implementation of such programs as compensatory education and training, and by the priority given to civil rights, affirmative action and regulatory legislation. Presidents Nixon and Gerald Ford, following Kennedy and Johnson, found it pragmatically necessary to acknowledge the validity of government's role in facilitating the economic well-being of its citizens—even as Nixon initiated private measures to forestall black advances.

Ronald Reagan was the first President since the advent of the New Deal to call for the dismantling of these domestic social programs. In his 1982 State of the Union Address, he could point to more than $44 billion in cuts in social spending, with an additional $19 billion planned. Asserting that he had inherited a system in which valuable resources were "going not to the needy but to the greedy," the President vowed that his economic program would "protect the needy while it triggers a recovery that will benefit all Americans."

Reagan's years in office are now history. If the economic policies he put into operation have benefited all Americans, that lesson has been lost on the millions of the old and newly dispossessed.

The consequences of Reagan's policies can be traced with precision. His elimination of a single program—CETA—meant the loss of tens of thousands of job opportunities for disadvantaged youth (and members of the middle class who infiltrated the program). That number was small compared to what was needed, but to it must be added the generation that grew from childhood to adolescence during the eight years of Reagan's reign. The results are currently reflected in the calamitous unemployment rates and desperate plight of black youths who are ineligible for the "safety net" Reagan promised to retain. The loss of CETA—plus massive cuts in job training programs—meant, for many, loss of the opportunity to enter the economic mainstream. Similarly—age and race aside—as the military budget swelled to $1 trillion over eight years, cutbacks in food stamps and related nutritional programs affecting both the working poor and the unemployed had a disastrous effect. The relentless attacks on these and other social programs have led directly to sharp increases in numbers of the hungry, the homeless, the jobless and, inevitably under such circumstances, the crime-ridden and terrified.

Many white middle-class citizens who are quick to join in the chorus of indignant voices castigating Great Society programs that help the poor would fight to keep the measures resulting from the civil rights movement that benefit them. When the Reagan Administration tried to eliminate or limit the educational acts pushed through by the Johnson Administration, there was a great hue and cry. Nor are such vitally important cultural institutions as the National Endowment for the Arts and the National Endowment for the Humanities, which offer special channels of opportunity to academicians, artists and intellectuals, normally subjected to catcalls, though they, too, have been targeted for budget cuts.

Medicare, the subsidized national health insurance for the elderly that is a major legacy of the 1960s, takes a substantial slice of the budgetary pie for domestic spending: at recent count, more than eight times the 2 percent allocated for Aid to Families with Dependent Children (A.F.D.C.), or "welfare freeloaders," as the recipients are so commonly regarded. Even Medicaid, its poor cousin, receives more than twice A.F.D.C.'s share. But whites who benefit from national health insurance rarely know that it is a by-product of the civil rights movement.

Traditionally, these programs have become relatively untouchable, while it is the programs that are perceived as helping blacks that are castigated. The most acute condemnation is reserved for black teen-age A.F.D.C. mothers, who are unable to make a case for themselves or to represent very much of a political threat. Among the programs of the 1960s of which blacks have been the primary beneficiaries, only Head Start is generally considered a success, though this program does not cover even half the eligible children.

Community action programs in particular have taken a severe beating. Initially, the intellectuals who dealt with the issues of poverty thought that what we now call "self-help"—that is, community initiative—could be promoted by having people who live in the community—the poor—come together with government encouragement to design activities and place pressure on the system to respond to them.

It was too good an idea to be permitted to live: The record shows that as soon as community action projects were organized and the people started responding, many of the proponents of the new programs turned tail. They came to understand that once the poor got together they might realize that nobody was really going to solve their problems. Once they understood that—and if they were given support and encouragement in organizing—they might demand more fundamental changes.

In point of fact, the policy-makers—politicians, academics and government officials—knew all along that the economy was not going to generate enough jobs to solve the problems of blacks and poor people. Everybody knew this, including the poor. But at least government could *appear* to be helping, and some people might be lifted from poverty in the process. At the same time, the tensions stimulated both by the movement in the South and by the rebellions in the Northern cities could be defused. The objective thus became to provide enough financial support for people to be maintained—and contained—without making too much noise. Job training might be given to some in the hope that they might eventually find some employment and so that, in any case, the claim could be made that something was being done to give them skills. Education of a sort might also pay off in the long run.

Thus, the real question of the 1960s and

1970s became: How do you maintain the poor? How do you preserve stability while doing as much as possible for *some* people in the hope they will be helped, and help keep others quiet? The only alternative was to do what no one in government was prepared to do: come up with a strategy that would have created enough good jobs for people adequately and meaningfully to maintain themselves.

It is at this point that no one—neither the reactionary detractors nor the defenders of the social programs under attack—can manage an answer. For the painful reality of the 1980s is that the economy still does not generate enough jobs, and because of racial discrimination blacks have limited access even to those.

Where, then, do we go from here? We must begin simply by being honest. The problem being evaded—the present structural inadequacy of the economy—should be acknowledged. As a corollary, the notice "'We' did something for 'them' and look at the result!" must be exposed for what it is. Until this country finds a way to generate enough jobs for people who want to work—and there are massive numbers of them—it simply won't do to go around blaming the poor as "immoral" or "lazy." Once this much is accepted, it will be possible to talk seriously about what people can do for themselves and, more important, what the society can do for them.

Talk of job training and welfare reform, for instance, is futile in the absence of jobs, whether in the public or private sector or, ideally, in both. In areas of high unemployment, it makes no sense to declare that "they" will get jobs if "they" are educated. If that is true, why are there so many educated people now in poverty-level or part-time jobs and on the unemployment lines? One area calls for immediate action. For ghettoized teen-agers, male and female, the economic and social crisis is so grave that programs should be devised to provide work through public and private means *while they are in school*.

Of course, all programs enacted will entail community action of the self-help variety. Black people have always, often under great duress, helped themselves. But no black private institutions, agencies or individuals can fulfill the macroeconomic role of generating widespread employment; it is simplistic, if not the cruelest deception, to speak of their being able to do so. The private sector can assist, but it is the Federal government that must take the lead in turning the faces of citizens once more toward the ideals and goals of a society both fair and just.

As Ray Marshall, Secretary of Labor under President Carter, put it:

> We know that a full-employment policy would be good business. With a jobs program, $15 billion could save the Federal government $30 billion. We've demonstrated that in the past. The main reason we don't do it now is the neoconservative mythology that it didn't work. We ought not to let them get by with that. The contrary evidence is overpowering.
>
> . . .
>
> We should not let people make abstractions of human suffering.... Rather what we should fear most, as citizens of the richest nation on earth, is the judgment of the world community and of history that we were unwilling to be good and faithful stewards of our resources, that we deliberately decided not to use our resources to try to improve the human condition.

Any other course will betray the committed Americans who participated in, and paid dearly for, the most ennobling struggle of our times. And this, ultimately, was the message that the relatives of James Chaney, Andrew Goodman and Michael Schwerner took to the White House on June 23.

CHAPTER 14

Diversity, Ideology, and the Struggle for Equality

64

Class Struggles

Robert Reinhold

This article details California's experience with multicultural curricular reform in kindergarten through eighth grade. The goals of the reform movement are presented, and criticisms are discussed. The author shows that the processes of curricular change and textbook development are related to political pressures, demography, and debates concerning the history of pluralism.

Exercises to Guide Your Reading

1. List the goals of multicultural curricular reform.
2. Summarize the criticisms of multicultural curricular reform.
3. Describe the strengths and weaknesses of the social studies textbooks adopted by California. Compare those books to the textbooks you used in grades K–eight.
4. Offer first a criticism and then a defense of the Houghton Mifflin social studies textbook series.

Reprinted by permission of *The New York Times Magazine*. September 29, 1991. pp. 26–29, 46, 47, 52.

On a leafy side street in the Los Angeles suburb of Glendale, parents and children are playing out the American ritual of going back to school. The youngsters, still adjusting to the unfamiliar surroundings of classes at the Columbus Elementary School, clutch glossy new textbooks. About 30 of them file into John Robertson's fifth-grade classroom, where the walls are decorated with Presidential portraits, diagrams of the 50 states and Navajo sand drawings. From all appearances, a traditional setting. But appearances are deceiving.

That becomes evident when Robertson addresses his charges, with names like Aram, Razmik, Sarkis, Su Chin, Pierre and Angela. The classroom, a typical one in the new California, is filled with immigrant children from Soviet Armenia, Mexico, El Salvador, Korea and Hong Kong, plus a few Americans. At the rear, a Filipino-American teacher's aide, Nanette Morales, prepares to help Armenian and Korean children learn English.

It is Robertson's task to bring these mostly foreign-born youngsters into the American fold, and one of his main tools is the new blue textbook that each child carries. It is entitled "America Will Be," and is one of a series of new schoolbooks published by the Houghton Mifflin Company. Robertson directs the children to start reading a literature selection from the book—a Cherokee Indian version of the tortoise and the hare fable.

These youngsters and Robertson are at the front edge of a revolution in the teaching of history and social studies, one that has been building in many states for years but has reached its fullest flower in California. Four years ago, the state Board of Education adopted a history and social studies "framework," or curriculum, devised by a team that included Charlotte Crabtree, a professor of education at U.C.L.A., and Diane Ravitch, an Assistant Secretary of Education who was then an adjunct professor of history and education at Teachers College, Columbia University. It then invited publishers to submit a series of textbooks based on the new framework.

By all accounts, it was an intimidating invitation. The framework called for stretching the study of world and American history to three years each, introduced social studies into the earliest grades, restored the study of religion as a key factor in world history, emphasized history as a dramatic chronicle to be taught as "a story well told," reintroduced literature in historical instruction and fully integrated geography with history. And it demanded that the public schools "accurately portray the cultural and racial diversity of our society" while emphasizing the "centrality of Western civilizations as the source of American political institutions, laws and ideology."

The new books are the most visible product yet of this campaign to inject new life and relevance into the teaching of history. The express purpose of the undertaking is to force a sharp reversal of the decades-old trend of watering down textbooks to avoid controversy and appeal to the widest possible market.

And where the history is spicier, controversy is sure to follow, as was evident at the San Francisco School Board's public hearing on the books this June at the Everett Middle School. As the packed meeting got under way, most people stood for the Pledge of Allegiance. Indians, Chinese Americans, blacks, Hispanic Americans, Jews, Christians and Muslims all fell silent, placed hands over hearts and intoned "One nation, under God, indivisible, with liberty and justice for all."

But the raucous hearing that followed was anything but indivisible. In four and a half hours of shouting, a parade of speakers stepped before the microphone to denounce the books. Mary R. Hoover, professor of black studies at San Francisco State University, asserted that the new books distorted the history of blacks and other minorities "so Europe could be celebrated."

Christina Edwards, a lecturer in American Indian Studies at San Francisco State, introduced herself with the Lakota name of

Cungleska Lutawin, and complained that the third-grade book trivialized Indian history. "It reduces our sun dance and medicine dance to a toilet-paper project," she said. She drew cheers when she envisioned the uproar that would follow if children were asked to make a crucifix out of two Popsicle sticks and a clay Christ figure daubed with ketchup.

A smaller number of witnesses stood to defend the books as better than anything ever before available to youngsters. They were jeered.

While its critics have been numerous and vociferous, the project has enjoyed the forceful support of California's pugnacious Superintendent of Public Instruction, Bill Honig. In an interview in his office in Sacramento, Honig stoutly defended the framework against what he calls "the victimization crew," the "tribalists" and "separatists" in universities who "make a livelihood on discrediting broader cultural ideas."

And despite widespread complaints about its purported insensitivities to minorities, subtle and not-so-subtle stereotyping and outright biases, the California framework has begun to make wide ripples across American education. With 3.7 million pupils in grades kindergarten through eighth, California represents 11 percent of the $1.7 billion national market for school texts. Already the texts tailored to the California curriculum are beginning to be adopted elsewhere, in West Virginia, Indiana, Arkansas and Oregon, as well as Newark and Dubuque, Iowa.

The process by which these books were written, debated, adopted, amended and refined sheds light on the enormous complexity and political contentiousness of teaching history in this polyglot country. It is a debate that has gained urgency in New York and many other ethnically diverse states but nowhere more than in California. By the turn of the century, according to various projections, well under half the children of California will be "Anglos," or people of European origin, and more than a third will be Hispanic and one in eight Asian.

The question for educators and parents is this: Can these children, from the earliest school years, be exposed to the full diversity of cultures and traditions that make up the United States and still arrive at the conclusion that we are united by ideals, bonds and legal instruments that support the national motto, E pluribus unum, or "Out of many, one"?

Alternatively, are those common ideals, and the immigrant-absorption model on which they are based, fundamentally white European formulations that have excluded and failed the people of color whose ancestors came not in steamers from Europe but in shackles from Africa or, in the case of Indians, were here long before Columbus?

Since the 1978 passage of Proposition 13, which limited the taxing authority of local governments, California schools have turned increasingly to the state government for money, greatly enhancing the power of the state board and the Superintendent of Public Instruction. California is one of 22 "adoption" states, in which the state government reviews books for statewide use. While local districts are not obliged to buy the state-approved books, they must spend 70 percent of the $28.90 a year the state supplies for textbooks for each pupil on the approved books. Their alternative is to seek a waiver or put the money aside for future spending on state-approved books. California has been using this considerable power in recent years to promote its new approach to teaching history.

Indeed, when the Glendale fifth graders opened their new history books, they unwittingly marked the end of a lengthy process that began even before California formally adopted the new framework in 1987. And closely watching the California process from the very beginning were representatives of Ligature Inc., a small company based in Chicago and Boston that specializes in textbook development.

Ligature and companies like it develop an idea for a book, engage the authors and then seek a partnership with a publisher. By

1987, Ligature, headed by co-owners Stuart J. Murphy and Richard M. Anderson, had already produced an outline for a history series and chosen three authors: Gary B. Nash, professor of history at the University of California at Los Angeles, a leading academic proponent of "multiculturalism"; Christopher L. Salter, chairman of the geography department at the University of Missouri, and a crusader for geography education; and Beverly J. Armento, the director of the Center for Business and Economic Education at Georgia State University, and an expert in teaching economics to elementary-school children.

After California announced the adoption of the new framework, Houghton Mifflin, with no existing history series and, thus, no investment to protect, quickly contracted with Ligature to produce the books. Calculating that the California market alone could yield sales of $52.9 million, the company provided more than half the working capital of $20 million. It also brought in a fourth author, Karen K. Wixson, professor of education at the University of Michigan, who is an expert on reading pedagogy.

The books' developers relied heavily on the latest visual techniques, according to Ligature's Murphy. "Some kids are visual learners," he says. "We attempted to give kids a real capability to learn from maps, variations in color." Whereas previous textbooks usually used pictorial material as decoration to break up blocks of text, these books often use it to deliver the main message.

To show children that history is not just a lot of dates, the books make extensive use of features like "A Moment in Time," a vivid full-page drawing of some typical person in history—like an 18th-century Parisian market woman in a muddy skirt, a 10th-century crusader in chain mail, a 19th-century Cherokee mother and son. "Not one page was done without a designer, writer and editor sitting together," Nash says.

Critics and admirers alike agree that the new books are superior to the soporific history texts used by generations of American students. Never before have elementary-school texts made such an effort to include the broad sweep of history and the divergent cultures that flow into the American mainstream. The series consists of one book for each grade from first to eighth, and a separate fourth-grade book for six other states, including California. Each is filled with colorful charts, graphs, time lines, maps and photographs in a format suggestive of the newspaper USA Today.

The first three grades depart from the traditional practice of focusing on the family in the first grade, neighborhood in the second and the larger community in the third. Instead, the first-grade text ranges from the school, to town and country, city and suburb and "all around the big world," including a train trip across Canada. As an exercise, students write a letter to a cousin in Mexico.

The second-grade book focuses on family and citizenship, celebrating American institutions like the Presidency. But it also branches out, discussing Cambodian immigrants and people like Roberto Clemente, the Puerto Rican baseball star and humanitarian who died in an airplane crash while trying to deliver relief supplies to earthquake victims in Central America. The third-grade book takes children across the American continent, a geographical excursion that touches on rivers, forests, Pilgrims, prairie dogs, Indians, farmers and steelworkers.

The California version traces the state's history from pre-Columbian Indians to modern-day smog problems. The national volume offers a broader view of the American land, touching on different regions, and detailing the development of highways and factories. The fifth-grade book traces American history from the Indians to early 20th-century industrialization.

In the sixth grade, children are given their first introduction to the ancient world, including Mesopotamia, Egypt, China, Greece, India and Rome. The seventh grade continues this journey, explaining the slave trade in the Kongo (the non-Anglicized spelling of Congo) and early American civilizations like the Mayas. And finally, the eighth-grade books bring all this together into a chronicle of the American experience from the early European settlement to the Bush Presidency.

The series tries to correct the traditionally Eurocentric views of older texts. For example, the fifth-grade book (entitled "America Will Be," after a Langston Hughes poem) covers early American history and plunges students into the American ethnic rainbow with devices like a two-page color spread of different kinds of bread: pita for Greeks and Syrians, matzoh for Jews, corn bread for Indians, tortillas for Mexican and Central American Indians and so on.

The fifth-grade volume devotes roughly 50 pages to slavery in the South, with vivid, firsthand descriptions of its cruelty, and contains fairly frank treatment of the brutality visited on American Indians by European settlers. Among the primary sources quoted are Olaudah Equiano (an African slave), Abigail Adams, Marco Polo, Black Hawk and Jane Addams, the founder of Hull House. It quotes the writings of an escaped slave, the Rev. Josiah Henson, who described his mother, on her knees, begging the man who had just bought her to buy her baby too; she was kicked senseless.

The seventh-grade book, "Across the Centuries," devotes 51 pages to the history of Sub-Saharan Africa, tracing the Bantu migration, the rise of the Zimbabwe State and the Kongo Kingdom. It also covers Asian, pre-Columbian American and other civilizations, as well as Europe in the Renaissance, Reformation and the ages of colonialism and imperialism.

The fourth-grade book, "Oh, California," on the state's history, tries to describe the cruelties the Spanish mission system visited on the Indians of California. The books sometimes go to amusing lengths to achieve political correctness. The fourth-grade book has a full-page picture of a "vaquera"—a Mexican cowgirl—at a rodeo in 1820.

In the spring of 1990, nine publishers submitted entries to the state board's Curriculum Commission, which set up three panels of teachers to evaluate them. Only Houghton Mifflin offered books for all grades through eighth. In the end, the commission approved just the Houghton Mifflin series and a single eighth-grade entry from Holt, Rinehart & Winston Inc., "The Story of America: Beginnings to 1914." But it insisted upon certain changes, which started a process known in publishing jargon as "corrigenda," literally a list of errors to be corrected before publication.

For example, the original fifth-grade book credited John Wesley Powell with being the first person to lead a group the length of the Grand Canyon. That was changed to read that he was the first white person to do so, since Indians had traveled the route for centuries. And some changes were made to accommodate Muslim sensibilities. They deleted three pictures of Mohammed—in Islam, literal images of Mohammed are considered blasphemous—and a suggestion in the teacher's manual to have children impersonate Mohammed and his family, suggesting instead that they interview a Muslim scholar.

Other changes were made to avoid misinterpretations. For instance, a sixth-grade lesson on the life of Jesus and the rise of Christianity was originally titled "An Age of Transition." To Jewish groups, this implied that Judaism was just a way station to Christianity. The lesson is now called "Religious Developments."

But the commission rebuffed numerous demands that it delete unhappy events or blemishes in history. "The purpose of history cannot be to expunge all such episodes from this record in the mistaken interest of filiopietism or children's self-esteem, but instead must be to help children to learn from them," the commission stated in its formal recommendations to the state board, which accepted the books last October.

The publishers were stunned by the bitterness of the protest that surrounded the process of public hearings and comment. That debate has now filtered down to nearly every one of the state's school districts, and even to every school in decentralized districts like Los Angeles Unified. Given little choice, most local boards have accepted the new books, with the notable exceptions of Oakland and Ravenswood City, a heavily minority school district in East Palo Alto. In those areas, they were rejected as insufficiently multicultural.

The debate this summer in San Francisco, where minorities make up 83 percent of the student population, typifies the controversy surrounding the books. While the school board ultimately voted 5 to 1 for adoption—joining the approximately 600 of California's 1,016 school districts that had approved the texts by Labor Day—it did so with no great enthusiasm. And it tacked on a lengthy supplementary reading list that included such titles as "Black Heroes of the Wild West," "Chinese Americans, Past and Present" and "Gays in America."

Even supplementary reading, however, is unlikely to placate all the critics, who understandably focus on religion and race issues as particularly problematic. Jewish groups complain about what they see as invidious comparisons between Judaism and Christianity. In one sentence about Jews, for example, the sixth-grade book refers to "their god," with a lowercase "g." Three paragraphs later, discussing Christianity, the text refers to "a vision from God."

Muslims say they would like to see more pictures of people and fewer of camels when their religion is discussed. "When it comes to Islam, there are virtually no people," says Shabbir Mansuri, director of the Council of Islamic Education, based in Tustin. "The faces of real people disappear in the text. There is no relevance to the student. They will come away thinking this is a religion that does not deal with the rational thinking of the modern day, the religion of the terrorists."

Critics also have attacked the treatment of the Spanish missions in California, citing passages like this one in the fourth-grade texts about Father Junipero Serra: "Father Serra would also teach the Indians farming skills and trade crafts so that they would be able to support themselves." The Indians had no trouble getting by before Father Serra destroyed their culture, critics note sarcastically.

And many opponents say the books, for all their improvements over past materials, remain essentially, if unintentionally, racist. One of the most determined of these critics is Joyce E. King, director of teacher education at Santa Clara University, who was a dissenting member of the state Curriculum Development and Supplemental Materials Commission that approved the books.

She cites the sixth-grade book's treatment of the early development of human culture, starting two million years ago with Homo habilis on the plains of eastern Africa. The original version of the text urged children to imagine themselves there as "two naked dark-skinned people walk down to the lake not far from you. . . . You point to your open mouth to show them you are hungry. . . . One person walks off toward a field. . . . Soon the first person returns with a bloody bone. . . . They invited you to eat the red marrow oozing from the bone." (After complaints, the published version omitted the words "dark-skinned," "bloody" and "oozing.") Three pages later, the text moves forward to 12,011 B.C. and shows a Cro-Magnon man, a handsome clean-shaven fellow in buckskins. A few pages farther on, the text says, "In terms of physical features, the Cro-Magnons looked like people today."

King, who is black, finds that objectionable, saying it draws unfavorable comparisons between the savage Homo habilis of Africa and the clean-shaven Cro-Magnon of Europe. "The chapter begins with an imaginary excursion to Africa," she says. "Then three pages later we have a shaved white guy near a cave in France. That juxtaposition was problematic. They deleted 'dark-skinned,' but those kinds of problems cannot be fixed. We are putting these books in the hands of children who already have stereotypes."

She also criticizes sections on slavery, saying they depict slaves as animals devoid of human thoughts and emotions, and the black migration to the northern cities and the ghetto life they met there. "The discussion of the experiences of African Americans in the urban North perpetuates a negative stereotype of black life," she says. "Black ghettos appear to be just naturally crime-ridden and dirty."

The starkest paradox of the tempest aroused by the books is that the principal historian, Nash of U.C.L.A., is a man with impeccable left-liberal credentials. His books, "Red, White, and Black: The Peoples of Early America" and "Forging Freedom: The Formation of Philadelphia's Black Community," have been widely admired by black and American Indian scholars. That Nash, who is white, should now be painted as a racist is a source of considerable frustration and pain to him. "If I'm the bad guy," he asks, "who are your allies?"

California casual in a sweatsuit one recent morning, Nash spreads the books over his dining-room table in the affluent Pacific Palisades section of Los Angeles. Nash counters the criticism about the Spanish missions by pointing out that the books also describe the whippings and other cruelties suffered by Indians at the hands of Father Serra. He concedes some of King's points but stoutly defends the overall treatment of African history and slavery.

"I had never heard of the Bantu migration and the rise of the Zimbabwe state when I got my Ph.D. at Princeton," he says. "We have 80 pages on African history for 12-year-olds. This is what bugs me. Joyce King and other critics will not take notice of this and continue to say this is a Eurocentric series."

Some critics have said the books should have omitted contemporary Southern arguments in favor of slavery. "I am not willing to make concessions on this," Nash says. "The Southern arguments are so patently false—the kids see this." He argues that the eighth-grade book offers as harsh a portrait of slavery as ever given in an elementary text, reprinting lengthy passages from the powerful autobiography of Frederick Douglass, an escaped slave. "I do not think anyone

reading this would think this trivializes slavery," he says.

Ultimately, Nash argues, the issue comes down to the political one of whose vision of America one accepts. "You can turn American history into a story of unremitting oppression of exploited minorities," he said. "That's just as distorted as the old view." Nash, at least, clings to the optimistic notion that all Americans can find common ground in the "ongoing struggle for greater equality and social justice—this society sooner or later must be what it says it intends to be."

This is where the books come under the toughest ideological attack from critics who argue that the immigrant model marginalizes people of color. Chief among them is a Jamaican woman, Sylvia Wynter, who holds a joint appointment in African and Afro-American Studies and Spanish and Portuguese at Stanford University. Her lengthy critique of the fifth-grade book, "America Will Be," argues that it tends to equate the prejudice once experienced by white immigrants from Europe with the racism suffered by black, brown and yellow peoples, thereby justifying their exploitation.

What is needed, she wrote in a commentary to the state Curriculum Commission, is an entirely new framework that "seeks to go beyond the model of a nation-state coterminous only with Euro-immigrant America, to one coterminous as a 'world' civilization, with all its peoples: and therefore, for the first time in recorded history, coterminous (as a land that's not been yet but yet must be) with humankind."

State Superintendent Honig bristles at such arguments. "They do not like the idea of common democratic principles," he says. "It gets in the way of their left point of view that this country is corrupt. This country has been able to celebrate pluralism but keep some sense of the collective that holds us together. Everything is not race, gender or class. The whole world cannot be seen just through those glasses.

"Democracy has certain core ideas—freedom of speech, law, procedural rights, the way we deal with each other," Honig continues. "If everything becomes hostile race and class warfare, we are going to lose this country. The issue is not multiculturalism. We agree with that. The question is, Are you also going to talk about the political and moral values that are essential for us to live together?"

The books are mostly welcomed by teachers and students in schools districts that have been testing the books for the last year. At the Oak Hills Elementary School in Agoura, a suburb about 40 miles northwest of Los Angeles, the principal, Anthony W. Knight, calls them balanced and, more important, interesting to children. "The old methods of social studies were clearly boring to children," he says.

One fifth-grade teacher, Enid Miller, says many of her pupils were startled to learn from the texts that they were *all* immigrants. She had them interview their own families, and the class became what she called a "tapestry" of different ethnic groups—Iranian, Israeli, Chinese, Korean and Indian, among many others.

She says the chapters on slavery and the treatment of American Indians made a particularly strong impression on her students. "They are very sensitive," she says. "They feel outraged when they see what it really entailed." The Oak Park Unified School District recently adopted the books with little if any protest.

The visuals and graphics earn universal acclaim. In Tustin, a bedroom suburb in Orange County, 11 teachers piloted the book last year. One spring morning at the Currie Middle School, Sue Kraus's sixth-grade class was working on a crossword puzzle about the ancient Israelites. The pupils seemed genuinely absorbed. "It explains everything better, like daily life and religion, so you have a better idea of what things looked like," says Sarah Angle, a student.

Sheralin Conkey, a seventh-grade teacher at the Hewes Middle School in Tustin, says she jumped directly to the chapters about Islam and the Middle East when American troops went to Saudi Arabia last fall. "I found the book so much more detailed and comprehensive than the others," she says. "This book had two chapters on Islam and even went into the Shiites and the Sunnis and the lines of succession from Mohammed."

But the reception has been rougher in heavily minority districts, most notably the Oakland Unified School District—91 percent minority, mainly black (57 percent) and with a dropout rate of about 35 percent. Despite some reservations, the teachers and administration recommended adoption. "They were not perfect, but they were much better than what we had been using," said Robert L. Newell, associate superintendent for the division of instruction.

But in June the seven-member school board decisively rejected the books. "Almost 92 percent of our students are persons of color," said one board member, Toni R. Cook, who is black. "These books did very little for those children. We have 74 languages spoken in our schools. This is what the 21st century will be like.

"It's important for youngsters to see themselves," Cook insists. "How do we balance what they see on TV, lots of violence and crime. Their self-esteem is way down. They are portrayed as Willie Hortons. Oakland's challenge is how to truly have a multicultural curriculum. Ninety-one percent of our children are not European. How do we best excite them to the learning process?"

Two weeks into the school year, however, many Oakland youngsters weren't seeing anything. Parents, educators and activists still had not agreed on a new curriculum, and many students faced the new year without any textbooks at all.

The issues that have been raised by multicultural education have rubbed the rawest nerves, even in an America that is fundamentally pluralistic. A sharp debate broke out in New York State in late June over a paper prepared by a special panel for the State Commissioner of Education, Thomas Sobol, that urged a new curriculum that de-emphasizes the centrality of European thought and influence in the American experience. Noisy dissent came from some members of the panel, especially the historian Arthur Schlesinger Jr., who complained that "Europhobia" and a "cult of ethnicity" were turning America into a "quarrelsome splatter of enclaves."

The problem, in the view of Laurie Olsen, a former history teacher who is now with California Tomorrow, an educational group that develops and runs programs to deal with the increasingly multi-ethnic nature of California, is not the texts themselves. Rather, she says, it is "how polarized we are, how much fear there is about diversity, and how the schools have become the battleground." Lewis H. Butler, an Assistant Sec-

retary of Health, Education and Welfare in the Nixon Administration and now chairman of California Tomorrow, says the whole episode has been a "rather sad event" that pits white liberals against black and Indian scholars. "People who thought they were good guys found themselves bad guys, called racists or separatists," he says.

If the concept of the melting pot is outdated, what is to replace it? History, some say, is a kind of property whose owner controls the future. From that perspective, the future in California still belongs, however tenuously, to the proponents of traditional Western values. The current debate suggests, however, that an increasingly polyglot America has yet to come to grips with the full depth of its diversity.

65

Don't Be Happy—Worry

Susan Faludi

This article analyzes the cultural backlash against the feminist movement and the quest for greater equality for women. The author describes how several scholarly studies (which were later found to be seriously flawed) became evidence in the case against feminism. Media behaviors contributing to the backlash are discussed.

Exercises to Guide Your Reading

1. Summarize the findings and major weaknesses of the Harvard-Yale study showing a shortage of marriageable men.
2. Compare the effects of marriage on the mental health of men and women.
3. Identify the elements of backlash in the criticisms of no-fault divorce laws and in the reports on women's depression or burnout.
4. Predict the effects of expanding employment and occupation choices on women's life satisfaction.

By the end of the '80s, many American women had become bitterly familiar with a number of trends that were supposedly growing out of the choices they were making about their lives. Among these "statistical" developments were:

- A "man shortage" endangering women's opportunities for marriage.
  Source: A famous 1986 marriage study by Harvard and Yale researchers.
  Findings: A college-educated, unwed woman at 30 has a 20 percent likelihood of marriage, at 35 a 5 percent chance, and at 40 no more than a 1.3 percent chance.
- A "devastating" plunge in economic status afflicting women who divorce under the new no-fault laws.
  Source: A 1985 study by a sociologist at Stanford University.

Findings: The average woman suffers a 73 percent drop in her living standard a year after a divorce, while the man enjoys a 42 percent rise.
- A "great emotional depression" and "burnout" attacking, respectively, single and career women.
  Source: Various psychological studies.
  Findings: No solid figures, just the contention that women's mental health has never been worse and is declining in direct proportion to women's tendency to stay single or devote themselves to careers.

These widely reported developments have one thing in common: They aren't true.

How is it possible that so much distorted, faulty or plain inaccurate information can become almost universally accepted? Close examination of these three developments suggests that the statistics behind the

Reprinted from *The Washington Post Magazine* and *Backlash* by permission of *Random House*. October 20, 1991. pp. 13–17, 28–32.

"trends" the popular culture chooses to promote most heavily are the very statistics we should view with the most caution. They may well be in wide circulation not because they are true but because they support widely held media preconceptions—biases that, in the last decade, have formed part of a broad cultural backlash against women's quest for equality.

Beginning roughly in the late '70s with the rise of the New Right, which championed an agenda noteworthy for its extreme anti-feminism, the backlash took root in the Reagan era, spreading into national politics and the press, popular culture, advertising, executive suites and mainstream social thought. As it surfaced in popular discourse, the backlash adopted a somewhat tempered rhetoric and a subtle profile, culminating in the late '80s in a commercialized vision of muted "New Traditional" women.

But whether delivered in fiery broadsides from the pulpits of televangelists or in discreet sound bites from the drafting boards of Madison Avenue, the message of the backlash remained the same: Women who seek true equality will sacrifice true happiness. Feminism, women heard time and again, has proved their worst enemy, stripping them of love, marriage and motherhood, and yielding only poverty, depression and drab wardrobes.

Under the backlash, as the cases explored here show, statistics became prescriptions for expected female behavior, cultural marching orders to women describing how they *should* act—and how they would be punished if they failed to heed the call. This "data" was said to reflect simply "the way things are" for women, a bedrock of demographic reality. The only choice for women was to accept the numbers and lower their sights to meet them.

THE MAN SHORTAGE: A TALE OF TWO MARRIAGE STUDIES

Valentine's Day 1986 was coming up, and at the Stamford (Conn.) Advocate, it was reporter Lisa Marie Petersen's turn to produce that year's story on Cupid's slings and arrows. Her "angle," as she recalled later, would be "Romance: Is It In or Out?" She went down to the Stamford Town Center mall and interviewed a few men shopping for flowers and chocolates. Then she put in a call to the Yale sociology department, "just to get some kind of foundation," she says, "You know, something to put in the third paragraph."

She got Neil Bennett on the phone—a 31-year-old unmarried sociologist who had recently completed, with two colleagues, an unpublished study on women's marriage patterns. Bennett warned her the study wasn't really finished, but when she pressed him, he told her what he had found: College-educated women who put schooling and careers before their wedding date were going to have a harder time getting married. "The marriage market, unfortunately, may be falling out from under them," he told her.

Bennett brought out the numbers: Never-married college-educated women at 30 had a 20 percent chance of being wed; by 35 their odds were down to 5 percent; by 40, to 1.3 percent. And black women had even worse odds. "My jaw just dropped," recalls Petersen, who was 27 and single at the time. Petersen never thought to question the figures. "We usually just take anything from good schools. If it's a study from Yale, we just put it in the paper."

The Advocate ran the news on the front page. The Associated Press immediately picked up the story and carried it across the nation and eventually around the world. In no time, Bennett was fielding calls from Australia.

In the United States, the marriage news was absorbed by nearly every outlet of mass culture. The statistics were showcased in most major newspapers and received top billing on network news programs and talk shows. They wound up in sitcoms from "Designing Women" to "Kate and Allie"; in movies from "Crossing Delancey" to "Fatal Attraction"; in magazines from Newsweek to Cosmopolitan; in dozens of self-help manuals, dating-service mailings, greeting cards and night-class courses on relationships.

Bennett and his colleagues, Harvard economist David Bloom and Yale graduate student Patricia Craig, predicted a "marriage crunch" for baby-boom college-educated women for primarily one reason: Women marry men an average of two to three years older. So, they reasoned, women born in the first part of the baby boom, between 1946 and 1957, when the birthrate was increasing sharply, would have to scrounge for men in the less populated older age brackets. And those education-minded women who decided to get their diplomas before their marriage licenses would wind up worst off, the researchers postulated—on the theory that the early bird gets the worm.

At the very time the study was released, however, the assumption that women marry older men was rapidly becoming outmoded. Federal statistics now showed first-time brides marrying grooms an average of only 1.8 years older. But it was impossible to revise the Harvard-Yale figures in light of these changes, or even to examine them—because the study wasn't published. This evidently did not bother the press, which chose to ignore a published study on the same subject—released only a few months earlier—that came to the opposite conclusion. That study, an October 1985 report by researchers at the University of Illinois, concluded that the marriage crunch in the United States was minimal. Their data, the researchers wrote, "did not support theories which see the marriage squeeze as playing a major role in recent changes in marriage behavior."

In March 1986, Bennett and his co-researchers released an informal "discussion paper" that revealed they had used a "parametric model" to compute women's marital odds. Princeton professors Ansley Coale and Donald McNeil had originally constructed the parametric model to analyze marital patterns of elderly women who had already completed their marriage cycle. Bennett and Bloom, who had been graduate students under Coale, thought they could use the same method to predict marriage patterns. Coale, asked about it later, was doubtful. "In principle, the model may be applicable to women

who haven't completed their marital history," he said, "but it is risky to apply it."

To make matters worse, Bennett, Bloom and Craig took their sample of women from the 1982 Current Population Survey, an off year in census-data collection that taps a much smaller number of households, than the decennial census study. The researchers then broke that sample down into ever smaller subgroups—by age, race, and education—until they were making generalizations based on what Census Bureau demographers said could be as small as several hundred women.

As news of the "man shortage" study raced through the media, Jeanne Moorman, a demographer in the U.S. Census Bureau's marriage and family statistics branch, kept getting calls from reporters seeking comment. She decided to take a closer look at the researchers' conclusions. A college-educated woman with a doctoral degree and a specialty in marital demography, Moorman was herself an example of how individual lives defy demographic pigeonholes: She had gotten married at 32, to a man nearly four years younger. . . .

Moorman sat down at her computer and conducted her own marriage study, using conventional standard-life tables instead of the parametric model, and drawing on the 1980 Population Census, which includes 13.4 million households, instead of the 1982 survey that Bennett used, which includes only 60,000 households. The results: At 30, never-married college-educated women had a 58 to 66 percent chance at marriage—about three times the Harvard-Yale study's predictions. At 35, the odds were 32 to 41 percent, seven times higher than the Harvard-Yale figure. At 40, the odds were 17 to 23 percent, an average of 15 times higher. And she found that a college-educated single woman at 30 would be *more* likely to marry than her counterpart with only a high school diploma.

In June 1986, Moorman wrote to Bennett with her findings. She pointed out that more recent data also ran counter to his predictions about college-educated women. While the marriage rate had been declining in the general population, the rate had actually risen for women with four or more years of college who marry between the ages of 25 and 45. "This seems to indicate delaying rather than forgoing marriage," she noted.

Moorman's letter was polite, almost deferential. As a professional colleague, she wrote, she felt obligated to pass along these comments, "which I hope will be well received." They were received with silence. Two months passed. Then, in August, writer Ben Wattenberg mentioned Moorman's study in his syndicated newspaper column and noted that it would be presented at the Population Association of America [PAA] Conference, an important professional gathering for demographers. Moorman's findings could prove embarrassing to Bennett and Bloom before their colleagues. Suddenly, a letter arrived in Moorman's mailbox. "I understand from Ben Wattenberg that you will be presenting these results at PAA in the spring," Bennett wrote; would she send him a copy "as soon as it's available"? When she didn't send it off at once, he called, and, Moorman recalls, "He was very demanding. It was, 'You have to do this, you have to do that.'" This was to become a pattern in her dealings with Bennett, she says. "I always got the feeling from him that he was saying, 'Go away, little girl, I'm a college professor; I'm right, and you have no right to question me.'" (Bennett refused to discuss his dealings with Moorman or any other aspect of the marriage study's history, asserting that he has been a victim of the overeager media, which "misinterpreted [the study] more than I had ever anticipated." Bloom also refused comment.)

Meanwhile, at the Census Bureau, Moorman recalls, she was running into interference from Reagan administration officials. The head office handed down a directive, ordering her to quit speaking to the press about the marriage study because such critiques were "too controversial." When a few TV news shows actually invited her to tell the other side of the man-shortage story, she had to turn them down. She was told to concentrate instead on a study that the White House wanted—about abuse of the welfare system.

By the winter of 1986, Moorman had put the finishing touches on her marriage report and released it to the press. The media relegated it to the inside pages, when they reported it at all. At the same time, in an op-ed piece printed in the New York Times, the Boston Globe and Advertising Age, Bennett and Bloom roundly attacked Moorman for issuing her study, which only "further muddled the discussion," they complained.

Bennett and Bloom's essay criticized Moorman for using the standard-life tables, which they labeled a "questionable technique." So Moorman decided to repeat her study using the Harvard-Yale men's own parametric model. She took the data down the hall to Robert Fay, a statistician whose specialty is mathematical models. Fay looked over Bennett and Bloom's computations and immediately spotted a major error. They had forgotten to factor in the different patterns in college- and high school-educated women's marital histories. (High school-educated women tend to marry in a tight cluster right after graduation. College-educated women tend to spread out the rate of marriage over a longer and later period of time.) Fay made the adjustments and ran the data again, using Bennett and Bloom's mathematical model. The results this time were nearly identical to Moorman's.

So Robert Fay wrote a letter to Bennett. He pointed out the error and its significance. "I believe this reanalysis points up not only the incorrectness of your results," he wrote, "but also a necessity to return to the rest of the data to examine your assumptions more closely," Bennett wrote back the next day. "Things have gotten grossly out of hand," he said. He blamed the press for their differences and pointedly noted that "David [Bloom] and I decided to stop entirely our dealings with all media," a hint perhaps that the Census researchers should do the same.

Still, Bennett and Bloom faced the discomfiting possibility that the Census researchers might publicly point out their mistakes at the upcoming PAA conference. They proposed to Moorman that the three of them all collaborate on a new study they could submit jointly to the PAA conference—in lieu of Moorman's. When Bennett and Bloom discovered they had missed the conference deadline for filing such a new paper, Moorman notes, they dropped the collaboration idea.

In the spring of 1987, the demographers flew to Chicago for the PAA conference. The day before the session, Moorman recalls, she got a call from Bloom. He and Bennett were going to try to withdraw their marriage study, he told her—and substitute a paper on fertility instead. But the conference chairman refused to allow the eleventh-hour switch.

When it was time to present the notorious marriage study before their colleagues, Bloom told the assembly that their findings were "preliminary," gave a few brief remarks and quickly yielded the floor. Moorman was up next. But, thanks to still more interference from her superiors in Washington, there was little she could say. The director of the Census Bureau, looking to avoid further controversy, had ordered her to remove all references to the Harvard-Yale marriage study from her conference speech.

Three and a half years after the Harvard-Yale report made nationwide headlines, the actual study, an analysis of why black women's marriage rates were declining more steeply than those of white women, was finally published—without the much advertised marriage probability statistics. Bennett told the New York Times: "We're not shying away because we have anything to hide." The famous statistics were deleted, he said, because "right now my colleagues and I don't know whether we can stand behind our results or whether they warrant alteration or what have you."

In all the reportorial enterprise expended on the Harvard-Yale study, the press managed to overlook a basic point: There was no man shortage. As a simple check of the latest census population charts would have revealed, there were about 1.9 million more bachelors than unwed women between the ages of 25 and 34, and about half a million more between the ages of 35 and 54. In fact, the proportion of never-married men was larger than at any time since the Census Bureau began keeping records in 1890. If anyone faced a shortage of potential spouses, it was men in the prime marrying years; between the ages of 24 and 34, there were 119 single men for every 100 single women.

A glance at past census charts would also have dispelled the notion that the country was awash in a record glut of single women. The proportion of never-married women, about one in five, was lower than it had been at any time in the 20th century except the '50s, and much lower than in the mid to late 19th century, when one in three women were unwed. If one looks at never-married women aged 45 to 54 (a better indicator of lifelong single status than women in their twenties and thirties, who may simply be postponing marriage), the proportion of unwed women in 1985 was, in fact, *smaller* than it had ever been—smaller even than in the marriage-crazed '50s. (Eight percent of 45- to 54-year-old women were single in 1950, compared with 5 percent in 1985.) In fact, the only place where a "surplus" of unattached women could be said to exist in the '80s was in retirement communities. The median age of women in single-person households in 1986 was 66. The median age of single men, by contrast, was 42.

Conventional press wisdom held that single women of the '80s were desperate for marriage—a desperation that mounted with every passing unwed year. But surveys of real-life women told a different story. A massive 1986 study of women's attitudes by Battelle Memorial Institute in Seattle, which examined 15 years of national surveys of 10,000 women, found that marriage was no longer the centerpiece of women's lives and that women in their thirties were not only delaying but actually dodging the wedding banns. A 1985 Virginia Slims poll reported that 70 percent of women believed they could live a "happy and complete" life without being married. In the 1989 "New Diversity" poll by Langer Associates and Significance Inc., that proportion had jumped to 90 percent. A subsequent Virginia Slims poll in 1990 found that nearly 60 percent of single women believed they were a lot happier than their married friends and that their lives were "a lot easier." A review of 14 years of U.S. National Survey data charted an 11 percent jump in happiness among 1980s-era single women in their twenties and thirties—and a 6.3 percent *decline* in happiness among married women of the same age. If marriage had ever served to boost personal female happiness, the researchers concluded, then "those effects apparently have waned considerably in the last few years."

In lieu of marriage, many women were choosing to live with their loved ones. The cohabitation rate quadrupled between 1970 and 1985. When the federal government commissioned its first study on single women's sexual habits, in 1986, the researchers found that one-third of the unwed women were living with a man. Other demographic studies calculated that at least one-fourth of the decline in the number of married women could be attributed to couples cohabiting.

The more women are paid, the less eager they are to marry. A 1982 study of 3,000 singles found that women earning high incomes are almost twice as likely to *want* to remain unwed as women earning low incomes. "What is going to happen to marriage and childbearing in a society where women really have equality?" Princeton demographer Charles Westoff wondered in the Wall Street Journal in 1986. "The more economically independent women are, the less attractive marriage becomes."

Men in the '80s, on the other hand, were a little more anxious to marry than the press accounts let on. Single men far outnumbered women in dating services, matchmaking clubs and the personals columns, all of which enjoyed explosive growth in the decade. In the mid-'80s, video dating services were complaining of a 3-to-1 male-to-female ratio in their membership rolls. In fact, it had become common practice for dating

services to admit single women at heavily reduced rates, or in some cases even through free memberships, in hopes of remedying the imbalance.

Personal ads were similarly lopsided. In an analysis of 1,200 ads in 1988, sociologist Theresa Montini found that most were placed by 35-year-old heterosexual men, and the vast majority "wanted a long-term relationship." Dating service directors reported that the majority of men they counseled were seeking spouses or long-term relationships, not casual encounters. When Great Expectations, the nation's largest dating service, surveyed its members in 1988, it found that 93 percent of the men wanted, within one year, to have either "a commitment with one person" or marriage. Only 7 percent of the men said they were seeking "lots of dates with different people."

These men had good cause to pursue nuptials: If there's one pattern that psychological studies have established, it's that the institution of marriage has an overwhelmingly salutary effect on men's mental health. "Being married," the prominent government demographer Paul Glick once estimated, "is about twice as advantageous to men as to women in terms of continued survival." Or, as family sociologist Jessie Bernard wrote in 1972:

> There are few findings more consistent, less equivocal, [and] more convincing than the sometimes spectacular and always impressive superiority on almost every index—demographic, psychological, or social—of married over never-married men. Despite all the jokes about marriage in which men indulge, all the complaints they lodge against it, it is one of the greatest boons of their sex.

Bernard's observation still applies. As Ronald C. Kessler, who tracks changes in men's mental health at the University of Michigan's Institute for Social Research, says: "All this business about how hard it is to be a single woman doesn't make much sense when you look at what's really going on. It's single men who have the worst of it.

When men marry, their mental health massively increases."

The mental health data, chronicled in dozens of studies that have looked at marital differences in the last 40 years, are consistent and overwhelming: The suicide rate of single men is twice as high as that of married men. Single men suffer from nearly twice as many severe neurotic symptoms and are far more susceptible to nervous breakdowns, depression, even nightmares. And despite the all-American image of the carefree single cowboy, in reality bachelors are far more likely to be morose, passive and phobic than are married men. Single men suffer from twice as many mental health impairments as single women; they are more depressed, more passive, more likely to experience nervous breakdowns and all the designated symptoms of psychological distress—from fainting to insomnia.

If the widespread promotion of the Harvard-Yale marriage study had one effect, it was to transfer much of this bachelor anxiety into single women's minds. In the Wall Street Journal, a 36-year-old single woman remarked that being unmarried "didn't bother me at all" until after the marriage study's promotion; only then did she begin feeling depressed. A 35-year-old woman told USA Today, "I hadn't even thought about getting married until I started reading those horror stories" about women who may never wed. In a Los Angeles Times story, therapists reported that after the study's promotion, single female patients became "obsessed" with marriage, ready to marry men they didn't even love, just to beat the "odds." The Annual Study of Women's Attitudes, conducted by Mark Clements Research for many women's magazines, found that the proportion of all single women who feared they would never marry had nearly doubled in that one year after the Harvard-Yale study came out, from 14 to 27 percent, and soared to 39 percent for women 25 and older, the group targeted in the study.

Thanks to the press's relentless retelling, the fairy tale of the "marriage panic" had finally come true.

THE NO-FAULT DISASTER: A TALE OF TWO DIVORCE REPORTS

In the 1970s, many states passed new "no-fault" divorce laws that made the process easier: They eliminated the moralistic grounds required to obtain a divorce and divided up a marriage's assets based on needs and resources without reference to which party was held responsible for the marriage's failure. In the 1980s, these "feminist-inspired" laws came under attack: The New Right painted them as schemes to undermine the family, and the media and popular writers portrayed them as inadvertent betrayals of women and children, legal slingshots that "threw thousands of middle-class women," as a typical chronicler put it, "into impoverished states."

Perhaps no one person did more to fuel the attack on divorce-law reform in the backlash decade than sociologist Lenore Weitzman, whose 1985 book, *The Divorce Revolution: The Unexpected Social and Economic Consequences for Women and Children in America,* supplied the numbers quoted by everyone assailing the new laws. From Phyllis Schlafly to Betty Friedan, from the National Review to the "CBS Evening News," Weitzman's "devastating" statistics were invoked as proof that women who sought freedom from unhappy marriages were making a big financial mistake: They would wind up poorer under the new laws—worse off than if they had divorced under the older, more "protective" system, or if they had simply stayed married.

This is Weitzman's thesis: "The major economic result of the divorce-law revolution is the systematic impoverishment of divorced women and their children." Under the old "fault" system, Weitzman wrote, the "innocent" party stood to receive more than half the property—an arrangement that she says generally worked to the wronged wife's benefit. The new system, on the other hand, hurts women because it is too equal—and even-handedness is hurting older homemakers most of all. "The legislation of equality," she wrote, "actually resulted in a worsened position for women and, by extension, a worsened position for children."

Weitzman's work did not say feminists were responsible for the new no-fault laws, but those who promoted her work most often acted as if her book indicted the women's movement. *The Divorce Revolution*, Time magazine informed its readers, shows how 43 states passed no-fault laws "largely in response to feminist demand." A flurry of anti-no-fault books, most of them knockoffs of Weitzman's work, blamed the women's movement for divorced women's poverty. "The impact of the divorce revolution is a clear example of how an equal-rights orientation has failed women," Mary Ann Mason wrote in *The Equality Trap*. "Judges are receiving the message the feminists are sending."

Actually, feminists had almost nothing to do with divorce-law reform—as Weitzman herself pointed out. The 1970 California no-fault law, considered the most radical for its equal-division rule, was drafted by a largely male advisory board, appointed by then-Gov. Ronald Reagan. The American Bar Association, not the National Organization for Women, instigated the national "divorce revolution"—to streamline the legal apparatus and make the process less adversarial. At the time of Weitzman's work, half the states still had the traditional "fault" system on their books, with no-fault only as an option. Only eight states had actually passed community property provisions like the California law, and only a few required equal property division.

Weitzman argued that because women and men are differently situated upon divorce—that is, the husbands usually make more money and the wives usually get the kids—treating the spouses equally winds up overcompensating the husband and cheating the wife and children. On its face, this argument seems reasonable enough, and Weitzman appeared to have the statistics to prove it: "The research shows that on the average, divorced women and the minor children in their households experience a 73 percent decline in their standard of living in the first year after divorce. Their former husbands, in contrast, experience a 42 percent rise in their standard of living."

These figures sounded alarming, and the press willingly passed them on—without asking two basic questions: Were Weitzman's statistics correct? And, even more important, did she actually show that women fared worse under the new divorce laws than under the old?

In the summer of 1986, soon after Lenore Weitzman had finished testifying before Congress on the failings of no-fault divorce, she received a letter from Saul Hoffman, an economist at the University of Delaware who specializes in divorce statistics. He wrote that he and his partner, University of Michigan social scientist Greg Duncan, were a little bewildered by her now famous 73 percent statistic. They had been tracking the effect of divorce on income for two decades—through the landmark "5,000 Families" study—and they had found the changes following divorce to be nowhere near as dramatic as she described. They discovered a much smaller 30 percent decline in women's living standards in the first year after divorce and a much smaller 10 to 15 percent improvement for men. Moreover, Hoffman observed, a lower living standard for many divorced women may be temporary. Five years after divorce, the average woman's living standard was actually slightly *higher* than when she was married to her ex-husband.

What baffled Hoffman and Duncan most was that Weitzman claimed in her book to have used *their* methods to arrive at her 73 percent statistic. Hoffman's letter wondered if he and Duncan might take a look at her data. No reply.

Hoffman called. Weitzman told him she "didn't know how to get hold of her data," Hoffman recalls, because she was at Princeton and her data was at Harvard. The next time he called, he says, Weitzman said she couldn't give him the information because she had broken her arm on a ski vacation. When the demographers appealed to the

National Science Foundation [NSF], which had helped fund her research, Weitzman relented and promised she would archive her data tapes at Radcliffe's Murray Research Center. But six months later, the tapes still weren't there. Again, Hoffman appealed to NSF officials. Finally, in late 1990, the library began receiving Weitzman's data. As of this fall, the archives' researchers were still sorting through the files, and they weren't yet in shape to be reviewed.

In the meantime, Duncan and Hoffman repeated Weitzman's calculations using the numbers from her book. But they still came up with a 33 percent, not a 73 percent, decline in women's standard of living a year after divorce. The two demographers published this finding in the journal Demography. "Weitzman's highly publicized findings are almost certainly in error," they wrote. Not only was the 73 percent figure "suspiciously large," it was "inconsistent with information on changes in income and per capita income that she reports."

The press response? The Wall Street Journal acknowledged Duncan and Hoffman's article in a brief item in the newspaper's demography column. No one else picked it up.

Weitzman never responded to Duncan and Hoffman's critique. "They are just wrong," she said later in a phone interview. "It does compute." She refused to answer any additional questions put to her. "You have my position. I'm working on something very different, and I just don't have the time."

Confirmation of Duncan and Hoffman's findings came from the U.S. Census Bureau, which issued its study on the economic effects of divorce in March 1991. The results were in line with Duncan and Hoffman's. "[Weitzman's] numbers are way too high," says Suzanne Bianchi, the Census study's author. "And that 73 percent figure that keeps getting thrown around isn't even consistent with other numbers in [Weitzman's] work."

How could Weitzman's conclusions have been so far off the mark? There are several possible explanations. First, her statistics, unlike Duncan and Hoffman's, were not based on a national sample. She drew the people she interviewed exclusively from Los Angeles County. Second, her sample was remarkably small—114 divorced women and 114 divorced men. (And her response rate was so low that Duncan and Hoffman and other demographers who reviewed her work questioned whether her sample was even representative of Los Angeles.)

Finally, Weitzman drew her financial information on these divorced couples from a notoriously unreliable source—their own memories. "We were amazed at their ability to recall precisely the appraised value of their house, the amount of the mortgage, the value of the pension plan, etc.," she wrote in her book. Yet memory, particularly in the emotion-charged realm of divorce, is hardly a reliable source of statistics.

To be fair, the 73 percent statistic is only one number in Weitzman's work. While the media fixed on its sensational implications, the specific figure had little bearing on her second and more central point—that women are worse off since "the divorce revolution." This is important because it gets to the heart of the backlash argument: Women are better off "protected" than equal.

Though Weitzman's book stated repeatedly that the new laws have made life "worse" for women, it strangely concluded by recommending that legislators should keep the new divorce laws with a little fine-tuning. And she strongly warned against a return to the old system, which she called a "charade" of fairness. "It is clear that it would be unwise and inappropriate to suggest that California return to a more traditional system," she wrote.

A closer reading explains why Weitzman was ultimately forced to contradict her own theory on no-fault divorce: She had conducted interviews only with men and women who divorced after the 1970 no-fault law went into effect in California. She had no comparable data on couples who divorced under the old system—and so no way of testing her hypothesis. (A 1990 study by two law professors reached the opposite conclusion: Women and children, they found, were slightly better off economically under the no-fault provisions.)

Nonetheless, Weitzman suggested she had two other types of evidence to show that divorcing women suffered more under no-fault law. Divorcing women, she wrote, are less likely to be awarded alimony under the new legislation—a loss most painful to older homemakers who are ill-equipped to enter the work force. Second, women are now often forced to sell the family house. Yet Weitzman failed to make the case on either count.

National data collected by the U.S. Census Bureau show that the percentage of women awarded alimony or maintenance payments (all told a mere 14 percent) is not significantly different from what it was in the 1920s. Weitzman acknowledged this in her book but argued that one group of women—long-married and traditional housewives—have been hurt most by the new laws. Yet her own data showed the opposite, that older housewives and long-married women are the only divorced groups who actually are being awarded alimony in *greater* numbers under the new laws than they were under the old. She reported a remarkable increase of 21 percent in the number of housewives married more than 10 years who are awarded alimony under the new laws.

Her other point was that under no-fault "equal division" rules, the couple increasingly is forced to sell the house, whereas under the old laws, she said, the judge traditionally gave it to the wife. But the new divorce laws don't require house sales and, in fact, the authors of the California law explicitly stated that judges shouldn't use the law to force divorced mothers and their children from the home.

The example Weitzman gave of a forced house sale is in itself harshly illuminating. A 38-year-old divorcing housewife wanted to remain in the home where the family had lived for 15 years. Not only did she want to spare her teenage son further disruption, she couldn't afford to move because the child support and alimony payments the judge

had granted were so low. In desperation, she offered to sacrifice her portion of her husband's pension plan, about $85,000, if only he would let her stay in the house. He wouldn't. She tried next to refinance the house and pay off her husband that way, but no bank would give her a loan based on spousal support. In court, the judge was no more yielding:

"I begged the judge," she told Weitzman. "All I wanted was enough time for Brian [her son] to adjust to the divorce . . . I broke down and cried on the stand . . . but the judge refused. He gave me three months to move . . . My husband's attorney threatened me with contempt if I wasn't out on time."

The real source of divorced women's woes can be found not in the fine print of divorce legislation but in the behavior of ex-husbands and judges. Between 1978 and 1985, the average amount of child support that divorced men actually paid fell nearly 25 percent. One study in the early '80s found that divorced men were more likely to meet their car payments than their child support obligations—even though, for two-thirds of them, the amount owed their children was *less* than their monthly auto loan payment.

As of 1985, only half of the 8.8 million single mothers who were supposed to be receiving child support payments from their ex-husbands actually received any money at all, and only half of that half were actually getting the full amount. By 1988, the Federal Office of Child Support Enforcement, which oversees state and local agencies' efforts to collect from delinquent parents, found that only $5 billion of the $25 billion in unpaid support owed by fathers had been collected. And studies on child support collection strategies are finding that only one tactic seems to awaken the moral conscience of negligent fathers: mandatory jail sentences.

At the same time, public and judicial officials aren't setting much of an example. A 1988 federal audit found that 35 states weren't complying with federal child support laws. And judges weren't even upholding the egalitarian principles of no-fault. Instead, surveys in several states found that judges were arbitrarily misinterpreting the statutes to mean that women should get not one-half but *one-third* of all assets from the marriage. Weitzman herself reached the conclusion that judicial antagonism to feminism was aggravating the rough treatment of contemporary divorced women. "The concept of 'equality' and the sex-neutral language of the law," she wrote, have been "used by some lawyers and judges as a mandate for 'equal treatment' with a vengeance, a vengeance that can only be explained as a backlash reaction to women's demands for equality in the larger society."

In the end, the most effective way to correct the post-divorce inequities between the sexes is simple: Correct pay inequality in the work force. If the wage gap were wiped out between the sexes, a federal advisory council concluded in 1982, one-half of female-headed households would be instantly lifted out of poverty. "The dramatic increase in women working is the best kind of insurance against this vulnerability," demographer Greg Duncan says, observing that women's recent access to better-paying jobs has saved a lot of divorced women from a far worse living standard. And that access, he points out, "is largely a product of the women's movement."

THE GREAT FEMALE DEPRESSION: WOMEN ON THE VERGE OF A NERVOUS BREAKDOWN

In the backlash yearbook, two types of women were named Most Likely to Break Down: the unmarried and the gainfully employed. According to dozens of news features, advice books and women's health manuals, single women were suffering from "record" levels of depression and professional women were succumbing to "burnout"—a syndrome that supposedly caused a wide range of mental and physical illnesses from dizzy spells to heart attacks.

In the mid-'80s, several epidemiological mental health studies noted a rise in mental depression among baby boomers, a phenomenon that soon inspired popular-psychology writers to dub the era "The Age of Melancholy." Casting about for an explanation for the generation's gloom, therapists and journalists quickly fastened upon the women's movement. If baby-boom women hadn't gained their independence, their theory went, then the single ones would be married and the careerists would be home with their children—in both cases, feeling calmer, healthier and saner.

The rising mental distress of single women "is a phenomenon of this era, it really is," psychologist Annette Baran asserted in a 1986 Los Angeles Times article, one of many on the subject. "I would suspect," she said, "that the great majority of any psychotherapist's practice—maybe two-thirds—is single women who have relationship problems." A 1988 article in New York Woman magazine issued the same verdict: Single women have "stampeded" therapists' offices, a "virtual epidemic." The magazine quoted psychologist Janice Lieberman, who said, "These women come into treatment convinced there's something terribly wrong with them." And, she assured us, there is: "Being single too long is traumatic."

In fact, no one knew whether single women were more or less depressed in the '80s; no epidemiological study has actually tracked changes in single women's mental health. As psychological researcher Lynn L. Gigy, one of the few in her profession to study single women, has noted, social science still treats unmarried women like "statistical deviants." They have been "virtually ignored in social theory and research." But the lack of data hasn't discouraged advice experts, who have been blaming single women for rising mental illness rates since at least the 19th century, when leading psychiatrists described the typical victim of neurasthenia as "a woman, generally single, or in some way not in a condition for performing her reproductive function."

As it turns out, social scientists *have* established one fact about single women's mental health: Employment improves it. The 1983 landmark "Lifeprints" study found poor employment, not poor marriage prospects, the leading cause of mental distress among single women. Researchers from the Institute for Social Research and the National Center for Health Statistics, reviewing two decades of federal data on women's health, came up with similar results: "Of the three factors we examined [employment, marriage, children], employment has by far the strongest and most consistent tie to women's good health." Single women who worked, they found, were in far better mental and physical shape than married women, with or without children, who stayed home. Finally, in a rare longitudinal study that treated single women as a category, researchers Pauline Sears and Ann Barbee found that of the women they tracked, never-married single women reported the greatest satisfaction with their lives—and single women who had worked most of their lives were the most satisfied of all.

While demographers haven't charted historical changes in single women's psychological status, they have collected a vast amount of data comparing the mental health of single and married women. None of it supports the thesis that single women are causing the "age of melancholy." On the contrary, study after study shows single women enjoying far better mental health than their married sisters (and, in a not unrelated phenomenon, making more money). The warning issued by family sociologist Jessie Bernard in 1972 still holds true: "Marriage may be hazardous to women's health."

Married women report about 20 percent more depression than single women and three times the rate of severe neurosis. Married women are plagued by more insomnia, trembling hands, dizzy spells, nightmares, hypochondria, passivity, agoraphobia and other phobias, unhappiness with their physical appearance and overwhelming feelings of guilt and shame.

A 25-year longitudinal study of college-educated women found that housewives had the lowest self-esteem, felt the least attractive, reported the most loneliness and considered themselves the least competent at almost every task—even child care. The Mills

Longitudinal Study, which tracked women for more than three decades, reported in 1990 that "traditional" married women ran a higher risk of developing mental and physical ailments in their lifetime than single women—from depression to migraines, from high blood pressure to colitis. Finally, when mental health researchers Gerald Klerman and Myrna Weissman reviewed all the depression literature on women and tested for factors ranging from genetics to PMS to birth control pills, they could find only two prime causes for female depression: low social status and marriage.

If mentally imbalanced single women weren't causing the "age of melancholy," then could it be worn-out career women? Given that employment improves women's mental health, this would seem unlikely. But the "burnout" experts of the '80s were ready to make a case for it anyway.

"Women's burnout has come to be a most prevalent condition in our modern culture," psychologists Herbert Freudenberger and Gail North warned in *Women's Burnout*, one of a raft of potboilers on this "ailment" to hit bookstores in the decade. "More and more, I hear about women pushing themselves to the point of physical and/or psychological collapse," Marjorie Hansen Shaevitz wrote in *The Superwoman Syndrome*. "A surprising number of female corporate executives walk around with a bottle of tranquilizers," Daniel Crane alerted readers in Savvy. Burnout's afflictions were legion. As *The Type E Woman* advised, "Working women are swelling the epidemiological ranks of ulcer cases, drug and alcohol abuse, depression, sexual dysfunction and a score of stress-induced physical ailments, including backache, headache, allergies, and recurrent viral infections and flu." But that's not all. Other experts added to this list heart attacks, strokes, hypertension, nervous breakdowns, suicides and cancer. "Women are freeing themselves up to die like men," asserted James Lynch, author of several burnout tomes, pointing to what he claimed was a rise in rates of drinking, smoking, heart disease and suicide among career women.

The experts provided virtually no statistical research, just anecdotes—and periodic jabs at feminism, which they quickly identified as the burnout virus. "The women's liberation movement started it" with "a full-scale female invasion" of the work force, *Women Under Stress* maintained, and now many misled women are belatedly discovering that "the toll in stress may not be worth the rewards." The authors warned, "sometimes women get so enthused with women's liberation that they accept jobs for which they are not qualified."

The message behind all this: Go home. "Although being a full-time homemaker has its own stresses," Georgia Witkin-Lanoil wrote in *The Female Stress Syndrome*, "in some ways it is the easier side of the coin."

Yet the actual evidence—dozens of comparative studies on working and nonworking women—all points the other way. Whether they are professional or blue-collar workers, working women experience less depression than housewives; the more challenging the career, the better their mental and physical health. Women who have never worked have the highest levels of depression. Working women are less susceptible than housewives to mental disorders—from suicides and nervous breakdowns to insomnia and nightmares. They report less anxiety and take fewer psychotropic drugs than women who stay home. "Inactivity," as a study based on the U.S. Health Interview Survey data concludes, ". . . may create the most stress."

Career women in the '80s were not causing a rise in heart attacks and high blood pressure among women. There was no such rise: Due to medical advances and health and fitness consciousness, heart disease deaths among women have dropped 43 percent since 1963; most of that decline has been since 1972, when women's participation in professional and managerial jobs took off. The incidence of hypertension among women has likewise declined since the early '70s. Only the lung cancer rate has increased, and that is the legacy not of feminism but of the massive mid-century ad campaign to hook women on smoking. Since the '70s, the total number of women smokers has dropped.

The importance of paid work to women's self-esteem is basic and longstanding. Even in the "feminine mystique" '50s, when married women were asked what gave them a sense of purpose and self-worth, two-thirds said their jobs; only one-third said homemaking. In the '80s, 87 percent of women said it was their work that gave them personal satisfaction and a sense of accomplishment. In short, as one large scale study concludes, "Women's health is hurt by their *lower* [emphasis added] labor-force participation rates."

By helping to widen women's access to more and better employment, the women's rights campaign couldn't help but be beneficial to women's mental outlook. A U.S. National Sample Survey study, conducted between 1957 and 1976, found vast improvements in women's mental health. The famous 1980 Midtown Manhattan Longitudinal Study found that adult women's rate of mental health impairment had fallen 50 to 60 percent since the early '50s. Midtown Manhattan project director Leo Srole concluded that women's increasing autonomy and economic strength had made the difference. The changes, he wrote, "are not mere chance coincidences of the play of history, but reflect a cause-and-effect connection between the partial emancipation of women from their 19th-century status of sexist servitude, and their 20th-century advances in subjective well-being."

If anything threatened women's emotional well-being in the '80s, it was the backlash itself, which worked to undermine women's social and economic status—the two pillars on which good mental health is built. As even one of the "burnout" manuals concedes, "There is a direct link between sexism and female stress." How the current counter-assault on women's rights will affect women's rate of mental illness, however, remains to be seen.

Who, then, was experiencing the baby boomer's "age of melancholy"? In 1984, the National Institute of Mental Health unveiled the results of its most comprehensive mental health survey, the Epidemiological Catchment Area (ECA) study, which drew data from five sites around the country and in Canada. Its key finding, largely ignored in the press: "The overall rates for all disorders for both sexes are now similar."

Women have historically outnumbered men in their reports of depression by a 3-to-1 ratio. But the ECA data, collected between 1980 and 1983, indicated that the "depression gap" had shrunk to less than 2-to-1. In fact, in some epidemiological studies of mental health, the depression gap barely even existed. In part, the narrowing depression gap reflected women's brightened mental picture—but, even more so, it signaled a darkening outlook for men. Epidemiological researchers observed a notable increase especially in depressive disorders among men in their twenties and thirties. While women's level of anxiety was declining, men's was rising. While women's suicide rate had peaked in 1960, men's was climbing. The rates of attempted suicide for men and women were converging, too, as men's rate increased more rapidly than women's.

While the effects of the women's movement may not have depressed women, they did seem to trouble many men. In a review of three decades of research literature on sex differences in mental health, social scientists Ronald C. Kessler and James A. McRae, Jr., with the University of Michigan's Institute for Social Research, concluded: "It is likely that men are experiencing more rapidly role-related stresses than are women." The role changes that women have embraced "are helping to close the male-female mental-health gap largely by increasing the distress of men." While women's improving mental health stems from their rising employment rate, the researchers said, at the same time "the increase in distress among men can be attributed, in part, to depression and loss of self-esteem related to the increasing tendency of women to take a job outside the home." For many men in the '80s, this effect was exacerbated by that other

well-established threat to mental health—loss of economic status—as millions of traditional "male" jobs that once yielded a living wage evaporated in a restructuring economy. Observing the dramatic shifts in the mental-health sex ratios that were occurring in manufacturing communities, Jane Murphy, chief of psychiatric epidemiology at Massachusetts General Hospital, wrote in 1984: "Have changes in the occupational structure of this society created a situation that is, in some ways, better for the goose than for the gander . . . ?" As Michigan's Kessler put it in an interview, researchers who focus on the female side of the mental health equation are likely missing the main event: "In the last 30 years, the sex difference [in mental illness] is getting smaller largely because *men* are getting worse."

Numerous mental health reports published in the last decade support this assertion. A 1980 study finds husbands of working women reporting higher levels of depression than husbands of housewives. A 1982 study of 2,440 adults at the University of Michigan's Survey Research Center finds depression and low self-esteem among married men closely associated with their wives' employment. A 1986 analysis of the federal Quality of Employment Survey concludes that "dual earning may be experienced as a downward mobility for men and upward mobility for women." Husbands of working women, the researchers found, had greater psychological distress, lower self-esteem, and greater depression than men wed to homemakers. "There lies behind the facade of egalitarian lifestyle pioneering an anxiety among men that cannot be cured by time alone," they concluded. The fact is, they wrote, "conventional standards of manhood remain more important in terms of personal evaluation than contemporary rhetoric of gender equality."

A 1987 study of role-related stresses, conducted by a team of researchers from the University of Michigan, the University of Illinois and Cornell University, makes the same connection and observes that men's psychological well-being appears to be significantly threatened when their wives work. "Given that previous research on changing gender roles has concentrated on women to the neglect of men," they wrote, "this result suggests that such an emphasis has been misleading and that serious effort is needed to understand the ways changing female roles affect the lives and attitudes of men."

This warning, however, went virtually unheeded in the press. When Newsweek produced its May 1987 cover story on depression, it put a grim-faced woman on the cover—and, inside, all but two of the nine victims it displayed were female too.

66

Equality: Why We Can't Wait

Adolph Reed, Jr., and Julian Bond

This article reviews several books and articles which epitomize the liberal explanation for the declining popularity of progressive social movements. The liberal position is analyzed from an historical perspective that recognizes the racial stratification of the American working class as well as the widespread white support for both occupational and residential segregation. The authors conclude with a call for a principled stand against racism and for social equality.

Exercises to Guide Your Reading

1. Explain the terms "racist opportunism" and "progressive social agenda." Give examples of each.
2. Paraphrase the liberal argument concerning the role of race in defeating the progressive social agenda.
3. Identify similarities between the cultural backlash against feminism and the opportunism of racial victim-blaming.
4. Give examples of historical revisionism.

A specter is haunting liberal-left intellectual life—the specter of racist opportunism. From prestigious sociology departments to *The Atlantic, The American Prospect, Dissent* and *In These Times*, from *Washington Post* pundits to *New York Newsday* editors, its victim-blaming message echoes: Liberal and progressive forces have fallen onto hard times in American politics because they have become too closely identified with the excessive demands of blacks, feminists, etc. and have failed to give proper weight to the concerns of the beleaguered white working and middle classes. This story is rapidly congealing into an unexamined orthodoxy, a ritual lament that seeks to justify what is at best a failure of nerve.

In this lament, progressive agendas lost credibility, and/or Democrats lost the White House, because they deviated from the old New Deal coalition's focus on universalistic programs and became identified with "special interests." This alienated the Democratic Party's white working- and middle-class constituency, which both carried the fiscal burden for the programs targeted to others and felt that many of the specific programs affronted their own "traditional values."

Versions of this tale have proliferated. Some, like Theda Skocpol's in "Sustainable Social Policy: Fighting Poverty Without Poverty Programs" (*The American Prospect*, Summer 1990) and William Julius Wilson's in *The*

Reprinted by permission of *The Nation.* December 9, 1991. pp. 733–37.

Truly Disadvantaged and "Race-Neutral Policies and the Democratic Coalition" (*The American Prospect*, Spring 1990), concentrate on bemoaning the alleged hijacking of liberal social policy in the 1960s by small-minded black militants who insisted on race-targeted programs and censored public discussion of social pathologies among the black poor. Others, like Jonathan Rieder's in *Canarsie: The Jews and Italians of Brooklyn Against Liberalism*, and Jim Sleeper's in *The Closest of Strangers: Liberalism and the Politics of Race in New York*, champion the cause of whites who feel threatened by feminist demands and liberal initiatives aimed at advancing racial equality. The most extensive and coherent statement of the new orthodoxy by far, however, is Thomas Byrne Edsall and Mary D. Edsall's new tract, *Chain Reaction: The Impact of Race, Rights, and Taxes on American Politics*. Because of its comprehensiveness the Edsalls' volume epitomizes the current vogue.

For the Edsalls the meter of history starts running in the mid-1960s. At that point Goldwaterite Republicans began what would become a successful polarization of American politics around the issues of racial liberalism, the proliferation of groups claiming institutionalized rights, and government spending—all three of which came to be identified with the Democratic Party.

The Goldwaterites were aided in this mission, the Edsalls say, by the "violent contagion of race riots in northern slums," the inflammatory antics of "black extremists" (who even taught right-wingers that "confrontation and rejection of accommodation were themselves mobilizing strategies") and the "reluctance of liberalism and the Democratic party to forthrightly acknowledge and address the interaction of crime, welfare dependency, joblessness, drug use, and illegitimacy with the larger questions of race and poverty." Although blacks' bad and insensitive behavior is pivotal in the Edsalls' story, others also contributed to the new polarization by "threatening the most entrenched traditions of the middle class"; among them were those who fought to se-

cure constitutional protection for criminal defendants, advocates of reproductive liberty and proponents of gay rights.

Having laid this foundation, the Edsalls adorn it with many of the standard pieces of the new line. They present Daniel Patrick Moynihan's racist, scurrilously misogynous 1965 report, *The Negro Family: The Case for National Action*, as an unfairly scorned work of prophetic insight, and they even attempt to legitimize it by linking it to W.E.B. Du Bois's 1899 study, *The Philadelphia Negro*—also a standard move at the moment. (They neglect to mention, however, that Moynihan called for correcting young black men's putative character defects by shipping them into a "world away from women" in the military, coincidentally just as cannon-fodder needs were increasing along with escalations in Vietnam.) The Edsalls' attempt to vindicate Moynihan is part of a general attack on those who have dissented from victim-blaming rhetoric, particularly regarding inner-city poor people. Worse yet, the Edsalls say, liberals and the left have been irresponsible not only in failing to face up to poor blacks' socially destructive behavior but also in pursuing divisive strategies of social engineering in struggles for the integration of schools and public housing in Northern cities like Boston and Chicago.

They adduce these actions to show how the spread of civil rights activism in the North created a "growing link between race and partisan allegiance"—the core of their argument that a "chain reaction" driven by race has transformed the white electorate. And who is to blame? Upper-status white liberals and "extremist" or undeserving blacks undermined the Democratic coalition by challenging "traditionally" Democratic whites who were affronted by civil rights agendas. This combination of black bad behavior and white liberal insensitivity produced an "ugly disenchantment" with black aspirations, reaching from "the bungalow wards of Chicago ... to prominent public intellectuals" like Norman Mailer.

In the context of this backlash, the Edsalls portray "ordinary citizens," the "average working man and woman" (to be "average" and "ordinary," of course, one must be white), as repelled by liberals' forsaking of "standardized merit-oriented criteria" for "racial preferences in hiring and in education." Listen carefully to their history of the period: "Lawsuits forcing court-ordered hiring and promotion in unions and in police and fire departments *were driving* a wedge between formerly Democratic white workers and . . . black competitors"; "affirmative action was forcing divisive conflicts between . . . Jews and blacks." [Emphasis added.]

But this formulation, in presuming a prior compatibility, denies the reality of explicitly racial stratification within the working class and a history of white working-class antagonism toward blacks—coexisting, certainly, with many exemplary instances of interracial solidarity—that stretches back through the 1863 New York draft riot. This antagonism was visible after Reconstruction in the widespread expulsion of blacks from occupational niches in cities both North and South, and active, often militant, support for occupational and residential segregation. Unfortunately, the Edsalls are so locked into an image of black demands as the root of all evil that they do not bother to consider why, after all, there was ever a need for aggressive anti-discrimination efforts in the first place.

Edsall and Edsall never explain why they choose to start their story when they do, why they focus it the way they do, why they tell it the way they do—despite the fact that alternative interpretations yielding different conclusions exist at every point. Take their view of deindustrialization: Jobs leave, local economies change and wage scales drop as a result of "economic forces." That construction sets the stage for jeremiads about the exigencies of "global competition," which leaves "little or no room for traditional liberal Democratic policies sheltering the disadvantaged." With that, they issue what amounts to a warning to the left to shut up and get with the program:

> Intensified international competition will exert increasingly brutal pressure on America's economic and political systems, and on policies offering special protection, preference, or subsidy to groups within the population—whether they be ethnic or racial minorities, unskilled workers, prisoners, elected officials, the elderly, the disabled, AIDS victims, or single mothers.

Yet this story's inexorability is a function of its narrow perspective. A different, more textured explanation of the foundations of the postwar governing synthesis and the tensions within it is provided by Alan Wolfe's *America's Impasse*; Barry Bluestone and Bennett Harrison's *The Deindustrialization of America*; and Samuel Bowles, David Gordon and Thomas Weisskopf's *Beyond the Waste Land*. These authors demystify the public sector/private sector distinction, demonstrating the ubiquity of government intervention to cement loyalties by using public policy to channel the flow of material resources. They illuminate the extent to which corporate choices and American public policy—foreign and domestic—are implicated in urban, regional and national deindustrialization. Had they taken this analysis into account, the Edsalls might have been constrained (a) to explain why only *certain* categories of domestic public spending become stigmatized as "welfare" and (b) to come out from behind their smokescreen of claptrap about the exigencies of global competition and affirm as their own the vision they project to be the ineluctable course of American politics and policy.

Similarly, they simply recycle the canard—legitimized by William Julius Wilson's black imprimatur—that the left was responsible for the backlash against antipoverty policy because of its refusal to confront the issue of social pathology among the poor. That charge is a complete falsehood, and one the Edsalls elide (like the blank in the Watergate tape) with the gaps in their bibliography. In fact, the pervasive spread of mean-spirited rhetoric about poverty in the 1980s was surprising precisely because careful and thorough liberal scholarship had so recently demolished its prior incarnation as "culture of poverty" ideology in the 1960s and 1970s. The Edsalls ignore Carol Stack's accessible and widely read *All Our Kin*, which directly challenged Moynihan's pathological-matriarchy thesis with ethnographic data, and fail to recognize Eleanor Leacock's *The Culture of Poverty: A Critique* and Charles Valentine's *Culture and Poverty*, which systematically refuted the culture-of-poverty idea on both theoretical and empirical grounds as anthropologically and politically bankrupt.

Because theirs is the most elaborate presentation to date, the Edsalls most clearly reveal the complex of distortions and mystifications on which the new orthodoxy rests. They write as if American society emerged in 1964 from a state of nature. Only by doing so can they represent white working-class and middle-class hostility to black aspirations as a post–civil rights movement phenomenon, or romanticize the old New Deal Democratic coalition as an entity neutral with respect to distinctively racial stratification. This convenient amnesia sustains the lie that the put-upon Joe Six-Pack and the "average family" are not directly implicated as beneficiaries of the racially stratified system.

The Edsalls insulate the absurdity of this view by packing around it a comparably mystified notion of the suburbs as a new, coherent political constituency. For them, the phenomenon of postwar suburbanization had nothing to do with pre-existing racial polarization, and thus the attitude of white suburbanites now is a reaction against what they see as the excesses of the inner city. But the desire to flee from impoverished inner-city populations (and from blacks in general) that the Edsalls describe long preceded post-war suburbanization and was, in fact, one of the forces that drove it. While it is true that not living within the same municipality certainly reinforces white separation from inner-city life, suburbanization is more the effect than the cause of polarization. In addition, there are suburbs, and there are suburbs. Invocation of "suburban" as a euphemism for white, or even

middle class, is not exactly accurate, as suburban life itself becomes increasingly diverse. Interestingly, the Edsalls demonstrate the polysemous character of the suburban image in their own stereotypes. On the one hand, they decry out-of-touch "suburban liberals" who ram race-mixing down the throats of the sturdy white working and middle classes; on the other, the suburb appears as a spawning ground for white racial impatience. Which is the real suburb, then—not to mention polyglot entities like East Orange, New Jersey; Mount Vernon, New York; Skokie, Illinois; Montgomery County, Maryland; De Kalb County, Georgia; Santa Clara County, California?

To their credit, the Edsalls note the major role of civil rights enforcement and government employment in accounting for the post-1964 rise in black income and occupational mobility. Yet they scold liberals for having aimed antidiscrimination efforts at unabashedly racial monopolies in building trade unions and municipal employment, efforts that "required whites to give up both customary privileges and substantial material rewards." They allow that those "practices clearly had discriminatory consequences, but they were also practices core to a host of craft unions across the country, unions that had been built not only as labor organizations, but as family and ethnic associations structuring community life." They veer from this sentimentality, worthy of any Old South apologist, to an ostensible pragmatism. True, they admit, exclusionary practices had meant "denial of jobs to blacks for several hundred years, but the remedies were often zero-sum solutions in which the gains of one group were losses for the other." They imply the existence of some other course, but they offer no hint as to what it might be. We might infer that blacks simply should have foregone economic opportunity in deference to those whites' traditional values, but once again the authors avoid coming clean.

It is instructive in this regard that the Edsalls identify race rather than racism as the pivotal issue. In so doing they reflect a longstanding sentiment that American politics and life would be better, neater, more pure if we could somehow get race out of it. This sentiment has been around since the Founding and has had adherents at all points on the ideological spectrum. In its milder forms it appears as a high-minded but naïve call to transcend race; its most virulent strains—seen most recently in David Duke's gubernatorial campaign—seek to expunge blacks (and/or other nonwhites) from the body politic. On the left it typically has been expressed in exhortations to subordinate the pursuit of racial justice to some other mission—building the (white) labor movement, advancing the agendas of petit-bourgeois white women, preserving the New Deal coalition, not hurting white people's feelings or their "traditional values." This sentiment rests on reluctance to admit the endemic and pervasive character of explicitly racial stratification in American society and thus reluctance to accept the equally explicit struggle for racial justice as a necessarily integral component of our political life. At bottom it stems from an inability to perceive black Americans as legitimate, full members of the polity. That is the ugly truth that hides within all the sophistry about universal versus targeted federal programs and leaks out in every reference to put-upon "average Americans"; blacks are construed as Americans with an asterisk, a problem for a non-black civic "us."

The contributors to this *Nation** special issue have come together around a conviction that the new orthodoxy and its premises must be challenged. We believe that it is not only wrongheaded and dangerous but also, in its essential particulars and overall interpretation, simply false. These contributions, therefore, present critiques of the orthodoxy's central components and provide richer, more credible accounts. The authors demystify the breezily nostalgic representation of an Edenic New Deal coalition and

*Special edition of *The Nation* was titled "The Assault on Equality: Race, Rights and the New Orthodoxy."

demonstrate ways that racial stratification continues to order the life chances of America's citizens.

Finally, at the risk of seeming defensive about our own pasts, we must take note of the curious circumstance that in virtually all versions of the narrative against which we write, the mid-1960s appear as the Fall. Some proponents of that view depict an era, moreover, most unfamiliar to those of us who were around at the time. In Theda Skocpol and William Julius Wilson's 1960s, for example, "black militants" were powerful enough to dictate the terms of federal social policy; in the Edsalls', only antiwar activists, not the war in Vietnam itself, caused domestic political conflict.

In some cases, perhaps, specific old personal grievances support this queer reading of 1960s radicalism. Perhaps it is also fed by beliefs that politics should not involve rocking the boat and convictions that minority poor people are a breed apart. Some liberals seem to be middle-aging into a tolerance of privilege that "just happens" to be racial. Across the board, though, this representation of the 1960s justifies a view that commitment to principle has little, if any, place in politics. It underwrites three strategic assumptions: (1) No price is too great to pay for the election of *any* Democrat to the presidency; (2) race is so monolithic and immutable a cleavage in American politics that progressive initiatives will inevitably fail if they openly endorse programs of racial justice; and (3) those "special interests" canonized in the 1960s—black Americans especially—must now do penance for the harm wrought by their profligate ways. We emphatically reject all three and insist that principle can indeed win.

One could just as easily look back to the 1960s and point the finger the other way. Many of us recall an understanding that part of the white left's mission was to organize and educate against racism within white middle- and working-class constituencies. That project obviously did not get very far, though many good people put a great deal of effort into it and continue to do so. Others either gave up or were fainthearted all along in their own commitment to the premise of racial equality. Thus we hear a *Realpolitik* that wants—in the mode of Liberal Republicanism in the 1870s—to "get beyond" the race issue by having minorities go away. That strategy is both obnoxious and doomed. Our only hope lies not in rejecting but in resuscitating the project of confronting racism in the white electorate for what it is and struggling with whites to overcome their commitments to racial privilege. Only then can we begin honestly and productively to discuss strategies for building a progressive movement that accounts for the complex and corrosive effects of racial stratification. No more euphemisms, no elaborate circumlocutions. Those who want to dispense with an egalitarian agenda should declare themselves forthrightly and stand on their convictions. That way we can all know who stands for what, and act accordingly.

67

The Bishops on the U.S. Economy

James R. Crotty and James R. Stormes

This article summarizes the economic report of the National Conference of Catholic Bishops and places this report in a sociohistoric context. The relationship between the pastoral letter and Pope John Paul II's encyclical *On Human Work* is explored. Suggestions for institutional change are reviewed.

Exercises to Guide Your Reading

1. Identify the moral aspects of economic activity.
2. Give examples of the immoral aspects of employer-employee relationships.
3. Discuss the strengths and weakness of economic democracy.
4. Evaluate the statement that "Human work has an ethical value of its own."

Several years ago, the National Conference of Catholic Bishops agreed to prepare a pastoral letter evaluating the U.S. economy from an ethical perspective. A group of thirty-odd influential conservatives (who christened themselves the Lay Commission on Catholic Social Teaching and the U.S. Economy) was "so worried by the expected anti-capitalist tone of the bishops' draft," according to the *Washington Post*, "that they launched a pre-emptive strike . . . in the form of [their] own economic statement." One of the bishops on the drafting committee, in turn, labeled the Lay Commission's letter "a panegyric of capitalism." Conservative columnist William F. Buckley called the draft pastoral letter a "sad . . . accumulation of lumpen cliches" while the *Wall Street Journal* complained that it "profoundly . . . misapprehends the nature of capitalism."

Such tension between the American Catholic hierarchy, powerful Catholic businessmen, and conservative intellectuals over the merits of our economy would have been un-thinkable twenty years ago. American bishops, it has been rightly said, used to bless the American economic system in the same way that they blessed battleships. The emergence of the bishops' critical perspective on the U.S. economy, we believe, can best be understood as the product of two distinct but related developments since the 1960s.

The first is the worldwide economic crisis of the 1970s and 1980s. These years have seen the onset of rising unemployment, economic instability, and secular stagnation in much of Europe and North America, along with a widening recognition among Church people that the crushing poverty of the great majority of the Third World's people will never be alleviated under existing economic and political institutional arrangements. The second is the profound change that has taken place in the way the Church understands its relation to "the world" since the Second Vatican Council of the 1960s. The Church has increasingly seen itself as an in-

Reprinted by permission of *Challenge*. March–April 1985. pp. 36–41.

tegral part of civil society; as such, it accepts a responsibility to help right the social evils that it sees around it. Recent Catholic teaching on peace and disarmament, as well as on the international economic order, reflects this development.

The bishops' pastoral letter should be seen in this light. Since it may represent the start of significant intervention by the Catholic hierarchy into the debate over U.S. economic policies, it deserves careful attention by economists.

WHAT THE BISHOPS' LETTER SAYS

"Economic policy, economic organization and economic relationships have a significance that goes beyond ... technical questions ... to profoundly human and therefore moral matters, including what we hope and believe about the destiny of humanity. Interpreting these moral aspects of economic activity in the light of the Gospel" is the task the bishops have set for themselves. Their letter evaluates the U.S. economy according to moral criteria drawn from Catholic social teaching; it indicates institutional arrangements where these criteria are not met and proposes alternative policies. (While a major part of the letter concerns the relationship of the U.S. economy to Third World countries and the world economy as a whole, in this article we will consider only the bishops' treatment of the domestic economy.)

The bishops use a summary question to judge economic institutions: "Do they permit all persons that measure of active social and economic participation which befits their common membership in the human community?" The fundamental concept of "active economic participation" has three aspects: access to a just share of economic benefits, opportunity for meaningful work, and involvement in decisions that affect one's economic life.

Catholic social thought holds that each person has the right to a just share of the goods of the earth, a teaching grounded in

the theology of creation. Creation is a gift given by God to all human beings because each shares in His dignity. Human dignity, the bishops write, "comes with human existence prior to any division into races or nations and prior to human labor and achievement." While the preferred way to obtain a just share of economic benefits is through fair remuneration for labor, when that is not possible (because of unemployment, illness, or childrearing responsibilities), the human community is still obligated to guarantee each of its members a standard of living in keeping with human dignity.

In light of this principle, the bishops judge that "the fact that so many people are poor in a nation as wealthy as ours is a social and moral scandal that cannot be ignored." They also state that "the distribution of income and wealth in the United States is so inequitable that it violates [the] minimum standard of distributive justice."

As the bishops see it, poverty and inequality are rooted in economic institutions and social structures; therefore, their substantial reduction will require fundamental structural change. The bishops cite several examples. First, traditional capital-investment priorities, which have caused entire communities to "fall victim to a downward cycle of poverty" because of plant closings, must give way to processes that value the "rights of workers over the maximization of profit." Second, an inhumane welfare system justified by a punitive attitude toward the poor must be replaced by adequately funded, participatory programs. Third, discrimination that keeps minorities and women from meaningful employment must end. Only economic institutions that support human dignity and enable people to take control of their own lives, the bishops argue, can guarantee a just division of economic benefits.

Creative and productive employment is the second vital form of participation in economic life. Through it, one can not only achieve a dignified standard of living, but also contribute to society and develop oneself. Unemployment destroys this form of participation, and the Church therefore condemns it as a social evil. Pope John Paul II's writings on the role of work have amplified Catholic teaching on this subject. In the pope's view, work is not simply income-producing activity. It is nothing less than human self-creation, the simultaneous fulfillment and transformation of one's material and spiritual needs. It is both a contribution to and a key form of integration into the life of the community. In the pope's words: "Human work has an ethical value of its own."

Applying this perspective, the bishops find any unemployment rate above a frictional level of 3 to 4 percent to be unacceptable; they consider recent U.S. unemployment rates "morally unjustified." They conclude that "the most urgent priority for U.S. domestic policy is the creation of new jobs with adequate pay and decent working conditions" and therefore recommend a number of policies, including the creation of long-term public service jobs and joint government-business programs of job creation using "tax policies, the allocation of credit, and other supportive services."

THE CALL FOR NEW INSTITUTIONS

The bishops recognize that sustained full employment will not be achieved as long as "the country shows no sign of making a full-scale commitment to the goal." Therefore, they recommend grassroots political activism to make full employment the top national priority. However, they are also aware that commitment alone will not get the job done. Meaningful work for all who seek it also requires the development of democratic and participatory institutions for economic decision-making.

This last demand is rooted in the view that social solidarity and mutual responsibility characterize any economy that respects human dignity. More explicitly, the right to participate in economic decision-making is seen as rooted in the intrinsic value of work, which the pope characterizes as an activity of "a conscious and free sub-

ject ... who decides about himself." Therefore, the bishops feel, "the development of social, economic and political means to exercise mutual responsibility is one of the most urgent challenges facing the U.S. economy today."

They take up this challenge with a call for "the creation of a new order ... of new ways of thinking ... of new institutions in a new 'American experiment' in economic democracy." This is essentially a call for democratic decision-making in the workplace and for democratic national economic planning. As such, it is certainly the most radical institutional demand in the letter.

At the level of the firm, the bishops want serious experiments with employee stock ownership, worker cooperatives, increased control of the quality of work-life, and so forth, all to be evaluated according to "their effectiveness in actually increasing the participation of employees in shaping decisions."

At the national level, planning is deemed a prerequisite to solving the problems of unemployment and poverty. While careful to state their opposition to "collectivist" and "statist" approaches to economic coordination, the bishops also reject the notion that the unimpeded market will guarantee economic rights. They propose an experiment, a search for new democratic and participatory models for establishing and implementing national economic priorities.

One implication of the bishops' letter is clear: when an economic system is judged to be incapable of providing minimally acceptable levels of participation, it is the economic system that must change, not the standards of participation. "All human beings," the bishops insist, "are ends to be served by the institutions which make up the economy, not means to be exploited for more narrowly defined goals."

THE BISHOPS AND THE POPE

Even this brief outline should make clear how opposed the bishops are to the priorities and policies of the Reagan Administration. The bishops are also far bolder in their demand for full employment and an expanded and reformed welfare system than the liberal wing of the Democratic Party. The pastoral letter places them far outside the mainstream of current economic and political thinking.

However, observers who have focused on the bishops' "radical" policy demands (conservative columnist George Will criticizes the "extremism" of the letter) or their call for more active government intervention (Michael Novak calls the letter "unabashedly statist") have overlooked the most significant and radical aspect of the letter—its wholehearted adoption of John Paul II's teaching, in his 1981 encyclical *On Human Work*, that human labor is the foundation of Catholic social thought. A *New York Times Magazine* article on August 12, 1984, just before the bishops' letter was released, is more insightful. It quotes Archbishop Weakland, the head of the committee that drafted the letter, as follows: "One of the most challenging statements in John Paul II's [*On Human Work*] is that the dignity of the workers demands that they have a part in the decisions that affect their lives." The article continues: "The Archbishop's emphasis makes it obvious that the current Pope's thinking, which some critics label as socialistic in its claims that workers have a right to share not only in the business profits but in the means of production as well, will have a strong influence in the letter's development."

The bishops' call for an experiment designed to build an institutional foundation for "economic democracy" in the United States reflects their acceptance of the pope's teaching. This new focus in social philosophy puts both the pope and the bishops—however reluctantly—in fundamental conflict with those who are committed to the priorities and processes embedded in basic American economic institutions. This being the case, it will be useful to review briefly those points of Catholic social teaching presented in *On Human Work* that have strongly influenced the pastoral letter.

In the introduction to the encyclical, John Paul II writes that "human work is a key,

perhaps the essential key, to the whole social question." It is only through work that a person "achieves fulfillment as a human being and indeed in a sense becomes 'more a human being.'" And since we are social beings, not fully human unless part of a community, we must develop institutions of cooperative labor—social organization, a division of labor, decision-making structures—through which our work can be made effective. The pope stresses the "self-realizing" or "self-creating" character of social labor. Through cooperative labor, people create a new material world, new social institutions, new knowledge, and a new consciousness; that is, through cooperative labor people create themselves and their society.

The pope—a philosopher by professional training—further develops his analysis around what he sees as the essential characteristic of human labor, its status as the "subject" of all economic activity. "Man is the image of God partly through the mandate from his creator to subdue, to dominate, the earth," he writes. If people are to share in creation and "dominate the earth," they must control or be the "subject" of economic activity; they cannot be objects controlled by external economic laws. As a worker, a person is "a subjective being capable of acting in a planned and rational way, capable of deciding about himself and with a tendency to self-realization." This, according to the pope (in a passage quoted by the bishops), "constitutes the fundamental and perennial heart of Christian teaching on human work."

Therefore, the pope contends, to be "right" and "morally legitimate" an economic system must conform with "the principle of the substantial and real priority of labor, of the subjectivity of human labor and its effective participation in the [organization and control of] the whole production process." Conversely, an economic system is morally illegitimate if it permits capital, or productive property, to be "an impersonal 'subject' putting man and man's work into a position of dependence" in economic activity. Seen in this light, the major systemic economic deformity of both the modern capitalist economies of the industrialized West and the "collectivized" or "statist" economies of the Soviet Union and Eastern Europe is their inversion of the appropriate subject-object (or ends-means) relationship between labor and the means of production. In both systems, workers are treated as instruments or objects of production; they are organized by those who control productive property through undemocratic, authoritarian processes in pursuit of self-serving economic or political objectives.

"SOCIALIZING" THE MEANS OF PRODUCTION

The institutional root of this inversion in both capitalist and communist countries, according to the pope, is the system of control of the means of production. Workers do not control the use of productive property in either system; therefore, they cannot act as the self-realizing subjects of economic activity in either system.

In Western capitalism, the basic structural problem is the private ownership and control of the means of production by one social class. As the pope sees it, the history of capitalist economies reflects an apparently irreconcilable conflict between private ownership of the means of production and effective and meaningful worker participation in enterprise management. Capitalism divides people into those "who do the work without being the owners of the means of production" and "those who act as entrepreneurs and who own these means or represent the owners." The owners' desire to maximize their profits, reinforced by the pressure of competitive markets, forces managers to treat labor "as a special kind of 'merchandise' or as an impersonal 'force' needed for production."

What the pope is criticizing here—the treatment of labor as an instrument of production—is, of course, an uncontroversial aspect of the neoclassical theory of the firm. In neoclassical theory, owners or their representatives exercise control of the labor process as part of their rights as private-property owners. The argument that at full employment workers are able to negotiate a wage equal to the value of their marginal product, and to receive compensatory wage differentials for accepting undesirable jobs, does not change the character of intrafirm decision-making; ownership/management is the "brains" of the neoclassical firm, labor a tool.

The pope finds this capitalist labor process to be morally unacceptable, and so do the bishops. They claim that "justice, not charity" demands that workers "be treated as persons rather than simply as a 'factor of production.'" The pope argues that it "is clear that recognition of the proper position of labor and the worker in the production process demands various adaptations in the sphere of the right to ownership of the means of production."

As the pope sees it, then, capitalist ownership rights must be revised "in theory and in practice." The purpose of this revision is the "socialization" of the means of production, by which he means the creation of a system of ownership rights that supports worker control of the production process. The pope goes on to say, however, that eliminating private ownership through nationalization of the means of production does not automatically lead to their "socialization." The means of production cannot be considered truly socialized unless each worker "is fully entitled to consider himself a part-owner of the great workbench at which he is working with everyone else" and is "able to take part in the very work process as a sharer in responsibility and creativity." Therefore, "statist" economic systems cannot be considered to have socialized their ownership structure; the pope and the bishops categorically reject them.

How, then, is capitalism to be "reformed," the means of production "socialized," and society empowered as the subject of economic activity? The pope and the bishops agree on the general outline of an answer: the economy must undergo an evolution that culminates in worker self-management and a democratic political order that ensures rational planning at regional and national levels.

How is this transformation to be achieved? The pope and the bishops agree that democracy in the workplace requires substantial worker ownership of the enterprise. The pope contends that the best way to achieve worker control of production is "by associating labor with the ownership of capital as far as possible." As explained above, the bishops endorse a number of "new institutions of economic partnership."

The pope and the bishops endorse national economic planning for two reasons. First, planning is an institutional prerequisite for attaining such goals as sustained full employment and distributive justice. Second, without effective planning institutions, people cannot attain their proper status as the "subject" of economic life; only through a democratic planning process can they be empowered to exercise conscious control over their economic destinies. As the pope argues, government "must make provision for overall planning ... a just and rational coordination, within the framework of which the initiative of individuals, free groups and local work centers ... must be safeguarded." Overly centralized and excessively bureaucratic planning is not what they have in mind; they stress democracy, diversity of influence, and participation. Relatively free markets would presumably continue to play an important allocative role under "economic democracy," but the bishops contend "competition alone won't do the job." They definitely leave the precise structure of the planning instructions unspecified, believing that they can only be decided through trial and error.

The bishops, then, proceed from deep-rooted and philosophical principles, including those emphasized in *On Human Work*, to the central conclusion a just economic system must be built on work democracy and effective national economic plans. Their message is cautious in tone and evolutionary strategy. However, no amount of caution and experimental openness on means can alter the fact that conclusion puts them in fundamental conflict with the theory and practice of the American economic system.

SHOULD ECONOMISTS TAKE THE BISHOPS SERIOUSLY?

The pastoral letter is a potentially significant intervention in the current debate over national economic priorities. It is a clear and forceful demand to replace self-interest with social solidarity and mutual responsibility as the guiding principle of political discourse. It is also a plea to open the debate to the serious consideration of alternative economic and political institution that would be more consistent with, and supportive of moral values and social solidarity than our present arrangements are. But the charge has been made that the bishops' letter is hopelessly confused about economic theory and insensitive to economic and political reality.

The bishops appear to be vulnerable to this charge. They do not confront in any direct way a whole series of complex questions about the theoretical coherence and practical viability of their policies and programs—questions that would occur to any economist who reads their letter. Moreover, two related complications make serious consideration of these questions difficult. First, the bishops consciously chose to avoid theoretical economic analyses in their letter. Second, they have taken the position that it is the responsibility of professional economists, not the clergy, to transform the guidelines developed in their letter into institutions consistent with their objectives. Despite these complications, we will deal briefly with a few questions about the effect that adoption of the bishops' proposals might have on efficiency or economic growth, and suggest a general line of argument that could be taken in defense of the analytical coherence of their program.

- Would the degree of authority required by a national planning agency to achieve objectives such as sustained full employment, together with the substantial reduction in economic incentives that would accompany a more egalitarian distributional policy, stifle entrepreneurial initiative and retard technological innovation? The bishops' statements on planning suggest that the role of markets and material incentives would be reduced in scope, not eliminated. Enterprises would still face pressure from domestic and international competition to be technologically innovative. And individual and collective material rewards for socially productive innovation would continue to provide economic incentives for entrepreneurial initiative. The bishops seem to agree with Keynes, who argued that a high degree of inequality is not required to induce entrepreneurs to play the game of innovation and risk-taking. Much smaller incentives than are presently available, he said, "will serve the purpose equally well, as soon as the players are used to (them)."

- Will the dissolution of managerial authority and the inefficient and costly decision-making processes of worker self-management lower labor productivity? Here the bishops might respond that experience with worker self-management, in the United States and elsewhere, suggests that labor productivity is more likely to rise than fall when democracy is established in the workplace. Worker self-management produces a sense of ownership and involvement that increases motivation, raises initiative, and uses the special knowledge of production processes that only workers possess.

- Will the heavy hand of the national planning authority allocate resources less efficiently than the free market does at present, thereby reducing the economy's growth potential? The letter suggests the following kind of response. Current allocative priorities favoring luxury consumption and military production are both socially irrational and immoral. Moreover, sustained full employment and high capacity utilization would move the economy closer to its production possibility curve than it tends on average to be under present arrangements. After all, there are many examples of economies that have both more central coordination and higher average growth rates than the United States.

Perhaps the most persuasive argument that can be made against the cavalier dismissal of the bishops' program as theoretically incoherent is not based directly on economic theory proper, but rather on a theoretically informed evaluation of certain other nations' experiences. Consider, for example, the Swedish economy. Sweden is an advanced social-democratic society that already incorporates, in well-developed or embryonic form, several of the institutions and policies the bishops espouse. It has a very progressive social welfare program, an active public-employment program in support of a full-employment goal, an impressive employment record, a legal system that limits management power over labor, and a program to increase worker ownership of the firms in which they are employed. There are also many lessons, both positive and negative, to be learned from Yugoslavia's experience with worker self-management, the coresponsibility of local governments for economic decisions that affect them, and the problems and prospects involved in an attempt to integrate national planning, markets, and workplace democracy.

Our main point is not that the bishops have proposed a demonstrably coherent and realistic set of specific policy objectives and institutional transformations: they have not. There *are* challenging questions that they have not adequately answered. Our point, rather, is that their proposals are certainly not demonstrably incoherent, either. We do not believe that rigorous, unbiased economic analysis can demonstrate that it is in principle impossible to conceive of, and in practice impossible to construct, a mix of planning institutions, market mechanisms, forms of workplace democracy, and progressive welfare programs that would satisfy the bishops' moral criteria. Any condemnation of their "experiment" as theoretically inconceivable thus seems to us to be more of an ideological than a scientific judgment.

Leonard Silk concluded a review of the

pastoral letter as follows: "Many economists will [conclude] that the bishops have brought together competent economic analysis and a clear-eyed view of actual conditions in the United States and other countries. They will applaud the bishops for hitting so hard and challenging the nation to rethink its policies in the name of the well-being of all people." (*New York Times*, November 24, 1984.) In our opinion, the nation would be well served if these economists were to take up the bishops' challenge and place their considerable technical skills in the service of a new American experiment in economic democracy, an experiment designed to create economic institutions that both support and reflect the sense of community and sense of human dignity that are the foundations of the pastoral letter.

Suggestions for Further Reading

CLASSIC WORKS ON RACE AND GENDER, ECONOMICS AND SOCIETY.

Amott, T. and J. Matthaei. 1991. *Race, Gender and Work: A Multicultural Economic History of Women in the United States.* South End Press. Boston, MA.

Becker, G. 1971. *The Economics of Discrimination,* 2nd ed. University of Chicago Press. Chicago, IL.

Bergmann, B. 1986. *The Economic Emergence of Women.* Basic Books. New York, NY.

Blau, F. and Ferber, M. 1992. *The Economics of Women, Men and Work.* 2nd ed. Prentice-Hall. Englewood Cliffs, NJ.

Cherry, R. 1989. *Discrimination: Its Economic Impact on Blacks, Women and Jews.* D.C. Heath. Lexington, MA.

Baran, P. and P. Sweezy. 1965. *Monopoly Capital.* Monthly Review Press. New York, NY.

Boserup, E. 1970. *Women's Role in Economic Development.* St. Martin's Press. New York, NY.

Bowen, W. and T. Finegan. 1969. *The Economics of Labor Force Participation.* Princeton University Press. Princeton, NJ.

De Beauvoir, S. 1952. *The Second Sex.* Alfred A. Knopf, New York.

Friedman, Milton. 1962. *Capitalism and Freedom.* Chicago: University of Chicago Press.

Genovese, E. 1966. *The Political Economy of Slavery.* MacGibbon and Kee. London, UK.

Goldin, C. 1990. *Understanding the Gender Gap: An Economic History of American Woman.* Oxford University Press, New York, NY.

Gould, S. 1981. *The Mismeasure of Man.* W.W. Norton & Co. New York, NY.

Haley, A. 1964. *The Autobiography of Malcolm X.* Grove Press, New York.

Hooks, B. 1981. *Ain't I a Woman: Black Women and Feminism.* Pluto Press. London, UK.

Murray, C. 1984. *Losing Ground: American Social Policy, 1950–1980.* Basic Books. Washington, DC.

Rothenberg, P. ed. 1988. *Racism and Sexism: An Integrated Study.* St. Martin's Press. New York, NY.

ABOUT RACE AND ETHNICITY

Allport, Gordon. 1954. *The Nature of Prejudice.* Addison-Wesley. Reading, MA.

America, R. 1990. *The Wealth of Races: The Present Value of Benefits from Past Injustices.* Greenwood Press. New York, NY.

American Enterprise Institute. 1987. Public Opinion: Special issue on prejudice, July/August.

Baron, H. 1975. "Racial Domination in Advanced Capitalism: A Theory of Nationalism and Divisions in the Labor Market." In *Labor Market Segmentation,* ed. Richard Edwards, Michael Reich, and David Gordon. D.C. Heath. Lexington, MA. 173–216.

Beck, E. 1980. "Labor Unionism and Racial Income Inequality." *American Journal of Sociology* 85:791–814.

Berry, M. and J. W. Blassingame. 1982. *Long Memory: The Black Experience in America.* Oxford University Press. New York, NY.

Bonacich, E. 1975. "Abolition, the Extension of Slavery, and the Position of Free Blacks." *American Journal of Sociology* 81:601–27.

Bonacich, E. 1976. "Advanced Capitalism and Black—White Relations in the United States: A Split Labor Market Interpretation." *American Sociological Review* 41:34–51.

Boris, E. and P. Bardaglio. 1987. "Gender, Race, and Class: The Impact of the State on the Family and the Economy, 1790-1945." In *Families and Work,* ed. Naomi Gerstel and Harriet Engel Gross. Temple University Press. Philadelphia, PA. 132–51.

Bowser, B. P. and R. C. Hunt. 1981. *Impact of Racism on White Americans,* Sage Publications. Beverly Hills, CA.

Butler, W. and J. Heckman. 1978. "The Impact of the Government on the Labor Market Status of Black Americans: A Critical Review of Literature and New Evidence." In *Equal Rights and Industrial Relations,* ed. Leonard S. Hausman et al. Industrial Relations Research Association. Madison, WI.

Cartwright, W. and T. Burtis. 1968. "Race and Intelligence: Changing Opinions in Social Science," Social Science Quarterly (December), pp. 603–18.

Cherry, R. 1976. "Racial Thought in the Early Economics Profession." *Review of Social Economy* 33:147–51.

Cherry, R. 1980. "Biology, Sociology, and Economics—An Historical Analysis." *Review of Social Economy* 37:140–51.

Cherry, R. 1985. "Textbook Treatments of Minimum Wage Legislation." *Review of Black Political Economy* 13:25–38.

Chinese Historical Society of Southern California. 1984. *Linking Our Lives: Chinese American Women of Los Angeles*, Chinese Historical Society of Southern California. Los Angeles, CA.

Clark, C. 1975. "The Shockley-Jensen Thesis: A Contextual Appraisal," The Black Scholar (July).

Commons, J. 1924. *Races and Immigrants in America*. Macmillan. New York, NY.

Dachter, L. "Race/Sex Differences in the Effects of Background on Achievement," in *Five Thousand American Families*, Vol. IX, eds. Martha S. Hill, et al. Ann Arbor, MI: Institute for Social Research, 1981.

Dalfiume, R. 1969. "The 'Forgotten Years' of Negro Revolution." In *The Negro in Depression and War*, ed. Bernard Sternsher. New York: Schocken, 298–311.

Danziger, S. and P. Gottschalk. 1986. "Work, Poverty, and the Working Poor: A Multifaceted Problem." *Monthly Labor Review*, September, 17–21.

Darity, W. 1980. "Illusion of Black Economic Progress." *Review of Black Political Economy* 10:355–79.

David, J. ed. *The American Indian: The First Victim*, William Morrow & Co., New York, 1972.

David, P. et al. 1976. *Reckoning with Slavery*. New York: Oxford University Press.

Drake, St. C. and H. Cayton. 1945. *Black Metropolis*. New York: Harcourt and Brace.

Fogel, R. and S. Engerman. 1974. *Time on the Cross: The Economics of American Negro Slavery*. Boston, MA.

Franklin, R. and S. Resnik 1973. *The Political Economy of Racism*. New York: Holt, Rinehart, and Winston.

Fairchild, H. 1917. "Literacy Tests." *Quarterly Journal of Economics* 31:447–51.

Fusfeld, D. and T. Bates. 1984. *The Political Economy of the Urban Ghetto*. Carbondale IL: Southern Illinois University Press.

Gee, E. (ed.). 1976. *Counterpoint: Perspectives on Asian Americans*, Asian American Studies Center, University of California, Los Angeles.

Giddings, P. 1984. *When and Where I Enter: The Impact of Black Women on Race and Sex in America*, Bantam Books. New York, NY.

Gotteredson, D. 1981. "Black-White Differences in the Educational Process: What Have We Learned?" *American Sociological Review* (October).

Green, R. and R. Griffore. 1981. "Standardized Testing and Minority Student," Educational Digest (February).

Gwaltney, J. 1981. *Drylongso: A Self-Portrait of Black America*, Vintage Books. New York, NY.

Harrison, B. 1977. "Education and Underemployment in the Urban Ghetto." In *Problems in Political Economy: An Urban Perspective*, ed. David Gordon. D.C. Heath. Lexington, MA 252–61.

Jacobs, P. and S. Landau. eds. 1971. *To Serve the Devil*, vol. 1, *Natives and Slaves*, vol. 2, *Colonial and Sojourners: A Documentary Analysis of America's Racial History and Why It Has Been Kept Hidden*. Vintage Books. New York, NY.

Kluegel, J. and E. Smith. 1983. "Affirmative Action Attitudes: Effects of Self-Interest, Racial Effect, and Stratification Beliefs on Whites," *Social Forces* (March).

Knowles, L., and K. Prewitt, eds. 1969. *Institutional Racism in America*. Prentice-Hall. Englewood Cliffs, NJ.

Lazear, E. 1979. "The Narrowing of the Black-White Wage Gap Is Illusionary." *American Economics Review* 69:553–564.

Leigh, D. 1978. "Racial Discrimination and Labor Unions: Evidence from the NLS Sample of Middle-Aged Men." *Journal of Human Resources* 13:227–41.

Leonard, J. 1984. "Anti-Discrimination or Reverse Discrimination?" *Journal of Human Resources* 19:143–61.

Leonard, Jonathan. 1984. "What Are Promises Worth: The Impact of Affirmative Action Goals." *Journal of Human Resources* 20:3–12.

Liebow, E. 1967. *Tally's Corner: A Study of Negro Streetcorner Men*. Little, Brown, and Company. Boston, MA.

Marable, M. 1985. *Black American Politics from the Washington Marches to Jesse Jackson*. Schocken, New York, NY.

Malveaux, J. 1985. "Comparable Worth and Its Impact on Black Women." *Review of Black Political Economy* 14:47–62.

Marshall, R. 1974. "The Economics of Racial Discrimination: A Survey," *Journal of Economic Literature* (September).

Massey, D. 1979. "Effects of Socioeconomic Factors on the Residential Segregation of Blacks and Spanish-Americans in the U.S. Urbanized Areas," *American Sociological Review* (December).

Masters, S. 1975. *Black-White Income Differentials*. Academic Press. New York, NY.

McKitrick, E. ed. 1963. *Slavery Defended: The Views of the Old South*. Columbia University Press. New York, NY.

Moody, A. 1986. *Coming of Age in Mississippi*. Dell Publishing Co. New York, NY.

Moraga, C. and G. Anzaldua (eds.) 1981. *This Bridge Called My Back: Writings by Radical Women of Color*, Kitchen Table: Women of Color Press. New York, NY.

Moynihan, D. 1965. *The Negro Family: The Case for National Action*. Office of Policy Planning and Research, U.S. Department of Labor. Washington, DC.

Murray, H. 1969. "The NAACP Versus the Communist Party." In *The Negro in Depression and War*, ed. Bernard Sternsher. Schocken. New York. 267–80.

Myrdal, G. 1944. *An American Dilemma: The Negro Problem and Modern Democracy*. Harper and Row. New York, NY.

Naylor, N. 1983. *The Women of Brewster Place*. Penguin Books, New York, NY.

Newman, D., et al., 1978. *Protest, Politics and Prosperity: Black Americans and White Institutions*, 1940–1975. Pantheon Books. New York, NY.

Rank, M. 1988. "Racial Differences in Length of Welfare Use." *Social Forces* (June).

Reich, M. 1977. "Theories of Racism." In *Problems in Political Economy: An Urban Perspective*. ed. D. Gordon. D.C. Heath. Lexington, MA. 183–87.

Reich, M. 1981. *Racial Inequity*. Princeton University Press. Princeton, NJ.

Reich, M. 1988. "Postwar Racial Income Differences: Trends and Theories." In *The Three Worlds of Labor Economics*, ed. G. Mangum and P. Phillips. M.E. Sharpe. White Plains, NY.

Rivera, E. 1983. *Family Installments: Memories of Growing Up Hispanic*. Penguin Books. New York, NY.

Shulman, S. 1984. "The Politics of Race." *Monthly Review*. 35:49–53.

Smith, B. 1983. *Home Girls: A Black Feminist Anthology*. Kitchen Table: Women of Color Press. New York, NY.

Smith, J. and F. Welch. 1986. *Closing the Gap: Forty Years of Economic Progress for Blacks*. Rand Corporation. Santa Monica, CA.

Snyderman, M. and S. Rothman. 1986. "Science, Politics, and the IQ Controversy." *The Public Interest*. (Spring).

Sowell, T. 1975. *Race and Economics*. David McKay Co. Inc. New York, NY.

Sowell, T. 1981. *Markets and Minorities*. Basic Books. New York, NY.

Spero, S. and A. Harris. 1968. *The Black Worker*. Atheneum. New York, NY.

Stampp, K. 1956. *The Peculiar Institution: Slavery in the Ante-Bellum South*. Vintage. New York, NY.

Szymanski, A. 1976. "Racial Discrimination and White Gain." *American Sociological Review* 41:403–14.

United States Commission on Civil Rights. 1970. *Racism in America and How to Combat It*, Washington, DC.

United States Commission on Human Rights. 1981. *Indian Tribes: A Continuing Quest for Survival*. Washington, DC.

Villemez, W. 1978. "Black Subordination and White Economic Well-Being." *American Sociological Review* 43:772–76.

Vroon, P. A., J. DeLeeuw, and A. C. Meester. 1986. "Distribution of Intelligence and Educational Level in Fathers and Sons," *British Journal of Psychology*.

Wagenheim, K. and O. J. Wagenheim. eds. 1973. *The Puerto Ricans: A Documentary History*. Praeger. New York, NY.

Washington, B. 1963. *Up from Slavery*. Doubleday. Garden City, NY.

Weaver, R. 1946. *Negro Labor: A National Problem*. Harcourt and Brace. New York, NY.

Welch, F. 1973. "Black-White Differences in Returns to Schooling." *American Economics Review* 63:893–907.

Welch, F. 1981. "Affirmative Action and Its Enforcement." *American Economics Review* 71S:127–33.

Wellman, D. 1977. *Portraits of White Racism*. Cambridge University Press. Cambridge, MA.

Williams, J. 1969. "Struggles of the Thirties in the South." In *Negro in Depression and War*, ed. Bernard Sternsher. Schocken. New York, NY. 166–80.

Wilson, J. 1965. "The Negro in Politics." *Daedalus* 94:972–77.

Wilson, W. 1980. *The Declining Significance of Race*. University of Chicago Press. Chicago, IL.

Wolfe, J. 1982. "The Impact of Family Resources on Childhood IQ," *Journal of Human Resources*. (Spring).

ABOUT GENDER

Andrea, C. 1971. *Sex and Caste in America*. Prentice-Hall. Englewood Cliffs, NJ.

Aptheker, B. 1982. *Woman's Legacy: Essays on Race, Sex, and Class in American History*. University of Massachusetts Press. Amherst, MA.

Barrett, Michele. 1980. *Women's Oppression Today: Problems in Marxist Feminist Analysis*. Verso. London, UK.

Baxandall, R., E. Ewen, and L. Gordon. 1976. "The Working Class Has Two Sexes." *Monthly Review* 28:1–9.

Beechey, V. 1978. "Women and Production: A Critical Analysis of Some Sociological Theories of Women's Work." In *Feminism and Materialism: Women and Modes of Production*, ed. Annette Kuhn and AnnMarie Wolpe. Routledge and Kegan Paul. London, UK. 155–97.

Beneria, L. and G. Sen. 1982. "Class and Gender Inequalities and Women's Role in Economic Development." *Feminist Studies* 8:157–75.

Beneria, L. ed. 1980. *Women and Development: The Sexual Division of Labor in Rural Societies*. New York: Praeger.

Bentson, M. 1969. "The Political Economy of Women's Liberation." *Monthly Review* 21:13–27.

Besharoc, D. and A. Quin. 1987. "Not all Female-Headed Families Are Created Equal," *The Public Interest* (Fall).

Bielby, W. and J. Baron. 1986. "Men and Women at Work: Sex Segregation and Statistical Discrimination." *American Journal of Sociology* 91:759–99.

Blau, F. 1977. *Equal Pay in the Office*. D.C. Heath. Lexington, MA.

Blau, F. 1984. "Discrimination Against Women: Theory and Evidence." In *Labor Economics: Modern Views*, ed. Williams Darity, Jr. Kluwer-Nijhoff. Boston, MA. 53–90.

Blau, F. and C. Jusenius. 1976. "Economists' Approaches to Sex Segregation in the Labor Market: An Appraisal." In *Women and the Workplace*, ed. Martha Blaxall and Barbara B. Reagan. University of Chicago Press. Chicago, IL.

Boris, E. and P. Bardaglio. 1987. "Gender, Race, and Class: The Impact of the State on the Family and the Economy, 1790–1945." In *Families and Work*, ed. Naomi Gerstel and Harriet Engel Gross. Temple University Press. Philadelphia, PA. 132–51.

Brown, C. 1981. "Mothers, Fathers, and Children: From Private to Public Patriarchy." In *Women and Revolution*, ed. Lydia Sargent. South End Press. Boston, MA. 239–68.

Chafetz, J. 1978. *Masculine, Feminine or Human?* F.E. Peacock Publishers. Itasca, IL.

Chevillard, N. and S. Leconte. 1986. "The Dawn Lineage Societies: The Origins of Women's Oppression." In *Women's Work, Men's Property: The Origins of Gender and Class*, ed. Stephanie Coontz and Peta Henderson. Verso. London, UK. 76–107.

Ebert, R. and J. Stone. 1985. "Male-Female Differences in Promotions: EEO in Public Education." *Journal of Human Resources* 20:504–21.

Ehrenreich, B. 1981. "The Women's Movement: Feminists and Antifeminists." *Radical America* 15:93–101.

Ehrenreich, B. 1983. *Hearts of Men*. New York: Doubleday.

Eisenstein, H. 1983. *Contemporary Feminist Thought*. Boston: G.K. Hall and Company.

Eisenstein, Z. 1979. "Developing a Theory of Capitalist Patriarchy and Socialist Feminism." In *Capitalist Patriarchy and the Case for Social Feminism*. ed. Zillah Eisenstein. New York: Monthly Review Press, 5–40.

Eisenstein, Z. 1984. *Feminism and Sexual Equality*, Monthly Review Press, New York.

Friedl, E. 1975. *Women and Men. An Anthropological View*. New York: Rinehart & Winston.

Fuchs, V. 1988. *Women's Quest for Economic Equality*. Cambridge, MA: Harvard University Press.

Gordon, L. 1976. *Woman's Body, Woman's Right*. Grossman Publishers. New York, NY.

Harding, S. and M. B. Hintikka. 1983. *Discovering Reality: Feminist Perspectives on Epistemology, Metaphysics, Methodology, and the Philosophy of Science*. D. Reidel Publishing Co. Boston, MA.

Hartmann, H. 1987. "Internal Labor Markets and Gender: A Case Study of Promotions." In *Gender in the Workplace*, ed. Clair Brown and Joseph Pechman. The Brookings Institute. Washington, DC. 59–91.

Huber, J. and G. Spitze. 1983. *Children, Housework and Jobs*. New York: Academic Press. New York, NY.

Humphries, J. 1977. "Class Struggle and the Persistence of the Working Class Family." *Cambridge Journal of Economics* 1:241–58.

Humphries, J. 1976. "Women: Scapegoats and Safety Valves in the Great Depression." *Review of Radical Political Economics* 8:98–121.

Hunt, J. and L. Hunt. 1987. "Male Resistance to Role Symmetry in Dual Earner Households: Three Alternative Explanations." In *Families and Work*, ed. Naomi Gerstel and Harriet Engel Gross. Temple University Press. Philadelphia, PA. 192–203.

Jones, J. 1982. "'My Mother Was Much of a Woman': Black Women, Work, and the Family Under Slavery." *Feminist Studies* 8:233–69.

Kingson, J. 1988. "Women in the Law Say Path in Limited by 'Mommy Track.'" *New York Times*. 8 August, A1.

Lipman-Bluman, J. 1984. *Gender Roles and Power*, Prentice-Hall, Englewood Cliffs, NJ.

Lloyd, C., and B. Niemi. 1979. *The Economics of Sex Differentials*. Columbia University Press. New York, NY.

Lowe, M. and R. Hubbard, eds. 1983. *Women's Nature: Rationalization of Inequality*. Pergamon Press. New York, NY.

Madden, J. 1973. *The Economics of Sex Discrimination*. Lexington Books. Lexington, MA.

Malveaux, J. 1985. "Comparable Worth and Its Impact on Black Women." *Review of Black Political Economy* 14:47–62.

Matthaei, J. 1982. *An Economic History of Women in America*. Schochen Books. New York, NY.

Mitchell, J. 1971. *Woman's Estate*. Vintage Books. New York, NY.

Mitchell, J. 1974. *Psychoanalysis and Feminism*. Pantheon Books. New York, NY.

National Research Center. 1981. *Women, Work, and Wages: Equal Pay for Jobs of Equal Value*. National Academy Press. Washington, DC.

Naylor, N. 1983. *The Women of Brewster Place*. Penguin Books, New York, NY.

O'Kelly, C. 1980. *Women and Men in Society*. D. Van Nostrand Co. New York, NY.

Polachek, S. 1979. "Occupational Segregation among Women: Theory, Evidence and Prognosis." In *Women in the Labor Market*, ed. Cynthia Lloyd, Emily Andrews, and Curtis Gilroy. Columbia University Press. New York, NY. 137–57.

Reskin, B. and H. Hartmann. 1986. *Women's Work, Men's Work: Sex Segregation on the Job*. National Academy Press. Washington, DC.

Reskin, B. and P. Roos. 1990. *Job Queues, Gender Queues: Explaining Women's Inroads into Male Occupations*. Temple University Press. Philadelphia, PA.

Roos, P. 1985. *Gender and Work: A Comparative Analysis of Industrial Societies*. SUNY Press. Albany, NY.

Rosaldo, M. and L. Lamphere (eds.). 1974. *Women, Culture, and Society*. Stanford University Press. Stanford, CA.

Rubin, L. 1983. *Intimate Strangers: Men and Women Together*. Harper and Row. New York, NY.

Sawhill, I. 1976. "Discrimination and Poverty among Women Who Head Families." In *Women and the Workplace* ed. Martha Blaxhall and Barbara Reagan. University of Chicago Press. Chicago, IL. 201–11.

Scott, H. 1974. *Does Socialism Liberate Women? Experiences from Eastern Europe.* Beacon Press. Boston, MA.

Smith, B. 1983. *Home Girls: A Black Feminist Anthology,* Kitchen Table: Women of Color Press. New York, NY.

Smith, J. ed. 1980. *Female Labor Supply: Theory and Estimation.* University Press. Princeton, NJ.

Smith, J. and M. Ward. 1984. *Women's Wages and Work in the Twentieth Century.* Rand Corporation. Santa Monica, CA.

Spender, D. 1985. *Man Made Language* (2nd Edition), Routeledge & Kegan, Boston.

Stoll, C. 1974. *Female and Male. Socialization, Social Roles and Social Structure.* Wm. C. Brown. Dubuque, IA.

Tilly, L. and J. Scott. 1978. *Women, Work and Family.* Holt, Rinehart, & Winston. New York, NY.

Treiman, D., and H. Hartmann. 1981. *Women, Work and Wages: Equal Pay for Jobs of Equal Value.* National Academy Press. Washington, DC.

United Nations. 1980. *The Economic Role of Women in the ECE Region.* New York, NY.

Welter, B. 1978. "The Cult of True Womanhood, 1820–1860." In *The American Family in Social-Historical Perspective.* Michael Gordon, ed. St. Martin's Press. New York, NY. pp. 313–33.

Youssef, N. 1974. *Women and Work in Developing Societies.* University of California Press. Berkeley, CA.

ABOUT CLASS

Boyer, R. and H. Morais. 1972. *Labor's Untold Story.* United Electrical, Radio & Machine Workers of America. New York, NY.

Brittain, J. 1977. *The Inheritance of Economic Status.* The Brookings Institution. Washington, DC.

Corcoran, M. and L. Dachter. 1981. "Intergenerational Status Transmission and the Process of Individual Attainment," in *Five Thousand Families,* Vol. IX, eds. Martha S. Hill, et al. Ann Arbor, MI: Institute for Social Research.

Dollard, J. 1957. *Caste and Class in a Southern Town.* Garden City, NY: Doubleday and Company, Inc.

Domhoff, W. 1983. *Who Rules America Now?* Simon and Schuster, New York.

Resnick, S. and R. Wolff. 1987. *Knowledge and Class: A Marxian Critique of Political Economy.* The University of Chicago Press. Chicago, IL.

Sennett, R. and Cobb, J. 1973. *The Hidden Injuries of Class.* Vintage Books. New York, NY.

Shalom, S. 1985. *Socialist Visions.* South End Press, Boston, MA.

ABOUT POVERTY AND INCOME DISTRIBUTION

Amott, T. 1987. "The Retreat from Welfare." *Dollars & Sense* 127:6–8.

Amott, T. 1988. "Welfare Reform: A Workhouse without Walls." In *The Imperiled Economy: Through the Safety Net.* ed. Robert Cherry, et al. Union for Radical Political Economics. New York, NY.

Bane, M. 1986. "Household Composition and Poverty," in *Fighting Poverty,* eds. Danziger and Weinberg. Harvard University Press. Cambridge, MA.

Bane, M. and D. Ellwood. 1986. "Slipping In and Out of Poverty." *Journal of Human Resources* 21:1–24.

Blank, R. and S. Blinder. 1986. "Macroeconomics, Income Distribution, and Poverty." In *Fighting Poverty: What Works and What Doesn't,* ed. Sheldon Danziger and Daniel Weinberg. Harvard University Press. Cambridge, MA. 180–208.

Blumberg, P. 1980. *Inequality in an Age of Decline.* Oxford University Press. Oxford, UK.

Cherry, R. et al. 1987. *The Imperiled Economy: Macroeconomics from a Left Perspective.* Union for Radical Political Economics. New York, NY.

Cherry, R. et al. 1988. *The Imperiled Economy: Through the Safety Net.* Union for Radical Political Economics. New York, NY.

Coe, R. 1982. "Welfare Dependency: Fact or Myth?" *Challenge* 25:43–49.

Congressional Budget Office. 1987. *Work-Related Program for Welfare Recipients.* Washington, DC: U.S. Government Printing Office.

Danziger, S. and D. Weinberg, eds. 1986. *Fighting Poverty: What Works and What Doesn't.* Cambridge, MA: Harvard University Press.

Danziger, S. and P. Gottschalk. 1985. "The Poverty of 'Losing Ground.'" *Challenge* 28:32–38.

Duncan, G., et al., *Years of Poverty, Years of Plenty: The Changing Fortunes of American Workers and Families,* Ann Arbor, MI: Institute for Social Research, 1984.

Eberstadt, N. 1988. "Economic and Material Poverty in the US," *The Public Interest,* (Winter).

Feldstein, M. 1973. "The Economics of the New Unemployment." *The Public Interest* 33:1–21.

Ferrara, P. and K. Hopkins. 1987. "Health Status of the Poor," ed. Hopkins, *Welfare Dependency*, Alexandria, VA: Hudson Institute.

Gallaway, L. and R. Vedder. 1986. *Poverty, Income Distribution, the Family, and Public Policy*, Report to the Joint Economic Committee, U.S. Congress, Washington, DC: U.S. Government Printing Office.

Goodwin, L. 1972. *Do the Poor Want to Work?* The Brookings Institution. Washington, DC.

Gordon, D. 1972. *Theories of Poverty and Unemployment*, D.C. Heath and Company. Lexington, MA.

Heineman, B., et al., 1987. *Work and Welfare: The Case For New Directions in National Policy*. Center for National Policy. Washington, DC.

Hopkins, K. R. ed. 1986. *Welfare Dependency*. Hudson Institute. Alexandria, VA.

Jencks, C. et al., 1972. *Inequality*. Basic Books Inc. New York, NY.

McLanahan, S. 1985. "Family Structure and the Reprodiction of Poverty," *American Journal of Sociology*, 90:4.

Okun, A. 1977. "Equity and Efficiency: The Big Tradeoff." In *Problems in Political Economy: An Urban Perspective*, ed. David Gordon. D.C. Heath. Lexington, MA. 28–33.

Piven, F. and R. Cloward. 1971. *Regulating the Poor*. Pantheon. New York, NY.

Plotnick, R., and F. Kidmore. 1975. Progress Against Poverty: A Review of the 1964–1974 Decade. Academic Press, Inc. New York, NY.

Podell, L. 1968. *Families on Welfare in New York City*. City University of New York Press. New York, NY.

Rodgers, H., Jr. 1979. *Poverty Amid Plenty*. Addison-Wesley Publishing Co., Inc. Reading, MA.

Sheppard, H. 1967. *The Effects of Family Planning on Poverty in the United States*. Upjohn Institute. Kalamazoo, MI.

Winter A., ed., 1971. *The Poor: A Culture of Poverty, or a Poverty of Culture*. Wm. B. Eerdmans Publishing Co. Grand Rapids, MI.

ABOUT CHILDREN AND FAMILIES

Bianchi, S. 1990. "America's Children: Mixed Prospects." *Population Bulletin* 45, no. 1.

Bogue, D. 1975. "A Long Term Solution to the AFDC Problem: Prevention of Unwanted Pregnancy," *Social Science Review* (December).

Garfinkel, I. and S. McLanahan. 1986. *Single Mothers and Their Children: A New American Dilemma*. Washington, D.C.: Urban Institute Press.

Hayes, C., J. Palmer, and M. Zaslow, eds. 1990. *Who Cares for America's Children? Child Care Policy for the 1990's*. National Research Council, National Academy Press. Washington, DC.

Huber, J. and G. Spitze. 1983. *Children, Housework and Jobs*. New York: Academic Press. New York, NY.

Kamerman, S. and C. Hayes. 1982. eds. *Families that Work: Children in a Changing World*. National Academy Press. Washington, DC.

Kamerman, S. and A. Kahn. 1988. "What Europe Does for Single-Parent Families," *The Public Interest* (Fall).

McLanahan, S. 1985. "Family Structure and the Reprodiction of Poverty," *American Journal of Sociology*, 90:4.

McLanahan, S. 1985. "Charles Murray and the Family." In *Losing Ground: A Critique*, ed. Sara McLanahan et al., Madison, WI: Institute for Research on Poverty, University of Wisconsin—Madison, 1–7.

Mead, L. 1985. *Beyond Entitlement: The Social Obligations of Citizenship*. The Free Press. New York, NY.

Mercy, J. and L. Steelman. 1982. "Familial Influence on the Intellectual Attainment of Children." *American Sociological Review* (August).

Novak, M. et al. 1987. *The New Consensus on Family and Welfare*. American Enterprise Institute, Washington, DC.

Omolade, B. 1986. *It's a Family Affair: The Real Lives of Black Single Mothers*. Latham, NY: Kitchen Table—Women of Color Press.

Orlitz, E., and B. Bassoff. 1987. "Adolescent Welfare Mothers: Lost Optimism and Lowered Expectations." *Social Casework* (September).

Podell, L. 1968. *Families on Welfare in New York City*. City University of New York Press. New York, NY.

Rubin, L. 1976. *Worlds of Pain: Life in the Working Class Family*. Basic Books. New York, NY.

Schultz, T., ed. 1974. *Economics of the Family*. A conference report of the National Bureau of Economics Research. University of Chicago Press. Chicago, IL.

Sheppard, H. 1967. *The Effects of Family Planning on Poverty in the United States*. Upjohn Institute. Kalamazoo, MI.

Vinovskis, M. 1988. "Teenage Pregnancy and the Underclass." *The Public Interest* (Fall).

ABOUT AGING

Burtless, G. (ed.) 1987. *Work, Health and Income Among the Elderly*. Brookings Institution. Washington, DC.

Clark, R., J. Kreps, and J. Spengler. 1978. "Economics of Aging: A Survey." *Journal of Economic Literature*, (September).

Congressional Research Service. 1981. *Retirement Income for an Aging Population*. The Committee on Ways and Means. U.S. Government Printing Office. Washington, DC.

President's Commission on Pension Policy. 1981. *Coming of Age Toward a National Retirement Income Policy*. U.S. Government Printing Office. Washington, DC.

Schulz, J. 1988. *The Economics of Aging*. 4th ed., Auburn House. Dover, MA.

Starr, P. 1986. "Health Care for the Poor: The Past Twenty Years." In *Fighting Poverty*, eds. S. Danziger and S. Weinberg. Harvard University Press. Cambridge, MA.

U.S. Senate, Special Committee on Aging. Annual. *Developments in Aging*. U.S. Government Printing Office. Washington, DC.

ABOUT WORK AND JOBS

Ballen, J. and R. Freeman. 1986. "Transitions between Employment and Unemployment." In *The Black Youth Employment Crisis*. eds. D. Freeman and H. Holzer. University of Chicago Press. Chicago, IL. 23–74.

Berg, I. 1970. *Education and Jobs: The Great Training Robbery*. Praeger. New York, NY.

Berlin, G. and A. Sum. 1988. *Toward a More Perfect Union: Basic Skills, Poor Families, and Our Economic Future*. Ford Foundation. New York, NY.

Bluestone, B. and B. Harrison. 1986. *The Great American Job Machine: The Proliferation of Low-Wage Employment in the U.S. Economy*. U.S. Congress. Joint Economic Committee. Washington, DC. (December).

Bowles, S. 1977. "Unequal Education and the Social Division of Labor." In *Problems in Political Economy: An Urban Perspective*, ed. D. Gordon. D.C. Heath. Lexington, MA. 238–52.

Coleman, J. 1966. *Equality of Educational Opportunity*. U.S. Department of Health, Education, and Welfare. Washington, DC.

Congressional Budget Office. 1977. *Inequalities in the Educational Experiences of Black and White Americans*. Washington, DC: U.S. Government Printing Office.

Doeringer, P. and M. Piore. 1971. *Internal Labor Markets and Manpower Analysis*. Lexington, MA: D.C. Heath.

Ferber, M. and B. O'Farrell, with L. Allen, eds. 1991. *Work and Family: Policies for a Changing Workforce*. National Research Council. National Academy Press. Washington, DC.

Freeman, R. 1973. "Decline of Labor Market Discrimination and Economic Analysis." *American Economics Review* 63:280–86.

Freeman, R. and J. Medoff. 1984. *What Do Unions Do?* Basic Books. New York, NY.

Goodwin, L. 1972. *Do the Poor Want to Work?* The Brookings Institution. Washington, DC.

Gordon, D., R. Edwards, and M. Reich. 1982. *Segmented Work, Divided Workers: The Historical Transformation of Labor in the United States*. Cambridge University Press. Cambridge, UK.

Gotteredson, D. 1981. "Black-White Differences in the Educational Process: What Have We Learned?" *American Sociological Review* (October).

Harrison, B. 1977. "Education and Underemployment in the Urban Ghetto." In *Problems in Political Economy: An Urban Perspective*, ed. D. Gordon. D.C. Heath. Lexington, MA 252–61.

Hopkins, K., J. Newitt, and D. Doyle. 1986. "Educational Performance and Attainment," In *Welfare Dependency*, ed. K. Hopkins. Hudson Institute. Alexandria, VA.

Huber, J. and G. Spitze. 1983. *Children, Housework and Jobs*. New York: Academic Press. New York, NY.

Killingsworth, M. 1983. *Labor Supply*. Cambridge University Press. Cambridge, U.K.

Markey, J. 1988. "The Labor Marker Problems of Today's High School Dropouts," *Monthly Labor Review* (June).

Miller, E. and S. Haugen. 1986. "Hourly Paid Workers: Who They Are and What They Earn." *Monthly Labor Review*. (February).

Piore, M. 1977. "The Dual Labor Market." In *Problems in Political Economy: An Urban Perspective*, ed. D. Gordon. D.C. Heath. Lexington, MA. 91–95.

Rosenburg, S. 1988. "Restructuring the Labor Force: The Role of Government Policies." In *The Imperiled Economy: Through the Safety Net*, ed. R. Cherry, et al. Union for Radical Political Economics. New York, NY.

Schiller, B. 1976. "Equality, Opportunity, and the 'Good Job,'" *The Public Interest* (Spring).

Solow, R. 1990. *The Labor Market as a Social Institution*. Basil Blackwell. Cambridge, MA.

Stone, K. 1974. "The Origins of Job Structures in the Steel Industry." *Review of Radical Political Economy* 6:61–97.

U.S. Commission on Civil Rights. 1982. *Unemployment and Underemployment Among Blacks, Hispanics, and Women*. U.S. Government Printing Office. Washington, DC.

U.S. Department of Labor. Annual. *Employment and Training Report of the President*. U.S. Government Printing Office. Washington, DC.